From Psychoanalytic Narrative to Empirical Single Case Research

Implications for Psychoanalytic Practice

Horst Kächele
Joseph Schachter
Helmut Thomä
The Ulm Psychoanalytic Process Research Study Group

Routledge
Taylor & Francis Group
New York   London

Routledge
Taylor & Francis Group
270 Madison Avenue
New York, NY 10016

Routledge
Taylor & Francis Group
27 Church Road
Hove, East Sussex BN3 2FA

Printed in the United States of America on acid-free paper
10 9 8 7 6 5 4 3 2 1

International Standard Book Number-13: 978-0-88163-489-1 (Softcover) 978-0-88163-488-4 (0)

Library of Congress Cataloging-in-Publication Data

Kächele, Horst, 1944-
    From psychoanalytic narrative to empirical single case research : implications for psychoanalytic practice / Horst Kächele, Joseph Schachter, Helmut Thomä & The Ulm Psychoanalytic Process Research Study Group.
        p. ; cm. -- (Psychoanalytic inquiry book series ; v. 30)
    Includes bibliographical references and index.
    ISBN 978-0-88163-488-4 (hardcover : alk. paper) -- ISBN 978-0-88163-489-1 (pbk. : alk. paper)
    1. Psychoanalysis--Research--Methodology. 2. Psychoanalysis--Case studies. I. Schachter, Joseph, M.D. II. Thomä, Helmut. III. Ulm Psychoanalytic Process Research Study Group. IV. Title. V. Series.
    [DNLM: 1. Psychoanalytic Therapy--methods--Case Reports. 2. Anxiety Disorders--therapy--Case Reports. 3. Depressive Disorder--therapy--Case Reports. W1 PS427F v.30 2008 / WM 460.6 K11f 2008]

RC506.K28 2008
616.89'17072--dc22   2008000451

Visit the Taylor & Francis Web site at
http://www.taylorandfrancis.com

and the Routledge Web site at
http://www.routledgementalhealth.com

Contents

Foreword

A little more than two decades ago, I had the occasion to write the foreword for the English language version of the first volume in what has become the professional lifetime project of Helmut Thomä and Horst Kächele, aided by a host of collaborators, originally German, but increasingly over time, truly worldwide,* a project to develop the theory and the practice of psychoanalysis on a basis "rooted in [empirical] research on the psychoanalytic process and its results" (Thomä and Kächele 1987 p. x).† In my foreword to that first joint volume (pp. v–viii) I cited what I felt were three guiding themes in the contents of that publication, *Psychoanalytic Practice, V. 1: Principles* (1987).

The conventional assumption has been that Freud had, uniquely in the world's intellectual history, fully succeeded in creating a science and a profession in which the theory (the road to knowledge) and the therapy (the road to cure) were inherently joined, and truly the same. Thomä and Kächele pointed oppositely, to a conceptual disjunction, that while the theory is predominantly concerned with the determinants of genesis (i.e., the past), the techniques of therapy are oriented to achieving the necessary and sufficient conditions for change (i.e., the future). That is, a central problematic has always been the dialectic—and the tension—between the evolving theoretical and the evolving clinical therapeutic developments.

A second theme, a consequence of this conceptual disjunction, is the inevitable consideration of the complicated relationship of psychoanalysis qua therapy—in Freud's hands, the *only* therapy—to the then burgeoning whole panoply of psychoanalytic psychotherapies, varyingly expressive and supportive, that represent applications of the same psychoanalytic theoretical understanding of the organization and functioning of the mind to the differentiated spectrum of psychopathology presented in our consulting rooms. That is, one theory generated varieties of technical applications addressed to the clinical exigencies of the varieties of mental and emotional

---

* See www.balint-stiftung.de.
† U.S. paperback version, 1994a, p. x.

disorders. How similar and how different is "pure" psychoanalysis, innovated by Freud, and all the derived and linked psychoanalytic psychotherapies devised to deal with those varied clinical exigencies in the varieties of patients not amenable to the classical method?

The third theme presented in that first volume, and linked, but not at all isomorphically, to the other two, was the breakdown of Freud's intention and lifelong effort to maintain a coherent and unitary structure in the psychoanalytic discipline and profession that he had almost singlehandedly brought into being, with the formation of his secret committee of the seven loyal ringholders, and then the creation of the IPA, all designed to establish the dimensions and the parameters of psychoanalysis against diluting or fracturing pressures from within or without. The failure of this effort began even in Freud's lifetime, with the rise of the Kleinian movement in Great Britain, with its differing metapsychology, and has now evolved worldwide with our consensually acknowledged multiple theoretical diversity, or pluralism as we have come to call it (Wallerstein, 1988; 1990).

Underpinning all of these organizing themes was the clarion call for the necessary turn to empirical research as the only valid way to truly resolve these entangled issues, and to properly enhance the established psychoanalytic knowledge base. In 1992, the same two authors, this time with an enlarged group of collaborators, including some from outside of Germany, brought out the companion volume, *Psychoanalytic Practice, V. 2: Clinical Studies,* the counterpart clinical application of the theoretical principles expounded in volume one.*

In 1988 *Psychoanalytic Process Research Strategies,* edited by Hartvig Dahl and the two German colleagues, Kächele and Thomä, was published—the report of a conference of American and German empirical researchers into psychoanalytic treatment processes held in Ulm, Germany in the summer of 1985, just prior to the 34th IPA Congress in Hamburg. This conference, bringing together many of the most prominent researchers in psychoanalytic treatments, each presenting his own work, deploying their individual concepts and instruments with the analytic case material that they individually had available, was a most impressive and successful demonstration of how such empirical studies could make significant progress toward answering the many questions that the two Thomä–Kächele volumes posed for the understanding of psychoanalytic conceptions and practices.

Now some two decades later—and after the intervening years of worldwide burgeoning conceptual advance, methodological sophistication, and empirical demonstration in psychoanalytic therapy research—Kächele and Thomä with a new co-editor, Joseph Schachter, have brought forth their capstone volume, bringing together the thinking and the findings of

---

* U.S. paperback version, 1994b.

a long, closely-shared professional lifetime devoted to the research ideals and research promises of the earlier book for which I had written the foreword—though, given the growing momentum of the Ulm psychoanalytic research enterprise, I fully expect this current volume to be but an interim, rather than a final, marker.

The guiding theme of this current volume is emblazoned in its title, *From Psychoanalytic Narrative to Empirical Single Case Research,* or how one translates case descriptions and case reports into incrementally established research knowledge. In what is arguably the most important paper on dream analysis since Freud's *Interpretation of Dreams,* Erik Erikson (1954) described a detailed re-examination of Freud's Irma dream, the first dream reported in Freud's dream book, from the point of view—well beyond Freud's intent—of showing that it could be conceived to reveal more than the basic fact of a disguised wish fulfillment derived from infantile sources; that it, in fact, could be seen to carry the historical burden of being dreamed in order to be analyzed, and to thus open the door to dream analysis on what Freud was to call the "royal road" to the illumination of the unconscious. With this in mind Erikson, in his title, dubbed the elaboration of the Irma dream *The Dream Specimen of Psychoanalysis.* In this same sense, Freud's famous case histories (Dora, Little Hans, the Rat Man, the Wolf Man, Schreber), and an array by a range of subsequent psychoanalysts listed in Table 3.1 in this volume, of "sizable treatment reports of single cases" can be taken as *specimen* single-case reports upon which this present volume not only builds, but vastly extends, into serving as vital grounding for intensive empirical therapy research. This is what the authors, following Freud's tradition and adding their own developed empirical research studies, call being "idiographic nomotheticists" who search out "complex probabilistic explanatory schemas, knowledge of which deepens and enriches our understanding". Their aims, like Freud's before them, are thus simultaneously both "idiographic and nomothetic", to reconcile or surmount the often seeming "opposition of intuitive understanding and scientific understanding", and to build what Meissner has called "the science of subjectivity". This search for what (research) study of what the specific, leading to the generalizable, can yield, as the path (or as a major path) in the development of psychoanalysis as a science—a science of the theory building *and* a science of treatment—is what this present volume is all about.

To accomplish this, the three editors and their contributing collaborators across the three worldwide regions of psychoanalytic activity have assembled and logically ordered a sequence of sections (some of them previously published and now updated) from theoretical rationale and framework, through a 100-page long clinical description of the case of Amalia X, treated by Helmut Thomä, and onto what they call a sequence of guided clinical judgments, followed by a further sequence of computer-based studies of the case material.

The patient, Amalia X, came to analysis as a single woman, a teacher who suffered with anxiety and depressive symptoms, religious scrupulosity and compulsions, plus central concerns about her social and sexual identity linked to a severe bodily hirsutism. Her 531-hour psychoanalysis covered a five-year span, with 517 sessions audio recorded and with five of them out of every 25 transcribed, all installed in the Ulm Textbank database and now available for study by qualified investigators. The case description in this volume, occupying about 100 pages, is of two kinds: first a longitudinal overview, spanning the entire analysis, built around changes over time in symptoms, manifest behaviors, object-relationships, and transferences, followed by more detailed cross-sectional accounts along all the same dimensions from each of the 22 sequential five session transcription periods. Because this method of presenting loses the two-person interactional quality of the actual clinical sessions—available in the transcribed sessions—it can make more difficult the linking of the exchanges around the therapeutic interventions (insight into therapeutic *process*) to the ultimate enduring changes in the described dimensions of functioning (assessment of therapeutic *outcome*).

Nonetheless, the sheer volume of the presented material and the circumstances under which it is provided—in this volume and in the available Ulm Textbank—certainly warrants the proud claim of the authors that it takes its place alongside the much studied patient of Dahl's, Mrs. C., as a specimen case for psychoanalytic therapy research. In this sense it fulfills a central criterion of the decade-long work of the Collaborative Analytic Multisite Program (CAMP) (Bucci and Freedman, 2007), that psychotherapy process and outcome research can take the next—quantum—step, when the separate investigators, with differing sociocultural and language contexts, differing conceptual frames, and different devised instruments, can all work together on a shared database of available transcribed psychoanalytic hours, and can thus contrast and compare their findings and their conclusions based on shared study of the same clinical sessions. In this way their similarities and differences can be spelled out, as well as where the same concepts are employed with different meanings, and where different languages describe the same meaning. In being available as a specimen case, Amalia X truly provides what the authors call a "road map" for all the kinds of formalized studies presented in this volume, and also for what the diverse worldwide cadre of psychoanalytic therapy researchers can devise.

It is just these kinds of studies, already accomplished with the material of Amalia X by researchers from around the world, that the entire second half of this volume presents. They are divided into two sections: Guided Clinical Judgments and Lingustic Studies. These studies are written by clusters of different authors and in every instance but one, including either Kächele or Thomä. The Guided Clinical Judgments section includes studies of change in emotional insight, self-esteem, attribution of suffering to external forces and/or internally to oneself, manifest dream portrayal, and reactions to regular breaks in clinical work (weekends, and then longer breaks for illness, trips, vacations, etc.). Only in the instance of attribution of suffering is an explicit effort made to link the therapeutic interventions and the exchanges around them to the personality changes achieved, making thus the crucial link of process to outcome, the ultimate goal of therapy research. To me this kind of linking represents a still unrealized potential of the overall therapy research enterprise, at least as portrayed in this volume. It can of course be made the direct object of scrutiny, with further examination of the verbatim transcripts of the Amalia X hours, in the Ulm Textbank itself.

This section also includes three studies of the Amalia X material by exponents of other process research concepts and instruments, Lester Luborsky's Core Conflictual Relationship theme, Joseph Weiss and Harold Sampson's Unconscious Plan built on their control-mastery conception of the psychoanalysis process, and Enrico Jones' Psychotherapy Process Q-Sort. This provides a major opportunity to contrast and compare the findings and conclusions of these different conceptualizations and methods with each other, and with the studies of the Thomä-Kächele Ulm group as well. This is actually done in preliminary ways in the presentation of the methods of the San Francisco Psychotherapy Research Group (SFPRG), led by Weiss and Sampson.

The Linguistic Studies section, which is built around the technological possibilities available within the Ulm Textbank, owes a great deal to another Ulm member, Erhard Mergenthaler, who is among the cluster of authors of five of the six separate presentations in this computer-assisted section. We can certainly credit the creation of the Ulm Textbank, with its many search possibilities for language studies, as demonstrated in the various studies presented here, as itself, both a signal achievement in the furtherance of the psychoanalytic therapy research enterprise, and as well, a major gift to the psychoanalytic research community. Investigators are welcome to use the Textbank to explore its database, and within their own language orbits, to emulate it.

What does my entire foreword add up to? The authors express their overall intent as follows at the very end: "We plead decisively for multidimensionality of empirical ways of access concerning the subject of psychoanalysis; namely to make research on the impact of unconscious processes on conscious experience and behavior. In this research process the systematic single case study takes its proper place—next to other ways of access." I would state more. This volume registers a major landmark achievement in the often slow and halting march of empirical research possibilities for the furtherance of psychoanalytic theory and practice. It points a major way for us all, as each reader will discover for him or herself.

Robert S. Wallerstein

REFERENCES

Bucci, W. and Freedman, N. (eds.) (2007), *From Impression to Inquiry: A Tribute to the Work of Robert Wallerstein*. London, International Psychoanalytical Association (pp. 67–134).

Dahl, H., Kächele, H., and Thomä, H. (eds.) (1988), *Psychoanalytic Process Research Strategies*. Berlin, Springer-Verlag.

Erikson, E. H. (1954), The dream specimen of psychoanalysis. *Journal of the American Psychoanalytic Association* 2: 5–56.

Thomä, H. and Kächele, H. (1987), *Psychoanalytic Practice, 1. Principles*. Berlin, Springer-Verlag; New York: Jason Aronson 1994a.

Thomä, H. and Kächele, H. (1992), *Psychoanalytic Practice, 2. Clinical Studies*. New York, Springer-Verlag; New York: Jason Aronson 1994b.

Wallerstein, R. S. (1988) One psychoanalysis or many? *International Journal of Psycho-Anal* 69: 3–21.

Wallerstein, R. S. (1990) Psychoanalysis: The common ground. *International Journal of Psycho-Anal* 71: 3–20.

Editors

Horst Kächele, M.D. is professor of psychotherapy and chair of the Department of Psychosomatic Medicine and Psychotherapy, Ulm University, and training and supervising analyst of the German Psychoanalytic Association (DPV/IPA). He has conducted research on process and outcome in psychotherapy and psychoanalysis, psychosocial aspects of bone marrow transplantation, eating disorders, and attachment. In addition to many publications in German and English, he is co-author with Helmut Thomä of the Ulm textbook *Psychoanalytic Practice,* which has been translated into more than 10 languages. Together with Dr. Thomä, he was awarded the Sigmund Freud Prize of the City of Vienna in 2002 and the Mary S. Sigourney Award in 2004.

Joseph Schachter, M.D., Ph.D. conducted neurophysiological and developmental research with newborn offspring of schizophrenic mothers when he was director of child psychiatric research at the University of Pittsburgh School of Medicine. He was a training and supervising analyst at the Pittsburgh Psychoanalytic Institute and is the author and co-author of many papers. He is the author of *Transference: Shibboleth or Albatross?* and the editor of *Transforming Lives,* which uniquely included patients' commentaries about their psychoanalytic treatment. Recent interests include the status of the psychoanalytic profession and the nature of unresolved epistemological problems of psychoanalysis. Now retired, he is a member of the faculty of the Columbia University Psychoanalytic Clinic for Training and Research and the William Alanson White Society.

Helmut Thomä, M.D. was chair of the Department for Psychotherapy, Ulm University (1967–1989). In 1968 he founded the Ulm Psychoanalytic Institute and was its director until 1989. He is past president of the German Psychoanalytic Association (1968–1972). He is a member of and training analyst with the International Psychoanalytic Association and was the first Privatdozent for Psychoanalysis at a German university, working at Mitscherlich's Psychosomatic Hospital in Heidelberg. His monograph

Anorexia Nervosa (1961) was the first German psychoanalytic mono-graph translated into English (1968). Together with Horst Kächele, he was awarded the Sigmund Freud Prize of the City of Vienna in 2002 and the Mary S. Sigourney Award in 2004. In 2006, he was awarded a *doctor honoris causa* by the University of Leipzig.

Contributors

The Ulm Psychoanalytic Process Research Study Group

Cornelia Albani, M.D., Ph.D. is board certified in psychosomatic medicine and psychotherapy, and is assistant professor in the Department of Psychotherapy and Psychosomatic Medicine, University of Leipzig. Her research interests include psychotherapy process research and epidemiological studies on interpersonal guilt, religion, social anxiety, and depression.

Gerd Blaser, Ph.D. is a clinical psychologist and psychoanalyst in private practice, certified in cognitive behavioral therapy and psychoanalysis. His research interests include psychotherapy process research and epidemiological studies on interpersonal guilt, religion, social anxiety, and depression.

Anna Buchheim, Ph.D. is a clinical psychologist and worked as research fellow at the Department of Psychosomatic Medicine and Psychotherapy and has been a lecturer in medical psychology, psychosomatic medicine, and psychotherapy at Ulm University. She is now chair of clinical psychology at University of Innsbruck, Austria. Her research spans attachment in mother–infant interaction in psychotherapy and in borderline patients, as well as neuroimaging research on borderline patients and on depressive patients in psychoanalysis.

Michael Geyer, M.D., Ph.D. is director of the Department of Psychotherapy and Psychosomatic Medicine, University of Leipzig, and is board certified in psychosomatic medicine and psychotherapy as well as in psychiatry and neurology. His research interests include psychotherapy process research, psychosomatic epidemiology, and public health research.

Hans-Joachim Grünzig, Ph.D. is a clinical psychologist in private practic since 1985 and was a research fellow of the Ulm study group (1974–1985). His interests include psychotherapy process and computer-assisted text analysis.

Roderich Hohage, M.D., Ph.D. is a psychoanalyst in private practice. He was a fellow in experimental hematology at Ulm University (1969–1973) and deputy chief of the Department of Psychotherapy, Ulm University (1974–1991), as well as training and supervising analyst at the Ulm Psychoanalytic Institute (DPV, IPA).

Michael Hölzer, M.D., Ph.D. is director of the Sonnenberg Klinik, Stuttgart, a hospital for psychosomatic medicine and psychotherapy, and director of the SINOVA Clinics, an association of psychosomatic departments providing inpatient treatment for psychosomatically ill patients. He received psychoanalytic training at the Ulm Psychoanalytic Institute (DPV, IPA) and has done psychotherapy process research, particularly with respect to the affective aspects of psychotherapeutic verbalizations (i.e., the Affective Dictionary, Ulm).

Judith Humbel, Lic. Phil. is a clinical psychologist in the Outpatient Multidisciplinary Pain Management Program, Department of Rheumatology and Institute of Physical Medicine, University Hospital, Zurich.

Uwe Jacobs, Ph.D. is a clinical psychologist, is director of Survivors International, and has an independent psychotherapy practice in San Francisco, California. Research interests include psychotherapy process research and outcome studies in torture rehabilitation.

Juan Pablo Jiménez, M.D., Ph.D. is director of the Department of Psychiatry and Mental Health East, Faculty of Medicine, University of Chile, and is a training and supervising analyst for the Chilean Psychoanalytic Association. President of the Latin-American Psychoanalytic Federation (Fepal) (2006–2008), he has also been a research fellow, Alexander von Humboldt Foundation (1985–1986), scientific collaborator, Department of Psychotherapy, Ulm University (1987–1990), vice president, Latin-American chapter of the Society for Psychotherapy Research (1992–1994), member of the Research Advisory Board, International Psychoanalytic Association (1994–2007), and member of the faculty, research training program, International Psychoanalytic Association and University College, London (2007).

Erhard Mergenthaler, Ph.D. is a professor and Director of Informatics in Psychotherapy, Ulm University. President of the International Society for Psychotherapy Research (SPR), he is a consultant for psychotherapy projects for the research advisory board of the International Psychoanalytical

Association. His interests include psychotherapy process research, and his computer-assisted approaches for transcript analysis are standards in the field.

Lisbeth Neudert-Dreyer, Ph.D. is a clinical psychologist and psychoanalyst (DPV/IPA) in private practice, and has worked in the Department of Psychology, University of Marburg, and the Department of Psychotherapy, Ulm University. Her main emphasis is in process research in long-term psychotherapy and psychoanalytic single-case studies.

Friedemann Pfäfflin, M.D., Ph.D. is a professor and Director of Forensic Psychotherapy, Ulm University, and is a training and supervising analyst of the German Psychoanalytic Association (DPV/IPA). President of the International Association for the Treatment of Sexual Offenders (IATSO), he is also past president of the International Association for Forensic Psychotherapy (IAFP) and the Harry Benjamin International Gender Dysphoria Association (HBIGDA). His research interests include transsexualism, treatment of sexual offenders, forensic psychotherapy, and history of psychiatry during Nazi times.

Dan Pokorny, Ph.D. is a mathematician, psychotherapy researcher, and methodical consultant at Ulm University. His research interests include process research, text analysis, core conflictual relationship themes, verbalized emotions, guided affective imagery, and exploratory statistical procedures.

Nicola Scheytt, M.A. is a clinical psychologist and music therapist at University Clinic for Psychosomatic Medicine and Psychotherapy, Ulm, and is a training und supervising therapist in a number of associations for music therapy. She is also in private practice.

Reto Volkart, Ph.D. is a clinical psychologist and psychotherapist and is head of the Center for Psychotherapy in Zurich (ZEPT), Switzerland, where he teaches several postgraduate courses. His interests include psychotherapy research.

Preface

In this book we document our longstanding work concerning the subject of psychoanalytical single case research. Systematic and broadly conceived empirical studies of individual psychoanalytic cases are rare. Many publications advise conducting individual systematic studies, yet few provide an example of their own. Obviously this is easier said than done. In the early 1970s we familiarized ourselves with the state of theoretical and empirical psychoanalytic research. It was necessary to screen the methodically orientated works that at that time were still rare. This includes the epochmaking work of Gottschalk and Auerbach (1966) pointing to directions about how to proceed. The rich paper by Wallerstein and Sampson (1971) reinforced our decision to choose the single case research approach. A thorough study of the first edition of the *Handbook of Psychotherapy and Behaviour Change* by Bergin and Garfield (1971), containing Luborsky and Spence's (1971) evaluation of "quantitative research on psychoanalytic therapy" was helpful. These inputs led to our first reports concerning the field of psychoanalytic therapy research. At the beginning of our endeavor we received support by correspondence with Hans Strupp, Donald Spence, Lester Luborsky, and Hartvig Dahl. This brought us into contact with the newly founded Society for Psychotherapy Research (SPR), which with its yearly conferences became an increasingly important forum for scientific exchange. The first international conference about psychoanalytic process research was conducted in Ulm in 1985 with the support of the German Research Foundation, and took place prior to the Hamburg International Psychoanalytic Association (IPA)-Congress. This documented the fruitful exchange between the American psychoanalytic researchers and the German participants. The works presented by Bucci, Dahl, Gill, Luborsky, and others concerning the psychoanalytic treatment of Mrs. C, which was conducted by Dahl himself under the supervision of Arlow, could be compared with our own first studies of the treatment of Amalia X. Dahl (1988a) in his introduction to the report published three years later—

known by insiders as the "blue book"—characterizes the paradigmatic achievement of this conference as follows:

> This is a book about the future that we hope will arouse the curiosity of clinicians and point a direction for researchers. It marks the surprisingly rapid evolution of psychodynamic psychotherapy research from an applied towards a basic science. (p.vii)

The prognosis was corroborated insofar as psychoanalytic treatment research became a field that attracted surprisingly many psychoanalytically oriented colleagues worldwide. The days of questioning whether or not such extraclinical research on clinical material was necessary and doable was definitively past.

Following an introductory chapter to the main topic of the volume, "Psychoanalytical Therapy Process Research," two chapters were prepared to identify the salient issues for our work. Chapter 2, first published in 1973 in German and two years later in English, presents the meta-science controversies of the 1970s; as they are still relevant today, we have now updated this work with preliminary remarks. Chapter 3 traces the fate of single case reports in the clinical psychoanalytic research. In Chapter 4, our paradigmatic case, the patient Amalia X is introduced. A comprehensive overview, in the form of a longitudinal and cross-sectional portrayal of her psychoanalytical therapy, is provided. In Chapter 5, guided clinical judgment studies are presented, and Chapter 6 reports on our efforts to implement computer-based content analyses. The individual chapters of this volume mention the main authors and the co-authors of the original publications, which were often published in English. We revised all the manuscripts; we partially shortened the text and where it seemed necessary we updated it.

A final impetus to collect this work of the Ulm Psychoanalytic Process Research Study Group in a single volume was Hartvig Dahl's invitation of members of the Ulm group to the George Klein Forum in the framework of the Midwinter Meetings of the American Psychoanalytic Association in 1997. There the senior author, the treating analyst of the patient Amalia X, documented his deep involvement in the undertaking. Adding a third author from the United States, Joseph Schachter, enriched our own debates. The collection of material compiled in this volume should also be looked upon as an open invitation for further studies on the specimen case. The records and transcripts are available to any serious student of psychoanalysis.

This volume is dedicated to Ms. Amalia X. Her consent to the usage of the verbatim recordings enabled us to do this research. We also thank the German Research Foundation (DFG), which supported this work for many years. For the helpful suggestions provided by our friends and colleagues we are especially grateful.

The English translation has been performed by Hilda Spiegel (Chapter 2), Peter Luborsky (Chapters 2 and 3), and Justice Krampen (Chapters 1, 4, 5, 6, and 7). All materials were finally edited by Joseph Schachter.

Horst Kächele
Joseph Schachter
Helmut Thomä
Ulm and New York

Chapter 1

Psychoanalytic Therapy Process Research*

INTRODUCTION

The case for psychoanalytic research is not academic; it is imperative. Psychoanalysis worldwide is under stress, and especially traditional American psychoanalysis is confronted by a simmering crisis reflected in decreased status and prestige. Although the roots of these crises are manifold, unresolved disagreements about fundamental theoretical and clinical tenets have resulted in a fragmentation of psychoanalysis that contributes to this decline (Hauser, 2002). For example, starting around 1960, questions were raised about the reliability and validity of the concept of "psychoanalytic process." Numerous attempts to achieve a consensually agreed definition all failed. Vaughan, Spitzer, Davies, and Roose (1997) conclude from empirical studies that analysts cannot judge analytic process reliably and question whether it is a viable construct on its own. Process definitions have to be related to the outcome. Sigmund Freud (1912e, p. 114) implied this when he coined his famous inseparable bond thesis.

Dialogues repeatedly have failed to resolve the lack of consensual agreement regarding theoretical or clinical issues. Wallerstein (2002) concludes the following:

> We are without warrant ... to claim the greater heuristic usefulness or validity of anyone of our general theories over the others, other than by the indoctrination and allegiances built into us by the happenstance of our individual trainings, our differing personal dispositions and the explanatory predilections then carried over into our consulting rooms. (p. 1251)

---

* Horst Kächele, Joseph Schachter, and Helmut Thomä.

1

It is time, Gabbard and Westen (2003, p. 338, italics in original) urge, that "we attempt to move from arguing about the therapeutic action of psychoanalysis to *demonstrating and refining it.*" The best possibility for resolving these differences and for developing some consensus about the fundamental tenets of psychoanalysis rests with empirical research generating relevant data that can provide a basis for consensual agreement about fundamental psychoanalytic principles (Schachter, 2005b).

For many years the Ulm Psychoanalytic Process Research Study Group has implemented a program to examine the material bases of psychoanalytic therapy. We were and are convinced that only the careful exploration of the patient's interaction with the analyst can illustrate the central aspects of psychoanalytic treatment and enable an empirically driven theory of the process. In a panel discussion about psychoanalytic process research at an annual meeting of the German Psychoanalytic Association on October 11, 1968, in Ulm, Germany, the senior of this group, H. Thomä articulated the necessity of systematic examination as follows:

1. The psychoanalytic and the relevant psychosomatic research seems, as one can learn from literature, to move mainly in two directions that can simply be described as "process" and as "outcome" research. Process research mainly concerns the scientific evaluation of psychoanalytic treatments of single cases. However, in examinations that mainly deal with results of therapies, greater numbers of treated and nontreated cases are compared with one another. The two research directions overlap in many points because Freud's (1937a, p. 256) "beneficient results" of the therapy are dependent on the course of the psychoanalysis. The differentiation of process and outcome dates back to the Marienbad Congress 1936 and in particular to a lecture by E. Bibring (1937).
2. However, "one of the famous claims of analytical work is that research and treatment coincide" (Freud, 1912e, p. 114); in another place Freud (1927a, p. 256) speaks about a "precious encounter," an "inseparable bond between healing and research." But it should not be concluded *eo ipso* that treatment and research are identical. There is no assurance that the observation of the analyst and his theoretical conclusions drawn from observation are really reliable.
3. Process research is the most original field in psychoanalysis. The psychoanalytic process is determined by the events in the psychoanalytic situation. The specific technical psychoanalytic means is the interpretation. In the interpretation, technique and theory are combined. Process research serves for the completion of the technique and the validation of the theory (Thomä, 1968).

It has been argued that clinical case reports, especially Freud's, have had a greater influence on psychoanalytic theory and practice than findings generated by formal research. That influence, however, has had negative as well as positive consequences. A number of case-report-based theories and practices have proven to be erroneous, such as the conception of infantile omnipotence, the conception of female sexuality, and the belief that homosexuality was intrinsically psychopathological. Clearly, plausibility of the clinical implications of case reports is not a solid basis upon which conclusions can be drawn (Schachter & Kächele, 2007).

Wallerstein and Sampson (1971, p. 47) conclude that it was necessary to conduct formalized and systematized examinations of therapeutic process in psychoanalysis: "Our central conviction is that the informal case study, in spite of its forceful power of conviction, has certain realistic and obvious scientific limitations." Several observers attested the lack of reliability of clinical inferences (Schachter & Kächele, 2007). Pulver (1987a) demonstrates that analysts with different theoretical convictions vary widely in the analytic inferences they derive from case material, and Fosshage (1990) and Streeck (1994) replicate this finding. Spence (1992, p. 562) observes, "The clinician ... tends to listen to the clinical material with a favorite set of theoretical predispositions." And he concludes, "Interpretations in a clinical setting have an unfortunate tendency to reflect the therapist's expectation rather than the underlying facts of the matter" (ibid., p. 559). Masling and Cohen (1987, p. 65), citing several clinical examples, even draw the conclusion that all psychotherapies generate clinical evidence that support their theoretical positions and so can be understood as "instances of therapists systematically rewarding and extinguishing various client behaviors."

In addition to these limitations in the usefulness of clinical case reports, there are analysts who cite the extraordinary difficulties in empirical study of psychoanalytic case material and believe that the result of such study is likely to be of little value to psychoanalysis (Green, 2000) or may well be damaging (Perron, 2006). Many analysts criticize nonclinical analytic research, arguing that formal research destroys the uniqueness of individual patients.

Since in scientific terms there are serious limitations to the value of clinical case reports, progress in psychoanalysis should not rest solely on such reports. Clinical findings need to be tested by empirical research. Those critics fail to recognize that some sacrifice of the uniqueness of phenomena and individuals is necessary in order to conduct empirical studies. Krugman (2007) articulates this in the field of economics, explaining why the abstract conception of "economic man" is useful. It is easy, he notes, to make fun of such abstractions:

You might ask, why not represent people the way they really are? The answer is that abstraction, strategic simplification, is the only way we can impose some intellectual order on the complexity of economic life. And the assumption of rational behavior has been a particularly fruitful simplification. (p. 27)

Comparable abstractions are necessary to impose some intellectual order in the complexity of psychoanalytic treatment. Ever since Glover undertook a questionnaire study with British analysts (Glover & Brierley, 1940) interpretation was the first subject of manifold efforts to examine aspects of the treatment process in a formalized and clinical manner. Thomä and Houben (1967), picking up the long debate on interpretations as a central aspect in the analyst's technique, registered the patient's reactions in order to estimate the effects and the ensuing reactions on the former. In the course of these examinations the problems concerning the effectiveness of interpretations and the related problem of truth resurfaced again and again.

To systematically evaluate the impact of interpretations, Thomä and Houben (1967) followed Isaacs's (1939) suggestion and designed a report-schema. This demanded that the analyst write an hourly protocol and localize his interpretations theoretically, and, in addition, to state exactly the patient's reactions (for a precise description see Thomä & Kächele, 1994b, pp. 22–23). In the course of the examinations it became obvious that the appropriate validation can be obtained only by empirical process and outcome research. In agreement with many authors the Ulm study group decided to perform a series of process studies within the intensive model design that is adequate to meet—as Bucci (2007) spells it out—the characterization of psychoanalysis as the science of inner experience, conscious and unconscious, or one might say the science of psychological representations and processes. Psychoanalysis is not a science of behavior, and not neuroscience. In cognitive psychology as in psychoanalysis, one makes inferences from what is observed to inner experience, including conscious and unconscious experience. Scientifically, one doesn't access inner experience introspectively, that is, through one's own subjectivity (Bucci, personal communication).

The positive assessment of the formal single case study in which Wallerstein and Sampson (1971) aim at the reconciliation between clinical impressions and research was the critical methodological suggestion in developing their research strategy. If one follows their recommendation, the systematic single case study provides the intersection of clinical and scientific work.

Davison and Lazarus (1994) also comment positively about the possible advantage of an intensive case study:

• A case study can raise doubts about a generally accepted theory.

- A case study can be a valuable heuristic for following better controlled examinations.
- A case study allows the examination, even if not really controlled, of a seldom but important phenomenon.
- A case study provides the possibility for new principles and ideas to be tested in a new way.
- A case study can in certain circumstances allow enough experimental control of phenomena to provide scientifically acceptable information.
- A case study can supply meat for a theoretical skeleton.

In exploring these arguments, the case-study methodology was rediscovered also in academic psychology (Bromley, 1986). Furthermore, new methodological approaches and the growing appreciation of qualitative research (Frommer & Rennie, 2001) have produced in the meantime a lasting impact on social science in general and on the field of treatment research in particular (Hill & Lambert, 2004, p. 102). Today there is more emphasis on what kind of questions must be examined by which methodological approach in order to find interesting answers that enrich the field (Kächele, 1986). The purpose of these approaches is both "to do justice to the subjective factor in social sciences and to focus research efforts on the individual fate" (Leuzinger-Bohleber, 1995, p. 446).

RESEARCH IN CONTEMPORARY PSYCHOANALYSIS

The psychoanalytic culture differentiates between *research in psychoanalysis* and *research on psychoanalysis*. Scientific investigations in psychoanalysis originate in the therapeutic situation. In a rather optimistic stance it is assumed that the clinicians apply the psychoanalytic method in a critical vein and thus fulfill the requirement of scientific thinking.

The English language allows a play of words: Wallerstein (2001) distinguishes between *search* and *research*. Analysts are constantly "searching," but to come from search to research a certain degree of formalization and systematic categorization has to be applied. In the prevailing vignette-culture most psychoanalytic authors limit themselves to the description of transference and countertransference processes, thus leading to the rather extreme stance of subjectivism.

The prevailing representation of treatment reports is characterized by reference to essential psychoanalytic concepts. Research-minded analysts differ from clinicians who prefer to remain "on-line" (an expression introduced by Moser, 1991) that characterizes an analyst's stance in the evenly hovering attention in the clinical situation; it is in contrast to the objectifying "off-line" position of a clinician outside the consulting room or of a researcher. Both figures of speech grasp the pendulum from subjective experience to objectifying reflection within and outside the session. Already when writing session notes the analyst leaves the on-line position, and when case reports are published another basis of collegial and interdisciplinary discussions is reached.

Research in psychoanalysis thus refers to the "mother ground" (Schlesinger, 1974) of the therapeutic situation and always includes the analyst, his thinking, and his actions, which is not only reflected from the outside by himself but also by others. Therefore, the contrasting of *research in psychoanalysis* and *research on psychoanalysis* separates what belongs together (Perron, 2003). Both perspectives refer to intraclinical research (in contrast to extra- or nonclinical research). To raise clinical reports to the rank of single case studies detailed and reliable criteria have to be made explicit.

Nonclinical empirical psychoanalytic research has two large realms, independent from each other. The application to all topics of culture knows no boundaries; therefore, the interdisciplinary exchange with all humanities covers a wide field, and we are unable to cover it here (see Section 6 of the recent *Textbook of Psychoanalysis* [Person, Cooper, & Gabbard, 2005]). However, we will mention some points with regard to extraclinical, experimental research about psychoanalytic topics.

Although the experimental approach is the most appropriate method for examining hypotheses (Campbell, 1967), manipulation of the examined object is not possible in the clinical situation. Nonclinical studies examining the diverse aspects of basic psychoanalytic theory, though often largely unknown to clinicians, have attracted many experimental psychologists (Shulman, 1990). Quite extensive compilations and secondary analyses by well-meaning critics have been compiled (Fisher & Greenberg, 1977, 1996; Hilgard, 1952; Kächele, Ehlers, & Hölzer, 1991; Kline, 1981).

There is no reason to view the clinical situation as a deficient version of the experiment; a formerly popular way of expressing this was to say that the psychoanalytical treatment situation is a quasi-experimental event. Shakow (1960, p. 88) criticizes this view and prefers to speak about the psychoanalytical interview as a seminaturalistic approach. The proper methods of examination are therefore not experimental methods but are methods of the systematic, social-science-based analyses of material as Allport (1942) documents. The single case study can be handled with exactness and procedures that are suitable to the examined materials. Edelson (1988, p. 231ff) especially emphasizes in his book *Psychoanalysis—A Theory in Crisis* the possibilities of the single case research to surpass the heuristic discovery oriented perspective. Generally speaking, it is remarkable how many papers are published about problems of doing research and how few substantial reports about systematic studies performed are available.

CONCEPTUAL RESEARCH

Recently a new genre has been created for which Dreher (2000, 2005) has coined the expression *conceptual research*. It is fair to say that conceptual clarifications have constituted not a small bulk of analysts' efforts to come to grips with the ongoing change of terms and their referents (e.g., Compton, 1972; Pine, 2006). A recent overview concluded that "if IJP accurately reflects the international viewpoint, conceptual research is a central issue in current psychoanalytic research" (Leuzinger-Bohleber & Fischmann, 2006, p. 1361).

Concepts characterize the cosmos of psychoanalytic theory and its change. Therefore, the range of concepts and their relationship to clinical experience, their operationalization in the widest sense of the word, has been in the center of the psychoanalytic profession for a century. Written definitions attempted to determine what pychoanalysis was and is. One easily can consult using a conceptual dictionary—for example, the highly appreciated *Vocabulary of Psychoanalysis* by the French analysts Laplanche and Pontalis (1967), the American Psychiatric Association sponsored *A Glossary of Psychoanalytic Terms and Concepts* (Burnes, Moore, & Fine, 1968), Klumpner's (1992) *A Guide to the Language of Psychoanalysis*, or *The Dictionary of Kleinian Thought* (Hinshelwood, 1989). However, what psychoanalysts make out of these definitions in their practical works remains opaque. In our view pure conceptual research without empirical underpinnings remains sterile and may even hinder progress.

THE CONTEMPORARY VERSION OF FREUD'S INSEPARABLE BOND THESIS

The scientific study of single cases, not the clinical reports, constitutes in our view the *Contemporary Version of Freud's Inseparable Bond Thesis*. In this sense Freud's beneficial effect—the therapeutic success—represents a pragmatic criterion of truth. It requires the clinician to spell out his hypotheses on structure and dynamics and to look for *independent* criteria to refute or confirm these.

Clinical inferences from the material of a case history may be valuable sources of hypothesis development—which Blatt (2004, p. 4) beautifully argues recently by pointing out the importance of his two initial psychoanalytic cases for his later thinking about anaclitic and introjective types of depression—but are not of scientific value for hypothesis testing, largely because clinical inferences are diverse and notoriously unreliable. Clinical material from a case history is almost invariably viewed very differently by different analysts. A prominent scientist notes that it is ironic "that psychoanalytic authors attempt to employ clinical data for just about every purpose but the one for which they are most suitable—an evaluation and understanding of therapeutic change" (Eagle, 1984, p. 163). However, for the assessment to be scientific it must be based on reliable measurements.

A first striking example was provided by Lester Luborsky (1955), who, working together with Raymond Cattell, introduced P-Factor-Analysis for intraindividual repetitive measurements in understanding psychotherapeutic change (see also his reevaluation in Luborsky, 1995). Twenty years later the Penn Study Group (Graff & Luborsky, 1977) reported on the study of four analytic treatments. Each treating analyst filled out a checklist assessing transference (defined as material overtly or covertly related to the analyst) and resistance (the patient's associations are general, defensive, or oppositional). Results indicated that two patients with favorable therapeutic outcomes showed rising transference (as defined here) and diminishing resistance over the course of the treatment. The two patients with poorer therapeutic outcomes showed more parallel curves for transference and resistance; the patient with the poorest outcome showed a high resistance curve.

The work of the research group of Joseph Weiss and Harold Sampson from the Mount Zion Psychotherapy Research Group became well known. Their first study examined two competing theories concerning defense analysis in the case of Mrs. C (Sampson, Weiss, Mlodnosky, & Hause, 1972). In the following years they applied their newly developed concept of the Control-Mastery Theory to the same case (Weiss, Sampson, & The Mount Zion Psychotherapy Research Group, 1986) as well as to shorter therapies (Silberschatz, Curtis, & Nathans, 1989). The former examination utilized the completely tape-recorded psychoanalytic treatment created by Hartvig Dahl (New York). A journalist, J. Malcolm (1980), was successful in seducing the analyst-author to claim the authorship for this first "specimen hour" that Dahl was to publish as "Anonymous" (1988).

Meanwhile, a good number of psychoanalytic scientists who cooperated with Dahl could use this material of his "specimen case" (Bucci, 1988, 1997; Horowitz, 1977; Jones and Windholz, 1990; Spence, Dahl, & Jones, 1993; Spence, Mayes, & Dahl, 1994). The most recent use of the collected materials was presented by Ablon and Jones (2005, pp. 554–558), who identify one notion of psychoanalytic process in terms of Jones's Q-sort methodology: alas, their definition is a function of selecting a homogeneous group of traditional analyst raters. One might wonder what a psychoanalytic cross-cultural comparison study on the notion of an "ideal psychoanalytic process" would look like. In any case, process research focusing on individual cases are timely as reported by Joseph, Anderson, Bernard, Father, and Streich (2004), Waldron et al. (2004a, 2004b), Lingiardi, Shedler, and Gazillo (2006), Porcerelli, Dauphin, Ablon, and Leitman (2007), and Bucci and Maskit (2007).

Overviews on the methodology of single case studies have been presented by Kazdin (1982, 1994, 2003), Hilliard (1993), and Fonagy and Moran (1993). The latter summarized the topic succinctly:

> Individual case studies attempt to establish the relationship between intervention and other variables through repeated systematic observation and measurement.... The observation of variability across time within a single case combines a clinical interest to respond appropriately to changes within the patient, and a research interest to find support for a causal relationship between intervention and changes in variables of theoretical interest. The attention to repeated observations, more than any other single factor, permits knowledge to be drawn from the individual case and has the power to eliminate plausible alternative explanations. (p. 65)

COMPARISON OF SINGLE CASE
AND GROUP STUDIES*

Inappropriate use of statistical methods with single cases led to the view that single case studies were not applicable for clinical research:

> In the clinical field the opinion persisted for a long time that comparisons between groups of patients are the sine qua non of the statistical valid scientific clinical research and the single case study is attributed at best to the status of intuition and clinical insight which is not accessible for statistical tests and attempts for validations.... (This opinion) has unfortunately immortalized the by nature superficial methodology as the only scientific prototype in clinical research. (Bellak & Chassan, 1964, p. 23)

Practical reasons led to a rediscovery of the single case methodology, which utilized new theoretical and statistical evaluations (Bortz & Döring, 1995). The single case study intensively examines individual patients in the psychoanalytical situation:

> The long-term commitment for therapy between patient and therapist and the regularity of the scheduled psychotherapeutic sessions, whether they be on a weekly, semi-weekly, or daily basis, provide an ideal opportunity for the collection of relatively large quantities of

---

* We are grateful to Dr. Pokorny for help with this part.

> data for the testing of hypotheses within one or another framework
> of psychoanalytic theory. (Chassan, 1979, p. 258)

In theoretical terms the single case study can be described as an "intensive model" in comparison with use of large samples that constitute an "extensive model" (Chassan, 1979). A prerequisite for the meaningful examination of the single case is that the examined feature varies over time, within the patient. The variable is observed under various conditions. Marginal conditions such as age, sex, personality, and previous experience of the patient remain relatively constant and are therefore better controlled than in a group sample. On the other hand, through intensive scrutiny of the case the marginal conditions are well known to the investigator, who can choose to include them in the examination. Chassan (1979) emphasizes that study of the single case can be arranged dynamically; the design of the study can be changed, side effects can be considered, and additional questions introduced, which in large samples requires considerable expenditure.

When studying group samples, even when a significant result is obtained, nothing can be said about the contribution of the individual patient and nothing about the variation in the examined variable of the individual patients. This limits the implications of any finding for enhancing treatment. As claims about whole populations are always based on limited samples, generalization of findings from group studies is limited. Furthermore, the information from group studies does not reveal individual differences, which is not the case with the single case study. Group studies, more than individual case studies, are subject to the complication of outliers, individuals whose data points fall far outside the distribution of members of the group. Judgment about how to deal with outliers is arbitrary and can profoundly influence the results for the group.

Chassan (1979) radically argues that if one specifies the variable in the single case study, the results can be generalized to a population with the same variable. The possibility to generalize is better in the single case because the variables are better known. The representativeness of findings derived from a sample depends on the randomness of selection of the examined groups, which in clinical research often is not assessed. Further, often the selection criteria for the sample are included in the examination, so that no population remains for reference. By case comparison and case contrasting the findings from an individual case can be extended to a population; however, one has to work step by step to avoid overgeneralization.

Our purpose is to warrant the utility of empirical single case research, not to assert that studies of population samples are of no value. Although the literature has had proponents of individual studies and proponents of group studies, there is no reason to consider these two approaches to be in conflict. They are complementary. Individual researchers may have a predilection for one or the other, but to assert that one is better in general than the other is unnecessary and seems unfounded. There is a clear need for a botanical phase in furthering the field; therefore, the call "back to single case research" by prominent scholar in the field Klaus Grawe (1988) was timely. The ultimate test is the demonstration by each approach of the production of findings that enhance psychoanalytic theory and practice. Perhaps one approach may be more effective with certain classes of variables and the other approach more productive with other classes of variables. To paraphrase Chairman Mao Zedong's aphorism, let both approaches bloom. Unlike by Mao, this is an honestly intended proposal.

The center of several methodological discussions about the problems of single case studies concerns the question of whether it is possible to draw valid conclusions from "one case" or from "$N = 1$" findings for the whole population. One has to note that the aims of a mathematically statistical analysis are considerably more modest and that the term *case* takes on quite a different meaning in the clinical and statistical context. In a psychotherapeutic single case study one often works with a sample of several sessions that are to be viewed as an observation of statistical cases. Through the sequence of the sessions the statistical samples carry the untoward dependence of the observed cases. The variable *time*, made operational, for example, by the date or the session number, offers at the same time the chance to control statistically this dependence (Grünzig, 1988). The population to which one refers by the help of statistical techniques is built through the entire amount of all sessions with the examined person (of the clinical case) during the therapy or the therapy phase. The significance level of the applied statistical tests informs us of the safety by which the conclusions can be drawn. The total sample is thereby represented through the examined object—that is, through the examined patient–therapist–couple.

Even in the case in which all sessions of the therapy are examined—and hence the sample coincides with the population—the view of the significance level reached gains a sound meaning, although another from a traditional one. It connotes rather relevance than significance of a finding. For a human observer it is generally difficult to differentiate between the lawful and the random and particularly to differentiate between the true patterns in the statistical data and random ones. Such patterns can represent changes in the time or differences between various session settings or circumstances. The human mind is trained to find sense even within the complex—or chaotic—structures. Who has failed to recognize humans, animals, or plants while observing white clouds in the sky? Who can be sure that observed amazing patterns in data are really meaningful? Fortunately, statistical procedures can give valuable help in this differentiation. Their technical construction is based on recognizing the nonrandomness in the observed structures. In the case *sample = population*, the formally significant result alerts the researcher: This result seems to be interesting;

it likely did not arise randomly and may be relevant to the investigated psychoanalytical process.

Part of the statistical results of a single case study presents the question of whether this is transferable to other clinical cases. This principally possible and desirable generalization is however no longer of mathematical statistical nature. The rumor that Freud's recordings of his own dreams grew to be the basis of psychoanalysis became a historical example in the well-regarded textbook of research methods for social scientists by Bortz and Döring (1995, p. 299).

The scope of the single case study can be characterized as follows:

> In a single case study a unit of examination is precisely investigated and described in which observational methods frequently play an important role. The qualitative single case observation helps in answering questions concerning individual processes and courses. Therefore it is very important in the clinical area to exactly observe the development of a patient during psychotherapy with the purpose of drawing conclusions about the success of the intervention. (Bortz & Döring, 1995, p. 298)

The case-specific and nontransferable part of the results possesses a complementary meaning. The group-orientated research namely focuses on the property that is common to most of the individuals of the examined population. The unique human phenomena constituting his individuality thereby fall, for example, on a common ground that is termed the *nonexplained variance of error*. To investigate and to appreciate this dimension of the unique and the individual is a task for which the single case study is especially qualified (Messer, 2007; Messer & McCann, 2005).

THE PRO AND CONTRA OF TAPE RECORDINGS

Namely it is an advantage for the clinical discussion if an analyst later on gives detailed information about how he feels and thinks during a session and records this in a written protocol; this also allows other colleagues to develop the possibility of alternative views. However, the systematic weakness of such reports was repeatedly noticed. The most recent statement about this issue puts that matter succinctly:

> Disagreements about the meaning of case material are commonplace in clinical work and constitute important grounds for criticism regarding the scientific status of psychoanalytic methods for acquiring knowledge. A particular problem is that clinical observers

may vary a great deal in the concepts they use in their descriptive language. Observers of the same case material may not arrive at the same conclusions; indeed, they may not even consider the same dimensions. This issue of handling differences in inference or judgment among clinical experts is particularly important since there are alternative theoretical models in psychoanalysis. (Ablon & Jones, 2005, p. 543)

The weaknesses in studies that are supported by nonformalized treatment protocols are by now sufficiently known. Spence (1986) shows that analytical narratives are often described on the basis of covert psychodynamic assumptions. In addition, it is very often impossible to extract the contribution of the analyst; generally only a few interpretations are communicated selectively. It is not possible to find out what has been omitted or reproduced differently. For scientific examinations it is not sufficient to rely on the memory of the analyst only—a viewpoint that should generate recorded evidence in analysts. Therefore, through the introduction of the tape recording in the psychoanalytical situation a new research paradigm was created. Providing a personal view Merton Gill (1994, p. 152) makes a strong plea that "process research should be done with some kind of recording of the original exchange. I believe that transcripts of audio recordings will suffice."

This device is no longer controversial in the scientific community of research-orientated psychoanalysts (Thomä & Kächele, 2004b, p. 26ff). Certainly one must agree with Colby and Stoller (1988, p. 42) that a transcript is "not a report about what really happened, but only a report of what has been recorded." Our answer to this warning limitation could only be to find out which picture of the "true" psychoanalytical progress can be reconstructed on the basis of transcripts. The main progress this tool provides is that it allows independent observers—may they be analysts or scientists of other disciplines—to make independent findings about what happens in the treatment room. From the outset it has been recognized that of the two participants, "the therapist is more chronically disturbed by the procedure. Unlike the patient he does not think of the situation as one in which exposure of himself is an intrinsic and necessary evil" (Knapp, Mushatt, & Nemetz, 1966, p. 404).

The advantage, however, is that a multitude of social scientific methods for the study of the psychoanalytical process can be applied. It is in this vein that Fonagy (2002) recommends the following:

Imaginative studies making use of the advances in recording and coding techniques and particularly phonetic and linguistic speech analysis could undoubtedly advance our understanding of the psychoanalytic process (Fónagy and Fonagy 1995). To ban such procedures outright is to tie our hands behind our back in competing with other psychotherapeutic procedures. To me the issue of recording depends strongly on the research question asked. (p. 23)

We certainly agree that one has to keep the perspective that it is one of many windows on the process; again, the question will be which kind of findings materialize from that particular window.

TESTING OF PROCESS MODELS

Beyond the basic aim of the Ulm group's research work to generate a self-sufficient access to the in vivo material of psychoanalytical treatments, the task was to examine aspects of the clinical psychoanalytical theory. In our view this entails finding out how analysts transform their thinking into the therapeutic situation. We must be able to provide a systematic description of what analysts say and feel and which role the patients play in this dialogue. For this the tape recordings provide a sufficiently good enough basis; more extravagant recording possibilities are certainly viable but for such questions are not compellingly necessary.*

First of all, one has to discuss many theoretical and methodological questions in view of the extra- or intraclinical testing of clinical hypotheses (Chapter 2 in this volume). In spite of many difficulties we have become convinced that many characteristic concepts of clinical psychoanalysis relate to areas that manifest themselves in the verbal mode. Although unconscious processes can be very well examined in experimental arrangements and have been examined diversely (Shevrin, 2000, 2005), the Ulm group examined natural nonexperimental material of psychoanalytical sessions. We basically make the assumption that in the course of treatments the data are produced that support or refute clinical assumptions (Hanly, 1992). Therefore, we decided to examine properly recorded psychoanalytical treatments.

Process models of a psychoanalytic treatment are not theoretical, abstract matters; they are factually more or less part of the day-to-day work of the psychoanalyst. These processual models are handed down from one generation of analysts to the next; they entail, often only in metaphoric expressions, unexpressed theories. Sandler (1983, p. 43) rightfully demands that the private dimension of these concepts should be explored.

---

* Video recordings as they are extensively used by Krause (1988; 1989) for face-to-face therapy are not yet convincing for couch analyses. The reason lies in the minimal activity in the face of the resting patient (oral communication F. Pfäfflin).

In the first volume of the Ulm textbook Thomä and Kächele (1994a, Ch. 9.3) illustrate a few common models of process; they sketch out their model of process, which is based on the *focus concept*. By a focus they mean the centrally created interaction topic of therapeutic work that is the result of the material of the patient and the understanding of the analyst. Since single focus points hypothetically remain connected through a central conflict with one another, this process model can be applied for shorter as well as for longer treatment. Beyond this, it is compatible with various theoretical conceptions. They conclude, "We conceptualize, therefore, psychoanalytic therapy as a continued, timely, not limited focal therapy with changing focus" (ibid., p. 347).

This concept of Ulm's model of process concerning the course of psychoanalytic treatment was the result of assimilating the findings of the developing field of systematic therapy research (Luborsky & Spence 1971, 1978). More than ever we are convinced that psychoanalytic process research must ignore the subjective position in which all theoretical approaches are regarded as equal in therapeutic potency. We think this conclusion by Pulver (1987c, p. 289) is premature. Clinical psychoanalysis must be freed from a "narrative self-misunderstanding"—to paraphrase Habermas's (1971a, Chapter 2, this volume) verdict regarding Freud's scientist self-misunderstanding—and become a science that works on therapeutic grounds with empirical methods (Kächele, 1990).

This goal requires descriptive examinations of the therapeutic interaction as well as examinations of the analyst's (Meyer, 1988) and the patient's inner thoughts and feelings, including specifically the process of internalizing the therapeutic experience as it is recorded in the intersession questionnaire (Arnold, Farber, & Geller, 2004; Orlinsky & Geller, 1993). Fundamental for this are studies of how unconscious fantasies are expressed both verbally and nonverbally (Krause & Lütolf, 1988; Krause, Steimer-Krause, & Ulrich, 1992). We see the necessity of thorough and reliable description as a basis of theoretical generalization and as a precondition of etiological reconstruction.

Examining the interactive foundation of the course of treatment not only involves our reacting differently to the same material but also includes analysts being personally touched by the patient's material. Expressed in clinical terms, we often find that the countertransference precedes the transference. In the language of research, one would say that the cognitive-affective conception of the analyst provides the semantic and pragmatic domain that the patient can use. The actual degree of an analyst's involvement can first be identified through tape recordings (Bouchard, Normandin, & Seguin, 1995). If an analyst hands over a transcript of a session to a colleague, it is amazing how many of the analyst's own problems become evident because the transcript exposes easily how much has evaded his self-evaluation. Schachter and Kächele (2007) concur with Renik's (1998, 2004) assertion that many elements of the analyst's subjectivity are unconscious at the moment of interaction and therefore can only be understood retrospectively. Further, this retrospective understanding becomes accessible only through the analyst's limited and restricted self-analysis or through consultation (Renik, 1998, 2004). For the analyst there is a significant discrepancy between his own professional ideal and his daily, routine performance. Kubie (1958) was the first to point out this; more recently, Fonagy (2005) speaks in the same vein.

Dahl, Rubinstein, & Teller (1978) demonstrates that analysts were selective in their perceptions of patient material and that attempts at free floating attention provide only limited protection from the effect of the analyst's expectation structures. Moreover, it can even promote unconscious effects concerning role expectations (Sandler, 1976). These various references on the problems of the development of the analyst's judgment and the creation of evidence substantiate the bipersonal foundation of the psychoanalytic situation in which valid descriptions versus fantasized descriptions are difficult to distinguish; they must be understood as constructions in a social realm (Gergen, 1985; Gill, 1994).

Inner psychic conflicts are expressed at least in part in the patient–analyst interaction, and they are, therefore, a function of the dyadic process. Its form is unique for every therapeutic dyad; each psychoanalytic treatment constitutes a singular history. However, many process models do not do justice to this historic uniqueness. Tolstoy (1996 [1868]) characterizes this uniqueness in literary style:

> They could not know the disease Natasha was suffering from, as no disease suffered by a live man can be known, for every living person has his own peculiarities and always has his own peculiar, personal, novel, complicated disease, unknown to medicine.... This simple thought could not occur to the doctors ... because the business of their lives was to cure, and they received money for it and spent the best years of their lives on that business. But, above all, that thought was kept out of their minds by the fact that they saw they were really useful, as in fact they were to the whole Rostov family.... The doctors were of use to Natasha because they kissed and rubbed her bump [like a child's soreness], assuring her that it would soon pass if only the coachman went to the chemists in the Arbaty and got a powder and some pills in a pretty box for a ruble and seventy kopecs, and if she took those powders in boiled water at intervals of precisely two hours, neither more nor less. (pp. 582–583)

Luyten, Blatt, and Corveleyn (2006) disagree about the importance of uniqueness, maintaining the following:

> Psychoanalysis is not (or at least is not only) a science of purely individual, idiosyncratic thought, affect and behavior, but rather studies regularities that can be observed across human beings.... Although every patient has his or her own "idiosyncrative narrative," any clinician will recognize regularities or "master narratives" in the particular story and dynamics of a patient. To deny this, and to act as if we approach each new patient as a tabula rasa, would be naïve. (p. 581)

They conceive that these regularities or master narratives arise intrinsically and independently from the patient's mind, not shaped by or influenced by the analyst, an immaculate creation. They fail to consider how the analyst's expectations of these master narratives may influence their presentation in the clincial context. This influence may explain why analysts are so rarely surprised by the shape and content of these master narratives. As we quoted earlier, Masling and Cohen (1987, p. 65) conclude that all psychotherapies generate clinical evidence that suppport their theoretical position by "systematically" rewarding and extinguishing various client behaviors. This uniqueness is confirmed by Luyten et al. (2006), however, citing the Ablon and Jones (2005, p. 592) Psychotherapy Process Q-Set study, which "revealed unique treatment processes in each [of two] case."

We acknowledge that diagnostic characteristics—one form of regularity across individuals—are associated with treatment responses (Blatt & Sharar, 2004). However, we are a long way from being able to parcel out the variance in treatment behavior between individual and group characteristics of the patient. It seems premature to dismiss the importance of the patient's uniqueness as naïve.

The range of conceptualizations can be illustrated by Freud's model of the treatment process. His comparison with the chess game (Freud, 1913c, p. 123) clarifies that rules of a game give rise to an infinite variety of moves. This influences the potential paths of the interactions that exist independently of each dyad's special circumstances. Chess is, after all, played all over the world by the same rules. Furthermore, there are strategies and tactics that can be useful in different phases of the game, such as the opening or end phase. This varies according to the individual technique of each player and influences the dyadic interactions in which the players gauge the expected strengths and weaknesses of each other. Freud wanted the rules of treatment to be the same for all patients so that psychoanalytic treatment would be regarded as a scientific enterprise (Schachter & Kächele, 2007). But chess is an inappropriate metaphor for psychoanalytic treatment. The goal of chess is defined and is simple and unitary; the goals of psychoanalytic treatment are not defined, should be mutually developed by patient and analyst, and are complex and multiple. Given the uniqueness of each analytic dyad it is to be expected that optimal methods (i.e., rules) would be unique. In addition, although it is controversial, some psychoanalytic groups are essaying modifications in the fundamental rules of the game (ibid.).

In psychoanalysis is there something like a fixed set of rules independent from the unique dyad? In chess it is easy to determine which moves conform to the rules and which break the rules; in psychoanalysis such differentiations are difficult (Thomä & Kächele, 1994a, p. 215). Many psychoanalysts still believe that the rules in the psychoanalytic situation can be determined regardless of the interactions in a particular dyad. Freud's (1913c) conception of psychoanalytic treatment describes how the transference neurosis develops independently of the analyst's behavior:

> He introduces a process of the disintegration of the existing repression; he can supervise, promote, remove obstacles and certainly also ruin much about it. In all, however, the process, once introduced, goes along its own way and neither lets itself be told the direction nor the sequence of the points it affects. (p. 130)

We find much ambiguity in Freud's assertion. Freud hoped to formulate technical rules that were as close as possible to an experimental ideal. Many analysts tried to maintain Freud's ideal, but that has not been possible (de Swaan, 1980). It was not ever and is not possible for the analyst to be a nonhuman, neutral entity who has no impact on the patient–analyst interactions, although for a long time this was the central utopian fantasy of psychoanalysts. We don't find useful the assumption that every analytic treatment runs in linear (developmental) phases from early to late as some process models imply. Instead of simple linearity, we conceive of a sequence of foci resulting from a bargaining process between the needs and wishes of the patients and the analyst's choice of interventions: This real issue is "what works at what time with what analyst" (Blatt & Sharar, 2004).

OUR METHODOLOGICAL APPROACH

The goal of the studies presented in this volume was to establish ways to systematically describe long-term psychoanalytic processes in various dimensions and to use the descriptive data obtained to examine process hypotheses. This entails the generation of general process hypotheses as well as the specification of single case process assumptions. It should go beyond general clinical ideas as to how a psychoanalytic process should unfold and specify for each patient what kind of material has to be worked on in order to achieve change in various dimensions of specified theoretical relevance in each particular case—be it structural properties or symptomatic (verbal) behavior.

Our approach did not include the recording of external measures in order to limit the intrusions on the clinical process (Kächele, 1988). Our methodological conception—inspired by Sargent's (1961) conception—consists of a four level-approach; on each level different material involving different levels of conceptualization is worked on:

A level: Clinical case study
B level: Systematic clinical descriptions
C level: Guided clinical judgment procedures
D level: Computer-assisted text analysis

This multilevel approach reflects our understanding that the tension between clinical meaningfulness and objectification cannot be creatively solved by using one approach only. A fairly similar approach has recently been detailed by Freedman, Lasky, and Hurvich (2003) mapping "two pathways toward knowing psychoanalytic process" that concatenates essentially clinical procedures with methods generating external validity.

For the A level we have provided typical examples on the patient Amalia X in the second volume of our textbook (Thomä & Kächele, 1994b).

For the B level we have exemplified our understanding of what constitutes a systematic clinical description in Chapter 4. In Chapter 5.1 the treating analyst contributes to this level by adding his advice on how to advance *comparative psychoanalysis,* illustrating this by excerpts from two significant sessions.

For the C level, clinical descriptions performed by two or more observers maintain the nature of the data on a qualitative level. In psychoanalysis the step from transforming the rich qualitative though unsystematic knowledge into quantitative assertions has barely begun. The tool to perform this transformation consists in a simple representation of a dimensional aspect of the concept under study on a scale. A scale is an elaborate version of the primordial "yes" or "no" distinction that marks the beginning of any measurement operation (Knapp et al., 1975). Luborsky (1984) aptly calls these operations "guided clinical judgment procedures," which catch the process of narrowing down the clinicians' capacity of recording complex data and thereby enable reliability of observations. On this level of our research approach various studies were performed.

The D level in our research model, text analysis, introduces the methodology of computer-based text analysis as tool. The use of the computer has developed from content analysis to text analysis, a process that has been described in detail elsewhere (Kächele & Mergenthaler, 1983, 1984; Mergenthaler & Kächele, 1988, 1993). Other linguistic methods also are placed on this level.

CONCLUSION

Psychoanalytical therapy research is still a stepchild of our profession; the number of those who seriously occupy themselves with this is not great. It is bound to scientific institutions since only there is the infrastructure that makes its implementation possible. Today its emphasis lies in the comprehensive comparative evaluation of various forms of psychoanalytical therapy as well as in the microprocess analysis of psychoanalytical action. A stringent empirical demarcation of "proper psychoanalysis" from other psychoanalytical treatments has not been demonstrated. Besides the existing variance within what is internationally designated as psychoanalysis, there exists great variability of the person-bound psychoanalytical technique that is implemented in bipersonal interaction structures (Ablon & Jones, 2005, 564ff.; Czogalik & Russell, 1995). The number of potential interaction structures is huge; the various combinations of patients and analysts provide for a psychoanalytic variability that only artificially can be divided into neat categories (Fonagy, Jones et al., 2002). It may be more helpful to identify essential dimensions of psychoanalytical therapeutic action and to find out, at each time for and with the patient, what mixture and which doses are good for him.

The individual psychoanalyst is called on to determine through careful, methodological and sophisticated case studies whether his intervention can be portrayed as well founded. Critical clinicians are then on their way to provide their contribution to making psychoanalytic therapy objective. Clinically based process-outcome research of single cases does not destroy the science, as Freud feared—on the contrary.

Chapter 2

Problems of Metascience and Methodology in Clinical Psychoanalytic Research[*][†]

ADDITIONAL REMARKS SOME 30 YEARS LATER

On re-reading this now more than 30-year-old paper, we are pleased to note that it has remained current and has received significant attention, as for example in Rubovits-Seitz' (1998) substantial work *Depth-Psychological Understanding: The Methodologic Grounding of Clinical Interpretation*. Such studies from years past have been of vital help in clarifying our position as clinicians and researchers. The following argument of John Wisdom (1970), a philosopher close to the Kleinian school, is one we have taken to heart:

> It seems clear that a clinician cannot handle research into clinical hypothesis without having his area demarcated from the rest. More importantly, a psychoanalyst who wishes to test his theories empirically … cannot begin his work, until the morass of theory, ontology, and *Weltanschauung* has been "processed" by philosophy of science. (pp. 360–361)

Without being aware of it, therapeutically successful clinicians are continually testing—in the broadest sense of the word—their theories. The problems of empirical therapy research on the single case are commonly underestimated. Hypothetically assumed causal connections between symptoms and their unconscious causes follow statistical probabilities and therefore cannot be deduced from scientific laws. This is one of the reasons why the Hempel-Oppenheim (1953) schema on the parity of post-

---

[*] Helmut Thomä and Horst Kächele.

[†] Preparation of this paper was aided by the *Deutsche Forschungsgemeinschaft* (German Research Foundation). This paper was originally published in 1973 in *Psyche* 27, pp. 205–236, 309–355. The English translation, by Hilda Spiegel, was published in 1975 in *Annual of Psychoanalysis* 3, pp. 49–119.

diction and prediction is not applicable to the human sciences (see section "Description, Explanation and Prognosis in Psychoanalysis"). This was pointed out already by the mathematician von Mises (1939; engl. 1951), with whose work we were not yet familiar in 1973: "it seems justified to point out that the totality of the observations in this field seems to correspond more to the assumption of a statistical than of a strictly causal correlation" (p. 238).

In this sense we were and remain empiricists and "idiographic nomotheticists" in Freud's tradition. In order to avoid misunderstanding, this paradoxical formulation requires some explanation. First, it must be emphasized that psychoanalysts are not lawgivers. The psychoanalytic method cannot be based on laws even if it is true, as Fonagy (2003) believes, that "facing the logical weaknesses of our position, we have tended to raise the status of 'clinical theories' to laws" (ibid., p. 19). It is misleading to deduce the behavior and experience of our patients from pseudo-laws. Freud discovered complex probabilistic explanatory schemas, knowledge of which deepens and enriches our understanding of psychopathology as a whole.

The probability that similar diseases will take similar courses makes it possible to establish a typology. Still, following the principle of trial and error, the single case lies at the center of an ongoing research process. Initially one can only base oneself on uncertain diagnostic and prognostic assumptions, and a degree of uncertainty always remains. With increasing life experience and specialized analytic knowledge, probabilistic assumptions made in the course of an analytic treatment gain in reliability and certainty. In this limited sense we regard ourselves as "nomotheticists of the single case" in our striving to find typical regularities given like cases. Psychoanalysis has made an essential contribution to overcoming the historical opposition of understanding and explanation in the human sciences.

To fully present our current position we must first comment on the work of Ricoeur (1970). It was only quite recently that we recognized the overwhelmingly powerful influence that Ricoeur has had on many adherents of French psychoanalysis. To our mind, the controversies between Green (2000) and Stern (2000) and Green (2005) and Wallerstein (2005a, 2005b) would remain incomprehensible without an awareness of Ricoeur's influence. Green "maintain[s] that as yet there is no serious study of Freudian thought by psychoanalysts. We had to wait for Ricoeur, a philosopher and a non-psychoanalyst to read such a work" (2005, p. 631).

Clearly Green considers Ricoeur's reading of Freud's *oeuvre* to be the only legitimate one. We share the view of Welsen (1987) that in its content Ricoeur's "reading of Freud" is borne by the thesis that psychoanalysis is an intertwining of energetics and hermeneutics; like a human science it reveals the meaning of psychic phenomena, while like a natural science it explains these by reducing them to conflicts of psychic forces. In this sense

Ricoeur asserts that " ... Freud's writings present themselves as a mixed ... discourse, which at times states conflicts of force subject to an energetics, at times relations of meaning subject to a hermeneutics" (Ricoeur, 1970, p. 65). Ricoeur attempts to prove that the dichotomy of energetics and hermeneutics dominates Freud's entire *oeuvre*—from the "Project for a Scientific Psychology" (1895) right to the "Outline of Psychoanalysis" (1940a). Thus Ricoeur's "energetics" contains essentially the economic aspect of metapsychology. This results in an intimate entanglement, a closed circle in fact, because the interpretation of latent, unconscious meaning is linked with metapsychological energy displacements. Ricoeur's failure to pose critical questions either regarding metapsychological energetics or the interpretation of meaningful connections results in the downright research-hostile position of many French psychoanalysts influenced by him (Perron, 2006). Research always begins with critical questions that arise out of everyday professional practice. Analysts work as therapists. For this reason, differing attitudes have great repercussions on the therapeutic process. In this connection there seem to be commonalities between Ricoeur and Lacan, to which Welsen (1988) has pointed: "Both Lacan and Ricoeur fail to know Freud in his own self-understanding, which is indebted in no way to linguistics or hermeneutics but to the natural scientific tradition of the 19th century" (p. 308). Freud saw in metapsychology "the consummation of psycho-analytic research" (1915e, p. 181). On the other hand Freud could not avoid a monistic utopia and even expected that as biology progressed, psychoanalytic hypotheses would one day be "blow[n] away" and replaced by physiological and chemical terms (Freud, 1920g, p. 60). In sum, it can be said that Ricoeur's hermeneutics is intimately bound up with economic assumptions without his having sufficiently come to terms with Habermas' (1971a) verdict on Freud's "scientistic self-misunderstanding."

What we as research-oriented clinicians criticize in particular are Ricoeur's erroneous judgments regarding the scientific position of psychoanalysis as therapy. The fundamental flaw in Ricoeur's argumentation is that he bases himself on a behaviorism that has now become obsolete even in modern behavioral therapy, a behaviorism that reduced psychology as a whole to the observable stimulus-response schema. This enables him to set up the thesis that psychoanalysis is neither a factual nor an observational science. Thus even a modified or revised form of operationalism, upon which the publications of Ellis (1956), Frenkel-Brunswik (1954) and Madison (1961) were based, can be designated by him as downright treasonous to the essential core of psychoanalysis. Many of Ricoeur's arguments, which form the basis for his strict separation of observed facts and their "meaning," coincide with the death of a primitive behaviorism. With the "cognitive turn" in behavior therapy came an acknowledgment of introspection and the problem of the "psyche of the other." Since then this "turn" has moved beyond the point of lip service and there has been a further rapprochement between the cognitive sciences and psychoanalysis (Bucci, 1997a). Ricoeur proceeded from a behaviorism that regarded the psyche as a "black box."

On one point we can agree with Ricoeur: analysts do not operate on the plane of behavioristic axioms, nor do they accept the methodology so constituted. They are concerned with observation and interpretation of the probability of certain reactions based on unconscious conditions which determine how a stimulus receives its meaning. But in our estimation all psychoanalytic statements are at some point connected with observable facts, among which we also count verbally communicable experience. To this extent we concur with Ricoeur's (1970) opinion:

> If we grant that the analytic situation as such is irreducible to a description of observables, the question of the validity of psychoanalytic assertions must be reexamined in a context distinct from a naturalistic science of facts ... [N]o art of interpreting would be possible if there were no similarities between cases and if it were impossible to discern types among these similarities. (pp. 373–374)

The insight that observation statements are theory-dependent means that no sharp dichotomy can be made between observation language and theory language without rendering distinctions impossible. In psychoanalysis as in everyday life, descriptions are made of phenomena that exist in a context. It is the context that changes with different points of view. With an altered perspective, different aspects of the phenomena also become visible. The more one distances oneself from the observable phenomena in depth-hermeneutics, the more difficult it becomes to justify interpretations. The associated methodological difficulties were pointed out by the above-mentioned British philosopher:

> [T]he unconscious is more like a root of a tree, and however much you develop the root into actual shoots, it can never be identified with the sum of the shoots that break through the soil. The unconscious always has more potential and is more than its manifestations. Its scientific status is like those high-level concepts in physics which are *never* open to checking by direct observation. (Wisdom, 1984, p. 315; italics in original)

Ricoeur (1970) raised a number of questions in the assumption that their empirical resolution was beyond the power of psychoanalysis:

> However, on what conditions is an interpretation valid? Is it valid because it is coherent, because it is accepted by the patient, because

it improves the condition of the patient? But a given interpretation must first be characterized by objectivity; this means that a number of independent inquirers have access to the same data obtained under carefully standardized circumstances. Next, there must be some objective procedures to decide between rival interpretations. Further, the interpretation must lead to verifiable predictions. But, psychoanalysis is not in a position to meet these requirements: its data are enmeshed in the individual relationship of the analyst to the analysand; one cannot dispel the suspicion that interpretations are forced upon the data by the interpreter, for want of a comparative procedure and statistical investigation. Finally, the allegations of psychoanalysts concerning the effectiveness of therapy do not satisfy minimum rules of verification; since the percentages of improvement cannot be strictly established or even defined by some kind of "before and after" study, the therapeutic effectiveness of psychoanalysis cannot be compared with that of some other method of treatment, or even with the ratio of spontaneous cures. For these reasons, the criterion of therapeutic success is unusable. (pp. 346–347)

In contrast to this catalogue of allegedly unanswerable questions, a bit further on one encounters a series of requirements set by Ricoeur which he himself appears to regard as satisfiable:

It is perfectly legitimate, therefore, to require the analyst to compare his percentage of improvements with the ratios obtained by different methods, or even with the ratio of spontaneous improvement. But it should be realized that one is at the same time requiring that a "historical type" be transposed into a "natural species"; in doing this, one forgets that a type is constituted on the basis of a 'case history' and by means of an interpretation that in each instance arises in an original analytic situation. Again, psychoanalysis cannot sidestep, any more than exegesis, the question of the validity of its interpretations; nor even that of a certain sort of prediction (what is the probability, for example, that a patient be accepted for therapy, or that he can then be successfully treated?). Comparisons must surely enter into the analyst's field of consideration; but it is precisely as a problem of historical science, and not of natural science, that analysis encounters and poses the problem. (pp. 374–375)

As can be gathered from a commentary by Grünbaum (1984, p. 48), Ricoeur (1981, p. 248) remained enmeshed in contradictions. On the one hand he adhered firmly to his conviction that "facts in psychoanalysis are in no way facts of observation," while on the other hand we read in the context of this passage:

> What is remarkable about psychoanalytic explanation is that it brings into view motives which are causes. ... In many ways his [Freud's] explanation refers to "causally relevant" factors. ... All that is important to him is to explain ... what in behavior are "the incongruities" in relation to the expected course of a human agent's action. ... It is the attempt to reduce these "incongruities" that ... calls for an *explanation* by means of causes. ... To say, for example, that a feeling is unconscious ... is to say that it is to be inserted as a causally relevant factor in order to explain the incongruities of an act of behavior. ... From this ... it follows ... that the hermeneutics of self-understandings take the detour of causal explanation. (pp. 262–264)

Here Ricoeur obviously acknowledged that psychoanalytic explanations are *causal* and are simultaneously intended to explain different types of behavior.

At this point we reproduce Grünbaum's (1984) comprehensive commentary in its entirety, because it contains considerable consequences for clinical research and for the most comprehensive documentation possible of it:

> Now, the imperative to furnish cogent evidence of the purported causal linkages invoked to explain the patient's case history is not lessened by the injunction (Ricoeur 1981: 266–268) to fulfill the "narrativity criterion" as well. The latter requires that the "partial explanatory segments of this or that fragment of behavior are integrated in a narrative structure" reflecting the individual analysand's etiologic life history (p. 267). But, as Ricoeur emphasizes, the psychoanalytically reconstructed scenario not only must be a "coherent story" (p. 267)—made "intelligible" by the explanatory segments—but must also aspire to being true, rather than merely persuasive and therapeutic. Quite properly, therefore, he enjoins that "we must not give up our efforts to link a truth claim to the narrativity criterion, even if this claim is validated on a basis other than narrativity itself" (p. 268). (p. 47)

In our opinion, in recent decades many psychoanalysts have endeavored in their case reports to optimize the connection between the claim to truth and the narrative criterion in the sense of Ricoeur's admonition. It should be particularly emphasized that Grünbaum, the sharpest living critic of psychoanalysis, here approves of a Ricoeur whom he otherwise excoriates:

Indeed, he elaborates (pp. 268–269) on "what makes a narration an explanation in the psychoanalytic sense of the term" as follows: "It is the possibility of inserting several stages of causal explanation into the process of self-understanding in narrative terms. And it is this explanatory detour that entails recourse to non-narrative means of proof. (p. 48)

Our own clinical efforts are thoroughly documented in volume II of the Ulm Textbook (Thomä and Kächele, 1994b). The empirical studies on the model case of Amalia X published in the present research volume have it as their goal to arrive at a comprehensive validation.

Regarding Ricoeur's reading of Freud and his influence on French psychoanalysis we could have formed an opinion 30 years ago. It is another matter with the work of Adolf Grünbaum, which did not yet exist in 1973. Grünbaum's auspiciously entitled book, *The Foundations of Psychoanalysis: A Philosophical Critique,* did not come out until 1984—close to the same time as the first German volume of the Ulm Textbook (Thomä and Kächele, 1985). The subtitle of his book carries no hint of the crushing conclusion at which his critique arrives. From the perspective of Grünbaum's theory of science, psychoanalysis has no reliably secured foundations. For the title to reflect the thrust of the book, it would at least require a question mark and would perhaps read: "Is Psychoanalysis Scientifically Founded?" The title as chosen and the laudatory blurbs piqued the curiosity of a readership reaching far beyond the precincts of psychoanalysis, psychotherapy and psychiatry. Grünbaum's devaluation of the clinical experiential foundation unsettled many psychoanalysts.

Faced with this theoretician's criticism that it is impossible to test the validity of psychoanalytic interpretations, analysts—according to Mitchell's (1998) observation—developed the following "Grünbaum Syndrome":

> ... several days of guilty anguish for not having involved oneself in analytic research. ... And may (also) include actually trying to remember how analysis of variance works, perhaps even pulling a twenty-year old statistics off the shelf and quickly putting it back. There may also be a sleep disturbance and distractions from work. (p. 5)

We remained unaffected by this syndrome, as we had long been acquainted with the themes discussed by Grünbaum. We think psychoanalysis can be validated according to our understanding of science as a *human* science and not a physicist's science. These same themes had been the subject of a historically prominent symposium of American philosophers and psychoanalysts that took place at the New York University Institute of Philosophy in 1958. In his talk there, Hook (1959b) raised the familiar issue of falsification and asked the analysts "... what kind of evidence they were prepared to accept which would lead them to declare in any specific case that a child did not have an Oedipus complex" (p. 214). The analysts in attendance were amazed and their answers were in part rather odd. Hook himself came to the conclusion that the oedipal phase is by no means universal:

> Many normal children do not manifest it. This would seriously invalidate one of Freud's central hypotheses. It would tend to indicate that the absence of the oedipal phase as well as variations in the extent, intensity, and mode of its expression are determined by social and cultural institutions. It suggests that the *significance* of the child's unlearned behavior depends upon the responsive reaction of adults and the institutional framework within which it is interpreted and channeled. (pp. 217–218)

That this description came from Hook and not from one of the attending representatives of psychoanalysis is astonishing in retrospect. Almost 50 years later in a book review, E. Kafka (2004) quotes Arlow, who held a lecture at this symposium himself and had the impression that the Hartmann period was coming to an end because the question raised by Hook could not be convincingly answered. Grünbaum was an active participant at this symposium and made brief remarks on the discussion. As is evident from the *festschrift* in honor of his 60th birthday, edited by Cohen and Laudan (1983), in 1958 he was still far removed from psychoanalysis. He was viewed as a theoretical physicist specializing in space and time issues and was dubbed "Mr. Space and Time of American Philosophy." As can be gleaned from the bibliography of the *festschrift*, it was in two later papers that Grünbaum launched his vehement science-theory critique of psychoanalysis.

Within a short time of its publication, his *Foundations* ... had elicited 39 responses. The author in turn responded to these with his article "Précis of the foundations of psychoanalysis" (Grünbaum, 1986a). Finally, in 1993 a collection of pertinent papers appeared under the title "Validation in the Clinical Theory of Psychoanalysis."

Looking back over his publications we find it noteworthy that Grünbaum has maintained his position almost unchanged for many years. He concedes only "... that I am no more inclined to put a cap on the ingenuity of intraclinical investigations than on that of extraclinical ones" (1993, p. 112). In the context of Grünbaum's convictions, this opaque sentence is essentially meaningless. He continues to praise Freud's brilliance to the skies while simultaneously denying his ideas the foundation of scientifically assured experience. In this connection a typical sentence of Grünbaum's deserves quotation:

> In the first place, I do *not* rule out the possibility that, granting the weakness of Freud's major clinical arguments, his brilliant theoretical imagination may nonetheless have led to correct insights in some important respects. Hence, I allow that a substantial vindication of some of his key ideas may perhaps yet come from well-designed extraclinical investigations, be they epidemiologic or experimental. Conceivably, it might even come from *as yet unimagined* new clinical research designs ... (p. xi)

With great reservations Grünbaum accepted the objection of Holt that tape-recorded and transcribed analyses could make possible a separation of valid from invalid data, to achieve a decontamination (1993, p. 111).

Grünbaum's logical exegesis can be reduced to a small number of concepts. He comes to the conclusion that Freud's "master proposition," the "necessary condition thesis" (NCT) for the genesis of neuroses, namely the causal role of repression, is unproven. The concept of repression represents the comprehensive theory of defense mechanisms. The NCT is coupled with the "tally argument" of treatment technique. According to Grünbaum, the complex psychoanalytic setting is so contaminated that it is impossible to make scientifically founded statements about the genesis and healing of psychological suffering. This judgment results from Grünbaum's critique of Freud's tally argument:

> The solution of his [i.e., the patient's] conflicts and the overcoming of his resistances can only be successful if one has given him *expectations* that are *in accordance* with his inner reality. Whatever was inaccurate in the physician's suppositions will fall away in the course of the analysis; they must be withdrawn and replaced by more correct ones. (Freud, 1916–17, p. 453, author's italics)

It should be noted that the *Standard Edition* translates Freud's phrase "*die mit der Wirklichkeit in ihm* übereinstimmt" (literally, "that *accord* with the reality in him") as "... *tally* with what is real in him." At this point Freud expresses the opinion that the therapy is successful only if the patient attains an accurate insight into the truth of his biographical and pathological history. The tally argument describes a problem of correspondence and not a claim to truth, as Freud had assumed.

Grünbaum (1984), who explored the problem of testing psychoanalytic theory on the couch in some depth, refers to the assertion that veridical insight leads to therapeutic success as the "necessary condition thesis."

This thesis is the most important assumption for the "tally argument"—
the argument that therapeutically successful analyses speak for the truth of
the analytic (dyadic) knowledge that is gained in these analyses and transmitted to the patient. Against the therapeutic effect of veridical insight,
Grünbaum asserts the following doubts: The therapeutic effect could also
stem from suggestion on the part of the analyst, being based for example on
nonveridical insights and pseudoexplanations; the therapeutic effect could
be a matter of a placebo effect evoked by faith on the part of analyst and
patient in the truth and efficacy of the insight generated through interpretation; the therapeutically desired changes could also derive from other
aspects of the analytic setting, as for example from the experience of a new
kind of human relationship, and not from the factor of "veridical insight."

Edelson (1984), in contrast, maintains the claim that objectively true
(veridical) insight on the part of the patient is the necessary prerequisite
for changes assessed as therapeutically positive in the framework of a psychoanalysis. At the same time however he concedes that veridical insight is
not a sufficient precondition for achieving therapeutic changes in analysis.
Edelson argues that analysis-specific goals and changes are all tied to the
patient's veridical insight and that it is possible to speak of a successful
and effective psychoanalytic treatment only if these goals and changes have
been achieved.

It is not hard to recognize that the controversy over the necessary condition thesis is really about the question whether Freud's assertion of an
"inseparable bond between cure and research" is valid for psychoanalysis
or not. Someone who simply accepts the "inseparable bond" thesis into his
argumentation as an undisputed fact (e.g., in the form of the tally argument) treats it as a natural law, forgetting that the role of "veridical insight"
has not been adequately studied in empirical research into the therapeutic
process (see Chapter 5) and that the concept of insight is fraught with methodological difficulties. Hence it would be premature to accept assertions of
a connection between veridical insight and therapeutic success as fact (and
thus comparable to natural law). Such caution is also justified in view of the
fact that empirical process research has recognized a whole array of other
conditions beyond veridical insight that play a significant role (Orlinsky et
al., 2003).

The question whether Grünbaum's contamination thesis is justified or
not must be decided on the basis of empirical process research and not
within the framework of philosophical discussions. The same is true of the
charge of suggestion, the legitimacy of which would have to be established
empirically in regard to psychoanalytic practice before it is raised with
the certainty often associated with it (Thomä, 1977). It must therefore be
demanded that the forms of changes specific to psychoanalysis be exactly
described and distinguished from other processes; further, that research
seek indicators of the changes in question, since as dispositions they are

only indirectly observable by way of these indicators; and finally, that not only the conditions for veridical insight be specified and investigated, but also what is needed beyond "veridical insight" in order to achieve the kind of personality changes envisioned by the goals specific to psychoanalysis (Edelson, 1984).

Grünbaum forcefully defends Freud's scientific position against philosophical and psychoanalytic hermeneuticists such as Ricoeur, Habermas and Gadamer on the one hand and Klein, Schafer and Gill on the other. Against Popper he argues convincingly in favor of the scientific status of psychoanalysis. Popper regarded psychoanalysis and Marxism as unscientific because, since both of them can be verified by anything at all, they fail to meet Popper's criterion of demarcation: falsifiability. On the basis of Freud's case histories, Grünbaum counters Popper's argument, asserting that there have indeed been refutations and falsifications of earlier hypotheses in the history of psychoanalysis, and these have been based on clinical experience and findings. The reader will share our surprise: In the controversy with Popper, findings have suddenly gained validity, although Grünbaum has denied them any force of proof. To speak with Grünbaum's own words, these modifications of theory are an eloquent testimony that Freud was responsive to *adverse* clinical and even extraclinical findings that *contradict* his theory. He quotes the lesson that Freud learned in 1926 from the circumstances of Wolf Man and Little Hans:

> It was anxiety which produced repression and not, as I formerly believed, repression which produced anxiety. ... It is no use denying the fact ... that I have on many occasions asserted that in repression the instinctual impulse is transformed into anxiety. *But now an examination of phobias, which should be best able to provide confirmatory evidence, fails to bear out my assertion; it seems, rather, to contradict it directly.* (1926d, p. 109)

Grünbaum (1984) gives a number of proofs on Freud's readiness to alter his view:

> Furthermore, we need only recall the very theme of Freud's 1937d paper "Constructions in Analysis," namely, just how he assures the intraclinical falsifiability of those clinical reconstructions that are avowedly the epistemological lifeblood of his whole theory! When Popper asks, "what kind of clinical responses would refute to the satisfaction of the analysts...psychoanalysis itself?" I ask in return: what is "psychoanalysis itself"? Is it the theory of unconscious motivations, or the psychoanalytic method of investigation? As to the former, Freud stressed its conjectural nature by espousing Poincaré's

view that the postulates of the theory are evidently undetermined free creations of the human mind. (p. 281)

In his controversy with Popper, however, in the last section of his book Grünbaum (1984) makes an about-face in a complicated chain of argument that at first appears to run in favor of psychoanalysis. He gangs up with Popper on the back of psychoanalysis:

> Since Freud's Tally Argument failed and no substitute for it is in sight, Popper is quite right that contamination by suggestion does undermine the probative value of clinical data. But I have argued that insofar as his case against the clinical confirmability of psychoanalysis *is* sound, it does *not* redound to the discredit of inductivism qua method of scientific theory validation. And I have documented that Freud had carefully addressed—albeit unsuccessfully—all of Popper's arguments against clinical validation. (p. 285)

With these few concluding sentences Grünbaum tacitly takes back the passionate defense of psychoanalysis as a science that he had offered Popper. The two philosophers, though at odds regarding inductivism, are in agreement in their verdict that Freud's efforts towards a clinical confirmation of the defense theory were without success. Thus Grünbaum places the founder of psychoanalysis in the ranks of failed geniuses.

Grünbaum, until recently (2001), failed to consider that all the essential insights of psychoanalysis were gained in the scientifically impure clinical setting—including those observations that prompted Freud to renounce previously accepted causal connections. It should be added: precisely *because* Freud did not succeed in creating the "social null situation" (de Swaan, 1980) that is a given in the experiments of natural science. It is to Freud's credit that he shied away from fully introducing the subject and its attendant scientific problems into medical practice and therefore swayed throughout his life between psychoanalysis as science and as therapy. Like Grünbaum, he was disturbed by contamination of the findings through the personal influence of the analyst, because of which "the therapy [could] destroy the science" (1927a, p. 254). The suggestion problem troubled him his entire life. In the Anglo-American literature this problem is referred to as "Fliess's Achensee question," as in Meehl's (1983) publication under the title "Subjectivity in psychoanalytic inference: the nagging persistence of Wilhelm Fliess's Achensee question."

In his search for contamination-free data, Grünbaum, the scientific philosopher of physics, radically bypasses the methodological problems of psychoanalysis. These are rooted in the fact that in a practical-therapeutic human science there can be no pure data. The seemingly neutral analytic stance intended to assure objectivity was accordingly incapable of excluding the "disturbing" influence of the observer in order to achieve objectivity. The current acknowledgment of contamination makes possible the distinction of different ways in which influence is exerted and different intersubjective processes.

Psychoanalysis is the only systematic psychopathology on the foundation of human conflicts (Binswanger, 1955). These latter cannot be simulated; their investigation and therapy must be conducted in a human relationship. In our judgment, the practical and scientific problems this entails can be solved more appropriately today than at Freud's time. The problem of contamination is soluble in modern psychoanalytic research. Due to his physicalistic orientation, Grünbaum declared scientific investigations of causal connections in the psychoanalytic setting to be impossible, and displaced them to the outside. As experimental investigation of unconscious processes and dream research (Shevrin, 2005; Leuschner and Hau, 1995; Holt, 2002, 2005) has shown, "extra-clinical" research has its own independent significance. But this cannot of course replace investigations of the "native soil" of therapy, which are so productive in both scientific and practical terms.

Some years ago an intensive exchange of ideas with Grünbaum helped clarify our own position. He drew our attention to a careless formulation in our earlier study (Thomä and Kächele, 1975) in which we had written:

> We agree with Rapaport (1960) that proving the validity of psychoanalytic theory is a task of the scientific community, which has to agree on the practical procedure of empirical science. Contrary to the restrictive limitation of general interpretations, psychoanalytic research and practice cannot be satisfied with a concept of the self-formative process that is as philosophically vague as it is rich in content, and from which confirmation of the theory should result. In any case, the logic of explanation through general interpretations points towards the specific way in which the confirmation of psychoanalytic statements can alone be obtained: this becomes clear in the linking up of hermeneutic understanding with causal explanation: "Understanding itself gains explanatory power" (Habermas, 1971a, p. 328). With regard to symptoms, constructions take the form of explanatory hypotheses with the aim of analyzing modes of behavior in causal terms. The *dissolution* of a "causal coherence" through interpretative efforts illustrates the efficacy of psychoanalytic therapy. The constructions are to be applied to the single case; they thus become theoretical statements from which singular prognoses can be derived. Generally speaking, these prognoses identify the conditions causally responsible for the neurotic state and claim that the therapeutic process must dissolve these conditions in order to induce

change. The disappearance of the efficacy of the supposed internal conditions—e.g., pathogenic unconscious fantasies—demonstrated itself in changes of symptoms and behavior. (italics added by authors in quotation)

Grünbaum was irritated by this careless formulation of ours, which he quotes out of context as follows: "The dissolution of a causal connection by means of the work of interpretation [in the treatment situation] illustrates the efficacy of psychoanalytic therapy." We were first made aware of this careless formulation in an oral communication with Grünbaum. Later, in the German translation of his major work (1988), he confirmed for us that in the Ulm textbook (Thomä and Kächele, 1985) we had assessed the matter correctly:

> In the meantime Thomä and Kächele have assessed the matter correctly... "In the end, the specific causes of the repression can fall away, i.e. become ineffective. This change dissolves the determined patterns and not the causal nexus as such – the latter, as Grünbaum (in *The Foundations of Psychoanalysis*) emphasizes, is in fact confirmed by the dissolution as a correctly surmised connection" (cit. Thomä and Kächele, 1985, p. 27). (p. 33)

Such proofs form the scientific foundations of psychoanalysis and we believe they have been abundantly supplied. Presumably Grünbaum would not allow this argument to stand. For example, he might counter: What is possible in principle collapses due to the contamination of all data in the execution. At this point Grünbaum could take recourse to his thesis of "necessary condition" and his "tally argument." As an advocate of unified science, he could maintain his position by claiming that it is impossible to apply the logic contained in it due to the inevitable contamination in the therapeutic situation. We honor this opinion within the context of the following motto: "Nobody has ever denied scientific status to psychoanalysis on the ground that it is not like physics. For we would then have to rule out the whole of biology as a science, which would be absurd." (Hook, 1959b p. 214).

As editor of the book *Psychoanalysis Scientific Method and Philosophy*, Hook made this statement at a famous conference of philosophers of science and psychoanalysts which took place in 1958. Careful readers of the 28 papers will discover that almost all points of view on the contemporary controversies about the scientific status of psychoanalysis were dealt with in one or the other of those papers. We were acquainted with the discussion already in 1973 when we wrote the paper here commented upon. Therefore, as mentioned above, we never suffered seriously from the syndrome baptized by Mitchell as "Grünbaum Syndrome." Probably Grünbaum's interest in the scientific status of psychoanalysis was born at that conference. He gave a one-page comment on Kubie's paper (Grünbaum 1959, p. 225). He became a very erudite reader of Freud and psychoanalytic literature. The proofs he offers that psychoanalytic therapy is not based on scientific foundations seem to be well argued as long as one accepts the position of a scientist according to Grünbaum's definition. Insofar, his argumentation collides with Hook's motto. Grünbaum's scientific ideal is the double-blind trial of the placebo-model (1993b). This model, of course, is the absolute opposite of psychoanalytic theory and practice. Grünbaum's (2006, 2007) very recent publications clearly demonstrate in his critique of Caws (2003) and Mills (2007) that he remains an adamant partisan of a very one-sided idea of science only applicable to natural sciences.

PSYCHOANALYSIS AS SCIENCE?

For many years a voluminous literature about the ranking of psychoanalysis among the sciences has been produced. The planning and carrying out of our research projects necessitated the clarification of our own ideas concerning the scientific status of psychoanalysis by discussing essential controversies. Here we want primarily to take up those points of view that influence methods of clinical research. The integration of psychoanalysis with the nomothetic or ideographic sciences, with natural, social, behavioral sciences, or the arts, must be considered an unimportant academic question, unless this question results in relevant consequences for research and practice.

It was Freud who discovered the role of the participant-observer and its far-reaching influence on the observational situation. Since it goes beyond "understanding" in its description of phenomena and its proposed theories of "explanation" about the observations it has obtained, psychoanalysis is situated in a border region of scientific theories.[*]

This position might account for the fact that there is hardly a modern philosophical movement that has not been concerned with psychoanalysis and its methodology of research. The exponents of "unity of sciences," those of the logical-empirical theory of analytical science, as well as the followers of the dialectic and hermeneutic movements in philosophy and sociology all find psychoanalysis to be interesting matter for discussion. It is remarkable that psychoanalysis will not fit into the hermeneutic claim, nor will it be forced into the Procrustean bed of the uniform scientific method

---

[*] In this translation the terms *understanding* and *explanation* are set in quotation marks when it is important to indicate their terminological rather than their colloquial character (see also Eissler, 1968; Hartmann, 1972, 1958).

of unity of science. It is not surprising that the exponents of unity of science cast doubts on psychoanalytic explanations because these can only be proven in an interpretive context, while on the other hand psychoanalysis as an "explanatory" theory is not hermeneutic enough.

We do not, however, intend to psychoanalyze the claims of the unity of science movement in order to have the last word in all matters of scientific truth. Rather, we will endeavor to turn the many valiant efforts and disputes concerning psychoanalysis to its own advantage. The application of scientific criteria (in the sense of the positivistic theory of science) such as the ability for replication, objectification, and validation poses special problems that have been discussed for a long time within psychoanalysis. The discussion of these problems encompasses a field between two extremes, which in their distribution and valuation can be seen to belong either to the Anglo-American or the French-German sphere. While we often too flippantly dismiss as positivism the effort to see psychoanalysis as an empirical and verifiable science, the group of behavioristic social scientists rejects "understanding" as a constituting element of the dialogue. If in psychoanalysis "understanding" is attained by the way of explanation, as stated by Radnitzky (1973, p. 244ff), there is the danger that its model will be distorted by exaggerated emphasis of one aspect to the detriment of the other. These diverse attitudes have considerable practical consequences for research and treatment in psychoanalysis because it is a behavioral science with highly theoretical implications. The history of psychoanalysis itself, up to the most recent arguments among psychoanalysts, shows how vulnerable and unsure it is in regard to "understanding" itself as a science.

HERMENEUTICS AND PSYCHOANALYSIS

We will critically illuminate those aspects of hermeneutics that are important for the interpretative technique of psychoanalysis. In this we will proceed along the lines of Apel (1955, 1971), Gadamer (1965, 1971a, 1971b), Habermas (1967, 1971a, 1971b), and Radnitzky (1973). Our theme will be limited to the relation between the hermeneutic and the psychoanalytic *technology of interpretation*; this limitation will determine our selection and our critical attitude toward its literature. We have arrived at our conclusions by including arguments from philosophy and the theory of science that have also entered into the dispute on the metascientific basis of sociology.* They prove useful for the resolution of certain methodological problems in psychoanalysis.

---

* This debate is called "Der Positivismusstreit in der deutschen Soziologie" (Adorno et al., 1969). It originated during an International Sociological Congress in Tübingen in 1952. Among others, Theodor Adorno and Kaarl Popper were the prominent proponents.

Within this fixed framework we will content ourselves with examining, from a historical point of view, those aspects of hermeneutics that are close to the interpretative technique of psychoanalysis in its psychology of "understanding." To facilitate communication, we would first like to give a definition in accord with Radnitzky's explanation. The term *hermeneutics** dates from the seventeenth century. It was formed from *hermeneutike techne* and means a procedure to interpret texts ("the teaching of the art of text interpretation"). In the Greek *technai logikai (artes sermonicales)*, hermeneutics was in close relation to grammar, rhetoric, and dialectic. Hermeneutics is the science of interpretation according to which interpretation is based on a previous comprehension of the complete meaning of what is to be interpreted and proceeds to the exploration of presumed situational contexts. It is thus circular theory. It indicates an indissoluble interplay between an "understanding" of the whole and an "understanding" of a part, or between a subjective precomprehension and an objective comprehension of the object. This circle implies a correction based on the feedback between the preliminary "understanding" of the whole text and the interpretation of its parts. The development of hermeneutics was essentially influenced by the exegesis of the Bible to which the theological background of our present discussion should be ascribed. The theological debate over the theory of hermeneutics is documented in (among others) the principle of Schleiermacher: Initially one does not usually arrive at an "understanding" but rather at a misunderstanding; so the problem of "understanding" becomes a theme of epistemology (the theory of knowledge), namely, that we have to already know—that is, we have to have a previous comprehension—in order to investigate something. The clearest expression of the hermeneutic procedure can be found in the arts, in the philology of the text interpretations. There, the basic question is, What meaning, what significance did and does this text have?

The step from the interpretation of old texts to the question of their present meaning adds a historical dimension to hermeneutics. Instead of practicing a precritical, normative, and dogmatic transfer and passing on of tradition, the art of hermeneutics nowadays claims to promote the mediation of traditions within a critical "understanding" of self and history.

---

* *Hermeneuo*: I denote my thoughts by words, I interpret, I explain, I expound, I translate. We assumed wrongly that there was an etymological relation between hermeneutic and Hermes because Hermes, the god of commerce, messenger of the gods, had the duty of an interpreter: He had to translate their messages. Professor K. Gaiser of Tübingen University, whose help in this and other matters we gratefully acknowledge, has given us the philological opinion that the coupling of Hermes and hermeneutics is based on popular etymology, that is, on the fortuitous resemblance of these words. *Hermeneuo* actually derives from a root with a meaning identical to *speaking*.

Hermeneutics has thus become the instrument of the arts. Hans Albert (1972, p. 15) affirms that it is a technology of interpretation having at its base unspoken assumptions about the regularity and legitimacy of insights in art. Only Martin Heidegger and his followers raised hermeneutics to a "universal outlook with its own peculiar ontological claims" (Albert, 1971, p. 106). This has significantly influenced the humanities.

From philological, theological, and historical hermeneutics, a line leads to "understanding" psychology. The common denominator that connects the psychology of "understanding" with the arts is the claim of putting one-self into somebody else's place, of empathy with a text or with the situation of the other. The sharing of experiences of another person is one of the pre-requisites that make psychoanalytic treatment possible. Introspection and empathy are essential characteristics of the technical rules of "free association" and of "evenly hovering attention," which supplement each other.

The sentence, "Each understanding is already an identification of the self and of the object, a reconciliation with the one who would be separate, if he were outside of this understanding; what I don't understand remains different and alien to me," when translated into contemporary language, could have been written by a psychoanalyst who concerns himself with the nature of empathy (compare, e.g., Greenson, 1960 and Kohut, 1959). The quoted sentence is from Georg Hegel, as quoted by Apel (1955, p. 170). Kohut (1959, p. 464) affirms that Freud utilized introspection and empathy as scientific instruments for systematic observation and discovery.

The relation between general hermeneutics and psychoanalytic situations works in two ways. The analyst starts to understand the patient's (up to now) incomprehensible behavior by retracing its development. Historically genetic "understanding" is thus accomplished—that is, the "understanding" of psychological or psychopathological phenomena in the greater context of a life history. Consequently, the problem of the relation of the parts to the whole and vice versa, as well as its interpretation, has to be solved. According to Gadamer (1965, p. 319), the interpretation starts "where the sense of a text is not immediately comprehensible. One has to interpret wherever one does not trust the immediate appearance of things. The psychologist interprets, not by evaluating life histories in their intended meaning, but by asking about what happened in the unconscious. The historian interprets the data of tradition in the same way, in order to grasp their true meaning, which is expressed and at the same time hidden by them."

In this statement, Gadamer (1965) seems to visualize a psychoanalyst; his description highlights depth psychological questioning. It was precisely the incomprehensible, the seeming senselessness of psychopathological phenomena, that would yield to understanding when it was traced back to its unconscious roots in childhood. The problem Gadamer presents is more than an unimportant little detail: It is the problem of disguised and encoded writing, one of the most difficult ones within hermeneutics. Here hermeneutical philology seems to arrive at a frontier similar to the one that the psychology of "understanding" could not transcend. It is a fact of scientific history that neither static nor genetic "understanding"—in Karl Jaspers's sense—has made essential contributions to the psychogenesis of neurotic or psychotic symptoms, or to their psychotherapy. We have to inquire, therefore, by what means the psychoanalytic method has achieved a larger degree of "understanding." Is the method of psychoanalysis a special, at times partially complemented, hermeneutical, interpretive science? Were the old traditional rules of interpreting only adapted by a special technique in order to conform to the conditions of psychopathology, or the psychotherapeutic relation of physician and patient? Do we have to look for the difference that first created the new technical means of interpretive understanding in practice, or is novelty a new theoretical, explanatory paradigm, as the historian of science, Thomas Kuhn (1962), put it?

There is no doubt that by accepting the unconscious, these new technical means, especially the ones concerned with treatment, have added another significant dimension: the dimension of depth to the philological and historical rules of interpretation. One could therefore call the interpretive technique of psychoanalysis *depth hermeneutics*. According to Habermas (1971a), psychoanalytic interpretation is concerned with those symbolic connections through which a subject deludes himself. Depth hermeneutics, which Habermas contrasts with the philological hermeneutics of Dilthey (1900), is concerned with texts that show the *self-delusions* of the author. Besides the obvious content and its connected indirect but intended comments, the texts document a latent part of the orientation of their author that is not available to him and from which he is alienated but that is nevertheless his own. Depth hermeneutics appear in this context as a process that marks the lifting of alienation, but Habermas states that the real task of hermeneutics, which does not limit itself to philological procedures, consists of combining the analysis of language with the psychological investigation of causal connections.

As we will show later, the subject and method of psychoanalysis, and especially its empirical steps of confirmation, are essentially very different from philological-theological or language-analyzing hermeneutics. Thus the concept of depth hermeneutics suggests too close a relationship between them. Surely, Freud had taken an understanding attitude:

> He had talked to patients he believed what they told him, instead of using objective methods. But what did he do? He developed methods, while looking at phenomena, that suited these phenomena, and these methods proved to be teachable: this means that a scientific method was created here which would never have originated if the phenomenon had not first been observed by a person endowed

equally with the wonderful gift of apprehending phenomena, on the one hand, and understanding them, on the other, with a very critical and very methodical intellect. (von Weizsäcker, 1971, p. 301)

THE LIMITS OF THE HERMENEUTICAL POINT OF VIEW

The digression into hermeneutics served to put the interpretive technique of psychoanalysis into a larger scientific and historical context. We have disregarded the fact that the psychoanalytic situation implies very special rules of interpretive technique. This accounts for the fact that its interpretive art is very different from all hermeneutical movements and schools. Philological and historical hermeneutics do describe the relationship of interpreter and text as a sort of dialogue, a kind of talk. It is evident, however, that the text, unlike the patient who interacts with the physician, can neither talk nor take an active position pro or con.

This difference becomes equally clear when one considers the methodological difficulties of psychoanalytic biography. In this field, the problem is that a solution of the biographical riddles, as Helene Deutsch (1928, p. 85) calls them, must be found "not by the psychoanalytic method, which can only be used directly and on the living person, but by being armed with analytic knowledge of the processes of mental life." The basic difference between a textual interpretation and a psychoanalytic situation could be defined by the fact that between physician and patient there exists not only an imaginary interaction as the one in the hermeneutic circle but also a mutual and real interchange of a very unique kind. From this arises the claim, we believe, that a psychoanalyst not only gives plausible interpretations but also develops an explanatory theory from which one could derive recommendations for actions that have the power to change behavior. As a result, the perception of the psychically alien, the "understanding," becomes integrated into a new function. No consequences for the text arise from its interpretation, be it right or wrong; the interpreter remains to the end bound to his separate world. But for the patient, who has to be understood, the consequences of a correct or incorrect interpretation of the psychically alien are far-reaching.

Ricoeur (1970) underlines the psychological "understanding" aspects of hermeneutics from the point of view of philosophy. In his work the difference between interpretation of texts and psychoanalytic technique runs the danger of being wiped out. Lorenzer (1970), a German psychoanalyst from the Frankfurt Sigmund-Freud-Institut, also tries to put reliable insight into the psychically alien on a hermeneutical and psychologically "understanding" basis. His thesis incorporates a fruitful revision of the psychoanalytic theory of symbols and an attempt to reinterpret psychoanalytic work as work about language that tries to comprehend the origins of symptoms and the deformation of language as "excommunication" of private contents from consciousness.[*] Such attempts to attach the psychoanalytic method unilaterally to *szenisches Verstehen*[†] (scenic understanding) and to hermeneutics are doomed to fail. It is by chance that psychoanalysis has always been used against the claim of universality by the philosophical advocates of hermeneutics. The "radicalization of the hermeneutical point of view" by Lorenzer (1970, p. 7) leads us to the limits of hermeneutics where its principal weaknesses become apparent. A discussion of Lorenzer's ideas will afford a special opportunity to further analyze the relation between interpretive practice and explanatory theories in psychoanalysis.

In the following discourse we assume that the psychoanalyst fulfills certain basic conditions and that the process of comprehension is achieved by empathy with the psychically alien. The importance of imagination in the process of insight can hardly be overestimated. As Paula Heimann (1969) states:

> We can imagine what and how somebody else feels and thinks; how he experiences anxiety, hope, desperation, vengeance, hate, love and murderous impulses; what kind of imaginations, fantasies, wish-dreams and impressions, physical pains, etc., he has and how he fills these with psychic content. (p. 9)

The psychoanalyst, however, would not only want to understand the thoughts and feelings of the other with the help of his ego functions, which Heimann (1969) believes to be the most essential parts of a soberly defined concept of empathy. Rather, he finds himself seeking for insights that are reliable. He is confronted here with a crucial problem of research into the processes of psychoanalysis. How to arrive at a *reliable* knowledge of the psychically alien is, in our opinion and that of Lorenzer (1970), a question of life and death for psychoanalysis as a scientific discipline.

Our preliminary answer to this question is that the psychoanalytic process has to be carried by empathic understanding because it would not otherwise occur. The question of the reliability of the understanding brings us to the problem of validation or falsification in the framework of explanatory theories. There is the question of how it will be decided if psychic and psychopathological phenomena and their genetic significance have

---

[*] Compare Stierlin's (1972) extensive review.
[†] *Scenic understanding*: a kind of intuitive perception of the whole gestalt by way of the findings of situations that are conserved in the unconscious in their original gestalt.

been rightly or wrongly "understood." Is it the "understanding" itself that assumes the decisive validating or falsifying function?

We know that according to its principal proponents (cf. the psychiatrist and philosopher in Jaspers, 1948) the psychology of *Verstehen* (understanding), though it has not developed a method of systematic observation similar to that of psychoanalysis and does not lay down any general or specific theories of psychogenesis, has to give proof through objective data: "Not by subjective or intersubjective evidence do we ascertain a 'comprehensible context,' but through objective data" (Jaspers, 1948, p. 251). In contrast to Jaspers, Lorenzer (1970) believes that, by transforming static to scenic understanding, the experiencing of evidence can be introduced as a decisive scientific test of reliability. Unlike most other psychoanalysts, by omitting explanatory theories from the treatment situation, he reduces the test of reliability almost completely to the intuitive experience of evidence.

According to Lorenzer (1970) the scenic understanding and the evidence in the psychoanalytic knowledge of the psychically alien occupy a special place next to the logical understanding and empathy. Indeed, in the course of a discussion about the process of psychoanalytic conceptualization, one really arrives at matters that cannot be resolved by any logical or psychological understanding of the psychology of consciousness. Scenic understanding embodies a large number of intrapsychic processes in both the analyst and patient as well as the interpersonal processes of transference and countertransference. In scenic understanding unconscious processes are involved and are described according to the principles of established models of interaction (Lorenzer, 1970, p. 109). The analyst makes sure of his understanding by the same psychic mode that occurs in a logical and psychological understanding under the name of experiencing of evidence. The experiencing of evidence in scenic understanding is attached to the models of interaction. These models of interaction make it possible to recognize the most varied events as the expression of one and the same scenic arrangement.

These concepts need closer scrutiny, inasmuch as Lorenzer (1970) makes them the guide to his treatment process and even uses them to ascertain the reliability of the recognition of the psychically alien. Since he denies the assumption that explanatory steps are integral parts in the formation of analytic understanding, he is the most exemplary and weighty exponent of putting psychoanalytic knowledge on a basis of pure "understanding" psychology. Lorenzer (1970) is convinced that his thesis—that psychoanalytic practice consists in a pure and self-contained process of "understanding" without explanatory steps—will be proven absolutely right by a discussion of the conceptual innovation of scenic understanding. This concept can undoubtedly incorporate elements of psychoanalytic insight into the mental life of others.

Scenic understanding finds its conclusive certainty as follows: "It proceeds in analogy with logical comprehension and empathy; it is guaranteed to the analyst through the experiencing of certainty." "Experiences of evidence are brought to correspond to the perception of good *Gestalten*" (Lorenzer, 1970, p. 114). By the help of the view of gestalt psychology, which Devereux (1951), Schmidl (1955), and, even earlier, Bernfeld (1934) had applied to explain the successful closure of interpretations, Lorenzer tries to prove the reliability of experiences of evidence. Indeed, there are some experiences that end up in a persuasive, possibly common "Aha" experience (a "co-variant of action") (Bühler, 1927, p. 87). Did the "Aha" experience end all doubt because an insight had become a meaningfully significant gestalt? But precisely what is such a gestalt that leads up to reliable evidence in the dialogue? Freud's (1896d, p. 205) analogy, in which he compared the interpretive construction of an infantile "scene" with fitting the pieces of a "child's picture puzzle" together, could perhaps be inserted into some theory of gestalt psychology.* For Freud the crucial step of the scientific procedure in psychoanalysis does not rest upon the subjective evidence, though it might be accompanied, for example, with convincing reconstruction of a traumatic scene; instead, it is rather that of "therapeutic proof," which is an observable change of behavior. The additional understanding of the "scene"—in 1895 this consisted of sexual traumas in childhood—could not by any means be justified as correct by itself but had to prove itself through the hypothetically required resolution of the symptoms and by "objectifying of the trauma." Lorenzer's (1970) abstention from securing more supportive evidence has serious consequences for the requirement of reliability. Sometimes he has doubts about the reliability of scenic understanding (ibid., pp. 150, 163). Thus, the question arises: When scenic understanding tries to pinpoint the original incident through all the falsifications of meaning, on what is it based?

Scenic understanding relates to psychoanalytic drive, for example, motivations theory, even if Lorenzer (1970) rejects the concept of motivation for psychoanalysis. He sees it as an alien element within psychoanalysis, especially because of its relationship to behavior. He even fears that the concept of motivation excludes the particular essential task of psychoanalysis (ibid., p. 27).† We don't have to further substantiate here that these theses cannot be sustained.

Loewald (1971, p. 71) further developed the psychoanalytic theory of drives into a theory of motivation, proposing the thesis that personal motivation is the basic assumption of psychoanalysis (p. 99). We believe that

---

* Kurt Lewin's (1937) gestalt theory is especially close to psychoanalytic theory. It seems very dubious to us that experiences of evidence could gain more reliability through gestalt psychological descriptions (see Bernfeld, 1934).

† Lorenzer (1970, p. 165) cannot help but speak of "the unconscious determinants of behavior" and so abolishes his own argument against the use of motivational and behavioral concepts.

in "scenic understanding," motivations and their unconscious antecedents are created figuratively through the imagination. It is through his imagination that the psychoanalyst, as Heimann described it, puts himself into the scenes the patient calls forth. However, since Freud's discovery of certain contents of psychic reality, we know that the scenes did not really happen in the way the patients could remember them if he could remember them at all.

Lorenzer seems to have this problem in mind when he speaks of falsification of meaning. In this context: what is meant by the thesis that the psychoanalyst should approach the original event through "scenic understanding"? We first have to assume the validity of the theory of trauma in its original and uncut form, "an original event." Out of this arise, among other things, several questions for empirical research: if one defines original events, which mean traumas, according to exterior characteristics, then one should endeavor to objectify these events after one has found them (Bonaparte, 1945; Freud, 1896c). If, on the other hand, one considers the inner, the psychic side, in shaping and displacing highly affective events or experiences, then the "scenic understanding" of these events ought to be proven by a newly created edition of these events in the treatment situation that are revealed also by a close scrutiny of written records of treatment until finally the full scene would be reconstructed through "try-out" interaction and language games in the psychoanalytic situation. However, the search for the original events, in the sense of the old trauma theory or of later psychoanalytic theories, is not an end in itself.

Rather, psychoanalytic theories advance the hypothesis that a change in behavior should occur after the release of repression and the working through of an incestuous wish and an imaginary castration threat in the transference neurosis. There is a definite "if–then" hypothesis implied; therefore, psychoanalytic theories can be clinically validated or falsified. The proverb *tertium non datur* is valid for a successful analysis. Here lies the possibility of validation through empirical studies of process, which will prove to be a stronger assurance against errors than Gestalt psychological, weakly supported "experiences of evidence." The latter have a more heuristic function, making possible the formation of hypotheses rather than the corroboration of them.

Dilthey (1894) ascribes the formation of hypotheses to "descriptive" as well as to "explanatory" psychology, if only in the various stages of the process of cognition: "Descriptive psychology ends with hypotheses, while explanatory psychology starts with them" (p. 1342). How far descriptive psychological or psychopathological-phenomenological comprehension is already governed by hypotheses and whether theoretical preconceptions have not always and predominantly directed the description and influences the selection of the phenomena to be described are questions that have no importance here.*Along the lines of Dilthey, Kuiper (1965) also wants to incorporate hypotheses into a decisive stage of the psychoanalytic process of cognition and in this way to assure its examination.

The problem then shifts to the question of whether psychoanalysis is an "explanatory" or an "understanding" psychology (Eissler, 1968, p. 187). Because of its methodological consequences, we will here discuss the kind of relationship that exists between "understanding" and "explanation" when they intermingle in psychoanalysis. Kuiper (1964) also regards his critical-historical works and those in the philosophy of science about "understanding" psychology and psychoanalysis as a contribution toward a methodological consideration of psychoanalysis. He writes:

> Without first accounting to oneself which form of psychology to use, one uses all sorts of methods, explanations and modes of thought indiscriminately. Empathic insight is employed alternatively with constructs that contain models; psychologically empathic connections are not sufficiently differentiated from speculation about the theory of drives: one proves hypotheses in one area with arguments that are taken from the other. (p. 32)

Kuiper (1964, p. 19) believes it especially dangerous if "experiences of evidence" are regarded as decisive. Psychological connections are not proven by a feeling of certainty, as is so often stated. Some have wanted to reserve empirical proof for basic correlations—for example, organic brain disease and dementia—and they have thought, in a narrow sense, that the experiencing of evidence would be sufficient for other psychological connections. This is, of course, false. The fact that we deem a connection to be evident does not at all mean that this connection is also valid for the patient whose attitude, or rather whose experience, we try to fathom. Material proof has to be given for satisfactory explanation; in any case, our opinion has to be supported by empirical inquiry. If we regard the "experience of evidence" as sufficient reason to accept a connection, then "understanding" psychol-

---

* Freud (1915a, p. 117) gives a remarkable example of his scientific thinking in which he describes the interplay between ideas and empirical trial and error:
The true beginnings of scientific activity consist rather in describing phenomena and then in proceeding to group, classify and correlate them. Even at the stage of description it is not possible to avoid applying certain abstract ideas to the material on hand, ideas derived from somewhere or other, but certainly not from the new observations alone. Such ideas—which will later become the basic concepts of the science—are still more indispensable as the material is further worked over. They must at first necessarily possess some degree of indefiniteness; there can be no question of any clear delimitation of their content. So long as they remain in this condition, we come to an understanding about their meaning by making repeated references to the material of observation from which they appear to have been derived, but upon which, in fact, they have been imposed.

ogy becomes a source of error. The "intuitively 'understood connection' stays hypothetical until proven in a definite case" (ibid.).

Kohut (1959), another author who has focused particularly on the special importance of introspection, affirms that the insights gained through empathy need many safeguards. We believe that for the same reason Eissler (1968) emphatically defines psychoanalysis as an explanatory theory because questions of validation of hypotheses as well as general scientific dialogue would cease with the acceptance of subjective certainty, just as all decisions would be attributed to individual and subjective infallibility. Although Eissler defines psychoanalysis as *psychologia explanans* and not as *psychologia comprendens,* a position opposite to Kuiper's (1964) strong affirmation of understanding, we find the two authors in agreement on most of the methodological points. Both ask for objectifying proof that has to go beyond the descriptive understanding of feelings or certainty. Eissler seems to think about this kind of understanding by saying that it could become the antagonist of scientific explanations. So long as understanding psychological statements claim that the proof of hypotheses is already rendered by exact descriptions, further scientific investigations would indeed be superfluous because the process of cognition would be ended. In our view, Eissler ranks psychoanalysis as a *psychologia explanans.* Like Kuiper, he asserts the provisional quality of descriptive understanding statements and affirms the necessity of proving hypotheses. As a result of the possibility of falsification of psychoanalytic theories Eissler predicts their reconstruction, which also means a partial refutation. That is why Eissler, as well as David Rapaport (1960), ascribes to various parts of psychoanalytic theory a longer or shorter life expectancy.*

In our opinion it is now clear why in the history of psychotherapy and psychoanalysis the question of whether psychoanalysis belongs to the explanatory or to the "understanding" psychologies recurs. For Freud and important theoreticians after him, such as Heinz Hartmann, David Rapaport, and many others, the claim that psychoanalysis is an explanatory theory implied a "mental science" (Hartmann, 1927, p. 13), thus requiring first of all the strict proof of its hypotheses along the lines of "natural science." As a result of the fact that the natural sciences and their contemporary norms were to be the principal models for proof, the methodological originality of the empirical, specifically psychoanalytic line of argument was neglected. On the other hand, the radicalizing of the hermeneutical point of view has not enlarged the empirical basis of psychoanalysis at all; on the contrary, it has narrowed it extremely. Abstention

---

* That Eissler (1971), on the other hand, tried to revive the generally discarded death drive, fits in well with his prognosis, because the ontological assumptions, hidden in the hypothesis of the death drive, are explained in their psychological significance. Briefly, Eissler is concerned with the psychological-existential meaning of death and not with its reduction to a drive.

from proving hypotheses has been replaced by the autarchy of an intuition that confirms itself by evidence.

According to Albert, the theological past of hermeneutics is obvious here, as it is with Heidegger. It is indisputable, according to authors of such different backgrounds as Abel (1953), Albert (1968, 1971, 1972), Jaspers (1948), Kuiper (1964, 1965), Stegmüller (1969), and Weber (1949), that understanding has a heuristic or helpful effect on treatment. But scenic understanding also requires additional proof; hence, Lorenzer (1970) cannot support his extreme thesis.

How Lorenzer (1970) himself views the failure of his hermeneutic radicalism and at which point of his argument he lets the explanatory theories of psychoanalysis enter into the concept of scenic intuition is typical. His argument, reduced to its bare essentials (p. 12), is that there is one place inviolate from all errors of theoretical language: psychoanalytic practice (p. 198). Here scenic understanding would be rounded off with a self-contained, flawless, ideal operation if the inevitable scotoma of psychoanalysts would not disturb their intuition. It is then assumed that there is one absolutely certain place for recognizing the psychically alien: psychoanalytic practice—if only the blind spots of psychoanalysts would not cloud their scenic understanding. The psychoanalyst, completely liberated from his scotoma, would know with absolute assurance, and therein lie the consequences of the theory of cognition of this psychological utopia—which experiences of evidence are true. Since in ordinary practice the ideal operation of the closed understanding circle is never achieved, the experience of certainty will prove more or less right. That way it would be left completely up to subjective judgment if an understanding curve has come to a convincingly right or wrong closure.

According to Lorenzer (1970), the psychoanalyst tries to fill the gaps in his understanding by bringing in explanatory theory as compensation. This helps him find the thread of understanding again. No doubt, theory can serve as a help in orientation whenever it functions from the beginning and not as we believe at the end or as compensation. The theoretical crutch could only help to point to the right way of perceiving the psychically alien if it no longer had to be examined concerning its empirical proof. According to Lorenzer, it seems to be sufficient that the explanatory theories of psychoanalysis can smooth over blind spots and close interrupted understanding curves. In this way the validity of theory is either presumed or is left to be proven by continued subjective scenic understanding. However, in order to make psychoanalytic practice the crucial place of where the proof of its explanatory theories is to be rendered—and we would not know where else they could be fully tested—one cannot rely on one single and, as one has seen, uncertain criterion. The radicalization of the hermeneutical point of view and the absolute refusal to objectify anything connected with it can serve neither as a practical nor as a scientific guide.

ON THE RELATIONSHIP BETWEEN THE INTERPRETIVE PRACTICE OF PSYCHOANALYSIS AND ITS EXPLANATORY THEORIES

The closing remarks of the preceding paragraph have a rather large impli-cation: We said that explanatory theories could find their decisive scientific proof nowhere but in psychoanalytic practice. If the psychoanalytic method is not employed and the process takes place outside of the treatment situ-ation, only those parts of a theory can be tested that do not need a special interpersonal relation as a basis of experience and whose statements are not immediately related to therapeutic practice.* So here, when we speak about explanatory theory, we mean clinical explanatory theory.

When clinical theories are concretely proven by a given dyad (patient–psychoanalyst), special problems result because method and theory have an especially close connection in psychoanalysis. From here on we will base our argument on the assumption that there is a close connection between practice and theory; we believe that the psychoanalytic art of interpretation needs theories as a guide. Paraphrasing Popper (1959, p. 423), we would say that interpretations of facts are always made in the light of theories. That the light of psychoanalytic theories can only illuminate each given case very insufficiently especially at the outset of a treatment is attributed not to the weaknesses of the theories but to the inevitable lack of information. How-ever, hypothetical assumptions by which the interpretive action is directed come into play at once. But there are other, even contradictory, opinions. MacIntyre (1958) claims that psychoanalysis as psychotherapy is relatively autonomous in relation to psychoanalytic theory. He adds for emphasis, "Freud's method of treatment is not altogether dependent—and this may be an understatement—on his theoretical speculation" (p. 86).

When one looks at the reasons given for the relative or even absolute autonomy of the technique, one finds a *mixtum compositum,* which is made up of presumably practical experiences and of judgments about the state of the theory. We will first present some condensed arguments for the first category—the practical.

> *Thesis No. 1:* There are successes in psychotherapy by physicians whose theoretical knowledge is minimal, not to say zero.
> *Thesis No. 2:* In the course of a treatment psychoanalysts often grope their way in the dark. In spite of insufficient and in some situations

---

* Rapaport (1960, p. 113) believes that experimental proof of psychoanalytic theory for the most part is dubious because "the overwhelming majority of experiments designed to test psychoanalysis propositions display a blatant lack of interest in the meaning, within the theory of psychoanalysis, of the propositions tested. Thus most of them certainly did not measure what they purported to; as for the rest, it is unclear whether they did or not."

even completely absent theoretical orientation, they do the right thing intuitively, as is so often said.

Both theses seem to be applicable. But the question arises: What are they advocating? Their arguments are not, as we will show, in favor of the autonomy of practice. Such observations, which are not by any means systematically researched, show that actions that are unconsciously influenced by theory also exist. In every interpersonal relationship the right word can appear at the right time without the necessity of any further theoretical derivations or deliberations. Psychotherapeutic interactions are no exception. To put this in psychoanalytic terms, as much can happen preconsciously in these interactions as in the psychotherapeutic learning process itself. Practical knowledge can also be gained during training because psychotherapy is not concerned with imparting theoretical knowledge but with imparting immediate experience, by which it might appear as if theory were abandoned. It is said, for instance, that no theoretical knowledge of neurosis or psychopathology is imparted by the training course in Balint groups. If this would be true, it would support the thesis of autonomy of practice because the undebatable therapeutic success of doctors instructed in Balint groups would by definition have been independent of theory. But the appearance is deceptive.

Anybody who has participated in Balint groups for a while, and especially anybody who has seen Michael Balint himself in workshops, knows that theoretical psychoanalytic models were created there in such an effective manner that they were transformed into "prescriptions for action." The most important element in the process of learning in the Balint groups is the fact that one's own action and its continuous correction are the focal point. A continuous effort toward trial and error is maintained in this manner, although its relation to theory is covered up. We would like to remark in passing that it is a rather poor process of learning when theories are only covertly transmitted to students, as if they are being implanted into the "preconscious," in the hope that they can be called forth to action at the right moment. The preconscious is neither the proper place of proof, nor has it the proper criteria for showing what constitutes error in the trials and where proof lies.

The untenable thesis of the relative or absolute autonomy of practice from theory contains the old theme of the role of intuition in technique. However, proof of theories by psychoanalytic methods does not require a previous clarification of the question of how the psychoanalyst arrives at interpretations in the course of his practical technique, whether or not they came about rationally or intuitively. The deciding factor is that the treating psychoanalyst or competent colleagues can agree, on the basis of consensus (see Seitz, 1966), as to whether or not theoretical guidelines are apparent in the interpretations given.*

Theory-testing research into process is further complicated by the combination of general and special variables. We make this distinction to separate the typical variables of the psychoanalytic process from nonspecific factors. Research in psychotherapy demonstrates that the mere expression of empathy and interest for the patient can be helpful and beneficial by itself. An understanding attitude toward the patient, as is demanded by the basic rule of psychoanalysis, can itself have a favorable effect, as we know from the investigations of the Rogerian school.

Empathy, "evenly suspended attention," and other typical patterns of ideal behavior, which the psychoanalyst should be able to adopt, are highly susceptible to disturbances. Countertransferences are unavoidable. An insurmountable countertransference can exert an unfavorable influence on the process of treatment, so that success or failure would not be attributable to theory in that particular case. It is completely conceivable that the psychoanalyst in such a case can explain the psychopathology of the patient very well and can give interpretations with correct content. The idea seems to be justified that therapeutic success or failure cannot be cited in the service of validation or falsification of a theory.

In the psychoanalytic situation, the light of the "theory" is deflected by the occurrence of subjective influences and by favorable or unfavorable therapeutic and patient variables—not to speak of external factors, which also can impede treatment. Therefore, it seems justifiable to think that successes or failures cannot be used for validation or falsification of theory. This frequently voiced opinion is partly right and partly wrong. Psychoanalytic theories can only be proven in their subjective form, which they take on in each dyad. Here, "understanding" in the commonly understood sense of the word comes to the fore. Without empathy, the situation would be so transformed that it would be a completely unsuitable setting for testing psychoanalytic hypotheses.

These reflections show that in psychoanalytic research, concerning treatment processes, those situational variables have to be encompassed that codetermine the course of the treatment in a nonspecific way. In order to give validity to the psychoanalytic data gained, scientific research has to be directed especially at the processes of interaction, for instance, phenomena of countertransference, which Perrez (1971, p. 226) points out. If, because of countertransference, the psychoanalyst deviates too widely from the typically ideal behavior pattern that the basic rule prescribes, then the ground of psychoanalytic technique has been abandoned, and neither falsification

---

* "Scientific objectivity can be described as the inter-subjectivity of scientific method" (Popper, 1944, p. 217).

nor validation of psychoanalytic theory can be derived from this study of the process.

The struggle to observe the basic rule (A. Freud, 1936), which marks one side of the psychoanalytic interaction, is not lost as long as the interaction is continued. This means that the minimal conditions are fulfilled, which means that the patient arrives and the psychoanalyst is there for him. The highlights of the struggle show in particular that the psychoanalytic situation serves essentially to clarify the disturbances of communication. Radnitzky's (1973, p. 235ff) stylized and pure dialogue, which proceeds by understanding alone, does not exist in practice.

Radnitzky (1973) speaks about quasi-naturalistic phases in psychoanalytic treatment, which should start at the limits of understanding. He believes that when the dialogue is interrupted, explanatory operations set in, which enlarge the understanding of the self and of the other. This artificial dismemberment seems to have contributed to the idea that explanatory operations, which prove hypotheses, find a satisfactory conclusion and corroboration only through understanding and resumption of an interrupted dialogue. Actually, the dialogue is disturbed from the first moment on, since psychoanalytic situation is asymmetrically designed to make the hidden distortions of communication clearly visible.

Psychoanalytic theory as a scientific system is, of course, already operative for the psychoanalyst at the outset of a dialogue with a patient. It offers a special terminology for causal connections and affords a comprehension of the modes of behavior that cannot be grasped without explanatory schemata.

We will now explore the question of the special means psychoanalytic theory employs. No doubt, the light of the theory shines where interpretations are given in the psychoanalytic situation. It is in the art of interpretation that psychoanalytic hypotheses become instrumental. We want to add a few qualifying remarks to these statements in order to avoid misunderstanding. We do not mean to say that theoretical explanations are given in the process of interpretation. In spite of the great variations in individual techniques in psychoanalysis, there is general agreement that theoretical explanations are not effective in therapeutics. Theory itself offers explanations for this fact, but we cannot take these up here.

It would certainly be simpler to prove the scientific reliability of theory if the derivation of interpretations could be easily recognized, if they were pure hypotheses. Thomä and Houben (1967) discuss the theoretical and practical difficulties in the employment of interpretations as a means of validating psychoanalytic theories. Our efforts and reflections since then have shown that the problem is even more complex than we had originally thought. It is the instrumental character of interpretations that complicates their functions in proving theory: "We intervene by interpretation in an existing setup with the intention of bringing about certain changes" (ibid., p. 681).

Due to the instrumental character of interpretation, Farrell (1964) denies this hypothetical basis. He tried to substantiate his argument by referring to Freud's (1909b) statements that psychoanalysis is not an impartial scientific investigation but a therapeutic measure. Its essence is "not to prove anything but merely to alter something" (Freud, p. 104). Actually, for a real change in the patient, there is no better proof for the theory than empirical findings; thus, Freud's words imply a true clinical as well as a scientific aim. Consequently, Farrell has to abolish his extreme point of view; he eventually concedes the following about an interpretation:

> [It] retains hypothesis-stating and hence declaration features. But these are apt to be overlaid by, and lost in, the complicated instrumental context in which this sort of statement functions. Consequently, even though such a statement has declaratory features, it may be difficult on many occasions to discover from its context just what its truth criteria are. (p. 321)

Indeed, it is most difficult, especially because it is not enough to test an interpretation within a session (Wisdom, 1967); each series of interpretive repetitions in the psychoanalytic process must be evaluated.

It does not mitigate against the central role of theory in scientific proof that interpretations as communications always contain more than their, at best, discernible guideline. Interpretations as verbal communications also have unspecified content, which might in a given case outweigh the special psychoanalytic point of reference. Therefore, empirical investigations show that many statements of an analyst cannot be considered interpretations in a narrower sense. To demonstrate the kind of conditions that have to be met in order to derive theoretical proof from interpretations, let us say that proof should be shown that prognosticated changes in a patient occur by interpretations referring to the hypothesis in fear of castration, but not by using interpretations referring to the hypothesis of separation anxiety. This way, falsification or validation would be possible only in individual cases. The proof would be limited by the special conditions of trial and error relative to the examination of two alternative hypotheses during a protracted phase of treatment.

These limitations result from the structure of psychoanalytic theory, which we will discuss later. We are also omitting here the problem of circularity. This problem exists because proof has to be established of just those theories from which hypotheses are to be derived with the help of interpretations, which in turn contain these hypotheses. We shall discuss the problem of circularity and the question of suggestion in the final part of this chapter. Here we want to remark that the proof has to be oriented to a standard of the prognosticated change in the patient. In this procedure, the role of resistance has to be considered in advance and not retrospectively. It does not have to be predicted, but it must be defined. Similarly, in other fields of medicine, one expects no change in a patient if he sabotages therapy.

For this kind of theoretical proof, it does not matter how the interpretations originate in the mind of the psychoanalyst. Along the lines of Levi's (1963) work, Loch (1965) presents a schema that emphasizes the rational root, the theory-related planning of interpretations, while fully considering the emotional relation to the patient. Lorenzer (1970), who wants to reduce his arguments to a common denominator, affirms in opposition to this that intuition is the origin of interpretations. Cautioned by the controversy between Theodor Reik and Wilhelm Reich, one is well advised to take into consideration as valid factors the personal bias of the psychoanalyst. Nothing needs to be added to the work of Kris (1951), who clarified the long-standing controversial issues of "intuition and rational planning" in psychoanalytic psychotherapy. Moreover, neither planned nor intuitive interpretations can take a preponderant place in the studies of process and interaction. Both have to prove themselves through given prognoses and by their effects, which can be objectified.

To this end, we presume that certain phases of treatment and their predominantly interpretive working-through can be recognized by the analyst himself or by consensual validation of other experts. If psychoanalyses are recorded, the psychoanalyst who interprets intuitively can afterward recognize the presumably theoretical and practical points that relate to his intuitive perception. We do not want to hide our own personal bias and would like to express our skepticism about an intuition that thinks that it can work on objective data and continuous validation without reassurance. Even retrospective explanation, after the analysis as a whole and after each session, remains in many instances hypothetical and is subject in the further course of analysis to trial and error. We believe that Freud (1912e) had the same idea when he cautioned analysts not to draw scientific inferences about a case before the treatment is ended. Freud even advised against interim reports so as not to limit either therapeutic or scientific openness. He seemed to fear that provisional theoretical explanations of the origin of symptoms could, once they are formulated, assume a status they cannot merit:

> The distinction between the two attitudes would be meaningless, if we already possessed all the knowledge (*or at least the essential knowledge*) about the psychology of the unconscious and about the structure of the neuroses that we can obtain from psychoanalytic work. At present we are still far from that goal and we ought not to cut ourselves off from the possibility of testing what we have already

learnt and of extending our knowledge further. (pp. 114–115, italics added for emphasis)

All this is concerning the provisional nature of theoretical assumptions and the creation of the best conditions for their proof. Besides the danger that premature theoretical explanations of neuroses, psychoses, and psychosomatic syndromes can amount to fixed prejudices, there exists another danger, equally unfavorable to therapy and science; this is a technique that overlooks its hypothetical nucleus and thereby the necessity of continuous practical and scientific validation. Technical interpretations in the course of treatment, because of their latent hypothetical component, are just as provisional as are theories. Practice reflects the imperfection of theory. At best, it can have the same reliability as theory; otherwise practice would be better than theory.

We see in "Freud's Methodology" (Meissner, 1971) that the advice to postpone explanatory synthesis until the end of treatment cannot be taken literally. Even during his education the future psychoanalyst learns something else. Interim reports that present unsystematic clinical proof of theory are currently given in the technical seminars of psychoanalytic institutes. Supervision also has, as its aim, to try alternative strategies of interpretation according to the behavior of the patient. It is the changes in the technique of interpretation, whether they have been intuitively or rationally arrived at, that in the course of a treatment or in relation to various symptoms afford the possibility of giving the clinical theoretical proof that Freud demands. One should strive to focus on a systematic approach analogous to the aims of brief psychoanalytically oriented therapy (see Malan, 1963). The awareness of the danger that Freud describes furthers clinical flexibility. Moreover, the repetitions of the transference neuroses will also help to prevent random interpretation and promote the use of a flexible system that can adjust to changes in the patient.

Keeping in mind the previously discussed limiting factors, pertaining to interpretations containing a possible hypothetical nucleus, we now take up the question of which kind of theories can be proven clinically.

Empirical inquiry of this type has to confront the problem of falsification. When and why does a psychoanalyst give up one "strategy of interpretation" (Loewenstein, 1951) in favor of another? Are the underlying theoretical explanations already refuted in this case only or in general? The behavioral and the social sciences have special problems of proving and refuting, which arise from their subject matter and which psychoanalysis confronts in an exemplary way: The combination of method and theory and the mediation by a subject have made it a paradigm for other disciplines (Kuhn, 1962). All this has made psychoanalysis the butt of criticism by theoreticians of science.

MacIntyre (1958, pp. 82–83) describes the difference between an experimentalist and a clinician as follows: The experimentalist would like to conduct experiments in which his hypotheses would be falsified and in which situations would arise that would show false hypothesis to be unserviceable. Since he is looking for flaws in his hypothesis, it constitutes a victory for him when he discovers a situation in which his hypothesis breaks down. In contrast to the experimentalist, the clinician's only interest is to promote healing, but it is not true that the clinician is only interested in matters that further the healing process. To the contrary, he is also very much occupied by the question of which factors stand in the way of healing. Thus the psychoanalyst looks for alternative hypotheses in a given case, even if these cannot be isolated in a way that would permit strict experimental disposition and proof, independent of the subject. MacIntyre then raises the question of what kind of refutation would be valid for psychoanalysts and what would move them basically to change theoretical conceptions. He answers along the lines of Glover (1947) that nothing would move psychoanalysts to change their conceptualizations. But a closer look at Glover's statements shows the reason for MacIntyre's error:

> The basic ideas of psychoanalytic theory could and should be employed as a discipline to survey all theoretical reconstructions of mental development and all etiological theories, which cannot be verified immediately by clinical psychoanalysis.... It is often said, that Freud was ready to change his formulations, if this was necessary for empirical reasons. This is true for some parts of his clinical theory, but in my estimation not for his basic ideas. (p. 1)

It is illuminating that MacIntyre (1958) leaves out a large part of the original. In the missing part Glover (1947) gives some examples of basic ideas: the mobility and quantity of energy of drives and memory traces. Glover is of the opinion that dynamic, economic, and topographic—namely the metapsychological points of view—can be reduced to three basic ideas. These are the ideas that, according to Glover, cannot be immediately proven empirically by the clinical method and, unlike clinical theory, have not been changed. It is not true, however, that the basic ideas, the metapsychological points of view, have never experienced any changes (see Rapaport & Gill, 1959). Even if these ideas had proved to be rather resistant empirically one would, first of all, have to explain the reason for it.

It is a fact that the psychoanalytic method can only indirectly examine the metapsychological points of view empirically. These are in no way the basis of psychoanalytic practice or clinical theory but are rather their "speculative superstructure" (Freud, 1925d, p. 32). Freud (1915b, p. 77) characterizes metapsychology throughout his whole work in this way, but the "witch" keeps on exercising a singular fascination on his whole thought. We believe we can attribute this to the fact that Freud never gave up the idea that the day would come when the psychological and psychopathological observations of psychoanalysis could be traced back to universal laws. Speculations about mental economy in particular show that Freud (1895a) never completely abandoned "his audacious thought" of the "Project for a Scientific Psychology ... of fusing the theory of the neuroses and normal psychology with the physiology of the brain" (Kris, 1954, p. 33).

Freud's (1914c, p. 79; 1920g, p. 60; 1925a; p 32) expectations that one day all theories, including the ones of psychoanalysis, could be reduced to microphysical theories also can be seen in the fact that his formulation of specific economic metapsychological assumptions is couched in such physicalistic terms such as *energy, displacement,* and *charge.* The farther metapsychological speculations move away from the plateau of observation of the psychoanalytic method, the less such observation will be able to substantiate or to refute the speculative superstructure. The distance between practice and theory can be measured by the terminology: The richer the physicalistic-neuro-physiological language of metapsychology becomes, the more difficult it is to determine its psychological nucleus.

It could be said in general that metapsychological assumptions have an empirical scientific significance only if they can be linked to observations by rules of correspondence (Carnap, 1950). Such rules do not furnish a complete definition of the theoretical concepts through the language of observation, but they give an empirical content that is good enough for applicability and examination. When one considers the dynamic, topographic, structural, genetic, or economic assumptions of metapsychology, along the lines of Rapaport's (1960) summary, it becomes clear that their proximity to observation varies widely. Their "survival potential" (ibid.) depends on their nearness to the plateau of observation; without rules of correspondence they atrophy, even if they seem to be unchanged. Their unchanged state can be a sign that they are not at all basic but, on the contrary, have been discounted in practice or have not been current or proven practical from the beginning.

The clinical research that led to the Hampstead Index (Sandler, 1962; Sandler et al., 1962) shows how important it is to establish rules of correspondence. The task of relating to the observational data of an individual case with the clinical theory of psychoanalysis, and possibly with its metapsychology, makes conceptual precision mandatory as a prerequisite for validation or falsification studies. The therapeutic flexibility of the psychoanalyst will not be narrowed by this; to the contrary, it will rather be widened because alternatives will be defined and systematized. But mainly it will become possible to determine more accurately which observational data agree with a clinical hypothesis and which ones refute it. Though the testing of alternative hypotheses is the mark of the psychoanalytic interpretive process, it is not its aim to definitely refute one or another clinical-theoretical explanation of a given case. The analyst, for technical reasons of treatment alone, has to keep himself open to the possibility that psychodynamic hypothesis considered as refuted in the present phase of the treatment could be revalidated later. Freud's (1915a) "A Case of Paranoia Running Counter to the Psycho-Analytic Theory of the Disease" points up casuistically some problems of falsification of theory in a single case, from which general refutations have to be derived.

The problems of falsification gave rise to an informative discussion between psychoanalysts and theoretical scientists (Hook, 1959a), in which Waelder (1962) later took part with a critical review. Hook (1959b, p. 214) asks some psychoanalysts what kind of evidence they would deem valid for ascertaining that a child has no Oedipus complex. Hook's question derives from a position within the theory of science that Popper (1959, 1963) introduced as "falsification theory." In his arguments with the logical positivism of the early Vienna Circle, Popper arrives at the conclusion that inductive logic does not provide a "criterion of demarcation" that would facilitate differentiation of the empirical, the metaphysical, the scientific, and the unscientific systems. On the basis of detailed arguments that we cannot take up here (nor can we go into critical considerations of the falsification theory by Kuhn, 1962), Popper (1959) concludes that the "criterion of demarcation" is not the verification, but the falsification of a system. Popper demands that the logical form of the system "shall be such that it can be singled out, by means of empirical tests, in a negative sense: *it must be possible for an empirical scientific system to be refuted by experience*" (p. 41; italics in original).

Psychoanalysts can agree with this definition of empirical sciences, as shown by a representative quotation from Waelder's (1962, p. 632) critical review: "If no set of observations is thinkable that would disprove a proposition, what we have is not a scientific theory but a prejudice or a paranoid system." In the light of this agreement in principle, it is rather surprising that psychoanalytic theory has been scientifically criticized from the point of view of the theory of falsification. This comes from demands for the creation of experiments of falsification. The theory of falsification grants scientific status only if *experimenta crucis* can be performed. Thus, the criterion for falsification consists in the fact that only those theories are empirically valid that expose themselves to the risk of experimental refutation. Those would be theories that would "permit" only a genuine subclass of all possible experimental results, while they would "forbid" all the others. Though Popper has shaken the foundations of scientific theories of the logical positivists of the Vienna Circle with the theory of falsification, he has—although in critical distance from them—followed the same interests, namely, to enthrone the method of experimental natural science as the only valid one. The type of theory that satisfies this requirement is the statement of universal laws. Statements of universal law can be useful for the deduction of limited prognoses that can be proven by planning new experiences, independent from any former ones.

We are coming back to Hook's (1959a) question and hope that by our remarks on the theory of falsification we can explain why the answers of the psychoanalysts could not satisfy his requirements for scientific theory. The given, fictitious, diagnostic description of a child without any signs of an oedipal experience or behavior possibly still contains a minimal percentage of the Oedipus complex. Waelder (1962) rightly points out that the scientifically and experimentally oriented falsification theory neither recognizes the logical structure of the Oedipus complex as a concept of types* (see also Chapter 3) nor values the possibilities of clinical refutations of theories, because of its restrictively normative conception of science. Besides absolute refutations there exist other ones, especially in the applied sciences which are so highly probable that for all practical purposes, one can call them refutations.

The clinical theory of psychoanalysis, particularly in its special part, contains descriptions of pathogenesis in autistic children or in pre-oedipal disturbed grownups, who practically refuted the Oedipus complex. So, one could say that the Oedipus complex was already refuted by the psychoanalytic method before Hook formulated his question on the basis of the theory of falsification. In fact, in testing clinical alternatives of pathogenic connections, considerations develop for conceiving a scale along which the Oedipus complex dissolves itself into its components and can thus be conceptualized as having zero effectiveness, as in the case of a paranoia of jealousy, "which went back to a fixation in the pre-oedipal stage and had never reached the Oedipus situation at all" (Freud, 1933a, p. 130). It is evident that in a diagnostic and prognostic evaluation of the case, for example, in the clinical validation of theory, positive and negative signs are compared and weighed against each other. Therefore, Hook's question is highly relevant because it could lead to a thoroughly necessary and desirable increase in the precision of the theory by its demand to provide a negative definition. It is, at any rate, not easy to explain, because of the different levels of abstraction in psychoanalytic theory, which one of its regions can be proved valid by interpretive practice.

In conclusion, we shall give a summary of the different levels of psychoanalytic theory, in order to mark the regions that are most relevant in empirical testing of the psychoanalytic theory. We will use Waelder's schema (1962).

---

* Compare the explanations of Hempel (1952).

The schema differentiates the following:

1. *Data of observation:* These are the data the psychoanalyst receives from his patient and that generally are not available to others. These data form the level of observation. They become subject to interpretation relative to their connection with each other and their relation to other modes of behavior or to conscious or unconscious contents. Here we are at the plane of *individual clinical interpretation* (Freud's individual "historic" interpretation, 1917, p. 270).
2. *Generalizations:* From the individual data and their interpretations derive generalizations, which lead to certain assertions in regard to patients, formation of symptoms, and age groupings. This is the level of *clinical generalization* (Freud's typical symptoms).
3. *Theoretical concepts:* The clinical interpretation and their generalizations permit the formulation of theoretical concepts, which can already be contained in the interpretations or which could lead to interpretations of, for instance, such concepts as repression, defense, return of the repressed, and regression. Here we have the *clinical theory* of psychoanalysis before us.
4. *Metapsychological concepts:* Beyond this clinical theory, without being able to draw a sharp line, are more abstract concepts like cathexis, psychic energy, Eros, death wish, constituting psychoanalytic *metapsychology.* Especially in metapsychology, or rather behind it, is Freud's personal philosophy (see Wisdom, 1971).

The schema makes a hierarchy of psychoanalytical theories visible; their respective values for scientific theory vary in empirical content. Interpretations relate mainly to clinical theory. They contain explanations, which permit prognoses, as we will point out later. How far the technological aspect of this theoretical area and its theoretical and scientific position apply to more abstract elements of psychoanalytic theory will be discussed in the following chapters.

GENERAL AND HISTORICAL INTERPRETATIONS

Whereas in our last arguments we stressed the explanatory character of psychoanalytic theories, Habermas, the prominent German sociologist of the "critical school of Frankfurt," presents quite a different view of Freud's scientific achievements.

What Habermas (1971a) sets as his task in his book *Knowledge and Human Interests* is concisely summarized by Nichols (1972) in a short review of that book:[*]

> First, to provide a critique of science on the basis of self-reflection—a critique he develops by tracing the various alternatives to positivism provided by idealism, historicism, and phenomenology; and second, to lay some of the foundations for an epistemology which satisfactorily connects knowledge (as theory) with human interest. (p. 18)

One of the sciences Habermas (1971a) deals with in great detail is psychoanalysis, as a representative example of a social science that has not yet found its proper philosophical underpinning. Right at the beginning of his chapter "Self-Reflection as Science," Habermas characterizes the traditional self-understanding of psychoanalysis as a scientistic self-misunderstanding (p. 246).

This wrong and misleading understanding of the metascientific status of psychoanalysis would especially concern the evaluation of psychoanalytic theory rather than its practice; for example, it would regard in particular the research efforts to validate the theory. The origin of this misunderstanding is reconstructed by Habermas (1971a) in the following way: The basic categories of psychoanalysis were "first derived from experiences of the analytical situation and the interpretation of dreams" (ibid., p. 252). The assumptions regarding the functional relations of the psychic apparatus and the origin of symptoms are "not only *discovered* under determinate conditions of a specifically safeguarded communication," but also "they cannot be displayed independently from these" (ibid., p. 307). From this, it follows that "psychoanalytic theory formation is embedded in the context of self-reflection" (ibid., p. 252). The connection of the structural model, which originally was derived from the communications between doctor and patient with the model of energy distribution, would then constitute the decisive and misleading step: that Freud "did not comprehend meta-psychology as the only thing it can be in the system of reference of self-reflection: a general interpretation of self-formative processes" (ibid., p. 252).[†]

---

[*] During the preparation of this English translation of our paper, we realized that we are in considerable agreement with most of Nichols's (1972) critical remarks.

[†] A self-formative process signifies the cultural correlate to the biological process of development from childhood to adulthood. It comprises the process of education, of training, and of growing self-awareness that can be summarized also in a concept of growing psychosocial identity. The category of *Bildung* (self-formation) is central to the philosophical idea of enlightenment and played a great role in Germany's cultural development during the last centuries.

According to Habermas (1971a), "it would be reasonable to reserve the name metapsychology for the fundamental assumptions about the pathological connection between ordinary language and interaction" (p. 254). A metapsychology thus conceived would not be an empirical theory but a methodological discipline that, as metahermeneutics, would have to explicate the conditions of the possibility of psychoanalytic knowledge. Whether Habermas has any use at all for the classical metapsychological points of view remains obscure.

We have already dealt with the role of metapsychology in the process of psychoanalytic insight (*Erkenntnis*) and with the question of clinical verification of metapsychological viewpoints. The notion that, for many metapsychological viewpoints, it is impossible to set up rules of correspondence implies that vast areas of metapsychology belong to the speculative superstructure of psychoanalysis, which can hardly be verified by empirical -clinical methods.*

In any case, between the various chapters in the building of psychoanalytical theory, there exist as we have seen, a great number of indirect connections, so that from the observations that can be made on the "ground floor," accessible to all, conclusion can be drawn for what is supposed to occur on higher or lower floors. Thus, on the one hand, metapsychology plays a much smaller role than Habermas (1971a) ascribes to it, and also it can be scientifically verified to a limited extent, though it belongs mostly to the speculative superstructure. In this state of affairs metapsychology does not lend itself at all to being used as a metahermeneutic approach.

The methodological discipline proposed by Habermas (1971a) is not affected by this criticism of the misunderstanding that, in our opinion, crept into Habermas's reception of the concept of metapsychology. We believe that the methodological position of general interpretations† would gain little if one gave it a superstructure (e.g., metahermeneutics) that is in some way related to metapsychology. To this superstructure would adhere, in our opinion, all those obscurities that characterize the relationship between clinical theory and metapsychology. The methodological significance of general interpretations is sufficiently independent. With these, Habermas describes strategies of research that are simultaneously self-reflective.

---

* Cf. Freud (1914c, p. 77): "But I am of opinion that that is just the difference between a speculative theory and a science erected on empirical interpretation. The latter will not envy speculation its privilege of having a smooth, logically unassailable foundation, but will gladly content itself with nebulous, scarcely imaginable basic concepts, which it hopes to apprehend more clearly in the course of its development, or which it is even prepared to replace by others. For these ideas are not the foundations of science, upon which everything rests: that foundation is observation alone. They are not the bottom but the top of the whole structure, and they can be replaced and discarded without damaging it."

† As we will specifically show later, the concept of *general interpretations* comes from Popper, who introduced it for historical explanations.

On the level of self-reflection, as distinguished from the logic of the natural sciences and humanities, something like a methodology separated from its content is not possible because the structure of the context of knowledge is one and the same as the object under examination. The general interpretations, however, are also distinguished by Habermas (1971a) from meta-hermeneutical statements:

> For, like theories in the empirical sciences ... general interpretations are directly accessible to empirical corroboration. In contrast, basic meta-hermeneutical assumptions about communicative action, language deformation, and behavioural pathology derive from subsequent reflection on the conditions of possible psychoanalytic knowledge. They can be confirmed or rejected only indirectly, with regard to the outcome of, so to speak, an entire category of process of inquiry. (p. 255)

Habermas (1971a) thus characterizes those laws, the metascientific status that we questioned in the beginning, as "general interpretations." It would be wrong to understand these to be psychoanalytic interpretations (*Deutungen*) in the technical sense in which the word is used in treatment. On the contrary, they can be conceived of as patterns of early childhood development that can be applied as interpretive schemas for individual life histories. They consist of "assumptions about interaction patterns of the child and his primary reference persons, about corresponding conflicts and forms of conflict mastery, and about the personality structures that result at the end of the process of early childhood socialization, with their potential for subsequent life history. These personality structures even make possible conditional predictions" (ibid., p. 258).

In this framework, general interpretations are developed that are the result of various and repeated clinical experiences. They have been derived according to the elastic procedure of hermeneutic anticipations (Habermas, 1971a, p. 259). The basic outline of the whole proposition developed here by Habermas, which alone makes possible the experiences outlined so far, is the consideration of the life history* as a self-formative process (*Bildungsprozess*) that, in the case of a patient, is characterized as disturbance. In line with this, the object of psychoanalytic treatment is "the interrupted self-formative process" that, by the experience of self-reflection, is brought to its end.

---

* Habermas places the reconstruction of the life history entirely in the center of his discussions. In fact, however, the working-through of the transference neurosis in the here and now plays a much greater role therapeutically than the reconstruction of the past.

Regarding general interpretations we now must keep in mind that, contrary to interpretations in the technical sense used in treatment as soon as an interpretation claims the status of "general," it is removed from the hermeneutic method of continuous correction of preliminary understanding by the text. Therefore, it is true of general interpretations that they are fixed, as distinguished from the hermeneutic anticipation of the philologist. By this Habermas (1971a) means that general interpretations have a theoretical anchorage, insofar as they imply at least generalizing statements that must be demonstrable in the individual case and that therefore are exempt from the permanent change through the hermeneutic circle. Therefore, general interpretations must be verified by derived prognoses. If further one takes into account that the reconstructive postdictions (statements after the fact)—which, with the model of the general interpretation, can as narrative forms be derived for the individual case—also have for Habermas the character of hypotheses, which are fallible, then we have found thus far in these discussions clear indications that the aforementioned sentence of Popper (1959) (*"It must be possible for an empirical scientific system to be refuted by experience"*) is also valid for psychoanalysis (p. 41).

So far, Habermas's (1971a) clarification of the metascientific position of psychoanalysis seems to offer the following advantages: Uncovering of the scientistic misunderstanding leads to the question of how far an imitation in psychoanalysis of the methods of the natural sciences that are not appropriate for their object has brought empirical research to an impasse. Insofar as the verdict of scientistic self-misunderstanding concerns many a metapsychological viewpoint—the model of energy distribution,* for instance—Habermas's critique corresponds well with similar conceptions held by quite a few psychoanalysts (i.e., Holt, 1962, 1965; Rosenblatt and Thickstun, 1970). The problems involved in the concept of "psychic energy" are, of course, discussed by many more authors than we can refer to in the context of this chapter (see Shope, 1971).

From Habermas's (1971a) argumentation, it follows that it would be misleading to look for the great X of psychic energy, which, as Freud (1920g) says, enters as an unknown into all our equations. The conclusion that psychoanalysis belongs to the humanities and not to the natural sciences could contribute to the stimulation of empirical research appropriate to psycho-

---

* We would have before us a law of natural science, if one succeeded in verifying empirically the psychoanalytic model of energy distribution, in showing measurable conversion (*Wandlung*) of energy, and in deducing prognoses with the knowledge of specific border conditions. There were fundamental reasons for the fact that the efforts undertaken by Bernfeld and Feitelberg (1930) in this direction had to fail. "The energy-distribution model only creates the semblance that psychoanalytic statements are about measurable transformations of energy" (Habermas, 1971a, p. 253).

therapy. Following Habermas, this research should refer to the general interpretations covering the realm of the clinical theory of psychoanalysis.

The characterization of psychoanalytic clinical laws as "general interpretations," as systematized historical knowledge, facilitates the understanding of the specific situation of psychoanalysis. Moreover, if one sees as central that the general interpretations must be tested against derived prognoses, then a clear dividing line to the philological-hermeneutic procedure has been drawn and empirical research has been secured to the extent of establishing expected behavioral changes—hopefully, in accordance with the theory. It is tempting to turn with this understanding to the verification of psychoanalytic theses. Habermas would then, with a difference in terminology aside, come close to Popper. To be sure, Habermas moves again in another direction when he deduces the degree of validity only from the patient's self-reflection.

In contrast to the instrumentalistic viewpoint of the purposive-rational organization of means or of adaptive behavior, the elementary events of a psychoanalytic dialogue are processes in a drama: The functional relationship of disturbed self-formative processes and neurotic symptoms must be understood in the light of a dramatic model. That is, the elementary processes appear as parts of a structure of interactions through which a "meaning" is realized. We cannot equate this meaning with ends that are realized through means, on the model of the craftsman. What is at issue is not a category of meaning that is taken from the behavioral system of instrumental action, such as the maintenance of the state of a system under changing external conditions. It is rather a question of a meaning that, even if it is not intended as such, takes form in the course of communicative action and articulates itself reflectively as the experience of life history. This is the way in which "meaning" discloses itself in the course of a drama (Habermas, 1971a).

> In the drama of the self-formative process, the subject is at once both actor and critic. The goal of the process is the capacity of the subject to relate his own history and comprehend the inhibitions that blocked the path of self-reflection. For, the final state of a self-formative process is attained only if the subject remembers its identifications and alienations, the forced upon him objectivities and the reflections it arrived at, as the path upon which it constituted itself. (p. 260)

While on the one hand Habermas (1971a) restores the relation to Freud's empirical-scientific thinking through the concept of general interpretations borrowed from Popper, on the other hand certain romantic elements, which are far removed from Freud's sober notion of education, seem to enter into the goal conception of the self-formative process. Albert's (1971, p. 55) plea for a critical rationalism could include Freud's intention insofar as he justly indicates a certain linking of hermeneutics and dialectics as "German ideology" and opposes this to Freud's natural-scientific maxims. In the following discussion, we shall take a look at the consequences that result from Habermas's argument for the verification of general interpretations. The minuteness with which we refer to Habermas's philosophical exegesis of psychoanalysis is justified by the radical consequences of the announced verification of the "general interpretations" that, according to Habermas, result from it.

The systematically generalized history of an infantile development enables the psychoanalyst to make "interpretive suggestions for a story the patient cannot tell" (Habermas, 1971a, p. 260). Because of this, the interpretation of a particular case proves itself "only by the successful continuation of an interrupted self-formative process" (ibid.). On the basis of this, Habermas can conclude that "analytic insights" possess validity for the analyst only after they have been accepted as knowledge by the analysand himself. For the empirical accuracy of general interpretations depends not on controlled observation and the subsequent communication among investigators but rather on the accomplishment of self-reflection and the subsequent communication between the investigator and his "object" (ibid., p. 261). By this, the general interpretations are marked off from statements regarding an object domain that are made in the context of general theories. While the latter remain exterior to the object domain, the validity of the former depends on the fact that "statements about the object domain [are] applied by the 'objects,' that is, the persons concerned, to themselves" (ibid.). The distinction between the empirical validity of general interpretations and that of general theories is characterized by Habermas as follows: In the behavioral system of instrumental action, the application of assumptions to the reality remains the concern of the inquiring subject. In the behavioral system of self-reflection, the application of statements is possible only via the self-application of the research object that participates in the process of insight. In short, general interpretations have validity only to the degree "that those who are made the object of individual interpretations know and recognize themselves in these interpretations" (ibid.).

Only now it becomes evident how clearly Habermas (1971a) tries to draw the dividing line between general theories, which can be falsified, and general interpretations, which must be tested by the reflexivity attained by the patient. This effort to draw a dividing line cannot, however, be maintained by Habermas himself, nor are psychoanalytic practice and research in agreement with him. The contradictions in which Habermas becomes entangled can be traced back to the fact that the general interpretations on the one hand move too far from such evidence as is required for general theories and on the other hand must prove their value in the distribution of clinical success and failure. These, however, following Habermas, evade intersubjective evaluation:

> The criterion in virtue of which false constructions fail does not coincide with either controlled observation or communicative experience. The interpretation of a case is corroborated only by the successful *continuation of a self-formative process*, and not in any unmistakable way by what the patient says or how he behaves. Here, success and failure cannot be inter-subjectively established, as is possible in the framework of instrumental action or that of communicative action, each in its way. (p. 266; italics added for emphasis)

We cannot understand how Habermas (1971a) relates the distribution of clinical success and failure to the patient's experience of reflection alone. Introspection and reflection are, precisely as psychoanalysis has shown, subject to serious self-deception. Whether the force of an unconscious motive is broken reveals itself objectively exactly there where it can be ascertained intersubjectively: in symptoms and changes in behavior. Besides, free association at first leads away from goal-oriented introspective reflection and expands it when it overcomes resistances. There is probably no analyst who bases the way in which he conducts his treatment only on the reflections of the patient or on his self-formative processes or takes it as the only proof of interpretive hypotheses. The experience of the patient, which he accumulates in the course of a psychoanalytic treatment and as a result of which he arrives at a new interpretation of his life situation, is one aspect in which the success of the treatment manifests itself to the patient. However, there is an evaluation of the success of the treatment in the sense of objective proof of a successful psychic change, which can be fairly well operationalized and subjected to scientifically controlled testing (Fonagy et al., 2002a).

Habermas's discussion introduces the leading utopian idea that an enlightened subject disposes of the history of his "becoming himself"; this is, in our opinion, overestimation of self-reflection. It is easily overlooked that the emancipatory character of psychoanalysis is documented not only by the gained or regained insight into oneself but also by changes in the capacity for human relationships. Many patients are unable, at the end of psychoanalytic treatment, to give an account of which changes and which self-formative processes have taken place in them: They are aware of a change in the immediacy of their experience and actions without being able to reflect philosophically on it in an adequate way (see Leuzinger-Bohleber, Stuhr et al., 2003).

The maxim "Where id is there shall be ego" cannot be understood to mean that the dynamic unconscious, the repressed, and that which unfolds its power behind the back of the subject lies permanently at the conscious disposal of the subject after the analytic treatment. We find Gadamer's (1971a, p. 312) criticism concerning this matter to apply here: "The idea of the elimination of a natural determination in rational, conscious motivation, is in my opinion a dogmatic exaggeration inappropriate to the '*condition humaine.*'" Habermas (1971a) fails to appreciate the necessity that psychoanalytically, the developmental process of the individual consists basically of psychic structures and functions that safeguard the ability to work and love. By this we do not mean a conforming adaptation to an ahistoric reality principle. This principle in our view has a regulatory function and is prone to historical change, which finds its respective sociocultural content in historical change.

Therefore, in the practice of psychoanalysis, we aim at a reasonable equilibrium between those poles that can be characterized as the pleasure principle and the reality principle. Ideally, the blind autoplastic subjection to the contents of the reality principle that are passed on by sociocultural tradition and its internalization in ego and superego functions should be replaced by reasonable alloplastic solutions. Here, a concept of the theory of therapeutic technique assumes significance, namely, "acting out." Acting out signifies such alloplastic, outward-directed efforts of change as are unconsciously drive directed. Insofar as the demands that only the environment should change are not accompanied by the willingness and ability to change oneself, one can usually assert psychoanalytically that in these one-sided alloplastic actions we often are dealing with acting out. That such acting out can often have vast social and historical consequences is one of the tragic paradoxes of the history of mankind. One could almost say that often petrified situations can only be changed when through certain misunderstandings of reality forces of acting out are liberated, which do not seem to know any limits. The tragic fact is that the changes then regularly take place through aggressive-destructive forces, which soon lead to similar disturbing countermovements (see Waelder, 1967). Thus, important insights into collective processes can be gained from the psychoanalytic method, since one can clearly discern in the acting out of the individual the disharmony in society: It is fought there instead of beginning with the individual's own self-formative processes.

The consequence of Habermas's effort to present psychoanalysis as the only tangible example of a science incorporating methodical self-reflection that furthermore should be a model for social reflection would be that the technology of clinical interpretative work thus would have to be rejected. Its methodological particularity, however—that it can be an explanatory science as well as an emancipating reflection—must be, in our opinion, the central issue determining its epistemological status. The multiplicity of psychotherapeutic-intervention techniques that can be derived from psychoanalytic theory and practice indicates an instrumental aspect of which no clinician is ashamed. "The very fact that, since Freud's time, the psychoanalytic method has been used in treating both children and psychotics—to neither of whom Habermas could really grant the capacity for self-reflection—would seem to substantiate this in an important way" (Nichols, 1972, p. 267).[*]

Habermas's (1971a) assertion that success and failure cannot be ascertained intersubjectively in treatment and that justifications based on the disappearance of symptoms are not legitimate fails when confronted with psychotherapeutic practice. Also Freud's emphasis that only the process of the analysis can decide the usefulness or uselessness of a construction does not exclude the confirmative force of changes in symptoms and behavior but comprises an expression of the self-formative process more than just the self-reflection of the patient.

Habermas himself says elsewhere (1963, p. 482) that one of the suppositions for the testing of theories is that repetitive systems can be made accessible to controlled observation. However, just such repetitive systems are present, for instance, in stereotypes of behavior that, through the repetition compulsion, manifest themselves in the various forms and contents of transference neuroses. Repetition and change both manifest in behavior are observed; these observations are reflected in the practice and theory of psychoanalysis. He admits that "single hypotheses can be taken out of the metapsychological context of interpretation and be tested independently" (1967, p. 189):

> Herewith is needed a transposition into the theoretical frame of strict empirical sciences.... In any case, Freud's theory contains assumptions which can be interpreted as lawful hypotheses in a strict sense; from this it follows that it also comprehends causal relations. (p. 190)

What Habermas (1967) seems to admit here is the content of the general and specific theory of neuroses; its confirmation by the experience of the reflection of the patient alone, however, seems to us insufficient. By this there is a task assigned to self-reflection that patients, again according to clinical experience, cannot accomplish.

We agree with Rapaport (1960) that proving the validity of the psychoanalytic theory is a task of the scientific community, which has to agree on the practical procedure of empirical science. Contrary to the restrictive

---

[*] As for the rest, the devaluating qualification that presents instrumentalism as the only knowledge of interest to the "real" sciences is pointed out by Albert (1971). According to him, such a reproach has, in the history of knowledge, always served the screening of specific articles of belief against criticism made possible by the natural sciences (p. 110).

limitation of the confirmation of general interpretations, psychoanalytic research and practice cannot be satisfied with a concept of the self-formative process that is as philosophically vague as it is rich in content and from which confirmation of the theory should result. In any case, the logic of the explanation through general interpretations points toward the specific way in which the confirmation of psychoanalytic statements can alone be obtained: This becomes clear in the linking up of hermeneutic understanding with causal explanation: "Understanding itself gains explanatory power" (Habermas, 1971a, p. 328).*

Transgressing the methodological antithesis of understanding and explaining by an "understanding explanation" or an "explanatory understanding" already can be found in the work of Max Weber. Following Albert (1971) Weber had tried by his conception of theoretical sociology as an understanding science that is directed to an understanding explanation of cultural realities, to overcome this antithesis. In our view the relevance of psychoanalysis in the history of science resides in this overcoming of the antithesis of understanding and explaining (Von Wright, 1994).

In regard to symptoms, constructions take the form of explanatory hypotheses with the aim of analyzing modes of behavior in causal terms. The dissolution of a "causal coherence" through interpretive effort illustrates the efficacy of psychoanalytic therapy. The constructions are to be applied to the single case; they thus become theoretical statements from which singular prognoses can be derived. Generally speaking, these prognoses identify the conditions causally responsible for the neurotic state and claim that the therapeutic process must dissolve these conditions in order to induce change. The disappearance of the efficacy of the supposed internal conditions (e.g., pathogenic unconscious fantasies) demonstrates itself in changes of symptoms and behavior.

In its logical form, however, explanatory understanding differs in one decisive way from explanation rigorously formulated in terms of the empirical sciences. Both of them have recourse to causal statements that can be derived from universal propositions by means of supplementary conditions: that is, from derivative interpretations (conditional variants) or law-like hypotheses. Now the content of theoretical propositions remains unaffected by operational application to reality. In this case we can base

---

* The reconciliation of the methodological antithesis between understanding (*Verstehen*) and explaining (*Erklären*) can be found *in statu nascendi* in Max Weber, in an "understanding explanation" or an "explaining understanding." According to Albert (1971), Weber tried, with his concept of theoretical sociology as an understanding science, which aims at an understanding explanation of the phenomena of cultural reality, to overcome the long-standing antithesis of explaining and understanding and with it the position of extreme historicity as represented by Dilthey (p. 137).

explanations on *context-free laws*. However, in the case of hermeneutic application, theoretical propositions are translated into the narrative presentation of an individual history in such a way that a causal statement does not come into being without this context. General interpretations can abstractly assert their claim to universal validity because their derivatives are additionally determined by context. Narrative explanations differ from strictly deductive ones in that the events or states of which they assert a causal relation are further defined by their application. Therefore, general interpretations do not make possible context-free explanations.

The contextual dependency of psychoanalytic explanations (so-called narrative explanations) argued by Habermas relativizes causal statements and renders impossible strict deductive derivations from laws. Among the few analysts drawing practical and scientific conclusions due to the probabilistic nature of all psychodynamic statements beyond the mere phenomenological descriptions, Benjamin Rubinstein (1980) deserves special mention. His simple but disquieting message is that psychodynamic statements contain hypotheses in need of confirmation; they may even be wrong in single instances. Fonagy (2003, p. 19) draws the same conclusion: "Facing the logical weaknesses of our position we tend to ascribe the clinical theories the status of laws" and tend to deduct behavior and experience from them. Actually clinical typologies allow only probabilistic statements. In a particular instance results can deviate from the probability statement that requires single case studies despite the well-known problems of generalizations from them. The formalized empirical evaluation of treatment reports moves beyond the heuristic, hypothesis-generating function of clinical descriptions and is able to secure objectively identified correlations by statistics (Schaumburg, Kächele, & Thomä, 1974). Obviously the transferability of findings is limited to similar cases. Assuming that all analysts are searching for explanations in order to understand their patients, the dividing line is not between hermeneutic science and empirical social science but in the attitude toward causality. In clinical practice only probability statements, only inductive statistical explanations are possible, but not deductive-nomological conclusions (von Mises, 1951; Ruben, 1993). Recognizing that (unconscious) motives function as causes, then enlightenment, in the sense of "causality of destiny," that Habermas took from Hegel, is rightfully a core issue of psychoanalysis.

From this follows in our opinion, in regard to the methodology of research, that it is of the utmost importance to examine the individual case in its concreteness. Both the self-formative process, as experienced by the subject of treatment, and his objectively recorded changes in conduct and behavior must and can be examined on verbal and preverbal levels and thus become the criteria for testing the clinical hypotheses.

To clarify still further the concept of general interpretation, which plays such a central role in Habermas's conceptualization, we shall now look for its original frame of reference. Popper (1944) introduces the term to distinguish between scientific and historical theories to make a qualitative difference:

> Now it is important to see that many "historical theories" (they might perhaps be better described as "quasi-theories") are in their character vastly different from scientific theories. For in history (including the historical natural sciences, such as historical geology) the facts at our disposal are often severely limited and cannot be repeated or implemented at our will. And they have been collected in accordance with a preconceived point of view; the so-called "sources" of history only record such facts as appeared sufficiently interesting to record, so that the sources will, as a rule, contain only facts that fit in with a preconceived theory. Since no further facts are available it will not, as a rule, be possible to test that or any other subsequent theory. Such historical theories, which cannot be tested, can then rightly be charged with being *circular* in the sense in which this charge has been unjustly brought against scientific theories. I shall call such historical theories in contradistinction to scientific theories, "general interpretations." (pp. 265–266)

The verifiability of these historical general interpretations is restricted insofar as there are no *experimenta crucis* in historical research and in psychoanalysis as there are in the natural sciences. Popper (1944) gives an elaborate argument for this, which leads him to give up the naive view "that any definite set of historical recordings can ever be interpreted in one way only" (p. 266). Hereby it becomes clear how closely Popper's falsifications theory is connected with the axiomatic sciences. He then introduces a number of relative proofs for historical interpretations, which suffice to determine probable and relative validity:

1. There are false interpretations that do not agree with the acknowledged recordings.
2. There are interpretations that need a number of more or less plausible auxiliary hypotheses to avoid falsification by the data.
3. There are interpretations that do not succeed in connecting a series of facts that are connected by another interpretation and are explained to that extent (p. 266).
4. Accordingly, considerable progress would also be possible in the area of historical interpretations. Besides, all sorts of intermediate stations between more or less general points of view and specific or singular historical hypotheses would be possible that, in the explanation of

historical events, play the role of hypothetic initial conditions and not the role of general laws (see Klauber, 1968).

It is obvious that the considerable qualitative distinction Popper (1944) makes between scientific theories and general interpretations is no longer present in Habermas (1971a), to whom general interpretations claim the same degree of validity as general propositions in the empirical sciences. Their decisive difference lies in the logical procedure of validating research. To become more acquainted with these differences, we now consider the problem of which relations exist between the general model of scientific explanation, general interpretations, and single forms of explanation as they occur in psychoanalytic work and research.

DESCRIPTION, EXPLANATION, AND PROGNOSIS IN PSYCHOANALYSIS

Allport (1937) characterizes scientific activity as the effort to understand, predict, and control. Of this triad, the role of understanding is likely to be underestimated; it bears too close a relationship to philosophical speculation, whereby one easily overlooks the fact that understanding as a hermeneutic principle is in every scientific activity the condition of further progress. In the preceding pages we have already dealt at length with the role that understanding has in the scientific process. The procedures of prediction and control as represented in Allport's viewpoint presuppose explanations. In its daily decisions, clinical practice deals with this immanent coherence as a matter of course. For our discussion, however, it seems useful to clarify here once again the principle of this coherence before we continue with a discussion oriented toward psychoanalysis. From a logical point of view, scientific predictions have the same structure as explanations. The event to be expected is deduced logically from given laws and auxiliary conditions, whereas explanations are a sort of post hoc reconstruction of how an event has come about. This deduction of the prediction goes back to Popper's (1959) description of the logical structure of causal explanations. Hempel and Oppenheim (1953) systematize the relationship between prediction and explanation in the model of scientific explanation named after them (the HO-model of scientific explanation). To facilitate the discussion we will repeat the relationships.

In an explanation, an *explanandum*—that is, a specific fact that has occurred—is presented. To explain it, one has to look for (at least) one law and the accompanying initial conditions. In a prognosis, however, the explanandum is not given; we know only the laws and the initial conditions. Table 2.1 clarifies this difference in graphic form:

Table 2.1   Differences of Explanation and Prognosis

Explanation		Prognosis
sought	law	given
sought	initial conditions	given
given	explanandum	sought

In the explanation as well as in the prognosis, an explanandum is deduced from (at least) one law and the initial conditions belonging to it. The only difference is that in each case different elements are sought and given. On the basis of our discussion in the section on "General and Historical Interpretations," it is clear that the HO-outline implies a type of explanation, which in psychoanalysis is only applicable by corresponding extension of the definition. Before we occupy ourselves with other forms of explanation, which according to Stegmüller (1969) can likewise come under the concept of scientific explanation, we must come to grips with a contrary position.

It is often said from various quarters that a great deal of Freud's achievements lie in his brilliant description of many aspects of human behavior. The most prominent representative of this position must be Ludwig Wittgenstein, who, according to Moore (1955, p. 316), emphasizes, "There are so many cases [in Freud's writings] in which one can ask oneself how far what he says is a hypothesis, and to what extent [it is] only a good manner of presenting the facts."

MacIntyre (1958, p. 61) arrives, in his effort to explain the concept of the unconscious, at a similar conclusion in this matter: "For Freud's achievement lies not in his explanations of abnormal behaviour but in his redescription of such behavior." When one tries to fathom where the basis for such judgments lies, as Sherwood (1969)[*] does, then one finds that Wittgenstein refers to "The Psychopathology of Everyday Life" (Freud, 1901) and that MacIntyre predominantly considers "The Interpretations of Dreams" (Freud, 1900). Both works indeed contain anecdotic material given to illustrate ways in which the psychic apparatus functions. Causal remarks, taken out of the clinical context, appear thereafter only as ways of presenting the facts and easily lose their explanatory character. If, however, the clinical context is restored, then what Sherwood says is true:

---

[*] See also the discussion of Sherwood's book by Eagle (1973), Rubinstein (1973), and Sherwood (1973).

> It is of course true that Freud described certain acts of the patient in a new way. But the important thing is that he tried thereby to explain them.... To give a new description in given contexts can indeed come close to an explanation. The distinction between these two procedures is not always sharp and in each case it depends on the context, the situation in which it takes place. (p. 187)

Even though MacIntyre (1958, p. 79) acknowledges elsewhere that a clarifying description can indeed count as a way of explaining, he feels that he has to again deny the title of explanation to Freud's efforts to explain the significance of dreams, which have to do more with a deciphering than with explanation (ibid., p. 112). The discrepancy that here clearly comes to the fore concerns the scope, the concept of explanation. Different types of explanation are certainly at the base of Freud's clinical presentations.

Sherwood (1969) points to the fact that Freud's explanations in the case histories of patients—he illustrates extensively with the example of the Rat Man—always concern, first of all, an individual patient, a specific case history (see Chapter 3 in this volume). The object of research is not a class of certain psychiatric symptoms and not a class of people who have a certain illness, but a single person. As the historian, Freud is interested in the particular outcome of events in order to perceive the typical. Accordingly, Freud uses generalizations about compulsion neurotics as a class. In the same way, there is a general theory of human behavior beyond the explanation of particular life histories (see Waelder, 1962).

A presupposition for generalization is that the explanations have been tested in a particular case. The other condition is self-evident: that the explanations tested in the particular case are present in a group of cases, whereby they become typical. The typical coherences are always only part of a case history; the particular explanations are woven into the whole. This context, which represents the comprehensive integrating moment, is characterized as "psychoanalytic narrative." Within this narrative various types of explanations can be isolated, which occur in different distributions. Hereby the narrative is to be regarded not simply as the sum (total) of these various explanations but as the integrating framework: "In short, giving an account of the resolution of a single symptom would in fact amount to the task of relating an entire case history" (Freud, 1896c, p. 197).

According to Danto (1965), representations that present events as elements in a history are called "narrative statements." Since psychoanalytic explanations lie within the totality of a life history, the denotation "psychoanalytic narrative"—which as far as we know was first used by Farrell (1961) in philosophical discussion—underlines the historical character of psychoanalytic explanations.

The Notion of Scientific Explanation

In the German-Austrian philosopher Stegmüller's (1969) fundamental elaborations on the concept of scientific explanation—still the most complete overview on the status of analytic philosophy in the German language—he first of all singles out scientific explanation from a multiplicity of everyday usages of the word. The explanation of the meaning of a word—which can also be called *definition*, the explanation as text interpretation, instruction on how to act, or detailed description and moral justification—these numerous meanings of the concept of explanation show hardly anything in common, and Stegmüller calls them at best a concept family in Wittgenstein's sense.

In the psychoanalytic models of explanation, as Sherwood (1969) shows, all those forms and explanations that are known from everyday language occur. It is a question of discovering the source of a feeling of "explaining" as if it were the origin of something strange. Herewith nothing is yet explained in the sense of the HO-explanation; only a more precise knowledge of the facts is achieved. The explanation of the genesis (origin) of a symptom already poses difficult problems of demarcation. If the observed transference behavior is reduced to an infantile attitude to the mother, then not only are facts that appear as disparate brought together, but also by way of trial, genetic explanations are accepted that must prove themselves as retrodiction. The multitude of phenomena and processes in the psychoanalytic situation requires different explanatory operations, which should not be, a priori, designated as scientific or unscientific. Sherwood concludes his illustration of the various types of explanation with examples from the case history of the Rat Man: "A psychoanalyst is called upon to answer a wider range of questions on human behavior, and his explanations can therefore be of very different sorts" (ibid., p. 202).

Indeed, the demarcation of different types of explanation from explanation in the strict sense of the HO-model, as is partly reflected in Sherwood (1969), does not take into regard the fact that, according to Stegmüller (1969, p. 336), "the concept of scientific explanations was introduced in such a way that it could claim for itself general applicability in all *empirical* sciences." To be sure, the form of the construction of the concept of explanation decides whether it is applicable: A narrow conception corresponds to the HO-model as we have briefly outlined it in the previous passages (under an explanatory argument should be understood a deductive conclusion, among the premises of which is at least one deterministic or statistic law hypothesis); if, however, the concept is taken in a larger sense, that of Stegmüller, then not only the search for grounds in reality or causes but also quite generally the search for a basis in reasons can enter into the search for an explanation.

This enlargement of the concept of scientific explanation draws particular historical, and consequently also some psychoanalytic, explanations into its scope. The language of the historian, as well as of the psychoanalyst who reports on his case, is full of expressions that indicate an effort to explain. Logical or inductive arguments of many theses, instead of causal arguments, are often given. The selective description of the historian becomes an initial explanation because the description is governed by hypotheses. To be sure, in historical explanations regularities that have a statistic or trivial character are often drawn; the explanatory argument is therefore often not mentioned. Stegmüller (1969) lists other qualities of historical initial explanations, which cause the historical scientist not to interpret his statements as explanations in the sense of the HO-model. As a superior point of view he introduces thereby, following Hempel (1965), the incompleteness of such explanations. Incomplete explanations, which are also called "explanation outlines," can be reduced to the following four roots:

1. The explanation has dispositional character.
2. The explanation contains self-evident generalizations from the commonplace, which are not specifically mentioned.
3. The explanation is incomplete because further derivation of a law must be explicitly renounced because its range would be exceeded.
4. The explanation is incomplete due to insufficient experiential material.

According to Stegmüller (1969) for the aforementioned reasons high demands on historical explanations cannot be materialized; he therefore proposes a broadly conceived definition of historical explanation in the sense of the HO-outline:

> An explanation of E on the basis of antecedents' data A1. A1 would accordingly be present, when the event-to-be explained is to be expected on the basis of its antecedents'-event and to be expected either in the sense of a purely intuitive and not further defined, or in the sense of a formally specified "confirmative concept" [*Bestätigungsbegriff*]" (p. 348).

The genetic statements of psychoanalytic theory can be covered—that is to say, with this form of historical explanations the present efforts to explain psychoanalytic developmental psychology can be so classified, at least formally. That hereby the degree of confirmation is attained with different precision is clearly shown in the various results of the longitudinal studies by Benjamin (1950), Escalona (1952), and others. Interestingly enough, William Langer, as early as 1957 when he was president of the American Historical Association, advocates "the use in the future, for the purpose of historical explanations, to a much greater extent than before, of ideas of psychoanalysis and related theories of depth psychology" (quoted in Stegmüller, 1969, p. 423). Langer pleads in particular for the use of dispositional explanations, because the model of conscious-rational behavior could not suffice for the historian.

The Concept of Dispositional Explanation

It is worthwhile to discuss in greater detail the concept of dispositional explanation, because, like functional explanation, it is of great importance for psychoanalysis. Statements such as "the glass breaks because it has quality X" are dispositional explanations. Because the dispositional quality of an object or individual has consequences in the nature of a law, Ryle (1949) classifies such explanations as "law-like" statements. Dispositional explanations concern that "category of cases in which the activity of the acting persons should be explained with the help of character traits, convictions, goal projections and other dispositional factors" (Stegmüller, 1969, p. 120). The patient brings to treatment certain modes of behavior and certain qualities based on subconscious conflict constellations, which we explain by dispositions. Since the patient unconsciously seeks a repetition of his infantile traumata, he constructs the transference situation in an analogous manner. The formation of the transference neurosis can be interpreted as the transposition of such dispositions in object relationships that are experienced anew. The overcoming of the transference neurosis will then lead to the dissolution of the unconscious conflicts that previously determined his behavior and with it, of the disposition of those conflicts as a lawful way of reacting. Dispositional statements are often not regarded as explanations, because their relation to basic laws is, as a rule, not made explicit.

The logic of functional explanations must still be discussed separately. Freud speaks of the dream as the guardian of sleep. Are we dealing here with a scientifically legitimate mode of explanation, or is the finalistic consideration here only a veil over an as-yet-unknown causal phenomenon? Or does the functional presentation represent only a descriptive coherence, without the claim of explanation? As a prototype of a functional explanation in psychoanalysis we propose Freud's (1926d) theory of symptom formation:

> Since we have traced back the generating of anxiety to a situation of danger, we shall prefer to say that symptoms are created in order to remove the ego from a situation of danger. (p. 144)

The manner in which Freud (1926d) expresses himself here is teleological. It seems almost as if what happens in symptom formation should be included in the outline of conscious goal-oriented action. But, as Stegmüller (1969) shows, the logical outline of the functional analysis provides an appropriate representation of the relations. System S is the individual in whom pathological symptoms form. Disposition D is the pattern of compulsive behavior that impresses like a symptom. The effects of disposition D can be indicated by N, which is in the case of symptom formation, the binding of anxiety. Herein, the functional explanation would be that, condition N is deemed necessary for a normal functioning of S, which in this case means that S can continue to live without serious psychic crises. As Stegmüller shows in his further examination, the testing of the empirical significance of such functional explanations presents considerable difficulties. These lie in the exact definition of the various parts of the explanation model. For the purpose of verification, *that* class of individuals must be specified for whom a defined disposition D lawfully has the effects N; that is to say, an empirical difficulty lies in the empirically meaningful definition of the system S for which the functional explanation is claimed. A further difficulty arises for empirical testing procedures when not only the disposition $D1$, but also another disposition $D2$ shows the same effects of the nature N, for the system is thus functionally equivalent to disposition $D1$.

Let us put this problem in psychoanalytic terms. Not only the defense mechanism of denial, but also that of isolation, of reversal, and so forth, can be utilized for the binding of anxiety of someone suffering from compulsion neurosis. The introduction of additional dispositions weakens, however reciprocally, the explanatory value of the original one. Thus, for instance, Bronislaw Malinowski's thesis that the effect of magic is necessary for the functioning of primitive society is reduced in its explanatory value because no proof is given that only this magic enables primitive man to overcome existential anxiety. The weakness of the functional analysis thus lies in its greater range of descriptive applications, concerning which the heuristic character is easily overlooked. If, in psychoanalysis, it can be shown that different dispositions are effective for different categories of individuals, then the functional explanation can also claim explanatory value.

Prognosis

After this orientation regarding different forms of explanations and their use in psychoanalysis, we ask ourselves what the position of prognosis is in psychoanalytic theory and research. Although not all of science lies in proof, and prognosis is not the only purpose, the prognostic power of a theory has acquired an important place in psychological research. In the history of psychoanalysis, prognosis has not been held in high esteem, neither as instrument nor as goal. Indeed, we must here distinguish between unreflexive-automatic clinical everyday use and theoretic reflection. "Every interviewer who exercises any kind of interpretative technique, predicts from one moment to the next," writes Meehl (1963, p. 71). Thus, in the practice of psychoanalysis, clinical experience and suggestions of therapy derived from it are from the very beginning practiced as applied prognostics. "To be sure, we know very little about the frequency of their success and their reliability and in how far the course of the interview depends on them," Meehl (ibid.) continues. The theoretical skepticism of the psychoanalyst was based on an opposition, pointed out by Freud (1920b), between analysis and synthesis, which proved to hamper the adequate reception of the prognosis as an instrument of scientific effort.

> But at this point we become aware of a state of things which also confronts us in many other instances at which light has been thrown on by psychoanalysis on a mental process. So long as we trace the development from its final outcome backwards, the chain of events appears continuous and we feel we have gained an insight, which is completely satisfactory or even exhaustive. But if we proceed the reverse way, if we start from the premises inferred from the analysis and try to follow these up to the final result, then we no longer get the impression of an inevitable sequence of events which could not have been otherwise determined. We notice at once that there might have been another result and that we might have been just as well able to understand and explain the latter. The synthesis is thus not as satisfactory as the analysis; in other words, from knowledge of the premises, we could not have foretold the nature of result.... Hence the chain of the causation can always be recognized with certainty if we follow the line of analysis, whereas to predict it along the line of synthesis is impossible. (pp. 167–168)

This presentation from the case report on female homosexuality appears to demonstrate convincingly that it is in principle impossible to predict the future development of a personality; hence, the range of genetic psychoanalytic statements is reduced to the *post-festum* analysis of the development of the personality. When at this point we apply the outline on explanation and prognosis previously reported, then the question presents itself whether in fact, with exactly the same border conditions, the explanandum could have been something other than (as in the case under discussion) female homosexuality. We believe that if one follows the patho-etiological road in the directions Freud records, other possibilities of development emerge in retrospect because other border conditions occur at the horizon of thought. Then it seems as if the development did not necessarily have to lead to female homosexuality. Moreover, the completing series, the etiological outline developed by Freud (1905d, pp. 239–240), contains border conditions that, if they are or were known, permit explanation. We are therefore confronted here with a problem that can perhaps hardly be solved in empirical ways but is not insoluble in principle.

Freud's formulations can lead to misunderstanding insofar as the knowledge of the presuppositions or, more precisely, the knowledge of all presuppositions must make the nature of the event predictable. In the aforementioned article, Freud himself explains the pessimistic result—that synthesis is impossible with the lack of knowledge about further causes. These causes are, however, nothing other than alternative border conditions, which, of course, looking back at the pathogenesis can never be known. Only a psychoanalyst endowed with the *Weltgeist* of Pierre-Simon Laplace could perhaps name all possible border conditions retrospectively. An illustration of the relation between the knowledge of possible border conditions and the prognostic results is given by Benjamin (1959) in his excellent work on the role of prediction in developmental psychology.

Although Freud's resignation concerns prediction only in the context of genetic psychology, we must remember that the claim of conditional predictions has been formulated with much reservation in other fields of psychoanalytic theory and practice as well. According to Rapaport (1960), this is related to the central position of the principle of overdetermination in psychoanalytic psychology:

> The psychoanalytic concept of *overdetermination* implies that one or several determiners of a given behavior, which appear to explain it, do not necessarily give its full causal explanation. This is not per se alien to other sciences, though a *principle of overdetermination* did not become necessary in any of them. Psychoanalysis' need for this principle seems to be due partly to the multiplicity of the determiners of human behavior and partly to the theory's characteristic lack of criteria for the independence and sufficiency of causes. The determiners of behavior in this theory are so defined in that they apply to all behavior and thus their empirical referents must be present in any and all forms of behavior. Since there is usually no single determiner which constantly assumes the dominant role in a given behavior, other determiners can hardly be neglected while a dominant determiner is explored. When favorable conditions make one determiner dominant, the investigator is tempted to conclude that he has confirmed a predicted functional relationship; as he indeed has. Regrettably, the attempt to repeat the observation or experiment in question often fails, because in the replication either the same behavior appears even though a different determiner has become dominant, or a different behavior appears even though the same determiner has remained dominant. (pp. 66–67)

On the basis of such considerations it seems logical to Rapaport (1960) that Freud overestimates the role of postdiction and underestimates the role of prediction in the construction of the theory. Waelder (1963) subjects the principle of overdetermination to a critical analysis, which brings a logical as well as a semantic clarification. With reference to a weighty place in Freud's (1910a) text, Waelder points out that the principle of psychic determinism and of overdetermination must be understood as a heuristic concept, which for methodological reasons requires for all psychic processes—whether they appear as unpretentious, arbitrary, or accidental—sufficient motivation: "As you already see, psychoanalysts are marked by a particularly strict belief in the determination of mental life. For them there is nothing trivial, nothing arbitrary or haphazard. They expect in every case to find sufficient motives" (Freud, 1910a, p. 38).

The introduction of determinism had therefore, first of all, the function of providing a secure methodological foundation for Freud's analysis. From the "belief" in the determination of psychic life, a series of methodological principles of the psychoanalytical technique of research can be derived. Besides, it follows from the citation that "to be determined" was for Freud equivalent with "to be motivated"; this permits Waelder (1963) to reject the philosophical debate about the question of determinism and free will. From here on the farther-reaching concept of overdetermination must also be considered. Let us first examine those places where Freud introduces the concept of overdetermination; in the "Studies on Hysteria" we find in the discussion of etiological questions the following references: "Almost invariably when I have investigated the determinants of such [hysterical] conditions what I have come upon has not been a *single* traumatic cause but a group of similar ones" (Freud, 1895a, p. 173, italics in original).

What Freud (1995d) illustrates here casuistically in the case of Elisabeth von R. is further explained in the theoretical chapter "The Psychotherapy of Hysteria": "He [the physician] is aware of the principal feature in the etiology of the neuroses—that their genesis is as a rule overdetermined, that several factors must come together to produce this result" (p. 263). In the same way it is true for the symptoms of hysteria: "We must not expect to meet with a *single* traumatic memory and a *single* pathogenic idea as its nucleus; we must be prepared for *successions* of *partial* traumas and *concatenations* of pathogenic trains of thought" (pp. 287–288).

The clearest definition of the extent of the concept is found in Freud's (1895f) discussion of Löwenfeld's critique of the anxiety neurosis: "As a rule the neuroses are *overdetermined*; that is to say, several factors operate together in their etiology" (p. 131). What can be summarized from these citations and what functions as "the principle of overdetermination" is therefore the idea that there is for the neurotic disorders and their symptoms not a single cause but many causes working together, the relationship among which cannot be seen as simply cumulative. The structural totality of this set of causes produces together the necessary and sufficient conditions.

In "The Psychopathology of Everyday Life," Freud (1901), in the discussion of promises, quotes Wundt, who in his *Völkerpsychologie* (psychology of nations) claims for slips of the tongue, a series of psychic influences that raise doubt about a single causal motivation of promises:

> In some cases too, it may be doubtful to which form a certain disturbance is to be assigned, or whether it would not be more justifiable in *accordance with the principle of the complication of causes,* to trace it back to a concurrence of several motives [Wundt, Völkerpsychologie, 1910, 380–381]. I consider these observations of Wundt's fully justified and very instructive. (pp. 60–61, italics in original)

Even if the principle was not new and is, especially today, recognized in all sciences that occupy themselves with more complex systems, it is nevertheless of special credit to psychoanalysts who as pioneers have consistently applied it. Sherwood's (1969, p. 181) criticism of psychoanalysts who claim to have "newly discovered" this principle and who want it understood as an essential concept that distinguishes psychoanalysis from other sciences, misses to that extent the heart of the matter. Psychoanalytic explanations have too often been criticized for their plasticity and vagueness. To no small degree, these criticisms stem from efforts on the part of psychoanalysts to take into account the multiple conditions and functions of psychic acts.

In any case, Sherwood (1969) justly indicates a misunderstanding of the concept of overdetermination to which Waelder (1963) also addresses. If one thus means that there are several causal "constellations" independent of each other and necessary and sufficient, as Guntrip (1961) seems to say, then the result is a logical impossibility.* Waelder (1963) tries to clarify the content of the concept of being overdetermined, which starts from the aforementioned logical untenable nature. The historical perspective Waelder gives in his reference to the origin of the concept is interesting. Freud's effort to conceive of psychic processes and results in neurophysiologic concepts brought the model of psychic causality into analogy with the processes of a single neuron: Stimulus-accumulation with threshold values was an adequate concept for the manner in which neurological processes are effective. The overdetermination necessary for neurological processes— namely to reach threshold values—was borrowed for psychic processes. Waelder corrects the basic misunderstanding by bringing out the meaning of the situation and introducing a new concept: The principle of the mul-

---

* Anyway, as Stegmüller (1969, p. 5) indicates, self-directed behavior-flexible systems can reach a similar goal along roads that are causally independent of each other.

tiple function of a psychic act implies no contradiction in regard to logic causality; it expresses the psychoanalytically central fact that any psychic act can simultaneously serve different needs and problem solutions.

While the confusing "overdetermination of the psyche" was one limitation of the possibility of prediction, so even after clearing away this misunderstanding, the question remains why we are incapable of predicting the nature of the result from knowledge of the presuppositions. In answer to this, Freud alleges that only qualitative and not quantitative etiological relationships are known. Only at the end of developmental process, one could say which of the psychic forces were the stronger, because only the outcome can inform us about the relationship between the forces. Particularly obscure relationships are present when human behavior is the result of a conflict of almost equal inner forces thus making different end results possible. Conflict solutions and steps of development are therefore decisive processes. The greater the number of border conditions, the more degrees of freedom exist and the factors of uncertainty in the prediction increase proportionately. However, predictions become reliable in those cases in which there is no conflict or in which one side is clearly stronger than the other.

In regard to this, Waelder (1963, pp. 90ff) mentions two marginal cases that render predictions possible: first, those in which the behavior is exclusively governed by the mature ego; or second, those under completely opposite conditions in which the governing by the mature ego is practically entirely eliminated and the action is therefore exclusively ruled by biological forces (drives) and the primitive efforts of solution of the immature ego—that is, when the wealth of determinants of human behavior is diminished.

Anna Freud (1958) further points out that predictions are possible not only in these two extreme cases but also in the numerous cases in which the components—primitive inner forces and sense of reality—exist in a stable relation characteristic for the individual concerned. Such stable mixtures would then constitute the essence of character (ibid., p. 92). More or less stable relations, that is, limited "degrees of freedom," always exist in the circumscribed range of psychic disturbances within the total personality. Psychoanalytic explanations and predictions concern these relatively closed systems.

Conceptual Vagueness or Principal Objections

With respect to the difficulties mentioned so far of deriving the possibility of prediction from the theory of psychoanalysis, the question now arises whether we here have conceptual obscurities or fundamental objections. The question is of particular interest in regard to practical necessity: "Thus prediction, or predictability, is in the analysis not accidental but belongs to its essence. And it is obviously true ... that our technique is constantly based on such tentative predictions. Without it a rational technique would be impossible" (Hartmann, 1958, p. 121).

For clarification we should first distinguish between different areas, in which prediction can be used, in order to examine in each case whether and to what extent predictions are possible. In its present form, psychoanalytic theory has hypothetic explanations ready for a wide range of social phenomena. Systematic verification of such explanatory efforts with the help of predictive techniques will be discussed here only for the therapeutic situation.

Escalona's (1952) skepticism of whether prediction is possible in clinical psychoanalytic research finds its origin in two considerations. The one, which refers to the conclusive force of an applicable prediction, does not directly belong here and will later be discussed separately. The other consideration compares the psychoanalytic therapeutic situation with the laboratory experiment and finds that in the therapeutic situation, for instance, the environmental variable cannot be controlled sufficiently to be able to make meaningful predictions concerning the behavior of the patient. Escalona overlooks that in psychoanalysis one has to do with *relatively* stable and permanent structures, which guarantee a high degree of evenness in the reaction to stimuli. Bellak and Smith (1956), in a pioneering experimental study, were able to show that the importance of the environmental variables is, in fact, considerably reduced by the reaction-readiness of the patient.

From the effort to make predictions concerning the next step in treatment—short-term predictions—one can reasonably distinguish the effort to make prognostic assertions concerning the outcome of treatment. For this, goals of treatment have to be formulated and written down at the beginning. To illustrate this with the model of prediction study of the Menninger Clinic, changes in behavior, adaptive changes (in Hartmann's sense), intrapsychic changes such as insight, changes in drive defense, constellations, or structural changes of the ego can be indicated. As Sargent and her coworkers (Sargent, Horwitz, Wallerstein, & Appelbaum, 1968) show in detail, the use of predictions as scientific instruments requires, in any case, a more precise explanation of the formal nature of predictions. Based on Benjamin's (1950, 1959) fundamental longitudinal studies of children, in which he specified prediction as an instrument to validate psychoanalytic-genetic assertions, a prediction model was outlined that permitted empirical testing of predicted changes after psychoanalytic treatment (see also Luborsky and Schimek, 1964, for a thorough study of these issues).

As we have been able to show, without specific reference to any of the studies mentioned, prediction as an instrument of examination can also be used in psychoanalytic therapy. The stability of neurotic processes permits us to regard the psychoanalytic treatment situation temporarily as ahistoric, even if it is embedded in the framework of systematically generalized history.

Structural Identity of Explanation and Prognosis

In conclusion, one question must still be raised that puts the significance of prediction in a larger context. Hempel and Oppenheim's (1953) outline of scientific explanation leads to the plausible conception to which we referred to previously: "that explanatory and prognostic arguments are similar in regard to their logical structure" (Stegmüller, 1969, p. 153). This would mean that we can only be content with an explanation when we can turn it around, as it were, and use it as an instrument of prediction. On the other hand, we know examples of correct predictions in which the explanatory coherence was not always already known. This theoretical self-evidence, as suggested by the HO-model, was annulled by Scriven (1959). In his analysis of the role of explanation and prediction in the theory of evolution, he shows that the explanatory force of Darwin's hypotheses is not reduced by the lack of prognoses of similar scope:

> Darwin's success lay in his empirical, case by case, demonstration that recognizable fitness *was* very often associated with survival and that the small random variations could lead to the development of species. He did not discover an exact universal law but the utility of a particular indicator in looking for explanations. (p. 478)

To a great extent, similar conditions seem to exist for psychoanalysis. Complete explanatory sets of laws and border conditions are seldom available enough so that they could be transformed into valid predictions. But very often psychoanalysis can demonstrate the explanatory power of particular indicators that sediment into well-known "rules of thumb" of which the daily clinical work draws its predictive capacity.

CIRCULARITY AND SELF-FULFILLING PROPHECY

Preface

The expression *self-fulfilling prophecy* was coined by R. K. Merton in 1957. He refers to the theorem of W. I. Thomas, the Nestor of American sociologists, which is basic to the social sciences: "If men define situations as real, they are real in their consequences." Merton adds:

> Were the Thomas theorem and its implications more widely known, more men would understand more of the workings of our society. Though it lacks the sweep and precision of a Newtonian theorem, it possesses the same gift of relevance, being instructively applicable to many, if indeed not most, social processes. (p. 421)

In any discussion on predictions in psychoanalysis, the question must be examined whether interpretations fulfill themselves therein. Therefore, we have to occupy ourselves with the problem of circularity. To make the theme explicit, let us look in our text for references to circle and circularity. First we hit upon the hermeneutic circle and then on circularity in historical explanations. We can further perceive a circular movement in the psychoanalytic art of interpretation, where certainly, to pick up a thought of Dilthey, one could speak of a "circularity of experience, understanding, and representation of the mental world in general concepts:—if we include under the latter the clinical theory of psychoanalysis" (Dilthey, *Collected Works*, VII, 145, as quoted by Apel, 1967).

Let us first maintain with Apel (1967, p. 147, italics added for emphasis) that the hermeneutic circle signifies "that we always already must have understood, in order to understand at all and to be able to *correct*, however, our preliminary understanding through the *methodic* endeavor of understanding." In this definition the demand for methodic correction of preliminary understanding seems to us essential, because the common bond of scientific proceedings is assured by it.

Apel thus sees in hermeneutics a "methodic" circle. With Gadamer (1965), who follows Heidegger, the circle has lost this meaning. If one simplified somewhat, one could say that in the philosophical hermeneutics of Gadamer and Heidegger the incomplete preliminary understanding is replaced by the "anticipation of completeness." In this anticipation of completeness the totality always seems to be already known, so that parts become understandable only when they appear in a complete unity of meaning. The philosophical-hermeneutic anticipation of completeness (Gadamer, 1965, p. 277) presupposes that hermeneutics is freed from the restrictions of the scientific concept of objectivity, as Gadamer emphasized (ibid., p. 250). The important thing for us is a correction of the psychoanalytic-psychotherapeutic preliminary understanding, which is in agreement with the empirical sciences and can be made objective. Thus, Gadamer's anticipation of completeness takes the place of an antithesis that cannot be regarded in an empirical-scientific way, because it is from the very beginning outside of its terrain and therefore enjoys a kind of extraterritorial immunity. Here, to simplify, one could say that the circle is completely closed from the beginning.

Circularity in a general sense exists in every scientific inquiry because a selective preliminary understanding enters into the formation of hypotheses. Radnitzky (1973, p. 215) discusses those aspects of the circle that one can render visible outside of hermeneutics. In the natural sciences, descriptions are governed by anticipated explanations. Before something can be explained, that which is to be explained (the explanandum) must be expressed in the language of the theory with which one hopes to achieve the more exact explanation. For instance, in order to explain planetary movements with Newton's theory, one must set the descriptions in a relevant form, but to do this, one must possess a certain preliminary understanding.

Preliminary understanding and correction, formation of hypotheses and verification, characterize every science and therefore cannot imply circularity in the sense of a vicious circle. Also, the process of knowing is in itself a circular process. It proceeds from ideas (hypotheses) to the facts and back again. To conceptually distinguish general circularity from its incorrect forms, we indicate the latter from now on as *vicious circle*, as faulty conclusion or the like. Then, when does preliminary understanding become faulty circularity? When is the reproach of circular conclusion justified? What proof can be found in the assertion of Popper (1944, p. 265) that it is unjust to accuse scientific theories of circularity, while in general interpretations, therefore, in historical explanations, circularity can be present in the pejorative sense of the word?

It is a question of eliminating faults that necessarily still characterize the preliminary understanding, by testing hypotheses with facts. Hereby one should be careful that the immanent faults in the preliminary understanding do not remain hidden by a preestablished choice of material, which would lead to an apparent confirmation. The fact that theory and method move in the same frame of reference would have to lead to a vicious circle only when the research directions were such that they could give answers that are already given by the theory. Theory and method must therefore be independent from each other to the extent that the observations can say "no" to the theory (see Meehl, 1973, pp. 114ff). A theory constructed according to the well-known proverb, "When the rooster crows, the weather changes or it remains the same," cannot be contradicted.

That it is possible for theory and method to move in the same frame of reference, while sufficient independence remains, is illustrated by Popper (1959) in a comparison of research and legal processes. In investigating a specific problem that need not concern us here, namely the establishment of so-called basic sentences, Popper shows, by the example of a classic trial by jury, the jury members' and judges' dependence on and independence from the penal system. Thereby the rules of procedure and jurisdiction, one could say plural controls, protect against errors (pp. 109–110). The rules of procedure, according to which the verdict is reached, are, however, not identical with the legal norms to be applied to the case, but both belong to the legal system. To this extent dependence exists on the legal system and the process moves within this circle.

It is not surprising that precisely this analogy of the research process with a legal process, likewise discussed by Radnitzky (1973, p. 216), played a role in the discussion between Habermas (1969) and Albert (1969) on the occasion of the so-called dispute on positivism (see Adorno et al., 1969, pp. 242, 278). Albert refers to the fact that in the relationship of rules and manner of procedure in the legal system one does not find a circle "in the relevant sense of the word." A "relevant circularity," as we may in any case understand Albert, would be a faulty conclusion implicit in the system or procedure. However, of greater importance is what Habermas (1969) concludes from the analogy between research and legal process: "Something like experimentally established facts by which empirical-scientific theories could fail, are constituted first in a preliminary context of interpretation of possible experience" (p. 243).

The reason we presented Popper's analogy* and the preceding discussion between Albert (1969) and Habermas (1969) is because the all-around relationship to the legal system must result just as little in faulty judgments there as do faulty conclusions in psychoanalysis. They occur because their interpreting practice depends on its explaining theories. To the contrary: All precautions serve to avoid, respectively correct faulty judgments in the one cases and faulty conclusions in the other.

The Psychoanalytic Easter Eggs

Since in the section on general interpretations we have already established that the testing of psychoanalytic theory takes place by the standard of changes that can be predicted under certain conditions, we can now turn to a further more fascinating problem. Let us assume that a patient suffering from anxiety neurosis would, in the course of psychoanalysis, show changes in his symptoms conforming to the theory. Since the theory, as we have shown, has influenced the technique of interpretation, the self-confirmation could be produced along this way (self-fulfilling prophecy). At this point one usually quotes what F. Kraus† is supposed to have said: The psychoanalyst finds the Easter eggs that he has first hidden himself (as quoted by Wyss, 1961, p. 372). Thus, it is supposed that psychoanalytic observations are not related to the real facts but owe their existence to the imagination of the psychoanalyst. Here, one attributes to the imagination a power that in fact it does possess: It produced reality long before Sigmund Freud discovered its constructive and destructive potential, and it was illustrated with a document that was completely independent from psychoanalytic technique—the Oedipus saga as described by Sophocles. As

---

* Since Popper (1972) otherwise illustrates the methodology of the empirical sciences almost exclusively with the natural sciences, this analogy has special significance: It shows that Popper himself cannot maintain the restriction of the concept of empirical science.

† Although this ironic remark could as well have come from the antipsychoanalytic and anti-Semitic mind of K. Kraus, who allegedly said that psychoanalysis is the illness that it pretends to cure, it was the German internist F. Kraus who, on the whole, was less antagonistic to psychosomatic medicine.

we read in Freud's (1953) biography (Jones, 1953), his discovery was connected with the fact that he had recognized oedipal wishes and fears in a personal form.

The discovery that the theme of self-fulfilling prophecy is explicit precisely in the Oedipus complex is obvious, not only because of its central position in psychoanalytic theory. After all, the Oedipus myth proves that the power of prophecies extends to their tragic fulfillment. It is for this reason that Popper (1963, pp. 35, 38, 123) proposed to always speak of an "Oedipus effect" in those cases where one wants to indicate the influence of a prognosis on the predicted event. Popper substantiates his proposal with the oracular pronouncements that set the "causal chain" of events in motion precisely by their prophesizing: Laius arranges for Oedipus to be murdered after having his heels pierced to prevent the prophesied patricide and incest. We may here assume familiarity with Sophocles' *Oedipus Rex* and turn to the context on which Popper founds his proposal. He emphasizes that the compelling force of the oracle's pronouncement has escaped the psychoanalysts, and he believes he can prove this. According to Popper, Freud overlooks the influence of the psychoanalyst on the patient and his communications, as well as the related methodological problems in theory testing, in the same way he overlooks the role of the oracle in the Oedipus saga. Thus, Popper suggests that psychoanalytic interpretations come close to the pronouncements of the oracle. At the same time, he diagnoses a partial reduction of the field of vision of the psychoanalyst, which prevents him from recognizing the proper interpretations of the "causal function."

This much is true: Oracular pronouncements are not set at the beginning of the causal chain in psychoanalysis. Insofar as one cannot credit the oracle with omniscience, one will have to raise the question where then the oracle can have received his information. We do not hesitate to answer: from Laius, Jocasta, and Oedipus. It is not the oracle that sets the law of destiny in motion: It is father, mother, and son who speak through the oracle. But how does Laius know that Oedipus may kill him? From himself, and his own unconscious destructive desires, directed against his son. At the hand of the fate of Laius, Jocasta, and Oedipus, Freud illustrates that human reality can be determined by conscious and *unconscious* psychological wishes, to a degree of complete necessity. In the first discussion of the Oedipus complex, on dream interpretation (Freud, 1900a, p. 263), one can, however, also read that oedipal conflicts can have a different outcome and that the complex in question is then structured by different specific initial conditions, for instance, in the area of family and social culture. One could say in short that man, on the basis of his psychophysical constitution in the oedipal phase lawfully gets into conflicts whose outcome is decided by initial conditions. In discovering the Oedipus complex in his patients, Freud was impressed by the biological lawfulness of its structure, although its dissolution took various forms.

Freud described the psychodynamic efficacy of these various forms of dissolution as registered in the experience and behavior of man. That the "initial conditions" responsible for these conflicts occupy so important a place was then revealed in experiences with neuroses, perversions, and psychoses in the various diagnostic categories and, last but not least, in anthropological field research (see Hall and Lindzey, 1968). Besides, in psychoanalytic therapy, it is not of primary importance to dissolve the particular form of the Oedipus complex into its components and to provide historical-genetic explanations. Rather, its influences on ways of feeling and behaving should be delimited from those of other unconscious dispositions. For instance, inferiority feelings and ideas of insignificance, as well as impotence representing possible forms of a fear of castration that has become unconscious, can be distinguished from the development of the same triad on the basis of disturbances in the oral phase or on the basis of narcissistic disorders. We have here one of those certainly still insufficiently solved problems of the clinical theory of psychoanalysis, namely to determine typical pathogeneses more precisely. It is here that the difficulties that we discussed in the section on general interpretations operate. It is a matter of indicating or refuting covariance in those areas for which, according to the theory, a broader context must exist, for example, repetition compulsion and its dissolution. Whatever wishes and fears related to the total complex are discovered means little at first. The decisive criterion in a given case is whether the hypothesis of a causal relationship between unconscious oedipal death wishes and experiences, for instance, and apparently unfounded and totally unintelligible guilt feeling can be proven or not (if X, then probably Y). Similar or content-wise different correlation statements are of the greatest importance for clinical theory and practice. In the steps from secured descriptive correlations to explanations, motives in their dissolution prove to have been causes that operated. While correlation statements about typical symptom or character configurations are not prognoses in the scientifically relevant sense, their dissolutions are predictable under certain initial conditions, and therefore they are not ex post facto explanations. The former, namely the correlations statements, make a diagnostic orientation possible and follow the proverb *ex ungue leonem* ("by his claw we know the lion"). To conclude from the claw to the lion is therefore, as Waelder (1962) notes— not a prediction, because from the occurrence of a specific sign one can only conclude the existence of another symptom, while predictions concern future changes in a situation. These are determined by conditions, which is why one also speaks in short of "conditional prognoses."*

Scientific prognoses are conditional in contrast to prophecies. Albert (1968, p. 130) gives, in line with the distinction stressed by Popper in particular, the following summary of the logically contrasting structures of prognosis and prophecy: A presupposition for the prognostic application of a theory would be an appropriate description of the end situation of the event-to-be-predicted (including the different interventions possible for the acting person) in the language of the theory in question. Such a description of the initial conditions of the proceedings would result in specific statements which, in contrast to the general hypotheses of the theory itself, concern a well-defined area in space and time.

Let us to this end consider once again the extremely simplified psychoanalytic example that has been given. End situation: guilt feelings. Explanatory hypothesis: unconscious oedipal death wishes. Determination of specific initial border conditions namely forms of resistance, which could annul the influence of psychoanalytic "interference" (interpretations), that is to say, make them ineffective. (The resistance argument obviously does not serve the *correctness* of the psychoanalyst, but it qualifies various end situations with different prognoses.) The positive or negative result of the prediction has, first of all, significance only for this particular case at this particular time.

We have dealt generously with the concept of initial conditions, which refers to the validity of a universal natural law and concerns its specific application. There is now no need for us to clarify which psychoanalytic assumptions can have nomological character. The deductive method of causal explanation is, according to Popper (1959, p. 146), also applicable when, in the uniqueness of events—and the psychoanalyst has to deal with these first of all—the typical can be discerned as it is generalized in psychoanalytical theory. Thus statements of probability can be derived from the theory and can be tested. For the rest, Albert (1972) does not hesitate either to grant to the alternatives of action, that is, to the possible interferences, the role of causally relevant circumstances, or to designate them as initial conditions (p. 130). When it is a matter of determining the influence of these initial conditions, of the operations of the acting person on

---

* The opposite of conditional prognoses is unconditional prophecies, while unconditional prognoses are those in which the conditions can with certainty be regarded as fulfilled. Popper (1963, p. 339) mentions the following example: "If a physician has diagnosed scarlet fever then he may, with the help of the conditional predictions of his science, make the unconditional prediction that his patient will develop a rash of certain kind." Here, however, it appears rather to be a variation of *ex ungueleonem.*

the proceedings, then alternative influence can be checked against the pre-suppositions; they can be either verified or falsified. To apply this logical structure in an empirical scientific manner means to test, in the context of the particular theory after the principle of trial and error, alternative inter-ventions against the predictions. The psychoanalytic procedure follows this rule whereby the place of manipulative interventions in experimental arrangements, which are independent from the experimenter as a person, is taken over by technical interpretations that are insolubly connected with the participating person.

Our comparative discussions can be summarized as follows: Psychoanal-ysis as technique and theory fulfills presuppositions to interrupt apparent vicious circles—that is, to recognize faults in the definition of the initial conditions (psychodynamic situational diagnosis) as well as in the influenc-ing operations (border conditions—technique of interpretation). One could even say that the course of treatment is characterized by a constant correc-tion of these faults. Since in every case the conditional prognosis is changed accordingly, a systematic testing of it is possible only when the conditions remain somewhat constant over a certain period of time. Sudden blows of fate, totally independent of the psychoanalytic process, can create a new situation, just as intervening exterior events can be suitable to call forth a fluctuation of themes in psychoanalytic sessions. However, sooner or later, those relatively stable situations with which psychoanalytic theory con-cerns itself in particular will again exist, because they constitute the core of nosologically and psychopathogenetic different disorders: We mean the repetition compulsion. That the repetition compulsion is a superordinate essential characteristic of psychic disorders is unquestionable. No theory deserves to be taken seriously that does not present testable hypotheses for the psychogenesis of the repetition compulsion, which characterizes all psy-chopathological symptoms. Freud's greatest methodological discovery is, in our opinion, that he discerns the repetition compulsion in the transference neurosis. In this connection Popper (1963a) cannot escape expressing his agreement with psychoanalysis:

> Psychoanalysts assert that neurotics and others interpret the world
> in accordance with a personal set pattern which is not easily given
> up, and which can often be traced back to early childhood. A pattern
> or scheme which was adopted very early in life is maintained
> throughout, and every new experience is interpreted in terms of it;
> verifying it, as it were, and contributing to its rigidity. (p. 49)

Popper (1963a) then gives his own explanations, based on his theory of neu-roses, for the repetition compulsion; most neuroses come about through the prevalence of a dogmatic attitude because a partial fixation of the development of a critical attitude has taken place. Their resistance against changes could perhaps on some basis, by which Popper terminates his considerations of his theory of neuroses, be explained as follows: On the basis of an injury shock, anxiety emerges and there is an increased need for confirmation and security. This process would be analogous to the injury of a limb. From anxiety one no longer moves it, and it becomes stiff. One could even maintain that the case of a stiff limb is not only similar to the dogmatic reactions but is an example of it.

We must deny ourselves the opportunity to translate Popper's (1963a) theory of neuroses into psychoanalytic concepts and subject it to Popper's own demands for refutations. This much can parenthetically be mentioned: The trauma to the limb* implies castration anxiety, and the stiffness refers (in Popper's own words) to character deformation; this is, to the results of unconscious, defensive processes. Here it is essential to note the agreement regarding the presupposition for psychoanalytic explanations and prognoses. Their presupposition is that in the repetition compulsion a repetitive system is present in which the conditions of its origin are conserved and strengthened—even via feedback (Popper here appropriately describes psychoanalytic experiences).† At the pivotal point of the transference neurosis, repetitions can be observed as nowhere else. This pivotal point is methodologically of particular interest. Given the case wherein the explanatory hypothesis says that a dogmatic attitude has come about as a protection against castration fear. From the hypothesis a technique of interpretation can be deduced that has the purpose of making the unconscious castration fears conscious. With this abbreviation of technical terminology, a complicated procedure is described that leads to an intrapsychic change of the, thus far, operative motivations. The conditional prediction that the dogmatic attitude will loosen when fears of castration no longer have their causal (motivating) power confirms or refutes the explanatory hypothesis concerning this relation. The psychoanalytic interventions address themselves to causes in order to change them and lead to a peculiar situation. Their disappearance becomes proof of their previous causality. With the annulment of the repetition compulsion, psychoanalysis justifies itself therapeutically and scientifically. This thesis means that explanations of psychopathological phenomena in neuroses, perversions, addictions, psychoses, and character disorders are verified and falsified (proven to be true or false) by the predicted change.

---

* We invite the reader's attention to the German pun: limb = *Glied*, *Glied* = Penis. Furthermore, *stiff* and *stiffness* are the most frequently used German terms for erection. Certainly Popper knows this pun, perhaps without "knowing" what role it unconsciously plays in his theory of neurosis.

† An interruption of the repetition compulsion can therefore be effected by psychotherapeutic work on the strengthening of the ego.

If one tries to arrange the explanatory steps formally according to the many possible meanings of explanation, we can say that the repetition compulsion on the observational level refers to a latent (unconscious) disposition as a theoretical concept; then we can describe the repetition compulsion in the first place as an essential characteristic of a disposition. This description provides, if confirmed by the case, the presupposition of a dispositional explanation. In the therapeutic dissolution of the disposition for a "repetition compulsion," typical relationships as they are systematized in clinical theory become observable relationships that, according to their logical structure, belong predominantly to the historical-genetic and probabilistic-genetic explanations, as well as to the functional analysis (see previous section).*

In historical explanations circular errors can be particularly great, in Popper's opinion. For psychoanalysis, however, these problems should be easier to solve than for historical science, as Freud (1937d, p. 259) shows in a comparison with archaeology. It is the repetitions in the transference of reactions from life history, originating in the early years, that permit the psychoanalyst to correct his explanatory outlines. This correction is accomplished in the practical application of life-historical constructions in the present and in prognostic testing, as we have described earlier. Historical interpretations are not verified by the fact that men in the present learn a lesson from history or do not. Genetic-psychoanalytic constructions, on the contrary, address themselves to the repetitive systems of man, who himself represents his history. If the goal of a limited change in the empirically examined case (symptom-bound repetition compulsion) is not reached, and if this was deduced historically and genetically from an unconscious fear of castration, then the construction must be regarded as refuted for this case and during this phase of treatment.

Psychoanalysis and the Problem of Suggestion

We conclude with a few remarks concerning the problem of suggestion (see Thomä, 1977). In the context of circularity and self-fulfilling prophecy, we must first set straight Popper's assertion that psychoanalysts have overlooked their own influence on the patient in the same way as the role of the oracle in the Oedipus saga has been overlooked. The opposite is true: Freud (1916–1917, p. 448; 1921c, p. 89) frequently concerns himself with the theme of suggestion. That the objectivity of the findings that are brought out can be questioned because of possible suggestive influencing has been

---

* To avoid misunderstanding, we draw attention anew to the fact that although psychoanalysts in general do not give patients a logical explanation of one kind or another, their rational manner of conducting treatment does indeed observe logical laws.

denied with good reason. The psychoanalytical method itself, as is known, originated in the failure of suggestive practices and of cases wherein these had proven to be ineffective. Most patients who come into psychoanalysis have behind them frustrating autosuggestive efforts, as well as all kinds of unsuccessful influences from others against their symptoms. It can therefore not be the usual suggestions that lead to a change in a structure that so far has remained stable (repetition compulsion).

Besides, the "suggestions" of the psychoanalyst are not aimed at the symptoms but at their motivations. For this reason, Freud distinguishes hypnotic and other kinds of suggestions from the psychoanalyst's sphere of influence, though he stresses that the latter obviously also depends on the capacity of being influenced as an essential characteristic of man; if such were not the case, psychoanalytic interference would also be impossible. Technical interpretations in treatment can be compared to operations in experimental arrangements without which the theory cannot be verified. In the objection that the psychoanalyst finds the Easter eggs that he himself first has hidden, one supposes a *vicious circle*, a self-fulfilling prophecy. Now, nobody will contest that symptoms are real and manifest themselves as the consequences of a psychopathogenesis.

We allude to Merton's 1957 theory and maintain the following: The patient defined his emotional experiences, wishes, and fears as "real" long before a psychoanalyst appeared on the scene. The psychoanalyst discovered the definitions; he did not create them. It seems to us that otherwise, one must make an absurd assumption: One would have to start from the fact that, in connection with the predicted symptomatic changes, freshly discovered pathogenesis was neither operative nor remained operative in the present via repetition compulsion; in other words, the elimination of the repetition compulsion takes place independently from its pathogenesis through suggestions of one kind or another. Nobody will seriously want to maintain such a complete separation. The fact that the psychoanalyst as a person has positive and negative influences on his patient should not be indicated by the loaded term *suggestion*.

Freud's often misunderstood recommendation that the psychoanalyst should conduct himself in regard to his patient as a mirror that only reflects is directed in particular against uncontrolled suggestions. It is an invitation to observe countertransference and to burden the patient neither with one's own personal problems nor with one's own ideologies. To this extent, the recommendation serves the interest of the patient; in it, however, is also expressed the scientific ideal of the experimenting researcher who would have his method entirely independent from the person. The precise quotation and its context are the basis for the following assumption: "The doctor should be opaque to his patients and, like a mirror, should show them nothing but what is shown to him" (Freud, 1912e, p. 118). Freud wants to purify the psychoanalytical method of all undesirable elements and, if one takes the quotation to the letter, of all personal elements. It is clear that this summons should not be taken literally. All witnesses tell us that as a physician Freud himself provides another example. If the psychoanalyst behaves only like a mirror and adds nothing to what is shown, then the psychoanalytic process can never get started (see Stone, 1961). The explanatory psychoanalytic theories pass their tests of verification in as far as the elimination of the repetition compulsion. That it is interrupted must be attributed to *new* experiences that the patient has in communicating with the psychoanalyst and that he tries out and enlarges. Verification and falsification of the theory are thereby complicated, particularly since the conditional prognoses depend on the question of whether or not new experience takes place.

Thus no testing of psychoanalytic theory is possible without considering that the method is embedded in human interaction. The transference onto the mirror characterizes *one* side of this interaction. What takes place in the psychoanalytic situation is more than the testing of a theory that refers to the psychopathogenesis up to the immediate present. The very title of Freud's (1914g) study on technique, "Remembering, Repeating, and Working Through," permits us to perceive that the working-through leads via remembering (past) and repeating (present) to the future. That the psychoanalyst, precisely in this working-through, acts as mediator to new experiences and makes positive identifications possible is self-evident. This is essential and constitutive for therapy, though it complicates the testing of the theory. There is no reason, however, to speak of suggestion where the psychoanalyst is acting as a person.

SUMMARY

In preparing our empirical research, we have reviewed the discussion concerning the scientific-systematic position and about the logical status of psychoanalysis in order to determine our own position within these controversies. Our work mediates between the attempts at methodological clarification, which have been made by psychoanalytic authors and the debate about the character of psychoanalysis—whether it is science or hermeneutic-dialectic procedure—that has been carried on by nonanalysts. The conception of psychoanalysis as "depth hermeneutics" has been criticized along the lines of Popper and Albert. In our opinion, the grounding of all psychoanalytic knowledge on the basis of a strict psychology of *Verstehen* would limit the empirical basis of psychoanalysis. Objectifying methods are an indispensable corrective in this regard. We have considered the relationship between psychoanalytic theory and therapy. Psychoanalytic data collection must be made reliable, the theoretical concepts sharpened, and the rules for translating them into empirical tests of falsification defined.

According to Freud, metapsychological concepts belong to a "speculative superstructure"; its relevance diminishes with increasing distance from clinical experience. In agreement with Waelder (1962) and Wisdom (1971, 1972), we distinguish the following steps in psychoanalytic theory: observational data; clinical generalizations; clinical theory; metapsychology, Freud's "personal philosophy." Objectification and falsification apply chiefly to "clinical theory."

We have discussed the dovetailing of general theories—chiefly the theory of neurosis—with interpretations as they occur in psychoanalytic therapy and with the theory of such interpretations. The concept of repetition compulsion refers to a psychic apparatus as a relatively closed system that is embedded in life history, and in its frame motives become effective in the guise of causes. The proof of any hypothesis under consideration consists of the elimination of those initial conditions that potentiated the repetition compulsion. Whereas Habermas contends that the patient's self-reflection is the sole criterion for the revision of disturbed formative processes, we criticize this view as a utopian-dogmatic overestimation of the role of knowledge. We have discussed the role of description, explanation, and prediction in psychoanalysis and have dealt with the problem of circularity of reasoning and self-fulfilling prophecy in psychoanalytic practice and its consequences for clinical research.

Chapter 3

The Significance of the Case History in Clinical Psychoanalytic Research[*][†]

FREUD'S CASE HISTORIES AS A METHODOLOGICAL PARADIGM

The discussion of psychoanalysis as a discipline has generated a host of quite controversial philosophical debate, as we have sketched out in the preceding chapter. The more it enters into general awareness that psychoanalysis as a psychological system has exerted and will continue to exert a tremendous influence on the psychosocial profession and on contemporary culture generally, the more remarkable it seems that decades after its inception, some of the most basic concepts of this theoretical and practical system remain controversial (cf. Meehl, 1973, p. 104). Yet surely it would not be an exaggeration to speak of Sigmund Freud's (1895d) first attempt to explain neurotic symptoms in a fundamentally different way from his contemporaries as a scientific revolution. Before Freud's attempts, hysterical symptoms were regarded by psychiatry as the result of a "degenerate constitution," the consequence of a somatic predisposition. Freud's critical contribution to the development of psychological research consisted in his formulation of two assumptions: that hysterical symptoms should be regarded primarily as psychic phenomena—though not necessarily conscious ones—and that as such they are to be viewed as comprehensible psychic structures. As Mayman (1973b) emphasizes, these postulates of psychologism and determinism remain the two most important postulates upon which psychoanalysis is based today.[‡]

The introduction of these two assumptions, which went hand in hand with the development of a corresponding method of observation, represents

---

[*] Horst Kächele and Helmut Thomä.
[†] Adapted from Kächele (1981).
[‡] Cf. Rapaport's (1967) discussion in his little-known lectures on psychoanalytic methodology.

a decisive turning point, a new methodological paradigm (Kuhn, 1962). It is one of the central paradoxes in the development of psychoanalytic theory and practice that while Freud has gone down in the history of scientific theory as a significant and incisive methodologist,* the yield of empirical psychoanalytic research has only recently begun to bear fruits.

The fact that the insights of psychoanalysis were caught in the critically assailed cross fire from the philosophy of science (see Chapter 2 in this volume) undoubtedly has to do with the nature of Freud's approach: The search for new hypotheses was far more important to him than painstaking examination of clinically verified information using empirical methods.

The continuous development of psychoanalytic theory over the 40-year course of psychoanalytic research that began with Freud himself can be traced most clearly by following the history of central clinical concepts, such as that of anxiety (Compton, 1972). Of course, not all concepts have always evolved to the current level of development in the field: Some, like the theory of dreams, have remained almost unaltered over long stretches of time (Edelson, 1972). This lack of consistency first became apparent during initial attempts at systematization, as those of Rapaport (1960), and it has remained a peculiarity of psychoanalytic theorizing. What is generally known as "psychoanalytic theory" is in fact more like a research program comprising many loosely connected theories whose status must be evaluated quite variously in terms of the philosophy of science. There are, for example, psychoanalytic theories of memory, perception, attention, consciousness, action, feeling, concept formation, and biographical development, to name but a few of the fundamental ones. These form the basis of the clinical theories, which themselves are conceived in a very loose fashion (compare, e.g., the theory of anxiety with that of narcissism or the theory of treatment, which would have to distinguish a theory of course from a theory of outcome). Moreover, the testing of each of the different components—the different subtheories—is a separate task that must be approached with the most varied methodological approaches. In regard to the clinical theory of psychoanalysis—and it is only in this regard that we will deal with the relevant questions here—quite divergent views still exist on the methodology of hypothesis-testing research.

The point of contention here, between psychoanalysis and academic psychology, is how the classical psychoanalytic method is to be evaluated as a research instrument. Its clinical significance is not in the same measure at issue, nor is it so controversial in the theoretical discussion. In terms of scientific logic, however, it is apparent that the meeting place of research and therapy (Freud, 1926c) is still a living issue, inasmuch as the testing

---

* See also Kaplan (1964), whose textbook on scientific theory incorporates Freud's argument against premature formalization and strict definition of the central conceptual bases of a theory.

of hypotheses is still an aim that is pursued. Sarnoff (1971) unequivocally formulates the experimental psychologist's response to the frequent assertion that the psychoanalytic situation is a quasi-experimental one:

> It does not logically follow that the conduct of psychoanalytic therapy is an ideal, necessary or sufficient method for the scientific testing of deductions from his (Freud's) conceptions of personality. Indeed, owing to the multitude of uncontrolled events that occur as patient and analyst interact within any psychoanalytic session, one can safely assert that such sessions cannot even minimally satisfy the scientific principle of control required to test a hypothesis deduced from a Freudian variable of personality. (p. 8)

It might seem logical to conclude from this that no single assertion based on the experience of the psychoanalytic setting can be accepted as valid until it has been verified experimentally. This view, however, is quite bluntly rejected by Kubie (1952):

> Many of these laboratory charades are pedestrian and limited demonstrations of things which have been proved over and over again in real life.... Experimental facilities should not be wasted on issues which are already clearly proved and to which human bias alone continues to blind us. The experimentalist should rather take up where the naturalist leaves off. (p. 64)

Kubie (1952) goes on to compare this situation to the introduction of the microscope by Leuwenhoek, arguing that it is sufficient to look through the microscope of analysis to convince oneself of the validity of the contested questions. Also there is little doubt that certain elementary phenomena, upon which psychoanalytic theory is built, do not require experimental testing. The fact that there are two kinds of mental processes, primary and secondary, requires little or no interpretation; it can easily be made evident that dream states or drug-induced states "bring to the fore mental processes which do not abide by the laws of ordered logical thought" (Rapaport, 1960, p. 112). As soon as one wishes to pass from these initial observations to more precise statements, however, one must strike out upon new methodological paths. The great number of sometimes contradictory schools of psychoanalysis makes it obvious that the analytic method as an observational instrument in the discipline of the social sciences cannot readily be compared with the microscope or other natural science observational instruments. According to Rapaport (1960, p. 111), the major body of positive evidence for psychoanalytic theory lies in the field of accumulated clinical observations: "The first achievement of the system was a phenomenological one: it called attention to a vast array of phenomena and to the relations between them, and for the first time made these appear meaningful and amenable to rational consideration."

On the phenomenological plane of ordering and establishing relationships, Rapaport (1960) sees the accumulated clinical evidence as eminently positive testimony for psychoanalytic systems. In regard to the theoretical propositions of the system, however—for example, the special theory of neurosis—there is no such assurance: "Because a canon of clinical investigation is absent, much of the evidence for the theory remains phenomenological and anecdotal, even if its obviousness and bulk tend to lend it a semblance of objective validity" (p. 111). Thus, the absence of an experimental canon of clinical investigation—not to be confused with clinical interpretative technique—appears to remain a central weakness in the testing of clinical research in psychoanalysis. "This makes it urgent to reinvestigate Freud's case studies with the aim of clarifying whether or not they can yield a canon of clinical research at the present stage of our knowledge" (ibid.).

The present chapter takes up this call and examines Freud's case histories in terms of the didactic and scientific principles in their presentation. Our attempt will be to show that Freud aims simultaneously at ideographic and nomothetic aspects that lead to the creation of clinical types. In conclusion, the historical development of psychoanalytic scientific reporting will be characterized as a transition from case histories to individual case studies.

In spite of Rapaport's (1960) demand, little attention has been given to the case presentation as a means of scientific communication in psychoanalysis. For this reason it is of particular interest that several studies have turned to the Freudian case history in an attempt to clarify the scientific status of psychoanalysis. In Sherwood's (1969) logical analysis of the explanatory principles in psychoanalysis, the story of the Rat Man, Paul Lorenz, occupies a central position. At the same time Sherwood does not fail to point to the peculiarity that "in perhaps no other field has so great a body of theory been built upon such a small public record of raw data" (p. 70).

Perrez (1972) analyzes the presentation of the Wolf-Man's infantile neurosis as to the formal logic of its structure. Both authors examine the validity of the steps of argumentation in the presentation of the cases (not questioning for the moment the validity of their content). While Sherwood (1969) is more interested in discovering which kind of logic* is appropriate for psychoanalysis generally, Perrez accepts only a generalizing nomothetic approach. Not surprisingly, in the process he finds gaps in the presentation, incomplete derivations, and sketchily outlined explanations instead of complete explanations that would satisfy the requirements of the Hempel-

---

* Schalmey's (1977) study appears to remain poorly known. Taking the case of Daniel Paul Schreber as an example, it analyzes the logic of argumentation and proof in psychoanalysis.

Oppenheim schema (cf. Stegmüller, 1969; see Chapter 2 in this volume). This limited fulfillment of scientific requirements is also surely due to the fact that Perrez bases his investigation on a case presentation. The implicit assumption that a published case history would provide a representative reflection of the actual occurrence and hence, that the scientific status of psychoanalysis could be determined by critical analysis of a *single* case history appears problematic. No one has ever systematically investigated the relationship of the case presentation to the course of treatment it portrays. Hence, it remains unclear if the incompleteness of a case history is due to the summary of the treatment itself or if the observational material in the treatment was insufficient. Furthermore, the choice of a case presentation that focuses on "refuting" the views then being put forth by Carl Jung and Alfred Adler forced a selective presentation in which more attention was given to the contested points while other uncontested assumptions were employed without examination.

Yet these objections do not invalidate Perrez's (1972) fundamental criticism. Rather, we need to inquire how a description of the psychoanalytic process might be constituted to avoid the deficiencies of the classical case histories. From the start Freud himself was aware of the imperfections of his case histories. In his "Studies on Hysteria" (1895d) we detect a note both of amazement and of self-justification in his remark that his case histories "read like short stories" (p. 160) and "lack the serious stamp of science" (ibid.). Yet in the very next sentence he also rejects any artistic ambitions: "I must console myself with the reflection that the nature of the subject is evidently responsible for this, rather than any preference of my own" (ibid.). Even if Freud occupies a high rank as a writer of scientific prose—this is underscored by his receipt of the Goethe Prize in 1930 and in Walter Muschg's (1930) essay of the same year—the fact that he was in the position of portraying life histories and human destinies did not blind him to the huge gap that divided him from the poet:

> I must now consider a further complication to which I should certainly give no space if I were as a man of letters engaged upon the creation of a mental state for a novel, instead of being a medical man engaged upon its dissection. (Freud, 1905e, p. 50)

Freud's talents as a writer certainly contributed decisively to the development of the case history in the psychoanalytic context. Wittels (1924), among others, reports in his biography of Freud, "Stekel informed me that Freud told him he would like to be a novelist someday so that he could bequeath to the world what his patients have told to him" (p. 13). Freud, as Kris (1954) emphasizes, was in an intellectual conflict:

> A new and unprecedented vista was opening before him—that of stating in scientific terms the conflicts of human psyche. It would have been tempting to base his excursion into this territory on intuitive understanding, to trace all case histories to their biographical roots, and to base all the insight on intuition, "of the kind we are accustomed to having from imaginative writers." (p. 15)

The literary self-assurance Freud demonstrates in the presentation of biographical material, which first came into its own in his "Studies" (1895d), inevitably made this temptation real and immediate. We know from his correspondence—the Freud-Fliess letters—that he was already able to penetrate literary motif-development psychologically. His analyses of two short stories by Conrad Ferdinand Meyer are the earliest attempts of this kind (Kris, 1954, p. 15). The opposition of intuitive understanding and scientific explanation can be called the crux of the aforementioned conflict and is by no means mitigated in theory or practice today. In 1928, Freud speaks of himself as one of those "who have to find their way through tormenting uncertainty and with restless groping" (1928b, p. 133) and compares himself with others to whom it is "vouchsafed ... to salvage without effort from the whirlpool of their own feelings the deepest truths" (ibid.).

Is the essay form of presentation merely a consequence of the "nature of the object" of psychoanalysis?

In spite of the appearance that the case histories may give, in Kris's (1954, p. 15) opinion there could never be any doubt on which side Freud stands: "He had been through the school of science, and it became his life work to base the new psychology on scientific methods." In his studies of Freud's methodology, Meissner (1971, p. 281) describes clinical psychology as a science of subjectivity, as an attempt to grasp experience and its modification in a controlled way. In the same vein Sherwood (1969) rhetorically asks his readers, "What is its (i.e., psychoanalysis'—author's note) subject matter; what is the principle focus of interest in this case?" According to Sherwood, Freud's attempt to explain the case history of the Rat Man emphasizes his uniqueness as an individual human being:

> Freud and ourselves as latter-day observers are confronted by a single sick individual whose life story presents a variety of incongruities—events and attitudes demanding to be explained, to be brought within the framework of understandable human behavior. Freud, like the historian, is interested in a particular course of events, namely, an individual's history. (p. 188)

However, this systematic determination of the aim of the individual case histories does not completely coincide with Freud's own intentions, for each case history contains unmistakable references to other patients with similar conflicts. Similarly, throughout we encounter comments regarding the general applicability of findings, as in this instance in the case of the Wolf-Man:

> In order to derive fresh generalizations from what has thus been established with regard to the mechanisms and instincts, it would be essential to have at one's disposal numerous cases as thoroughly and deeply analyzed equally to the present one. (Freud, 1918b, p. 105).

The decisive point in favor of Sherwood's (1969) accentuation seems to be that any new gain in knowledge about the individual case is possible only out of its totality. In this way the special methodological nature of clinical investigative technique, as it has developed, converges on the single case history—a fact that Meissner (1971, p. 302) also emphasizes: "Analytic methodology is ultimately forced to rest upon the single case history." This insight determines the function of the case history as the explanation of singular events, in this way thematizing the ideographic element of the psychoanalytic narrative (Farrell, 1981). The problem of determining the theoretical position of psychoanalysis is rooted in this complication, which was created by the introduction of the subject. This was already noted by Hartmann in 1927 in the introduction to his historically significant book *Die Grundlagen der Psychoanalyse (Foundations of Psychoanalysis)*:

> Historically, psychoanalytic psychology is characterized by having grown out of the seemingly unbridgeable gap that separated a scientific, chiefly experimental psychology of elementary psychical processes from the "intuitive" psychology of the writers and philosophers. The historical significance of psychoanalysis for psychology consists in its having made accessible to scientific contemplation those regions of psychical life that formerly had been relegated to occasional observation and to the psychological apercu, which is not only scientifically more or less irresponsible but also tends to make value judgments. (p. 8)

To understand the significance of the case history in clinical psychoanalysis, it must be recalled that in the early decades of psychoanalytic research it was also an important medium of communication for psychoanalysts practicing essentially in isolation. This didactic aspect apparently had a much stronger conceptual influence on psychoanalytic training programs and thus also on the training of later researchers than is generally realized (Tuckett, 1994).

The centrality of the case history in psychoanalytic training can easily be confirmed by studying the catalog of lectures at a variety of psychoanalytic institutes. The six case histories that Freud presents in greater detail function here as introductory material to clinical practice in psychoanalysis—material that is worked through again and again by new students. As Jones (1955, p. 257) says regarding the Dora case, "This first case history of Freud's has for years served as a model for students of psychoanalysis." The close ties among therapy, research, and training led to the creation of a traditional form of communication so that the short case report came to seem a natural form; initially its relevance to research was certainly brilliantly confirmed.

For this reason the problems that were gradually systematized by the developing empirical research of the social sciences, the problem of the reliability of clinical observation to name but one, were addressed only belatedly and hesitantly by the psychoanalytic research community. The six detailed Freudian case presentations had been raised to the level of paradigmatic models: "But these six essays of Freud's far excel, both in presentation and original content, anything any other analyst has attempted" (Jones, 1955, p. 255).

Even without this idealization it seems incomprehensible why at least the thoroughness and exactness of Freud's studies did not inspire a large number of further case histories that might be considered a treasury of psychoanalytic observation today. There were only a few attempts made to compose comprehensive clinical studies. Before we take up Rapaport's (1960) suggestion and consider several of Freud's case studies from the methodological point of view, we will mention several biographical points that we believe were of great significance in the development of the case history in Freud's work.

Freud's own training at first completely followed the paths dictated by his natural scientific studies at Brücke's Laboratory. His further training as a neuropathologist initially strengthened his empirical experimental orientation. Then, he began his theoretical separation from the Helmholtz school, in particular starting with his "Aphasia" (Jones, 1953, p. 215). Jones goes on to point out, however, that while Freud had proven himself a good clinician, an extremely skillful histologist, and an independent thinker, he was essentially unsuccessful in experimental physiology.

Jean-Martin Charcot may be taken as the model for Freud's emphasis on well-rounded description.* Freud (1893) writes of him:

> As a teacher, Charcot was positively fascinating. Each of his lectures
> was a little work of art in construction and composition; it was perfect

---

* Frommer and Langenbach (2001) follow in this evaluation our earlier study (Kächele, 1981).

in form and made such an impression that for the rest of the day one could not get the sound of what he had said out of one's ears or the thought of what he had demonstrated out of one's mind. (p. 17)

In his obituary of Charcot, Freud (1893f) especially stresses Charcot's clinical thrust, which he had particularly developed through his unique talent:

He used to look again and again at the things he did not understand, to deepen his impression of them day by day, till suddenly an understanding of them dawned on him. In his mind's eye the apparent chaos presented by the continual repetition of the same symptoms then gave way to order; the new nosological pictures emerged, characterized by the constant combination of certain groups of symptoms. The complete and extreme cases, the "types," could be brought into prominence with the help of a certain sort of schematic planning and, with these types as a point of departure, the eye could travel over the long series of ill-defined cases—the *formes frustes*—which, branching off from one or other characteristic feature of the type, surrender to indistinctness. He called this kind of intellectual work, in which he had no equal, "practicing nosography," and he took pride in it. (p. 12)

Thus, to Freud (1893f, p. 12) Charcot was "not a reflective man, not a thinker: he had the nature of an artist, a *visuel*, a man who sees." And in this description of the man he revered, we get a hint of the traits that Freud, probably not yet very consciously, may have seen as central to himself.

References to Freud's failures in experimental studies that he conducted during his student years, in contrast to his descriptive histological studies of the same period, address this distinction: "There are two sides to this preference of the eye over the hand, of passively seeing over actively doing: an attraction to the one and an aversion to the other. Both were present" (Jones, 1953, pp. 52–53). This orientation might have been one of the factors that prompted Freud to turn away from the various active therapeutic techniques such as electrotherapy or hypnosis: "He preferred to look and listen, confident that if he could perceive the structure of a neurosis he would truly understand it and have power over the forces that had brought it about" (ibid., p. 53). It can be only roughly gauged how great Charcot's influence may have been on Freud's clinical research—Charcot, who never tired of "defending the rights of purely clinical work, which consists in seeing and ordering things, against the encroachments of theoretical medicine" (Freud, 1893f, p. 13). In a letter written from Paris to Freud's fiancée, the conclusion is that Freud's switch from neurology to psychopathology can be largely ascribed to Charcot's influence.* From Charcot, Freud adopts not only the clinical method but also the rehabilitation of hysteria and its significance in researching neurotic disease pictures:

> The first thing Charcot's work did was restore its dignity to the topic; little by little people gave up the scornful smile with which the patient could at that time feel certain of being met: she was no longer necessarily a malingerer, for Charcot had thrown the whole weight of his authority on the side of the genuineness and objectivity of hysterical phenomena. (p. 19)

There is little doubt that Freud's empirical but nonexperimental approach developed on the model of the great master Charcot: When Freud went to Paris, his anatomical interests at first felt closer to him than clinical questions. According to Jones (1953, p. 211), the decision to quit working at the microscope in Paris was essentially taken for personal reasons and because of Charcot's scientific influence.†

As far as we know, no exact comparison has been made of Charcot's and Freud's descriptions of their patients. Nevertheless, the description of Charcot's nosographic method could easily be applied as well to the form in which Freud presents his clinical work. After all, the linking of typical processes in the life of the psyche is central to analytical work. The focus of attention has shifted from the symptoms to the psychic mechanisms; this is Freud's decisive step beyond descriptive psychopathology.

We have already mentioned Freud's (1895d, p. 124) justification of the special character of his case history, with which he prefaces the discussion of Elisabeth von R. The first of the case histories presented in the "Studies" (Frau Emmy von N.) still is very far from resembling a short story. Formally it is much like a continuous record of treatment presented almost with-

---

* In a letter dated October 21, 1885 to Martha Bernays, Freud writes, "I believe I am changing a great deal. [Let me tell you what it is that is affecting me.] Charcot, who is both one of the greatest physicians and a man whose common sense is of the order of genius, simply demolishes my views and aims. Many a time after a lecture I go out as if from Nôtre Dame, with a new [sense of the Perfect.] ...Whether the seed will ever bring forth fruit I do not know; but what I certainly know is that no other human being has ever affected me in such a way" (Jones, 1953, p. 185). [Brackets include portions of German text omitted by Jones.—translator]

† There is a historical point in relation to Freud's quitting working at the microscope. He was unable to get an academic appointment in Vienna because he was a Jew, and since he was married and about to have children, he needed to earn an income; for that reason he went into neurological practice—he later acknowledged (to Kardiner 1957) that he wasn't interested in therapy. I find it ironic that if he had not been a Jew and had gotten an academic appointment—he was certainly bright enough—he would have continued with his neurological research and might never have discovered psychoanalysis (personal communication by J. Schachter).

out revision. The language is sober and objective and keeps largely to the observational level. Many years later, the author of this case history himself looks back on this presentation with compassion for the novice:

> I am aware that no analyst can read this case history today without a smile of pity. But it should be borne in mind that this was the first case in which I employed the cathartic procedure to a large extent. (addendum 1924 to Freud, 1924d, p. 105)

Whether the "novice" really needs our pity is another question. A thorough study conducted by a Chicago research group (Schlessinger et al., 1967) of Freud's scientific style at the time of "Studies on Hysteria" makes it plain that even these early case histories are exemplary:

> Freud presented clinical evidence and theoretical propositions at various levels of abstraction, which could be derived from the observational data by inductive reasoning. His hypothesis formation through deductive logic was clearly labeled and sparingly employed. He used deduction to validate his theories by making clinical predictions, which could then be tested in the consulting room. (p. 404)

Statements found in Freud's work about the methodological difficulties of his case presentations show that he was fully aware of the problems associated with the use of case histories as a form of scientific communication and that he always emphasized the heuristic nature of these communications. We shall now examine several of these points as they appear in the various great case histories.

Dora

Freud (1905e) introduces "Fragment of an Analysis of a Case of Hysteria" with the following words:

> In 1895 and 1896 I put forward certain views upon the pathogenesis of hysterical symptoms and upon the mental processes occurring in hysteria. Since that time, several years have passed. In now proposing, therefore, to substantiate those views by giving a detailed report of a case and its treatment, I cannot avoid making a few introductory remarks, for the purpose partly of justifying from various standpoints the step I am taking, and partly of diminishing the expectations to which it will give rise. (p. 7)

Freud's (1905e) guiding objective is to "bring forward some of the material" on which his conclusions are based and to "make it accessible to the judgment of the world." However, he immediately admits that considerable technical difficulties in the process of reporting will have to be overcome. The doctor must not make notes during the actual session with the patient "for fear of shaking the patient's confidence and of disturbing his own view of the material under observation. Indeed, I have not yet succeeded in solving the problem of how to record for publication the history of a treatment of long duration" (pp. 9–10).

In the Dora case, two fortunate factors for reporting came together:

> In the first place the treatment did not last more than three months; and in the second place the material which elucidated the case was grouped around two dreams (one related in the middle of the treatment and one at the end). The wording of these dreams was recorded immediately after the session, and they thus afforded a secure point of attachment for the chain of interpretations and recollections which proceeded from them. (p. 10)

Thus, it was possible for Freud to wait to set down these case histories until the treatment was concluded. As a motivating element for this feat of memory he does not omit to emphasize that his memory was enhanced by the interest in publication.

The Dora case has become the object of many clinical secondary analyses (e.g., Deutsch, 1957; Erikson, 1962, 1964; Kanzer, 1966; Langs, 1976; Levine, 2005; Mahony, 2005). From a methodological point of view Marcus (1976) points to the poetic qualities of the text and its persuasive powers; Spence (1987, p. 123) qualifies it as a tour de force in the art of persuasion: "The appeal of the Dora case and its undoubted standing as a literary masterpiece make us aware of the influence of what might be called rhetorical craft and the subtle power of the clinical narrative."

Spence (1987, p. 133) also refers to a study by Hertz (1983), who uncovers a disturbing parallel between Freud and Dora: "They were both reticent; neither told the whole story; and finally we find a certain vagueness about the source of both Freud's and Dora's knowledge" (p. 133).

Little Hans

Freud's (1909b, pp. 5–149) next case history deals with the "Analysis of a Phobia in a Five-Year-Old Boy" known as Little Hans. Here the presentation is based on stenographic notes taken by the patient's father who, as we know, conducted the treatment himself. Freud himself makes comments on the treatment and follows it with a discussion in which he examines the series of observations from three points of view:

> In the first place I shall consider how far it supports the assertion which I put forward in my *Three Essays on the Theory of Sexuality.* Secondly, I shall consider to what extent it can contribute towards our understanding of this very frequent form of disorder. And thirdly, I shall consider whether it can be made to shed any light upon the mental life of children or to afford any criticism of our educational aims. (p. 101)

In the context of our present methodological questions regarding the significance of the case history as a practical and scientific means of communication, the report stands out for its relatively clear separation of observation and explanatory commentary. This is due to the allocation of roles in which the father—as the therapist—reports, while Freud (1909b)—as the control analyst—provides the commentary. While the father's interest in the analysis apparently supports attentiveness to the material being sought, at the same time a clear distinction remains in the text. It may be partly owing to this circumstance that this case of horse phobia lent itself to different interpretations by psychologists of different provenance. It speaks well of a case presentation in that it allows for alternative explanations at all. Among the psychoanalytic commentaries and alternatives that have been proposed are those of Baumeyer (1952) and Loch and Jappe (1974): Using a number of indications scattered throughout the text of the case history of Little Hans, they revealed more about the close connection between symptom formation and early suppression. However, the same case also has served to criticize the way psychoanalytic evidence has been generated (Wolpe and Rachman, 1960). In any case Gardner (1972) praises Little Hans as the most famous boy in child psychotherapy literature (p. 24). Recently centennial reviews and reconsiderations have reexamined the case in the light of newer theory (Blum, 2007; Fingert Chused, 2007; Munder Ross, 2007; Stuart, 2007; Wakefield, 2007).

The Rat Man

In the same year as the work about Little Hans, Freud published another comprehensive case history. In fact, his "Notes upon a Case of Obsessional Neurosis" (1909d) contain far more than the modest title might lead one to expect. The case of the Rat Man, Paul Lorenz, is the only one of the six long case reports to present a complete and successful treatment. This case presentation can be called exemplary in many respects. The technical difficulties in reporting, about which Freud still complains in the Dora

case—how a lengthy treatment could possibly be retained in memory—
were resolved. The case report is based on the daily notes that Freud was in
the habit of setting down each evening. Interestingly, it is precisely in this
case that Freud warns against the following:

> ... the practice of noting down what the patient says during the actual
> time of treatment. The consequent withdrawal of the physician's
> attention does the patient more harm than can be made up for by any
> increase in accuracy that may be achieved in the reproduction of his
> case history. (p. 159, note 2)

Yet the daily notes form the indispensable fund on which subsequent scientific processing can draw. Nevertheless, as Freud was in the habit of destroy-
ing both the manuscript and the preparatory notes and also warned against
settling on explanations before conclusion of a treatment, the opinion is
often heard that psychoanalytic case histories can rightly emerge from the
head of the analyst at the conclusion of treatment like Athena from the head
of Zeus. The tacit assumption here is that the entire relevant material will
have gathered and taken form in the analyst's "head" (i.e., unconscious).
However, Freud prefers to make very thorough notes:

> By some odd chance, however, the day-to-day notes of this case,
> written every evening, were preserved, at least those for the best
> part of the first four months of treatment, and James Strachey has
> edited and published a translation of them in conjunction with the
> case history itself. (Jones, 1955, p. 230)

It is worthwhile studying this case history in detail, since its organization
particularly reveals Freud's dramaturgic skill in structuring the dialogue
between the reader and himself. In the introduction, Freud emphasizes two
functions of the "following pages": first, to give *"fragmentary extracts*
from a case history of obsessional neurosis"; second, in connection with
this case but supported by other previously analyzed cases, to offer *"dis-
connected indications of an aphoristic character* upon the genesis and the
finer psychological mechanism of obsessional processes ..." (Freud 1909d,
p. 155) (italics in original). Freud justifies the fragmentary nature of this
case history by pointing to his duty as a doctor to protect the patient from
indiscrete curiosity, particularly in a capital city. On no account should
it be thought that "I regard this manner of making a communication as
perfectly correct and one to be imitated" (p. 155). Similarly, the aphoristic
nature of the theoretical indications is not intended to function as a model
but is connected with Freud's confession that he has "not yet succeeded in
completely penetrating the complicated texture of a *severe* case of obses-

sional neurosis ..." (p. 156). To help the reader follow the structure of the case history, we provide the following breakdown of its contents:

1. Extracts from the Case History
   a. Beginning of the Treatment   (first session)
   b. Infantile Sexuality   (first session)
   c. The Great Obsessive Fear   (second and
                                                                          third sessions)
   d. Initiation into the Nature of the Treatment   (fourth session)
      (deepening, elucidation by Freud of the
      psychological differences between the conscious
      and the unconscious)   (fifth session)
      (a further childhood memory)   (sixth session)
      (the same topic)   (seventh session)
   e. Some Obsessional Ideas and Their Explanation
   f. The Precipitating Cause of the Illness
   g. The Father Complex and Solution of the Rat Idea

2. Theoretical
   a. Some General Characteristics of Obsessional Structures.
   b. Some Psychological Peculiarities of Obsessional Neurotics: Their
      Attitude Toward Reality, Superstition, and Death.
   c. The Instinctual Life of Obsessional Neurotics and the Origins of
      Compulsion and Doubt

The detailed development of the theme in this work (Freud, 1909d) is introduced in strict chronological order. The reader is able to look over Freud's shoulder (or through the one-way screen).* As the clinical teacher, Freud stops at particular points to summarize and explain to the reader the meaning of what he has presented: "The events in his sixth or seventh year which the patient described in the first hour of his treatment were not merely, as he supposed, the beginning of his illness, but were already the illness itself" (ibid., p. 162). With these words he might then go on to introduce a critical discussion of infantile sexuality. There follow anticipated theoretical conclusions by way of explicating the knowledge gained thus far: "A complete obsessional neurosis, wanting in no essential element, [is] at once the nucleus and the prototype of the later disorder....". Thus, Freud's technique of presentation consists in oscillating among very careful description,† a rather short section of material, and a thorough theoretical discussion of it.

---

* Mahony (1982) dedicates a whole chapter to elaborate on this aspect of Freud's style (pp. 73–101).

† It is no accident that Freud points out in a footnote to this presentation that what he is writing is based on his notes from the day of treatment.

This theory-related clarification not only applies to the foregoing material but also leads to hypotheses that will determine the further course of the clarification process:

> If we apply knowledge gained elsewhere to this case of childhood neurosis, we shall *not be able to avoid a suspicion* that in this instance as in others (that is to say, before the child had reached his sixth year) there had been conflicts and repressions. (p. 164; italics added for emphasis)

Starting in the second session the patient introduces the actual experience that prompted him to seek out Freud's help. Freud's technique of winning the reader for his presentation of the patient is once again to alternate between his function as the treating physician and as a reporter: "This 'both' took me aback, and it has no doubt also mystified the reader. For so far we have heard only of one idea ..." (Freud, 1909d, p. 167). The "we" draws the reader into the consulting room, into the analytic case-conference. After presenting the precipitating event in the third session, Freud takes the patient's relating of another event in the fourth session as occasion to explain the nature of the treatment to him. His continuing explanation in the fifth session of the mode of action of analysis is of particular interest regarding the establishment of what is known today as the working alliance, the relationship plane that must be cultivated at the inception of treatment. The patient is so pleased by the acknowledgment that Freud shows him (ibid., p. 402) that in the sixth session the patient brings out more infantile material of great importance. The theme of his death wish toward his father dominates the seventh session as well. After that, Freud concludes his exposition of the case history, not without explicitly noting that the course of treatment covering 11 months essentially corresponds to the sequence that he outlined in the first sessions.

At this point Freud (1909d) the author changes his technique of presentation. Instead of giving a continuous description, he first summarizes several obsessional ideas (E), explains the precipitating cause of the illness (F), and clarifies the father complex with his solution to the idea of the rat (G).

In these parts of the essay, exemplary symptoms are analyzed—pars pro toto—and traced back to their causative constellations. These examples are already inserted into a more general context. Thus, wherever the opportunity presents itself, distinctions and differentiations vis-à-vis hysteria are discussed, or references to other patients are made. At the same time Freud (1909d) also attempts to discuss the question of whether the mechanisms he has analyzed can be generalized:

Compulsive acts like this, in two successive stages, of which the second neutralizes the first, are a typical occurrence in obsessional neuroses. The patient's consciousness naturally misunderstands them and puts forward a set of secondary motives to account for them—*rationalizes* them, in short. But their true significance lies in their being a representation of a conflict of two opposing impulses of approximately equal strength: and hitherto I have invariably found that this opposition has been one between love and hate. Compulsive acts of this sort are theoretically of special interest, for they show us a new type of method of constructing symptoms. What regularly occurs in hysteria is that a compromise is arrived at, which enables both the opposing tendencies to find expression simultaneously— which kills two birds with one stone; whereas here each of the two opposing tendencies finds satisfaction singly, first one and then the other, though naturally an attempt is made to establish some sort of logical connection (often in defiance of all logic) between the antagonists. (p. 192)

This lengthy quotation from the case history under discussion is intended to demonstrate the degree to which Freud unites clinical demonstration with a vigorous examination of the concept. The sureness of his theoretical discussion, which is also reflected in the detail and skill of his interpretation, reminds the reader that the example under analysis here is not the only one of its kind but that the author is using this case to test his own conceptions.

In the second part of the treatise, the relation of practice to theory is reversed. Initially the clinical deliberations were examined for their theoretical content and thus established, while now the theoretical considerations occupy center stage and the clinical example serves only to exemplify them. The regular processes of compulsion neurosis that can be abstracted from the individual case and established as having their own independent existence are presented in terms of their significance for the development of psychoanalytic theory. Here we are shown how theory can lay claim to an ability to make statements of broad validity, reaching the level of hypotheses about human culture and developmental history. From considering that "a tendency to taking pleasure in smell, which has become extinct since childhood, may play a role in the genesis of neurosis" (1909d, p. 247)—a tendency that he has discovered in other neurotics, compulsives, and hysterics—Freud begins to wonder "... whether the atrophy of the sense of smell (which was the inevitable result of man's assumption of an erect posture) and the consequent organic repression of his pleasure in smell may not have had a considerable share in the origin of his susceptibility to nervous disease. This would afford us some explanation of why, with the advance of civilization, it is precisely the sexual life that must fall a victim to repression" (1909d, p. 248). It is characteristic of Freud's case histories that while they perform a concrete analysis of the given case, at the same time they provide the setting for far-reaching hypotheses that bring to fruition the great riches of clinical thought.

The day-to-day notes previously mentioned deserve separate consideration. In 1955 they were made available to the public in volume X of the *Standard Edition*. Elisabeth Zetzel, however, discovered them only in 1965 when she consulted the *Standard Edition* instead of the customary *Collected Papers* in preparing a paper. Her discovery led to an important addition to Freudian interpretation: In these clinical notes there are more than 40 references to a highly ambivalent mother–son relationship, which were not adequately considered in the Freudian case history as it was published in 1909 (Zetzel, 1966). These notes underscore the great importance of separating clinical observation from theory-bound interpretation. Freud (1909d, p. 255) himself notes with astonishment that the patient, after being informed of the conditions for treatment in the first interview, had said, "I have to ask my mother." This reaction of the patient, though surely important, is not to be found in the case report itself. Other interesting treatments and reappraisals of the Rat Man case incorporating Freud's notes are found in Shengold (1971), Beigler (1975), Holland (1975), and Mahony (1986). Recently Freud's technical omissions—from today's point of view—have been critically discussed by Schachter (2005a).

The Wolf-Man

The excerpt "From the History of an Infantile Neurosis" (Freud, 1918)—the most detailed and most important of all Freud's case histories—deals with a relatively short period of treatment. After the analysis had been going on for four years without making any significant progress (Jones, 1955, p. 275), Freud (1918) set a deadline on the treatment:

> Under the inexorable pressure of this fixed limit his resistance and his fixation to the illness gave way, and now in a disproportionately short time the analysis produced all the material which made it possible to clear up his inhibitions and remove his symptoms. (p. 11)

According to Freud's (1918b) own indications, the clarification of the infantile neurosis that he describes in this study derives almost entirely from these last months—from the setting of the deadline to the end of treatment. Requested by the patient to "write a complete history of his illness, of his treatment, and of his recovery," (p. 8) Freud refuses because he regards this as "technically impracticable and socially impermissible." (p. 8) The "fragmentary" report—a bit of self-irony, since Freud surely saw how it compared in volume with his other case histories—represents a combination of a treatment and case history and is organized as follows:

1. Introductory Remarks
2. General Survey of the Patient's Environment and of the History of the Case
3. The Seduction and its Immediate Consequences
4. The Dream and the Primal Scene
5. A Few Discussions
6. The Obsessional Neurosis
7. Anal Eroticism and the Castration Complex
8. Fresh Material from the Primal Period—Solution
9. Recapitulations and Problems

As is known, one of the aims of this publication was to combat a new form of resistance to the results of psychoanalysis. Jung and Adler had undertaken reinterpretations aiming to "ward off the objectionable novelties.... The study of children's neuroses exposes the complete inadequacy of these shallow or high-handed attempts at re-interpretation" (Freud 1918b, p. 9). As Freud's (1914d) presentation in his "On the History of the Psychoanalytic Movement" reveals, the polemic nature of this confrontation is noticeably subdued; instead, he attempts an "objective honoring of the analytic material." In his review of Gardiner's (1971) anthology *The Wolf-Man by the Wolf-Man*, Kanzer (1972, p. 419) stresses that Freud, inspired by his experiences with the wolf dream, required his students to collect and report similar dreams indicative of early sexual experiences. The reaction to this, he says, encouraged direct observation and analysis of children. In his opinion this is to be regarded as a milestone in psychoanalytic methodology, since it has underscored the importance of collaborative research. This statement is remarkable when one recalls that Freud (1918b) repeatedly emphasizes the impossibility of "in any way introducing into the reproduction of an analysis the sense of conviction which results from the analysis itself" (p. 13). The methodology of psychoanalytic research was by no means oriented a priori toward a successful description of individual cases. The addenda hoped for from later treatment reports on the Wolf-Man and the descriptions of adult neurosis in the famous patient of psychoanalysis, remain disappointing. Even the Wolf-Man's own autobiographical remarks contribute little to an elucidation of a childhood, which has been charged with such a great burden of proof.* Mahony (1986)—specialist in matters of Freud's literary style—dedicates a whole monograph on the Wolf-Man.

---

* A very clear and didactically well-organized survey of the structure of argumentation in the Wolf-Man is given by the French authors Lebovici and Soulé (1970).

Freud's (1920a) sixth case history, "The Psychogenesis of a Case of Homosexuality in a Woman," can be omitted in the context of this methodological discussion, since in it Freud presents only "the most general outlines of the various events" and "the conclusions reached from a study of the case," because the requirements of medical discretion made it impossible to report it in greater detail (p. 147).

The Schreber Case

The fourth case history of 1911, Freud's (1911) "Psychoanalytic Notes on an Autobiographical Account of a Case of Paranoia (Dementia Paranoides)" generates a methodological discussion since it relates to a patient whom he had never seen, so in the strict sense it is not a case history at all.[*] Thus, Freud seems to feel the need to provide a justification for the fact that "the analytic investigation of paranoia presents difficulties of a peculiar nature to physicians who, like myself, are not attached to public institutions" (p. 9). Because the therapeutic prospects were judged to be poor, as a rule Freud was unable to obtain sufficient analytic material to "lead to any analytic conclusions" about the structure of the cases. A clever maneuver drawing on what was already known about paranoia changes this unfavorable situation into an excellent one:

> The psychoanalytic investigation of paranoia would be altogether impossible if the patients themselves did not possess the peculiarity of betraying (in distorted form, it is true) precisely those things which other neurotics keep hidden as a secret. Since paranoiacs cannot be compelled to overcome their internal resistances, and since in any case they only say what they choose to say, it follows this is precisely a disorder in which a written report or a printed case history can take the place of personal acquaintance with the patient. (p. 9)

What was first introduced as a justification proves to be a great advantage. Freud (1911) can tell readers to look up all the places in Schreber's (1903) *Denkwürdigkeiten eines Nervenkranken* (Memoirs of my illness) that support his interpretations and read the patient's own words for themselves. The demand that was previously impossible to fulfill—actually to provide the potential critic with the original data—was now met for the first time. This resulted in the English translation by MacAlpine and Hunter (1955). Dissatisfied with the therapeutic results of the then traditional thesis of

---

[*] Cf. also Adler's (1928) case of Fräulein R.

a homosexual conflict of the paranoid psyche, they turn to the "original text," which was more quoted than actually read:

> We therefore read Schreber's memoirs and subsequently published a study (MacAlpine and Hunter, 1953) in which we showed that projection of unconscious homosexuality, though playing a part in the symptomatology, could not account for the illness in course or outcome, phenomenologically or aetiologically. (p. 24)

Based on this experience MacAlpine and Hunter (1955) decide to translate the memoirs, not hesitating to praise this report from the methodological and didactic point of view as well:

> For all students of psychiatry, Schreber, his most famous patient, offers unique insight into the mind of a schizophrenic, his thinking, language, behavior, delusions and hallucinations, and into the inner development, course and outcome of the illness. His autobiography had the advantage of being complete to an extent no case history taken by a physician can ever be: its material is not selected or subject to elaboration or omission by an intermediary between the patient and his psychosis, and between both and the reader. Every student therefore has access to the totality of the patient's products. Indeed the memoirs may be called the best text on psychiatry written for psychiatrists by a patient. (p. 25)

Freud's report on senate president Schreber was initially taken up by a number of psychoanalytic authors and utilized further. Abraham (1914) studied a case of neurotic light phobia, which until then had not yet been specifically treated in the literature: "And yet it contains ... an important clue to our understanding of them" (p. 172). The indication refers to Schreber's delusion that he could look at the sun for minutes without being dazzled. If a delusional misapprehension of the danger of being blinded can be accepted in the psychotic, Abraham proceeds to assume in the neurotic an anxiety an exaggerated fear of the risk of being blinded.

For the history of research it is of particular interest to see the development of an entire Schreber research program that, like MacAlpine and Hunter (1955), does not confine itself to the sections excerpted by Freud. Until this point the Freudian report had been taken up and discussed by a number of psychoanalysts (Abraham, 1924; Bonaparte, 1927; Brenner, 1939; Fenichel, 1931; Spielrein, 1912; Storch, 1922). Starting in 1945 we observe the growth of an independent Schreber research, which in American psychoanalysis was carried particularly by the studies of Niederland (for a summary see Niederland 1974), Katan (1959), and Nunberg (1952). A number of others participated in the discussion, among them White (1961, 1963) and Meissner (1976).[*] An unexpected development occurred in 1946 when Baumeyer (1956, 1970) became medical director of the hospital in which Schreber had been hospitalized and came upon a great quantity of new material, which he published in the following years. Next to the contributions of Katan and Niederland, those of Baumeyer are the most important ones that have contributed to an understanding of the psychoanalytic aspects of the case. At Jacques Lacan's instigation a French translation of the memoirs was prepared, which was studied in the seminars of the Lacan circle. Lacan himself produced a linguistic structural analysis of the book, which especially deepens our understanding of Schreber's "basic language" (Lacan, 1959). Recently contributions by Israels (1989) and Lothane (2005) have enriched the controversial debates.[†]

The fruitfulness of the decision to choose a publicly accessible case history as the starting point is further corroborated by the fact that this work became the object of scientific analyses outside of psychoanalytic circles. Thus, Elias Canetti (1962, p. 434) proclaims that "there is no richer or more instructive document." To him, examination of this one system of paranoiac delusion leads to the conclusion that "paranoia is an *illness of power* in the most literal sense of the words" (p. 448, italics in original).

By placing Freud's 1911c analysis of the Schreber case at the end of this survey of case histories, we wish to show that a particularly favorable constellation is present here for further research: There is a clear division between the original and its interpretation, and new interpretative initiatives could be taken again and again. Certainly there are other valid approaches to studying the significance of Freud's case histories and their methodological peculiarities. Literary scientist Steven Marcus (1976) analyzed the Dora case as a work of art and finds that the case histories represent a literary genre: "They are creative narratives that include their own analysis and interpretation in themselves" (p. 441).

Our interest here resides in the creative opportunity that is open to later researchers to correct previous attempts at interpretation and explanation using the case histories.

This discussion of the case history as a communication medium in Freud's writing has been oriented around his six lengthy case histories (Jones, 1955, pp. 255ff). The boundaries between this form and other clinical communications of Freud's are not precise and certainly have not been drawn using

---

[*] The list is by no means exhaustive. Further references are found in Niederland (1974).

[†] Little known in this discussion is an effort to use computer-based content analysis to solve some of the riddle of this case report (Laffal, 1976).

any explicit distinguishing criteria. The case histories in question are those that presented individual patients in a thorough way and at the same time were intended to illustrate general principles.

FROM THE CASE HISTORY TO
THE SINGLE CASE STUDY*

The central scientific and didactic function of the case history is to bring out the type in the manner that Freud (1933a) evidently adopted from Charcot's nosographic method: "Progress in scientific work is just as it is in analysis. We bring expectations with us into the work, but they must be forcibly held back" (p. 170). Thus, the oscillation between conjectures/hypothesis and the testing of them is crucial. Frommer and Langenbach (2001, p. 60) in their discussion of "the psychoanalytic case study as source of epistemic knowledge" follow Schwartz and Wiggings (1987) in calling such early stages of knowledge that have abductive and inductive elements "typifications." Amid the plethora of "formes frustes" one must be able to "read" the ideal type and then give it succinct form in an example, and this ability may account for the efficacy of a convincing case history. For this reason, we feel it is crucial for psychoanalytic and particularly clinical researchers to acquaint themselves with the concept of the type as a conceptual instrument of the highest order. The following discussion regarding the establishment of types as an ordering operation is based on the type concepts proposed by Hempel (1952).

The first and simplest type is designated by Hempel (1952) as the classification type. It arises when the individuals to be classed by type are assigned to different categories. The assignment is made according to the criteria of completeness, unambiguousness, and exclusivity. Although this form of classification is very popular in the thinking of everyday clinical practice, the necessary conditions are seldom met. To characterize patients by "typical interaction patterns" or to refer to a "typical anal" or "typical suicidal" patient is misleading if the classificatory type is intended. In this kind of pragmatic type assignment for everyday use, which is especially common in psychoanalytic characterology, the genetic/dynamic aspect is ignored. Dictated by clinical needs, it is essentially a simplification of the cognitive contents that enter into the diagnostic decision-making process. According to Hempel, the classification type is most applicable during the early stages in the development of a science. Classification types function here as ordering structures by which the phenomenal world can be organized. They are

---

* This section is dedicated to A. E. Meyer, whose polemic "Down with the Short Story—Long Live the Patient-Therapist Interaction Story" (1994) breathed new life into our aspirations.

present, however, only when the mentioned conditions are actually met. Yet in this respect clinical psychoanalytic phenomenology (i.e., systematic description) is more than unreliable. Indeed, it is a distinguishing mark of many theoretical discussions that their empirical basis is not unambiguously described.

A methodologically more demanding type (i.e., one belonging to a higher logical level) is designated by Hempel (1952) as the extreme type. This type is defined by two extremes that are rarely or never encountered in reality. Between the two extremes, subjects are characterized according to their closeness to or distance from one of the poles (see Rosch's [1978] "principles of categorization"). In practice, transitional forms are conceivable between classification and extreme types, but in theory there is no gradual transition. In psychoanalytic clinical practice, this type makes little sense. While we may speak of a patient being more or less "anal," as a purely empirical feature-class "not at all anal" or "extremely anal" is not reasonably conceivable. A concept such as "anal" or "anality" is essentially an ideal type (see following) although specifically for research purposes it may be useful to make extreme-type application of certain concepts.

While the classification type and the extreme type are empirical in nature—that is, they can be established by empirical features—the ideal type is a model that unites observable phenomena and concepts in an interpretive or explanatory schema. And herein lies its difference from the concept of *gestalt*, which embraces only empiric-phenomenal aspects. With this type, occupying the highest logical level of the three, the issues surrounding the concept of type altogether now become visible. It makes evident the amount of theory that as a rule goes into conceptualizing such types; thus, it becomes clear that the concept of the ideal type leads to examination of theory—a demand that is implicit in psychoanalytic case study.

This discussion of the significance of the type in psychoanalytic case study brings out a useful point of distinction vis-à-vis the biographical method, namely the generalizing thrust to which psychoanalytic case studies have always laid claim. Certainly the ability to discern types within the multiplicity of the phenomenal world is of tremendous heuristic value, yet it still must be asked if beyond this, the case-study approach has also been adequately worked through from a methodological point of view to permit an evaluation of clinical typology (Wachholz and Stuhr, 1999). In the following section, the research connected with this question is examined under the theme of the transformation of the case history into the single case study.

We now trace a development in the way clinical matters have been communicated in psychoanalysis since Freud's case histories. The first "genres" to establish themselves in the organs of scientific communication were more or less artfully drawn clinical miniatures, excerpts of treatments, single observations, and dream analyses. Excellent examples of these can be found in Ferenczi's (1927[1964]) *Bausteine der Psychoanalyse* (Fundamentals of psychoanalysis), vol. 2, *Praxis* (Practice), in which the reader can still feel the enthusiasm for the newly revealed world that was now to be understood and communicated. The story of Little Hahnemann, which is subliminally reminiscent of Little Hans, dates from 1913. Another typical report for these years is a case presented by Schilder (1927) on a psychosis following a cataract operation:

> The psychoanalyst seldom has the opportunity to publish the entire material on which he bases his conclusions. The psychosis on which I wish to give a brief report presents such clear and unambiguous findings after a short period of observation that a documentary presentation is possible. This alone is reason enough to justify a detailed presentation of the case history. (p. 35)

After this introductory justification for providing a "detailed presentation"—the entire study is only about nine pages long—Schilder (1927) reports on a 53-year-old female patient who develops a condition of psychotic agitation in the aftermath of a cataract operation. Schilder describes the productive symptoms, which are dominated by images of her body being injured and portions of her own or her doctors' flesh being cut out, and then offers the following summary:

> This gives rise to the overall picture that the eye operation activates in the patient the general concept or general consciousness of injury to the body as a whole, within which concept an injury to the genitals is particularly dominant.... The fact that it is an eye operation that evokes the psychosis is especially noteworthy inasmuch as it is well known that the eye frequently stands for the genitals. It should also be emphasized, however, that other operations, both in men and in women, will evoke a castration complex. (p. 42)

From then on Schilder (1927) is engaged in comparing and classifying this single case history:

> The psychosis has the type of Meynert's amentia. Formally it appears to be essentially indistinguishable from the majority of published observations of psychoses following cataract operations, to the extent it is at all possible to make a judgment on the basis of short case histories. (p. 43)

Now several additional types of operations are mentioned to which the literature ascribes a castrating action, and Schilder (1927) concludes his presentation with the following words: "I have no doubt that the castration complex is significant in the genesis of postoperative psychoses and believe that a general significance must be ascribed to the results of the study of this case" (p. 44).

The sense of entitlement with which Schilder (1927) takes the step from discussion of an individual case to generalization is presumably based on a great number of other widely known experiences, but these are *not cited*. This is a characteristic of the clinical research tradition that Rapaport (1960) describes as clinically impressive yet not valid. We are left wondering if psychotic episodes occur more frequently after eye operations than after other operations—which one is inclined to assume given the towering importance of the eye as a sexually symbolic organ—or if this finding is not rather a product of wishful thinking.

With a change of style in scientific communication came the attempt to make verbatim transcripts of treatments accessible to the public. The need for this became evident as partial reports began to be published on such impressive successes that doubts seemed appropriate. Thus, in his review of a book by Sadger (1921) titled *Die Lehre von den Geschlechtsverirrungen auf psychoanalytischer Grundlage* (Theory of sexual aberrations on a psychoanalytic foundation), Boehm (1923) writes:

> If the author wishes to assert that after just four sessions he has achieved a permanent cure by dissolving the mother bond (p. 96), this will raise doubts in the circles of Freud's pupils. On the other hand, if this accomplishment, standing alone, is supposed to be beyond doubt, then there is a significant omission in the text: A presentation of the technique that made it possible to dissolve the mother bond in four sessions would necessarily revolutionize the entire field of psychoanalytic therapy as it has been known. (p. 538)

The critic was fortunate in this case. Sadger (1921) had based his treatment reports on in-session stenographic notes, and these voluminous and detailed presentations made it possible for Boehm (1923) in his review to make a clear criticism of the treatment technique and thus also of the theoretical relevance of Sadger's conclusions:

> The case histories read like essays or novels that patients might write about the origin of their ailments after having read some part of the psychoanalytic literature and understood it poorly. They keep giving attempts at explanation, interpretations, questions, while symptoms presently manifested are simply "traced back" to their "source" in conscious childhood impressions and portrayed as repetitions and mere habituation: "This might have its source in" ... is a stereotypical

phrase in all of them.... It struck me that Sadger's patients use the same expressions, the same German as Sadger himself uses in his text. The longer I worked with these case histories, the stronger became my conviction that all of Sadger's patients were under a strong suggestion from the author—probably unconsciously to him—and for his sake made no resistance to "associating" whatever attempts at explanation they assumed from their reading and from suggestive questions might please the doctor. Consequently these case histories, published as they are on the basis of stenographic records, unfortunately have no value as scientific evidence; furthermore they do not provide the uninitiated with an accurate picture of a psychoanalytic treatment. (p. 539)

There could hardly be a clearer illustration of the advantages of providing stenographic or even verbatim accounts of treatments, as they allow for an evaluation not solely based on the evidence of the analyst, who is describing himself. Why Freud never published his notes—why he limited his discussion of technique to a small number of essays, most of which relate to the first 10 years of psychoanalytic work—will not be considered here in detail.*

What is surely a significant development in this regard occurred in 1939: Confronted with the virtual unanimity of psychoanalysts regarding their method—after all, Freud himself had most clearly described it—Edward Glover felt sufficiently uneasy as to undertake an empirical survey within the British Psychoanalytic Society (Glover and Brierley, 1940). Using quite simple questions such as, "When in the session do you engage in interpretation?", "How much interpretation do you do?", and "What do you interpret?" the results of the study revealed that as an ideal construct the psychoanalytic method allows psychoanalysts a great deal of empirical freedom, of which they take full advantage. As Michael Balint (1950) shows, these multifarious variations in technique stem at least partially from "changes in the therapeutic goals" of psychoanalysis, which in turn are derived from a differing reception of theoretical developments. Thus, Glover's attempt can also be seen in the context of the tensions that had arisen in the British Society with the development of the various schools. Even today there appears to be a considerable difference between the theory needed for the technique and the theory actually available, as can be

---

* Brody (1970, 1976) compiled a demographic evaluation of Freud's patients based on all patients mentioned in Freud's works. The assumption that this would capture a representative sample of Freud's clients, however, appears highly problematic. The simple fact mentioned by Brody that the number of published case histories declines rapidly after 1900 means that the patients presented in "Studies on Hysteria" (Freud, 1985d) receive a qualitatively undue weight in the development of psychoanalysis.

observed in the disagreement with the French analysts. A good example of this is given in Widmer-Perrenoud's (1975) review of the 1972 study by Kestemberg and Decobert titled "La faim et le corps":

> Whoever turns to the case descriptions expecting to gain a better understanding of the theory and learn a specific technique for dealing with anorexics will be disappointed.... In other words, there is a discrepancy between the subtle theoretical considerations regarding the narcissism of anorexics and the application of these insights to treatment. (p. 587)

As a bibliographic exercise Kächele (1981) reviewed the post-Freud psychoanalytic literature for treatment reports of a certain size, searching for presentations that cover, using a rough measure, more than 30 pages in published form. He tabulated as a synopsis those reports that at the time of the study met this criterion (Table 3.1). Though some publications may have escaped the search, the synopsis ought to be informative and representative on the whole. Of the examples that are listed, we will be able to discuss only a part, placing emphasis on those cases that seem most important to us.

The synopsis lists the author and identifies the patients (whenever possible citing their age, sex, and any names by which they might be known in the literature), the dates and length of treatment, to the extent that this could be ascertained from the reports, as well as indicates the type of record and the approximate page count of the report in published form. Looking at the dates of publication in this sample, its incompleteness must be emphasized once again. One is struck by the fact that from 1930 to 1959 there were 6 reports, while from 1960 to 1979 there were 20.

These data certainly may not be reliable statistically, but they confirm the impression that the study of the literature gave us: An increasing number of in-depth case reports are being made available to the public. It is interesting to note that in some cases treatment and publication are separated by a relatively long time. Also, 11 of the 26 reports concern children or adolescent patients—quite a high number when one considers that the quantitative proportion of child therapists is doubtless quite a bit lower. Furthermore, almost all of these children suffer from psychotic or prepsychotic illnesses. The length of the reports cited here varies from the arbitrary lower limit of 30 pages to more than 600 pages of text. With few exceptions these reports were written after the sessions. Verbatim transcripts were used only by Robert Stoller (1974), although Paul Dewald's 1992 report, which was based on stenographic writing during the session, probably approaches the exactness of a verbatim transcript. It is obvious that the more recent reports have demonstrated more concern on methods of reporting clinical material

Table 3.1 Extended Case Reports

Author	Case	Date of Treatment	Duration	Date of Publication	Type of Record	Size (Number of Pages)
Adler	"Fräulein R."	—	—	1928	after-session notes	146
Taft	7-year-old boy	—	31 sessions	1933	in-session notes	161
Wolberg	42-year-old man "Johann R."	1940	4 months	1945	after-session notes	169
Berg	young man	ca. 1940	—	1946	in-session notes	ca. 240
Sechehaye	18-year-old woman	1930	10 years	1947	after-session notes	107
McDougall and Lebovici	9-year-old boy "Sammy"	1955	166 sessions	1960	in-session notes	270
Klein	10-year-old boy "Richard"	1944	93 sessions	1961	after-session notes	490
Thomä	26-year-old woman "Sabine"	1958	304 sessions	1961	after-session notes	70
Parker	16-year-old boy	1955	200 sessions	1962	after-session notes	355
Bolland and Sandler	2-year-old boy "Andy"	ca. 1960	221 sessions	1965	weekly report after-session notes	88
Boor	22-year-old man "Frank A."	ca. 1960	580 sessions	1965	after-session notes	30
Pearson	12-year-old boy "adolescent"	—	6 years	1968	after-session notes	140
Milner	23-year-old woman "Susan"	1943-1958	15 years	1969	after-session notes	410
Dolto	14-year-old boy "Dominique"	1968	12 sessions	1971	after-session notes	160
Balint	43-year-old man "Mr. Baker"	1961	29 sessions	1972	after-session notes	130
Dewald	26-year-old woman	ca. 1966	304 sessions	1972	in-session notes	620
Winnicott	30-year-old man	ca. 1954	—	1972	after-session notes	240
Argelander	35-year-old man	—	ca. 600 sessions	1971	after-session notes	75

Table 3.1 Extended Case Reports (continued)

Author	Case	Date of Treatment	Duration	Date of Publication	Type of Record	Size (Number of Pages)
Stoller	30-year-old woman	—	—	1974	in-session notes	400
Winnicott	2-year-old girl "Piggle"	1964	14 sessions	1978	after-session notes	200
Firestein	25-year-old woman	—	—	1978	after-session notes	30
Goldberg	25-year-old man "Mr. I."	—	—	1978	after-session notes	108
Goldberg	31-year-old woman	ca. 1966	600 sessions	1978	after-session notes	98
Goldberg	22-year-old man "Mr. E."	ca. 1972	2 years	1978	after-session notes	134

(Klumpner & Frank, 1991). This preliminary overview should facilitate the subsequent discussion of several of these treatment reports, in which we shall limit our commentary to the authors' methodological approach.

We shall begin with the report of the British psychoanalyst Charles Berg (1946), who was also active at the Tavistock Clinic. Before the war he saw a young man whose unusual symptomatology struck him: He was practically normal but still felt the need to consult a psychoanalyst. Berg bases his decision to make the case report on this:

> It was on this account that I was tempted to record his analysis stage by stage in the hope that I would be able to convey to others interested in the subject the insight gained from a study of this clinical material. (p. 9)

The presentation of this treatment report is based on in-session notes and is ordered chronologically; the selection of the material is made according to clinical progress. Thus, to a certain point Berg follows the exposition that Freud exemplifies with the Rat Man, but he does not explicitly refer to Freud. The preliminary interview is presented in great detail, and the first sessions even more exactly.

Gradually a condensation process sets in, and the selection is largely determined by the thematic structure. Certain climaxes (e.g., the beginning of transference, the regression to childhood, the father-fixation) determine the further course of the presentation. It is a play in three acts under the overarching themes of father, mother, and son, for which the report is even divided into three "books."

The fate of a treatment report by Donald Winnicott deserves to be noted. At the 27th Conférence des Psychanalystes de Langues Romains in Paris in 1954, and a year later to the British Psycho-Analytical Society, Winnicott reported on the analysis of a schizoid man who experienced states of "withdrawal and regression" during analysis, an understanding of which proved critical for the further course of this treatment (Winnicott, 1954). In 1972 Winnicott's notes of the last six months of this treatment appeared hidden away in a comprehensive book by Giovacchini (1972) on issues of treatment technique under the title "Fragment of an Analysis" (Winnicott, 1972). Interestingly, the extended written version of the lecture including the case material, which appeared in German in *Psyche* in 1956, already contains the following unmistakable indication: "It so happens that for the last four months of this part I made a verbatim report, which is available to anyone who wishes to read back over the work to-date with the patient" (Winnicott, 1956, p. 207) [Translation from German].

Surely it is an indication of a special communication problem among psychoanalysts that this offer of Winnicott's (1956) could only be taken up posthumously. Since then the report on this treatment has been published separately (French edition 1975; German edition 1982). Annie Anzieu's (1977) sensitive critique in the *Bulletin of the European Psychoanalytic Federation* (No. 11) immediately shows the virtue of such a publication in promoting discussion. In contrast to the admiring attitude of the American editor Giovacchini (1972), Anzieu criticizes the analyst's penchant for interpretation, which makes it impossible to experience the unbroken speech of the patient: "The situation does not appear to be the kind to which a French analyst would usually refer" (p. 28). To Giovacchini, it is just this perceptible activity on the part of the analyst that they find of positive significance:

> The benefits derived from the detailed presentation of an analytic case are emphasized by this example. Not only do we learn about Dr. Winnicott's clinical-theoretical orientation, which has had and will continue to have, in our opinion, considerable impact on psychoanalytic theory and practice, but we are also made aware of how really exciting and rewarding the actual treatment of a patient can be. We particularly want to call the reader's attention to the way in which Dr. Winnicott has integrated fantasy and dream material with reports of routine daily activities, in the service of the analysis. (pp. 455–456)

Given the particular personal transmission of theory and technique in psychoanalysis, we must acknowledge it as a great exception that the process notes from a treatment by a significant psychoanalyst are available at all, allowing us to get at least a step closer to a direct impression and to make independent judgments on technique and theory.

A similar legacy is found in Melanie Klein's (1961) report on a child analysis, which she compiled shortly before her death. She provides an explanation of the aims of this voluminous publication herself:

> In presenting the following case history, I have several aims in view. I wish first of all to illustrate my technique in greater detail than I have done formerly.... The day-to-day movement in the analysis, and the continuity running through it, thus become perceptible.

> I took fairly extensive notes, but I could of course not always be sure of the sequence, nor quote literally the patient's associations and my interpretations. This difficulty is one of a general nature in reporting on case material. To give verbatim accounts could only be done if the analyst were to take notes during the session; this would disturb that patient considerably and break the unhindered flow of

associations, as well as divert the analyst's attention from the course
of the analysis. (p. 11)

The short duration of the treatment is not simply due to a favorable
course; in fact, as the editor informs us, it was made clear from the beginning that only four months would be available. It is important that Klein
(1961) feels able to assure us that this analysis does not differ in any way
from an analysis of normal duration.

One might think this report would especially lend itself to research, as it
contains notes on exactly 93 sessions with an average length of five pages
each. Yet apart from Geleerd's (1963) exhaustive discussion, the only other
investigation we are aware of is the recent detailed study by Meltzer (1978),
which provides a systematic description of the course of this treatment.

Joyce McDougall and Serge Lebovici (1969) report on the analytic treatment of 9-year-old Sammy which took place in the mid 1950s in Paris.
The lad himself initiated the exact report on the treatment, since for a long
period he refused to speak except if the analyst took down every word he
said: "Now write what I dictate. I'm your dictator," he would shout (p. 1).
After eight months the treatment of this psychotic child was terminated,
apparently with significant improvement, yet the reports of the parents
from subsequent years, which are included in the publication, make it clear
that this fragment of a child analysis was really only a beginning: "Sammy
left for New York the following day. Thus his analysis after only eight
months' treatment, still in its beginnings, came to an abrupt end" (Commentary of the analyst in her notes on the last session, No. 166 of 9/9/1955,
McDongall and Lebovici, 1966).

As mentioned before, treatments of children seem more likely to be published than those of adults.* One, the case of 2-year-old Andy, was published by Bolland and Sandler (1965) of the Hampstead Clinic. Covering
a period of 50 weeks, 271 sessions are presented in weekly summaries. In
addition, this treatment report exemplifies the way the Hampstead Index
works. In the preface of this study, Anna Freud explains that by index-
ing analytic material (i.e., by putting it into schematic form) the research
group at the Hampstead Clinic seeks to "create something like a collective
analytic memory, a store of analytic material that makes a wealth of data
gathered from many colleagues available to the individual researcher or
author" (p. x).†

Another report is that of Francoise Dolto (1971). Her 14-year-old Dominique is "cured" of his psychotic regression in 12 sessions. Dolto too seeks

---

* The ethical issue of children giving "informed consent" to publication must be
bypassed here.
† The use of the index as a research instrument is described by Sandler (1962).

justification in referring to Freud's case histories, particularly the child case histories such as Little Hans, and expresses criticism:

> Contemporary literature offers a multitude of short or minute extracts drawn from a series of several hundred sessions. These represent selections from the dreams, the words, or the behavior of patients, and mostly serve to justify technical research or some discussion of transference or counter-transference. The clinician is left to wonder about the basis of their selection. (p. 3)

In addition, Dolto (1971) makes a plea for the presence of third parties in the treatment situation, such that "one of the psychoanalytically trained individuals present records everything that is said on either side, by both the patient and the analyst" (p. 8). As it happens, this condition is not fulfilled in the Dominique case, and the process notes are made by the therapist herself.

Without these exact records, it is unlikely that the negative criticism directed at this case report by the American reviewer Anthony (1974) could have been so objective or so outspoken in declaring that "each nation [seems] to cultivate its own psychoanalytic garden" (p. 684). The German reviewer Haas (1976) seems to prefer a garden à la Lacan.

This critical discussion deserves high marks because it makes it possible to reduce ideological differences to their demonstrable empiric substance. This appears to be why Dolto's (1971) demand for "extremely detailed notes" is not controversial, to the extent that they are in fact published and made available for didactic and theory-demonstrating purposes. Unfortunately, a great number of reasons speak against this, reasons that cannot be lightly dismissed. Protection of the patient and the need of the analyst for protection as well are without doubt the prime ones, which is why we often see the problematic issues surrounding a publication dwindle with the passage of time. Thus, it is probably no accident that Winnicott's records became accessible only after 20 years, that Klein's treatment of Richard was not published until 1961, or that Balint's presentation of his focal therapy did not appear in print until 10 years after completion of the treatment. We learn from David Malan (1975) that Balint decided only quite late (around 1952) to take on cases himself. The first two cases he treated, as reported by Malan (p. 116), "were singularly unsuccessful," but the third attempt led, through its literary use, to a new type of psychoanalytic treatment: focal therapy.

> This book is based on Michael Balint's treatment of the patient Mr. Baker, written by him (Chapter 5). Unfortunately, the comments at the end of each session report are "asymmetrical." The reader should

be aware that Michael Balint dictated his notes right after each session and that originally these notes were not meant for publication. He later decided to include them in their original form with only very minor stylistic and grammatical changes here and there. (Ornstein, 1972, p. vii)

The aim of this joint work, which took gradual form over the course of time, was "... to use the history of the treatment of Mr. Baker to study in detail the interactions between the patient's associations and the therapist's choice of interventions. From the theoretical point of view this interaction can be summed up not only as the study of the treatment as a process, but also as a study of the developing doctor-patient relationship" (Balint, Ornstein, & Balint, 1972, p. 2).

When one considers this study from the point of view of the public nature of its observational data, several questions arise that Balint himself posed and immediately answered:

The material for this study is the collection of session reports, which were as a rule dictated to a secretary immediately after each session. No notes were made during the treatment sessions. The therapist relied entirely upon his memory. We know that this method has many drawbacks, and a number of purists will find it inadequate for meaningful research.

We readily admit that in a way recall from memory is not as reliable as a record on tape. On the other hand, we maintain that the internal cohesion within any single session and the whole series of sessions taken together is enough to demonstrate the validity and usefulness of this particular method.

Here we would only like to indicate that the method of recording used in this treatment facilitates the clear emergence of both the patient's character and the nature of the therapeutic technique, whereas otherwise both would have to be laboriously extracted from the collection of raw data provided by tape-recordings. Furthermore, no tape-recording can give any information about "interpretations thought of, but not given", the atmosphere of the session, the therapist's initial expectations, or his changing views regarding outcome and his afterthoughts and so on; on the other hand, all these important data are provided by the design of the method used. (Balint et al., 1972, p. 2)

Balint et al.'s (1972) argument emphasizes that in psychoanalysis, the publicly accessible raw data go beyond the verbal utterances of the patient and therapist. Only the crudest behaviorist could deny that the therapist's considerations, intentions, and attitudes have a potent existence in the therapeutic process. Balint et al.'s suggestion introduces the subjective dimension of this process into research, thus opening up a great number of vital issues to it for the first time.

In this connection, an important formal aspect of the described treatment is that a structuring element enters into the description of the sessions: Prior to treatment a *schema* was established, setting in advance the thematic points to be covered. In this way a relatively systematic documentation of this course of treatment was achieved.

In fact, such a schema for describing a course of treatment was introduced earlier, in 1951, by Alexander Mitscherlich at the Heidelberg Psychosomatic Clinic. In 1947 in his monograph *Vom Ursprung der Sucht* (The origin of addiction), he had already presented three case histories in which the presentation of the course of treatment is organized almost entirely within the framework of a dream analysis.[*] This "Systematic Case History" was intended to complete the "biographic anamnesis" in order to capture the process aspect of treatments. How many such "systematic case histories" were in fact written is difficult to determine today. To date only one has been published in the *Festschrift* for Mitscherlich: "Although only a small number of patients and their disease courses have been systematically studied, for many reasons it is more than justified at this moment to recall a work from the pioneer era" (Thomä, 1978, p. 254).

Doubtless inspired by this conception but not directly determined by it are the extensive case histories involving patients suffering from anorexia nervosa presented by Thomä (1961).[†] Regarding the scope of the case Sabine B., Thomä writes:

> Even a report as extensive as the following one presents only a selection of the observations and considerations that were gone through in 304 treatment sessions. In order to get at what was essential, we proceeded from the experiences of transference and resistance, which became the guideline for our presentation. (p. 150)

---

[*] This may be compared to French's (1952) monograph, which bases its clinical proofs on an extensive series of dreams of a female patient (on the use of dream series, cf. Geist & Kaechele, 1979).

[†] See also de Boor's (1965) monograph on the psychosomatic aspect of allergy, which also contains several lengthy case histories and treatment reports.

Subsequently Thomä (1961) apologizes for the "considerable" length of the report (approximately 70 pages), without pointing to the dearth of thorough treatment presentations as a justification for going into such detail. The presentation of this treatment is divided into 16 sections, the longest of them covering a period of 38 sessions and the shortest 9 sessions. A methodological discussion as to how this division of the treatment was arrived at is limited to the statement that the treatment sections are described according to "main themes." It would certainly be a worthwhile undertaking to make a careful investigation of the decision-making processes that lead to such segmenting of the psychoanalytic process (cf. Knapp et al., 1975).

In Hermann Argelander's (1971) case study "Der Flieger" (The pilot), we begin to see a noticeably more positive attitude toward comprehensive reporting. The chronological presentation of a course of treatment is expanded to include a theoretical introduction and a concluding summary with critical reflections; as to his procedure in selecting the material, Argelander writes, "In documenting the analytic material I shall alternate between a summarizing report form and excerpts of verbatim transcripts, especially at points that appear important for my theme" (p. 10). Since the presentation was intended as a contribution to the ongoing discussion of narcissism, the theme was focused in the tradition of the psychoanalytic case history.

Argelander's (1971) explicitly formulated reflections on the form of his presentations, his chronological recording of the events in the analysis, his strictly systematic inclusion of numerous verbatim quotes, and his summarizing reports, which appear very objective and free from theoretical and personal bias, all reveal the author's endeavor to allow for more transparency in his case presentation than was often true of earlier case histories. At the same time it must be noted that Argelander had to strike a selection and make descriptive summaries of long sections to keep down the length of the work.

The issue of the length of the case presentations studied here deserves special mention; the argument is too easily made that the importance of a work surely cannot be measured by its length. In fact, to the extent that clinical observations are being presented, the length of a treatment report does give an indication of the closeness to clinical reality of the observations presented.

It is useful in this regard to look at the case of Mr. Z first described by Kohut (1979a) that for good reason was not included in our tabulated list of cases. In it the course of two psychoanalyses is presented, one differing considerably in technical approach from the other.

Even though the clinical details provided in the German translation of "The Restoration of the Self" (Kohut, 1979b, pp. 172–216) are more complete than in the English journal version (Kohut, 1979a) a conclusion such as Kohut's calls for a far more comprehensive presentation. For example, the conclusion, based on this case, that "the new psychology of the self is helpful in the clinical area, that it allows us to perceive meanings, or the significance of meanings, that were formerly not perceived by us, at least not consciously" (Kohert 1976a, p. 26), should be supported with documentation that enable it to be tested.

Recently a biography on Kohut (Strozier, 2001) clarifies that Mr. Z's second analysis was an artful invention to illustrate how his second analysis should have been. In 1984 Kohut reinforced his satisfaction with the first fictive psychoanalysis worldwide. Indirectly he sharply criticized his training analyst, Ruth Eissler, whom he had chosen for tactical reasons after his application for training at the Chicago Psychoanalytic Institute was rejected. In his own appreciation he glorifies the changes by the self-psychological theory. Nothing else Kohut (1979a) did illustrates more clearly his heroic sense of himself. The two analyses of Mr. Z, published as genuine case material in the profession's most respected journal, reveal his deep psychoanalytical understanding and experience (Strozier, 2001, p. 308). Even in his last work *How Does Analysis Cure?* (Kohut, 1984) in a final debate with his critics he wrote:

> The case not only highlights the way theoretical changes enable the analyst to see new clinical configuration, but further demonstrates how the analysts' apprehension of the self-object transference affects his handling of clinical material via the enpanded empathy that results from the new theoretical frame. (p. 91)

The two analyses of Mr. Z are also a telling demonstration that even distinguished journal editors are unable to differentiate valid clinical dynamics from theoretical, hypothetical dynamics; how then can any analyst determine whether the dynamics developed with a patient are valid or theoretical?

Further detailed cases provided as support to Kohut's theory are found in a casebook edited by Goldberg in 1978. It presents relatively lengthy case reports, primarily of those patients who appear in short vignettes in Kohut's books. Thus, the book represents a "response to a persistent and clear request from a large number of clinicians" who have concerned themselves with Kohut's concepts (Goldberg, 1978, p. 1). The presentation of the analyses of Mrs. I and Mrs. A, each over 100 pages long, certainly allows for an excellent clinically oriented discussion.

Yet the need for even more detailed presentations of treatments seems to be felt by the treating analysts and the researchers alike. Thus, Paul Dewald decided to document an entire psychoanalytic treatment by making careful notes during the sessions. Introducing his intention at a workshop of the American Psychoanalytic Association in April 1972, Dewald stresses that "... most experienced analysts can conduct a reasonably effective psychoanalytic treatment with our current understanding of the process, and our traditional methodology of anecdotal description has resulted in the accumulation of a considerable body of knowledge" (quoted in Dorpat, 1973, p. 170). "Nevertheless," Dorpat comments, "if we are to have an impact, scientifically, beyond our profession, further research in this area is essential" (p. 171).

Dewald (1972) describes a treatment that was conducted initially without any scientific aim. Its systematic elaboration was undertaken only a year after conclusion of the treatment. Nevertheless, Dewald has to make detailed, almost verbatim notes of the dialogue while treatment was in progress, and he attempts to incorporate nonverbal elements of the communication into them. It is interesting that the "verbal interventions" of the analyst are cited separately, as if it were odd for the analyst to have a part in the psychoanalytic dialogue.

As might be expected, the note-taking becomes a technical problem. Still, Dewald (1972) assures us that as a rule his taking notes was accepted by the patient as belonging to the overall psychoanalytic situation as part of the treatment arrangement. Furthermore, it was found that the patients' reactions to it could be analyzed exactly as other reactions to the analyst's reality. The patient whom Dewald introduces is a young woman suffering from a classical mixed neurosis with multiple phobias, free-floating anxiety, depression, and frigidity. As it developed, the patient quickly grew accustomed to the analytic situation and proved an understanding partner in the work. Thus, the treatment lasted only 24 months (347 sessions) and led to improvement of the symptoms as well as a structural transformation of her personality.

About a year after the conclusion of treatment, Dewald began to transcribe his notes using a Dictaphone, making a particular effort to be true to the patient's idiomatic traits. When it came to publishing the notes, however, he had to select a sample as the material was too voluminous in its entirety.

This argument points to a certain contradiction between the scientific demand for revealing the original data and the practical limitation resulting from the impossibility of publishing even relatively short psychoanalyses in toto. Psychoanalytic process research suffers between the scylla of shortening and the deep blue sea of "systematical acoustical gap" (Meyer, 1981). What is "impossible," of course, is a determination that must be agreed upon by scientists. Only when such notes have been established as major data sources are these "impossibilities" likely to change.

Dewald made a decision to present unabridged session process notes of certain time blocks of the treatment. In addition he rounds out each set of in-session notes with summaries that enable the reader to gain insight into the analyst's thoughts. For those periods of treatment not presented in full, highly compressed summaries are inserted. Table 3.2 is intended to provide an overview of the distribution of the total publication into the several treatment sections and types of presentation:

Table 3.2   Dewald's Sampling

Length of treatment	24 months = 347 sessions
Verbatim record of these	107 sessions
Sample: months	1 + 3; 11; 13; 15; 23 + 24
Total volume of clinical material	656 pages
Portion of this in verbatim text	510 pages
Portion of this in summaries	146 pages

What was Dewald's aim in keeping notes of this treatment? The presenter at the workshop gives the following explanation:

> Dewald's aim in publishing this case record was to provide an overview of the psychoanalytic process from a clinical perspective, with demonstration and documentation of psychoanalytic data. Now that these data are published, it is possible to study them from a variety of different perspectives. Other researchers could try to validate through consensus on just what constituted the analytic process in this case. The same data could also be approached predictively by someone who has not previously studied the case and who would therefore not be biased by his advance knowledge of what happened in the analysis. (Dorpat, 1973, p. 172)

On par with Dewald's (1972) report in scope and importance is that of Stoller (1974), who has been studying questions of psychosexual development for years. In the introduction to his 400-page report on this unusual patient, Stoller, too, takes a position regarding the undertaking that makes room for both sides: the advocates of the classical case study who follow in the footsteps of Freud, and the experimentalists who have learned to doubt the value of individual clinical studies. The following passage exemplifies the style of the foreword to this book, which is essentially a plea for comprehensive case presentation:

> Despite the importance of discovering the psychodynamic sources of human behavior and the extensiveness of the literature to date, there is not a single psychoanalytic report in which the conclusions are preceded by the data that led to them. If such data are not available,

critics can be forgiven for not being convinced of the validity of the conclusions.... You and I never know when reading someone's report whether he is right because he is brilliant, imaginative, and agrees with noted authorities, or whether he is right because his conclusions follow from his data; we cannot know because we have not had access to his data. (p. xiii)

This foreword also strikes a now familiar refrain. What should interest us, however, is that these are not methodological outsiders speaking but experienced clinicians who themselves have cultivated the traditional style of communication for years and decades. The question as to whether the examples gathered here will be style-setting or not hinges on whether clinical needs will require making more information on treatment available than has traditionally been the case. The desire to get a real look into the psychoanalyst's workroom is no longer disparaged as voyeurism or infantile curiosity but has gained clinical, didactic, and scientific respectability in recent years.

By its nature, psychoanalysis can be experienced and learned only within a human relationship; for a long time this peculiarity resulted in putting a low priority on publishing treatment reports. The general feeling was that the important elements of a treatment could not yet be demonstrated or communicated. When one reads the enthusiastic reviews of treatment reports of experienced psychoanalysts, however, the opposite is regularly shown to be true. Thus, James (1979) writes regarding Winnicott's (1978) *Piggle*:

Remarkably enough there are few accounts of clinical work which tell to the new, and to the learning, analyst, how others who are believed to be successful work. "The Piggle" is one of those *rare open descriptions which establish a style.* (p. 137; italics added for emphasis)

Our hope is that a style-setting influence will be felt not only from Winnicott's (1972) treatment technique but also from the openness practiced by him and others. At the same time there does seem to be a certain risk associated with such openness. Margaret Little's (1990) personal record of her analysis with Winnicott in the early fifties describing psychotic anxieties and their containment was courageous. Harry Guntrip's (1975) report on his two analyses with Fairbairn and Winnicott, for example, appeared only after his death, and the attempt of living, particularly younger analysts to report on their "apprenticeship on the couch" (*Lehrjahre auf der Couch*; Moser, 1974), cannot be an easy undertaking. In his discussion of Moser's "confessions," Lowenfeld (1975) clarifies the special requirements that must apply to a treatment report of this kind composed by a professional colleague. With reports by patients it is easier to accept each of them for its particular nature and motivation. Homages to Freud (Blanton, 1971; Doolittle, 1956; Wortis, 1954) or reports on therapeutic experiences* possessing special literary charm, as those of Hannah Green (1964) and Marie Cardinale (1983), more easily win our sympathy. Attempts to write a common report, in which the patient and the therapist together reflect on the treatment, are still so uncommon as to arouse curiosity (Yalom & Elkin, 1974). A recent example was provided in Schachter's (2005c, see ch. 5) collection of treatment reports. However, Mary Barnes's (1971) *Two Accounts of a Journey Through Madness*, an overtly enthusiastic report from R. D. Laing's therapeutic community Kingsley Hall in London, also raises doubts about the therapeutic function of such shared reports. In her review, Curtius (1976, p. 64) speaks of a "new literary genre of the patient *Bildungsroman* or the therapist-patient novel in letters."

Since the publication of Kächele's study in 1981 it is obvious that in recent years detailed case reports are being published more and more frequently. Some of them have even reached television audiences. The growth of public interest in what goes on in psychotherapy is paralleled by psychoanalysts' growing interest in communicating their clinical experiences to each other in greater detail. The topic of the "analyst at work" rightly moves metapsychological discussions into the background.

A more recent example underscores that the problems of adaequate reporting still carry moments of tensions. In 1981, Casement reported at the International Congress in Helsinki on a technical problem ("Some pressures on the analyst for physical contact during the re-living of an early trauma"), which was published in the following year (Casement, 1982). Later, the author published an enlarged version of the paper in two books (Casement, 1985, 1990) and compiled important opinions from discussants of diverse theoretical orientations (Casement, 2000). In the meantime, as Boesky (2005) points out more than 25 authors have taken position to the original report; the publication of such discussions has become a kind of "cottage industry" (p. 842). Boesky's conclusion of his methodological critique focuses on the lack of understanding of clinical evidence formation: "If we truly wish to reap the benefits of pluralistic psychoanalysis, we are well advised to refine our understanding of what information about the patient has been used to support the conclusions reported" (p. 860).

This problem of how an analyst gains and refines his working model of the patient and of the transference–countertransference situation and how he is in a position to adaequately report about this has been studied

---

* Only recently the diary of a 27-year-old patient on her treatment with Freud for 80 sessions in 1921 was published by the granddaughter of the patient, the Swiss psychoanalyst Anna Koellreuter: www.werkblatt.de Nr. 58 (DIE ZEIT vom 2.8. 2007).

in a Hamburg-Ulm collaborative project (Meyer, 1988); following up this research road into an analyst's mentation, König (1993) delivers a unique example studying a single session by detailed cross-examination of the analyst based on the transcript of the session.

To conclude our study of the transformation of clinical vignettes and traditional case histories into formalized single case studies of the course of a treatment, it should be pointed out that, beyond the didactic clinical advantages of the latter, they also open up possibilities for systematic studies using social science research methods. Whether they are published in complete form or simply in the form of samples, the inclusion of treatment process notes arranged by observation and conclusion can provide a valuable and adequate fund of material for further study, though with limitations. As Thomä and Houben (1967) point out:

> ... extensive case-history material that we have collected in technical seminars over the years proves inadequate for scientific evaluation in its present form. Too often the psychoanalytic case presentations have remained on the level of "uncontrolled" clinical description. That means that in these reports observation and theorizing are still too closely interwoven. (p. 664)

Therefore, to ensure systematic documentation of courses of treatment, the use of mechanical devices, whether video or audio, to record the dialogue is indispensable today. This creates new problems, starting with concerns on the part of the therapists (cf. Bergmann, 1966; Fonagy, 2002; Gill, Simon, Fink, Endicott, & Paul, 1968; Perron, 2003) and extending to the issues involved in evaluating the material that has been gathered. To solve them, new technologies have been integrated into psychoanalytic research, which provide it with the necessary help. The implementation of computer-assisted archives, as Luborsky and Spence (1971) called for, has been put into practice for some time now in Ulm (Kächele & Mergenthaler, 1984; Mergenthaler & Kächele, 1993; see ch. 6.2) and at a few other places by now (e.g., Luborsky et al., 2001; Waldron, 1989), thus facilitating qualitative and quantitative text analyses.

The process of transformation that we have attempted to highlight with a series of examples was first set off by increasing criticism of the scientific value of clinical case presentations. Freud's case histories owe their life and success to a captivating synthesis of the observational material they present and the theoretical conclusions they draw from it.

Nevertheless, or perhaps *because,* Freud's case histories are so captivating that they contributed to an overestimation of the methodological value of such presentations, a struggle is now taking place over this core issue: Can clinical research continue to consist solely in such informally structured treatment reports, or should it be complemented by more formalized research strategies? Our answer has been that an increased formalization and intensification of research is both desirable and necessary in course and outcome research.

Finally, let it be stressed that the traditional method of psychoanalysis, which in its original form we owe to Freud, was sufficient to earn it the highest place among the scientific endeavors that have enriched our anthropological knowledge. The German philosopher Heinz Kunz (1975, p. 45) expressed this clearly: "No other discipline in our age has concerned itself so intensively and comprehensively with the human being, his experience and behavior as psychoanalysis."

Yet we cannot overlook the fact that this achievement of Freud must now be reattained bit by bit in this phase of "normal scientific activity" (Kuhn, 1962). As to the further development of clinical psychoanalytic research, we are convinced that the methodological requirements have grown and that intensive investigation of the single treatment case has opened new territory. This will include the "role of the psychoanalyst" (Sandell et al., 2007; Thomä, 1974), since long the dark continent of clinical-analytic research. The review presented here hopefully will further contribute to the transformation of the case history into the single case study, thus securing the foundation for a new stage in clinical psychoanalytic research.

Chapter 4

Amalia X

The German Psychoanalytic Specimen Case[*]

WHY SPECIMEN CASES?

Why do we need specimen cases in psychoanalytic research? As we have shown in Chapter 2, in psychoanalysis, oral tradition documented by case studies constituted the major means of reporting the insights gained by introducing the therapeutic situation as a field for discovery-oriented research. We also have pointed out that Sigmund Freud's case reports have attained the status of specimen cases. They still frequently fulfill the function of an introduction to his work. Jones (1955, p. 288) emphasizes "that the Dora case for years served as a model for students of psychoanalysis, and although our knowledge has greatly progressed since then, it makes today as interesting reading as ever."

However, increasing criticism both of Freud's explanations of etiology in his case histories, and of his technique as described in his treatment reports, has instigated Arlow (1982, p. 14) to express his concern about the psychoanalytic ties to objects belonging to the past. He recommends that we should simply say goodbye to these "childhood friends" who served us so well, put them to rest, and get back to work.

That and how Anna O., Little Hans, Dora, President Schreber, the Rat Man, and the Wolf-Man became our childhood friends is definitely very important, as is knowing the conditions under which each friendship developed. Training institutes mediate these friendships, in this way familiarizing the candidates with Freud's work as a therapist, scientist, and author.

So now we have to take up Arlow's (1982) advice and get back to work. One solution among many is, for example, Michels's (2000) discussion about the multiform use of case studies, which could be to develop a series of so-called specimen cases. What are specimen cases? In the first edition of the *Handbook of Psychotherapy and Behavior Change*, Luborsky and Spence (1971) point to the paucity of primary data:

---

[*] Horst Kächele, Marianne Leuzinger-Bohleber, and Helmut Thomä.

We need data accumulated during actual analytic sessions. Ideally two conditions should be met: the case should be clearly defined as analytic, meeting whatever criteria of process and outcome a panel of judges might determine; and the data should be recorded, transcribed and indexed so as to maximize accessibility and visibility. To date no sets of data exist that meets these conditions. (p. 426)

This claim was made more than 30 years ago. In Germany the implementation of the Ulm Textbank formally starting in 1980, based on many years of tape recording of psychoanalytic and psychotherapeutic sessions, has demonstrated the feasibility of such an instrument on an international scale (Mergenthaler & Kächele, 1993). Today the availability of the case of Mrs. C studied intensively by a number of U.S. researchers and the establishment of the Psychoanalytic Research Consortium (Waldron, 1989) and the Penn Case Collection (Luborsky et al., 2001) in the United States have also implemented this research tool.

We shall objectify the claim that the case of patient Amalia X, which we introduce soon, does qualify to be called a "specimen case" in the sense of the Luborsky and Spence (1971) argument. The case has been tape recorded, the material is principally available to researchers via the Ulm Textbank and the criteria that a panel of analysts would have to decide whether it was a "true analytic case"* or not was not part of our decision since the treating analyst, Helmut Thomä, was at the time a well-respected psychoanalyst. An uneasy topic in the development of an open research atmosphere has been the disclosure of the analyst's identity. There are certainly excellent clinical concerns for protecting the patient's privacy. Most of us still seem to be afraid to disclose the identity of being the therapist in a research case; however, in terms of promoting research we feel that it is counterproductive for furthering the scope of research. We feel that the analyst's participation is a fruitful enrichment of the research perspective.

THE PATIENT AMALIA X†

Now we would like to familiarize our readers with the patient called Amalia X.‡ She was 35 years old at the onset of her psychoanalytic treatment

---

* Dewald (1972).

† Adapted from Thomä & Kächele (1994b).

‡ The patient has given her written consent to tape recording and its later use for empirical studies, which at the time of her treatment, had not been specified. In 2003 when the patient, after more than 25 years, returned for a short clinical intervention she was invited to read through all that had been done with her recordings. We thus followed Stoller's (1988) recommendation to familiarize patients with the materials. Her comment to the exposure: "I am surprised at what you had done with all of this; to me this is the past." She consented to take an AAI, which we shall present later in this volume.

and was a teacher living on her own. However, she felt obliged to keep quite close contact to her parents, especially to her mother. She came for treatment because of increasing depressive complaints and corresponding low self-esteem. She suffered from religious scruples with occasional obsessive/compulsive thoughts and impulses, although she had turned away from the church after a phase of strict religiosity in her twenties. Respiratory complaints arose for periods of time. Occasionally she suffered from bouts of erythrophobia in special circumstances. In the order of siblings, Amalia came between two brothers, one two years older and the other four years younger, to whom she felt and still feels inferior. Her father was absent for her entire childhood—initially due to World War II and later for occupational reasons. By profession he was a notary public who as a private person had great difficulties in communicating emotionally. His rigid and compulsive state of mind prevented any intense contact with all his children. Amalia described her mother differently: She was impulsive, had many cultural interests, and suffered from the emotional coolness of her husband. Concerning her early years Amalia described herself as a sensitive child yet much devoted to childhood games. She especially liked to paint. While the father was away during the five years of wartime, Amalia X took on the role of father and tried to be a replacement to her mother for her missing partner. At the age of 3 Amalia contracted a mild form of tuberculosis and was bedridden for six months. Then, because of her mother's more severe case of tuberculosis when Amalia was 5 years old, she was sent away, being the first of the siblings to go and live with her aunt. There she remained for about 10 years. The two brothers had to follow her and at the end of the war joined her to live with their grandma and aunt, since their mother was in and out of hospital repeatedly.

She was dominated by the religious strictness and puritanical upbringing to which she was subjected by her aunt and grandmother. After the war the father could not find a suitable job in their hometown and only appeared on the weekends. As a schoolchild, Amalia always was one of the best pupils and shared in the interests of the boys in class and at home. She did not get on well with girls; even at more than 60 years of age, during the Adult Attachment Interview (AAI) interview she still remembered vividly an episode of rivalry with a girl that was less intelligent but more attractive than she. Amalia used all kinds of achievements to fulfill her religious demands. During puberty, the relationship to her father deteriorated, and she withdrew from him even more. When she was in her late teens she had a friendly, affectionate relationship with a boy of her age. She was considering engagement, but this ended abruptly due to strict parental prohibitions. Since puberty Amalia had suffered from an idiopathic hirsutism, which is an abnormal growth of hair due to unknown biological causes.

The patient's entire development and social position, especially her early ideas to become a nun, were affected by the stigma of this virile syndrome that could not be corrected and that she tried in vain to come to terms with. Among its effects came a disturbed sense of self-worth, deficient female identification, and social insecurity. This made personal relationships difficult and rendered it impossible for Amalia to enter into any close sexual relationships. Although it had been possible for her to hide her stigma—the virile growth of hair all over her body—from others, the cosmetic aids she used had not raised her self-esteem or eliminated her extreme social insecurity in the sense of Goffman (1974). Her feeling of being stigmatized and her neurotic symptoms, which had already been manifest before puberty, strengthened each other in a vicious circle; neurotic compulsion scruples and multiple symptoms of anxiety neurosis impeded her personal relationships and most importantly kept her from forming closer heterosexual friendships.

Since the patient Amalia X gave her hirsutism a prominent position in her subjective understanding of the causes of her neurosis, we have to consider the status of this somatic disturbance from which we derive the specific changes that may constitute one goal of the analysis. The hirsutism probably had a double significance to the patient: On the one hand it impeded her feminine identification, which was problematic in any event because of her constant unconscious desires to be a man. For her, femininity was not positively considered but rather associated with illness—that is, her mother's. Moreover, she felt that her brothers received preferential treatment. Her increased hair growth occurred in puberty, a period when sexual identity is labile. The appearance of masculinity provided by her body hair strengthened the developmental revival of oedipal penis envy. Of course, the latter must have already been at the focus of unresolved conflicts, because it would otherwise not have attained this significance. Signs of this can be seen in the patient's relationship to her two brothers, whom she admired and envied, although she often felt discriminated against. As long as the patient could fantasize that her penis desire was fulfilled, her hair growth corresponded to her body schema. Yet the fantasized wish fulfillment only offered relief as long as the patient managed to maintain it, which was impossible in the long term because virile hair growth does not make a man out of a woman. This raised the problem of sexual identity once again. It was on this basis that all cognitive processes connected with feminine self-representations became a source of conflict for the patient, causing distress and eliciting defense reactions. On the other hand, her hirsutism also acquired somewhat the quality of a presenting symptom, providing her with an excuse for generally avoiding sexually enticing situations. However, she was not consciously aware of this function of her physical disturbance.

The analyst offered to treat this woman, who was hard working in her career, cultivated, single, and quite feminine despite the way she felt about her stigma, because he was relatively sure and confident that it would be possible to change the significations she attributed to her stigma. In general terms, he proceeded from the position that our body is not our only destiny and that the attitude that significant others and we ourselves have toward our bodies can also be decisive. Freud's (1912d, p. 189) paraphrase of Napoleon's expression to the effect that our anatomy is our destiny must be modified as a consequence of psychoanalytic insights into the psychogenesis of sexual identity. Sexual role and core identity originate under the influence of psychosocial factors on the basis of one's somatic sex (see Kubie, 1974; Lichtenstein, 1961; Stoller, 1968).

Clinical experience and empirical data* justified the following assumptions. A virile stigma strengthens penis envy and reactivates oedipal conflicts. If the patient's wish to be a man had materialized, her hermaphroditic body scheme would have become free of conflict. The question, "Am I a man or a woman?" would then have been answered; her insecurity regarding her identity, which was continuously reinforced by her stigma, would have been eliminated; and self-image and physical reality would then have been in agreement. It was impossible for her to maintain her unconscious fantasy in view of physical reality. A virile stigma does not make a man of a woman. By identifying herself with her mother, regressive solutions such as reaching an inner security despite her masculine stigma revitalized the old mother–daughter conflicts and led to a variety of defensive processes. All of her affective and cognitive processes were marked by ambivalence so that she had difficulty, for example, deciding between the different colors when shopping because she linked them with the qualities of "masculine" or "feminine."

Two clinical expectations can be derived from these thoughts that can serve as goals for a successful treatment. The patient would not be able to accept social and sexual contact until first she had attained a sufficiently secure sexual identity and overcome her self-insecurity and second had given up her feelings of guilt about her desires.

Both points of this prognosis were confirmed. Amalia X significantly increased her capacity to establish relationships and had lived with her partner for a longer period of time without being restricted by any symptoms. Her conscientiousness, which initially was often extreme, mellowed although the demands she placed on herself and those around her continued to be very high. In discussions she became livelier, showing more humor and apparently getting more pleasure from life. Can these changes be traced back to the fact that both of the causal conditions have demonstrably lost their effects as a consequence of her psychoanalytic treatment? We answer this decisive question in the affirmative although space prevents us from discussing the reasons in detail. The proof of structural changes

---

* Psychological studies on women with hirsutism have been reported by Meyer and von Zerssen (1960) and Meyer (1963).

requires detailed descriptions of the psychoanalytic process. We can say, in conclusion, that despite her virile hair growth, Amalia X found a feminine identification and freed herself of her religious scruples and feelings of guilt toward her sexuality in accordance with the prognosis.

The claim that this case can be used as a specimen case also requires that systematic psychometric evaluations before and after treatment are available. For the interested reader we give some of the findings resulting from data assessed by psychological tests applied outside the therapeutic situation. As outcome measures we used the Freiburg Personality Inventory (FPI; Fahrenberg, Selg, & Hampel, 1978) and the Giessen Test (Beckmann & Richter, 1972). These inventories were presented to the patient at the start of treatment, at the end of treatment, as well as two years after the treatment had ended. At the last follow-up point of investigation the patient was given in addition the questionnaire on experience and behavior (Zielke & Kopf-Mehnert, 1978).

The results of the psychological tests, performed by an independent clinical psychologist as a check of success at the beginning and after the termination of treatment and also as part of the follow-up two years later, confirmed the clinical evaluation of her analyst that the treatment was successful. A comparison of the profiles in the FPI* (Fahrenberg et al., 1978) showed that the values at the end of treatment were more frequently in the normal area and less frequently at the extremes than at the beginning of treatment. This tendency had become more pronounced on follow-up.

Especially on the scales on which the patient had shown herself to be extremely (= standard value 1) irritated and hesitant (scale 6), very (= standard value 2) yielding and moderate (scale 7), very inhibited and tense (scale 8), and extremely emotionally fragile (scale N), the values returned to the normal area. On a few scales the patient diverged positively from the norm after the completion of treatment. Amalia X described herself as psychosomatically less disturbed (scale 1), more satisfied and self-secure (scale 3), more sociable and active (scale 5), and more extroverted (scale E).

The standard value of 8 on scale 2 at the end of treatment deserves special attention because it expressed that the patient experiences herself as being spontaneously very aggressive and emotionally immature. At this point in time she may still have been anxious about her aggressive impulses, which she did not have such strong control over at the beginning of treatment; on follow-up this value had returned to normal. The patient seemed to have gained the security in the meantime that she no longer needed to fear an aggressive outburst. Conspicuous is also the extreme value on scale 3 on follow-up; Amalia X, whose desire for treatment was the result especially of depressive moods, described herself here as extremely satisfied and self-secure.

---

* Similar to the Minnesota Multiphasic Personality Inventory.

The values on the psychoanalytic-oriented Giessen Test for the patient's self-image were within the norm on all three tests. Beckmann and Richter (1972), who developed this procedure, have commented about it: "At its conception great weight was placed on experiencing how a proband describes himself in psychoanalytically relevant categories" (p. 12).

The correlation between the two profiles (at the start and at the end of treatment) is remarkably high ($r = 0.92$), but the *level* of the profile had changed. The corresponding coefficient of similarity (Cattell, Coulter, & Tsujioka, 1966), which reflects the absolute level of the scores in each profile, is consequently much lower ($r = 0.35$) and is statistically significant at the 10% level. Profile comparison yields the striking finding that the high value in the depressive scale at the start of treatment has decreased to a "normal" value and that the "normal" dominance at the start of treatment has clearly increased. The more extreme values diverging from the normal range simply demonstrate the initial self-description to be relatively depressed (scale HM [hypomania] vs. DE [depression]) and the concluding one to be rather dominant (scale DO [dominance] vs. GE [composure]). The profiles especially demonstrate a shift showing that the patient experienced herself after treatment to be more dominant, less compulsive, less depressive, and more permeable (more open; more capable of contact). On follow-up the profile of her self-image was completely inconspicuous.

Of note regarding the image that the analyst had of the patient at the beginning of treatment (Giessen Test of Imputed Image of Others) was that the analyst considered her to be more disturbed than she did. In his eyes she was significantly more compulsive, depressive, retentive, and socially restricted. In these dimensions the image attributed to others was outside the normal range. According to Zenz, Brähler, and Braun (1975) such a clear discrepancy is frequently observed after the initial interview. This discrepancy disappeared at the end of treatment, when the analyst considered her to be just as healthy as she did. Somewhat larger differences persisted on only two scales: The analyst viewing her to be more appealing and desirable as well as more compulsive that she did.

In summary, it can be said that the personality structure remained the same, although a change in level emerged insofar as the patient presents herself at the end of the treatment as more dominant, less obsessive, less depressive, and more in touch with unconscious contents and mechanisms. The follow-up profile is almost identical to the one at the end of treatment.

In addition, the *Veränderungsfragebogen des Erlebens und Verhaltens* (Questionnaire on changes in experience and behavior) (Zielke & Kopf-Mehnert, 1978) was presented at the follow-up stage of the investigation. This questionnaire consists of 42 items that ask directly about changes. In working through this questionnaire, the patient is asked to evaluate the changes between the start of treatment and the present day. This questionnaire yields one total score; there are no subscales. The patient's total of

245 out of 250 possible points corresponds to striking positive change (*p* < 0.001). "Positive change" means an increase in self-assertiveness, in contentedness, and in social abilities but a decrease in anxiety and agitation.

The results of the psychological tests supported the analyst's clinical evaluation, and those on follow-up confirmed the continued positive development in the postanalytic phase.

Some years later she returned to her former therapist for a short period of analytic psychotherapy because of problems with her lover, many years her junior.

At a recent follow-up—more than 25 years past her initial treatment and at over 60 years of age—it turned out that life events had caused some difficulties, and she asked for help. We referred her to a female analyst of her age not connected to the research team; however, we took the opportunity to invite her to be interviewed by an attachment researcher (see Chapter 6). Amalia X had a few sessions with the colleague we referred her to: No clinical information whatsoever was disclosed by this colleague besides informing us that she had left the consultation and that she was able to make peace with her situation as it was.

THE PSYCHOANALYTIC TREATMENT OF AMALIA X*

Clinical Narrative or Systematic Description?

Two individuals meet in a highly professionalized situation in order to bring about a change by exploring the biography of one of them and actualizing it interactively in the therapeutic relationship. This clinical investigation process is tied to the two-person situation. As the reporter or presenter of a treatment, the analyst is always on one side—how could it be otherwise? When he leaves the dyadic situation after each session and after the termination of treatment he finds himself alone in dialogue with himself about his experience with this single other human being, whom he has come to know only through his own subjectivity.

What becomes of the field of investigation when the patient has left the consultation room and the analyst goes to his desk? The moment the analyst and the patient separate, the phase of field work is over. The analyst has come home from the "field"—whether we wish to see it as a jungle or a desert—and is now engaged in clinical research at his desk. Yet if this contemplative activity is to merit the name of research, we need to know if the particular analyst has the ability to play differentiated roles. Is he able

---

* Based on Kächele H, Schinkel A, Schmieder B, Leuzinger-Bohleber M, Thomä H (1999): Amalia X, Verlauf einer psychoanalytischen Therapie. *Colloquium Psychoanalyse* (Berlin) 4: 67–83. Translation by Peter Luborsky.

to act as a researcher upon himself? Can he depart from the directorship principle aiming to maximize evidence and develop alternative interpretative schemes for his research process with a patient, as demanded by Edelson (1988)? In this phase of reflective ordering of experience, the balanced attention of the psychoanalytic attitude is suspended. The psychoanalyst becomes a writer of a kind of specialized literature, which may become the object of scientific evaluation itself as Marcus (1976) convincingly demonstrates for the Dora case.

This kind of clinical research by an isolated working analyst transmits an individual's reflected experience in oral or written form to his professionally qualified reference group. In fact, during the reflection process most likely the group is already present as a model of professional expertise in the analyst's mind and all too frequently determines what is publicly communicated. Perhaps our way of working necessitates referring back to a group of colleagues, but then we should come to a more conscious agreement about it than we have done so far. A crucial problem with the group-bound research process is that the narrative structure of the transfer of knowledge makes it more difficult, if not impossible, for any non-system-immanent criticism to occur (Kächele, 1986).

For all their skill, the clinical case histories have systematic errors stemming from this background—errors we have discussed in Chapter 3. Here we have chosen a different approach based on complete recording of the treatment process using a tape recorder. Of course we recognize that tape recording does not capture the "whole" process, in case this holistic viewpoint is raised in objection. Like a radio play, a genre unto itself that no one would expect to convey all aspects of a drama, a tape recording cannot reasonably be expected to be all encompassing. The audible verbal exchange is registered more exactly than it can be by a participating therapist; that is all. What is important, however, is what these recordings have enabled us to do: to transcribe, at considerable effort, a systematic sampling of sessions. According to the time scheme we established, periods of 5 sessions were transcribed with 25-session intervals between them, resulting in 22 reporting periods, which comprises about a fifth of the 517 sessions recorded. On the basis of these verbatim transcripts, a preliminary draft of the course of this analysis was compiled by two female medical students[*] and then revised and supplemented by the authors of this chapter.

Beyond the scientific significance of this undertaking we expect enormous clinical benefits from having access to the perspective of uninvolved third parties as the basis for further deliberations with a new level of depth. Whatever the third party may determine, for the moment we should be ready to accept that it represents something of clinical significance derived

---

[*] At first, to mention the gender of the students reading the bulky material seems neccessary.

from verbatim transcripts: a systematic longitudinal and cross-sectional description of a treatment process.

The making of a systematic description requires establishing chief headings under which the material is to be categorized. The primary ones are dictated by the general aspects of treatment technique that would have to enter into the description of any treatment; beyond these, case-specific aspects will need to be included as well.

In the present case we have selected the following categories:

- Present external life situation
- Present relationships
- Symptom domain (e.g., bodily feeling, sexuality, sense of self-worth)
- Relationships with family in present and past
- Relationship with the analyst

Unlike a narrative presentation, in which a holistic picture of the processes is constructed where moments of chronological concentration and episodic expansion are unavoidable, an objective course description of this kind will focus on determinations that can be made from the recordings by an uninvolved third party. Only what is readable in the transcripts—this is what has actually become manifest in the dialogue—can enter into these descriptions.

By means of this longitudinal presentation it is possible, for example, to demonstrate the thesis that we proposed in chapter 9 of the first volume of the Ulm textbook (Thomä & Kächele, 1994a, pp. 345ff), namely that psychoanalytic therapy is "a continuing, temporally unlimited focal therapy with changing focus." Other studies may be dedicated to investigating the internal logic of the dream series in this treatment or evaluations may focus on the course of the symptoms, in particular the patient's somatic complaints. Diving even more into the details, excerpts from a specimen session may be presented, thus giving the analyst the opportunity to demonstrate his way of technique with accompanying reflective remarks (see Chapter 5 in this volume). Systematic description of a case thus allows for a diversity of studies sharing the same public data base that in turn furthers the standing of psychoanalysis as scientific discipline.

A Topical Longitudinal Overview*

Table 4.1, which presents a summary of the course of treatment, prepared as previously mentioned from a systematic process description based on a systematic time sample of the verbatim transcribed sessions. The longitudinal organized reports summarize the development of the analysis along the topics of the "External Situation," "Symptoms (Hirsutism)," "Sexuality,"

---

* Adapted from Kächele et al. (1999).

Table 4.1 The Observation Periods of the Course of Treatment

I Sessions 001–010	II Sessions 026–030	III Sessions 051–055
IV Sessions 076–080	V Sessions 100–105	VI Sessions 126–130
VII Sessions 151–155	VIII Sessions 177–181	IX Sessions 202–206
X Sessions 221–225	XI Sessions 251–255	XII Sessions 282–286
XIII Sessions 300–304	XIV Sessions 326–330	XV Sessions 351–355
XVI Sessions 376–380	XVII Sessions 401–404, 406	XVIII Sessions 421–425
XIX Sessions 444–449	XX Sessions 476–480	XXI Session 502–506
XXII Sessions 510–517		

"Sense of Self-Worth" (Guilt theme), and "Object Relationships" (family, extrafamilial, with the analyst). These in turn were enriched as the texts were read repeatedly by the group of authors.0

These observation periods were described one after the other; the following summarizing description longitudinally portrays the sequence of events for each of the categories.

External Situation

At the outset of treatment, the analysand is engaged in her teaching career. Topics from the occupational sphere, such as conflicts with superiors, colleagues, and "subordinates," are frequently brought up in the sessions, and she often goes into the minutiae of conflict situations that bother her, seeking relief in the analyst's approval of her behavior.

At the outset of the analysis, the analysand begins hormone therapy in hopes of effecting a change in her hirsutism in this way as well.

She lives alone in an apartment and spends weekends and vacations (such as the one around the 25th session) with her parents and relations. There are very few changes in the external circumstances of the analysis for most of the time.

In observation period X (sessions 221–225) she has an automobile accident that very much preoccupies her, as she is under the impression that she caused it (an elderly man drove into her car).

Interruptions in the analysis, such as the one of two months' duration following session 286, upset her a great deal.

After the 300th session of the analysis, the patient makes an active effort to come into contact with men (e.g., by placing a personal ad). Then she enters into a series of relationships, some of them sexual. After the 420th session she enters into correspondence with a man with whom she hopes to develop a close relationship. Around the 450th session she meets this friend for the first time.

After the 500th session the conclusion of the analysis is brought up. The analysand still works as a teacher. She also mentors teacher trainees and has great difficulties with some of them.

Symptoms (Hirsutism)

The initial period of the analysis is largely taken up with the patient's confrontation with her body hair. She clearly feels the stigma of mannishness it carries and doubts if a change in attitude could ever remove this. Hence, she places great hopes on hormone treatment and thus, from a psychodynamic point of view, devalues any possible success of the psychoanalysis.

The meaning of the hirsutism comes out in a dream (observation period I) in which the analysand offers herself sexually to a man and is rejected by him. A woman figures in this dream whose body is completely covered with hair.

Having what she experiences as a "defective" body in comparison with other women is painful to her; only in comparison with an overweight colleague does she feel she "comes off well" (10th session). In a dream (29th session) she has to clean a toilet in which plants and moss are growing. She compares these plants, which she has to clean even though they are "not her mess," with her hair, which she can do nothing about but still has to live with.

In the next two observation periods (sessions 51–55, 76–80), she never directly refers to her hirsuteness. By relating two dreams with obvious sexual symbolism she, however, addresses the associated uncertainty about her sexual identity. In another dream (session 102), she is lying with her brothers on a meadow. Suddenly her brothers are girls and have a much more attractive bust than she does. This dream makes her realize that she cares how she compares physically with others. A film about people of short stature gives her another occasion to come to terms with her physical difference. She wishes she could transcend the limits that her body imposes on her.

A dream connected with transference fantasies occurs in observation period VII (sessions 151–155). She dreams she has been murdered; a man has undressed her and cut off her hair. Once again her hirsutism figures very directly in the manifest content of dreams during observation period VIII (sessions 177–181). In one dream, she wants to marry two men. She is standing in front of the bed of one and the moment has come to take off her bra. She tries to explain to him that she has body hair in abnormal places; this frightens her and she wakes up.

In the next sessions of the analysis the theme gradually recedes. In the 222nd session she still has a diffuse recollection that she dreamed of "something to do with hair" but cannot remember it in detail. In its place, the analytic work increasingly focuses on the issues involved in coming to terms with her body more generally. Finally, in observation period XII (sessions 282–286), it becomes possible to illuminate the connection between her body hair and her sexuality: if the hair were gone, she would be (in her fantasies) completely at the mercy of sexual violation.

We see it as an indicator of improved self-acceptance on her part that in period XIII (sessions 300–304), in the context of reproaching herself for having concealed her body hair in her ad, she says, "Sometimes it (the hair) bothers me, but sometimes not, and then I find myself quite acceptable." In period XV she explains that at the start of therapy she often felt undressed by herself. She would be walking next to herself like a second person, observing herself through her clothes as though they were transparent. Then she would be frightened just by the sight of herself. Since then, she has been able to dream of herself in a transparent nightgown and find herself attractive. She is not disturbed by the fact that she is with a man in her dream. In this way she is testing, in her dreams, the possibility of having an attractive body. In reality she continues to suffer from contact and exhibition anxieties.

Finally she enters upon an explicitly sexual relationship with her friend (sessions 376–380); and although she mentions often feeling inhibited during sexual intercourse because of her hair, increasingly the issue is coming to terms with her feelings about her body quite generally; the hirsutism seems to have moved to the background. In another relationship with an artist, her fears of being rejected aesthetically because of her hair come to the foreground again, but she takes comfort in the thought that her hair is something in the order of a test, a hurdle that her friend has to jump over like the wall around a boarding school.

The focus of coming to terms with her body in connection with her sexuality becomes more and more central. In period XIX (sessions 444–449), she still brings up the concern that she continually allows her hirsuteness to rock her sense of sexual identity, even though her partner directly signals that he is not troubled by her hair.

A critical event in this context is a dream from period XXI (sessions 502–506), in which her hair turns into roots. She feels like root wood with threads that she spins around her friend, trapping him in a hedge. Thus she possesses a woven framework that can bear weight, and this makes her feel glad. Now her hair is accepted and no longer felt as troublesome.

In the final period (session 510–517), the analysand dreams of a lady in the circus who suddenly rides out through the water on a bicycle with her blouse open, revealing a beautiful bust and spraying water around in all directions. This dream gives her occasion to return to her envy of "full femininity" and also of the unblemished, odorless skin of her grandmother (and of the analyst).

Sexuality

From the start the topic of sexuality assumes a central role in the psycho-analytic dialogue. In the initial sessions she informs the analyst that she masturbated at least between the ages of 3 and 5. However, her strict religious upbringing, represented in particular by her aunt, led her to attach feelings of guilt to sexual impulses.

These impulses express themselves all the more vehemently in her dreams: She now relates a dream in which she experiences herself as a beautiful, sensual "Raphael Madonna" who is deflowered by a man and as a nursing mother. As a day residue of the dream, she is afraid of losing her virginity as she attempts to insert a tampon. In the initial sessions she expresses her desire to affirm sexuality and to find it beautiful in order to experience it to the full, but her hirsutism gets in the way as well as her doubts as to whether she is a real woman at all. She mentions in passing that sexuality was always connected with "excess" for her.

This conflict continually reemerges. In period III (sessions 51–55), for example, she wonders why as an unmarried woman she should have anything to do with sexuality. In her dreams she experiences pleasant sensations as she reviews the history of her sexual life at confession. She is able to speak to her younger brother about her sexual desires. She reacts with confusion, however, when the analyst interprets a dream (period IV, sessions 76–80) in which this brother crawls through a stove pipe by suggesting that the stove pipe might represent her vagina and that perhaps she desires coitus with this brother.

In the next period (sessions 101–105), once again the focus is increasingly on her guilt feelings about her masturbation. She experiences strong ambivalence toward the analyst. On the one hand she fantasizes that he accepts her sexuality but is being "conciliatory" and on the other hand that he may in fact secretly condemn her. In sessions 151–155, hidden sexual fantasies regarding the analyst become apparent. She is occupied (sessions 177–181) with her fear that the analyst might consider her frigid and emphasizes what a lovable, cuddly, and also sensual child she was, but ultimately she comes around to her own fear that she might be a nymphomaniac. The suggestion that her fear of sexuality might not only have to do with her hair is met with vehement rejection on her part at this point.

Period X focuses on the confrontation with her fears and wishes regarding castration: She is afraid a pigeon could peck her eyes out or that she could injure herself masturbating. She dreams of a car accident in which a huge truck drives into her car and speaks openly of an almost compulsive fantasy she used to have that priests "had something going on down there even though they looked the same in front and in back." Her castration wishes toward men become clear in a fantasy: Among certain Indians it is the custom for mothers to suck on the penis of their male infants to satisfy them. In the analysand's fantasy, this turns into biting off the penis. Later (sessions 251–255) a dream in which she sees a woman shot by a man reveals masochistic and voyeuristic needs.

The tremendous feelings of guilt associated with sexual impulses for her become ever more evident. In period XIV (sessions 326–330), she mentions the criticism of a colleague, who spoke of her patting a trainee as "immoral contact." She herself rationalizes this, making a clear distinction between affection and sexuality. Working through the issues around her guilt feelings makes it possible for her to take up a sexual relationship with a man (sessions 376–380); what stands out here is how strongly she resists a passive feminine position and tries for an active role in sexuality. As mentioned already, her conflict over feminine sexual identity remains the focus of the analytic work in the subsequent sessions. Among other things there is a concrete need to come to terms with her genitalia and the associated sexual fantasies. The precipitating event for this is that she was slightly injured in coitus with her friend, which makes her incapable of reaching orgasm either in sexual intercourse or in masturbation. She is preoccupied with how "rich female sexuality" is compared with "pitiful male sex acrobatics." At the same time it becomes apparent how threatened she feels by nearness to her friend; her present anorgasmia (sessions 444–449) is also connected with it. Since her friend maintains relationships with other women as well, she is confronted with jealousy, with the feeling of "being made a whore by him," and so forth. Her struggle to come to terms with these facets of sexuality as "experienced in reality" lead to an observable consolidation of her acceptance of her own body and her own sexuality (sessions 502–506).

Sense of Self-Worth and Guilt Issues

Parallel to the change described already in the realm of sexuality, there is also a change in the analysand's initially labile sense of self-worth, dominated as it is by archaic guilt feelings. Initially she manifests pronounced weakness of her self-esteem, often feeling rejected by those around her; her students label her an "old maid," and in the analytic situation she is dependent on positive responses from the analyst.

The experience of being accepted by the analyst/authority figure leads to a visibly heightened sense of self-worth as early as period III (sessions 51–55). She finds it possible to accept validation from her students. As transference intensifies, however, her sense of self-worth is subject to renewed ups and downs, primarily because she is plagued by doubts that that analyst might reject her because of her deficiency in feminine identity (sessions 76–80, 101–105). In sessions 126–130 it becomes clear that this instability is also connected with her relationship to her father: He failed to give her sufficient experience of validation and affection and as a rule preferred her brothers.

In the next observation period it becomes possible to approach the associated guilt feelings, partially of oedipal origin, by looking at transference fantasies (e.g., sexual fantasies about the analyst). In a later phase of the treatment (sessions 251–255), it becomes apparent that the intensity of the guilt feelings is also connected with the impulsivity of the analysand: She now often speaks about the tension between her excessive wishes and fantasies and what is officially permissible and "normal." The boarding school years are a frequent object of her reflections. An important step toward developing a more stable sense of self-worth is made with her decision to take the initiative in seeking a partner (e.g., by placing ads). She imagines being able to do without the analyst and "swim on her own" in the holidays, taking a vacation trip without her parents (sessions 300–304).

Her decision to step into a heterosexual relationship repeatedly evokes feelings of self doubt and insecurity; yet through the analytic relationship it proves possible for her each time to avoid withdrawing from relationships because of frustrations and wounds. Thus, she is able to have real experiences (including sexual ones) that can become the basis for developing a higher sense of self-worth. These form a counterweight to the frequent pangs of guilt she feels particularly toward her mother, whom she experiences as judging her as a whore. These guilt feelings are a repeated focus of the analytic work.

In the last section of the analysis, the analysand's growth in terms of a stable sense of self-worth is impressive. She is able to admit to herself without feeling guilty that she is "a strong woman." This impression was empirically substantiated by Neudert, Grünzig, and Thomä (1987, ch. 5.3).

Familial Object Relationships

It was mentioned above that at the onset of the analysis, the analysand's real familial object relationships figure largely in her life. For example, she spends her weekends and holidays with her parents and relatives. She portrays her relationship to her father with definite ambivalence: On one hand, she wishes to be a loving and caring daughter to him who, as her mother—"a quiet and patient woman with father"—would not wound him or be aggressive toward him; on the other hand, she is aware of intense feelings of hatred toward him. To her brothers she is connected by a close relationship as well. With the elder she feels and has always felt like a "satellite," while the younger is an object of her admiration and envy, in part because of his autonomy in relation to their parents.

The first change that she registers in this realm is an increasing and relieving distance from her mother (sessions 51–55). She also gains distance from her younger brother, particularly in terms of the sexual attraction he exerts on her. Later (sessions 76–80) she reveals the degree to which her mother took her into her confidence, always advising her not to criticize her father openly. Later on (sessions 126–130) it comes out how much he conceals his feelings from her and hurts her in this way. She used to hold her father responsible for everything ugly (even for her hair). She experiences him as bothersome in her relationship with her mother.

In period VIII (sessions 177–181) the thrust of her reproaches switches: She complains vehemently that her mother didn't take enough care of her, blaming her for everything wrong with her including her "hysterical development." At the same time she unites with her mother in criticizing the analyst. Later (sessions 251–255) it becomes clear what an "asexual" influence her mother has on her. It also becomes obvious that she is extensively involving her mother in the analysis through conversations with her. Only in the session 300, fearing that her family may interfere in her search for a partner, does she make it clear that this is coming to an end. Subsequently the role of the family gradually diminishes, disappearing for long phases of the analysis. In period XVI (376–380), however, conflicts increasingly begin to arise again, mostly in conjunction with her rebellion against her parents' treating her like a minor. Finally the discussion broaches oedipal desires for the love of her father that she has shifted onto her brother (sessions 444–449). As she begins to realize the extent of the conflicts and loss in quality of life she has suffered through the rigidity of her parents, particularly her mother, she begins to become aware of intense feelings of hatred toward them (sessions 476–480). In the final sessions, she draws parallels between the difficulties she had separating from her parents in adolescence and the impending separation from the analyst.

Extrafamilial Object Relationships

At the onset of analysis, the patient's chief extrafamilial object relationships are with her colleagues. She complains that she is always the one who has to invest in them and is used by the others as a "rubbish bin." In period II (sessions 26–30) it becomes evident that she is practically incapable of going into social situations alone and establishing contacts. One of the first successes of the analysis that she registers is that she feels somewhat more independent of what others think of her; now she can even go for a walk alone (sessions 51–55). In the following sessions her director continually enters into the discussion: She is afraid, for example, that he holds the analysis against her (sessions 101–105). As before, she feels inhibited in relation to her colleagues (sessions 126–130), yet her extrafamilial contacts continue to be limited almost exclusively to them (sessions 221–225). She feels mocked as an "old maid" and is full of envy toward married female colleagues. During the analyst's vacation (before the 300th session), she receives several responses to her personal ad from men, among them a doctor who is undergoing psychoanalytic training himself, which occupies her fantasy life a great deal. In the end, in spite of great reservations and difficulties she in fact takes up a sexual relationship with one of the men (sessions 376–380). At work she is now able to accept warmer and less conflicted relations with colleagues and "subordinates": She is touched at the love and care they show her by visiting when she is at home in bed with a disc injury. After another ad (sessions 421–425), in spite of many fears she takes up contact with an artist, wishing to have the feeling that she is now ready for a nonbourgeois world. In period XIX (sessions 444–449), she is concerned with a long-standing relationship she has had with a man going through divorce. In spite of all conflicts she feels connected to him. At the same time she would like to try out a number of relationships with men before committing herself and posts a new ad (sessions 476–480). In the last sessions of the analysis she reports on a fascinating relationship with a "polygamous man," whom she experiences as highly egotistical. Her fantasies of separating from him come up in conjunction with the impending end of analysis.

Relationship with the Analyst

The initial relationship with the analyst takes form in the context of her social isolation. She is preoccupied with how close she is allowed to get or *should* get to the analyst. In one of her first dreams, she is an au pair girl in the home of her analyst. At a family celebration she searches desperately for the analyst's wife. Next to several "shriveled up" old women she finds a young and very beautiful but distant-seeming girl. She finds it impossible to accept this girl as the analyst's wife and so turns her into his daughter. She competes with this woman and envies her for her youth and beauty. The analyst orders her to clean the toilet, in which she discovers not excrement but plants. She resists this demand because the "mess in the toilet" does not come from her.

Her associations show that up to this point (sessions 26–30), she has related to the analysis as a test and is afraid of being rejected because of "her mess" (e.g., her excessive hair growth). In the next observation period (51–55) she is making an obvious effort to make a closer connection with the analyst. She also wants to listen and to interpret. In response to her questions she wants answers from the "specialist," not silence. She wants the analyst to demonstrate exact recall of situations from earlier sessions and so forth. Some initial manifestations of transference appear in her comparison of the analyst to her mother: With both of them she fears they could get angry at her. In sessions 76–80, the analysand's attitude to the treatment frequently becomes the focus of attention. She sees herself as having begun the analysis "naive" and "pure." Now she is looking into books and informing herself in more detail about psychotherapy. Her insecurity becomes apparent: She finds lying on the couch unnatural and compares the analysis to a game at which she always loses.

She also levels specific reproaches at the analyst, criticizing him for always just interpreting but never explaining to her how he arrives at his interpretations. Besides, he never goes into her questions. Her relationship to the analyst preoccupies her so much, she says, because it is so one-sided. She feels humiliated, like a victim. She wants to "put up a savage fight." In a dream, she portrays the punishment she fears for this resistance: She is sitting with him, his 8-year-old daughter, and her own mother in a garden. The analyst is upset with her because she has told his daughter, "You are a darling."

She is mistrustful of his neutral analytic attitude and wants to be told directly how he has really taken her criticism. In sessions 101–105, a pronounced ambivalence toward the analyst becomes evident: On the one hand he is "the most important person"; on the other she wishes to be independent and suffers from feelings of dependency on him. She looks into publications by the analyst and his wife to find out what kind of person he is and what he might consider normal.

Finally (sessions 126–130) the development of father transference becomes recognizable as she compares her situation of lying on the couch at the mercy of the analyst to her feelings of powerlessness toward her father. The following observation period (sessions 151–155) as well is dominated by her relationship to the analyst. She openly criticizes his interpretations, particularly when they focus on her sexuality issues. She has the feeling that the analyst already knows beforehand "where it's headed" and feels found out and humiliated on her detours and digressions. She often experiences the analyst as hard, unfeeling, and detached and has a strong desire to be important to him. The ambivalence is even more obvious in sessions 177–181: She reports a number of dreams in which she runs (or drives) after the analyst, becomes his accomplice in a murder and scrubs his toilet. She speaks of her idea of kidnapping his children someday and interrogating them about the family. At the same time her resistance to the analytic work is great: She accuses the analyst of not understanding her correctly, of always just hinting at things that he actually knows perfectly well, and in so of being unfair. She wants to force the diagnosis out of him but finds no way to get at it. Later on (sessions 221–225) she associates the idea of being in "treatment" with being under the analyst's "control";* this is one reason why she fights tooth and nail to preclude increasing closeness to the analyst. After the anxieties connected with this have been worked through, she is better able to settle into the analytic relationship. She imagines being able to sleep peacefully during analysis and wishes the analyst could be the guardian over her dreams (sessions 251–255).

---

* The expressions she associates are "Behandlung" (treatment) and "in der Hand haben" (to have under control); translator.

In this context the impending two-month separation is difficult for her to bear (sessions 282–286). She feels abandoned by her "Papa" and is jealous of everyone who has anything to do with him. She considers simply picking up and leaving. In the next observation period (sessions 300–304), she is very aggressive and upset at the analyst because of the impending separation, which also triggers great anxieties. She feels as if she was "on the scaffold," rejected and condemned to impotence. She also fears that he will reject her for her attempt to find men by posting personal ads. This issue gains vivid expression in a dream in which the analyst sets madmen on her who want to hang her and whom she is supposed to shoot. Meanwhile he stands to the side and washes his hands in innocence while she has to grapple with the black passions that he unleashes upon her; he leaves on a trip for two months, leaving her to fight alone. Plainly oedipal fantasies also come into play: She is jealous of his wife, whom he is taking with him on the trip and thus being unfaithful to her (the analysand).

In a session of the next period (421–425), she brings the analyst a bouquet of flowers to apologize for the demeaning thoughts she had about him and to thank him for everything he has made possible through the analysis, above all her relationships to men. She is practicing saying goodbye to him.

Sessions 476–480 are characterized by intense transference feelings: for one, her feeling that the analyst, like her father, never really provided her with a sense of security and strength; for another, she is in the throws of vehement sexual desires toward the analyst: At home she made a wish that in the next session she would seduce the analyst, simply draw the curtains and undress. She is afraid that the analyst would react to this with horror. In her imagination, he has to be a "consummate lover." In her mind she makes threats toward him if he does not pass this test. She justifies her sexual desire with the thought that it would do him good to start a new relationship with a woman for once.

The concluding sessions are dominated by the topic of separation. In a dream she first must "outsmart" the analyst to get away from him before he notices that she has already managed to grow roots—the capacity to continue living on her own. To do this she must find her own way through a hollow tree—the acceptance of her vagina—and then can run away on her roots. Then she is able to state, "Probably you are bored by what I am telling, but it's my time now." In the end she leaves the analyst starving and emaciated on his mountain: She is now the stronger one. What is important to her is that it becomes clear that she is afraid the analyst, like her parents, could be disappointed by her way of saying goodbye.

It is also interesting that she is now no longer jealous of her companion analysands: She is no longer bothered by the "prewarmed couch." She can swim on unperturbed in the "warm water" without feeling crowded out by the other patients.

Countertransference

Many readers would want to have a similar presentation of the analyst's countertransference; alas, there are limitations to the materials that served as the basis for this exposition. We have asked the treating analyst, and he has given the following answer: "I have been able to tame my unavoidable countertransferences and have been able to use them in the service of the progression of the patient."

After presenting this longitudinal view of the psychoanalytic treatment of the patient Amalia X, in the next chapter we present a cross-sectional presentation of the course of treatment that goes into detail and depth. Readers that want to study individual (German) sessions are invited to ask for copies from the Ulm Textbank where the whole material is stored.

AMALIA X IN CROSS-SECTION

After this longitudinal section evaluation of the psychoanalytical treatment of the patient Amalia X, we would like to invite our readers to get involved in an in-depth, detailed cross-sectional oriented illustration of the course of treatment.

Period I, Hours 1–10

The first description is based on a time span of 10 hours in order to obtain a sufficient extent in the recording of important guidelines.

External Situation I

The 34-year-old patient is unmarried and lives alone but is still closely bound to her parents. She is active in an educational profession, which if viewed realistically she practices competently and reliably.

Symptoms I

There are few statements to be found concerning physically related symptoms; instead there are mainly remarks reported about the psychosocial situation.

Physical Image I

Her remarks concerning her body occur mostly in close connection with sexuality and the comparison with the looks of other women. Obviously a subjectively very tormenting male-type covering of hair determines her thinking and feelings, especially since she can already anticipate that the analysis will only change her attitude toward this but will not change the covering of the hair. The meaning of this hair becomes concrete in a dream in which the patient offers herself sexually toward a man and is rejected by him. A woman appears in this dream whose body is covered all over with hair. However, she can compare her looks with a fat colleague and compares well if she emerges feeling her covering of hair against being fat.

Sexuality I

The patient remembers that she had masturbated at least from her third to her sixth year of life. From early childhood on up to puberty she experiences sexuality as sinful under the influence of ecclesiastical sexual taboos and an aunt who then represented her mother and strictly prohibited every sexual activity. In dependence of ecclesiastical norm expectations—which she integrated very much into her superego—she sees it to be the most important inhibition on the way toward the realization of a heterosexual relationship. All the more fiercely her intensive wishes find a breakthrough in her dreams.

> Dream: She experiences herself as beautiful, a very sensual "Raffael-Madonna," who is being deflowered by a man, and at the same time as a breastfeeding mother. The dream was preceded by the effort to try to insert a tampon into the vagina.

On the one hand, the patient has the wish to affirm sexuality and to find it nice and to be able to live up to it completely; on the other hand she sees herself confronted with the reality of her body hair and doubts that she is a real woman. She says that for her sexuality is always connected with excess.

Self-Esteem I

This is essentially negative. In her eyes, the students regard her as an "old maid." In the effort to be accepted she holds back her aggression against her environment. The feeling of being out of control is therewith strongly occupied with fear. For her own decisions she needs the confirmation through the judgment of other persons of authority; this she expects in the analysis from the analyst.

Present Relationships I

In particular in the relationships with her colleagues at her workplace, the patient experiences herself as the one who always has to invest and is used as a "trash can." Her wish for total understanding with someone with whom she can talk stands opposite the feeling to expose herself, to undress, if one is talking about one's problems.

Family and Story of Life I

The relationship toward the father is clearly ambivalent. She describes him as an extremely sensitive, often aggressive reacting, fearful, and reserved person. She wants to be toward him a loving, caring daughter who does not hurt him and is not aggressive toward him. In this she compares herself with the mother who is a quiet woman who tolerates the father. At the same time she mentions long-standing, clear feelings of hatred toward the father ("At the age of 14, I once said, 'I hate you'"). Since the beginning of her childhood she has not felt like she has been taken seriously by her two brothers. Professionally, because of her female sex and being without a man, she is inferior to them. As a child she often took the parents' punishment instead of the brothers. She sees herself as a "satellite" of the older brother. She admires her younger brother; he is controlled, balanced, and patient. He pushes through his autonomy toward the parents and occupies himself little with the problems of the parental house.

Psychodynamics I

Based on the first 10 sessions two main conflicts can be established. The first is the relation to sexuality: The patient is incapable of normal heterosexuality; this is connected strongly with anxiety and feelings of guilt. And second, one can assume that the hirsutism has had an amplified effect on her insecurity concerning her female role.

In view of the problem of being accepted, one can find in the patient essentially negative self-esteem and a strong fear of being accepted by the environment in various areas of life.

Period II, Hours 26–30

External Situation 2

Professionally nothing has changed essentially for the patient. A few weeks before these sessions the patient had a vacation with the parents, her aunt, her uncle, and their daughter.

Symptoms 2

She reports compulsive feelings of guilt toward ecclesiastical norms. The patient develops an intensive fear that her needs and fears are being observed and recognized by her environment.

Body Hair 2

In a dream (29th hour) the patient has to clean a toilet in which plants and moss grow. She compares the plants, although they are not "her dirt," with the hair for which she cannot be blamed but nonetheless has to live with.

Guilt Topic 2

The patient compares the attitude of her uncle and her cousin toward church with that of her own. Her uncle is religious and occupies himself with theology. However, he has a progressive-liberal standpoint toward church and creates for himself a free space in his own life, opposite to the principles represented by the church. Also her cousin, in spite of strict upbringing, lives not under the pressure of commandments and compulsion. She holds her strong will responsible for making it possible to endure her upbringing.

The patient cannot realize this attitude for herself. She develops hatred toward the church, which is interfering with her private life. At the same time she is helplessly at the mercy of the commandments and compulsions and must let herself be tormented by them.

Relationships 2

The patient mentions that a friend of hers, whom she became acquainted with through a newspaper ad, is going on vacation and that because of that she will often be alone in the evenings and on the weekends. Therewith she expresses that she is almost incapable of going into unknown company and making contact. Other humans could see that she is alone and that she longingly and desperately searches for contact. On one hand she feels isolated and pushed aside; on the other hand the glances of her surroundings penetrate her even in her most intimate realm and make her become ashamed and blush. She mentions that she continuously feels unprotected and exposed to her surroundings and that from an early age on, especially in confession, she had to "open her most inner realm." In this time massive anxiety and guilt feelings were cultivated in her. Her negative self-esteem is above all connected to the difficulties in finding contact and her deficit on the level of emotions.

Family 2

In this period she mentions only briefly the relationship toward her father. She relates to the vacation time long ago in which she had a good understanding with her father since the object of his critical remarks was the mother. In a dream the patient sees how her cousin turns somersaults on a lawn with an acquaintance. She envies her cousin because of her light-heartedness but finds her, in contrast to herself, naïve and insensitive, particularly toward sexual relationships.

The patient develops feelings of guilt because she is allegedly being favored by her boss. She is competing with a colleague for the goodwill of the boss but at the same time fearfully declines his offerings.

Relationship with the Analyst 2

The previously described problematic is actualized in the relationship with the analyst. She relates to the analyst a dream in which she wanted to build a relationship with him and later feels this to be too personal. She feels hurt.

In the dream she was an au pair maid in the family of the analyst. At a family party she desperately searched for the wife of the analyst. Next to a few old and "withered" women, she found a young, very beautiful, but reserved girl. She could not accept this girl as the wife of the analyst and therefore made her his daughter. She competed with this young woman and envied her because of her youth and beauty. The analyst ordered her to clean the toilet in which she did not find excrement but plants. She refused this order, because the "dirt" in the toilet was not hers. She felt as if the behavior of the analyst was such that he pushed her nose into her own "dirt" and in addition also blames her for the "dirt" of others. The relationship toward the analyst was to be realized only if the "dirt" (i.e., her hair) would disappear. She feels deeply hurt by her analyst because he rejected her and blamed her for her hair for which she had no blame. Further, he also stated that he himself was happy.

Still, she feels the analysis to be a test situation. In another dream she was obliged to do a test held by the analyst.

Period III, Hours 51–55

External Situation 3

There are no essential changes.

Symptoms 3

For two days the patient has light "asthma," which she blames on weather sensitivity.

Body Hair 3

In this session the patient does not speak at all about her problem concerning her body hair.

Sexuality 3

Altogether, the patient shows very conflicting behavior toward her sexuality: She did not masturbate for quite some time and asks herself what she should have to do with sexuality in her situation (unmarried). Still, in her dreams she occupies herself vividly with it.

In a dream she confesses toward her brother, pictured as a monk-doctor, about her previous sexual life in which she has pleasant feelings. She admits that she would like to have a sexual relationship with her brother.

The conflict shows, moreover, as in her second dream she associates a dream with a situation in her everyday school life: On the one hand she barely can say a sexually vulgar word (fuck); however, on the other hand she reports proudly that she had given a good sex education to a class.

Family 3

Toward the mother she now experiences a reserved relationship in which she feels better. In comparison with the parents of her students, who do not give any sex education to their children, and her own mother toward whom she could express everything, her mother comes across better. However, this mother was horrified because at the age of 15 the daughter used a sexually vulgar term for no reason.

Toward the younger brother she has built up some distance in the meantime because he arouses sexual wishes in her. She imagines him as a good, considerate lover. She evades this problem by breaking off contact.

Relationships outside the Family 3

In her relationships the patient feels more independent from the judgment of others: She can go again for walks alone and resumes painting.

Self-Esteem 3

The self-esteem has risen in comparison with her situation in the beginning of the analysis—she feels altogether better. She experiences several acknowledgments: A student accompanies her for a part of her way home; she paints again, drives the car again in order to go for a walk.

Relationship toward the Analyst 3

In this period the patient makes an effort to come into a closer relationship with the analyst. She wants to also listen herself, to interpret, and wants to have answers from a "professional" to her questions and no silence; she wants the analyst to remember exactly the situations from earlier sessions.

It shows in the transference: The patient compares the analyst with her mother. In this she expresses fear that he is angry because she tries to create a different level of conversation with him and to express her own opinion about a situation. At the same time she discovers that she can also clear up something for herself and does not have to "run" to the analyst for everything.

Period IV, Hours 76–80

External Situation 4

Nothing has changed concerning the professional situation. During this period she attended a conference in which psychotherapeutic topics were also discussed. She reads books about psychotherapy.

Symptoms 4

There are no specific statements to be mentioned except concerning her physical feeling.

Body Hair 4

The body hair is not directly mentioned in this period. In the interpretation of two dreams, which are related in this period, genitals are referred to—concretely vagina and uterus.

The content of the first dream is that the patient must climb up a very narrow tower toward her apartment. She has dreamed this dream frequently. Previously she always had to crawl through a narrow door opening into her apartment; this time she does not manage. The tower and the tiny door opening are interpreted as a symbol for the vagina. First, the patient reacts with disbelief and defense toward this interpretation because she, as a woman, cannot have the feeling to penetrate into the vagina, and the uterus is invisible for her. Further, this interpretation makes her deep insecurity concerning her sexual role obvious; she says that with that she would be half a man.

Sexuality 4

In connection with the aforementioned dream she remembers another dream in which her brother crawls through an oven tube. The thought that the oven tube represents her vagina and that that would mean that she had intercourse with her brother confuses and frightens her.

Family 4

The patient has discussed social problems with her older brother, her sister-in-law, and her dentist. In doing this she obviously has clearly argued her opinion and was insulted by her brother as an inhibited socialist and by her sister-in-law as being envious of her brother. She did not let herself be intimidated by this and called her brother and her sister-in-law cold blooded.

The patient says that she never related well with her older brother. In the argument, concerning her relationship toward the analyst, the patient addresses the triangular relationship of mother/father/daughter. She respects her mother for having always been very open toward criticism. At the same time she asks for her mother's advice concerning her insecurity of the critique toward the analyst. She mentions that her mother always advised her not to criticize the father openly and not to counter an unpleasant situation in a verbal way but instead to do it indirectly. Her help and protection seeking relationship with her mother expresses itself in that she interprets the aforementioned dream as her sometimes wanting to retreat into a cave—into the uterus of the mother.

Other Relationships 4

The patient learns, mainly through her profession, about the social situation of lower classes in the population. She defends their needs and is outraged about their material and political/legal situation. She feels the better position of the intellectual middle class in comparison with that of the workers is unjust.

Self-Esteem 4

The patient is rather confused in several sessions. It is difficult for her to be open. Her self-esteem is expressed mainly on the level concerning the relationship with the analyst. On the one hand she is very afraid to be disregarded, to be helpless, and to be looked at stupidly; on the other hand she tries to bring herself into a stronger position through the analysis. She criticizes the analyst, defends herself from him, and demands concrete answers to her questions.

In her identification with the female role it becomes clear that she is massively insecure in her femininity and she is half a man. She mentions anew that she had, in earlier days, often to undress herself (e.g., confession). She can look at herself undressed in front of a mirror; however, others would, after an initial positive attitude toward her, soon be scared away by her bad and negative sides.

Relationship with the Analyst 4

A topic extensively spoken about in this period is the attitude of the patient toward the analysis. The patient finds that she went naively and untarnished into the analysis. She occupies herself more intensively with psychotherapy by means of books. Through this a strong insecurity in relation to her behavior in the analysis becomes clear. She feels it to be unnatural that she has to lie on the couch and does not see the reactions of the analyst. She compares the analysis with a game in which she always loses.

The patient concretely reproaches the analyst. She criticizes him for always interpreting only and not making it understandable how he comes upon these interpretations and that moreover he does not answer her questions. She illustrates her own situation in that she intensively tries to obtain from the analyst an understanding of his thoughts and has herself searched for the interpretations that fit the schemata of the analyst. By this she adapted to the analyst and began to treat herself the way in which he treated her. At the same time she made a prerogative for various problems belonging to her and for which she would like to find an answer and also feels that an interpretation of the analyst would be disturbing. The relationship of the analyst causes her "trouble," especially since it seems to her one-sided. She feels humiliated and a victim. The patient rebels strongly against this situation and is very determined to defend herself against that.

In the 79th hour she reports a dream in which she sits in the yard with the analyst and his approximately 8-year-old daughter and her own mother. In this dream the analyst shows the reaction that she expected concerning her critique or fear. He is angry because she says to his daughter, "You are a treasure."

The patient mistrusts the neutral behavior of the analyst and insists on an answer to her question. She wants to know how he has really understood her critique.

Period V, Hours 101–105

External Situation 5

A test in several classes puts the patient under much pressure.

Symptoms 5

The patient does not show any pronounced symptoms in this period.

Body Hair 5

The problem of the body gains current meaning through a dream. The patient lies on a lawn with her brothers. The brothers are suddenly girls and have a much more beautiful décolleté than her. She determines by means of this dream that bodily comparison with other humans is important to her—also with her students.

Through a movie about undersized persons she occupies herself with her being physically different. She also wants to be able to accept to leaping over the boundaries that her body supposedly sets.

Sexuality 5

The patient still has guilty feelings concerning her masturbation. She tries to fight them in that she searches for her sexual norm and standard. Her own ambivalence comes forth clearly: She, on the one hand, reproaches the analyst who does not condemn her sexuality for only pretending that her sexual activity does not disgust him; on the other hand she thinks that he has an overly generous standard and too much tolerance for her.

The problem of a standard appeared already in her earlier life in her confessions as the minister expressed, "It is all not so bad," "If you pray off your unchastely thought," and so forth. Also here she searched for the punishing authority, not the appeasing.

In the analysis she hoped to find this critical view in the analyst's secretary. This woman transcribes the sessions and the patient assumes has a stricter standard and therefore must condemn her. The thought about this condemnation and that the secretary has knowledge of her appears for the first time in this period, but it does not disturb her.

Family 5

In reference to the dream with her brothers a few childhood memories come to her mind that above all revolve around her relationship with her younger brother. She has loved him very much, although he was more favored than she. She does not begrudge him for that—he was more handsome than she, although she is similar to him in some facial features. In the evening they often kissed each other, played with one another, and told each other stories. She emphasizes that there was never any seduction in this but also puts value into the realization that she was a very sensual child.

Relationships outside the Family 5

A former girlfriend who had to marry some time ago, although she is very attractive and charming and at first wanted to give birth to her child alone, plays a role in this period. Now this friend is in a "bad situation" with her husband. The patient feels superior to her and says to herself, "See it leads to this if one gets involved with men."

The patient feels strongly that her boss in the school begrudges her for the analysis and makes her work especially hard—above all, work that she actually does not have to do—and he wants to get rid of her. She feels that she is not taken seriously at this point, which is important to her: her psychological problems. This feeling reflects in the relationship with the analyst as well.

Idea of Norm 5

The patient came to the conclusion that every human has his own norm so she has to search and find hers. In that she orientates herself strongly by her surroundings—the analyst, his secretary, and her girlfriend—and feels again and again insecure between the wider and narrower norms with which she is confronted.

Self-Esteem 5

In this period the patient needs confirmation of her person from the analyst. She is very insecure, above all concerning her sexuality. She feels rejected by her boss in the school and, in the analysis, rejected by the analyst. Only toward her girlfriend does she feel superior.

Relationship toward the Analyst 5

The relationship with the analyst is marked by the search for a norm that meets her own standards (also in sexuality). Her own ambivalence reflects this. Therefore, she also reads works from the analyst because she wants to know what kind of human he is. In this, the reactions of the analyst concerning her statements play an important role: She feels easily rejected, not accepted and repeats the emotions which she has toward her boss. At the same time the analyst is the most important person for her whose answers and reactions she imagines outside of the analysis as well. She wants to become independent but must, however, discover that she becomes dependent by the trust that she gives someone; the feeling of rejection by the analyst is actually all right with her. Again a strong ambivalence comes forth: At the same time she is afraid to become annoying to the analyst.

Period VI, Hours 126–130

External Situation 6

Between the fourth and fifth hour in this period lies a longer vacation for the patient. Important for the course in the analysis is that she had recently read a book by T. Moser that concerns his experience in teaching analysis.

Symptoms 6

No symptoms reported.

Body Hair 6

In this period the patient talks little about her body; the problem of her hair becomes current again in this connection. The patient goes to a gynecologist who prescribes a new hormone preparation for her. The patient puts a lot of hope into this preparation and compares the probable success of the medical treatment with that of the analysis. The analysis can only change the attitude toward the hair but not the existence of the hair and seems therefore dissatisfying to her. She occupies herself with the diagnosis given by the analyst—"idiopathic hirsutism"—and thereby feels that the analyst does not take her hair seriously enough. According to her, he cannot do this in any event because he has never seen with his own eyes the extent of the hair.

In the course of updating the relationship with the father, the patient finds that she has inherited everything ugly and disturbing from him. He is also responsible for the male stigma of her hair.

Family 6

The relationship of the patient toward her father is the main topic in this period. For the patient it is of great significance that her father has seldom showed real affection and generally covered his feelings toward her. She feels misunderstood by him and punished by withdrawal of love. In contrast to her brother, he only sees negative properties in her.

She remembers that she always held her father responsible for everything ugly particularly for her hair. At the same time she cannot negate the father within herself because without his parts she would be only "half or quarter."

In the relationship toward her mother the patient feels the father to be disturbing. The feeling of the patient at home is strongly dependent on the behavior of the father. If he takes care of her she feels liberated and relaxed.

There is insecurity in her judgment about her father and probably also about how her father should be. This expresses itself in a dream in which her father holds a scientific lecture and is praised by professors.

Relationships outside the Family 6

In contact with her colleagues and acquaintances the patient has the feeling of being inhibited and unable to react spontaneously. There she can talk little about herself and her problems and difficulties.

Idea of Norm 6

In her grandmother's personality the patient crystallizes her ideal self-image. The grandmother is, in her eyes, an understanding, good, humorous woman of action in whom she has always found help and support. She could counter religious coercions maintaining a sovereign posture. Fascinating for the patient is the toughness of the grandmother toward herself and her emotional coldness. The meaning of the grandmother for her self-ideal becomes most clear in these two sentences: "Basically I only love my grandmother," and "I am like my grandmother."

Self-Esteem 6

The self-esteem of the patient is presently very unbalanced. The taking up of the relationship with the father contributes to the negative self-esteem: too little confirmation and affection and the experience that her brothers were favored.

In the competing conflict between her "self" and the position as the patient of the analyst, she feels inferior concerning her looks but equal concerning her mental abilities.

The patient experiences the book by Moser as reinforcement for showing more about herself in the analysis and for talking more openly.

Relationship toward the Analyst 6

The patient currently passes through a phase of transfering the relationship of the father onto the relationship with the analyst.

Departing from a conversation with colleagues the patient asks the analyst the question of whether he likes his patients as he likes all of his children. She fears that the affection of the analyst can be bought with money and therefore is not real. Further, she expresses fear that the experiences from her relationship with her father are repeating with the analyst. She compares her situation of lying on the couch and being at the mercy of the analyst to the helplessness toward her father.

The patient tries to break through the distance that is put on in her analytical situation in that she calls the analyst several times at his home. At the same time, she hopes that the analyst will not give in to her "blackmailing" efforts and that he will not give her forced and involuntary affection. With that the patient makes it clear that she has a great desire for narcissistic input.

The patient develops jealousy and rivalry feelings toward another patient of the analyst. She fears that the analyst prefers this patient and that she herself cannot live up to this woman. She is insecure as to whether the analyst only practices his function as an analyst or if he would play along in such a game (see also Family 6).

Period VII, Hours 151–155

External Situation 7

This is unchanged.

Symptoms 7

Lightly depressive annoyance: The patient is generally downcast and without initiative. She feels internally cold and empty. She wants to flee from her surroundings, break up everything, and go away.

Body Hair 7

The body hair is mentioned in connection with a dream during which she was murdered. A man took off her clothes and cut off her hair. She has no further fantasies concerning this dream.

In the preoccupation concerning the head of the analyst she thinks less about the external, the face, and more about the content of the head—about thinking. The hand, however, expresses for her bodily touch and caress.

In connection with the school topic the patient mentions the biblical quote, "An eye for an eye; a tooth for a tooth." To evade punishment she would have to rip out both of her eyes and become blind, because otherwise she would always see something forbidden.

Sexuality 7

The problem of female identity is only mentioned briefly, although the patient concludes that at the moment, just as she did at the time when she went into a convent, she often questions whether something is female or not—up to the color of the toothbrush. In the relation to the analyst, hidden sexual fantasies are expressed.

Relationships 7

The patient mentions only briefly her aunt as an exemplary Christian.

Topic of Guilt 7

The patient still suffers from massive feelings of guilt that are updated in this period in the relationship toward the analyst. The Bible prohibits a closer emotional and sexual relationship with the analyst. She has the feeling that the claim of not being allowed to say or do anything forbidden means to her to put an end to life. The patient thinks again of returning to the convent and fleeing from the relationship with the analyst—thus to flee from a "struggle down to the knife."

Self-Esteem 7

The self-esteem of the patient is rather negative. She doubts that she is acknowledged by the analyst—that she means something to him. She feels that she is asked to fulfill demands that she cannot fulfill. At the same time, however, she is able to criticize the analyst and to express her aggressive wishes.

Relationship toward the Analyst 7

The patient expresses a fear of burdening the analyst too much with her problems. She fears that he will not withstand her aggressive wishes—that he falls down and cannot handle it. Behind this, one can assume the fear of the violence of her aggressive wishes that could lead up to the desire to kill, as well as the fear of losing the analyst.

The patient preoccupies herself in a detailed manner with the relationship toward the analyst. Her open critique concerning his interpretations is a sign of her dissatisfaction with the relationship, probably primarily on the level of emotional expression. For example, the patient is concerned with the fact that the analyst laughs very little and that his relationship toward her is reserved, hard, and cold. His "lack of understanding" toward her feelings expresses itself in that he only answers her with the phrase "it rains again" in response to her guilt feelings concerning the starving humans in Africa.

The patient has the intensive wish to have a meaning for the analyst—that she herself lives within him. She imagines giving him her watch as a present, which in his hands would become beautiful again and wonderfully strike every hour for him. At the same time it is difficult for her to accept a positive relationship of the analyst as a genuine feeling toward her.

In her imagination she breaks through the distance in the relationship in that she throws herself toward the analyst, grabs him by the neck, and wants to hold him very tightly. The patient occupies herself further with the head—the thinking of the analyst. She imagines hitting a hole into the head of the analyst in order to penetrate into his head and to measure it. She envies the analyst for his head and would like to exchange it for hers.

The patient has the feeling that the dogma of the analyst, the "Freud Bible," cannot be unified with the ecclesiastical Bible. The much sharper contradiction, however, consists between her thoughts and wishes for a closer (sexual) relationship with the analyst on one hand and the joint prohibition of the two bibles on the other hand. This is also expressed in that the patient tries to put her thoughts and needs into the center and to defend them from both bibles. The wish to not only look into the head of the analyst with her eyes but to touch it and to caress it, as in her fantasy, and to lie with the analyst on a bench in a park, proves her physical-sexual needs.

At the same time the patient develops a fierce defense against interpretations of the analyst that indicate a sexual problematic. She has the feeling that the analyst already knows exactly ahead of time "where to go" and feels humiliated and caught in her detours and distractions.

Period VIII, Hours 177–181

External Situation 8

This is unchanged.

Symptoms 8

No symptoms mentioned.

Body Hair 8

The problem of the hair appears in connection with a dream. Two men want to marry her: Suddenly she stands at the bed of one of them and should take off her bra. She tries to explain to him that she has hair on body parts where others do not. With that, she is frightened and awakens.

She thinks that her hair is her greatest problem and is horrified about the remark of the analyst who says that she could dream the hairs away. Her conclusion is that he does not want to sufficiently understand what her hair means to her.

She complains about her mother because of the hair and attributes to the hair a great deal of her difficulties to find contact and also the fact that she has not found a partner as of yet. Further, she remembers that in puberty she was disgusted by every touch and that her piano teacher always used to caress her arms.

Sexuality 8

The patient mentions her sexuality particularly in relation to the analyst: She is afraid that he could find her frigid, ice cold; therefore, she emphasizes that she used to be a very lovely, affectionate child (up to puberty). She misunderstands the analyst in that she thinks that he definitely emphasizes thinking of her being the opposite of frigid; however, she did not ask until the following session about what he understands concerning this matter. Then she expressed imagining herself being like a nymphomaniac.

Interpretations of the analyst that her fears could be the result of some-thing other than her hair; however, she rejects.

Relationships 8

The relationship toward her mother is of great importance in this period: The patient reproaches her that she has cared too little for her and is respon-sible for all her problems and her "hysterical development." Basically she wishes her mother's death but at the same time reproaches herself for that strongly. She compares herself with the mother who, according to her, used to be a fashionable young girl with many admirers; in contrast, she was seen as a *"Blaustrumpf."*[9] She is bothered that her mother simply sits still when she reproaches her and barely reacts. At the same time she bonds with her mother against the analyst: The mother already wanted to call the analyst and tell him her opinion about the analysis of her daughter. The patient claims that her mother understands her much better than the analyst. She repeatedly mentions a cousin, a medical student, who strictly rejects the analysis.

Fear 8

During this period, the patient has uncertain feelings of fear that she can, however, only make objective in relation to her hair. This fear appears espe-cially clear in a dream in which she suddenly glides on a swaying ground above an abyss.

Self-Esteem 8

She finds herself inferior in comparison to others but wards this off in that she blames others (her mother, her respective contact person).

Relationship toward the Analyst 8

This relationship is marked by a strong ambivalence of the patient toward the analyst: She vacillates between the wish of the most possible approach and strong defense.

The wishes for an approach express themselves in several dreams in which she walks and drives after the analyst, becomes an accomplice in a murder, and cleans his toilet. She expresses the thought to kidnap his children and to question him about his family. She has a great fear that he could find her frigid.

Her defense shows itself above all in the relation to the behavior of the analyst during the analysis. She reproaches him for not understanding her correctly and because he always only makes allusions about things of which he actually knows about exactly; therewith, to her he is unfair. She feels that his thoughts are an interference to removing something of importance to her. She wants to take the diagnosis out of his head by violence but does not find an entrance. Therefore, she plays with the thought to break up the analysis. At the same time she has a great fear that the analyst would want to withdraw from her; in that he would take an important professional position and therefore no longer would be available to her.

Period IX, Hours 202–206

External Situation 9

This is unchanged.

Symptoms 9

The patient suffers from a continuous urge to urinate and connects this with a massive fear of damage. At the same time she complains about unrest and sleeping disorders.

Body 9

In view of the main problem in this period, the fear of having damaged herself while masturbating, the topic concerning her body focuses on genital matters.

The patient feels pressure that can be localized in the urethra and extends to the uterus and the anal region. She describes a feeling that reminds her of bursting air bubbles in water. In her fantasy she sees medical drawings with muscles, tubes, and bubbles. The patient tries to create an image with the help of anatomy books of her genital region that she can view and judge by applying a mirror.

Sexuality–Masturbation–Topic of Guilt 9

Due to the fear of damage, the patient expresses a very insecure and guilty attitude toward masturbation. She fears to have done something wrong in the act of masturbating. She does not answer the analyst's question explicitly concerning whether she has the feeling by touching her genitals that something is damaged or incomplete. While masturbating, she has conflicting feelings: on the one hand something destructive closely mixed with feelings of guilt and on the other hand, positive feelings. She remembers that in confession, masturbation played a big role and that the father confessor pressed statements from her concerning masturbation. Also the imagination of the patient to stand on the scaffold expresses her feelings of punishment and condemnation. The patient finds, perhaps as an excuse, that lately masturbation did not play such an important role as it did for her earlier.

Fear 9

The patient concretely imagines to have damaged a muscle while masturbating through pressing and rubbing, as in a difficult birth the sphincter of the bladder can be damaged. The patient is impaired very much by this fear. She suffers from sleep disorders and disturbances in work. In school she fears that the pupils could discover wet spots on her trousers. She has the feeling that everything is wet and that she is swimming in water.

Family 9

The patient asks her brother for advice concerning her complaints but cannot talk to him about the fear of damage. In this period she develops an admiration and envious attitude toward her brother. In comparison with him she feels little and ugly and completely damaged. Impressive is the phrase, "I almost would say that I want to be like that."

Relationships outside the Family 9

At the time the patient does not feel accepted in the school and by her colleagues. She feels like she is misunderstood and abused by everyone. On the one side she compares herself to a "little rubber dog" on which everyone steps, suppresses, halfway ridicules, halfway despises—in short the old virgin. On the other side, there are female colleagues who have a family, have children, have birthdays, and are admired by their colleagues and their boss.

Exponent of this other side is a female colleague who the patient calls "princess" and whom she admires, envies, and at the same time hates. This colleague is described by the patient as an attractive woman, having a mixture of sovereignty and humanity. In her relationship toward her boss the situation of competition comes out openly. On the one hand she envies the colleague for the capabilities of winning the boss to her side. But on the other hand she categorically refuses the methods that entangle the boss and make him weak.

On the basis of her own role, standing apart, she sees in this relationship boss/princess only the side that excludes others by such behavior. Strengthened through injustices and privileged attitude among her colleagues, the patient accumulates a helpless feeling of anger against all authorities, especially the boss, the analyst, and the "princess." The boss is, according to her, incapable of resolving the problems of the school; he is like her father, weak and "one-legged."

Relationship toward the Analyst 9

The relationship of the patient toward the analyst is based on an attitude of trust. The fact that the analyst at one point gives an explanation for his technique is understood by her as a proof of trust. She has the feeling that she no longer has to drill into the head of the analyst in order to have insight into his well-kept treasure. At the same time this leads to her reacting essentially more sensitive upon separation from the analyst, and, for example, she feels the end of a session to be an expulsion as well as a feeling of love withdrawal.

The patient can speak openly to the analyst about her fear of damage. She pressures him to give her an answer if it is medically possible to have damaged herself while masturbating. The analyst's answer causes her to feel relief at first; however, at the same time she also feels to have black-mailed him with this statement.

In this connection she remembers a former teacher from whom she obtained a "very good" grade in comportment in an underhand manner. In the following session it becomes obvious that the answer of the analyst illustrates not the hoped for relief but rather threatening danger. She has the feeling that the analyst would lead her somewhere where everything is allowed, because in his view of the world there may be no guilt.

The patient sways between two ideas, which she fears or unconsciously expects, to be in the person of the analyst: on the one hand, the role of a seducer and on the other, the role of a moral judge.

The exit from this threatening situation without borders being within herself bringing confusion upon everything and wrecking everything is the confession; the minister who draws clear borders, also coinciding with her ideas of commandment and prohibition.

Period X, Hours 221–225

External Situation 10

The patient has in this period a car accident for which she is not at fault, although this accident preoccupied her very much.

Symptoms 10

No symptoms mentioned.

Body Hair 10

On this topic the patient speaks of a dream that she has had. She remembers to have dreamed very graphically about something concerning her hair. This dream, however, was suppressed by the anger she felt.

Sexuality 10

Through this whole period there is the topic of castration and fear of damage; however, at the same time there is also the imagination of penetration into her body. In the first session of this period she recounts the fear that she felt when a dove was lying in the corridor of her house: the fear of something flying toward her and being damaged; to have the eyes pecked out.

For a long time she has had the fear and disgust specifically of birds and generally of animals. She could not look at images of animals—for example, worms—since she had the feeling of being eaten and bitten. In the convent she sometimes had to pluck chickens and cook them, which disgusted her so much that to this day she no longer cooks chicken. The fear of being attacked and pecked at by the dove increased as she tried to chase it away with a broom (i.e., a weapon). Therefore, it becomes even more dangerous when she tries to defend herself from the threatening damage. To be castrated, but also to be deflowered is expressed in a further point.

She dreamed about a car accident: A very big truck drives into her car without her being allowed or able to defend herself. Following this, she really has an accident: An old man damages the front of her car. She reports that she really watched as he was driving his big car into hers and wrecked everything in the "front." The other car was not damaged — only hers was. She feels guilty of having wanted this accident and additionally feels this as being very sexual—as if the man had deflowered her with a great metallic phallus. The other aspect of the accident, which is to be castrated (damaged in the front), appears in the next dream: Her car is being damaged completely by many men in cars from all sides. Then she dictates to these men the conditions of restitution she wants. But as she says, "And now they have to sign an absolute declaration of transfer to myself," there is laughter: "You can say a lot, stupid!" The men do not want to give away their penis because they have "wrecked the front and the back" of her car—in other words, castrated it.

To accept this is difficult for her. Men have something that she does not have, and they withhold something from her. In earlier times she had great difficulty when she saw a priest. They were toward the outside "the same in the front and in the back," but through the priestly gown she always saw the penis.

This feeling of fear to be damaged she, however, denies very strongly. She represses a lot from the time that she had the idea of having damaged herself while masturbating. The analyst remembers that she was afraid that someone could see something—a wet spot on her pants or something similar. At first she does not want to accept this memory.

Her wish to castrate men, to have their penises resigned to her, she concretely makes in an image that forces itself upon her: In an Indian reservation the mothers suck the penises of their toddlers to satisfy them. In her fantasy this results in pulling off the penis. This fantasy she has already had in an earlier session but did not have the courage to speak about it.

In the dream in which many men damage her car a woman also crashes into her. The patient then takes away this woman's dollhouse for compensation. However, in her further thoughts she does not mention this woman again. Perhaps the dollhouse is a symbol for the children whom the patient fantasizes to be a confirmation of her femininity and therefore a compensation for castration. In her dream, however, this dollhouse is taken away again by this woman, and so once more she stands there empty-handed.

Guilt 10

The patient has strong feelings of guilt because of the car accident. She has the feeling of having wanted the accident and therefore to have caused it. Spontaneously she even has the urge to take all the guilt upon herself in front of the police.

In this period she occupies herself for a long time with a book by the theologian Küng. He writes about unselfish love, and she does not feel to be able to do this; she is only willing to give or to do something if she gets something in return.

Family 10

In this period the patient speaks about her family only briefly in that she remembers that in earlier times she had to pretend that she did not have a fear of animals.

Relationships outside the Family 10

The relationships outside the family are limited to the school and mainly connected with it. She is angry about the other teachers. One of them lives beneath her and did not help her dealing with the dove even though she pleaded for help; another one sat in a concert next to her and pretended as if he did not see or know her. She imagines that she could deal better with such a situation if she were together with another person. Then she could disregard other people better. So, however, it offends her when she is over-looked; in the school this happens often with her colleagues. To this she says, "I am powerless against birds and teachers.... Teachers are, however, worse." They also neglect her and damage her: "her face, her self-esteem."

In her dream she is also being let down by her colleagues: One is playing a game; one should let himself be killed. She wants to accept this if the others go along with it. She lets herself be killed and then sees that the others do not even think about having themselves killed. There is no solidarity.

She, however, can only give solidarity toward others if she is also allowed to make demands from them; she cannot love unselfishly. She can only love where there is also sympathy and this without second thoughts. Therefore she is impressed by a movie by I. Bergman where the man says to his wife, "I love you; however not with an ideal, unselfish love, but with a small, earthly, egotistical love." She herself treats her students according to her feelings differently and cannot treat everyone the same.

Relationship toward the Analyst 10

Before this period the patient has tried to break through the barrier between the couch and the stool of the analyst in that she gave a letter to the analyst. By doing this she experienced something like an electrical shock, she now reports. This feeling she already had once before when she gave him photos; now she is addicted to this. The barrier is broken through in the first hour of this period also because it is a Saturday hour and the analyst is there in leisure clothes and without a tie. At first she was very jealous that he had had no time on Friday; he thought he would want to go back to his wife and children, but then he chose her by offering this hour. This choice has inspired her even just as a thought; he would not have had to have given her the hour in reality—although she is so inspired she has the feeling of a serious struggle between her and the analyst. This struggle is about the love of the analyst tied into the thoughts concerning unselfishness.

She asks herself if the analyst would continue the analysis if the insurance would not continue to pay. The patient is very disturbed about the analyst getting money for caring for her like the Good Samaritan cared for the wounded. Basically he prostitutes himself for money since he earns his bread by the needs of his patients. She had once read a paper about psychotherapy which is when one cares for another or when the one who is cared for believes that he is cared for. For her this means that she is the cheated one in any case: the dumb prostitute's client who believes that one cares for him and loves him. If money is in the game, however, then it is not about pure love anymore but about power.

In this struggle for the love of the analyst it also bothers her that she had to go to him in order to ask if there was still a place free for her. Nobody came to her and asked her what her needs were and showed interest in her. The trouble of this struggle she projected onto the dove so that it became very horrible.

The German word *Behandlung* (treatment) sounds to her like "to be in someone's hand." That is all the more horrible because the analyst actually does not need the money and could live from his salary; therefore, the analysis is a game for him, a private hobby. However, she does not judge him to have a gambling nature, so he has her "in his hands" ice cold. Also he has withheld something from her, has overheard things and did not listen to things that were important for her; because of this she could not go on with them. He is therefore also not different than other men, although she often tried to make him a genderless being. However, she had to again and again find out that he has "something in the front"—that he is not a priest who would have to frighten her in her dreams and thoughts. He is a man who has her in his hands and to whom she must leave something, just like his other patients; from these she tries to read from their faces, what they have left behind.

Period XI, Hours 251–255

Body II

The attitude of the patient toward her body is viewed by the patient from different viewpoints in this period. The patient occupies herself with the problems of a boy in her school who suffers from being essentially shorter than his co-students. She can understand the situation of this student well because she must also live with physical defects.

The patient remembers that she had in her childhood once asked her mother if one would have to go to bed naked as a married woman. This shows that already then she had a great fear of the idea of showing herself naked in front of others. The patient finds that today a naked body such as that of a colleague on vacation does not disturb her anymore and that she can also show herself naked more easily.

In a dream it becomes clear that the patient hopes to be freed through the analysis from physical self-consciousness. She sees how a woman is freed and happy after analysis and expresses this feeling in a dance. In dancing the patient also expresses the need to be looked at by others and to be admired.

Sexuality II

The patient sees in a dream how a woman is being shot by a man. The scene takes place at her home. She also has to fight with the murderer and screams for the help of her father.

The patient associates with movies in which women are raped. She describes how she can, by watching these movies, live through the feelings of the man as well as those of the woman. In the masochistic role of the woman, the patient feels like the rape is a sexual "game" in which the woman only seemingly defends herself because it has for her erotic overtones. Concerning the sadistic role of the man—the strength and security and in particular that the man has no feeling of shame—impresses her.

The patient sees herself as a voyeur. However, her hidden presence and her profiting thereof without the participants wanting this burdens her. The fact of having viewers while in the sexual act has for the patient something attractive and at the same time alarming.

Guilt II

In this period the patient experiences extreme tension between her excessive wishes and fantasies, on the one hand, and the officially allowed and seemingly normal ones on the other hand. From this the thoughts of the convent develop again; there the conflict was defused in that the standard was set from the outside.

Family II

The patient imagines that it would be a relief for her if her mother would also have the fantasy of getting raped. This would, however, not fit her mother because she is, in her eyes, an almost asexual woman who does not allow herself any excesses.

Relationships outside the Family II

The patient recounts that she was asked by female colleagues why she is not married yet. She felt this situation to be embarrassing and could not answer the question.

Relationship toward the Analyst II

The relationship of the patient to the analyst in this period is ambivalent. The patient pursues a better understanding of what happens in the analysis. This is derived through an insecurity concerning the success of the therapy.

The patient reads an article, which she only partially understands, from the analyst in a newspaper. She feels helpless because the analyst has better insight into the analysis than she. She fears forgetting important matters of the analysis. The patient doubts that the analyst understands what it means to live with physical damage. She has the feeling that the analyst, with his questions, oversees her possibly unsolvable need—that he orders and categorizes her problems and therewith destroys them in their serious meaning.

The patient asks herself how long the analyst will endure being confronted with unchangeable things and wants to spare him powerless failure. She fears that the analyst could, because of being powerless, break up the analysis.

Next to the previously described fear it becomes clear in this analysis that the patient feels well and secure with the analyst. She imagines being able to sleep calmly during the analysis and wishes the analyst to be the guardian of her dreams.

Period XII, Hours 282–286

External Situation 12

There is a longer separation from the analyst ahead. The analysis is interrupted for two months because the analyst leaves for research assignments outside the country.

Body Hair–Sexuality 12

Through the hair, the patient expresses in this period her great ambivalence toward her sexual wishes: She fantasizes that she could get raped. With this her hair would become visible (i.e., known), and she is very ashamed of that. At the same time this hair would be a good protection against rape. Were the hair gone, she would be at the mercy of the sexual wishes of men and would no longer have the excuse: "Nobody likes me this way, not even a rapist." The protection from her sexual wishes and fantasies is no more.

In a dream her mother eats her wig. Thereby the mother also becomes defenseless. In this dream the patient wears a wide red skirt. She remembers that she once possessed such a skirt. At the time, her mother had dreamed that the patient was dressed in that skirt and was pregnant; the protection therefore had failed. Now she describes this skirt as common. She connects to it the idea of demimonde. She is very ashamed of this demimonde and imagining to be brought into connection with it. Since she had to go to the social worker, in the framework of her initial interview on street X, she was very careful that nobody she knew would see her go into this street. Formerly there was a brothel on that street. She was pleased that none of her pupils lived nearby and might have seen her.

In two further dreams she occupies herself with the topic of hair (i.e., sexuality). She dreams that one is not allowed to touch one where there are hairs. (In this, surely the feelings of guilt she has while masturbating also play a role in connection with the pubic hair.) One man was then allowed to touch her. However, he "also had a defect"—that is, a weakness—and basically cannot harm her. The kind of defect that this could be is illustrated in another dream in which a wrinkly old woman (who is therefore also defective) is together with a young man who, however, cannot penetrate with his penis.

With this dream she develops a great fear that she could also become this old and wrinkly and this ugly without having ever slept with a man. Her great defect, the hair, which only allows her to meet with "men having a defect"—that is, meetings in which sexuality is excluded—disturbs her very much. Her sexuality is diminished; this is the other side of her ambivalence in this period.

Family 12

The question concerning discretion about the topics in the analysis, which are brought into the analysis by the analyst, occupies her further. She has once talked in detail with her mother about the analysis and now is in conflict when the mother asks her about the analysis. On the one hand she feels this to be a breach of confidence; on the other hand she also occasionally needs someone to talk to about what she cannot say in the analysis.

Her mother has told a friend that her daughter is undergoing an analysis that she feels to be a great violation against discretion.

In a dream she is very angry about her father.

Relationships outside the Family 12

She refers only briefly to her colleagues: She has had trouble with one colleague because she insinuated that she had spread the rumor about another colleague being a lesbian. She rejects this and does not want to talk any further about this topic, upon which her colleague is angry.

Pupils and parents complain that she is indiscrete and cynical and that she helps good students to improve whereas she lets down the bad students. This reproach hurts her deeply. Extensively she illustrates the individual cases in order to have the analyst confirm that she is not that way.

Relationship toward the Analyst 12

In this period the analyst will do only research work for two months. He tells the patient that he will, during this time, probably appear in the newspaper; he would get an honorable assignment, which, however, he probably will not accept. She should handle this knowledge discretely. Therewith, a new dimension in her relationship toward the analyst arises: The analyst asks her for something; she must occupy herself with a topic that is brought about by the analyst (see also "Family 12").

Concerning the topic of discretion, she associates the book on training analysis by Tilman Moser that does not have this discretion about analysis. She believes that Moser was in a good position because he could write down the things that he could not say in the analysis.

It is difficult for her to think about the longer separation, which the analyst forces upon her. She has developed something akin to a Rockzipfelgefühl (hanging on the apron strings) and finds that she will very much miss the three fixed points in the week: the analytic sessions. She will then no longer have someone with whom she can talk to about the events of the day that occupy her, and she is also alone in the evening. She feels left alone by "Papa" and is jealous about all who have something to do with him. She contemplates simply running away.

She has a foretaste of being deserted as the analyst comes late into a session. (She was late, and at that point the analyst left again.) She had the feeling that the analyst would actually rather get rid of her. However, it comforts her somewhat that she believes to know things about the analyst that nobody else knows: She senses much by his voice and his way of listening.

The fear of being deserted breaks through in a session as she believes that he falls asleep while she is telling an important dream. Because of this she suddenly breaks up the session. She could not forgive this weakness, this disinterest concerning her, if he would really fall asleep. So she tries to find out whether he likes her or not. Being loved by the analyst plays a big role for her. She compares his behavior with that of hers toward her pupils: If she does not like a class then she also comes late.

Period XIII, Hours 300–304

External Situation 13

The patient for the first time places a personal ad looking for a (sexual) partner in a newspaper.

Symptoms 13

No symptoms mentioned.

Body Hair 13

With her decision to search for a partner through an ad in the paper the patient occupies herself also with her body. She dreams that her two brothers had said that she had lied in the ad because she did not mention her body hair.

The patient says about her hair, "Sometimes it disturbs me; sometimes I find it completely acceptable." This shows that in the meantime the patient has positive self-esteem concerning her body; nonetheless, her hair can shatter this self-esteem once again.

Family 13

In connection with having fear about the reaction of the analyst concerning her search for a partner, the patient speaks about the situation in the family. The fact that her brother has recognized her ad in the paper amplifies in the patient the feeling of having to protect herself from the interference and the judgment of her brothers and parents. The aforementioned dream lets one conclude that the patient does not feel accepted as a woman by her brothers.

The patient mentions that last winter she had often slept in the matrimonial bed next to her mother and that she had felt it pleasurable to have lied in the bed, which was warmed by her mother.

Relationships outside the Family 13

The patient is pleased that a teacher in her teaching staff is particularly nice and open toward her; she attributes her euphoric mood in the first session of this period back to this. The patient occupies herself intensively with this but does not have the courage to speak to this colleague about this because she fears becoming embarrassed.

In the time when the analyst was on vacation the patient decided to post an ad in the paper for a partner. Upon doing so she received several answers. The patient tries to imagine the men who have answered her as concrete as possible in order to make an image of them for herself. In this she is, however, very insecure and mistrusts the first impression. Mostly she occupies herself with a university graduate who, at the same time, is also undergoing psychoanalysis. On the basis of a letter she has received from the mother-in-law of a widowed man with three children, she tries to imagine herself in the role of a mother.

Self-Esteem 13

The fact that the patient does something on her own to find a partner is to be evaluated as a further positive step toward a positive self-esteem. The patient illustrates that during the absence of the analyst she had the feeling of being able to move into a free direction. She could go into vacation alone without being dependent on the parents. Behind her openly aggressive behavior toward the analyst hides the fear to be rejected by him as well as the feeling to be able to show independence toward him.

Relationship toward the Analyst 13

In this period the patient is very aggressive and angry toward the analyst. Essentially this is to be understood that on the one hand she wants to break free from the analyst; however, on the other hand she has great fear to have to separate from the analyst or even to be expelled by him. This is valid except for the first session in the period that takes place in the late afternoon and in which the patient has the feeling of entering into the private hermitage of the analyst. She feels this to be very pleasant.

The patient recounts a fairy tale in which it fascinates her that a girl from a poor home conquers a king and marries him. She puts this opposite the situation in the analysis in which she has difficulty to speak openly toward the analyst and to uncover herself. She wants to talk about quitting the analysis without having to give consideration to the analyst. The patient has the feeling that the analyst is not open and keeps the negative a secret. Therefore, she also does not know where the analyst feels aversion toward her analysis and toward her. In the following session, the patient no longer wants to lie down on the couch. She insinuates that the analyst has said that she tries to please him and does not show herself as she really is. Because of this the patient feels very upset. To have been moving in the analysis, on the level of wanting to be pleasant, means for her that the whole work was senseless. The patient wants to struggle with the analyst; in her eyes he tries to evade this. She feels rebuffed because the analyst only asks questions and does not position himself. The aggressions of the patient are tied with a massive fear of rejection. It seems to her as if she were on a scaffold, rejected and condemned to helplessness. She remembers once having seen how a patient came out of the room of the analyst with a face covered with tears.

The fear of the reaction of the analyst concerning her search for a partner plays an important role. She fears the analyst could object to this and reproach her for being hasty, not to have confidence in her taking this step or to view this as disturbing for the analysis. It would be painful to her if the analyst would be on another track concerning this question.

In imagining that the analyst would dislike everything she wrote in the ad and would stick a number onto every part of her body, her insecurity and also the fear of the judgment of the men who answered the ad is expressed.

The patient compares the difficulties of communicating with the analysts to the relationship she has with her father, who reproaches her for complicating everything and says she expresses herself incomprehensibly.

Period XIV, Hours 326–330

External Situation 14

The patient placed a second ad in the paper, and the first answers are coming. She still has contact with the university graduate from another city, who is also undergoing analysis.

Symptoms 14

No symptoms mentioned.

Body Hair 14

There is only a brief mentioning of this topic. The patient dreams of a bald-headed brutal man who wants sexual intercourse with her. However, before she is undressed, he goes away and says, "We do not fit together."

This rejection, this "naked truth" (i.e., bald-headed) she cannot handle. The contrast "bald-headed/her hair" disturbs her very much; she is disgusted by him. She draws no conclusions in how much this could have to do with her own hair.

She still does not feel old, does not want to have an old body. She buys, against the will of her mother, a "courageous dress," which nobody believes her to be capable of doing.

Sexuality 14

Sexuality appears only in one dream (see "Body Hair 14"). There she is rejected, as she herself has sexual wishes. She is rejected without a real reason: "He did not even try to see if we would fit together." This rejection hurts her deeply; however, then she remembers that this man actually seemed ugly to her and that she could not stand him.

Also in a further dream she has feelings of guilt and fear. In this dream a child is kidnapped and stays in her apartment together with the kidnapper.

Family 14

The patient feels rejected by her parents and thinks that the mother would like her to continue to be the "small gray mouse." She cuts words from the catchy paper ad and makes an average ad out of it. Also as she wants to give flowers to the analyst the mother advises not to do this: "A lady does not give flowers to a man." Then, however, she discusses in detail with her how she should present the flowers and where it would be best to put them down. In buying clothing the mother tries to advise her to buy a dress for a 45-year-old lady, which makes her very angry.

She is angry about her father who in earlier times often did not introduce her. In earlier times she could then play the "enfant terrible"; today she can no longer do this when she feels neglected.

Relationships outside the Family 14

The patient occupies herself intensively with the newly made acquaintance. In doing so she has the fear that the problems, which brought her to the analysis, however now bring forth that in the analysis everything is only changing seemingly; however in reality things only shift so that she is becoming only seemingly more independent and self-reliant. She wants to play being the superior toward this acquaintance but is not able to do so.

Everywhere she feels intensively as an outsider and not accepted, thus only standing apart. Much comes to her mind about this: In earlier times the father has often only introduced the mother but not her when they went out together; the co-headmaster makes derogatory comments about a colleague, who is also undergoing psychoanalytical treatment; in an event at the university she feels like an intruder into a closed society and feels to be completely in the wrong place and does not know what to talk about with the persons who are present. However, she has the strong urge to join in, while at the same time she is afraid that one could notice this. Positively though, she sees the relationships with her pupils; they are much freer and have better relationships than those she used to have toward her teachers. Former pupils also greet her on the street, she states proudly.

Self-Esteem 14

The patient feels rejected and pushed deeply into her problems by the analyst without receiving any help to come back out. Her effort to play being the superior concerning acquaintance X fails, but she succeeds with the analyst in one session: She simply leaves.

Relationship toward the Analyst 14

Also here neglect is important: The patient feels betrayed and neglected by the analyst in an event held by the society of the university. She has the impression that he left her standing there alone. Three analysis sessions later she leaves the session early and does not want to continue talking but wants to have something that she must solve on her own.

This same neglect she feels when in one session someone knocks at the door. The first time she feels very disturbed and neglected by the people who do not want to wait and who do not want to read the "Please do not disturb" sign. The second time she wants to maintain her place and settle the competition: "Sorry, now the place is mine; the younger brother must wait."

For several sessions she occupies herself with wanting to give flowers to the analyst. But she does not know how she should hand over the flowers to him. He could become embarrassed, and also she could become embarrassed. In any case there would enter a bit of privacy into the session. Finally she brings him a bouquet; however, the bouquet must, as a present from her, be placed in his analyzing room, and he is not allowed to take it home. The fear that the bouquet is rejected occupies her further.

> Dream: She dreams about an old road where flowers are missing and she wants to have flowers for herself. If (the flowers) remain with the analyst then she has, in fact, something from it. Striking is that in buying the bouquet two persons are being confused: The analyst and acquaintance X. Suddenly she no longer knows which of the two she actually wanted to give the bouquet to.

The patient begins on her part to interpret the analyst: She talks about the newest book by H.E. Richter[10] and thinks that her analyst should actually be envious of this colleague, who is writing so many wonderful books, whereby the analyst at the best could only publish his works in specialist journals. She would like to see in him a strong, shining father, who also can do something like that, but then immediately wards off this image leading her into the realm of childhood dreams. She is also afraid of this strong father: As she leaves the session early she is afraid that the analyst would want to press or tear something out of her, which she does not want.

Period XV, Hours 351–355

External Situation 15

The patient continues to teach in the school. A trip to America is ahead for the analyst.

Symptoms 15

No symptoms mentioned.

Body Hair 15

The patient still has contact fears that also show in dreams: She shuns away from showing her hair and of allowing herself to be touched; she is very ashamed and suffers from strong feelings of inferiority as a friend of her mother wants to pet her. She is very hurt as a cousin, consciously or unconsciously, addresses her hair.

She likes to touch others, for example, a little pupil; she feels well doing so.

At the beginning of the therapy she often felt undressed and as if she was walking next to herself as if she were a second person. She viewed herself as if she were dressed in transparent clothing. She was shocked by her own sight. Meanwhile she can dream of herself being in a transparent nightgown and find herself attractive, and it does not disturb her that she is in this dream with a man. In her dreams she tests the possibility of having an attractive body.

The feeling of being a hermaphrodite with hairs on the breast and of being more of a man than a woman intensifies through a television show in which a woman appears who had a sex change. She cannot imagine how this woman can now have men touch her and have them pet her and how she can cope with the still existing hair. She has not solved this problem as of yet; this former man, however, has accomplished this easily.

She herself has already felt like a man—as a brother among brothers. She cannot imagine that a man would like to encounter her hair while petting her.

Family 15

Family relations play almost no role in this period. The patient, however, remembers that her parents only once did not want her to simply go on vacation without a plan but instead thought she should make an exact traveling route; at the same time she compares the analyst to her younger brother who often simply kept silent but with whom she would have liked to have had a sexual relationship. An uncle compares her with his own children and says she was "a virgin," very well behaved, and so forth.

Relationships outside the Family 15

The patient feels strongly disturbed by the move of the department for psychotherapy into another building: If she parks there she is more conspicuous, is being questioned as to what she wants there, and must search under more difficult circumstances for a parking place and so forth. She still has difficulties feeling accepted completely. In the school she feels attacked and made ridiculous because at the door of her room, only her name is posted without "Mrs.," as is the case with her female colleagues. She was especially hurt as she complained to her boss, who then forgot the matter. Her difficulties to directly complain she also cannot overcome in a dream: She asks the janitor very ironically about the sign on her door, and he simply does not understand it; so she again feels like the stupid one. In reality she manages to eventually ask the janitor, but nothing changes.

Sexuality 15

The patient does not directly talk about sexuality in this period. She only occupies herself indirectly with it because a colleague addressed the caressing of a pupil as indecent touching. She herself says that she only felt the need to comfort; this was the case also as she caressed a big, vital, strong boy who had a toothache.

In this period she seems to separate strongly between tenderness and sexuality, feeling only tenderness, but admits to no feelings of sexuality.

Self-Esteem 15

Being an unmarried woman, the patient still is easily hurt and feels like she is not taken seriously. She also fears not to be able to compete with others in their relationship with the analyst. In a dream she, however, already sees herself more positively and begins to accept her body.

Relationship toward the Analyst 15

In the sessions the relationship toward him is the main topic in this period and emerges once again; all other topics are brought into relationship to it.

The impending trip of the analyst to the United States, which is the problem of being deserted, determines much in this period. Also, the relationship toward the analyst has gained a strong oedipal connotation.

The analyst becomes for the patient a powerful father who, however, only wants to care for his own biological children: She fantasizes that he has managed to move the department for the reason of having it easier to bring his children to the school that is near the new building. She herself has to suffer from this: She has to leave a familiar surrounding, drive somewhere else, accept a more uncomfortable room, and endure the noise of construction. He does not give her enough affection, just as her father never drove her to school; she always had to walk alone.

Further, she laments that the analyst does not even leave enough time for her so that he could bring her something back in the form of new insights—new knowledge. For this, five weeks are too short. As an actual present, however, she wants that he would disclose his basic principles and give her his knowledge and also step out of the usual pattern and perhaps caress her.

Instead, in a dream he sends her maniacs who want to hang her and whom she should shoot; he stands aside and washes his hands in innocence as she is fighting with her dark passions that he brings upon her. He escapes to America and leaves her struggling alone.

The analyst cannot give her any rest; otherwise she would not dream that badly. He cannot provide any external peace as in one session there is loud construction noise. However, he has someone call down and ask for a break of the noise, but it is to no avail.

The oedipal relationship toward the analyst is shown in the strong jealousy she feels because of the wife of the analyst. He goes with her to America and will be unfaithful to his patient.

She is convinced that his wife is jealous of the female patients and tries to influence the relationships of the analyst toward them, makes fun of them, and despises them. The patient could "for years" forget about the wife of the analyst and view her as nonexistent and without life; now the wife of the analyst appears very real and takes her beloved father away from her and to America. She is left behind as a child and does not even know if he takes her seriously. He makes her into a Miss and does not even address her with Mrs.; she is afraid to annoy him with her talking and that she is not satisfying his expectations. So she can only imagine him as being without life and face, like a white plate behind her head—as someone who never, as other analysts and patients, could blush. He remains cold and lifeless.

She feels measured by the standard of the "super patient Moser" who was rewarded with having a talkative analyst. However, she must struggle for every word of her analyst. In order to be able to compete with this, she ponders whether she should also write a book on psychoanalysis. In this the analyst would not have to violate his basic principles. She would then describe his life as a "super paradise picture of wholeness and quiet," in which he has it easy. He can close the curtains and care intensively for another person, and he can also relax. However, she must deal with many pupils and parents and by doing so almost lets herself be torn apart just as by the maniacs in the dream. In the analysis he can set the distance and the direction; these are things that she would also like to do.

She does not want to lie on the couch, in the pit of the analyst, who had his nap on it. She can get closer only when he is in the United States; then she wants to move into the building of the department.

She herself wants to determine when the analytic session is over; therefore, she always goes a few minutes early. That way she is not being kicked out and has a private triumph. At the same time she has the possibility of giving the analyst a present and pleasing him. She could not handle asking for more time; it would seem too overbearing for her. She would not be able to handle it, even if she would receive only five minutes of free time. Also she has not managed the monstrous fear of time in the analysis. In this period she speaks about this for the first time, as if she would hope to keep the analyst by this and to move him to return to her.

Period XVI, Hours 376–380

External Situation 16

This period is interrupted by Christmas vacation after the 378th hour.

Symptoms 16

No symptoms mentioned.

Body Hair 16

In this period there are barely any references to the physical image concerning the body or the hair. She has hurt an intervertebral disc and suffers from the pain, has sick leave, and receives massages from the mother as if she were a baby.

Sexuality 16

The patient has a sexual relationship with a man, and that occupies her. She does not agree with her role in this relationship and would like to be more attractive. She has the feeling of being in part only an object when he, for example, taps on her thighs while she must drive the car. She says, "I am not prudish, but would then also like to be allowed to be active in any way."

She pushes the guilty feelings she has because of having a sexual relationship as an unmarried woman onto her mother: She is not allowed to tell her about it; it would hurt her. Surely the mother would find this bad.

She also has feelings of guilt toward the analyst because of this; he could be bored by the bed stories, which she actually finds immature. However, she knows from her female colleagues that also they talk about bed stories, occupy themselves with sexuality, and in part are mean toward their men in a way in which she does not agree with; although as previously mentioned she emphasizes several times that she is not prudish.

Guilt 16

The patient has strong feelings of guilt concerning her mother because she does not know anything about her sexual relationship with a man.

Family 16

In the first session of this period the patient remembers briefly her younger brother with whom she sometimes felt to be quite close, without inhibition, and could be expansive. This she compares with the analyst to whom she often cannot get close.

The relationship toward the mother plays an important role. The point of reference concerning her inner occupation in relation to her mother is her sexual relationship. In her imagination the mother can only be prudish and condemn all sexuality outside of marriage. Her own internalized feelings of guilt show, as she recounts how much she would like to talk to her mother about this relationship. But she is not permitted to do so, because it would hurt her mother. She does not feel good about lying like this and says that if the mother would be curious she could learn rather a lot about her in her apartment. She would like to detach herself from her mother and would like to say, "I am now completely adult," but the mother takes care of her and treats her like a baby.

She cannot comprehend that her mother answers her question of whether she would be against it if she would sleep with a man without being married with, "No, on the contrary." According to her, this does not fit the image of her mother, who always seemed asexual to her.

By her mother's presence in the city where the patient lives, the analysis is being questioned. The mother wants, by all means, to drive back home together with the patient on Wednesday morning so that the Wednesday afternoon session would be canceled. The patient is willing to cancel the session rather than to make her mother angry.

Relationships outside the Family 16

Her relationships outside the family can be divided into two groups: (1) her relationships toward men; and (2) her relationships in her working life at school.

Relationships toward Men 16

The patient is friends with a man with whom she also has a sexual relationship. In this relationship she has rather conflicting feelings: On the one hand she feels rather positively, but on the other hand she feels used as an object. This she describes with the example of a walk in which they walked 3 meters apart from one another. Afterward they drove back together. She was steering the car, and he touched her thighs. Because she had to drive, she felt excluded. She would like to be more active sexually but would also like to be accepted in this activity.

With another young man from L, she arranged a noncommittal meeting. In spite of the noncommittal nature "thoughts were creeping into the back of her head." This man has given her a calendar in which there were many pious pictures. He says that this is a response to a card of hers. However, she had written this card with completely different motives.

In addition the topic analysis emerged in the relationship. This man wrote to the analyst requesting a possibility for analysis and received from the analyst the address of a female therapist. Therewith a good piece of the analysis came into a private relationship; the therapist also puts a mark on this part of her life.

School 16

In school with the children she has the feeling of accordance and togetherness, which she misses in her other relationships. "Her" children care for her very kindly when she is ill due to her intervertebral disc. They even visit her at home and are disappointed that she was at the doctor. The children think and feel in the class exactly that which she intends and even see ice flowers at the window that are not there.

In a dream a female colleague of hers appears, for whom she was for some time a mentor and with whom she had a good understanding. However, the mother of this colleague had something against this relationship.

In the dream the patient puts up her own pictures that she likes in the unfinished house of her colleague's mother. Her colleague's mother comes and rips the pictures off the wall and then paints her own pictures there. While doing this she says, "This is my house, my room; there my pictures are going to be put up." After awakening this woman appears to her still for a long time as a "nightmare"; her harmony is disturbed again.

Relationship toward the Analyst 16

The separation caused by the Christmas vacation plays an important role in the relationship toward the analyst. This time the patient tries to escape his "tentacles and nets," to be an adult, relaxed, and go with a lot of zest in to the Christmas vacation and not to be completely destroyed for three days. She tries to accomplish this in that she makes the effort to drop the last hour before the vacation because her mother wants to be driven home by her. The analyst then offers her many possibilities for appointments so that she eventually has to accept one. In the session at 8 o'clock in the morning she emphasizes several times that she is in a bad mood during the morning and that today one can do nothing with her.

In the course of the session the patient remembers a session in the former building that the analyst had granted her on a bank holiday. At the time the patient had the feeling that everything was a "rendezvous"; she wanted to go for a walk with the analyst. But she turns down the pleasant memories immediately. Today she does not want to go for a walk. The session ends with the sentence, "Today you have really disturbed me." (pause) "I now wish you a pleasant Christmas!" Initiated by the brief separation from the analyst through the vacation and, maybe to better pass the time, she addresses the topic of "separation" at the end of the analysis. However, by doing so she tries to create a rendezvous-like atmosphere. She admires the analyst for having worked on her fantasy for almost four years and that he once and again finds the main point. He has always offered his session so precisely to her that she was and is tempted to simply drop one. She even fantasizes that he could be angry with her if she would not do this once. He also now prevented her efforts, in that he formally forced the session upon her. He does not agree with her separation ideas, which makes her very angry. In this period the analyst is for her the master and the prince from the mountain, in the castle. She wishes that he would also climb down and be with the people and convey his wisdom not only to his 12 children and a few students. He should also notice something about the people, such as the prince was once lured away from the mountain by the coarse behavior of the people.

In this point she feels superior to him: the "Hieronymus in the building." She was able to make an experience of another dimension, a different and worldlier world of feelings, and would like to, as his leader, bring this closer to him and with that also to become closer to him. Up on the hill where the new department building is located she senses great distance toward him, cannot come closer to him, and even fears that he exploits her by using her as an object: she imagines that after every session he runs to his writing desk and makes a note of the things by which she has given him confirmation in his scientific theories.

The distance is symbolized by the distance of the parking lot barrier at the site of the building where the analysis takes place; the insiders can enter during the whole week and park on their designated places whereas the outsiders such as her must park at the bad muddy and slippery places, when unlucky. This parking lot symbolizes for the patient the power of the insider and also of the analyst for whom on top of this mountain she cannot be important and who is not so dependent on her as she is on him.

She even must fear that she bores him with her "bed stories" and that he secretly despises her and finds her immature and prudish and that he cannot understand and accept her like the mother. After the vacation she feels very positively toward the therapist. She feels like she is in good hands but also wants to pay him accordingly for this. She fears that she is still getting the sessions for the old price. On one hand this would mean that she rose in the row of the siblings to the first place; however, on the other hand, it would hurt her and his feeling of value if she would not have to pay him accordingly. Then, as the analyst agrees with her thought, she is shocked and ponders whether or not he is greedy and how she can protect herself and him from this. This also means for her that he is no longer enchanted and thus becomes the "prince who descends from the mountain." If she can pay him for the job then he is no longer so dangerous and becomes more sober and real.

Suddenly she understands his earlier quiet struggle against demands made by the university toward his "children." She remembers her indignation about the patronization; today she can accept his past behavior.

Period XVII, Hours 401–404 and 406

External Situation 17

The patient has placed another ad and received a few answers—mainly from northern Germany—with which she occupies herself.

Symptoms 17

No symptoms mentioned.

Body Hair 17

The body and her "hair wall" gain in importance through the (at first only written) contact to a man from G, who is an artist. She wishes for a speedy personal contact and at the same time fears the sharp view of an artist: How will he receive the admittance that she has hair where others do not have hair? The fear that he could, as an artist, feel repelled makes her occupy herself again more strongly with beauty norms. She leads a fierce discussion as to how important the looks are but thereby has the feeling of losing ground. Everything she has gained in her attitude toward her hair is breaking down. However, she comforts herself with the following thought: If the acquaintance can surpass the "hair wall," then this is like a test, just as she must surpass the wall of the convent.

Sexuality 17

The patient remembers how she was always hampered in her sexuality: as she wanted to receive her first kiss a brother disturbed her rendezvous. At home she was guarded well. Her most beloved wish to sleep with her brother she certainly was not allowed to express. Incest is strictly forbidden. Now her potency is requested in the relationship toward G, the new acquaintance. She is not sure whether it is only the sexual or also the mental potency that is requested; however, she has the tendency to mean only the mental.

Family 17

Especially the family has always hampered her in her personal development, misjudged her, and oppressed her. Her younger and beloved brother now misjudges her again. He disturbs her very much in that he gives her good advice for an ad in the paper, which contradicts her character. He views her too much like the gray mouse; she neither can nor is allowed to express her incest wish.

The "men in the house" always stuck together when it was about keeping her under surveillance and letting her search her way without any knowledge, thus following behind those who have knowledge. She was not allowed to wear pants at the table, was not allowed to take charge over her dolls that were operated on by her brothers. She was not allowed to ask about anything, because then she was ridiculed.

Only when the brothers had trouble with their girlfriends was she allowed to intervene as a "family inventory piece having a female sex" and thus had to be there in a helping manner.

In this period the contact to a cousin, whom she had not seen for a long time, plays a role. He portrays the analyst with the critical view of a medical student at the analyst's medical school.

Relationships outside the Family 17

Through the newspaper ad the patient has had written contact with several men, and she is particularly interested in two of them. The one, G, is a fascinating artist who has high demands, and the other one is a good, secure, and stupid one.

She feels to be at the crossroads between a bourgeois and a freer development. However, she is also afraid of a freer development, because she fears that she would not have enough strength. But she is also afraid that she would bury herself alive if she would now agree to a good, solid life. Because of this, she is pleased that this man declines. In the letters to the other man from G, she tries to be very smart and equal to him. She writes in a way that only someone who has a sense for hidden powers would recognize her true potency. However, she is also afraid to be seen falsely and to show herself in a false way: without her hair and as a human who can withstand the north. Instead she fears that in the north her "Swabian marrow" would be pulled out of her bones and her Swabian soul and personality would be sucked out.

She has great fear that her feelings, which were locked up for so long, will break out, as a sensitive artist would surely be able to bring about. So she is afraid of the first meeting and is satisfied with telephone, photo, and letters.

Self-Esteem 17

The patient vacillates very much in her self-assessment and would like to move out of her present world, which she finds bourgeois, and into another freer world. On the one hand she thinks of being capable of this; on the other hand she has great fear of being too bourgeois after all.

Relationship toward the Analyst 17

In this period the analyst gets another flower bouquet. This bouquet contains a strong symbol: First, the bouquet was actually meant for G; the analyst must fill in for him. Second, the bouquet serves as an apology for the disrespectful thoughts of her cousin and another professor of neurology concerning the analyst. The cousin finds the analyst awkward in his expression; the neurologist even says that every psychoanalyst is a mentally ill doctor. Also she finds the analyst awkward. She puts to a halt with the bouquet the question of what would be if he would really be crazy and thus lead her toward the wrong way. She thanks the analyst for having learned to do many things, which she would not have done without the analysis. She can hold on to this so that she does not lose ground under her feet and that she does not feel like the nun to whom someone suddenly says, "Your loving God does not exist."

She feels like the flowers, is afraid that the analyst does not care for them, and does not give them enough water and nourishment. In spite of that the opinion of the cousin strengthened something within herself and gave her a sense of superiority toward the analyst. The analyst does not talk to her on a second or third level, which would be too high for her; he is simply awkward, does not express himself clearly. Through this superiority, she can also say how important his face is to her and how much his eye contact and his smile means to her. She can herself come up with topics from which she was at first afraid.

Toward the end of this period the analyst becomes an old man who tiredly sits in front of the house and slowly grows into the ground; he becomes unimportant as a support and does not have anything to say anymore. The patient tries out the farewell and finds that she still does not feel quite secure, that she would like to choose the time, and that she still needs the analyst.

Period XVIII, Hours 421–425

External Situation 18

The patient has made written contact with another man through a newspaper ad. She wants to build a relationship with him.

Symptoms 18

No symptoms mentioned.

Body Hair 18

In this period the patient does not occupy herself with her own body. Instead the topic of her hair is addressed in the following connection: The patient is angry about a very secure-seeming patient of the analyst. He has a beard, and she says that men with beards are hiding something. In this context she remembers that also her friend P has a beard in the photo she has of him.

Sexuality 18

The patient asks herself the question (which is for her frightening) whether she wants to sleep with P when he visits her and also if he would like to. This is connected with insecurity about the sexual identity ("what is there, where one touches"). In this context she remembers that an acquaintance of hers allegedly took more than 10 years to notice that her husband is a transvestite.

Family 18

Concerning her own role (i.e., to be steadfast, to assert oneself or to fall over) the patient characterizes her father and her grandfather as humans who cannot assert themselves, are weak, and fall over. Her mother and grandmother, however, she experiences as dominating personalities who by all means try to be right. This quality also finds expression in the current mother relationship. The mother is the criteria for a good housewife; she determines "how the cake will be baked."

The patient describes that she, particularly in her puberty, would have liked to have had a strong father such as the analyst. Her father, however, always had to be supported by her. He was also never proud of her. He was proud only of her brothers. Everything went a lot slower with her, but because of this she made fewer mistakes and thought through many things more exactly.

Relationships outside the Family 18

The patient occupies herself with the relationship to P and with the fact that he wants to visit her together with his children.

The insecurity of whether she will be accepted and loved by P or whether she only will be used as one among many women burdens her. She is also not clear about her own feelings; she cannot find the right connection to him.

First she reacts aggressively when P decided on his own to come together with his children. According to her, the visit requires efforts by the children and her. She bonds with one of P's children, who is on the one hand still in need of protection but on the other hand also observes and experiences a lot. With this, she also expresses that she herself is in need of protection and very sensitive about how P deals with her.

The fact that he, when he visits her, cannot be there for her and that he comes by so "en passant" and in addition lets her wait for a long time hurts her self-esteem—"Who am I, I , I...?"—with whom one can do something like that. "I will show him who the master in the house is." She feels P to be dominant but says, however, at the same time that she feels superior to him.

Anxiety 18

Next to the fear of losing the affection of the analyst, the patient illustrates the fear of not being accepted by P and being humiliated by his children. She feels eight eyes looking at her. The oldest son of P she describes as a "model of self-reliance"; she is more afraid of his judgment than that of P's.

Self-Esteem 18

The self-esteem of the patient reflects in her discussion concerning her female role. At a birthday party she comes into contact with the husband of a colleague whom she describes as a "green youth," having no idea what life is about. She asks herself whether she should discuss with him, "to fight with the head," or if she should show herself as the nice host. On the one hand she wants to make her intellectual abilities known; on the other hand she wants to be the beautiful, attractive woman. She has the feeling that she cannot be herself.

In the mental confrontation with the children of the friend, it becomes clear that the patient does not feel capable of filling the role of a mother. Her self-esteem toward P vacillates. She feels like he is dominating but tries, at the same time, to assert her claims and to be steadfast.

The patient feels, as an unmarried woman at her age, disadvantaged compared with men. Men who are as old as she can easily "grab" for a young girl without being in conflict with society's norms. She absolutely thinks that she needs to get to know an older and also taller man.

Relationship toward the Analyst 18

In this period the analyst personifies the wish of the patient for a strong and helpful father who leads her (i.e., "I have always wished for such a father"). She wants to find out how old the analyst is.

The patient develops an enormously intense rivalry with the daughter of the analyst who, in her eyes, has a magical, mystical character. She is an angel at the piano, a fascinating dream being, disturbing, and overpowering like the stone on the desk of the analyst. She has an advantage from the beginning: the right of heritage, which her own brothers also had in relation to their mother. The analyst accompanied his daughter with his right hand—for the patient there remains, at the most, only his left hand.

Period XIX, Hours 444–449

External Situation 19

During this period the patient meets her friend P, after longer written contact.

Symptoms 19

No symptoms mentioned.

Body 19

In this period the patient occupies herself in detail with her physical self-esteem, her hair, and her sexual experiences, fears, and wishes. She has the wish that P would caress her neck and would emphasize that she has a very nice and smooth neck and that she is easily aroused there. However, she avoids the touch at her neck, because P could possibly feel a "stub hair" at the chin. Although the friend tells her that she should keep the hair on her body and on her legs, the hair is still a problem for her, and she has the feeling that he does not caress her on the body areas that have hair. It becomes clear in this period that the hair is an aspect through which she is being shattered again and again in her sexual identity. She would like P to have more hair. It disturbs her that he has such "female skin." Basically, he is more the woman and she more the man.

The patient identifies her hands with those of her parents. She has two completely different hands. The right hand, "the most awful one," equals the ugly hand of the father. The left hand is nicer and equals the hands of the mother. Simultaneously, however, she emphasizes that the father actually has very tender hands whereas the hands of the mother are raw like a "brush." Her right hand is dangerous, guilty, and nice at the same time; she can use it to hit but also touch her body and her clitoris.

The patient observes that P likes to look at the breasts of other women and is afraid that he would not like her breasts, even though he tells her that she has very nice breasts. She compares her looks with that of other women—in thoughts, especially also with those of the wife of her friend. In doing so she does not fare very well.

A central point for the patient is the fact that she is not aroused while having sexual intercourse with P and has no orgasm. Concerning this she looks for various answers. When she is within a certain distance to P (e.g., while driving the car) she is very aroused. However, as soon as sexual intercourse becomes possible and is wished by him, "she becomes cold." She is not herself and feels to be miles away from her body. Although she is very tender toward him, she has the feeling of abstracting herself from herself—to give herself up. She experiences sexual intercourse with P in a way in that he only sleeps with her body but not with her. He is not active, tender, and sensitive enough. Basically she is the man, and he is the woman. The patient is worried that she talks while having sexual intercourse and gets into ecstasy. She asks herself if this is love of herself.

She describes that to feel satisfied she must be penetrated up to her throat—that the feeling must go completely through her and that she must be "eaten up."

She blames P for not being able to have this feeling during sexual intercourse. She emphasizes that she has a "very big clitoris" and that therefore everything must be very easy. On the other hand she is very insecure about whether her genitalia is built right. This is amplified because P says to her that she is "built faultily" and "too big" for him. In this context the patient recounts that in the beginning P has hurt her during sexual intercourse and that she was bleeding even days afterward.

Since the patient has a sexual relationship with P, she also has no orgasm when masturbating. She reasons that this relates to her changed physical sensation. She also ponders if the hormonal preparation with which she is being treated leads to frigidity.

Another great problem for the patient is the fact that P also has sexual relationships with other women and probably still loves his wife. She is angry about this and is jealous and insecure about the question of which place she takes in the row. She also feels that P has made her to be a whore. In his bed she feels like she is in a "brothel."

Under great resistance she recounts that P wants her to buy sexy underwear. On the one hand she describes this to suit her fancy because she had already thought of this earlier—of wearing stockings to cover the hair on her legs; on the other hand it becomes clear that she comes into conflict with her morals because of this and is shattered in her self-esteem. She is forced to emphasize that it was not about "whore's underwear" but instead "solid sexy underwear."

Also the need to buy a book about positions in sexual intercourse is an acute problem for the patient. The patient notices that although she did not consciously try to suggest a pure image to P and also has spoken to him about masturbation, she, however, wants to see and show herself as "pure."

Family 19

At first the patient keeps her relationship with P a secret from her mother.

She dreams that she rode a train twice and did not return home. The third time she returned home but did not find the courage to ring the bell and instead threw stones at the window. She asked her mother to ride away with her because a man was shot. On the way there the mother broke in through a roof.

The patient interprets the dream herself as such: She was "shot through" by a man and now became in the eyes of her mother a whore. The mother has always warned her not to "throw herself away" for a man and argued that, as a woman, one is only used by men.

Marginally the patient recounts that P found her mother on a photo as a young girl very pretty and that the mother also always had an orgasm. The patient intensively yearns to sleep with her brother. In her imagination he must be the most tender lover. In this, she feels that her father is also involved in some way—"disturbing or stimulating."

Relationships outside the Family 19

Through another newspaper ad the patient has made contact to another man, probably more so to document to P that she is also interested in other men.

She is still not sure about the affection from P. Even when he visits her, he is first of all interested in divorcing his wife. She thinks that he cannot separate from his wife and that he needs several women at the same time to satisfy his needs and to compensate for the rejection of his wife. As one of these women she feels degraded into an object and made into a "corpse." This causes her to have mistrust, resignation, and, above all, aggression so that she can imagine killing P; in this she also sees that the source of these feelings is due to the influence of her mother who always warned her about men.

Simultaneously the patient looks for confirmation of herself in relationships. She sees herself as the "woman of his life" who is the only one who can give him security and strength and who brings the patience, which the mother was never capable to provide for the father. According to this idea she makes P the offer to "leave him in peace," to not see him anymore until he is divorced from his wife. By doing so, she basically plays the role of her previous life, always to be a good and fair comrade and not to claim anything; however, at this time, she is trying to let go of this previous role. Contrary to this she has the need to be so attractive for P that he also does not want to separate from her, even for only some time.

Sexuality 19

As the patient describes which feeling an orgasm would have to have for her, she remembers that she experienced her first tongue kiss as something awful and forbidden. At the time she thought "this must be like sexual intercourse." In confession she was punished harshly by a priest. After this experience she was capable only of a completely asexual relationship with a friend at that time.

The patient has feelings of guilt concerning her sexual needs. She has made herself dirty and has become a whore. In this, the mother plays an important role as a judge of morality and immorality.

Self-Esteem 19

The self-esteem of the patient in this period is ambivalent and considerably determined by her physical feeling. Through the experience with her body and the body of her friend, during sexual intercourse, she is once more insecure in her female identity. Simultaneously it becomes clear that she, even though it is a slow process, more so accepts her development. She is furthermore capable of not only seeing her herself as the origin of problems in the sexual area but also to see P as responsible for this; she wants to express her claims and needs.

The patient describes situations in which she experienced P as dominating and with that has the feeling "of shrinking toward a zero point"; only through hatred can she find herself again.

In this period particularly one conflict becomes clear in which the patient stands before herself in her imagination. Her life role so far was to be a fair comrade and to abstract herself from her own needs. Mainly, toward P, she takes up this role. She herself speaks about her mother position, which burdens her particularly when she meets P in her role as a woman in her sexuality. The other role—to be the pleasant, attractive, and passionate woman—is considerably burdened with insecurity.

Relationship toward the Analyst 19

The patient transfers the rejection that she feels internally by P and the fear to be used, disappointed, and betrayed to the relationship with the analyst. In the analysis she can easily express her hatred and her impatience.

She reproaches the analyst for not interpreting a dream of P which she recounted in the analysis and also that he does not tell her clearly what he thinks of the relationship and what she should stop doing. Once he says that time is on her side, and another time he tells her that she actually does not have time anymore. Just like P, also, the analyst holds something back from her. She imagines that he knows exactly which mistakes she does and that he does not understand that she is waiting for so long and throws herself away. She hates him and could shoot him dead.

In the following session she finds that she no longer has the need to hate the analyst and that for the first time she has the feeling to be right.

Period XX, Hours 476–480

External Situation 20

This is unchanged.

Symptoms 20

No symptoms mentioned.

Body 20

The patient is furthermore preoccupied with her body, her physical sensation, and the sexual problems. The hair is only directly mentioned in so far as the patient says that she has been, during sexual intercourse with P, often inhibited because she feared he could feel the hair on her body.

She sometimes feels her skin as being a strange cover, which she cannot lose.

The patient no longer experiences an orgasm since she has been hurt by P during sexual intercourse. She asks herself if, during the long time without having sexual intercourse, everything "has grown back together" again.

Previously she imagined having a virgin-like, narrow, and enclosing vagina. At the same time she emphasizes that the vagina was not important to her back then—only the clitoris. She has a nice, big clitoris—"as big as a tree." Since being injured during intercourse the vagina is, in her imagination, a "wide open fish mouth," a "wide cave from which everything falls out.... It is as if the operating doctor forgets the forceps in the stomach, leaving something behind, which changes the patient." This idea contradicts itself in that the patient, while touching, still finds an unchanged, narrow vagina; in spite of this it is the idea of her body that she has to deal with.

The fact that she also does not experience an orgasm while masturbating strengthens her in the idea that her genitals have changed psychologically. There must be a barrier between the clitoris and the vagina so that there is no longer any "flow." The patient imagines, for example, that her labia by reason of frequent masturbation became longer and bigger and now are in the way. Later it becomes clear that the patient's fantasy of wanting to close in and hold everything with her "upper and lower lips" is burdened with strong feelings of guilt.

The idea of the vagina being too big continues in the fantasy of being able to swallow everything, to have sexual intercourse with many men at the same time, to be so big that she can only be filled up by the whole world. Along with this is the idea of the patient having a very fat belly, to be the mother of the whole world and to be the Demiurge. The patient describes the orgasm as a special feeling, as something total—a feeling that must go through "from top to bottom and from bottom to top." This idea of feeling is closely related to the need of her vagina being filled up completely, that the touch of the clitoris is not enough because the center of arousal is, according to her, much deeper in the body.

The patient is worried because, unlike in earlier times, she can no longer be aroused purely visually. Further, she addresses the fear of being slightly lesbian. She would like to know how other women look and would like to touch their bodies.

The patient currently reads the Hite-Report and feels in this generally supported in her critique concerning the sexual behavior of men. It is obviously the norm among men that they only care about the sexual act itself without foreplay and after-play. Men are miserable sex acrobats; their sexuality is rough and not differentiated; they are only dependent on their impulse and overestimate their penis. They are afraid of tenderness, and only the woman can teach them how sexuality can be really beautiful. In this characteristic of male sexuality she sees an unchangeable fact of Western culture. However, the patient emphasizes that female sexuality is much stronger and more differentiated.

Also P was, as a lover, only average. He was egocentric, could not get involved with her, and was not tender enough.

In her need for tenderness the patient experiences the society here as a society of "visual contacts" in which physical touch is a taboo.

Family 20

Departing from her need for affection, safety, and tenderness, the patient illustrates the situation in her family. In her parental home, feelings were not seen as something nice; they were downplayed, suppressed, and made a taboo. This experience fills her with great hatred toward her parents. She experiences it as a great disappointment that she cannot even talk with her mother about her sexual problems. The mother has no idea of this and only cares about her work and cannot express wishes.

The patient had to do without physical affection and sexuality for a long time and now goes through much of what other women have experienced already by the age of 20. For this she first of all blames her father. She is angry at him, could hit him in his face, and have a screaming fit when she sees him. Besides, her father belongs to the men who cannot satisfy the sexual needs of a woman.

The patient mentions again the intense wish to sleep with her brother. In her imagination he is, next to the analyst, the best lover in the world.

Relationships outside the Family 20

The patient places a new ad. She says that among the applicants are a stubborn professor and a bachelor bound to his mother. Moreover, she received a letter from a man in Brazil who looks very good and, above all, looks like her brother. She is fascinated by the idea of going to Rio de Janeiro, into fairyland, to travel to a distinguished man even if this need contradicts her republican attitude. The patient imagines trying several routes, but to not mix them up.

As before, the patient deals with her relationship to P; she is about to detach herself a bit and clearly expresses aggressive feelings toward him. In spite of this she still hopes to be able to live with him. She imagines that it would be good for him to look for another woman in the midst of his life.

According to her, P belongs to the category, as Erich Fromm expresses, of motherly bound neurotics who only love in their own interest. He is not capable of getting involved with another human. The need for the caring mother is most important to him. This expectation raises in the patient all her motherly instincts. It satisfies her need to care for someone in a motherly way.

Now the patient is also extremely interested in how P is doing and how he is dealing with the relationship to his wife. She would like to go to him and support both in solving their problems.

The patient is also visited by a former pupil. She envies her because she already has, as a young woman, a sexual relationship with a man—because she gets want she wants ("She gets her orgasm delivered").

Self-Esteem 20

The self-esteem of the patient is ambivalent. By her reactions to the former pupil who visited her, it becomes clear that it is difficult for her to accept her slow development—that she is afraid at her age of not finding a man and of not being sexually attractive anymore.

So she decides that she has to change her life in the next years decisively: She wants to leave the school, move away, and build a life as a couple.

The patient still has to struggle with the problem that she has guilty feeling when she accepts something from someone else, when she is doing well, when she enjoys something. Then she suddenly feels a "barrier" within herself and directs everything accordingly in order to do something good for the other one.

In her open critique about the sexual behavior of P and men in general it simultaneously is expressed that she is more capable of putting her needs into the foreground and of claiming herself as a woman with her sexuality.

Relationship toward the Analyst 20

The patient recounts that she is reading a book by Fromm titled *The Art of Loving*. In connection with her statement, which the analyst probably finds too primitive, she describes how she experiences her current needs according to the situation in the analysis. She feels as if she were in a space empty of air in which it is impossible to "live elementary," in which above all any physicality is prohibited. Her wish to hold the analyst, to cling to him, and to begin crying cools down in this atmosphere—already in her imagination. She compares this to her relationship to her father who was never able to give her the feeling of safety and strength.

At home the patient had wished to seduce the analyst in the following session, to simply close the curtains and to undress. She fears that the analyst would react shocked. In her imagination he must be a perfect lover. Internally she threatens him if he does not master this test. The patient legitimizes her wish in that it might be also good for the analyst to once again start a new relationship with a woman.

In spite of many limits within the analysis the patient feels safe with the analyst. He has warm hands, a stabile, reliable face, an "I-am-there face." She can now also handle the idea that there are also other women who admire the analyst and give him flowers.

Period XXI, Hours 502–506

External Situation 21

The patient receives a letter from a school administration, which signifies the end of the analysis: She has to present herself to a physician working for this administration.

Symptoms 21

No symptoms mentioned.

Body 21

The hair of the patient turns to roots in a dream; she feels to be root wood with strings that spin P into a bush and hold him tight. Through this she has a carrying weave and feels this to be pleasing. Now the hair is accepted and no longer felt as disturbing.

The male–female problem resolves in the fantasy of getting a penis put between the breasts. This, for her, an already very old fantasy, would be the highest symbol of fertility, nurturing, and insemination of a furrow and of being earth bound. Especially between her own breasts she can, according to the form of her thorax, imagine a penis very well. This fantasy she could not even put into reality with P, although she does not know of any taboos with him. Therewith, she would be powerful. P admires and envies her for being a woman and being able to give birth and being productive.

In this whole period there is a feeling of accepting her body and sexuality. Also the fantasy to sleep with the analyst, as another not-so-stiff form of therapy, can be expressed without fear.

Family 21

The relationship with the parents is only talked about in connection with the separation from the analyst: The parents expected sadness from her as she left the house to study. But she could not feel sadness at the time of departure and did not get homesick until later.

She is afraid that the analyst could possibly expect, before the farewell, something other than a feeling of strength.

Relationships outside the Family 21

For the patient the relationship with P is important, although she does not want this at all. She constantly thinks about him, knows his timetable by heart, yearns for him, and even cries over him. In the beginning of this period she describes him mainly as a grandiose egoist with breaks in communication. She is weak against this and measures other men only in contrast to him; he, the individual player, awakened her passion for play. She is pleased by his phone calls, although she later dreams that children are being cut through their throats because of the telephoning. She does not want to further continue the friendship because of his polygamy and his egoism. She feels also used sexually: As she refuses to sleep with him on a lawn because she wants to talk, he says, "Then I put you by the tree."

In the course of this period, however, she increasingly finds her own strength, her carrying weave, and her roots, which can suck out others. She feels P to be weak and also feels in the relationship to him departure emotions. However, she does not simply cut off contact to P as he advised her to do for the end of the analysis.

Self-Esteem 21

The patient does not feel any guilt in feeling strong and the simultaneous acceptance of her own needs. Through the feeling to have roots, to be able to live forever, her self-esteem rose; she can accept herself and her body.

Relationship toward the Analyst 21

Also in this relationship the farewell and the becoming strong gains in importance. In a dream she first has to "trick" the analyst so that she can get away before he notices that she has already gotten the roots and the ability to live on. Thereby, she must search her own way through a hollow tree, the acceptance of her vagina, and can then run away on her roots.

Then she manages to say, "Probably you are bored by what I recount, but it is my time." Eventually she leaves the analyst starving, thin on his mountain, as she has become the stronger. She compares the analyst with P; the analyst is more considerate, not cool, without affection and understanding, as she is being told in a dream. The fear that the analyst could, like her parents, be disappointed by her way of farewell is soon recognized as transmission.

The patient is no longer jealous toward her "siblings," who lie on the couch before or after her; she no longer feels any rivalry. She is pleased when also the others feel well with the analyst and the analyst with them. The warmed couch no longer disgusts her; she can comfortably swim on in the "warm water" and does not feel pushed aside.

Period XXII, Hours 510–517

External Situation 22

The end of the analysis is agreed upon.

The relationship with P loosens; the patient wants to end it. In the school she has an intern with whom she does not get along.

Symptoms 22

No symptoms mentioned.

Body Hair, Sexuality 22

In a dream the patient experiences a lady in a circus who suddenly appears in an open blouse with very nice breasts and rides a bicycle through water, whereby water splashes in all directions.

Through this she becomes very envious and would also like to have such nice breasts to show and to be such an "erotic serpent priestess," who can exhibit herself; she would like to be able to show her nakedness, like an older woman with whom she once was on vacation. The patient associates the splashing water with protein, sperm, and procreation; she is astonished that this no longer is disgusting to her. The patient also relates the grandmother with nice skin, who starting at the age of 70 had little hairs on the chin, which the patient was allowed to pull out. The grandmother was completely without odor, without human odor—just like the analyst.

The patient remembers that she as a child, while playing with dolls with girlfriend Claudia, sometimes had strong sexual feelings. This girlfriend was also the only one with whom she could talk about sexuality during her childhood. However, it never came to any sexual touch.

Family 22

In this period the family does not play any role; only childhood memories appear, which go into the relationship with the analyst.

The mother appears as a strong, red-cheeked woman who conveys a feeling of reliance, although she once let her as a child stand at a train station and forgot about her. The earlier memories are those of a pale, serious, stern porcelain-like mother who is powerless.

In connection with beautiful bodies and her schoolmate C, the very beloved grandmother also appears who had nice skin and was without odor, as if without body. She was the only one in the family who had strong feelings against Claudia; all the others only said, "It is your own fault" when there was a quarrel. They did not support her; only the grandmother sent C away from the garden.

The father is mentioned only briefly because of a dream in which she uses a shoehorn; her father also used to have such a shoehorn.

Relationships outside the Family 22

Through the invitation of her arch enemy Claudia to a class reunion intensive feelings of hatred awaken within the patient. She would like to beat and kick Claudia and remembers that she already in earlier times wanted to stab her. Claudia was always so self-confident and always dominated her although they were friends in childhood. By the letter of decline and the intense feelings of hatred, which she can now allow herself, the patient goes a step further toward her inner strength. A further role in declining attending the meeting is the fact that all are married except her. She cannot handle this disgrace and does not want to have anything to with this disgusting class anymore.

A further need for the preoccupation with rejection and negative feelings and aggressions toward others is provided by the intern E at school, who is uninhibited in her aggressions and criticism and always attacks. The patient feels that she is being treated unfairly and feels inferior to E because E refuses to give lessons; E even ignores her and does not pay attention during class. The patient does not accomplish putting herself in the right light and praising herself next to the so self-confident E; for her that would be a bad self-compliment. It is, however, important to her to get along with E as proof of her own ability. So she is very relieved as it comes to an understanding.

The working on the relationship with P goes along parallel with the working in the analysis situation. In the relationship to P the patient is torn: On the one hand she wants to break up the relationship and no longer adapt herself and accept what is being put into her, no longer lose herself (she fears that maybe something similar has happened in the analysis); on the other hand P is for her the man of her life, and she does not want to be without him. He might give her a steady place, which the analyst fails to give to her. She let P torment her psychologically, let herself be changed painfully and invested patience, just as in the analysis.

The effort to try to detach herself from P is being made more difficult because he has become closer to her again. He needs her to unload his problems, but she cannot convert this for herself and so needs the analyst.

The topic of the upcoming end of the analysis goes through this whole period. The patient still reports having toilet dreams. In the analysis she wants to "stink alone" and no longer wants the assistance of the analyst.

The patient thinks about how she would like to arrange the last session; most of all she would like to make a completely normal day out of it, arrive as always and not simply cancel the session, lie on the couch as always and not sum up. She is convinced that she now can be successful in her idea of the farewell and that the analyst does not force his idea upon her and takes her by the leash.

Her friend P has told her that she should embrace the analyst for the farewell; then she could, without fear, run up the steps of her house in a lively manner.

In spite of all concrete thoughts concerning the farewell, there is also the idea about what could come afterward: the for her peculiar three days in the week without the analyst, the falling away of a steady place, a reliability that she does not want to miss and that she would like to have secure.

According to her view the farewell means to the analyst a successor who is already putting flowers on his table. He will no longer be viewed through her eyes, and she will symbolically build him a new apartment and his own stairway. Maybe he will no longer have any influence on her when he is no longer concretely present for her.

Within the thoughts concerning the end of the analysis are a mix of fear, jealousy, and hatred. She must try to make the analyst less powerful and to have no influence on her. She is afraid about ending the analysis too early like Moser. This shows in Moser's book *Gottesvergiftung* (The poisoning of God) in the fear of losing the fixed place, to stand alone even when the analyst sometimes by his silence radiates something such as death, as poisoned.

Feelings of jealousy and hatred are put onto the lucky successors; first she wards them off, but then she lets the analyst slide down from his castle in which he used to be integrated so nicely and locks him on a chair—the analytical "ear seat": tied up, kept warm, without being able to move and powerless. She would really like to strangle him, never give him away anymore. So she must make him to an old impotent man who, while recounting of bosoms falls asleep.

She knows that the relationship toward the analyst will somehow end emotionally, but she tries to hold him through new things: For the first time she tells him of her fear of steep stairs, which she had never mentioned before. The stairs to the analyst are especially bad. Also she likes neither tea nor coffee and does not like to pep herself up.

In her strong, aggressive feelings, the patient tries to make herself more independent from the analyst; she interprets much herself and also thinks that she does not need a confessional father and can encourage herself and "stink alone." She never totally followed the basic rule to say everything. Now she forgets her dreams, which she wanted to remember for the analysis, but interprets those of others, which is a further decrease of the power of the analyst. Maybe in 20 years she will build him a monument or write a book.

Now she can only find that her character did not change because of the analysis, that she did not become another human, did not become a saint. The question concerning change has become unessential; symptoms were not checked off in a row.

The analyst actually never was a strong father to her; she is overwhelmed by the hatred toward a neurology professor who once massively criticized her analyst. So she would like to embrace the analyst and protect him. But he has his wife for support. She was for the patient at first an unreachable problem then a strong woman who dominated the analyst. However, the patient never wanted to be like her.

The final thoughts in the last session are those that bring comfort into the separation; the patient and the analyst think the same in some things and are occasionally connected in their thoughts.

CODA

We provide this longitudinal and cross-sectional descriptive work to demonstrate what is feasible when tape recordings and verbatim protocols are available and can be examined by objective observers of the analytic process. Based on a time sample of 22 periods over the course of treatment, external reviewers were able to portray the treatment course with a minimum of psychoanalytic jargon. This clinical description conveys vividly the quantitative modifications in self-experience that constituted structural changes as characterized by Kafka (1989, p. 81). This clinical-systematic background may serve as a roadmap for the formalized studies that will follow.

Chapter 5

Guided Clinical Judgments

5.1   COMPARATIVE PSYCHOANALYSIS ON THE BASIS OF A NEW FORM OF TREATMENT REPORT*

Comparative Psychoanalysis

Although making comparisons (i.e., judging similarities and differences) is part and parcel of our life and of our professional thinking and acting, the phrase *comparative psychoanalysis* has recently made its way into our professional vocabulary (Scarfone, 2002). It refers to a qualitative comparison of various forms of psychotherapy, psychoanalysis among them. In view of the official recognition of psychoanalytic pluralism brought about by the courage of Wallerstein (1988, 1990, 2005a, 2005b), we are now obliged to compare various psychoanalytic techniques and theoretical assumptions with each other. To make the comparison reasonable, reliable, and fruitful, shared criteria are needed. In membership papers and published case reports, criteria are usually only implied, if not totally missing.

A corollary of "comparative psychoanalysis" is the growing interest in different ways of documenting clinical facts. Within the last decade an impressive number of original papers on this topic have been published. In his foreword to the special 75th anniversary edition of the *International Journal of Psychoanalysis*, devoted to "Conceptualization and Communication of Clinical Facts in Psychoanalysis," Tuckett (1994) wrote:

> After 75 years it is time not only to review our methodology for assessing our truth, but also to develop approaches that will make it possible to be open to new ideas while also being able to evaluate their usefulness by reasoned argument. The alternative is the tower of Babel. (p. 865)

---

* Helmut Thomä and Horst Kächele.

Therefore, to make "comparative psychoanalysis" a fruitful enterprise, it is essential to evaluate how the treating analyst applies his professional knowledge in specific interactions.

In many respects, psychoanalysis is an applied science based on clinical observation, but for all kinds of practical reasons the analyst as participant observer would be overburdened by having to combine his therapeutic task with being at the same time the researcher. Therapy research in psychoanalysis is a most complex endeavor far beyond the capacity of the treating clinician working in isolation.

Only a team can do the job implied by Sigmund Freud's "inseparable bond" thesis, namely that of testing the validity of causal connections observed in the analytic situation (see Chapter 1 in this volume). The psychoanalytic literature abounds in vignettes about new discoveries that often even lack a convincing description. The "contemporary countertransference subjectivism" seems to solve all practical and scientific problems: If the emotions of the analyst indeed mirrored the unconscious of the patient correctly, if the "third ear or eye" heard or saw the unconscious voices and scenes (as Johann Wolfgang von Goethe imagined the "Urphaenomene"), then without further ado psychoanalysts would be in a unique godlike position. Although we enjoy similar fantasies, we don't think they offer solutions.

To bring symptomatic—let alone structural—changes into correlation with intersubjective processes and eventually with unconscious schemata as their determining conditions is a difficult undertaking. In other words, microanalytic descriptions of intersubjective processes have to be related to whatever unconscious clichés generate typical patterns of symptomatic conflict resolution. We will demonstrate the relationship between hypothesized unconscious processes and detailed interpretations in two session reports of Amalia X.

Our interpretation of the *Junktim* stresses the responsibility of the treating analyst. Clinical research originates in the analytic situation; everything depends on the participation of the analyst. To this extent there is some truth in the inseparable bond thesis, especially if the context of the phrase is taken seriously. The Junktim is only fulfilled if its "beneficent effect" (German *wohltätige Wirkung*) is proven. Our emphasis that treatment reports have to be centered on processes of change is once more justified. As those processes refer to manifest experiences and behavior and their assumed unconscious roots (Freud's template or schema), it is essential to discuss their relationship to the intersubjective processes in the psychoanalytic situation. Only parts of the patient's experience can be expressed in a "language of observation," but to deny such a language to psychoanalysis, as Ricoeur (1970 pp. 366ff) did, is from our point of view unjustified.

Introductory Comments to the Audio Recording of Analytic Treatments

It is remarkable how many problems an analyst has to cope with when he gives a colleague the data from his work—even more so if the dialogue is audiotaped and transcribed. Colleagues confirm more or less bluntly what one's self evaluation actually cannot overlook, namely that there can be a significant discrepancy between one's professional ideal and reality. The very idiosyncratic style of interpreting of any analyst makes some editing of the original text necessary.

Tape recording is a relative neutral procedure with respect to the contents of recording; it will not miss spoken words as long they are loud enough to be recorded. Transcripts often seem paltry in comparison with the recollections that the analyst has of the session. When reading a transcript or listening to a tape one has to revitalize the clinical situation by identifying with both the patient and the analyst. It is the rich cognitive and emotional context that adds vitality to the sentences expressed by the patient and the analyst. It certainly will be a matter of training to fill in the gaps with the aid of one's imagination and one's own experience (like musicians able to read scores). In the traditional presentation of case material, which in general contains much less of the original data, this enrichment is provided by the author's narrative comments. Even the use of generalizations, for example, of the abstract concepts that are regularly employed in clinical narratives probably contributes to making the reader feel at home. The concepts that are used are filled—automatically, as it were—with the views that the reader associates with them. If a report refers to trauma or orality, we all attribute it a meaning on the basis of our own understanding of these and other concepts that is in itself suited to lead us into approving or skeptical dialogue with the author.

For Sandler and Sandler (1984, p. 396) the "major task for future researchers" is "to discover why it is that the transcribed material of other analysts' sessions so often makes one feel that they are very bad analysts indeed." They qualify this by adding that this reaction "is far too frequent to reflect reality" and ask "can so many analysts really be so bad" (ibid.)? It is remarkable that Sandler and Sandler made this comment in a special issue of the Psychoanalytic Inquiry, devoted to Merton Gill's innovative contribution to psychoanalytic technique. Our somewhat ironic rejoinder to this observation is the following: Sandler and Sandler would belong to those bad analysts, if they had presented audiotaped dialogues without giving their thoughts and feelings to put the flesh on the verbal skeleton. In other words, oral reports convey some of the emotional climate of the analytic situation to the audience, but without additional editing, and an augmentation of the transcribed material by the treating analyst, the pure written record alone is, indeed, paltry.

In retrospect we can say that the introduction of tape recordings into psychoanalytic treatment was linked with the beginning of a critical reappraisal of therapeutic processes (Gill, Simon, Fink, Endicott, & Paul, 1968; Rosenkötter & Thomä, 1970). This simple technical tool was, and still is, the object of a subsiding controversy among psychoanalysts (Wallerstein, 2003).

We believe that the introduction of research into the psychoanalytic situation is of great benefit to the patient. It enables the analyst to learn more than from any other kind of supervision. Clinical discussions based on audiotaped sessions come very close to the heart of the matter, if the analyst gives background information. A transcript creates the impression of being one-dimensional: The analyst's interpretation and the patient's answers do not automatically reflect latent structures, although typical interpretations disclose which school the analyst belongs to. Some 20 years after our empirical investigations of audio recordings of psychoanalytic dialogues (Kächele, Thomä, Ruberg, & Grünzig, 1988) we would like to encourage our colleagues to use that instrument to improve their therapeutic capacities.

Two Sessions of the Case of Amalia*

The Need for Annotation

In order to enrich the understanding of the following sessions I shall give each intervention some background information. These "considerations" are subsequently added to the exchange between patient's and analyst's responses. It is obvious that in arriving at my interventions I was led not only by the ideas described in the text. Whatever way interpretations have been created, any interpretation actually made must be aligned along "cognitive" criteria, as demanded by Arlow (1979). My comments refer to the "cognitively" and "rationally" determined "end products" (the interventions themselves) and neglect the intuitive, unconscious components in their genesis. Therefore, I rarely refer to my countertransference. I am an eclectic psychoanalyst and an intersubjectivist (Thomä, 2005). With regard to the countertransference I am as old-fashioned as Melanie Klein. I do not believe that countertransference is brought about by projective identification. There may be typical interactional patterns of transference and countertransference, but I think it is the responsibility of the analyst to make the best for the patient of his emotional reactions.

The source of each of my analytic thoughts remains an open question. If we assume that the analyst's perceptive apparatus is steered by his personality, values, and hopefully theoretical knowledge, which may have become preconscious, then it is very difficult to trace the genesis of interpretations

---

* Note the change in the style of our text. The treating analyst (H.T.) speaks now in the first person.

back to its starting point. For example, theoretical knowledge about displacement also facilitates preconscious perception; it pervades the analyst's intuition and blends with his emotional reactions. These "considerations" are my second thoughts. For all clinical and naturally controversial discussions, I recommend taking the background information as the starting point of our exchange. In other words, I hope that my considerations are coherent enough to be critically discussed. Such a coherence is important because it supports my hypotheses about the patterns in the patient.

Some Remarks about the Psychodynamic
Background of the Two Sessions

When structuring the psychoanalytic situation and dealing with problems of the described type, the analyst must pay extra attention not to let the asymmetry of the relationship excessively strengthen the patient's feeling of being different.

This is important because the idea of being different—that is, the question of similarity and difference, of identity and nonidentity—forms the general framework within which unconscious problems appear. In this case the analyst and patient succeeded relatively quickly in establishing a good working relationship, creating the preconditions for recognizing during the development of the transference the internalization of earlier forms of interaction with primary reference persons (e.g., parents and teachers). The correction that was achieved can be seen in the changes in her self-esteem, in her increased security, and in the disappearance of her symptoms (see Neudert-Dreyer et al., this chapter, Section 5.3).

In retrospect, almost 30 years later, I have the following afterthoughts about my personal understanding of the psychoanalytic method at the time. I think I was quite successful in establishing a helping alliance that made it possible to make transference interpretations with regard to processes of "displacement and condensation." The head is the symbol for understanding and communication and simultaneously a symbolic expression of the penis and the phallus in the sense of Jacques Lacan.

The two excerpts of sessions given herein are linked by the fact that each is concerned with enabling the patient to make new identifications as a result of the analysis of transference. The analyst's "head" became the surrogate of old, unconscious "objects," and its contents the representative of new opportunities. The representation of the "object," which is simultaneously a self-representation, made it possible to establish a distance, because the analyst made his head available and kept it too. Thus, he became a model for both closeness and distance. This example clearly demonstrates the therapeutic effect that insight into unconscious connections mediated by the analyst's interpretations can have. I think that my fantasies and thoughts tallied with the psychic reality of the patient.

I have selected this material because in my opinion it is suited to provide several lines of support to my argument. Although the head acquired sexual importance as a result of the process of unconscious displacement, this displacement did not alter anything regarding the primacy of emotional and intellectual communication between the patient and the analyst about what she was looking for as if it were hidden inside my head. The search for knowledge was directed at sexuality. This secret and well-guarded (repressed) treasure was assumed to be in the head (as the object of transference) because of the unconscious displacement. The revelation of "displacement" brought something to light that was "new" to the patient.

The two sessions are taken from a period of the treatment (No VII) when the patient explicitly experienced severe feelings of guilt, which were actualized in her relationship to me. The biblical law of an eye for an eye and a tooth for a tooth was reinforced in her experience because of her sexual desires. Her life-historical role model for the contents of her transference was a fantasized incestuous relationship to her brother. The increase in inner tension led the patient on the one hand to reconsider the idea of dedicating her life to the church as a missionary and on the other to contemplate committing suicide. (As a young girl she had wanted to become a nun and nurse but gave up this idea after a trial period because the pious confinement became too much for her. Leaving also helped her to establish some distance from the strict biblical commandments.) Now she wielded her "old" bible against me "in a fight to the finish." This fight took place at different levels, and the patient invented a series of similes for them. She had the feeling that the analyst's dogma, the "Freud Bible," could not be reconciled with her Christian bible. Both bibles, however, contained a prohibition of sexual relations with the analyst.

The patient struggled for her independence and needs, which she defended against both of these bibles. She developed an intense defense against my interpretations, and she had the feeling that I knew in advance exactly "what's going to happen." She felt humiliated because her detours and distractions had been detected. She had the intense desire to mean something to me and to live in me; she thought about giving me an old, lovely, and wonderful clock that would strike every hour for me (and for her).

In this phase of the treatment one topic took on special significance and intensity: This was her interest in my head. What had she learned from measuring my head? In a similar situation Amalia X had once said that for a long time she had thought that I was looking in her—of what was already there—in books, in my thoughts, in my head. She wished that something completely new would come out. She herself looked for interpretations and made an effort to understand my ideas.

Transcripts of Parts of Sessions 152 and 153

At the beginning of the session Amalia reported an uncanny dream in which she was stabbed in the back by a man; thus, she introduced the general topic of a fight between a man and herself with all the different levels and meanings of fights between the sexes. Then Amalia changed her role as a victim and became a perpetrator. In the next session she remembered that she had completely forgotten that she had looked on me as a young man with a head symbolizing a phallus. Her momentary forgetting is a beautiful example of Luborsky's (1967, 1996) attention to small parapraxes as symptoms. At first Amalia, reporting about her chief, fell into a role of masochistic subordination, and I commented by saying:

> Analyst (A): You presume that I'm sitting behind you and saying "wrong, wrong."

Consideration: This transference interpretation was based on the following assumption. The patient attributed to me a "superego function." This interpretation took the burden off her and gave her the courage to rebel (the patient had recognized long before that I was different and would not criticize her, but she was not sure and could not believe it because she still had considerable unconscious aggressions against old objects). I assumed that she had much more intense transference feelings and that both the patient and I could tolerate an increase in tension. I repeated her concern that I could not bear it and finally formulated the following statement: "Thus it's a kind of a fight to the finish, with a knife" (not specifying who has the knife). I made this allusion to phallic symbolism to stimulate her unconscious desires. It was an overdose! The patient reacted by withdrawing. Assumption: self-punishment.

> Patient (P): Sometimes I have the feeling that I would like to rush at you, grab your neck, and hold you tight. Then I think, "He can't take it and will suddenly fall over dead."

> A: That I can't take it.

The patient varied this topic, expressing her overall concern about asking too much of me and of my not being able to tolerate the struggle.

> A: It's a kind of a fight to the finish, with a knife. (This interpretation alludes to Amalia's dream about being stabbed, reported at the beginning of the session.)

> P: Probably.

She then reflected that she had always, throughout the years, given up prematurely, before the struggle had really begun, and withdrawn.

P: And I don't doubt any more that it was right for me to withdraw. After such a long time I have the urge to give up again.

A: Withdrawal and self-sacrifice in the service of the mission instead of struggling to the end.

P: Exactly, nerve-racking.

Consideration: She was very anxious about losing her object.

A: Then I would have the guarantee of being preserved. Then you would have broken off my test prematurely.

We continued on the topic of what I can take and whether I let myself be carried along by her "delusion." The patient had previously made comparisons to a tree, asking whether she could take anything from it and what it would be. I returned to this image and raised the question of what she wanted to take along by breaking off branches.

Consideration: Tree of knowledge—aggression.

P: It's your neck, it's your head. I'm often preoccupied with your head.

A: Does it stay on? You're often preoccupied with my head?

P: Yes, yes, incredibly often. From the beginning I've measured it in every direction.

A: Hum, it is …

P: It's peculiar, from the back to the front and from the bottom. I believe I'm practicing a real cult with your head. This is just too funny. With other people I'm more likely to see what they have on, just instinctively, without having to study them.

Consideration: To create shared things as primary identification. [This topic was discussed for a long period of time, with some pauses and "hums" by the analyst.]

P: It's simply too much for me. I sometimes ask myself afterwards why I didn't see it; it's such a simple connection. I am incredibly interested in your head. Naturally, what's inside too. No, not just to take it along, but to get inside your head, yes above all, to get inside.

Consideration: The partial withdrawal of the object increased her unconscious phallic aggressiveness.

The patient spoke so softly that I did not even understand "get inside" at first, mistaking it for "put inside." The patient corrected me and added a peculiar image, "Yes, it's so hard to say in front of 100 eyes."

P: Get inside, the point is to get inside and to get something out.

Consideration: I saw this getting inside and taking something out in connection with the subject of fighting. It was possible to put the sexual symbolism, resulting from the displacement from the bottom to the top, to therapeutic use by referring to a story that the patient had told in an earlier session. A woman she knew had prevented her boyfriend from having intercourse with her and had masturbated him, which she had described by analogy to headhunter jargon as "head shrinking." The unconscious castration-intention dictated by her penis envy created profound sexual anxiety and was paralleled by general and specific defloration anxieties. These anxieties led in turn to frustration, but one that she herself had instinctively caused, as a neurotic self-perpetuating cycle. The repression of her sexual and erotic desires that now occurred unconsciously strengthened the aggressive components of her wanting to have and possess (penis desire and penis envy).

A: That you want to have the knife in order to be able to force your way in, in order to get more out.

After we exchanged a few more thoughts, I gave an explanation, saying that there was something very concrete behind our concern with the topics of getting inside, head, and the fight to the end with a knife.

A: The woman you mentioned didn't speak of "head shrinkers"* for nothing.

P: That's just the reason I broke off this line of thought. [For about 10 minutes the patient had switched to a completely different subject.]

---

* The derogatory colloquial "headshrinker" (=psychiatrist) has no German counterpart and is unknown to Amalia. Her expression "Schrumpfköpfe machen" refers to a custom of Polynesian cannibalistic warriors who dry up the heads of enemies they have killed.

After expressing her insight into her resistance to an intensification of transference, she again evaded the topic. She interrupted the intensification, making numerous critical comments.

> P: Because at the moment it can be so stupid, so distant. Yes, my wishes and desires are the point, but it's tricky, and I get real mad, and when head and head shrinking are now ...

She laughed, immediately expressed her regret, and was silent. I attempted to encourage her.

> A: You know what's in your head.

> P: Right now I'm not at all at home in mine. How do I know what will happen tomorrow? I have to think back. I was just on dogma and your head, and if you want to go down ... [to a shrunken head]. It's really grotesque.

Consideration: I first mentioned the shrunken heads because I assumed that the patient would be more cooperative if the envious object relationship could be replaced by a pleasurable one.

Then the patient came to speak of external things. She described how she saw me and how she saw herself, independent of the head, which then again became the focus of attention in a general sense.

> A: By thinking about the head you're attempting to find out what you are and what I am.

> P: I sometimes measure your head as if I wanted to bend your brain.

The patient then described the associations she had once had when she had seen my picture printed somewhere.

> P: I discovered something completely different at the time. There was an incredible amount of envy of your head. An incredible amount. Now I'm getting somewhere at any rate. Whenever I think of the dagger and of some lovely dream.

Consideration: The patient obviously felt caught. She felt humiliated by her own association, as if she had guessed my assumption as to what the envy might refer to. In this case I would have rushed ahead of her, so to speak.

A: Humiliating, apparently to you, as if I already knew which category to put it in when you express envy, as if I already knew what you are envious of.

P: That came just now because you had referred to the shrunken heads, which I didn't even make. But what fascinated me is this fight to the finish, for the knife, to get to the hard part.... Yes, I was afraid that you couldn't take it. My fear that you can't take it is very old. My father could never take anything. You wouldn't believe how bland I think my father is. He couldn't take anything.

Consideration: A surprising turn. The patient's insecurity and her anxiety about taking hold developed "unspecifically" on her father.

A: It's all the more important whether my head is hard. That increases the hardness when you take hold.

P: Yes, you can take hold harder ... and can—simply—fight better.

The patient then made numerous comments to the effect of how important it was that I did not let myself be capsized, and she returned to her envy. Then she mentioned her university studies again and how she used to "measure" the heads of the others. Then she introduced a new thought.

P: I want to cut a little hole in your head and put in some of my thoughts.

Consideration: An objectivistic image of "intellectual" exchange as a displacement?
  The patient's idea about the two-sided nature of the exchange led me to recognize another aspect of this fight. It was also an expression of how important it was to me that she remains a part of the world (and in contact with me), and digress neither into masochistic self-sacrifice nor into suicide.

P: That came to me recently. Couldn't I exchange a little of your dogma for mine. The thought of such an exchange made it easier for me to say all of this about your head.

A: That you continue coming here so that you can continue filling my head with your thoughts.

Consideration: Fertilization in numerous senses—balance and acknowledgment of reciprocity.

P: Oh yes, and mentioning really productive ideas.

The patient returned to the thoughts and fantasies she had had before the session, about how she had been torn back and forth—whether she had a future at all and whether she shouldn't withdraw in some way or other and put an end to it all.

At the beginning I had attempted to relieve her intense feelings of guilt with regard to her destructiveness. I picked up the idea once again that her thoughts about my stability were in proportion to her degree of aggressiveness. The patient could only gain security and further unfold her destructiveness if she found strong, unshakable stability. The topic of dogmatism probably belonged in this context. Although she criticized it—both her own bible and my presumed belief in the Freud Bible—it also provided her security, and for this reason the dogmatism could not be too rigorous or pronounced.

A: Naturally you wouldn't like a small hole; you would like to put in a lot, not a little. The idea of a small or large hole was your shy attempt to test my head's stability.

My subsequent interpretation was that the patient could also see more through a larger hole and could touch it. She picked up this idea:

P: I would even like to be able to go for a walk in your head.

She elaborated on this idea and emphasized that even earlier (i.e., before that day's session) she had often thought to herself how nice it would be to relax in me, to have a bench in my head. Very peacefully she mentioned that I could say when looking back on my life when I die that I had had a lovely, quiet, and peaceful place to work. (My office was opposite a very old cemetery, now used as a park.)

Consideration: Quiet and peacefulness clearly had a regressive quality, namely of completely avoiding the struggle for life.

The patient now viewed her entering the motherhouse as if a door had been wide open and she had turned away from life. She then drew a parallel to the beginning of the session, when the door was open.

P: I really didn't have to drill my way in. Yes, there I could leave the struggle outside, I could also leave you outside, and you could keep your dogmas.

A: Hum.

P: And then I wouldn't fight with you.

A: Yes, but then you and your dogma would not be afraid of mine. In that setting of peace and quiet everything would remain unchanged, but the fact that you interfere in my thoughts and enter my head shows that you do want to change something, that you can and want to change something.

About five minutes into the next session (153), the patient returned to my head and measuring it and to the fact that it had disturbed her that I had started talking about the shrunken heads.

P: I told you so. Why do you simply want to slip down from the head?

She then described how she had hardly arrived at home before she recalled the thoughts she had had when she had said hello but then had completely forgotten during the session.

P: To me, he [the analyst] looks as if he is in his prime, and then I thought about the genitals and the shrunken heads. [But she quickly pushed this thought aside, and it was completely gone.] When you started with the shrunken heads, I thought, "Where has he got that again?"

The next topic was the question of my security and my dogmatism, and it was clear that the patient had taken a comment I had once completely undogmatically made about Freud and Carl Jung (I have forgotten what it was) to be dogmatic. She then thought about living a full life, about the moment when everything stopped for her and she became "ascetic," and about whether everything could be revived. Then she again mentioned fighting and my head.

P: I was really afraid of tearing it off. And today I think that it's so stiff and straight, and I think to myself, "I somehow can't really get into my head. I'm not at home. Then how should I get into yours?"

The patient then began to speak about an aunt who was sometimes so very hard that you might think you were facing a wall. She then continued about how hard and how soft she would like her head to be. Her fantasies revolved, on the one hand, around quiet and security; on the other hand, she was concerned about what might be hidden in her head and the danger of it consuming her.

Consideration: This obviously involved a regressive movement. The patient could not find any quiet and relaxation because her sexual desires were linked with pregenital fantasies, which returned in projected form because they were in danger of being consumed. These components were given their clearest, and in a certain sense also their ultimate, expression in an Indian story the patient later associated, in which mothers gave pleasure to their little sons by sucking on their penises but bit them off in the process.

The comparisons of the heads and their contents always revolved around the question of whether they went together or not.

> P: The question of how you have your thoughts and how I have mine …. Thoughts stand for many things….

> A: How they meet, how they rub off on one another, how far they penetrate, how friendly or unfriendly they are.

> P: Yes, exactly.

> A: Hum, well.

> P: You said that a little too smooth.

The patient thought about all the things that scared her and returned again to the shrunken heads.

> P: There I feel too tied to sexuality. The jump was too big.

The topic was continued in the question of her speed and of the consideration I pay to her and her speed.

> P: But it is true; naturally it wasn't just your head but your penis too.

Amalia X was now in a position, with phases of increasing and receding anxiety, to distinguish between pleasure from discovering intellectual connections and sexual pleasure. The couch became her mental location of sexual union, and her resting in my head the symbol of pregenital harmony and ultimately the location of shared elements and insight. This aspect became even clearer a little later.

Discussion

Comparative Evaluation

The claim of this communication was to provide data for a comparative evaluation. In the center of the psychodynamic focus of the two sessions is the process of displacement within the patient's body image into the transference. The head is used as a transference object. At the same time the patient uses the analyst's thought processes localized in his head as new experience in order to overcome transference repetitions. Substantially, the two sessions contain changes brought about by the offer of the thoughts and feelings of the analyst as a new object (Gabbard and Westen, 2003; Loewald, 1960). From a microanalytic point of view the verbatim protocol contains details that cannot be covered by the molar abstraction of the session.

An alternative conceptualization, based on the Weiss and Sampson (1986) plan analysis of the patient's material (see Section 5.7), pointed to traumatizing experiences of early upbringing. The analyst, although knowing about these early experiences, gave less weight to these early experiences in his case conception. He was convinced—whatever the early experiences had been—that the salient impact would had to have come from a corrective emotional experience within a new subject–object relationship in order to attain new internalized structures. In this sense we fully agree with Weiss's (1994) ideas about unconscious efforts of patients to disconfirm their unconscious, pathogenic, grim beliefs.

The comparative evaluation of these two case conceptions in the case of the specimen session 152 leads to an interpretation that the patient's wish to reside peacefully in the analyst's head not only signifies a phallic intrusion—as some discussants of the case presentation in New Orleans have pointed out—but also could represent the patient's pregenital wish for reunion with her mother. This unconscious fantasy could reflect the reparation of the early cumulative traumatizing separations experiences. The experimentum crucis consists in identifying behaviors and experiences of the patient that could be weighted for or against these two macroconceptions. However, the psychoanalytic proposition of overdetermination would not rule out that both interpretations have their own justification for which empirical referents have been identified. Therefore, the concept of minimodels in smaller or more extended form linked up to our concept of focal conflicts points to a crucial issue: Without such signposts marking meso-working models the analyst easily gets lost in almost infinite microscopic states of mind. Taking into account the conscious activity has a time window of about 3 seconds, it becomes obvious that such models are operating below consciousness and are guiding the analyst's listening and observational capacities. A beautiful example of such an unconscious model of psychic function has been spelled out by Spence, Mayes, and Dahl (1994) that describes the monitoring process.

Collegial Discussions

As this material was presented at a panel held at the 43rd Congress of the International Psychoanalytical Association in New Orleans, we quote from the final panel report by Wilson (2004):

> Jimenez discussed the issues along four dimensions: (1) what made agreement difficult was that everyone defines clinical material from

a very different point of view; (2) everyone struggled with how to discuss clinical material in a respectful way and avoid the temptation to "supervise" the technique of the Ulm-based presenters; (3) an exuberance of theory and scarcity of empirical observations; (4) there was a wide consensus throughout the panels, that, no matter what the difference in theoretical perspective, the patient-analyst dyad was proceeding in a way that could be described as characterized by a "psychoanalytic process" and what was interesting was that panelists of different persuasions provided different descriptions of how the sessions were evolving, although all agreed that a psychoanalytic process was present. (p. 1269)

Beyond this friendly bonfire of agreement that was not shared at all by all panelists (Ireland, 2004), we felt that Akhtar's (2007) discussion of the technical points of this presentation was quite enlightening:

Like his developmental understanding, Dr. Thomä's technique shows flexibility, resilience, and broad-mindness. It is centered upon helping the patient achieve ego freedom through interpretation and transference resolution. However, it incorporates a variety of listening attitudes and a broad range of interventions that can be seen as preparatory for, as well as in lieu of, the interpretive enterprise.

Forming a helping alliance: Dr. Thomä emphasizes that forming a "helping alliance" (Luborsky, 1984) is an important therapeutic task in the beginning phase of the analysis. Far from fostering regressive dependence, encouragement of realistic hope and assistance in developing unused mental abilities goes a long way in enhancing the "working alliance" (Greenson, 1967) and thus the analysis of transference. The analyst's open acknowledgement of the inherent awkwardness of the psychoanalytic situation, for instance, paradoxically causes the patient to relax. The analyst's explanatory attitude toward pauses in the flow of their dialogue serves the same function. Discussions of how the analytic dialogue differs from social discourse, how free association facilitates the discovery of hidden meanings, and how the analyst's not providing factual answers to the patient's questions also lead to the patient's greater participation in the analytic process (Thomä and Kächele, 1994b, pp. 35–38). Helping to get analyzed and analyzing are not enemies; they are friendly cousins.

Titrating the asymmetry gradient: Dr. Thomä acknowledges that a certain asymmetry within the dyad is essential for the analytic process to occur. However, the gradient of this asymmetry needs to be carefully titrated lest it add to the patient's feeling inferior and alienated. All this is important because the patient must experience both affinity and difference within the dyad; the former facilitates trust and self-revelation, and the latter helps in learning about oneself and assimilation of insights. In Stone's (1980) words, the former meets the condition of "resemblance" that is necessary for the development of transference and the latter places the analyst in a position to interpret the transference.

Dr. Thomä's equanimity and his viewing a patient's desire to read his papers and books as quite natural, even healthy, is a testimony to his respect for the patient's need for affinity. His stance on accepting gifts from a patient also exemplifies this point. He is opposed to categorically rejecting all such offers. In opposition to the prevalent view that accepting gifts derails analysis of such a gesture, he posits that "rejecting presents often prevents analysts from recognizing their true meanings" (p. 301). He acknowledges that accepting gifts can complicate matters but emphasizes that rejecting them can increase the asymmetry of the dyad to a painful extreme and the consequences might sometimes be irremediable. It is in the same spirit that Pine (1998) reminds us that the usually helpful aspects of psychoanalytic frame (e.g. couch, time limits, not giving information about where one is going for vacation) can be traumatic to some individuals, is in the same spirit.

Correcting major distortions of reality: As analysts we constantly bear and "contain" (Bion, 1967) patient's distorted views of us as well as of external reality. We hope that a piecemeal deconstruction of such scenarios would provide the patient a greater ego dominance over internal realities. Dr. Thomä certainly concurs with this stance but adds that the analyst must provide corrective information when there is a genuine matter of ignorance (e.g. in the treatment of fresh immigrants, an example he does not mention but I think would find agreeable) and when the patient's reality testing is getting seriously compromised. (p. 694ff)

The analyst, Thomä, commented on this evaluative statement as follows:

Dr. Akhtar's evaluation is gratifying. Indeed I was surprised about his capacity to discover my psychoanalytic attitude as expressed in the verbal communication. It is a very rare event in my professional career that a colleague just by reading a few transcribed sessions is able to describe in a colourful language the theory of a colleague's technique. He attested to me flexibility, resilience and broad-mindedness. Of course I am pleased about it and even more so for a very special reason: I started this analysis about 35 years ago, long before I met Merton Gill and before I was influenced by his turn towards intersubjectivity. Akhtar's evaluation is therefore especially noteworthy as a proof of my independent development towards relational psychoanalysis.

Akhtar (2007) extracts a most important issue of my psychoanalytic thinking, which is documented in these two sessions: The head is the autonomous location of the individual mind and in so far the organ of individual perspective on transferences and countertransferences. At the same time, the head can be used by mechanisms of displacements to differentiate various aspects of the intersubjective processes in the psychoanalytic situation, which is a permanent task. These sessions are good examples for displacement within the body image and a demonstration of beneficial therapeutic action in the psychoanalytic encounter.

5.2   EMOTIONAL INSIGHT[*]

Introduction

The mechanism of therapeutic change in psychoanalysis has long been a matter of discussion (Luborsky & Schimek, 1964). On the one hand the analysis of resistance and the uncovering of unconscious conflicts or of repressed memories is expected to result in changes of cognitive styles and of manifest behavior. On the other hand the patient will approach this task only in the framework of actual interactions with his analyst (Gill, 1982). Monadic and dyadic points of view are mixed up even in theories of transference and of the therapeutic relationship, as Thomä and Kächele (1994a) point out.

Insight is regarded as one of the central concepts of psychoanalytic treatment: Therapeutic change should result from gaining insight and not from behavioral training or from suggestions of the analyst. However, it has been difficult to define and to put into operational terms the concept of insight for empirical studies (Fisher & Greenberg, 1977; Messer & McWilliams, 2007; Roback, 1974). The concept sometimes refers to a goal of treatment (Myerson, 1965), to a prerequisite of change (Segal, 1962), to a personality attribute, or even to an epiphenomenon of therapeutic change (Fonagy, 1999a). These debates are summarized neatly by Connolly Gibbons, Crits-Christoph, Barber, and Schamberger (2007):

---

[*] Roderich Hohage and Horst Kächele.

> One central question that has not been addressed is whether the task
> of therapy is to make patients generally more insightful, or whether
> what is crucial is obtaining insight about one or a few central
> issues. Arguments could be made in both types of gains in insight.
> Psychotherapy may function, in part, by teaching the skills of
> acquiring insight…. To the extent that such skills are acquired, there
> is a greater likelihood that an important specific insight is obtained,
> leading to improvements in symptoms and functioning. (p. 161)

The most recent agreed upon definition by an impressive number of
researchers from all diverse kinds of therapy runs as follows:

> Insight usually is conscious (as opposed to unconscious or implicit)
> and involves both a sense of *newness* (i.e., the client understands
> something in a new way) and in making *connections* (e.g., figuring
> out the relationship between past and present events, the therapist
> and significant others, cognition and affect, or disparate statements).
> Hence, most of us agreed that we could define insight as a conscious
> meaning shift involving new connections (i.e., "this relates to that"
> or some sense of causality). (Hill, Castonguay, & Angus, 2007, p.
> 442)

This corresponds to agreement among psychoanalytically oriented scientists that a kind of integrative activity of mind is a predominant feature of insight (Kris, 1956). Melvin Scharfman (see the panel report by Blacker, 1981, p. 660) presented a very short definition: "Insight is bridging different levels of mind." The term *emotional insight* refers to the fact that self-knowledge is not sufficient to produce changes in patients. Emotional aspects have to be integrated with cognitive aspects of self-awareness.

We regard emotional insight as integration of different frameworks of self-perception. Inner experiences can either be perceived on a framework of emotional reactions or on a framework of cognitive judgments (Caspar & Berger, 2007). The patient deals with self-perceptions in an insightful manner if he is able to integrate the emotional access with a cognitive access to inner experiences. If we define insight in this way there are striking similarities between insight and the concept of tolerance of ambiguity (Frenkel-Brunswik, 1949). Different frameworks of a self-perception have influence similar to the stimulus ambiguity of outer perceptions, and they may provoke certain psychic conflicts (Hohage, 1986). As Kafka (1971) points out, tolerance of ambiguity in self-perception and in social interaction is a prerequisite of emotional growth.

Method: The Rating Procedure

The Emotional Insight Rating Scale is a content analysis approach using verbatim transcripts of psychotherapeutic sessions. The raters do not have to be clinically trained because the judgments are based on the language characteristics and not on clinical inferences. The rater has mainly to follow his intuitions based on his knowledge of the natural language and his common sense.

Coding units are single significant statements by the patient with a minimum length of 10 lines of text. A significant statement is delimited either by the analyst's statements or by pauses of a minimum of 10 seconds.

I   Extent of Experiencing

The coding units are rated on a six-point scale (gwE-Scale) according to the extent of experiencing included. There are two points of view that must be taken into account. First, experiencing requires references in the patient's statements to his "inner world"—to his thoughts, feelings, fantasies, and wishes. If he only deals with concrete interactions or with descriptions of other people or of situations, there is no reference to experiencing. It must be possible to reformulate his statements in a meaningful way according to a statement such as, "The patient is internally ... or internally does ..." Second, statements of the patient refer to experiencing only if the patient focuses his attention on this inner world. He has to deal with it consciously and to refer directly to it. The nature of insight requires that the patient recognizes internal acts. This operationalization of experiencing has important consequences: Even if a patient is accusing another person in an emotional way, his statements are not rated as revealing experiencing unless he refers consciously and directly to his own feelings. If the coding unit does not refer to any experiencing, it is excluded from further ratings.

2   Emotional Access

The emotional access to experiencing is determined by rating on a five-point scale to assess how much the patient is immersed in his experiences (Sub-Scale E). We choose the phrase *immersed in experiences* because it has connotations of "feelings," "lack of control," and even "overwhelmed." By analyzing portions of text that obviously showed a strong emotional access to experiencing we found three main factors indicating modes of being immersed:

a) The intensity and vividness of the experienced feelings
b) The extent of imaginative plasticity of the experiences
c) The extent of the spontaneity and presence of experiencing

The first indicator refers mainly to the patient's affectivity while the second and the third indicators refer more to the primary process thinking or to the concept of regression in the service of the ego. The following statement may illustrate how the patient is immersed in her experiencing:

> Oh, that girl, Cathy! I think sometimes I wanted to kill her! I guess she is the only person I would like to put my hands around her throat and choke—where really I must be aware not to have really bad wishes toward her; really bad, you know. She is so, so domineering and haughty, when I imagine how she walks and how she writes her name. I know about each piece of her hair and her skin and I detested her. I hated her like nobody else.

3   Cognitive Access

The cognitive access to experiencing is determined by rating on a five-point scale, the degree to which the patient is at a distance from his experiences (Sub-Scale C). Again, by analyzing typical statements, we isolated three factors indicating that the patient is at some distance:

a) The extent to which the patient observes his experiencing, wonders about it, and describes it ironically or expresses it in abstract terms
b) The extent to which the patient evaluates his experiencing by classifying, by judging, by summarizing, or by confronting it with reality
c) The extent to which the patient tries to give logical explanations or to analyze his experiences

The cognitive access to experiencing is illustrated by the following statement:

> In a certain way I suspect that this behavior of mine is sort of tricky and that it always plays a role. But when I reflect on this, and when I try to find my own way of living, then I am aware that it is necessary to keep on this way, and that I have to clarify my point of view, and strengthen my convictions. I think in the area of sexuality I've changed my mind in recent years, and the only problem is that I can't discuss this point of view in the right way.

4   Rating of Ambiguity

The raters were instructed to judge the coding units on Sub-Scale E and Sub-Scale C independently, although the scales are in some respect antagonistic. Normally opposites do not vary independently. However, the independent rating procedure opens the possibility that the emotional as well as the cognitive access to experiencing is integrated and therefore present at the same time. In this case we regard the contradictions to be logical ones and integration of this contradiction is synonymous with logical ambiguity. The following statement represents this kind of logical ambiguity:

> The water in that dream, so much water! That was incredibly exciting, how this woman pulled the wagon through the water and it splashed around and she had trouble keeping the wagon on track. That was a—Oh, the water! (Laughs) Now I know, oh I know what it means, the water and splashing, and before that the snake as a symbol. Oh I don't have to go on. Lately I've been very fascinated reading a report that described the origin of life, proteins, sperm, procreation … extraordinary and fascinating!

The combination of two subscales denoting opposite dimensions includes four extreme positions, as shown in Figure 5.1.

Polarization reflects a position in which only one access to experiencing is present. Logical ambiguity reflects a position where both kinds of access are present at the same time. If neither an emotional nor a cognitive access is present in the given text, the patient is in a neutral position. The scores of subscale E as well as of subscale C indicate some kind of active involvement of the patient. In a neutral position there is no involvement at all. We assess the total involvement of the patient by adding the scores of the subscales E and C (IN-Score = E/2+C/2)

In principal, ambiguity can be calculated by multiplying the scores of both subscales. By definition no ambiguity is observable when one subscale has a zero score; multiplication therefore is an adequate operation.

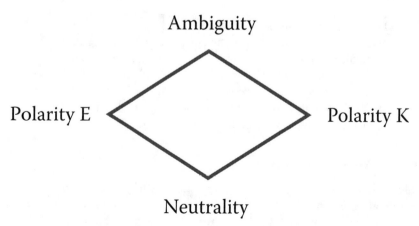

Figure 5.1 Extreme positions obtained by the combination of subscales E and C.

We observed, however, that sometimes by chance there are high scores on both scales without any integration, because being immersed and being at a distance are not related to each other. To avoid such pseudo-ambiguity, the rater has to judge the extent of ambiguity on a separate five-point rating scale (EC-Scale). He has to especially take into account the degree of tension between being immersed and being at a distance at the same time.

In summary the rater has to answer the following questions regarding the manual instructions:

1. Which are the coding units?
2. How important is the experiencing reported according to the weighting scale?
3. How intense are the emotional access and the cognitive access to experiencing?
4. What is the extent of ambiguity?

The verbatim transcripts are judged by three raters. They obtained five scores from each statement: gwE-Score, E-Score, C-Score, EC-Score, and the IN-Score.

Empirical Investigations

We now report on changes of emotional insight in the course of the psychoanalysis of Ms. Amalia X, our research case. We compared the initial phase of the treatment—that is, the first eight sessions—to the eight sessions just before termination. As the treatment was successful according to clinical judgment as well as psychodiagnostic test results we expected that there would be more insight at termination than at the beginning. Therefore, all significant statements of the initial phase and of the termination phase were rated on the emotional insight scales. The rates doing this job were blind to the location of the session. Table 5.1 shows the reliability of these ratings. Following thorough training, three raters showed a high degree of agreement based on $n = 216$ ratings, with reliabilities ranging between 0.85 and 0.88.

Table 5.1 Reliability of Statement Scores

	Cronbach's Alpha Coefficient (Pooled for Three Judges)
E-Score	0.87
C-Score	0.87
EC-Score	0.85
IN-Score	0.88
gwE-Score	0.88

In comparing the initial phase of this treatment to the termination phase, we had to take into account that there are time-series dependencies among the statements during each session, so that for statistical evaluation we could not treat the single statements as independent test samples. No time-series dependency, however, was detected when we compared not single statements but the mean scores for each session.

Table 5.2 shows the average of eight mean scores of the initial sessions and of eight termination sessions. The table reveals that there is significant increase of the emotional access, of ambiguity, of involvement, and of experiencing. The scores for the cognitive access show a slight decrease at the termination phase. We determined the p-value from the t-test (one-tailed). Although the number of cases is only eight in each sample, the differences are statistically significant with the exception of the C-Scores.

The data indicate that the emotional insight increased, as we expected. The increase in the emotional access is of special clinical interest also because the patient, as described before, reacted in a self-conscious, often obsessive-compulsive manner, which is reflected in the high C-Scores in the initial phase. In this case particularly, the increase in emotional involvement appears to be an important indicator of therapeutic change.

Discussion

We have reported on a method for assessing certain aspects of emotional insight and we have demonstrated changes in emotional insight in the course of early and late sessions taken from psychoanalysis.

This approach consists of a quantitative assessment not only of insight itself but of the emotional and the cognitive involvement of the patient as well. Of course therapeutic change is reflected not only by different insight scores. Nonetheless it may indicate an important step if the patient begins to deal with himself and not only with other persons. In such cases an increase in the extent of experiencing is a relevant result. The patient described in this report, however, seems to be psychologically minded and often deals with her own thoughts and feelings. Therefore, changes in the experiencing score here are of less importance. On the other hand, under the impact

Table 5.2 Average of Eight Mean Scores of the Initial Phase and of Eight Mean Scores of the Termination Phase

Mean Score of Sessions	E-Score	C-Score	EC-Score	IN-Score	gwE-Score
Sessions 1–8	1.04	1.24	0.31	1.14	1.42
Sessions 510–217	1.63	1.16	0.68	1.39	1.79
n = 16	$p < 0.01$	n.s.	$p < 0.01$	$p < 0.05$	$p < 0.01$

of psychic conflict this patient seems to strengthen her cognitive access to experiencing, and it is therefore an important therapeutic change that, under the pressure of termination, she is able to remain emotionally involved. This finding is supplementary to the finding of increased insight scores.

By rating not only integration but the emotional and the cognitive access separately as well, we differ from other content analysis approaches that quantify related phenomena, such as the Meaningfulness Scale of Isaacs and Haggard (1966), the Productivity Scale of Simon, Fink, and Endicott (1967), and especially the Experiencing Scale, provided by Gendlin and Tomlinson (1962). The Experiencing Scale has some striking similarities to our approach, but the cognitive dimension is neglected, as criticized by Wexler (1974). Another recent interesting measure is the Rutgers Psycho-therapy Progress Scale (RPPS; Messer & McWilliams, 2007, p. 21) "that was designed to measure patient progress using context that precedes the material to be rated."

One has to take into account, however, that this approach only deter-mines certain aspects of insight, not insight itself. By focusing on the patient's access to experiencing, the concept of insight as an increase in self-knowledge or of insight as awareness of unconscious motives is neglected. We cannot rule out that the patient may report in an insightful way but about insignificant matters or that she draws the wrong con-clusions. The correctness of her conclusions or the significance of her thoughts can be decided only by clinical judgment, and this judgment may itself be right or wrong. On the other hand, a decrease in emotional insight as well as an increase in resistance, if observed in the course of psychoanalytic treatment, cannot simply be regarded as a step backward. The psychoanalytic process has more than one dimension and becoming more insightful is only one among many targets of the process. In the ser-vice of therapeutic progress it may be necessary that the patient develops resistances and activates conflicts. Only if it is impossible to overcome such resistances and to work through relationship problems, will the ther-apeutic effect be questioned. We offer the emotional insight scale to help study such developments and thereby contribute to the understanding of the therapeutic process.

5.3   CHANGES IN SELF-ESTEEM[*]

Self-Esteem as a Concept in Treatment Research

In the personality research of recent years, self-esteem and a number of related concepts have played an increasingly important part, as Cheshire and Thomä (1987) show. This development has continued; at present clini-cal aspects are discussed as well (Bracken, 1996). Stipulated by the theory

---

[*] L. Neudert-Dreyer, H-J. Grünzig, & H. Thomä; adapted from Neudert et al. (1987).

of mentalization—the theory-of-mind discussion in developmental psychology—a psychoanalytic highly relevant discussion was opened (Fonagy et al., 2002).

In systematic empirical psychoanalytic research, such concepts as self-esteem largely have been neglected. Nevertheless, it is precisely this concept that can, in our opinion, most readily create meaningful links between process and outcome research, because it is a variable, equally relevant to both process and outcome. If the process of therapy is understood as a gradual acquisition of certain attitudes and abilities, and if outcome is assessed in terms of the possession and availability for action of these very attitudes and abilities, then it follows that the researcher should gather information about those features of the patient that are reflections of this process of acquisition and its stability of outcome.

In psychoanalytic theory construction, and also in clinical practice, self-esteem was for a long time regarded as an epiphenomenon without greater psychodynamic importance. Freud (1914c) uses the concept not so much as a technical term but somewhat colloquially, though in close connection with the idea of narcissism. He mentions three factors that constitute self-esteem:

1. Everything a person possesses or achieves, every remnant of the primitive feeling of omnipotence that experience has confirmed
2. The fulfillment of the ego-ideal, which represents the lost narcissism of infancy
3. The satisfaction of being loved in the context of a narcissistic object-choice

Self-esteem acquired theoretical and clinical importance in connection with the wider dissemination of the concept of narcissism and its revised formulation (Kohut, 1971, 1977). But also, independently of its involvement in narcissism theory (and consequently also in drive theory), increasing attention was being paid within psychoanalysis to the self and self-esteem, especially since self-psychology can be seen as a consequential development of ego psychology (Dare and Holder, 1981; Thomä, 1980).

In client-centered psychotherapy, the concepts of self-esteem and self-acceptance, respectively, are of major importance for the underlying theory of personality and psychotherapy. Rogers's (1959) process model assumes that the client will increasingly be able to develop self-esteem by means of the unconditional positive regard of the therapist. Acceptance by others, however, does not lead directly to self-acceptance but rather creates a secure atmosphere free of fear. The client can experience, reevaluate, and thus diminish incongruities between experiences and self-concept in such a climate without feeling threatened.

The increase in self-esteem in turn makes it possible for the client to integrate experiences, which until now were not, or not correctly, symbolized. Cheshire and Thomä (1987a, p. 127) discuss how Rogers's (1959) concept of the therapist's "regard" relates to specifically psychoanalytic hypotheses about the functioning of the transference and the "helping alliance"; and they also indicate how some of Rogers's assumptions have been tested empirically.

We supplement this clinical framework by a model derived from general psychological self-concept research, which seems appropriate for generating process hypotheses (Epstein, 1979). According to this model, a distinction has to be made between global self-esteem and a situation or area-specific type. In our investigation we had data on the external situation at our disposal, but these data were altered by the subjective reaction of the patient. We therefore refrained from dividing between these two criteria of classification (i.e., external situation versus subjective quality of emotions) and started from the assumption that overall self-esteem is constituted by components of self-esteem drawn from different life areas or problem areas. With these theoretical considerations established, we now turn to our empirical process study.

Case Description and Hypotheses

The study aims at testing process hypotheses related to changes in self-esteem in the course of the psychoanalytic treatment of the patient described in Chapter 4 in this volume. However, it is timely to remember the important investigation of Meyer and von Zerssen (1960), who studied women with idiopathic hirsutism. Those researchers, both psychoanalysts, pointed out that the combination of genetic factors and stress reactions may lead to an increase of the level of androgens. In women suffering from hirsutism in absence of distinct genetic disposition the handling of stressful situations most likely is not very favorable (see Fava & Sonino, 2000).

This assumption is favored by the circumstance that neurotic disturbances that are independent from the hirsute symptomatology are seen more frequently in these women. Speculating on the ground of their empirical findings Meyer and von Zerssen (1960) assume that a hirsute endocrine disturbance in females reactivates a widespread unconscious wish to be a man. As a sequelae, many women suffer from problems of acceptance. Meyer (1963) clearly distinguishes between a decrease of subjective acceptance (can I love me as I am?) and an assumed rejection by significant others (can he or she love me as I am?).

Therefore, we take up the consideration and state the following:

a) Hirsutism reactivates the wish to be a man and therefore leads to problems in female identity.
b) Women with hirsutism suffer from a problem of acceptance.

Hypotheses

In investigating changes of self-esteem in the psychoanalytic process, we are especially interested in three areas: (1) changes in general self-esteem, and in area-specific self-esteem as a function of the therapeutic process; (2) the impact of acceptance by important objects, especially the psychoanalyst, upon changes in self-esteem; and (3) the identification of intrapsychic conditions that are obstacles to an increase in self-esteem.

In explicitly formulating the hypotheses, it is assumed that these phenomena can be subject to objective assessment only insofar as they are openly verbalized by the patient. With this restriction we are formulating hypotheses about both general and area-specific changes in self-esteem.

General Hypotheses

A person's self-esteem is decidedly dependent upon his feeling accepted by significant others (acceptance by others). This relationship between self-esteem and acceptance by others is of essential importance for determining the *level* of self-esteem and also contributes to the actual genesis and maintenance of self-esteem in the first place. Consequently, the patient's capacity for developing solid self-esteem in the course of therapeutic treatment depends upon his capacity for experiencing acceptance by others; and in the realm of psychoanalytic treatment, the psychoanalyst is of course regarded as a paradigmatic "significant other" for the patient. A successful treatment process should therefore display an increase in the experience of acceptance by others and, consequently, an increase in self-esteem.

This acceptance by others is experienced first of all in the therapeutic relationship. This repeated experience of being accepted in therapy enables the patient to question his hitherto unfavorable and negative self-estimation. This is regarded as a prerequisite for the patient's new experiences outside therapy, namely those to do with feeling accepted by others. This new experience of feeling accepted by others consequently enables the patient to accept himself.

This therapeutic strategy is above all aimed at reducing the discrepancy between the experienced self and the ideal self and, therefore, aimed at reducing self-esteem. In addition, psychotherapy must supply for the patient relief from his threatening superego, and this may be achieved by working through the feared consequences of those sexual and aggressive wishes that the patient is regarding here and now as equally dangerous as he did in his childhood.

Area-Specific Hypotheses

We restricted ourselves to three essential problem areas for this patient: (1) the area of body, sexuality and female identity; (2) the area of achievement and success; and (3) the area of aggressivity and assertiveness. Our formulations related to the patient's psychodynamics and to the derivation of process hypotheses for each of the three problem areas were as follows.

Problem Area: Body, Sexuality, and Female Identity—Psychodynamic Considerations

The virile body hair leads to insecurities on the patient's side concerning her female identity. Real or assumed rejections decrease the patient's self-esteem, which is a further negative feedback for her attitude toward her body and her sexuality: Of special importance in this respect is her anticipation of rejection by men. Therefore she is doomed to fail, both with respect to her ego-ideal, by which she is obliged to be a valuable woman with an integrated sexuality, and with respect to her superego, which prohibits the fulfillment of her sexual needs.

Another most important influence in this area is the patient's relationship to her mother. Besides needing acknowledgement by men, a positively experienced female identity can only result out of the fact that mother figures are positively perceived in their female identity and that these present good objects of identification. In the case of this patient, it is to be expected that her insecurity with respect to her identity as a woman is connected with a negative attitude toward mother figures.

Process Hypotheses

Since the patient's sexual needs are closely related to feelings of guilt and to castration fantasies, an elaboration and eventual realization of her sexual needs can be expected only when the themes of guilt and punishment have been worked through. An indispensable step is the acceptance of her autoerotic needs. These psychodynamics will play an important part in the transference neurosis. Her insecure female identity can be overcome to the extent that she is able to perceive positive elements in her "mother figures."

Problem Area: Achievement and Success— Psychodynamic Considerations

The patient's low self-esteem is expressed, among other things, in her low confidence in successfully achieving something. This especially relates to her work and to the social field. The patient's unconscious fear of envy and of consequent aggression from others can be traced back biographically to the relationship to her brothers, from whom she had actually experienced such consequences of achievement on her own part. With her low self-esteem, she is highly dependent upon acceptance by others. Therefore, she experiences the danger of being rejected or attacked as especially danger-ous. The patient can be seen to be in the following dilemma: If she achieves too little, her self-esteem decreases, but if she achieves more than others, then she has to be afraid of their envy and aggression.

Process Hypotheses

In this problem area it is necessary to work through her feelings of guilt about achievement; she has to become independent of valuation and appre-ciation from her brothers to be able to be successful without constantly fearing envy and aggression; in addition, she has to gain the experience that she can tolerate envy and aggression if they occur.

Problem Area: Aggressivity and Assertiveness— Psychodynamic Considerations

This problem area overlaps to some extent with the previous one. If she is not able to be assertive in an aggressive manner toward others, her self-esteem decreases. If, by contrast, she does try to be aggressive, feelings of guilt emerge out of her fantasy that her aggressivity could mutilate or (even worse) destroy others. There is a discrepancy in this problem area, too: On the one hand, she wants to be able to pursue her needs aggressively, but on the other hand she feels that such dangerous aggressive tendencies are prohibited.

Process Hypotheses

These problems can be worked through directly in the therapeutic relation-ship. Experiencing acceptance by the analyst, even though she has aggres-sive fantasies, is a prerequisite for accepting her aggressivity herself.

Sample and Method

Sample

From the treatment, which consisted of 517 tape-recorded sessions, a sample of 115 verbatim transcribed sessions was used in this study. This sample of sessions was made up of 21 separate periods of consecutive ses-sions taken from different stages of treatment: namely, the first 10 and the last 10 sessions, plus 19 five-session periods taken at regular intervals in between. The reason for choosing longer runs of sessions at the beginning and end of treatment was that we wanted to have a broader database for making comparisons between the beginning and the end of treatment.

The Category System for Content Analysis

To test the hypotheses, we created a category system for content analysis consisting of 23 categories. When defining these categories for the purpose of a coding manual (cf. Neudert & Grünzig, 1983), we were careful to stay as close as possible to direct observation, which is an important condition for getting reliable judgments from nonexperts, because it minimizes the need for inference and interpretation. The 23 content categories, as used in the main study, together with their resultant reliability values are listed in Table 5.3. (Details to the definitions of the categories are presented in the original paper.)

Table 5.3 Reliability Values Derived from Combined Ratings According to the Formula of Spearman-Brown (Lienert, 1969)

Number	Category	Reliability Value
1	Positive self-esteem	0.81
2	Negative self-esteem	0.92
3	Positive acceptance by others	0.95
4	Negative acceptance by others	0.76
5	Positive view of motherly significant others	0.83
6	Negative view of motherly significant others	0.94
7	Motherly significant others (neutral view)	0.95
8	Fatherly significant others	0.97
9	Analyst	0.96
10	Female peers	0.98
11	Male peers	0.97
12	Brothers	0.99
13	Body	0.90
14	Body hair	0.98
15	Sexuality	0.97
16	Real heterosexuality	0.98
17	Imagined heterosexuality	0.96
18	Autoeroticism	0.98
19	Security concerning female identity	0.73
20	Insecurity concerning female identity	0.73
21	Achievement, success	0.90
22	Aggressivity, assertiveness	0.88
23	Feelings of guilt, fear of punishment	0.88

Evaluation

In order to test the trends we used Forster and Stuart's (1954) "record-breaker" and a linearity test (Cochrane, 1954); for the frequency of categories we used a test for change in level (ibid.); and in the case of the correlation coefficients, we computed product-moment values and tested their significance.

Although the most powerful model for describing time-series fluctuations is autoaggressive integrated moving average (ARIMA) (Box & Jenkins, 1976), we had to give it up in the end for two reasons. First, our data took the form of frequency counts with many zero values, and this seemed inappropriate to the parametric algorithm of ARIMA. Second, our time sampling is made up from a number of separate blocks, and it became apparent that the five-session blocks were too short to allow us to compute both ARIMA-based time dependencies and our process-dependent hypotheses.

Results and Discussion

Results of Process Study

The two central hypotheses about changes in overall self-esteem could be confirmed. That is, positive self-esteem increased during the course of treatment ($p < 0.01$), but the trend did not set in right at the start of treatment but only after wide fluctuations over the first 100 sessions; negative self-esteem, on the other hand, showed a continuous decrease from the beginning of treatment ($p < 0.01$). However, the hypotheses to do with changes in acceptance by others were not confirmed, because there were no systematic trends. Nor were the hypotheses to do with the relative incidence of different categories before and after focal working through confirmed. But with regard to hypotheses about differences between correlations among categories, there are indeed two confirmatory results: Self-esteem in connection with imagined heterosexuality improved according to expectations ($p < 0.05$), and negative self-esteem in connection with autoeroticism decreased as predicted ($p < 0.05$).

Comparison between the Beginning and the End of Therapy

In addition to our investigation of the continuous treatment process, we present a comparison between initial and terminal stages of the treatment, and we establish a connection between research on the treatment process and that on treatment outcome. We are referring here to the same variables as we used in the process study and are supplementing them by the use of typical standardized personality questionnaires.

As a sample for this comparison of initial and terminal treatment periods, we used the first 10 treatment sessions and the last 10 treatment sessions that were evaluated by means of the same content-analysis system. It is necessary to state that the raters were blind for the location of the sessions within the treatment. For statistical purposes, we are assuming the independence of these two samples. This assumption seems plausible since an objective period of five years has passed in the course of treatment, during which the essential problems of the patient have decidedly changed.

For each of the content-analytic categories, a test was done on the differences between the means of the two samples. Those eight variables whose significance value is $p = 0.10$ or less were included in a multivariate analysis of variance (MANOVA) (discriminant analysis). As was expected, the two samples were sharply discriminated by these variables ($F = 20.8$; d.f. = 41.15; $p < 0.01$), although only four of these variables contributed substantially to the discriminant function because of high intercorrelations (Table 5.4). These four variables are the categories "positive self-esteem" (1), "negative self-esteem" (2), "fatherly significant others" (8), and "analyst" (9).

Let us briefly summarize these findings. The level of the patient's self-esteem at the end of treatment is considerably higher than at the beginning. She talks less often about father figures and more often in contrast about the analyst and about peer men. Her brothers have lost their importance to a considerable extent at the end of treatment, as also her negative experience of mother figures decreased. She does not mention her body hair anymore and is more secure in the realm of the autoerotic as well as in that of her female identity.

Compared with her state at the beginning of therapy, the patient is presenting herself as a woman who has succeeded in her psychic separation from parents and siblings and who is able to establish relationships with

Table 5.4 The Eight Statistically Significant Categories for the First 10 and Last 10 Treatment Sessions: Means, t-Values, and Probabilities (p) for t

Number	Category	First 10	Last 10	p	t (Two-Tailed)
1	Positive self-esteem	2.4	5.8	−2.67	0.02
2	Negative self-esteem	20.4	7.7	7.07	0.00
6	Negative view of motherly significant others	2.0	0.6	2.41	0.03
8	Negative view of fatherly significant others	8.5	2.6	2.08	0.06
9	Analyst	5.6	14.5	−3.77	0.00
11	Male peers	7.4	15.2	−2.80	0.01
12	Brothers	9.2	2.3	3.22	0.00
14	Body hair	1.1	0.0	1.72	0.10

people who are of significance for her reality life and for the further development of her life circumstances.

Theoretical Considerations

Our conception of overall self-esteem as being composed of a number of area-specific elements, which had the advantage of lending itself readily to objective testing, was always perhaps somewhat simplistic and only one of various possibilities. Another of these possibilities, which is more consistent with our results, is that area-specific and general self-esteem are in fact a good deal more independent than we had supposed. Our results on the topic of overall self-esteem may reflect something more akin to Bandura's (1977) conception of "self-efficacy," which consists in a fundamental sense of being able to bring about changes in one's life but is entirely consistent with having problems in specific areas of self-esteem and consequently bringing them into therapy. It may well be this essential independence, which has been captured in our observation, that ratings of area-specific esteem fluctuate much more widely over the sessions (perhaps because they are relatively situation-specific and cognitively monitored), whereas overall self-esteem (which may reflect a more fundamental emotional property) stays relatively constant over time.

Furthermore, it is perhaps to be expected that during the course of therapy the patient's problems with overall self-esteem will be analyzed out into more specific areas that then become individually the focus of attention at different times and with different degrees of attendant anxiety or other emotion. Since also a main function of therapy, at least from the patient's point of view, is to deal with difficulties and malfunctions in various areas, it is not surprising that what she actually talks about (and what is therefore recorded in the categories) does not show either an increase in general positive self-evaluation or a decrease in its negative counterpart.

Our study also set out to clarify how favorable changes in self-esteem might be brought about in therapy, and for this purpose we paid attention both to its presumed infantile origins and also to here-and-now experiences of being accepted by others. Accordingly, we assumed that the analyst would function as a catalyst for both these sorts of feeling, by serving as a projection screen in the transference and by exemplifying acceptance by others in the reality-situation. We were unable, however, to draw any conclusions on this point from the category scores, since there were too few references to acceptance by others (in only 15 out of 115 sessions) to allow us to compute their correlation with references to the analyst, as would have been necessary to serve as the evidence relevant to our hypotheses. Two suggestions may be made about why this was the case.

First, the analyst's acceptance of the patient would have been communicated largely, and even exclusively perhaps, by nonverbal means, which the patient would have acknowledged and responded to not by explicit verbalization but by, for example, being able to relax and produce more material that she felt able to release in the atmosphere of acceptance. It will be evident from this that we were conceptualizing the therapist's acceptance as a quite specific factor in the treatment of patients suffering from disturbances in self-esteem and not simply as part of a generally facilitating background.

The second possibility is that the patient had internalized rejecting objects from the past so effectively that she was unable to perceive any acceptance in some contexts of her present situation even when it was there. This impression is given by many passages of the verbatim transcript, including one where she indicates that it is self-evident to her that every man will experience her hairiness as repulsive, without her ever having taken the risk of encountering this judgment in reality. From this point of view it might be expected that such obstructive internalizations gradually become to be recognized for what they are, in the course of therapy, and are eventually tested out in reality against the perceived judgments of currently significant others—in which case, an increase in the categories to do with acceptance by others is to be expected. But this result would be observed only if the testing out were explicitly reported in therapy, as opposed to being alluded to or symbolized in the latent content of various utterances or taking the form of an improvement in interpersonal perceptions and social skills. To clarify these questions further it would be important to establish whether the therapist did in fact give, for example, nonverbal indications of acceptance, which were simply not recognized as such by the patient, or whether such cues were unclear, inconsistent, or infrequent.

A second general purpose of our study, apart from that of trying to monitor changes in self-esteem, was to use the category data to test a model of the therapeutic process according to which it is seen as a succession of focal working through of particular psychodynamic themes. To this end we formulated a number of hypotheses about changes in three problem areas that might be apparent after relevant focal working through had taken place. But these hypotheses, which were couched in terms of differences between mean values of category usage and changes in correlation values, were supported by the data in only two instances.

Therefore, our findings do not in themselves support such a model, but we are aware that our method of identifying a therapeutic focus (see Section 5.6), although appropriate enough in itself, may have been invalidated by the fact that our sampling left out 80% of the total data. As far as the process model itself goes, even changes that do set in after certain themes have been worked through focally cannot be expected to do so at once, let alone to be revealed immediately in overt verbal behavior. In any case, we suppose that focal working through may be only a necessary, and not a sufficient, condition for lasting psychological change. It may simply lay the foundations for revised patterns of information processing and cognitive structuring, which in turn are the basis for acquiring alternative ways of behaving. In this case, to base calculations on data from sessions immediately after a therapeutic focus is to fail to give such complex processes time to develop.

These are all points to be borne in mind for future studies of the complex processes that contribute to beneficial change, such as was observed in this case, over the course of interpretive psychoanalytic therapy.

5.4   SUFFERING FROM ONESELF AND FROM OTHERS*

Theoretical Remarks

All psychotherapeutic schools agree that a patient's motivation to seek therapy depends decisively on the degree of suffering at the beginning of treatment. However, opinions differ as to how important suffering becomes in the course of therapy. Moreover, within psychoanalysis one finds contradictory views.

In "Lines of Advance in Psycho-Analytic Therapy" Freud (1919a) took a strong position on this question:

> Cruel though it may sound, we must see to it that the patient's suffering, to a degree that is in some way or other effective, does not come to an end prematurely. If, owing to the symptoms having been taken apart and having lost their value, his suffering becomes mitigated, we must reinstate it elsewhere in the form of some appreciable privations; otherwise we run the danger of never achieving any improvements except quite insignificant and transitory ones. (p. 163)

The technical means by which Freud (1919) tried to achieve this was the rule of abstinence in order to frustrate the patient's instinctual wishes. The energy, finding no discharge, would flow back to its infantile origins and bring their representations to consciousness, leading to the conflict being recalled instead of being acted out. From this point of view the patient must suffer in order to improve.

These considerations, anchored in Freud's theories of energies and instincts, have influenced psychoanalytic practice until today. The rule of abstinence, more than any other of Freud's technical recommendations, was set up as an absolute by many psychoanalysts and often has become a synonym for the psychoanalytic attitude. This frequently created an unhealthy

---

* Lisbeth Neudert-Dreyer, Hans-J. Grünzig, and Helmut Thomä; adapted from Neudert et al. (1987).

climate in psychoanalytic treatments so that even in 1967 Greenson warned in his popular textbook against excessive frustration of the patient because this would produce "interminable or interrupted analyses" (p. 278). Of course, many psychoanalysts soon started to justify the rule of abstinence not so much by theoretical but by technical considerations, because they were getting more and more skeptical of the economical aspects of the libido theory. Abstinence was no longer to maintain the suffering of the patient but to guarantee the objectivity of the psychoanalyst—objectivity as seen from a positivistic ideal of science.

There is one approach that in our opinion deserves particular interest: the control–mastery theory (Weiss, Sampson, & The Mount Zion Psychotherapy Research Group, 1986). In this theory the patient's transference behavior is defined as an instrument of reality testing: In the relationship with his psychoanalyst, the patient wants to test whether his unconscious pathogenic beliefs are true. These beliefs are the result not of instinctual wishes but of a primitive theorizing originating in conflict situations of childhood. Being influenced by these theories the patient sets aside important life goals and establishes defense mechanisms, inhibitions, and symptoms. It depends on the behavior of the psychoanalyst whether these infantile theories will appear confirmed or refuted. To be abstinent in this context means to pass the patient's test—that is, to *not* fulfill his pathogenic expectations.

In regard to the patient's suffering, the control-mastery theory predicts that the psychoanalyst, by means of being abstinent according to this theoretical view, refutes the threatening beliefs and thus meets the unconscious hope that led the patient to seek help in analysis. Instead of suffering more, the patient will feel relieved and relaxed because of his psychoanalyst's passing the test. This model of the psychoanalytic process was empirically tested against the process model derived from the theory of instincts repeatedly and turned out to be superior (cf. Weiss et al., 1986).

We think that often different sources of suffering related to the psychoanalyst get mixed up. First, it may be the expression of a patient's specific conflict. Second, he may suffer due to specific characteristics of the psychoanalyst's personality, because every negative transference reaction has a larger or smaller component that is focused on the specific personality of the psychoanalyst and how it has been shaped during his professional education, a point emphasized by Gill (1982). And last, the patient may eventually experience suffering due to the psychoanalyst's *technique*. Only this is the context of the suffering related to abstinence.

Unfortunately, neither critics nor defenders of a particular psychoanalytic view present empirical data to support their opinions. This single case study is an attempt to offer data on this subject. We are interested in the following questions:

a) Which part of the patient's suffering during psychoanalysis is related to his psychoanalyst? Which part has other sources? What are those?

b) How does the suffering in regard to the psychoanalyst change in the course of treatment? Is it constantly present as one would expect according to Freud? Is it worse at the beginning, while the therapist's behavior is still unfamiliar and strange? Or is there a crisis in the course of treatment? If so, what causes it?

c) How much suffering related to the therapist is in fact due to his abstinence?

d) What does the therapist do when he becomes the object of the patient's suffering?

Methods

Since we have previously described the method (Neudert, Kübler, & Schors, 1985) we can be brief. We investigated a single case because only this kind of study permits an examination in detail of the variability of suffering during the psychoanalysis. It also offers the opportunity to gather complex and differentiated information, including qualitative clinical data that enable the generation of more adequate hypotheses about the psychoanalytic process. The study was carried out on verbatim transcripts of psychoanalytic sessions by means of content analysis methods. Since none of the available content analysis instruments for measuring painful affects (Dollard & Auld, 1959; Dollard & Mowrer, 1947; Gottschalk & Gleser, 1969; Knapp et al., 1975; Mahl, 1961) was suitable for our questions, we developed two special content analysis manuals.

Manual I was used by independent judges to identify all sequences in the verbatim transcripts in which the patient verbalized painful or unpleasant feelings. In a second step the judges scored the degree of suffering and the way of dealing with it as it was expressed in the pertinent sequences. This manual consists of four distinct categories and four rating scales. In this chapter we refer to only two of the rating scales:

a) A five-point rating scale for judging the *intensity of suffering* in every sequence of the text where suffering was expressed. The various values of intensity from one session are added up to yield a sum score of "global suffering" (GS) for each session.

b) Another five-point scale on which the independent judges mark the degree of the patient's *helplessness in dealing with his suffering* for every pertinent sequence.

After having been corrected according to the Spearman-Brown formula (cf. Lienert, 1969, p. 119), Pearson's r as the coefficient of reliability between judges was .85 for both rating scales.

Manual II was used to measure what the patient suffered from or what he "blamed" for his suffering. The coding units were the same sequences that were identified according to Manual I. The main categories are "self" and "environment." The judgment is made on a five-point scale with the poles labeled "the suffering is exclusively related to self" and "the suffering is exclusively related to environment." If the environment is involved (i.e., when the raters check off one of the scale points between 2 and 5), they additionally have to choose one of the following subcategories:

Human environment (h)
Therapist (th)
Extra-human environment (e) (e.g., weather, fortune, animals)

When the raters are not able to decide who the patient blamed, they are to choose the category "unclear."

The measures of agreement were also very adequate for Manual II: Pearson's r (again corrected according to Spearman-Brown) for the rating scale "relatedness of suffering" was .92 ($n = 342$), and the Kappa coefficients (Cohen, 1960), which we used to compute the agreement on nominal data, were .76 for the three types of environment and .75 for the category "unclear."

Our *sample* consisted of 7 blocks of 8 consecutive sessions each for a total of 56 sessions. We chose this type of sample in order to be able to explore thematic connections across several sessions as well as examine medium-term effects of therapeutic interventions. The 7 blocks were spread over the entire treatment at varying intervals to avoid periodically recurring effects. For a discussion of sampling problems in time series see Grünzig (1988).

Results

Given the independent psychometric evaluations (Chapter 4 in this volume) we assumed that our process data would also show a successful course of treatment. For this purpose we used a nonparametric trend test for dichotomous data according to Haldane and Smith (1947–1949). The course of each variable can be described as a negative monotonic trend, that is, "global suffering" ($z = -2.14$; $p < 0.05$) as well as "helplessness" ($z = -3.67$; $p < 0.001$) decreased significantly during treatment. Further serial dependencies according to an ARIMA model (cf. Box & Jenkins, 1976) did not exist. Figure 5.2 shows the course of global suffering and displays two potential trends.

A simple linear trend may be good enough to catch the overall decrease of GS; however, visual inspection suggests modeling the course of suffer-

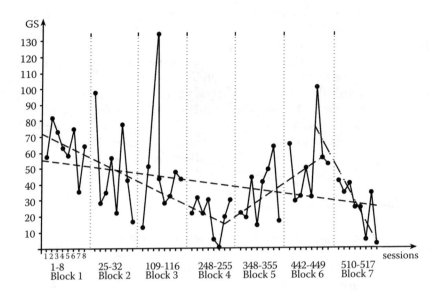

Figure 5.2 Course of Global Suffering: Values of intensity summed over all of the sequences of the session.

ing in a nonlinear fashion: A first negative trend prevails in the first half of the analysis; then there is an increase from Block 4 to Block 6, which then returns to a decreasing negative trend. Statistical check allows to formulate that the simple trend explains only 11% of the total variance, whereas the more complicated three-phase trend model explains 40% of the variation of GS.

Now what are the main sources of this patient's suffering during her psychoanalysis? Figure 5.3 shows the percentages of the different types of suffering for the entire treatment. 40.6% of the total suffering is predominantly or exclusively related to the environment. Here people outside the therapy seem most often to be the source of her suffering—30.5% compared with the therapist's 7.2% and the "extra-human" environment's 2.9%. For 35% of the time the patient's source of suffering is predominantly or exclusively herself, and 11.1% of her total suffering is evenly divided in relation to her environment and herself (scale point 3). 13.3% of the total suffering was categorized as "unclear."

To compare the proportion of the suffering related to the psychoanalyst with the total suffering, we selected all sequences in which the patient's suffering was predominantly (scale point 4) or exclusively (scale point 5) related to the therapist (Figure 5.4).

The mean score for the whole treatment is 7.2%. In six of seven blocks the suffering in regard to the therapist is less than 10% and in three blocks

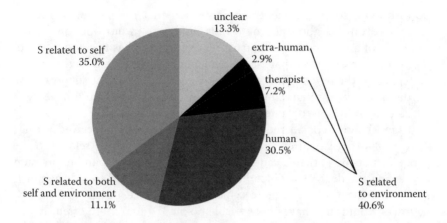

Figure 5.3 Percentage of the different types of suffering during the entire treatment (total suffering = 100%).

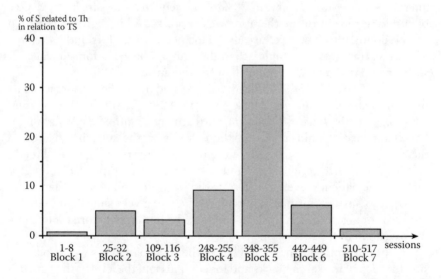

Figure 5.4 Mean percentage of suffering related to the therapist per block (total suffering = 100%).

less than 5%. Only Block 5 presents a totally different result with 34.3%. For that reason we will later explore this block in more detail from a clinical-qualitative point of view. One could argue that it might have been difficult for the patient to complain about the therapist; she either may not have talked about this delicate matter at all or tried cautiously to hint at it. But not to talk about one's suffering seems hardly compatible with the successful course of treatment. The objection that the patient might not have risked talking about it would only hold true in our opinion for the beginning of a treatment until a trusting relationship has been established. The second possibility—that the patient might have hinted at the suffering related to the psychoanalyst only very cautiously—is not supported by our data. It is likely that cautiously expressed suffering would have been reflected in an increased value of the category "unclear."

So far we have considered only those sequences that received ratings of 4 and 5—that is, suffering predominantly or exclusively related to the therapist. But the patient's cautiousness might still have found expression in reducing the degree to which her suffering was related to the therapist, thereby increasing the degree to which it was related to herself—that is, the raters would then have chosen scale points 2 and 3 more often. It was possible to test this alternative by examining those sequences in which the patient spoke in this toned-down manner about the analyst on the one hand and on the other hand about people who were not present and about whom she could presumably talk more easily. The data do not confirm this alternative. On the contrary, in 78% of the sequences in which any degree of suffering related to the therapist was expressed, this degree was scored as "predominantly" or "exclusively." This percentage of 4s and 5s related to the therapist was even higher than the comparable 63% for sequences of suffering related to people other than the therapist.

In Block 5 (sessions 348–355) suffering related to the therapist reached its peak immediately *following* Block 4 (sessions 248–255) in which the *total suffering* was the *lowest* for the entire treatment (Figure 5.2). What might have happened? Could it be that the increase in the suffering related to the psychoanalyst was the result of the psychoanalyst having taken Freud's call for abstinence seriously? Could it be that the therapist, intending to increase the patient's level of suffering, did so by becoming more abstinent? We tried to answer this question with the help of a very simple and reliable indicator of abstinence, namely, a count of the number of words spoken by the psychoanalyst per session.

Comparing both the mean number of the psychoanalyst's words per session for each of the seven blocks and for comparison, the level of the patient's suffering related to the psychoanalyst for each session gives a clear answer.

The therapist's mean number of words for the Block 5 in question is 855, which is higher than the average of 779 words across the entire treatment. The striking increase of the suffering in regard to the therapist was evidently *not* caused by the psychoanalyst's silence. In fact, if one looks at the entire course of the treatment, it was not true that the patient's suffering related to the therapist was a function of his silence. On the contrary, there is a small, not quite significant *positive* correlation ($r = .21$, $n = 56$, $p = 0.06$) between the number of words spoken by the psychoanalyst and the patient's suffering related to him, suggesting, if anything, that the more he talked the more the patient appeared to suffer at his hands.

What then might account for the surge of suffering related to the psychoanalyst in Block 5? An explanatory hypothesis occurred to us when we took a close look at the variation in all the types of suffering over the course of the seven blocks, as shown in Figure 5.5.

The diagram concerning the sources of suffering (Figure 5.5) makes clear that, for the first time in Block 5, the suffering related to the environment evidently replaces the suffering in regard to herself. Until then the patient apparently had been primarily occupied with her own insufficiencies, insecurities, and inhibitions. Now she began—as our data suggest—to tackle her environment, even though it was painful for her. And the psychoanalyst as a significant part of the environment became the primary and, according to the Weiss et al. (1986) control-mastery theory, *safe* object for her painful conflicts. The usefulness of this hypothesis will now be examined in the light of a more detailed qualitative consideration of clinical material from Block 5 (sessions 348–355).

Qualitative Results and Discussion

The following clinical descriptions are meant to complete the quantitative results and stick as closely as possible to the text of the verbatim transcripts. Our purpose is to make *plausible* relations among events, which seem to be

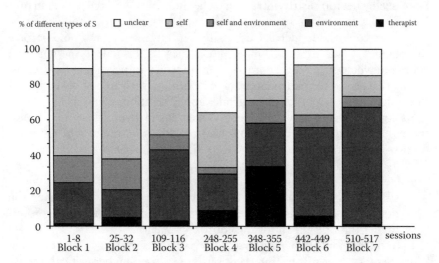

Figure 5.5 Mean percentages for each block of the categories: Unclear, suffering related to self, suffering related to both self and environment, suffering related to environment, suffering related to therapist (subcategory).

of importance for the psychoanalytic process. Our understanding of and reasoning about the material will proceed primarily along commonsense lines. When we use specifically psychoanalytic interpretations we shall do so explicitly.

The external situation during the sessions in question was the following: At the beginning of this period (Block 5) the psychoanalyst had moved his office. The consistency of the setting was disturbed; a previously unknown part of the psychoanalyst's personal life became visible to the patient.

In five out of eight sessions of this block the patient manifestly deals with topics of suffering that may be understood as paradigmatic complaints about abstinence. She complains that the psychoanalyst is silent so much and that he does not pick up on her offerings. She regards him as inaccessible and not interested in her. On the other hand there are many other sequences that contain no reference to suffering from the psychoanalyst's abstinence. The complaints in these sequences focus on a number of topics. The therapist's move has created confusion. She feels unprotected from his gaze because there are no curtains to dim the light in the new office. And here he also sits too close behind her. He expects too much from her. He asks too many questions about her holidays. And most of these complaints are based upon the patient's *assumptions* about the psychoanalyst rather than on his actual behavior (e.g., he does not express any overt expectation of her, at least not verbally).

The psychoanalyst focuses on the patient's concern about both his distance (too silent, not interested, inaccessible) and his getting too close (sitting too close, seeing her too clearly, intruding on her holidays). And the patient in turn is very eager to explain why she is concerned with his getting too close. She might lose control. Her defects (especially her unwanted hair) would become too obvious. And, above all, physical closeness is forbidden: She tells of a colleague who criticized her for touching someone. In psychoanalytic terms, during this period the patient appears to be dealing with an oedipal conflict if this is defined as a conflict about gender and generational boundaries.

So far the psychoanalyst has been looked at only from the patient's perspective. What did he actually do in this block? An evaluation of his interventions shows the following:

a) He does not intervene less than in the other treatment blocks in which suffering in regard to the therapist seldom occurs. Remember the quantitative finding that the number of the psychoanalyst's words is higher than his mean for the entire treatment.

b) In the sessions with a high score for patient's suffering in regard to the therapist, most of his interventions are focused on her critical, accusing, and irritated comments about him. He explicitly encourages the patient to complain about him. When the patient's complaints are directed toward a specific behavior he does not attempt to neutralize them (e.g., via a transference interpretation) but confirms their realistic aspects—in the manner suggested by Gill (1982). In one sequence the psychoanalyst even accepts the patient's reproach that he once used the word *dumb* in connection with her, although this term could not be found in the verbatim transcript.

c) A smaller group of the interventions seems to connect several of the patient's themes. For instance, he links her fear of staying in the session too long with her fear of her boundaries being violated by a forbidden touch. But very few of his interventions are interpretations in a stricter sense (i.e., connections with infantile wishes or hints at deeply unconscious content). More often, but only in certain sequences, the psychoanalyst focuses on latent meaning.

d) Frequently the psychoanalyst intervenes by introducing alternative ideas. For example, he suggests that silence could mean approval, not just criticism, as interpreted by the patient.

In summary, one can state that during this treatment period the therapist absolutely avoided defending himself. If he had had a defensive attitude he might have glossed over the patient's criticism and suffering or have doubted their justification. Although he was not abstinent in the sense of formally complying with a rule, he handled the principle of abstinence in a functional way (according to Thomä & Kächele 1994a, p. 218) that is against the background of a case-specific psychodynamic understanding: To be abstinent in regard to *this* patient during *this* phase of the psychoanalytic process means that the psychoanalyst had to avoid, even indirectly through an interpretation, personally defending himself.

Of course, the way the patient experiences the psychoanalyst's behavior is of crucial importance for the development of the therapeutic process. How then did she respond to this therapist's particular form of abstinence—that is, to his abstaining from being defensive? Fortunately, we can get a clear answer to this question by examining the last hour of this block when the patient begins to talk about how she had recently perceived the psychoanalyst. She had repeatedly complained about the bright daylight in the new office. But suddenly, since the previous session, curtains have been put up. She realizes that the psychoanalyst must have known that this has been planned but hadn't mentioned it when she had complained about the lack of curtains. She then becomes aware that his not telling her was just what made it possible for her to clearly experience what it feels like to be subjected to someone looking at her. And she gets some insight into the benefits of the psychoanalyst having withheld this information. She feels at ease and relieved by his calm reaction to her attacks. She describes the "impersonal" in the therapeutic relationship as a welcome protection. This sense of "impersonality" becomes so strong that she suddenly can no longer remember exactly what her therapist looks like.

Finally, from a psychoanalytic point of view, one can assume that the patient perceived her psychoanalyst's calm reaction as a relief not only in regard to her aggressive attacks but also in regard to her wishes to be close, even if she still experienced these wishes predominantly as anxieties. The analyst's abstinence did not manifest itself as a rigid clinging to a rule but was based on a correct understanding of her conflicts. Obviously he passed her test, as predicted by Weiss et al.'s (1986) control-mastery theory, by reacting in a calm way in both her criticism of him and her fear of being too close. The patient reacted according to the theory's prediction: She talked about her feelings of relief and relaxation. The "total suffering" is very low in this session, and her suffering in regard to the therapist completely disappeared.

5.5   DREAM SERIES ANALYSIS AS PROCESS TOOL*

Dream Series in Clinical Practice and in Research

Even if most discussions about dreams in clinical practice are focused around a single dream it is evident that reporting of dreams during a psychoanalytic treatment belongs to one of the most regular and repetitive phenomena of that kind of therapy. Patients dream more or less, and analysts differ in the extent they use the dreams offered by the patient. As a compromise formation a nonconscious, nonintentional agreement on the relevance of dreams for the treatments between patient and analyst is established: "Analytic therapy finds the analyst drawn into the intrapsychic as well as external communicative system of the dreamer" (Kanzer, 1955, p. 265).

Depending on the agreement a treatment may be based wholly on the analysis of the dream material or the dreams are treated like any other material (Fliess, 1953, p. 123). The first analyst to emphasize the use of dream series for the evaluation of the course of treatment has been Stekel: "The dreams in their totality have to be studied like a novel in progress (Fortsetzungsroman). There is no such thing as an individual interpretation of dreams, there is only a serial interpretation" (Stekel, 1935, p. 12). Without following Stekel's idea of the "prospective tendency" that he thought he would find in this serial interpretation, it remains clinically impressive how the repeated observation is able to strengthen the understanding of a patient's dynamics.

In the United States one of the first to systematically study manifest dream content per se was Saul (1940): He discusses the "utilization of early current dreams in formulating psychoanalytic cases." Later Saul and Sheppard (1954, 1956) attempted to quantify emotional forces using manifest

---

* H. Kächele & M. Leuzinger-Bohleber; adapted fromLeuzinger-Bohleber & Kächele (1988) and Kächele et al. (1999).

dreams. This track was also taken up by Beck and colleagues (Beck & Hurvich, 1959; Beck & Ward, 1961).[7]

Pioneering work on dream series was achieved by Thomas French, who from 1952 onward published his three volumes on *The Integration of Behavior* (French, 1952, 1954, 1958). In the second volume using a dream series of more than 200 dreams he shows "that every dream has also a logical structure and the logical structures of different dreams of the same person are interrelated, and that they are all parts of a single intercommunicative system" (French, 1954). In the third volume he applied this understanding for a thorough description of the reintegrative process within one psychoanalytic treatment (French, 1958).

Our own experience with dream series analysis began with demonstrating the usefulness of the spotlight analysis of Hall and van de Castle (1966), studying two levels of transference constellations in a dream series in the case Christian Y* (Geist & Kächele, 1979). Later the study group by Leuzinger-Bohleber and Kächele (1988) implemented a project to study cognitive changes based on dream reports in five psychoanalytic treatments. In that investigation we used dreams from the beginning phase (sessions 1–100) and the terminal phase (100 sessions before the end) comparing the cognitive functioning by a content analytic tool that was based on an integrative model on dreaming based on computer simulation models by Clippinger (1977) and Pauker, Gorry, Kassirer, and Schwartz (1976). In this first study on dreams we did not evaluate the development over the whole of the treatments—a task we have taken up in this study. We shall use the available dream material of the patient Amalia X that has been clinically summarized in Leuzinger-Bohleber's (1989) writeup of the whole project in her second volume (see Chapter 4 of this volume).†

Theoretical Model

Our first study used a theory-guided content analysis of cognitive processes based on computer simulation models to investigate changes in dreams processes of a patient in long-term psychoanalytic treatment. Although the latest fashion in neuroscience is based on connectionist models, especially neuronal networks (Spitzer, 1999), we have found it useful for our purpose to remain with the old descriptive model of cognitive-affective problem solving:

> Clippinger's theory of cognitive processes was convincing to us because it embodies the conception of conflictual processes taking place inside a black box, just as the structural theory in psychoanalysis

---

* The patient Christian Y has been discussed in Thomä & Kächele (1994b).
† A study on Amalia X's dreams using another qualitative strategy has been reported by Spiegel & Boothe (2006).

does. That is, it conceptualizes cognitive processes as being determined by the interaction of separate cognitive modules. The processes (programs) running in one module can complete, modify or inhibit and interrupt those running in other modules. Among other things this leads to characteristic structures in the interaction of the different modules and specific ways of perceiving and processing information. (Leuzinger-Bohleber & Kächele, 1988, p. 292)

A modified version of Clippinger's (1977) and Pauker et al.'s (1976) models that was developed by Leuzinger (1984) defines the six modules shown in Figure 5.6.

These modules perform the following tasks:

- MOZART selects what is attended to.
- CALVIN represents the superego and the patient's values and acts as censor.
- MACHIAVELLI develops problem-solving strategies.
- CICERO translates cognition into verbalizations.
- MARX perceives and tests reality.
- FREUD introspects and performs specific ego functions.

The model assumes reciprocal pathways of communication among the cognitive modules; for a detailed discussion of the operation of the model see Clippinger (1977). Its basic assumption is that unconscious motivations consist in cognitive processes, and it is the manifestation of these in the transcripts of what patients verbalize on the couch that we study.

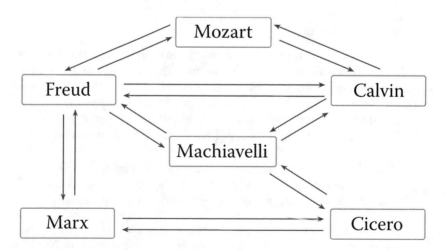

Figure 5.6 Model of cognitive functions.

In all that follows it should be understood that we use a very broad definition of *cognitive processes* as inner processes of perceiving and processing information that are always connected with physiological and emotional processes and cannot be studied separately (Pfeifer & Leuzinger-Bohleber, 1986).

Another theoretical input came from Moser, Pfeifer, Schneider, and von Zeppelin's (1980) work on sleep-dream simulation; there they have developed a very detailed item list for the description of the manifest content of dreams with respect to what Clippinger (1977) terms the functions of the MOZART module. This is described in detail in the doctoral dissertation of Merkle (1987) that was part of our first project. Our second study uses the same instrument yet applies it to a longitudinal data base of the patient's dreams.

Results of the First Study

Comparing dreams from the opening phase with dreams from the end phase of Amalia X's analysis, the main findings were as follows (Leuzinger-Bohleber, 1989).

Changes in Problem-Solving Cognitive Processes: Interactions among Cognitive Modules

The problem-solving cognitive processes of the patient comparing beginning and end of the treatment can be characterized by a high degree of flexibility; by an enlarged cognitive range and an associative and "gestalt-like" way of thinking; and by a capacity for a functional and realistic style of problem solving. Different information could be perceived and worked on at the same time and led to a process of generating and testing hypotheses that could compete with, modify, or contradict each other. Cognitive dissonances were recognized, reflected, and influenced, among other things, the decision-making process.

Unpleasant affects had an important function as signals indicating cognitive processes to be taken into account in the problem-solving process. In terms of our model, we found (1) increased cognitive and affective knowledge used in a functional way in different modules; (2) interrupted programs that functioned well and corresponded better to reality; and (3) an uninhibited interaction of cognitive processes in the different modules.

Changes within the Cognitive Module MOZART: Changes in What Was Attended to

The later the sessions in the successful treatment, the more the following changes were observable:

- More of the text of the dreams was attended to and worked over cognitively.
- The context of the dreams was taken into account.
- The analyst's interventions were part of the patient's dream associations.
- The patient pursued hypotheses about her dreams more systematically.
- The process of generating hypotheses took place easily, without much hesitation.
- The patient considered more than one hypothesis about the meaning of a dream.

In a separate assessment Merkle (1987) observes the following systematic changes in three dimensions of the manifest dream content, based on the model by Moser et al. (1980) comparing beginning and end of treatment: (1) expressed relationships; (2) dream atmosphere; and (3) problem solving.

Expressed Relationships

- The dreamer expressed better relationships with both her objects and herself.
- The range of interactions in these relationships was increased (e.g., in the late dreams she was more often alone) as well as interacting with one or more partners.
- Although the relationships were more often tender and friendly than in early dreams, to our surprise, they were also seldom neutral and included conflict relations—an indication to us that the range had been increased.

Dream Atmosphere

- The variety and intensity of affects in the manifest dream content was increased.
- The atmosphere was more positive with less anxiety, but aggressive, sad, and frightened moods were also expressed. This contradicted our original hypothesis that a single positive mood would prevail.

Problem Solving

- More problem-solving strategies were recognizable.
- Problem solving was more successful than not, and the dreamer was more active in doing it and seldom avoided it.
- The range of problem solving was greater than in early dreams.

Summarizing the beginning and end phases of five analyses comparing successful with the less successful cases we found less concern with the major psychopathological symptoms in the patient Amalia X. In the later dreams the content was more personal, with a greater variety of expressed activities. Moreover, the patient's dream interpretations were more "dialogue oriented," more convincing, and more directed at understanding the unconscious meanings of the dream. The associations were more constricted early and more varied in the late sessions. These are hints that the range of attention to dream material of the patient Amalia X was enlarged.

Similar are the findings of a replication study with a dream coding system, developed by Moser and von Zeppelin (1996) and reduced to 35 codes by Döll-Hentschker (2008), who tested the codes for reliability and validity. Comparison of dreams from beginning and ending phase shows a greater tolerance and integration of different affects like anxiety, anger, guilt, and shame, an increase in affect regulation capacities.

Method: Theory-Guided Complex Ratings and Hypothesis

The second study on which we now report utilized the total dream materials that we could identify in the transcribed sessions. The tool for the description of the dream material consists of three parts.

Part A: Relationships

- A.1: How does the marker happen to be in the dream? (active = 3; passive = 2; as observer = 1; not at all = 0)
- A.2: Are there human partners in the dream? (none = 0; one = 1; more than one = 2)
- A.3.1: What kind of relationship between dreamer and dream partner do you find in the manifest dream? (eight categories: loving, friendly, respectful, conflictual, clinch, neutral, sexual, indecisive)
- A.3.2: Describe the relationships of the dream partner among them. (eight categories: loving, friendly, respectful, conflictual, clinch, neutral, sexual, indecisive)

Part B: Dream Atmosphere

- B.1: Does the dreamer comment upon the atmosphere of her dreams? (yes = 2; no = 1)
- B.2.1: How do you judge the atmosphere in the manifest dream? (eight bipolar adjective items, scale 1–5)

- B.2.2: How do you judge the atmosphere in the manifest dream? (four unipolar items from "more" to "less")

Part C: Strategies of Problem Solving

- C.1: Is there one or more problem-solving strategies? (cannot judge any = 0; none = 1; one = 2; more than one = 3)
- C.2: Is problem solving successful? (eight categories: yes, no, partially, indecisive, trial with support, trial with hindrance, problem solved, passive solution)
- C.3: What kinds of problem-solving strategies do you find in the manifest dream content? (deferred = 1; avoiding = 2; active = 3)
- C.4: Are the problem-solving strategies reflecting upon by the dreamer? (scale 1–5; a lot = 5; very little = 1)

This study explores the issue of whether the aforementioned pre- and post-design in our first study—comparing the dreams from the beginning to the termination phase—is able to generate reliable statements on the development of psychological functioning that needs time to develop. Do we have to observe the development over the course of treatment? Particularly for the long-term treatments, what kind of models do we have to map the process? In our work in the long-term processes we have seen different courses for different variables (Kächele & Thomä, 1993); however, we assume that a linear trend model for changes in basic cognitive functioning is the most plausible.

To test this assumption we need more than data covering the course of the analysis from beginning and end phases of a treatment. Therefore, this study fills a gap in our understanding of cognitive changes process in long-term treatments. At least in using a single case design we might find out which of the descriptors are most likely to follow the linear trend model.

Description of the Material

At the time when we performed this replication study we had a large number of transcribed sessions: Out of 517 recorded sessions, 218 had been transcribed for various studies. We divided the total sample into portions of 100 sessions each to check for an adequate coverage of the treatment:

- Part 1: Sessions 1–45, 51–55, 61–62, 71–80, 98–99 (a total of 63 sessions)
- Part 2: Sessions 100–105, 109–116, 126–130, 150–157, 172–179, 181 (a total of 33 sessions)
- Part 3: Sessions 202–209, 213, 221–225, 236–237, 241–243, 246–256, 276–280, 286–287, 297–299 (a total of 43 sessions)

- Part 4: Sessions 300–304, 326–330, 335, 339, 343–346, 348–357, 376–383 (a total of 34 sessions)
- Part 5: Sessions 401–404, 406, 421–425, 431–433, 435, 442–449, 476–480, 482, 489, 501–508, 510–517 (a total of 45 sessions)

In these sessions a student rater (M.E.) identified all dreams; the dreams in part 1 and part 5 already had been localized by our former study. A total of 93 dream reports were identified with some sessions containing multiple dreams; so the total number of dreams used in this replication study was 111:

- Part 1: 63 sessions; Dreams 1–18
- Part 2: 33 sessions; Dreams 19–34
- Part 3: 43 sessions; Dreams 35–54
- Part 4: 34 sessions; Dreams 55–70
- Part 5: 45 sessions; Dreams 71–111

The Reliability Study

Three raters—two of them medical students (M.E. and M.B.) and one of them a psychoanalytically experienced clinical psychologist with more than 10 years of clinical experience (L.T)—were intensively trained to understand Clippinger's (1977) and Moser's and Zeppelin's (1996) models of cognitive processes. In several pretests they were acquainted with the kind of material to be rated. The training was very time consuming; the interrater reliability achieved was quite impressive: The three raters jointly judged one third of all identified dream reports ($N = 38$ out of 111 in 93 sessions):

- Items B2.1, B2.2, C4: Kappa 0.82–0.89
- Items A1, A2, C1, C3: Kappa 0.90–1.0
- Items A3.1, A3.2, B1, C2: Kappa 0.47–1.0

It is noteworthy that 84% of all values are beyond 0.7.

Results

The replication study focused on the three aspects from the study by Merkle (1987); the new results were as follows.

Expressed Relationships

A.1: How does the dreamer appear in the dream action?

Most frequently during the whole course of the treatment the dreamer is actively involved in the action. This is more surprising since the patient came with a depressive basic mood to analysis. In contrast to Beck and Ward (1961) findings, this patient never gave up the pace-making function—at least in her dreams.

A.2: Do dream partners occur in the dream?

Again, the patient is heavily involved with more than one partner all the time. A clinician might "see" in the data a slight increase of dyadic relationship, probably reflecting the patient's gain in intimate relationships of which one is the relationship with the analyst.

A.3.1: What kind of relationship occurs between dreamer and dream partner?

Statistically there are more loving, friendly, respectful relationships and less neutral relationships. We see this as a shift to the development of more pronounced positive qualities in relationships.

A.3.2: What are the relationships between the dream partners?

The findings point to the same development as in A.3.1.

To summarize the findings we use graphical illustrations to make our point that the overall impression of these items, along the course of the analysis, allows quite straightforward conclusions. There is less dramatic change and more stability as the findings from the Merkle (1987) study suggests (Figure 5.7).

Dream Atmosphere

B.1.1: Does the dreamer comment about the atmosphere of her dreams more often?

No obvious change.

B.1.2: If yes, how does she comment?

The findings are presented as a ratio of neutral-positive in relation to the total amount of sentences where she comments about the atmosphere in the dream (Table 5.5). There is a definite increase in the second half of the analysis of neutral-positive comments in regard to the dream atmosphere. From our clinical knowledge we find this is in good correspondence to the development of her personal life.

B.2.1: How do you judge the atmosphere of the manifest dream?

By Spearman rank correlations of time and bipolar adjective list we find rather impressive systematic changes in time in some of the bipolar adjectives like pleasurable/nonpleasurable (−0.56), euphoric/depressive (−0.64), harmonic/disharmonic (−0.42), hopeful/resigned (−0.70), happy/sad

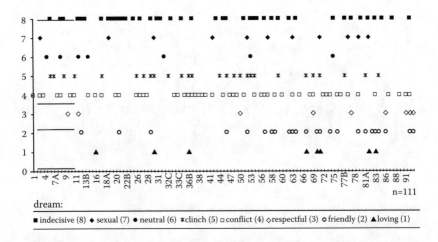

dream:

■ indecisive (8) ◆ sexual (7) ● neutral (6) ✻clinch (5) □ conflict (4) ◇respectful (3) ○ friendly (2) ▲loving (1)

Figure 5.7 What kind of relations do you find between the dreamer and the dream partner in the manifest dream content?

Table 5.5 Atmosphere in the Dreams

Phase/Sessions	Dreams	Sentences with Neutral-Positive to Total	Percentage
I 1–99	1–18	1/11	9
II 100–199	19–34	3/14	21
III 200–299	35–54	5/16	31
IV 300–399	55–70	6/08	75
V 400–517	71–111	6/10	60

(–0.58), easygoing/painful (–0.61), peaceful/dangerous (–0.52), and happy/desperate (–0.68); all of these correlations are < 0.001 *p*-value.

B.2.2: How do you judge the atmosphere of the manifest dream?

By Spearman rank correlations we also find rather impressive systematic changes with time in some of the unipolar adjectives such as anxiety ridden (–0.43), neutral (–0.26). However, aggressive atmosphere remained the same shifting from very low to very high level along the treatment. The category lustful exhibited a more complicated relation to time: At the beginning there was very little; then it peaked.

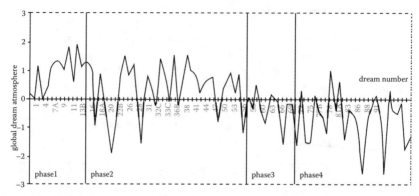

Figure 5.8 Global dream atmosphere: General factor: negative (high) versus positive (low) emotions.

By factor analytic technique* we identified a strong general factor that demonstrated the development of dream atmosphere over the course of treatment from negative to positive.

Keeping in mind the diverse findings on the level of single items an orthogonal varimax rotation was performed. The outcome of this operation pointed to two components. The factor "negative me" using Dahl, Hölzer, and Berry's (1992) system of classification of emotions incorporates the self-emotion states and displays a decreasing trend from whereas the factor "negative it" assembles the aggressive and anxious states that are object oriented showing an up and down across treatment.

Problem Solving

C.1: Are there one or more problem-solving strategies?

One or two problem-solving strategies are equally distributed across the treatment. There is no substantial change.

C.2: Is the problem solving successful?

The percentage of successful problem-solving strategies is increasing, and the unsuccessful strategies are decreasing; furthermore, partially successful solutions tend to be increasing.

C.3: What problem-solving strategies do you find?

The patient throughout the analysis is actively seeking solutions of problems; there is a slight increase in deferred actions. A clinician might be surprised by this result.

---

* We acknowledge the statistical assistance of Dr. Pokorny.

C.4: Are the problem-solving strategies reflected upon?

There is a powerful increase of the reflection upon these strategies continuously taking place over the course of the analysis. This finding is well represented in a graphical representation (Figure 5.9). The changes occur in a continuous nondramatic fashion along the continuum of treatment.

Discussion and Summary

The overall hypothesis of this replication study focused on the issue of whether the changes can be modeled as linear trends or whether other, non-linear models are necessary. Here the findings are very unequivocal: Either we find stationary processes with variations in intensity (e.g., in aggressive or anxious feelings), or the changes are either inclines or declines that are patterned along the time axis in a linear fashion.

Some surprises in the findings have to do with the patient's particular capacities that she already brought to the treatment. From the start she brought the capacity to actively organize relationship patterns in her dreams; however, the change occurred in the quality of these relationships: They became more friendly and caring.

The impressive findings concern the systematic change in dream atmosphere along the time axis: "negative me" emotions decreased, but "negative it" emotions display a stable variability. Another impressive finding is the systematic tendency for the capacity to shift from unsuccessful to successful problem strategies along the analysis.

Our conclusion is that the process of change in psychoanalysis in basic psychological capacities takes place all along the way. If the textual material

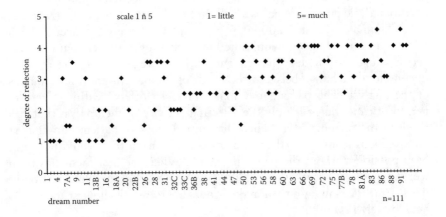

Figure 5.9 Reflection of problem solving.

dreams are made of is considered a valid extract from the patient psychic life, then this study has demonstrated the following:

a) Intrapsychic change does occur.
b) Intrapsychic change mainly takes place in a linear trend.
c) Relationship, atmosphere, and problem solving are valuable dimensions of capturing a patient's intrapsychic change process.

5.6 STUDYING THE CORE CONFLICTUAL RELATIONSHIP THEME (CCRT)*

Introduction

The great volume of material that is brought to light in the course of a psychoanalytic treatment must be reduced to what is most significant. Events are not significant in themselves, however: Significance is given to them. What an analyst considers significant in the analytic process depends on the criteria for meaningfulness that he or she applies to the course of the psychoanalytic process. One idea of process will be more differentiated or more explicit than another, yet as a fundamental premise no treatment can be upheld unless the therapist is in possession of conceptual models of courses of therapy, which suggest ways of proceeding and criteria for evaluation.

A psychoanalytic treatment can be characterized in a great number of ways. Freud compares the analytic process with a chess game and makes analogies between the activities of the archaeologist, the painter, and the sculptor and those of the analyst. Freud's work, however, provides no definite conception of process beyond specifying a beginning, middle, and final phase (Glover, 1955a). To this day the number of coherent models of the psychoanalytic process remains small. In the Ulm Process Model (Kächele, 1988; Thomä & Kächele, 2004a), psychoanalytic therapy is conceptualized as a continuing, temporally unlimited focal therapy with a changing, interactively developed focus. The sequence of foci is regarded as a result of an unconscious exchange between the needs of the patient and the resources of the analyst. The patient may make various "offers" within a certain period of time, but it is only the selecting activity of the analyst that can result in the forming of a focus. The mutual work of patient and analyst on one focus leads to further areas of concentration that would not have been possible without the preceding work. When the first focus has been worked through, access is gained to a second one; thorough exploration of the second focus may in turn make it possible to revisit the first focus in a qualitatively new way.

* C. Albani, D. Pokorny, G. Blaser, M. Geyer, & H. Kächele. The study was supported by the Deutsch Forschungsgemeneinschaft (DFG).

The thematic "offers" made by the patient may be understood in terms of what French (1958) calls "focal conflicts," which represent unconscious infantile conflict constellations (thematized by French as "nuclear conflicts"): In other words, they are the solutions generated under the pressure of the problem at hand. French, however, is left with an unresolved problem: "Still, searching for the patient's focal conflict is an intuitive art which cannot be completely reduced to rules" (p. 101).

The Core Conflictual Relationship Theme method developed by Lester Luborsky (Luborsky, 1977; Luborsky, Albani, & Eckert, 1992; Luborsky & Crits-Christoph, 1998) offers a way of making such focal and core conflicts operational. The aim of the present study is to investigate how effective the CCRT method is in depicting the therapeutic course of a psychoanalytic treatment according to the Ulm Process Model.

Current Status of Research and Aim of the Study

Although a considerable number and a great variety of studies have been conducted with the CCRT method (for an overview, see Luborsky et al., 1999), to date there have been very few that follow courses of therapy with the CCRT method. The studies known to us are of short-term therapies (Albani, Pokorny, Dahlbender, & Kächele, 1994; Anstadt, Merten, Ullrich, & Krause, 1996; Grabhorn, Overbeck, Kernhof, Jordan, & Mueller, 1994; Luborsky, Crits-Cristoph, Friedman, Mark, & Schaffler, 1991). To our knowledge there have as yet been no investigations of long-term psychoanalytic therapies using the CCRT method. The aim of our exploratory study was to describe the course of the 517-hour psychoanalysis of the patient Amalia X by the CCRT method. A guiding intention behind the study was to determine if and in what form the Ulm Process Model can be demonstrated in a psychoanalytic treatment.

Clinical Notes

The clinical evaluation of the case has been detailed in Chapter 4 of this volume. Here we only repeat the systematic description of the transference themes as they will be used in this study as a clinical anchoring point (Table 5.6).

It is not difficult to "invent" such descriptions, even as a nonspecialist reading the transcribed sessions. Yet it is in fact a painstaking process: The texts were first read and reread with the utmost care by two medical students (A.S. and B.S.), who then prepared an extract, which was in turn checked against the text for accuracy by two psychoanalysts (H.K. and R.H.). As a form of qualitative research, the resulting product is now finally gaining greater respect (Frommer & Rennie, 2001). From the beginning, the CCRT method has occupied a middle position between qualitative

Table 5.6 Clinical Transference Configurations

Clinical Transference Configurations	Therapy Phase	Session Numbers
Analysis as confession	I	1–5
Analysis as a test	II	26–30
The bad mother	III	50–54
The offer of submission and secret defiance	VI	76–80
The search for norms of one's own	V	100–104
The disappointing father and helplessness of the daughter	VI	116–120
The distant, cold father and the incipient longing for identification	VII	151–155
Ambivalence in the father relationship	VIII	176–180
The father as seducer or moral judge	IX	202–206
He loves me—he loves me not	X	226–230
Even father cannot make a son out of a girl	XI	251–255
The apron-strings feeling	XII	276–280
The poor maiden and the rich king	XIII	300–304
Fear of rejection	XIV	326–330
Helpless love for powerful father and jealousy of his wife	XV	351–355
Active separation and resisting abandonment	XVI	376–380
Discovery of her own critical powers, recognition of the analyst's deficiencies, new attempt at leave-taking	XVII	401–404, 406
The daughter held on the left hand—rivalry with the firstborn for the mother	XVIII	426–430
Hatred for the bountifully giving analyst and growing out of this expectation	XIX	445–449
The art of love is to endure love and hate	XX	476–480
Mastering leave-taking: having worked through the oral-aggressive fantasy about the analyst	XXI	501–505
Farewell symphony: the return of many fears and discovery of many changes	XXII	513–517

evaluation and exact quantification. Let us now look at the first application of this method to a psychoanalytic therapy.

The CCRT Method

The CCRT method makes it possible to show internalized relationship patterns. It is based on an analysis of narrative episodes of the patient's relationship experiences. As these "relationship episodes" are the foundation of the method, the first step is to identify them. Three types of components are then determined: wishes, needs, and intentions (W-component); reactions of the object (RO-component); and reactions of the subject (RS-component). Positive and negative reactions are categorized. Initially, formulation of the categories is kept as close to the text as possible ("tailor-made formulation"). Since the current American standard categories and clusters of the method have more than once been criticized (e.g., Albani et al., 1999), a reformulation of the category structures of the CCRT method was undertaken (for details see Albani et al., 2002; Albani et al., 2008). Unlike in the old system, a directional dimension was introduced into the wish component showing whether the activity comes from the object or the subject (WO—"What I wish the object to do for me" and WS—"What I wish to do for the object [or myself]"). This addition has proven relevant in initial studies.

In contrast to the old categories, the structure of the reformulated system has a consistent logic to it: All three dimensions are coded on the basis of the same predicate list, which is hierarchically structured. Reactions of the subject and object are analogous, and there is a complete analogy between wishes and reactions; both of the object and of the subject (e.g., cluster A, "Being attentive to someone"; WO, "The other should be attentive to me"; WS, "I want to be attentive to the other"; RO, "The other is attentive"; RS, "I am attentive to the other"). In the resulting reformulation there is a predicate list of a total of 119 subcategories grouped into 30 categories, which in turn are grouped into 13 clusters. In the present study, the evaluation was done on the subcategory level, while the results were presented on the cluster level (for names of the clusters, cf. Table 5.7).

The CCRT is composed of the most frequent wish, the most frequent reaction of the object, and the most frequent reaction of the subject.

Sample and Statistics*

The data were provided by the session transcripts of this completely taped psychoanalytic treatment that are accessible in the Ulmer Textbank. A systematic time sampling was made of the transcripts by selecting blocks of 25 consecutive sessions with a 25-session interval between each block. In the present study we evaluated only the first and last time blocks, here designated as therapy phases and numbered with Roman numerals. These were sessions 1–30 and 510–517. In addition, beginning with the 50th session, blocks composed generally of five sessions were analyzed at 50-session intervals. When a block was not found to contain at least 10 relationship

---

* The sample description of the transcribed text of Amalia X (Kächele et al., 1999) is based on 22 transcribed blocks of five sessions each, selected at 25-session intervals. The sessions analyzed here by the CCRT method were selected from half of the available sessions. For the sake of clarity and maintaining the connection to the other Ulm studies, we chose the numbering of 1–22 here as well. Thus the therapy phases examined here are the odd-numbered ones.

episodes, further sessions were added until a minimum of 10 relationship episodes was reached. Our sample includes 11 of the 22 available blocks but has 92 sessions in it.

Evaluation of the sessions was carried out in random order by an experienced CCRT evaluator on the subcategory level. Subcategories were not assigned to the clusters until statistical evaluation was undertaken.

Because of our rich database, it was possible to analyze not only the absolute frequencies but the complex structure of the data as well. On a two-dimensional contingency table, the variable "therapy phase" is set over against one of the CCRT variables (wish, reaction of the object, and reaction of the subject). As the null hypothesis, the observed frequencies of the individual dimensions are noted (e.g., wish clusters and therapy phases), and it is assumed that the two dimensions are independent (i.e., that the frequency distributions of the CCRT components are the same in all therapy phases). The alternative hypothesis then is that some categories occur more frequently in certain therapy phases than might be expected from the observed frequencies of the individual dimensions.

This hypothesis of the homogeneity of the therapy phases is first globally tested by the generalized Fisher Test (Monte-Carlo method).

In the following exploratory stage, using a one-tailed classical Fisher test, the CCRT categories are determined, which occur more frequently than expected in a particular therapy phase. Thus both the absolute highest-frequency categories as well as the more-frequent-than-expected categories are presented. (For details of this process, see Albani et al., 1994; Pokorny, 2008.)

Results

Reliability of the CCRT Evaluation

The CCRT evaluation was carried out by an experienced evaluator. In order to check for reliability and to avoid rater drift, during the evaluation process, one session out of the 11 evaluated blocks was selected at random to be evaluated by a second evaluator. In this we followed the approach of Luborsky and Diguer (1990). In the first step, agreement in the marking of the relationship episodes was checked, the criterion being an agreement within seven lines at the beginning and seven lines at the end of an episode. The percentage of agreement was 72% for the beginning of an episode and 69% for the end of an episode. In the relationship episodes in which marking was in agreement, agreement regarding the object of the episode reached 99%.

In the second step the relationship episodes were known, and agreement in the marking of the components was checked based on the criterion of seven words at the beginning and at the end of a component. The agreement at the beginning and the end of the component came to 76% for wishes, 96% and 95% for reactions of the object, and 94% and 96% for reactions of the subject. In the third step, the components were already given, and

the agreement regarding assignment to the standard categories and evaluation of the valence of the reactions was checked. Agreement regarding the
valence of the reactions was a kappa coefficient of .78. For assignment to
the standard categories (on the cluster level), the mean kappa coefficient
was .68 (W = .58, RO = .60, RS = .70).

Results of the CCRT Evaluation

In the 92 hours, altogether 579 relationship episodes were found, containing 806 wishes, 986 reactions of the object, and 1103 reactions of the subject. The positivity index (number of positive reactions in relation to the
sum of positive and negative reactions) came to 15.1% for reactions of the
object and 23.9% for reactions of the subject.

Table 5.7 gives an overview of the frequency distribution of the categories on the cluster level.

The CCRT (most frequent categories of all) for the entire therapy is
as follows:

WO: Others should be attentive to me (WO C1 A).
WS: I want to be self-determined (WS C1 D).
RO: Others are unreliable (RO C1 I).
RS: I am dissatisfied, scared (RS C1 F).

Table 5.7 Frequency Distribution of CCRT Variables: Object-Related Wishes
(WO), Subject-Related Wishes (WS), Reactions of the Object (RO), and
Reactions of the Subject (RS)

	Cluster	WO	WS	RO	RS
		n = 518	n = 288	n = 986	n = 1103
A	Attending to	46.3	12.5	4.2	3.3
B	Supporting	26.6	4.9	5.1	2.4
C	Loving/Feeling Well	14.3	19.8	4.4	6.0
D	Being Self-Determined	10.0	27.1	6.9	7.2
E	Being Depressed	0	0	.3	6.4
F	Being Dissatisfied/Scared	0	0	1.7	24.2
G	Being Determined by Others	0	.3	5.3	15.3
H	Being Angry/Unlikable	0	0	4.7	15.5
I	Being Unreliable	0	.3	19.3	.1
J	Rejecting	0	8.7	19.2	6.1
K	Subjugating	.2	6.2	13.6	1.4
L	Annoying/Attacking	0	2.8	7.3	1.4
M	Withdrawing	2.5	17.4	8.2	10.7

Note: Relative frequencies in %; n = 579 relationship episodes.

Table 5.8 Core Conflictual Relationship Theme (CCRT) in the Course of Therapy

Absolute Highest-Frequency Categories	More-Frequent-than-Expected Categories[a]
Therapy Phase I, Sessions 1–30, n = 30	
WO CI A "Others should be attentive" (112/ 55)	**WO CI A** "Others should be attentive" (112/ 55)
WS CI D "I want to be self-determined" (42/ 37)	**WS CI D** "I want to be self-determined" (42/ 37)
RO CI J "Others reject me" (82/ 24)	**RO CI J** "Others reject me" (82/ 24)
	RO CI G "Others are weak" (24/ 7)
RS CI F "I am dissatisfied, scared" (116/ 27)	**RS CI F** "I am dissatisfied, scared" (116/ 27)
	RS CI G "I am determined by others" (77/ 18)
	Negative RS 335/ 82
Therapy Phase III, Sessions 50–55, n = 5	
WO CI A "Others should be attentive" (9/ 41)	
WS CI M "I feel like withdrawing' (4/ 21)	
RO CI J "Others reject me" (10/ 20)	**RO CI F** "Others are dissatisfied, scared" (4/ 8)
RS CI F "I am dissatisfied, scared" (11/ 26)	**RS CI C** "I feel good" (7/ 16)
Therapy Phase V, Sessions 100–104, n = 5	
WO CI B "Others should support me" (12/ 44)	**WO CI B** "Others should support me" (12/ 44)
WS CI C "I would like to love and feel good" (5/ 36)	
RO CI I "Others are unreliable" (12/ 23)	**RO CI M** "Others withdraw" (9/ 18)
RS CI F "I am dissatisfied, scared" (25/ 42)	**RS CI F** "I am dissatisfied, scared" (25/ 42)
Therapy Phase VII, Sessions 151–157, n = 7	
WO CI A "Others should be attentive" (7/ 78)	
WS CI J "I want to reject others" (3/ 43)	**WS CI J** "I want to reject others" (3/ 43)
RO CI I "Others are unreliable" (6/ 27)	
RS CI F "I am dissatisfied, scared" (6/ 37)	**Negative RO** 22/ 100
Therapy Phase IX, Sessions 202–206, n = 5	
WO CI A "Others should be attentive" (8/ 33)	**WO CI D** "Others should be self-determined" (6/ 25)
WS CI M "I feel like withdrawing" (4/ 31)	
RO CI I "Others are unreliable" (11/ 26)	
RS CI F "I am dissatisfied, scared" (11/ 22)	**RO CI D** "Others are self-determined" (7/ 16)
Therapy Phase XI, Sessions 251–255, n = 5	
WO CI A "Others should be attentive" (7/ 33)	
WS CI A "I want to be attentive to others" (4/ 67)	**WS CI A** "I want to be attentive to others" (4/ 67)
RO CI I "Others are unreliable" (7/ 27)	
RS CI F "I am dissatisfied, scared" (10/ 32)	

Table 5.8 Core Conflictual Relationship Theme (CCRT) in the Course of Therapy (continued)

Absolute Highest-Frequency Categories	More-Frequent-than-Expected Categories[a]
Therapy Phase XIII, Sessions 300–304, n = 5	
WO CI A "Others should be attentive" (6/ 40)	
WS CI M "I feel like withdrawing" (3/ 43)	
RO CI J "Others reject me" (6/ 23)	
RS CI F "I am dissatisfied, scared" (9/ 36)	
Therapy Phase XV, Sessions 351–355, n = 5	
WO CI A "Others should be attentive" (19/ 54)	
WS CI M "I feel like withdrawing" (5/ 36)	**WS CI K** "I want to subjugate others" (3/ 21)
RO CI I "Others are unreliable" (14/ 25)	
RS CI H "I am angry, disagreeable" (17/ 28)	**RS CI H** "I am angry, disagreeable" (17/ 28)
Therapy Phase XVII, Sessions 401–404, 406, n = 5	
WO CI C "Others should love me" (7 30)	**WO CI C** "Others should love me" (7/ 30)
WS CI J "I want to reject others" (2/ 50)	
RO CI J "Others reject me" (12/ 27)	
RS CI G "I am determined by others" (9/ 25)	
Therapy Phase XIX, Sessions 445–449, n = 5	
WO CI B "Others should support me" (17/ 33)	**WO CI C** "Others should love me" (13/ 25)
WS CI C "I would like to love and feel good" (11/ 37)	**WS CI C** "I would like to love and feel good" (11/ 37)
RO CI I "Others are unreliable" (25/ 23)	**RO CI M** "Others withdraw" (18/ 17)
RS CI F "I am dissatisfied, scared" (28/ 23)	**RS CI M** "I withdraw" (25/ 20)
	Negative RS 42/ 91
Therapy Phase XXI and XXII, Sessions 501–517, n = 17	
WO CI A "Others should be attentive" (40/ 45)	
WS CI D "I want to be self-determined" (20/ 33)	**WS CI L** "I want to annoy, attack others" (5/ 8)
RO CI I "Others are unreliable" (46/ 21)	**RS CI H** "I am angry, disagreeable" (45/ 19)
RS CI H "I am angry, disagreeable" (45/ 19)	**RS CI D** "I am self-determined" (37/ 16)
	RS CI J "I reject others" (23/ 10)
	Positive RS 87/ 37

Note: Absolute/relative frequencies in percent in relation to the given phase of therapy.

[a] Fisher Test, two-tailed, $p = 0.05$, W: $n = 806$, RO: $n = 986$, RS: $n = 1103$.

Table 5.8 presents the typical categories for each phase of therapy.

In order to connect the CCRT findings to the clinical description we used French's distinction between "nuclear conflicts" and "focal conflicts." We were able to determine that across all phases of the treatment one basic theme becomes clear in each of the most frequent categories of the CCRT procedure: Amalia's wish for attention (WO C1 A) and support (WO C1 B) from others; her experience of the others as rejecting (RO C1 J) and unreliable (RO C1 I); and her dissatisfaction and anxiety (RS C1 F). In each of the phases of therapy, the subject-related wishes are distinct.

The more-frequent-than-expected categories are characterized by the themes that distinguish the particular therapy phase from the other phases.

Initial therapy phase I (sessions 1–30) is characterized chiefly by Amalia's wish for kindly attention from others (WO C1 A). She speaks of her colleagues, by whom she feels "used" as a "dustbin" (RO C1 J) but with whom she cannot speak about her problems. Amalia envies her female colleagues for their relationships. She feels insecure in relation to her students (RS C1 G), thinking they regard her as an old maid (RO C1 J), and there are conflicts in which she does not feel properly supported by her director (RO C1 G). She describes her father as a sensitive, fearful, and inaccessible person (RO C1 J, RO C1 G) and is disappointed at their distant and irritable relations (WO C1 A). A relationship episode with her father follows:

> P: For example, when I come home, by car now, he won't even come out. I know from my colleagues that they have fathers much older, and they pick them up and carry their bags in and so on, and he doesn't even come. So when I get home, and maybe my mother opens the door, then I might go to the bathroom or something, or I'm taking off my coat and standing in the entryway, he doesn't come, he doesn't move. Or I go into the living room, and he'll be sitting in the other room, you see he somehow can't take a step towards a person.

In relation to her brothers she feels inferior and not taken seriously, either by them or by the family as a whole. She makes a theme of her dependence on the norms of the church, the opinions of others and on her mother though her mother is the one she talks to. On the other hand, Amalia has the feeling she needs to be available for her mother and has feelings of guilt when she distances herself from her:

> P: Sometimes I really need my Sunday to just, well, and then there'll be something I have to do again, and then you see, my parents, they come around often, you know, my mother will call up and then she'll say, then, she'll just say, "Come" and I've simply never managed yet to say, "Please don't. I don't want you to," or, "It won't work out," or …

Her wish for change is expressed in her wish for autonomy (WS C1 D), which results from her experience of herself as dependent and weak, unable to set limits, and dissatisfied. For this phase of the therapy, the high proportion of negative reactions on the part of the patient herself is particularly characteristic.

In the ninth session, Amalia reports the first relationship episode with the analyst (out of a total of only four episodes in the initial phase):

> P: (pause) You know, anyway today I was awfully, I am so dreadfully tired, I've said that before and then today I really didn't have time to catch my breath from yesterday. The whole evening I was—well, I had a girl student visiting, who wanted something and so I didn't get to give it any thought, but just the same I started realizing some things yesterday and in that.... Sure in a certain sense it was finished too, and what I'm left with as a question is always the same thing. Fine, I see it now, but what I am supposed to do and how is it supposed to go on and, and, and what, I really didn't mean to say that, right.
>
> A: With the students and the grading problem, you mean, if that is supposed to go on?
>
> P: No, I mean here, how is this supposed to go on, when I lie here and tell you something and I try to understand it and you summarize it, then of course some things become clear, and nevertheless then I tell myself, what am I supposed to do with that, that's what was going through my head, and that's what I didn't want to say, because somehow it, because, I keep asking myself, if you recognize it, to what extent can you guide your actions by it.
>
> A: How it will go on?
>
> P: And how it will go on, right, that was really the question. Somehow at the moment I experienced that as an insult to you, and therefore I couldn't say it.

This episode illustrates the description of the clinical transference configuration of these therapy phases: the analyst as father confessor and examiner, in front of whom Amalia is careful, reserved, and uncertain but also beginning to come to terms with "authority." What is striking is that Amalia reports a great many relationship episodes in the initial sessions (on average 11 episodes per session), which makes sense from the clinical perspective: In the initial phase, the therapeutic relationship is being established and biographical material occupies a greater space.

In *therapy phase III* (sessions 50–55), Amalia describes episodes chiefly reflecting her wish to withdraw (WS C1 M), which she in fact succeeds in doing in relation to her mother and younger brother. The following episode with her mother gives a picture of the clinical description of this phase of the therapy as "the bad mother" but also shows that Amalia is exploring alternative types of behavior:

> P: No, otherwise on the weekend I actually have uh; well yes of course my mother called up again and wants, and would very much like me, uh, to come next weekend, or rather she would like to come, but I told her I wasn't sure yet what my plans were, and asked her to please wait, I mean, two or three weeks ago I would really have just, said, or let's say four weeks ago, uh please come and I have often said, yes please come, even when it wouldn't be convenient at all for me, and I just see that it, that it, uh would be perfectly ok alone, that I, um, I really don't need to get so, so worked up all the time because now, now I'm sitting here all alone and so forth, and of course it would be nice, not to be sitting all alone that way all the time well it's not always but a great deal of the time for sure but, um, I could make a lot more of it, not that I didn't used to read before or didn't do this or that too, but I just feel better about it, um, I can honestly say.

Amalia is feeling better and experiencing moments of self-confirmation (she is driving alone again taking walks, painting again; RS C1 C), although there are confrontations with the parents of her students.

Her relationship to the analyst is also becoming a more frequent topic (in 17% of the episodes). She demands answers instead of silence from the professional authority (RO C1 J) and would like to give her own interpretations as well.

Therapy phase V (sessions 100–104) is marked especially by Amalia's wish for support (WO C1 B). She feels that her director is judging her and discriminating against her because of her therapy (RO C1 J). She also is expressing her wish that the analyst should give her clear answers and be open and honest with her. She experiences the analyst as the "most important person" (38% of all episodes deal with the analyst) but feels rejected by him. She is unsure who he is and what he thinks of her and complains of his changing the subject and of his keeping the rules secret (RO C1 M):

> P: You know, just this business with my boss, really went to show how difficult it is, uh, what with the self-assessment that you make of yourself, and the assessment others make of you, which you can always somehow sense or see, to hold the balance there, when the two of them clash. And that's where I feel you are someone I can assume, um—right, I just feel—it's simply something like trust, and, and nevertheless, after all that's why I went running to the well, I didn't actually run to the bookstore, but I, I wanted to read it, because you see

I keep wanting to know who you are, and uh, you, you can't help asking yourself the whole time, "So who is this person that you are putting your trust in, and, and what kind of picture is he forming of you"—and, I mean, all those things that we've already spoken about ...

A: Um-hmm.

P: ... came back to me really powerfully—because—naturally I want to know: What kind of man is this, who has a profession like that, and a wife who also has a similar profession, uh, all that, that is somehow important. And then when you, if I can put it that way, to me it seems you change the subject, then I can't help asking myself, "Why, why is he changing the subject—is he embarrassed—well, why is he embarrassed by that?"—or is it that he wants me to be independent, ok, right. It, of course it has to do with that. But, I just think it's kind of going down different tracks. I mean, if I trust a person, of course I am dependent in a way—thank God, I would say and, and yet again at the same time I have to ...

A: Um-hmm.

P: I just need—at least here—to feel I have the right to sound you out, who you are and who I am—or rather I didn't put that quite right—who you are—it strikes me as very important, that, uh, why does he listen to me, right, it's another one of those questions. "Why does he do that? What is interest in a person?"

A: Um-hmm.

P: What's behind it?

According to the assessment by the CCRT method, the patient's "search for norms of her own," which was identified as a theme in the clinical description, appears to take place in two ways: on the one hand in coming to terms with her disappointed wishes for support but also in her confrontation and identification with the analyst.

Amalia's wish to reject others herself (WS C1 J) becomes important only in *therapy phase VII* (sessions 151–157). Amalia is dissatisfied (RS C1 F) and is considering entering a convent. Alongside of her relationship to her father (who is the object of interaction in 4 of 14 episodes of this phase), the focus of these sessions is the therapeutic relationship (the therapist is the object in 6 of the 14 episodes of this phase). On the one hand she is afraid she is asking too much of the analyst; on the other hand she criticizes his interpretations and finds, for example, that he does not laugh enough. During a visit by her parents she is disappointed that her younger brother is favored (WO C1 A), bringing back memories of her lifelong envy of her brother. In no other phase does Amalia portray the reactions of others so negatively as in this phase.

The wish that others should be self-directing (WO C1 D), characteristic of *therapy phase IX* (sessions 202–206), is aimed largely at her director, who lets himself be manipulated (RO C1 I) by a female colleague with whom Amalia is in rivalry and to whom she feels inferior (RO C1 D). From her analyst, Amalia wishes a direct answer to her concern that she might have caused herself damage in masturbation. She receives it (with some delay), in which process the therapist (by father transference) becomes a seducer and moral judge, as the clinical description emphasizes.

In *therapy phase XI* (sessions 251–255), Amalia succeeds for the first time in initiating a date with a male colleague (WS C1 A). She wishes she were able to speak openly about sexuality with her mother (WO C1 A), recalling her cautious attempts to question her mother, and wonders about her mother's sex life. Amalia wants to understand what happens in analysis—she attends lectures by psychotherapists and reads publications by her analyst but finds no answers, is unable to understand many things, and feels inferior to the analyst (RS C1 F). The clinical description of therapy phase XI, "Even father cannot make a son out of a girl," strongly reflects the therapeutic conception of the analyst, who focused on the patient's penis envy. The evaluation by the CCRT method, on the other hand, reveals above all Amalia's (new) openness ("I want to be attentive to others") in this therapy phase—both in the way she forms her relationships and in the way she confronts her own sexuality and femininity as she takes steps toward her mother.

During a three-week break in *therapy phase XIII* (sessions 300–304), Amalia decides to place a personal ad in a newspaper and receives several answers to which she in turn responds. She is afraid of how the analyst will react to this (WO C1 A), fearing his reproaches (RO C1 J):

P: In the weeks that you were away or unavailable, eh, I suddenly had the feeling I could "swim on my own" now. And then came my resolution that I will definitely not go on vacation with my parents this summer, that I'd do something on my own. I had answered this personal ad and made the decision to place one myself. And that was actually what I didn't want to tell you, because I was afraid you would interrogate me up and down and then you'd get angry and say, and then I was awfully afraid of what would come next and of course I've transferred that fear, but still it is sitting down there like an elemental force, that you will make an awful angry face and though you won't in fact forbid it, you'll say, "So all has been for naught, you've understood nothing, and this treatment here just gets in the way of your doing what you want"; that was it I think.

The fact that her younger brother recognized her ad in the paper strengthens her wish to protect herself from her brothers' and parents' interference and judgments (WS C1 M), also intensifying her dissatisfaction and feelings of inferiority, as comes out clearly in the image of the "poor maiden" given in the clinical description.

In *therapy phase XV* (sessions 351–355), Amalia is disturbed (RS C1 H) by outward alterations (e.g., her analyst's department has moved, there is a new therapy room, noise from building site). She feels unprotected by the analyst (WO C1 A) and jealous of his own children (RS C1 H):

> P: ... That you only moved up here to make it easier for you to take your children to school.

> T: What do you mean easier?

> P: Because I keep imagining your children will be going to school now in the, on Hochsträß and uh, and at first that made me, I mean, really furious.

She feels put under pressure both by her analyst and her father and thinks that there are expectations she has to fulfill. In her school, Amalia has confrontations with the janitor and her director (WS C1 K), in which she is able to adopt a more active posture and defend herself (RS C1 H). Her (unfulfilled) longing for her analyst's attention and her rage in its disappointment are also expressed in the following clinical description: "helpless love for the powerful father and envy of his wife."

In *therapy phase XVII* (sessions 401–404), the analyst receives a bouquet of flowers, which holds manifold symbolism. The bouquet was actually intended for a correspondent who had answered Amalia's next ad. At the same time it is an apology for the negative judgment of the analyst by Amalia's nephew, who knows the analyst from lectures and with whose criticisms of the analyst Amalia in part identifies (as also becomes clear in the clinical description). Amalia also identifies with her flowers, fearing that the analyst will not take good care of them (WO C1 C):

> P: I always really find it wonderful when someone knows how to take care of flowers. Most people take them and ram them in like a post in the earth and let them sit in the vase till they hang their heads. No, you know, these ones especially began to droop last time, and I thought uh-oh ....

> T: I didn't understand, you were saying?
>
> P: They were beginning to droop last time.
>
> T: They?
>
> P: They, the flowers began to droop.
>
> T: The flowers, right.
>
> P: Right, and so I thought, oh he's doing something wrong, that shouldn't be happening. And so naturally I was very glad today that you, that you did understand after all how to give them the right amount of water and food.

Through her correspondence with various men, Amalia explores her relationship to men and recalls her brothers' air of superiority and the lack of validation she experienced through her father (RO C1 J):

> P: It was never a climate of affirmation; it was always, how it all comes back to me, oh God. It was always, if I wanted to be a girl, I was stopped, and if I wanted, I remember once, I put on ski pants and my father said then, "I don't happen to have three sons, I should like to request, not at the table, go get changed." So I wanted to be a boy or to pretend it wasn't so important. It was always such an exclusive thing, the boys, I always had the feeling that my brothers, in spite of the connection I have to my younger brother, they did a better job of affirming each other and, and stayed together. Somehow behind my back they stuck together. After all they were the men and they were ok, and they were in the majority. Predestined from eternity to eternity. I don't know; it was just that way. A troublemaker and a liar, that's what I was, right and, ok yes. I have the feeling they were always watching to see what would come of it. They wanted to know just exactly what was different and what was going to come of it. And at the same time they always knew it in advance, what came of it. They just always knew everything better.

Therapy phase XIX (sessions 445–449) reflects Amalia's ambivalent experiences in her first relationship with a man. She wishes for a close, intense and also sexually satisfying relationship (WO C1 C, WS C1 C), but she is not sure of the affection of her partner (who still is attached to his ex-wife and also has other relationships) and is disappointed by his distance (RO C1 M, RO C1 I, RS C1 M):

P: ... And then he said, "Listen, when it comes down to it, you know, our relationship doesn't justify such a thing, you basically have no right, uh, hmm, to keep me away from other relationships. It would be a different thing if we wanted to start a family and have children, then it is bad to go around with other women." That's more or less what he said, and in retrospect it really shocked me terribly. And then when he called up on Monday, I had thought I wouldn't call again till Thursday, if he wants anything, let him do it, and then when he called on Monday, just as I had imagined.

T: First he wanted to put an end to it on Monday ...

P: Monday was absolute rock bottom.

T: Hmm.

P: I thought, I really have to put an end to this. And on the telephone I was absolutely icy and didn't say an extra word but then of course he called again about the pills. So then we talked. And that's when he probably got the impression that I was, about putting an end to it, he probably sensed something, I don't know. I don't know. I never actually said, "I'm through." And I never said, "Don't touch me again" or anything like that. Yes, indeed, we sure, oh we had such, talked so much on the telephone.

Insecurity, doubts about her physical attractiveness, and guilt that she fails to live up to her mother's ideas of morality are the main traits of Amalia's feeling life, as becomes clear in high proportion of negative reactions in this phase. Here again, the clinical description and the CCRT evaluation contrast: While the clinical description chiefly emphasizes Amalia's ambivalent relationship to her analyst ("Hate directed at the bountifully giving analyst, and an incipient turning away from this expectation"), the CCRT focuses on her new relationship experiences outside of the therapeutic relationship.

In the *concluding phases XXI and XXII* (sessions 501–517) of her therapy, Amalia is chiefly occupied with coming to terms with the experiences of her last relationship and of a new one that is in the offing, though emotionally she still feels very strongly attached to her previous partner (WO C1 A). Set off by an invitation from her arch-enemy to a class gathering, intense feelings of hate awaken in Amalia, but she is able to come to terms with them (WS C1 L). In the professional sphere, despite a particular challenge from two teacher trainees whom she experiences as very pushy, she is able to assert her will (WS C1 D) and is proud of that (RS C1 D, RS C1 J,

RS C1 H). The conclusion of the analysis and parting from the analyst are chief themes in this phase:

> T: I mean is there an idea, one that you have, as to what my way, my idea of coming to an end is?

> P: That one's easy for me. Mine is quite bold. I just thought you would adapt yourself to me.

> T: Um-hmm.

> P: And it was just in these last sessions that I got that feeling. It was really a feeling that, yes of course, he'll do what I want. Whereas before, there was this kind of tugging, I felt like I was being tugged on a leash and I had the feeling, he doesn't understand a thing, he has some kind of peculiar idea of his own of how to finish. He won't tell it to me of course, so I don't know it. And it was like a real tugging. And now, for about three or four sessions I think, I haven't been counting, my mind is the way I was just telling you. It'll simply work that way. I'll be sitting in my tortoise shell, and the harvest will come in. Like I told you.

> T: Um-hmm.

> P: I'll just get up and go, and I liked that so much that I thought, there's nothing he'll be able to do but go along. That fact that it isn't quite his idea of things, and if he finds something more thematically, that is his problem. Because there will always be something to find
> ....

What is striking is the great number of positive reactions by Amalia in the concluding phase. The clinical description speaks of a "farewell symphony: the return of many fears and the discovery of many changes"; and this is powerfully evident in the CCRT evaluation of the concluding phase, which illustrates Amalia's newly acquired freedom of action.

Discussion

Within the framework of our study, it has become possible for the first time to examine a long-term psychoanalytic therapy with the CCRT method during its course. Thus, compared with previous studies of single cases using the CCRT method, it offers the most comprehensive sample to date.

The relatively great number of reactions of the subject compared with other CCRT studies may be due to the fact that this was a psychoanalytic therapy and the patient was particularly encouraged to reflect on her feelings and thoughts. The results of the evaluation by the CCRT method underscore the clinical assessment of the success of the therapy and support the results of previous studies done on this material. Though the negative reactions of the objects and of the patient still predominate in the final phase of the therapy, a significant increase in positive reactions of the patient becomes apparent. The patient also described the reactions of the objects as more positive at the end of the therapy, but these changes could not be statistically established. The component "subject-related wishes and reactions of the subject" reveals that in the course of the therapy the patient was able to expand her freedom of action and acquire new competencies and that her depressive symptoms decreased.

The increase determined by Neudert, Grünzig, and Thomä (1987, Ch. 5.3) in positive feelings of self-worth and the decrease in negative feelings of self-worth in the course of the therapy match the content changes of the subject's reactions in the present study. Moreover, the distinct increase in positive reactions of the patient herself further supports this finding. Starting in therapy phase VII Amalia is in a position to perceive and express aggressive wishes, and starting in therapy phase XV these gain relevance in action. Particularly when this is contrasted with the dominant feelings of dissatisfaction and fearfulness at the inception of the therapy, the change in Amalia becomes apparent.

Alongside of a basic theme manifested in each of the absolute highest-frequency categories ("nuclear conflict"), each of the therapy phases also showed typical categories that characterize thematic foci in the sense of French's (1952) "focal conflicts" and that can be operationalized by the CCRT method. Thus the CCRT method makes it possible to structure material by content.

Being confined to narrative material, the CCRT method manifests a limitation when compared with the clinical description, particularly in the initial phases: While the clinical description of the first two phases focuses on the meaning of the treatment ("Analysis as Confession," "Analysis as a Test"), the CCRT method can access such aspects only through relationship episodes with the analyst. Such episodes in particular, however, are rarely reported by Amalia at the beginning of the therapy.

In contrast to the clinical description, which uses metaphorical language to highlight a theme according to the subjective assessment of the judges, investigation of the therapy phases by the CCRT method makes possible a more differentiated (and less subjective) analysis of the themes, as is seen in therapy phase III. In the clinical description, the "bad mother" takes center stage, while in the CCRT evaluation other aspects emerge: "I feel good" (regarding the patient's newly gained/regained freedom of action). While the clinical description is limited to the transference configuration, the CCRT method makes it possible to access interpersonal aspects inside and outside the therapeutic relationship.

Both the strengths as well as the limits of the CCRT method stem from its confinement to reports on relationship experiences by the patient herself. In other words, the investigation remains limited to those relationship experiences that the patient has perceived and verbalized. The method provides no way of including unconscious material (apart from the repetitive schemas that patients—often unconsciously—follow in describing the course of relationships) or of assessing defense mechanisms. Hence, the evaluation remains very close to the clinical material, though it does reflect intrapsychic processes in the narratives of interactions.

Parallels between the patient's descriptions of her relationship with the therapist and other objects can be examined by means of the CCRT method. Thus, the method makes it possible to capture structural aspects of the clinical transference concept. Nevertheless, the interactive transference currently in progress will not enter into the evaluation.

Although the method is called the Core *Conflictual* Relationship Theme, Luborsky leaves the concept of *conflict* unclarified. Conflicts in the analytic sense between wish and defense, between different systems or levels, or between drives (Laplanche & Pontalis, 1967) are not captured by the method. The wish component makes it possible to describe conflicts between two wishes that occur simultaneously and are mutually exclusive. It might be most accurate to say that the CCRT captures the theme of the most frequent wish without immediately revealing the associated conflict itself. Therefore, the CCRT should rather be understood as an indicator for capturing the patient's conflict. On the other hand, interpersonal conflicts are registered with great clarity and differentiation in the form of wish–reaction schemas. The ongoing interaction, however, is not captured, nor are the communicative and interactive functions of the narrative investigated within the therapeutic interaction.

With the CCRT method itself it is not possible to clarify how therapeutic changes have come about. In their studies, Crits-Christoph, Cooper, and Luborsky (1998) show a connection between the "accuracy" of the therapist's interpretations of the CCRT and the success of therapy.

It is now an uncontested fact that the quality of the therapeutic relationship is of critical importance for the success of therapy. On the whole, the relationship of the patient to her therapist seems to have been satisfying and positive for her—no other relationship is described with such a high rate of positive reactions toward the object of interaction.

The present study shows that the CCRT method makes it possible to capture clinically relevant interpersonal aspects of the psychoanalytic process, from the patient's point of view, that support the Ulm Process Model. The analyst's contribution, however, is reflected only in the patient's narratives regarding her relationship to the therapist. Use of the CCRT method provides for structuring of clinical material, for development of clinical hypotheses, and for checking on therapeutic focus during the course of therapy. The method is easily learned for clinical application, and the time required in formulating the psychodynamic connections for clinical use is minimal so that the method can accompany treatment throughout.

5.7   THE UNCONSCIOUS PLAN*

Introduction

The long-term systematic work of Weiss et al. (1986) is a sensible response to Gill's (1994, p. 157) observation: "While it is true that systematic research in psychoanalysis presents major obstacles, pitiful small percentage of work in our field is devoted to the development of methods that will allow for informed selection among our competing claims." The empirically based theory of the psychotherapeutic process developed by Weiss (1993) has become known as the control-mastery theory. This cognitive-affectively oriented psychoanalytic theory represents an important contribution to recent developments in psychoanalytic treatment theory and the research inspired by it.

The Control-Mastery Theory

The control-mastery theory is based on Freud's late ego psychology (1936, 1926d, 1937c) but also includes concepts drawn from object relation psychology (Fairbairn, 1952; Winnicott, 1965) and interpersonal theory (Sullivan, 1940), attachment theory (Bowlby, 1969, 1973, 1980), as well as from recent infant research (e.g., Stern, 1985).

Weiss (1993) views the striving for security and the avoidance of danger as fundamental principles regulating the unconscious mental life. In order to maintain a sense of security, according to Weiss defense processes last as long as there is an unconscious assumption that the perception and experience of the resisted contents represent a threat. This reveals the central significance accorded by Weiss to unconscious, planful and adaptive processes—conceptualized as unconscious ego functions in Freud's structural theory—for the regulation of defense strategies. The goal of therapy is to acquire a higher degree of control over these unconscious defense strategies and increasingly place them in the service of the patient's goals ("control-mastery"). Weiss attributes to the patient a strong unconscious wish to collaborate with the therapist in solving her problems and believes

* Cornelia Albani, Reto Volkart, Judith Humble, Gerd Blaser, Michael Geyer, and Horst Kächele. Adapted from Albani et al. (2000). The study was supported by the Deutschen Forschungsgemeinschaft and the Zurich Center for Psychotherapy (ZEPT).

that reenacting biographically acquired conflictual relationship patterns in the transference relationship serves as a way of testing their validity and finding alternative means of overcoming—that is, mastering—them. Weiss sees this mastery motivation as central to an understanding of the neurotic repetition compulsion and the therapeutic process.

Central to the theory is the existence of unconscious pathogenic beliefs, which are typically acquired in childhood or arise as a result of unconscious attempts to cope with traumatic experiences. Pathogenic beliefs make it possible to maintain relationships with important reference persons and aid in coping with traumatic experiences by diminishing feelings of helplessness (cf. Volkart, 1995).

Guilt feelings assume particular importance in Weiss's (1993) approach. Various forms of guilt are distinguished. Guilt at personal success or happiness that is felt to have been gained at the cost of other family members is referred to as "survivor guilt," a concept also found in Modell (1965) and Niederland (1981). Guilt at having injured others by one's own striving toward autonomy Weiss designates as "separation guilt."

To disconfirm pathogenic beliefs, the patient *tests* them in the relationship with the therapist. From this point of view, transference is not a pathological phenomenon to be seen as resistance to treatment but is an active unconscious strategy on the part of the patient to make use of the sheltered therapeutic relationship in order to come to terms with previous experiences and to have new relationship experiences. If the "test" is passed, the patient reacts with relief, introduces new material, works more intensively, or initiates a new test that exposes him to greater danger. In agreement with Alexander and French's (1974) concept of corrective emotional experience, Weiss (1993) emphasizes the active role of the therapist, which provides the patient with a positive experience of relationship in the ongoing therapeutic relationship so that therapeutic change can take place even without bringing resisted contents to consciousness.

The purpose of interpretations, according to Weiss, is to allow the patient to feel safe, to become aware of his pathogenic beliefs, and to understand his development and psychopathology. In this sense interpretations can also be evaluated empirically according to whether or not they serve the patient's unconscious plan. (For a critical discussion see Eagle, 1984, pp. 95ff.)

The Plan Formulation Method

With a view toward formulating their case conceptions and testing their concepts empirically, Weiss et al. (1986) developed the plan formulation method (Caston, 1977; Curtis & Silberschatz, 1986; Curtis, Silberschatz, Sampson, & Weiss, 1994; Curtis, Silberschatz, Sampson, Weiss, & Rosenberg, 1988). A first version, called plan diagnosis, included only four categories: goals, obstructions, tests, and insights. Later the method was supplemented to include a fifth area: traumas.

1. *Goals*: These are the therapeutic goals of the patient—that is, modes of behavior and experience, affects, and abilities that the patient would like to attain. They may be quite specific and concrete (e.g., to marry) or general and abstract (e.g., to gain the ability to withstand feelings of guilt). Goals can be conscious to varying degrees or unconscious.

2. *Pathogenic beliefs (obstructions)*: These include irrational pathogenic beliefs and associated fears, anxieties, and guilt feelings that are for the most part unconscious at the onset of therapy and prevent the patient from reaching his true goals.

3. *Tests*: This category lists tests by which the patient in therapy can attempt to disconfirm her pathogenic beliefs by testing the therapist and observing the latter's reactions.

4. *Insights*: This category comprises knowledge and experiences that can help the patient reach her goals. In particular, this includes insights about the genesis of the pathogenic beliefs in connection with traumatic experiences.

5. *Traumas*: Here all traumatic experiences are noted. These may be single traumatizing experiences or enduring negative relationship experiences from childhood.

Using the transcripts of the intake interview and the first therapy sessions, the judges independently determine items for the five categories. Typically the transcripts of three sessions are used for this purpose. The number of items is not limited. Items formulated include both especially typical ones as well as those that are possible but appear less relevant. All items of the individual judges are then gathered into a master list in random order. In a second step, the judges use this master list to rate, on a five-step scale, how relevant each of the items appears to them for this case. Using these ratings, the reliability is determined for each category.

For the final plan formulation, the mean values are determined per item and for one category across all judges. All items of one category of which the relevance rating falls beneath the median are dropped. The remaining items are checked for redundancy and edited for content by other judges. The plan formulation consists of a description of the patient, her current life situation and complaints, as well as the goals, obstructions, tests, insights, and traumas that have been ascertained.

Results on the Reliability of the Method

The SFPRG studies employed three to five judges. The reported intraclass coefficients (ICC) for the five categories fall between .14 and .97 for the single rater pairs, but the mean comes to between .78 and .9 (.78 for tests, .9 for goals, .86 for obstructions, and .9 for insights; Rosenberg, Silberschatz, Curtis, Sampson, & Weiss, 1986). The ICCs across all raters come to between .91 and .93 (Curtis et al., 1988; Person, Curtis, & Silberschatz, 1991). (For a detailed discussion of reliability, see Rosenberg et al., 1986.)

To date there has been only a single reliability study of another working group using the plan formulation method (Collins & Messer, 1991), and here too the ICCs for the various categories fall between .86 and .93.

Results of Empirical Research Using the Plan Formulation Method

In recent years Weiss et al. (1986) conducted extensive empirical studies of their theoretical concepts. The following selection is intended merely to provide an overview. For detailed information, the reader is referred to the original literature.

Studying the psychoanalysis of Mrs. C, Weiss et al., 1986) confirmed the hypothesis that even without interpretation, the patient was able to become conscious of previously repressed contents when she felt sufficiently sure of herself and did not react to these contents with heightened anxiety. This contradicts the classical psychoanalytic view that patients in all cases display a resistance to becoming conscious of repressed contents, which can be overcome only by interpretation, and that the elimination of repression is associated with anxiety.

The study of Silberschatz, Sampson, and Weiss (1986) examined three short-term therapies to investigate whether certain case-specific interpretations lead to immediate progress. The Plan Formulation Method makes it possible to adequately evaluate aspects of plans on a scale (Plan Compatibility Scale; Bush & Gessner, 1986) if an interpretation is helpful ("pro-plan") or unhelpful ("anti-plan") to the patient. Statements made by the patient immediately before and after the interpretation were rated on the Experiencing Scale (Klein, Mathieu, Gendlin, & Kiesler, 1970), which contains (among others) scales for evaluating the degree of insight, resistance, and associative freedom. The higher an interpretation is rated as "pro-plan," the greater and more positive the change on the Experiencing Scale.

Another study, based on seven 16-session short-term therapies (Norville, Sampson, & Weiss, 1996), demonstrated positive correlations between the mean value of the plan compatibility of all interpretations and the total result of the therapy at termination and in a follow-up after six months.

Using three 16-session short-term therapies, Silberschatz et al. (1986) investigated whether and in what way the plan compatibility and type of interpretation was predictive of the immediate changes in the patient's behavior after the interpretation. All interpretations were classified according to the typology devised by Malan (1963), which distinguishes between transference interpretations and nontransference interpretations. In determining the immediate change, three-minute segments preceding and following the interpretation were rated on the Experiencing Scale (Klein et al., 1970). The results failed to show either immediate effects of transference interpretations or connections between the number of transference interpretations per session and the mean experiencing score for that session. However, plan-compatible interpretations did lead to higher experiencing scores. When only those transference interpretations are considered that are rated as "pro-plan," no higher experiencing scores are found than after interpretations that were rated simply as "pro-plan" but not as transference interpretations.

Silberschatz and Curtis (1993) studied two short-term therapies and one psychoanalysis (Mrs. C; Silberschatz, 1986) to investigate how the therapist's behavior in the session influences the patient's therapeutic progress. They identified tests in the course of therapy and evaluated the appropriateness of the therapist's reactions and the immediate reactions of the patient to these using various scales (Relaxation Scale—Curtis et al., 1986, p. 200; Boldness Scale—Caston, Goldman, & McClure, 1986, p. 289; Experiencing Scale—Klein et al., 1970). In the two short-term therapies, 69 and 45 tests were ascertained and, in the first 100 sessions of the psychoanalysis, 46 tests. Positive changes were found on all three scales when the therapist passed the test.

Weiss's (1993) theory gives particular significance to interpersonal guilt. O'Connor, Berry, Weiss, Bush, and Sampson (1997) developed a questionnaire based on the control-mastery theory in order to measure interpersonal guilt: the Interpersonal Guilt Questionnaire (IGQ; O'Connor et al., 1997), whose 67 items form four scales: "survivor guilt," "separation guilt," "omnipotence responsibility guilt," and "self-hate." The connection between interpersonal guilt and psychopathology has been examined in some studies (e.g., Menaker, 1995; O'Connor, Berry, Inaba, Weiss, & Morrison, 1994). We are presently working on the development of a German version of this instrument.

Plan Formulation of Amalia X

To date there have been few German-language studies employing the Plan Formulation Method. Volkart (1995) uses the Weiss concept and the Plan Formulation Method for a detailed interpretation of a transcript. In the single case study of Volkart and Heri (1998), the facial action coding system (FACS, Ekman and Friesen 1978) method was used to study emotional processes relating to the affects shame, guilt, rage, disgust, and joy and to interpret them in connection with case-specific pathogenic beliefs.

Volkart and Walser (2000), again in a single case study using the FACS (Ekman & Friesen, 1978) for coding of mimic reactions, demonstrated that a female patient reacted with various nonverbal signals to a passed test and a failed test. These mimic signals were given almost immediately (i.e., within seconds).

Overcoming a wide geographical distribution, our group came into being out of a common interest in the Control-Mastery Theory, with which the various members have been familiar for some years. Visits to San Francisco, California, had given us (R.V. and C.A.) an opportunity to familiarize ourselves with the method and to discuss cases with San Francisco Psychotherapy Research Group (SFPRG) members. We began with a training phase on a transcribed case, which was made more difficult because the three raters (C.A., R.V., and J.H.) were able to come together as a group only once for a thorough clinical discussion. This meeting took place after the rating of the sample case, its purpose being to discuss the ratings and to arrive at as unified a case conception as possible.

For the final reliability study of the present research project, we chose the well-documented single case of Amalia X. Since for technical reasons the first interviews were not available, five therapy sessions from the initial phase of the therapy served as the data foundation, as well as several "stories about relationships" ("relationship episodes" in the CCRT method) taken from later sessions. We also had access to a compilation of case history data.

Results of the Reliability Test

The three judges first determine items for the five categories independently of one another. These are then combined into a master list and rated by each judge on a five-point scale (0 = not relevant to 4 = very highly relevant). In all, 252 items were rated by the three judges.

Table 5.9 gives an overview of the results of the reliability test that correspond to the results of the SFPRG and can be considered quite good given the minimal common training of the judges.

Structuring of the Items by Content

Using the ATLAS/ti text interpretation program,* items of similar content were assigned by consensus to certain categories on a similar level of abstraction. Only those items were used whose relevance rating (mean value of three judges) exceeded the mean value of all items per category. This procedure corresponds to the content analysis technique of "content structuring" described by Mayring (1993). In Tables 5.10 through 5.14 these categories are presented, each with one highly rated sample item. The categories are arranged according to the height of the mean value of the relevance rating of the items belonging to them.

---

* Thomas Muhr, available from Scolari, Sage Publications, London.

Table 5.9 Interrater Reliability for the Five Categories in the Plan Formulation of Amalia

Category	ICC	n	M	n,>M
Goals	0.93	65	2.61	39
Pathogenic Beliefs	0.82	57	2.36	31
Traumas	0.90	56	2.32	37
Insights	0.89	46	1.94	31
Tests	0.94	28	2.67	20

Notes: ICC, Intraclass correlation, two-way random effects model, average measure reliability (Shrout & Fleiss, 1979). n, number of items in total; M, mean value across all items and judges; n,>M, number of items above the mean value.

Plan Formulation for Amalia

Amelia X is a 35-year-old, single, employed woman who has sought treatment for worsening depressive complaints. She is socially isolated and maintains close contact with her family, particularly with her mother. Amalia has been unable to enter into sexual relationships up to this point.

Biography (Table 5.10, "Traumatic Experiences"): In the sibling order, Amalia is between two brothers, to whom she has always felt inferior. Her father was absent throughout her childhood—first due to the war and later for occupational reasons. At an early age, Amalia takes on the role of father, attempting to act as a substitute for her mother's missing partner. At the age of 3, Amalia contracts tuberculosis and remains bedridden for six months. When her mother's life is endangered by a serious case of tuberculosis, Amalia, age 5, is the first of the siblings to be put in the care of an aunt, with whom she remains for about 10 years. Here she is subjected to a strictly religious, austere, and puritanical upbringing at the hands of her aunt and grandmother. Since puberty Amalia has experienced great subjective suffering from an idiopathic hirsutism (pronounced body hair), though it is scarcely remarkable from an objective point of view.

The "Pathogenic Beliefs" in Table 5.11 reveal a markedly negative self-image. Amalia sees herself as ugly, bad, and burdensome to those around her. This is aggravated by keenly experienced autonomy issues: She hardly permits herself to dissociate herself from others and feels especially responsible for the well-being of her mother. Amalia experiences her own wishes as dangerous and morally reprehensible, particularly her sexual needs.

Important "Goals" in Table 5.12 of therapy are the perception and realization of personal wishes, particularly the need for a sexual relationship with a man but also other social contacts. Amalia would like to be able to set her own course independently of outer norms and to maintain a sense of

Table 5.10 Traumatic Experiences, Content Categories, and Sample Items

Content Category[a]	M	n	Sample Item	M
Functioning as substitute partner	3.67	4	The children were "substitute partners" for their mother (due to her unsatisfying marriage and the absence of her husband).	4.00
Mother's serious and protracted illness	3.67	1	Her mother was affected by protracted life-threatening illness during Amalia's childhood.	3.67
No contact with peers	3.67	1	Her close relationship with her mother and her role as substitute husband hindered contact to her peers.	3.67
Close relationship with mother	3.56	3	She always had to be there for her sick mother and assume the role of her passive father in caring for her.	3.67
Sent to live with aunt at age 5	3.56	3	Because of her mother's tuberculosis, at the age of 5 she was the first of the siblings to be sent away, living in the care of her grandmother and aunt for 10 years.	3.67
Wartime absence of father	3.46	5	During her first 5 years her father was absent because of the war.	3.33
Puritanical, dogmatic religious upbringing	3.33	7	She grew up in a strict, conservative, religiously fanatic environment, where any sensuality was prohibited.	3.67
Father cool, distant, compulsive and rigid	3.13	5	Her father is cool, distant, and emotionally unexpressive and has a compulsive, rigid attitude that makes it impossible to have a discussion with him.	3.67
Hirsutism	2.83	2	She has had abnormal body hair since childhood.	3.33
Aloneness within family	2.80	5	She felt like a complete outsider in her family, alone and not understood.	3.00
"Reasonable" and restrained behavior expected of her	2.75	4	The aunt requires Amalia to be "reasonable," because as a girl she "should understand."	3.00
TB at age 3	2.67	2	In her 3rd year of life she contracted TB and was bedridden for 6 months.	2.67
Experiences criticism and undervaluation in the family	2.67	2	She was often criticized or devalued.	3.00
Domination by brothers	2.67	1	She suffered greatly under her brothers' domination, unable to stand up to them or assert her own will.	2.67

[a] Items may be assigned to multiple categories.

separateness from others. In particular, she would no longer like to feel so responsible for others. Amalia wishes to find greater acceptance of herself and her body and become surer of herself.

Among the "Helpful Insights" in Table 5.13 are interpretations, which clarify for Amalia the problematic situation she entered into when she took on the role of her absent father in her mother's house. Alongside of this masculine identification, longing for her father is an important theme. A central focus is processing feelings of guilt and shame, by which Amalia experienced her aloneness as a deserved punishment and which continue to prevent her from forming close relationships. Also connected with the female identity problem stemming from identification with her father is Amalia's negative body image and self-image. With it Amalia attempted to explain to herself why she had been left alone by her parents and why she would be repulsive to any possible partner. Also important are insights that make Amalia aware that she withdrew from and subordinated herself to others because she always feared that independence on her part could become intolerable or dangerous to others.

In the "Tests" in Table 5.14, on the one hand Amalia displays defensive modes of behavior in therapy, expressing her pathogenic beliefs affirmatively. She acts quite reserved toward the therapist and presents herself as ugly and weak. On the other hand she risks offensive behaviors in which she directly casts her pathogenic beliefs into doubt, such as speaking with increasing directness about sexuality, showing curiosity, challenging the therapist, and introducing her own concerns.

Comparison with a Different Psychoanalytic Case Conception

By way of comparison let us turn to the case conception of Amalia X presented by Thomä and Kächele (1994b):

> Our clinical experiences justify the following assumptions: a virile stigmatization strengthens the penis wish or penis envy, reactivating oedipal conflicts. If the wish to be a man were fulfilled, the patient's hermaphroditic body schema would be free of contradiction. The question "Am I a man or a woman?" would then be answered and the identity issue, which is continually exacerbated by the stigmatization, would be eliminated. Self image and body identity would then be in harmony. However, the unconscious fantasy cannot be maintained in the face of the bodily reality: a virile stigmatization still does not make a woman into a man. Regressive solutions of attaining inner security in spite of the masculine stigmatization, through identification with

Table 5.11 Pathogenic Beliefs, Content Categories, and Sample Items

Content Category[a]	M	n	Sample Item	M
No right to a life of her own	3.67	2	She believes she has no right to impose her concerns on the family and therefore holds herself back.	4.00
A burden to others	3.48	7	She believes that she is a burden to others and must therefore make all decisions by herself, be perfect and never make mistakes.	4.00
Responsibility for mother	3.45	6	She believes that she is responsible for the well-being of others, particularly for her mother, and therefore finds it hard to dissociate herself from them.	4.00
Deserves isolation	3.39	6	She believes that she deserves being left alone and hence she thinks she has to do everything herself.	3.67
Wish for closeness is bad	3.34	3	She believes she should be ashamed of her longing for closeness and understanding and restrains herself in her wishes and needs.	3.67
Sexuality is bad	3.34	2	She believes that to enjoy sexual pleasure or long for a man makes her guilty and therefore she resists all sexual impulses.	3.67
Autonomy on her part harmful to others	3.11	3	She believes that it is painful and hurtful to others if she sets limits from them, and therefore takes exaggerated care to do the opposite.	3.33
Her personal wishes endanger others	3.00	4	She believes that her wishes, needs, and concerns pose a danger to others and therefore leads a socially isolated existence.	3.33
Competition endangers others	3.00	4	She believes she has to play the role of the "failure" (e.g., not earning an academic degree, remaining without male companionship) in order not to offer competition to others, and sabotages herself in both her private and professional life.	3.33
Sees self as ugly and bad	2.89	3	She believes that the sight of her ugliness must be unbearable to others, and therefore has to keep herself covered.	3.33

[a] Items may be assigned to multiple categories.

Table 5.12 Goals, Content Categories, and Sample Items

Content Category[a]	M	n	Sample Item	M
To experience satisfying sexuality	4.00	6	She would like to be able to enter into a sexual relationship with a man without feeling guilty.	4.00
To accept her own body	4.00	2	She would like to change her attitude toward her body and her virile body hair in a positive direction.	4.00
To perceive and realize her own wishes and needs	3.89	6	She would like to be able to articulate her wishes and stand up for her needs.	4.00
Self-determination, self-reliance, and independence from norms and persons	3.78	9	She would like to be able to define her own sphere of freedom and be able to move within it independently of the standards of the church, the doctrinaire views of the educated, or conventional norms.	4.00
To be able to express rage, annoyance, and other feelings openly	3.67	2	She would like to be able to communicate her annoyance without having to suffer feelings of guilt afterwards.	3.67
To feel less responsible for others	3.67	2	She would like not to feel responsible for others any more.	3.67
To trust herself, find security in herself, be self-accepting	3.50	2	She would like to develop greater security and confidence in herself.	3.33
To be able to compete with other women	3.33	2	She would like to be able to enter into competition with other women more openly.	3.33
To have relationships and social contacts on an equal footing	3.29	7	She would like to enjoy friendships on an equal footing, in which mutual interest and mutual support can be taken for granted.	3.67
To enjoy professional success	2.67	1	She would like to be professionally successful and also enjoy her success.	2.67

[a] Items assigned to only one category.

Table 5.13 Helpful Insights, Content Categories, and Sample Items

Content Category[a]	M	n	Sample Item: To become aware that ...	M
Assuming the role of her father	3.50	2	... she feels responsible for the well-being of her mother, has assumed the role of her father and is identified with a masculine self-image.	3.67
Wish for father	3.33	5	... she had a bad conscience toward her mother because she imagines that by her intense wish for her father she made her mother ill and drove her away.	3.67
Church as a substitute for father	3.33	2	... she had a great longing for a strong father and transferred this longing to the authority of the church.	3.33
Negative body- and self-image	3.27	5	... she experiences herself as unbearable, ugly, and unworthy of love, and therefore avoids social contact and does not express her wishes and needs.	3.67
Assumes guilt for absence of parents, aloneness as punishment	3.17	4	... she experienced the absence of her mother and father in her childhood as very bad and felt it was her fault and took her aloneness as her deserved punishment.	4.00
Avoidance of relationships out of guilt and shame	3.17	4	... she experiences herself as unbearable, ugly, and unworthy of love, and therefore avoids social contact and does not express her wishes and needs.	3.67
Guilt feelings, responsibility, identification with mother	3.09	7	... due to guilt feelings she feels intensely responsible for her mother and believes she has no right to dissociate herself from her.	4.00
Problematic identity as a woman	3.07	5	... she wished she had a masculine father who was involved in her life and was not afraid of her feelings or her femininity.	3.67
Avoidance of competition	3.00	1	... on top of her father's problematic personality she herself actively contributed to the lack of relationship to him because she was afraid this might be a threat to her mother.	3.00
Others unable to tolerate autonomy on her part	2.53	5	... she continues to maintain such a close relationship to her mother and avoids entering into friendships or a relationship with a partner because she is afraid her mother would not be able to bear a greater degree of independence on her part and would feel abandoned.	3.00

Table 5.13 Helpful Insights, Content Categories, and Sample Items (continued)

Content Category[a]	M	n	Sample Item: To become aware that ...	M
Subservience	2.33	5	... she continually puts herself into the role of an outsider or Cinderella in order to fulfill other people's needs for superiority.	2.33
Compulsive actions out of guilt feelings	2.00	1	... her compulsive ideas and actions were an attempt to assuage her tormenting feelings of guilt.	2.00

[a] Items may be assigned to multiple categories.

the mother, reawaken old mother-daughter conflicts and lead to a panoply of defense processes. (pp. 79ff)

Discussion

Comparison of these two case conceptions shows that Thomä and Kächele (1994b) orient themselves on the model of penis envy and diagnose the conflict on an oedipal plane. The plan formulation based on the control-mastery theory includes oedipal themes but prefers to diagnose a disturbance of "early triangulation" (Abelin, 1971), in which the existing dependence of the patient on her mother is understood not as a regression but as an inhibited development of autonomy caused by specific pathogenic beliefs. Clinically the two case conceptions would have different consequences for the interpretative work and possibly also for therapeutic interventions. From a Weissian viewpoint, chiefly one would have to thematize Amalia's feeling of responsibility for her reference partners and the resulting feelings of guilt, which ultimately serve to maintain the attachment to her mother and her resisted wish and longing for her father.

A comparison exploring which of the two conceptions is capable of clarifying which aspects of the therapeutic process must be left to future studies.

Even if our study is limited to a single case, we have been able to show that the plan formulation method can be reliably applied outside of the group around Weiss and Sampson and the English-speaking world, which represents a contribution to establishing the method.

In contrast to the SFPRG, in order to reduce the content of items lying above the mean value of the raters we chose a structured content analysis procedure enabling categorization on selected levels of abstraction for the final plan formulation. For future studies, as a further methodological refinement one might consider empirical verification of the assignment of the items to the categories. A disadvantage of this procedure is that the very specifically formulated items are lumped together in categories that seem rather general.

Table 5.14 Tests, Content Categories, and Sample Items

Content Category[a]	M	n	Sample Item	M
Thematizing sexuality	3.67	2	She will speak to the therapist of her sexual desires in order to test if he will condemn, punish, or pillory her for them morally as the church did.	3.67
Speaking more openly and directly	3.67	2	She will give herself more leeway in the course of therapy, speaking more openly and freely in order to test if the therapist tries to limit her and put her in her place.	3.67
Showing annoyance	3.67	1	She will explicitly express her annoyance (at a thing or person) in order to test if the therapist tolerates this or puts her in her place.	3.67
Showing curiosity, interest, and desire	3.67	1	She will ask the analyst about the reason for the setting (no eye contact) in order to test if she is permitted to be curious and eager.	3.67
A self-restrained and careful opening	3.62	7	She will cautiously open up to the therapist in order to test if he remains benevolent and does not condemn her.	4.00
Thematizing hirsutism	3.50	2	She will return repeatedly to the subject of her virile body hair as a symbol of her ugliness, in order to test if the therapist can still tolerate her in spite of it.	4.00
Expressing concerns and problems	3.33	1	She will confront the therapist with her worries and concerns in order to test if he shows as little interest as her father.	3.33
Checking the clock	3.17	2	She will look at the clock in order to test if the analyst is not getting tired of her and if she should take over the responsibility herself and do everything herself.	3.33
Emphasizing personal faults and weaknesses	3.00	1	She will continually bring up her faults and weaknesses in order to test if the therapist confirms her badness.	3.00
Challenging and provoking the therapist	3.00	1	She will challenge and provoke him in order to test if he is just as passive as her father, or if he is capable of taking an active stand.	3.00

[a] Items assigned to one category only.

An explanation for the high reliabilities obtained is, first of all, that complex formulations are reduced to simple, clearly structured categories, with the judges rating only single items, not complete formulations, and second that the judges share the same theoretical orientation (Curtis et al., 1988).

Unlike other methods of recognizing interpersonal patterns using standardized categories, the plan formulation method does not allow for interpersonal comparability. It does, however, offer the advantage of an individual, case-specific formulation that keeps very close to the text while also making possible inferences and clinical conclusions.

A particular strength of the method is the high clinical relevance of the different categories (Curtis & Silberschatz, 1986; Silberschatz & Curtis, 1986). The items gathered for the categories of traumas, pathogenic beliefs, and insights represent the essential foundation for the interpretive work. The predicted tests can help the therapist become conscious of possible transference–countertransference enactments and develop helpful, patient-specific therapeutic interventions.

The goals ascertained in the plan formulation make possible course control and facilitating goal attainment in the course of psychotherapeutic treatment and can serve as a guidepost for the therapist in the practical therapeutic work.

In addition, the method offers the possibility not only of ascertaining therapeutic success by the symptoms and by general procedures such as questionnaires but also of investigating the underlying psychological processes that lead to lasting changes using case-specific instruments. The Plan Attainment Scale developed by Silberschatz, Curtis, and Nathans (1989) makes it possible to judge the extent to which the patient has reached her specific goals and overcome her pathogenic beliefs and if she has succeeded in acquiring essential insights.

The plan formulation determined by this method can be understood in terms of a changing focus and serves as a way of structuring a case and generating hypotheses, which will require continual review and supplementation in the course of treatment (cf. Thomä & Kächele, 1994). Much as in Caspar's (1995) plan analysis, in which a hierarchy of plans is determined, the relevance of the items ascertained with the plan formulation method changes with the phases of therapy and of life.

Beyond the five categories covered in the plan formulation—traumas, goals, tests, pathogenic beliefs, and insights—other areas are conceivable that are not yet systematically captured by this method (e.g., resources of the patient).

Weiss sees patients as active collaborators in the therapeutic process—as interested in a solution to their problems, wishing to gain insights, seeking corrective emotional experiences by way of tests in the therapeutic process, and unconsciously but "planfully" working to disconfirm their pathogenic beliefs. His general theory of psychotherapy is based on clinical observation and is supported by extensive empirical findings. Admittedly, Weiss's claim regarding the general validity of his theory of the therapeutic process still awaits empirical validation in the clinical material of other forms of therapy (Eagle, 1984, p. 105). Nevertheless, the studies of the SFPRG are an impressive example of how theorization can be grounded and enriched by empirical research.

5.8   THE REACTION TO BREAKS AS AN INDICATOR OF CHANGE*

Loss–Separation Model

Through its own peculiar method, psychoanalysis has generated a great number of hypotheses related to the different fields of the psychoanalytic theory. The important heuristic value of psychoanalytic methods contrasts greatly with the weakness of its external validation. Both inside and outside psychoanalysis, we observe a growing interest in the validation of hypotheses by using methodologies unrelated to the psychoanalytic method borrowed from the social sciences. Lately we have been working on validation with empirical methodology of some hypotheses of the loss–separation model in the theory of psychoanalytic therapy.

The assumption on which this study is based is that the analyst, in his therapeutic work and interpretative actions with the individual patient, builds and deploys "working models" in which the most varied and disparate levels of psychoanalytic theory and technique crystallize (Bowlby, 1969; Greenson, 1960; Peterfreund, 1975). The patient too has working models, which have gradually become structured during the course of his or her life and in accordance with which he or she *interprets* his or her relationship with the analyst and develops expectations in regard to him (Bowlby, 1973). Within these working models, for patient and analyst alike, the loss–separation model occupies a position of paramount importance.

The theme of loss and separation is to be found at all levels of psychoanalytic theory and technique and goes beyond differences between schools. It may be said to have become a clinical commonplace. As such, it is found in the following:

1. In the explanatory theory of the genesis of psychic and psychosomatic diseases—in the hypothesis of the pathogenic potential of the early

---

* Juan Pablo Jiménez, Dan Pokorny, and Horst Kächele. This study was part of J.P. Jimenez, doctorial dissertation at the Ulm University Faculty of Medicine.

separation traumas

2. In the theory of psycho-sexual development—in the conceptions of Melanie Klein and M. Mahler
3. In the theory of transference—in the idea of the repetition in the analytic situation of the early processes of separation from and loss of primary objects
4. In the theory of personality when maturity and trait differentiation become dependent on the inner "separation" level of self and object representations
5. In the theory of therapy—in the association between working through and work of mourning

The loss–separation model is also a psychoanalytic process model. This view was formulated explicitly by J. Rickman long ago, as follows: "The week-end break, because it is an event repeated throughout the analysis, which is also punctuated by the longer holiday breaks, can be used by the analyst ... in order to assess the development of the patient" (Rickman, 1950, p. 201). He adds, "the week-end and holiday interruptions of the [analytical] work force up transference fantasies; as the [analytical] work continues these change in character in correspondence with the internal pattern of forces and object relations within the patient" (ibid.).

Notwithstanding its central position in the theory of technique as a psychoanalytic process model, the evolution of the reaction to breaks has not hitherto formed the subject of a systematic empirical study. Every process model always has two aspects (Thomä & Kächele, 1994a, ch. 9): a *descriptive* one—that is, it serves to describe the course and development of the treatment—and a *prescriptive* one, which guides the analyst in his interventions in the process and enables him to devise interpretative strategies.

This investigation is limited to the *description* by empirical means of the evolution of the reaction to breaks in an individual female patient's therapeutic process. The central hypothesis of the study may be formulated as follows:

The evolution of the reaction to breaks during the course of a psychoanalytic treatment is an indicator of the structural change being achieved by the patient through the therapeutic process.

This general hypothesis breaks down into two particular ones:

1. The working model of loss–separation can be detected in chronological correlation with breaks in the analytical treatment, in the material of the sessions (strictly speaking, in the verbal interaction between patient and analyst).
2. In a successful analysis, this model must evolve as envisaged for psychoanalytic theory.

An individual case is considered here because only a study of this kind allows a detailed examination of the evolution of the reaction to breaks during the analysis.

Amalia's psychoanalysis comprised 531 sessions extending over nearly five years. Of the 531 actual sessions, only 517 were recorded on tape, and of these, 212 had been (at the time of this study) transcribed according to the transcription rules of the Ulm Textbank (Mergenthaler & Stinson, 1992). The study was based on the 212 transcribed sessions fairly evenly distributed over the treatment.

Material and Method

The method of an empirical study should be consistent with what it is desired to find—with the hypotheses made and also with the available material—in this case, a sample of 212 verbatim transcripts of sessions in Amalia's psychoanalysis.

The first hypothesis of our study is that the transcripts of the sessions that relate to breaks in the treatment should contain the theme of loss–separation. Hence, the first requirement is to define formally what we mean by a break. Second, we have to test whether the loss–separation model appears predominantly in the transcripts of the sessions related in time to a break and not arbitrarily in any session within the sample. Once this relationship has been demonstrated, we shall turn to the second hypothesis and analyze the content of the sessions, which we shall from this point on call *separation sessions* and shall consider whether the transference fantasies appearing in the material of these sessions evolve during the course of the process and if so, how?

From the foregoing, three stages of this research can be identified, each of which will require a different method appropriate to its particular aims. The aim of the first stage is to formally define a break in treatment. The second sets out to determine the correlation between a *break session*, defined operationally, and an appearance in the material of the theme of loss and separation. The third stage of the research seeks to demonstrate an evolution in the patient's transference reactions which is reflected in the content of the material of the separation sessions.

For an initial definition of a break in the treatment, we adopt operational empirical criteria. On the basis of the attendance card, we draw up a histogram of the treatment, which we shall analyze herein.

At a second stage we try to establish the correlation between break sessions and separation sessions, because not all break sessions necessarily show a significant increase in the incidence of the loss–separation theme. If a correlation is found, we shall check what kind of break session may also be regarded as a separation session.

For a substantial description of the break sessions, we use the *Ulm Anxiety Topic Dictionary* (ATD; Speidel, 1979), which is a computer-assisted instrument for content analysis. The ATD comprises four thematic categories—guilt, shame, castration, and separation—operationalized as lists of individual words, each presumed to represent one of these categories. A computer program is used to analyze the verbal content of the analyst's and the patient's texts, taken separately for each session in the analysis, the result being values reflecting the relative frequency of text words belonging to each of the thematic categories. This procedure yields values for the categories of guilt, shame, castration, and separation, for the patient and the analyst, respectively, a comparison of which from session to session gives an approximate idea of the extent to which these themes were touched upon in each session. The dictionary was used in this study only as a crude instrument for the detection of themes and not to detect specific affects or anxieties.

To understand our point we should consider that 90% of the values found in the sessions with this instrument range, in the case of our patient, between 0.1% and 1.2% for the different categories. For example, if in a given session ATD yields a value of 0.75% for the category *separation-patient*, it means that 0.75% of the words used by the patient in that session—an average of 22 words in 2933—belongs to the semantic field of separation. It is therefore clear that values are mere indicators of spoken themes.

From this stage we hope to identify the sessions relevant from the point of view of the reaction to breaks—that is, sessions which show the impact of the session-free intervals on the analyst–patient dyad, as reflected in the four themes defined by the dictionary.

The sessions so identified—or rather a sample of these sessions where there are many—can be analyzed at a third stage by a method closer to the clinical method, with a view to examining in detail the evolution of the reaction to breaks throughout the treatment. In this part of the study we use the method devised by Luborsky (1977) to evaluate the transference (CCRT).

The CCRT method of evaluation of the transference and aspects of this method's reliability and validity have been described in various publications (Luborsky & Crits-Christoph, 1998). Being oriented toward description of the content of the transference, this method is highly suitable for evaluating the evolution of the transference fantasies appearing in the patient in relation to breaks during the treatment.

The first step of this method is identification by independent judges of *relationship episodes* (RE) in the session transcripts. These relationship episodes are nothing other than small narrative units in which an interaction with another person is described. The second step is for the CCRT judges to evaluate the relationship episodes, identifying the following three components in each:

1. The patient's principal wish, need, or intention in relation to the other person *(W, wish)*
2. The actual or expected response from the other person *(RO, response from other)*
3. The subject's (patient's) reaction to this response *(RS, response from self)*

The CCRT is the representation, summarized in a few sentences, that makes complete sense of the types of components appearing with the highest frequency throughout the sample of relationship episodes.

Results

Stage 1: Formal Definition of a Break

We define a break in the treatment by operational empirical criteria. The histogram reproduced in Figure 5.10 shows the following: Among the 531 actual sessions (of which 517 were recorded) there were 530 session-free intervals, of which we measure the duration in days (e.g., there is an interval of one day between a Monday session and the next Tuesday session). The histogram revealed five blocks of session-free intervals. Block 1 represents the shortest intervals and reflects the "ideal" timing (in this case, three times a week). These shortest intervals were defined as *nonbreaks*. Block 2 contains the weekend breaks. Block 3 comprises short breaks due to illness on the part of the patient or absences of the analyst for attendance at congresses or other reasons. Block 4 comprises breaks for Christmas and Easter holidays. Finally, Block 5 represents three summer holidays taken by the patient and the analyst at the same time, two breaks due to nonsimultaneous summer holidays, and two prolonged absences by the analyst for trips abroad.

On the basis of these blocks of breaks, it was possible to define which sessions correlated with which break and the type of correlation with the relevant break (whether before or after, and at what distance).

Results. Stage1: Histogram of Amalia's treatment

Number of intervals

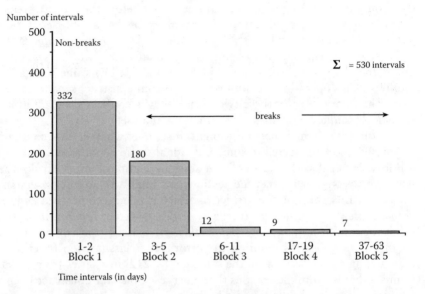

Figure 5.10 Stage I: Histogram of Amalia's sessions free intervals.

Stage 2: Identification of Separation Sessions

According to our hypothesis, the loss–separation model should appear in sessions correlated in time with the breaks (break session).*

To investigate the correlation between break sessions and separation sessions, we divide the sessions of the sample into groups in accordance with their correlation with the breaks: According to the duration of the break, whether they preceded or followed the break, and the number of sessions between the relevant session and the break. We compare the different groups formed in this way with a group of nonbreak sessions ($N = 86$). This group of 86 nonbreak sessions proved to be evenly distributed throughout the treatment.

---

* The relationship between the loss–separation model in the verbal records and the *break sessions* is not necessarily absolute and automatic. Theoretically it is also possible for the separation theme to occur in sessions which are not associated with real external break, such as those which are centered on an internal separation or on a certain distancing from the analyst during a particular session. On the other hand, breaks can occur that do not provoke in the patient a verbal reaction of separation that shows in records: there may be a non-verbal reaction that will obviously not appear in the verbal records. However, it is most likely that if the separation theme does appear in the verbal content of the session, it would do so in sessions associated with breaks.

The comparisons made among the different groups of break sessions and the group of nonbreak sessions reveal significant differences (t-test: $p < 0.05$) only in the group of sessions immediately before the longest breaks. In this group we find significantly higher values for the variable *separation-patient* and significantly lower values for the variable *shame-therapist*.*

These results enabled us to define operationally a *separation session* as one with a high value for *separation-patient* and a low value for *shame-therapist*. This operational definition specifies our construct *separation session*. The importance of these two variables was confirmed by additional statistical techniques such as discrimination analysis.

The question, which naturally then arose, was whether this construct might not also be detected in some individual sessions not associated with the longest breaks—for example, in sessions before or after breaks that were not so long, or in weekend sessions, or, finally, in nonbreak sessions. To answer this question, an artificial variable, called technically a *canonical variable*, was formed on the basis of the construct *separation session* (high *separation-patient*, low *shame-therapist*). Using the computer, this canonical variable was required to perform the classification function of rearranging all the sessions in the sample ($N = 212$) in a series from plus to minus—that is, from the sessions that most resembled the construct *separation session* to those that were least like it.

The next step was to compare the extreme groups of the sessions thus rearranged with the actual dates on which they took place. The result of this comparison again confirmed the hypothesis that the separation sessions tended to be grouped around the breaks: Of the first 20 sessions arranged in accordance with the canonical variable (i.e., the sessions most similar to the separation construct), 19 corresponded to sessions directly correlated with a break or to the period of termination of the analysis, while only one was a nonbreak session. The majority of these 19 break sessions preceded a prolonged break. Examination of the group of 20 sessions at the opposite extreme (i.e., those at the nonseparation end) showed that the majority of these were nonbreak sessions and the remainder weekend sessions.

On the basis of these results it can be asserted that the separation construct is *unstable* but *consistent*. This means that it does not always appear in the case of a real separation between analyst and patient (i.e., a break in the continuity of the treatment) but that, when it does appear, its probability of appearance is greatest when the relevant session immediately precedes a prolonged break.

The separation construct so far suggests that in this treatment (i.e., with this analyst–patient dyad) the reaction to breaks appears to be correlated

---

* This does not mean that *separation sessions* do not occur in association with shorter breaks such as weekends for example; it simply means that *as a whole* the group of sessions immediately before a long break are clearly different from *nonverbal sessions*.

with themes of separation and shame. More precisely, the analyst mentions the theme of shame less in the separation sessions than in the treatment in general.* If we consider only the 20 separation sessions in the last third of the analysis—specifically, from session 356 onward—the analyst ceases to speak about shame and the variable *shame-therapist* is practically zero. This might mean that toward the end of the treatment the analyst stopped relating the themes of separation and shame or that the analyst felt that shame was no longer a concern of the patient.

The rearrangement based on the canonical variable previously described enabled us to select a sample of 20 sessions containing material we knew to contain allusions to separation and that could be analyzed by the CCRT method in the third part of the study. These 20 sessions extend over a long period within the overall process (from session 14 to session 531, the latter being the final session of the treatment).

Stage 3: Evolution of the Separation Sessions

Of the 20 separation sessions obtained during the course of the first part of the study, we selected a smaller group for the application of the CCRT method to evaluate the content of the transference, using the following criteria:

1. We disregarded sessions containing reports of dreams, as the application of the CCRT to reports of dreams was shown to be problematical (Popp et al., 1990).
2. We chose a set of sessions that spread roughly over the entire process.

On the basis of these criteria, we selected from the beginning of the analysis two sessions immediately preceding the first prolonged break (recorded sessions 21 and 22) and from the end the last three sessions of the analysis (recorded sessions 515 to 517). We also selected two in the second third (recorded sessions 221 and 277) and two in the last third of the treatment (recorded session 356 and 433).

The CCRT allows a quantitative analysis of the relative frequency of its different components. However, our sample of six observations is too small for conclusions of statistical value to be drawn. None of the differences

---

* It is highly likely that the separation content may lead to a general working model and that the shame aspect points to a dyadic-specific content. If so, this is merely a trivial fact, namely that Amalia experiences separations within the framework of her personal neurosis where shame plays a special psychopathological and psychodynamic role (given her hirsutism and erythrophobia). We can think of many possible combinations. For example, the separation anxiety can be defeated by sexual shame anxiety; or the patient may feel depressive shame vis-à-vis her analyst because of her painful feelings of isolation and abandonment; on the other hand, separation from the analyst by a break can be experienced by the patient as humiliation and as a sign of shameful dependence, etc., and all this can develop in the course of analysis in different ways.

found, in fact, reached the level of significance, although it was possible to detect very clear trends.

It is clear from a direct reading of the selected sessions that a break as such was accepted by Amalia as a fact, although at first she may not have shown awareness of a transference reaction to this. With regard to this external factor—weekends, holidays, or the analyst's trip abroad—the patient reacts by expressing wishes and expecting from the object, or actually receiving from him, the fulfillment or the rejection of the wish. With regard to her wishes or demands, and in view of the object's responses, Amalia reacts with different emotions and fantasies which also range from positive to negative. The evolutions of the CCRT components in the course of the analysis reflect the development of Amalia's reaction to breaks.

The various components of the CCRT evolved as follows:

1. Relationship episodes (RE) in which the interaction partner was some person extraneous to the treatment, declined as the treatment progressed, while those in which the analyst was the partner and in which the patient herself was the subject and object of the interaction (i.e., self-reflective episodes) increased. This means that the transference and self-reflection became increasingly intense or, in other words, that the patient was increasingly on his way in recognizing the character of the transference relationship in parallel with an intensification of the processes of internalization and self-analysis.

2. With regard to the actual or expected response of the object (RO) to the patient's wish, positive responses increased slightly, while negative ones fell. This means that in general the object to which the demand or wish was addressed was seen as possessing increasingly benevolent and decreasingly frustrating features. In the patient's reaction (RS) to the object's response, the changes were much more intense: The subject's negative reactions clearly decreased as the analysis progressed, while the positive reactions increased. This means that Amalia was reacting to the breaks with less and less of a fall in her self-esteem and confronting them with increasingly positive expectations.

3. The patient's principal wish (W) activated by the break, in general and at a high level of abstraction, fell within the conflict between autonomy and dependence. However, this conflict evolved during the course of the therapeutic process.

In relation to the first break (sessions 21–22), the wish for harmony, to be accepted and respected by others and by herself, predominated in Amalia during the last session before the first summer holidays. The wish to be cured and to be independent also appeared, although to a much less important extent. The object's response was predominantly negative, and the patient perceived rejection, lack of respect, devaluation, utilization, and avoidance. Amalia reacted to this response with separation anxiety, helplessness, disillusionment, resignation, shame, avoidance, withdrawal, and insecurity. All this was experienced by the patient in direct relation to her parents and family; there was hardly any allusion to the therapist. Her separation verbalizations may have referred to feelings focused on her family rather than on her analyst.

In the second break (session 221), before an extended weekend, a change in the balance of forces in the conflict between autonomy and dependence was noted. Although the principal wish was still for closeness, harmony, and recognition, the wish for greater autonomy appeared more frequently, expressed in a desire to dominate the interpersonal situations that overwhelmed her and caused her anxiety. The object responded negatively, with remoteness, rejection, and lack of consideration, leaving the patient in the lurch. The patient reacted to this response with feelings of helplessness, panic anxiety, revulsion, and withdrawal (i.e., with intense separation anxiety and shame). This session marked the beginning of the appearance of transference allusions and also positive reactions by the patient to the negative response of the object; for instance, she acknowledged herself to be internally divided and full of jealousy and asked for help. With effect from this session, Amalia openly recognized the transference dimension of her wishes and reactions—that is, she began to experience the breaks in terms of her relationship with the analyst.

In the third break (session 277), immediately before another long weekend, the conflict between autonomy and dependence continued to evolve. The poles of the conflict came closer together and began to merge, now constituting a single desire for reciprocity, which could be formulated as a wish for closeness, in a relationship of mutual belongingness and equality of rights. This was accompanied by an explicit wish to talk to the therapist about traumatic separation: The patient spoke directly about death and the fear of a premature termination of the analysis. The object's response to these wishes was predominantly positive; the patient perceived interest on the part of others and of the analyst and felt herself to be understood and engaged in a process of interchange. At the same time, however, she felt that the analyst was resisting entering into a relationship of mutuality with her. Amalia reacted to this response with anxiety due to loneliness; she felt very isolated and abandoned but began to show signs of rage, mourning, and also hopes of permanence beyond loss.

The fourth break examined in our study corresponded to the last session (356) before a 40-day trip abroad by the analyst. In the second part of the study, the ATD shows that the analyst stopped relating the themes of separation and shame. The CCRT shows that in this session other people disappeared as interaction partners; the majority of the relationship episodes had the analyst as partner and some of them the patient herself. It was therefore an intensely "transferential" session. The patient had a single desire, representing the overcoming of the conflict between autonomy and dependence: Amalia wanted actively to place her needs and wishes in the framework of a relationship of mutuality. The object (analyst) responded to this wish without ambivalence, positively only, with acceptance and "giving permission" to Amalia to satisfy her wishes. The patient reacted with guilt feelings and loss anxiety, which gave rise to dissatisfaction and helpless rage. The positive reaction was represented by the hope of permanence in spite of the loss and by fantasies of struggle to assert herself in reality. This constellation suggests that the patient was undergoing a depressive reaction in this session. The object, being idealized, was not affected by projections, and the patient recognized that she herself was solely responsible for her difficulties and dissatisfactions. The analyst's references to her shame disappeared; as a reaction formation, this had performed a defensive function against anxiety and the pain of separation. Starting with this session, the process entered upon the phase of resolution; other people, outside the analytical situation, again began to appear—this time as the possible objects of wishes and demands.

The fifth break corresponded to the session (433) immediately before the last summer holidays. In this session, the wish for a relationship of equality took on a new dimension. Amalia saw this relationship in a man–woman context: What she wanted was a sexual partner with whom to establish a mutually satisfactory human relationship. The object's response to this new wish was unequivocally negative, and Amalia was rejected. In terms of the transference, this rejection represented an implicit recognition of the impossibility of forming a sexual relationship with the analyst. However, she reacted positively to this rejection, and, beyond her angry renunciation of the wish and her feelings of disillusionment and insecurity, Amalia was thinking hard about suitable alternatives for the satisfaction of her wishes and needs.

At the end of the analysis (sessions 515–517), what was unequivocally predominant was the wish to assert a vital identity as a woman, in a real relationship of mutuality with a man. A wish related directly to the termination also appeared: Amalia wanted to be able to continue the internal dialogue (self-analysis) she had achieved in the treatment, beyond the termination. The object's response was ambivalent: On the one hand, the object showed itself to be rejecting, incapable, unworthy of trust and inconsiderate; at the same time, however, it appeared as a model that offered support, with self-confidence, vitality, and generosity. Amalia's reaction was predominantly positive; she felt more realistic, more confident, and independent; she felt that she had changed positively, was not afraid of the separation, had something enriching inside her, and was ready to seek new experiences and to achieve self-realization. However, Amalia also showed negative emotions, such as pain at renouncing the relationship with the analyst, and felt that she still had a tendency toward masochism and an antagonistic passivity.

Discussion

Our study successfully demonstrates the evolution of Amalia's reaction to breaks although early in the analysis they were focused on her family and later in the analysis on her analyst. This evolution refers only to the transference fantasies that were verbalized. The method used, of analysis of verbal content, does not allow us to take account of nonverbal reactions. However, Amalia was a neurotic patient with a good capacity for symbolization, and it is therefore justifiable to suppose that her verbal behavior was a good expression of her internal world.

We must consider all components of the CCRT as the patient's reaction. That is to say, the wish, the object's response and the patient's reaction together constituted Amalia's reaction to breaks. The CCRT in the form applied does not distinguish between the actual and expected response of the object, so that the question remains open as to the extent to which the object's response corresponded to perception of the analyst's actual behavior or that of others toward Amalia and how far it is to be attributed to projections by the patient. In any case, the relative increase in relationship episodes in which the patient herself was an interaction partner showed a general tendency toward introjection, which ought to have been accompanied by an improvement in the reality sense. The evolution described conforms to analytical theory in its different versions. For instance, according to the Kleinian conception, Amalia attained "the threshold of the depressive position" (Meltzer, 1967) around session 356, the rest of the process being a working through of that position. On the basis of attachment theory (Bowlby, 1973), Amalia may be said to have reacted to the loss by the following sequence: first, with protest, in which separation anxiety predominated; then, with despair, in which she began to accept the loss and embarked on the work of mourning; finally, with detachment, the phase in which Amalia decided to renounce the transference satisfaction of her wishes and needs and turned toward external reality. In terms of ego psychology, the fact that Amalia showed less object-loss anxiety toward the end of the analysis than at the beginning suggests that the mental representations of the object had achieved greater independence of the instinctual wish and need for it (Blanck & Blanck, 1988).

Blatt and Behrends (1987) study the nature of the therapeutic action with regard to the processes of separation and individuation proposed by Mahler (1969) and with regard to the internalization phenomena. They point out that "progress in analysis appears to occur through the same mechanism and in a way similar to normal psychological development. Therapeutic change in analysis occurs as a developmental sequence which can be characterized as a constantly evolving process of separation-individuation including gratifying involvement, experienced incompatibility, and internalization. Patients gradually come to experience the analyst and themselves as separate objects, increasingly free of distortion by narcissistic needs and/or projections from the past relationships" (p. 293). Incompatibility experiences refer not only to real separations (breaks) but also to all interaction in analysis, which fails to gratify a patient's wish or need. Basing themselves on this concept, Blatt and Behrends propose the hypothesis that "important changes in the analytic process frequently occur shortly before or subsequent to a separation (break). Early in treatment, changes in psychological organization and representational structures will occur after a separation or a major interpretation. Later in analysis changes may also occur in anticipation of separation rather than only as a reaction to it" (ibid.). In Amalia's case the reaction was always in anticipation. In terms of this hypothesis, it must be concluded that Amalia's psychic structure is basically neurotic, and in which the "separation" on the representation of the object and the representation of the self is clearly established. For this reason the emotions evoked by separation have the characteristics of an "affect-signal."

However, the results of our study have no prescriptive value. We mean by this that it cannot be deduced from this study that Amalia improved *because* the analyst interpreted the emotions aroused by separation. Authors such as Meltzer (1967) postulate that analysis of the anxieties and defenses concerned with separation are the "motor of analysis." On the other hand, Etchegoyen (1986, p. 474, italics added for emphasis) states that "the task of the analyst consists, to a large extent, in detecting, analysing, and solving the separation anxiety.... Interpretations which tend to solve these conflicts are *crucial* to the progress of the analysis." But our study shows something different: in the material investigated, although the analyst interpreted the reaction to breaks, he did so cautiously, infrequently, and unsystematically; rather, he seemed not to set great store by the loss–separation model in the choice of his interventions. Indeed, the variable *separation-therapist* in the ATD proved irrelevant to the detection of separation sessions. If we study the separation-therapist variable throughout the 20 separation sessions selected, it can be seen that in actual practice in the first and in the final third of the analysis, the analyst dealt with the separation theme more than the patient did; in the middle third, on the other hand, the analyst practically ignores the theme. Since the value of the variable is an average value, this value was never significantly higher than the average of the nonbreak sessions. Naturally, this can lead to the hypothesis of a countertransference reaction on the part of the analyst because of unconscious feeling of guilt since at that time he interrupted the treatment to make two long trips abroad. Nevertheless, the reaction to breaks evolved in accordance with the psychoanalytic theory of therapy.

This seems to agree with Blatt and Behrends (1987), who state that, together with interpretation, incompatibility experiences—and breaks are only one instance of this—have an independent therapeutic action that motivates interiorization processes:

> Experienced incompatibility can take many forms in analysis besides interpretation, such as interruption of the cadence of hours because of the absence of the therapist or patient, failures in communication and empathy, or the patient's own increasing dissatisfaction with his or her level of functioning. It is important to stress that experienced incompatibility is not only externally imposed by the analyst through interpretations or by events such as the therapist's absence, but it can also originate with the analysand who may become increasingly dissatisfied with a particular level of gratifying involvement. (p. 290)

From the idea that analysis consists fundamentally in interpreting anxieties and defenses with regard to separations (breaks), the notion emerges that "the frequency ... of the sessions is an *absolute* constant.... Five [sessions per week] seems to be the most suitable number since it establishes a substantial contact time with a clean break at the weekend. It is very difficult for me to establish a real psychoanalytic process with a rhythm of three times per week, although I know that many analysts are able to do so. Such an inconsistent and irregular rhythm as an every-other-day analysis *does not allow the conflict of contact and separation to emerge strongly enough*" (Etchegoyen, 1986, p. 474; italics added for emphasis). Apart from the previous contradiction, if "many analysts are able to do so," frequency cannot be an absolute constant. Our research shows that in Amalia's psychoanalysis, with a frequency of three times a week, the contact–separation conflict not only emerged, as it did in the long breaks and in a percentage of the weekend sessions, but also developed as predicted in theory of the therapy. This empirical fact deprives frequency of its absolute quality, and supports Thomä and Kächele (1994a, p. 254) in the sense that a frequency should be established, which allows for evolution of the analytic process and which varies specifically with each analyst–patient dyad.

The final conclusion is that the evolution of the loss–separation phenomena as a reaction to breaks cannot continue to be considered as a direct result of specific interpretation or as a primary or independent cause of change in the patient. Our results suggest that the reaction to breaks evolves as an *indicator of change*—that is, as a *result* of highly complex analytical work.

Finally, a few words on the technical consequences of this study. The existence of schools in psychoanalysis presupposes a unilateral emphasis on certain aspects of analytical theory. For example, the Kleinian school stresses the importance of working through of primary mourning, which would almost naturally become activated by the different breaks occurring in the framework of the analysis. Consequently, the technical importance of immediately interpreting fantasies, anxieties, and defenses related to breaks between sessions, at weekends, and others is overemphasized. The danger of these interpretations becoming stereotype is maximized. Rosenfeld (1987, ch. 3) describes in detail how the interpretation of separation anxiety can be used by the analyst as a defense to ignore destructive fantasies, which emerge in the patient when in session with the analyst. Etchegoyen (1986, p. 528) points out that "patients frequently tell us that interpretations of this kind sound routine and conventional; and they are often right." In the light of the results of this study, it is possible to claim that one of the reasons for this stereotyping lies in the confusion between *indicator* of change and *cause* of change.

5.9   THE PSYCHOTHERAPY PROCESS Q-SORT*

Introduction

From early on in psychoanalytic research methods were sought after that would allow the description of different therapeutic processes without being too heavily oriented in favor of a specific theoretical orientation, but without being too general and able to identify the specifics of a concrete therapeutic operation. The first risk was illustrated by intervention catalogs as the one created by Isaacs (1939) that was used by Thomä and Houben (1967); the second risk was typical of many studies using the *Bales Interaction Catalogue* (Bales, 1950) from small-group research. A first example for a transtheoretical instrument was provided by Strupp (1957), who then performed a series of even experimental studies on the technical behavior of therapists (Strupp, 1960). Later Benjamin (1974) conceived the Structural Analysis of Social Behavior (SASB) that found its way into many studies on process (Benjamin, 1985).

Another major step was the development of Jones's Q-Sort methodology sorting patient and therapists typical and untypical contributions in a session that first was used in the landmark psychoanalytic case study titled "Toward a Method for Systematic Inquiry" (Jones, 1993; Jones & Windholz, 1990). Meanwhile, the Berkeley Psychotherapy Research Group has assembled an impressive array of comparative studies (e.g., Ablon & Jones, 1998, 1999; Jones & Price, 1998; Jones & Pulos, 1993; Jones, Hall, & Parke, 1991). The most recent description of the achievements of the Psychotherapy Process Q-Sort (PQS) is presented by Ablon and Jones (2005).

---

* Cornelia Albani, Gerd Blaser, Uwe Jacobs, Michael Geyer, and Horst Kächele; adapted from Albani et al. (2002).

Fonagy (2005) speaks of a debt of gratitude we owe to John Ablon and Enrico Jones for the humility they bring to our work:

> They bring reality to the psychological therapy we practice and believe in. The achievement of the paper is … its very simplicity: the approach expounded by Ablon and Jones makes the complexities of psychoanalytic thought and technique understandable and accessible to all. They have mastered that most difficult dialectic between the Scylla of an illusory of understanding generated by reductionism and simplification and the Charybdis of creating mystique and religion, where the innocent questions can no longer be asked and the truth is buried under layers of false sophistication. (p. 587)

Blatt (2005) in his commentary points to the method's contribution to large-scale research comparing different groups as well as to the analysis of a single case; he raises a number of critical points regarding the construction of a psychoanalytic prototype:

> It is important to keep in mind that the prototypes of the various treatments defined … appear to focus primarily on the activities of the therapist…. Yet the definition of any treatment is also contingent on the activities of the patient…. The style and nature of therapeutic interventions may vary not only among analysts but even within a particular analyst with different patients, or with the same patient at different phases of the therapeutic process. (p. 574)

This last point is illustrated by our findings on Amalia X.

Data and Methodology

In the present study, we applied the German version of the PQS (Jones, 2000). Jones's method attempts to create a uniform language with a clinically relevant terminology that can describe the psychotherapeutic process in a manner independent from various theoretical models and thus allows a systematic and comparable evaluation of therapeutic interactions across different therapy methods. The PQS consists of 100 items that are applied according to a rating system of nine categories (1 = extremely uncharacteristic; 9 = extremely characteristic) following the thorough study of a transcript or videotape of an entire therapy hour. The distribution of items according to the nine categories is fixed in order to approximate a normal distribution.

The database for the study was the first and last five hours of the psychoanalytic treatment of Amalia, which was conducted by an experienced analyst. The analysis according to the PQS serves to describe the characteristic elements of this treatment and to allow a comparison of the two phases in order to illustrate the relevant differences. The evaluation of the sessions was performed by two raters in randomized order and resulted in a mean interrater agreement of $r = .64$ (.54 to .78).

Results

Characteristic and Uncharacteristic Items for All 10 Hours

First, we will describe which items were rated as particularly characteristic and uncharacteristic for all 10 hours. A rank order of means was calculated. A further criterion for inclusion was that these items showed little or no difference in their means between the beginning and termination phases ($p < 0.10$, Wilcoxon-Test). These items thus provide a general description of the behavior of the patient, the therapist, and their interaction in the beginning and termination phase of the analysis.

The attitude of the therapist is described as empathic (Q 6), neutral (Q 93), conveying acceptance (Q 18), tactful (Q 77), not condescending (Q 51), and emotionally involved (Q 9). The therapist's own emotional conflicts do not intrude into the relationship (Q 24), and the therapist does not emphasize the patient's feelings (Q 81). The patient has no difficulties beginning the hour (Q 25); she is active (Q 15) and brings up significant issues and material (Q 88). The patient talks of wanting to be separate (Q 29), she accepts the therapist's comments and observations (Q 42), and she feels understood by the therapist (Q 14). The interaction is characterized by a specific focus (Q 23), for example, the self-image of the patient (Q 35), her interpersonal relationships (Q 63), and cognitive themes (Q 30).

These findings correspond partially to what the ideal psychoanalytic prototype of Ablon and Jones (2005) puts at the top of its list. There the key features are item 90: The patient's dreams or fantasies are discussed, followed by item 93: The analyst is neutral, followed by item 36: The analyst points out the patient's use of defensive maneuvers, followed by item 100: The analyst draws connections between the therapeutic relationship and other relationships. The fifth item is 6: The analyst is sensitive to the patient's feelings, attuned to the patient—empathic (ibid., p. 552).

Characteristic and Uncharacteristic Items Separating the Beginning and Termination Phases

In order to describe the differences between the beginning and termination phases of the therapy, the first and last five hours were pooled into separate blocks and the means of the ratings of the most characteristic and uncharacteristic items for both raters were calculated (Tables 5.15 and 5.16).

Jones (2000) established the practice of identifying the respective 10 highest and lowest ratings. Subsequently, the means were tested for statistical differences (Wilcoxon-Test, Table 3).

Description of the Beginning Phase Using the PQS

In the beginning phase of the therapy, the patient has no difficulty beginning the hour (Q 25), initiates themes, is organized, clear, and structured (Q 54), and brings up significant issues (Q 88). She accepts the therapist's comments and observations (Q 42) and feels understood by him (Q 14). The patient predominantly talks about her wish for independence (Q 29). The therapist's attitude conveys a sense of nonjudgmental acceptance (Q 18) and emotional involvement (Q 9) and is characterized by tact (Q 77). The therapist's remarks are aimed at facilitating patient speech (Q 3), and he is not condescending to her (Q 51). Countertransference reactions do not intrude into the relationship (Q 24). The therapist clarifies (Q 65), but he does not encourage the patient to try new ways of behaving with others or give her tasks (Q 85, Q 38). Dialogue has a specific focus (Q 23); the self-image of the patient (Q 35), her interpersonal relationships (Q63), and ideas or beliefs (Q 30) are central themes.

Description of the Termination Phase Using the PQS

Several characteristics of the therapy remain the same in the termination phase. The patient brings up relevant issues (Q 88), is active (Q 15), and feels understood by the therapist (Q 14). The therapist conveys a sense of nonjudgmental acceptance (Q 18); he is tactful (Q 77) and does not patronize the patient (Q 51). The self-image is still a focus (Q 35). There are differences from the beginning phase: In the termination phase the patient is animated (Q 13) and controlling (Q 87), and the therapist does not actively exert control over the interaction (Q 17) and is neutral (Q 93) and empathic (Q 6). The patient does not achieve new insight (Q 32), but she also does not rely upon the therapist to solve her problems (Q 52). In the last sessions termination of therapy is discussed (Q 75), love relationship is the topic of discussion (Q 64) and the dreams of the patient (Q 90). The therapist does not clarify (Q 65), does not interpret defense maneuvers (Q 36), and does not reformulate the patient's behavior during the hour (Q 82).

Items That Distinguish the Phases of the Therapy

Table 5.17 lists the items that distinguish the two therapy phases.
Typical of the beginning phase is that the therapist asks for information (Q 31), clarifies (Q 65), facilitates the patient's speech (Q 3), and identifies a recurrent theme in the patient's experience (Q 62). It is more characteristic

of the termination phase that the therapist does less reformulation on the actual behavior of the patient in the hour (Q 82) and reduced focus on the patient's feelings of guilt (Q 22). He is less active in exerting control over the interaction (Q 17). In the beginning phase of the therapy, the patient has a clearer and more organized expression (Q 54), feels shyer (Q 61) and inadequate (Q 59), and expresses shame or guilt (Q 71). In the beginning phase she relies more upon the therapist to solve her problems (Q 52) but is more introspective (Q 97) and achieves more new understanding (Q 32). In the termination phase the patient is controlling (Q 87), provocative (Q 20), and resists examining thoughts, reactions, or motivations related to problems (Q 58). She is more able to express angry or aggressive feelings (Q 84).

In the beginning phase the discussion was more centered on cognitive themes (Q 30). In the termination phase, the termination of therapy (Q 75), the love relationship (Q 64), and the dreams of the patient (Q 90) were discussed, and more humor was used (Q 74). The beginning phase was different in that it was especially typical that there was a less erotic (Q 19) and a less competitive quality (Q 39) to the therapy relationship.

Discussion

The items that were identified as characteristic for both phases of the therapy are not items one might call "typically psychoanalytic." This can be accounted for by the fact that the selected hours are from the beginning and termination phases of the therapy, where the analytic work is only begun or coming to a close. The patient appears to be constructively engaged in the work, and the behavior of the analyst aims at establishing or maintaining a working alliance. Relevant themes are worked through—in particular the patient's self image and interpersonal relationships, as well as her wish for independence. The high rating of PQS item 23, "The dialogue has a specific focus," is consistent with the assumption that the treatment was conducted according to the Ulm Process Model (Thomä & Kächele, 1994a). This model considers psychoanalytic therapy to be an interpersonally orientated nontime-limited focal therapy in which the thematic focus changes over time. The description using the PQS items conveys the impression of intensive therapeutic, albeit not (yet) prototypical psychoanalytic, work.

Using the PQS items in comparing the beginning and termination phase yields a vivid description of the differences between these treatment phases. In the beginning phase, the therapist interacts very directly and supportively with the patient. One can surmise an interactive influence between the patient's self-accusations, her embarrassment, and feelings of inadequacy and the behavior of the therapist, who inquires and facilitates her communication. The therapeutic technique contains clarifications but also confrontations that are aimed at labeling repetitive themes and interpreting current behavior. This corresponds to the patient's willingness to express herself clearly and to reflect on thoughts and feelings. The description of the beginning phase with the aid of the PQS supports the assumption that this treatment was successful in establishing a stable working alliance, which was most likely a decisive factor in its success.

In the termination phase, the patient is able to express angry feelings and appears less burdened by guilt, which can be considered a positive treatment result. The fact that the patient was able to engage in a love relationship during the course of treatment is another indicator for success, even though the relationship ultimately failed. Thus, in the final hours the theme of separation becomes important in the working through of that relationship and the termination of the therapy. The patient discusses dreams during the final sessions and talks about her ability to interpret them, which can be seen as an identification with the analyst's functions.

While seven items that were rated as typical for the beginning phase described the behavior of the therapist and patient, the items rated as typical for the termination phase were exclusively items that describe the patient and the interaction. The therapist leaves the control of the hour mostly to the patient and keeps a low profile.

The description with the PQS illustrates the differences between the two treatment phases and the way in which patient and therapist influence each other's behavior in a close interaction. The findings illustrate that—as Blatt (2005, p. 574) points out—Ablon and Jones's (2005) idea of a psychoanalytic prototype might not be easy to stabilize given the diversity of the analyst's techniques during phases in treatment. It is clear that to generate a systematic time sample along the course of the treatment is high priority as a next step.

The PQS does not provide complete information about the content of the therapeutic discourse. Therefore, a PQS rating does not allow the investigation of competitive treatment formulations. The description of a case by means of the PQS items has to reduce the richness of the clinical material but provides a framework for working models concerning the patient and the therapeutic interaction. The PQS does allow the testing of hypotheses concerning therapeutic processes and their relationship to treatment success.

Jones and Windholz (1990, p. 1012) discusses the PQS method as follows: "As a descriptive language, the Q-technique provides a set of categories shared across observers, guiding observers' attention to aspects of the clinical material that might have otherwise gone un-noted, and allowing them to emerge from the background."

Formal research in psychoanalysis started with the investigation of technique (Glover & Brierley, 1940) trying to identify the operations that create the psychoanalytic situation; it may be no surprise that the PQS brings the field closer to that aim.

Chapter 6

Linguistic Studies

6.1   INTRODUCTORY REMARKS*

The relationship of "psychoanalysis and language" was in the center of many theoretical and clinical discussions ever since Sigmund Freud (1917) had declared the following:

> Nothing takes place in a psycho-analytic treatment but an interchange of words between the patient and the analyst. The patient talks, tells of his past experiences and presents impressions, complains, confesses his wishes and his emotional impulses. The doctor listens, tries to direct the patient's processes of thought, exhorts, forces his attention in certain directions, gives him explanations and observes the reaction of understanding or rejection which he in this way provokes in him. (p. 17)

In contrast to the clear recognition of psychoanalysis as discursive activity—as Lacan (1953) espouses it succinctly—for quite a time the main stream activity on the relation of psychoanalysis and language was focused on Freud's theory of symbols. Language and the development of the ego was a favorite topic in the New York study group on linguistics (Edelheit, 1968). As Freud had developed his own rather idiosyncratic way of understanding symbols, some conceptual work with the different usage of the term *symbol* had to be done. Victor Rosen (1969) in his paper on "Sign Phenomena and Their Relationship to Unconscious Meaning" demonstrates that the work of the psychoanalyst can be conceptualized as a process of differentiating conventional symbols from sign phenomena. Understanding meaning by common sense has to be completed by understanding the additional unconscious meaning any concrete piece of verbal material may carry. The technical rule for the analyst of evenly hovering attention is directed to just this process. Listening to his patient's associations the analyst receives the

---

* Horst Kächele and Erhard Mergenthaler.

conventional meaning of what he listens to. Suspending his reaction to this level of meaning he then tries to understand potential meanings beyond the everyday meaning. By interpreting the analyst usually uses a perspective that is not immediate in his patient's view.

However, Forrester (1980, p. x) expresses in his introduction of his book *Language and Origin of Psychoanalysis* astonishment that there were only a few treatises on psychoanalysis, which dealt directly with the role of language in the course of treatment. Detailed studies concerning "spoken language in the psychoanalytical dialogue" were just beginning to blossom in the eighties of the last century (Kächele, 1983a).

Praising the Freudian dictum many a times psychoanalysts—often unintentionally—have been followers of the philosopher Austin (1962), who in his theory of speech acts, proceeds from the observation that things get done with words. In the patterns of verbal action, there are specific paths of action available for interventions to alter social and psychic reality. In psychoanalysis, writes Shapiro (1999, p. 111), "the prolonged interaction between patient and analyst provides numerous opportunities for redundant expression of what is considered a common small set of ideas in varying vehicles and at various times, designed to get something done or to re-create an old pattern." However, speech, if it is to become effective as a means of action, is dependent on the existence of interpersonal obligations that can be formulated as rules of discourse. These rules of discourse depend partly on the social context of a verbal action (those in a court of law differ from those in a conversation between two friends), and, conversely, a given social situation is partly determined by the particular rules of discourse. Expanding this observation psychoanalytically, one can say that the implicit and explicit rules of discourse help to determine not only the manifest social situation but also the latent reference field (i.e., transference and countertransference).

If the discourse has been disturbed by misunderstandings or breaches of the rules, metacommunication about the preceding discourse must be possible that is capable of removing the disturbance. For example, one of the participants can insist on adherence to the rule (e.g., "I meant that as a question, but you haven't given me an answer!"). In such metacommunication, the previously implicit rules that have been broken can be made explicit, and sometimes the occasion can be used to define them anew, in which case the social content and, we can add, the field of transference and countertransference can also change.

The compulsion arises from the fact that analyst and patient have entered into a dialogue and are therefore subject to rules of discourse, on which they must be in at least partial (tacit) agreement if they want to be in any position to conduct the dialogue in a meaningful way. It is in the nature of a question that the person asking it wants an answer and views every reaction as such. The patient who is not yet familiar with the analytic situation will expect the conversation with the analyst to follow the rules of everyday communication.

The exchange process between the patient's productions, loosely called "free associations," and the analyst's interventions, loosely called "interpretations," most fittingly may be classified as a special sort of dialogue. The analyst's interventions encompass the whole range of activities to provide a setting and an atmosphere that allows the patient to enter the specific kind of analytic dialogue (the general principle of cooperation enunciated by the philosopher Grice [1975]):

> If any kind of meaningful dialogue is to take place, each partner must be prepared (and must assume that the other is prepared) to recognize the rules of discourse valid for the given social situation and must strive to formulate his contributions accordingly. (quoted by Thomä & Kächele, 1994b, p. 248)

The special rules of the analytic discourse thus must be well understood by the analysand lest he wastes the time not getting what he wants. Therefore, he has to understand that the general principle of cooperation is supplemented by a specific additional type of metacommunication on part of the analyst. As we have already pointed out the analyst's interventions have to add a surplus meaning beyond understanding the discourse on the plain everyday level.

How does one add a surplus meaning? Telling a joke is a good case for working with a surplus meaning not manifest in the surface material. Jokes have a special linguistic structure and most often work with a combination of unexpected material elements and special tactic of presentation. Reporting clinical examples from the literature Spence, Mayes, and Dahl (1994) suggest that the analyst is always scanning the analytic surface in the context of the two-person space, consciously or preconsciously, weighing each utterance against the shifting field of connotations provided by (1) the course of the analysis; (2) his or her own set of associations; and (3) the history of the analysand's productions (p. 45). An experimental way to detect the generation of such add-on meanings was Meyer's (1988) effort via postsession free associative self-reports to find out "what makes the psychoanalyst tick", p. 273

For such questions that are basic for the psychoanalytic enterprise the development of conversational and discourse analytical methods was crucial moving the pragmatic use of language as speech on empirical grounds. When Sacks, Schegloff, and Jefferson (1974 p. 696) propose a "simplest systematics for the organization of turn-taking behavior in conversation" it is obvious that such tools would be of high relevance to psychotherapy as an exquisite dialogic enterprise.

336 From Psychoanalytic Narrative to Empirical Single Case Research

Although Mahony (1977) gives psychoanalytic treatment a place in the history of discourse, Labov and Fanshel (1977) probably were the first to apply such concepts to empirical investigation of psychotherapy sessions. In Germany the linguist Klann (1977, 1979) connected psychoanalysis and the study of language, no longer focusing on the traditional discussion on symbols but focusing on the pragmatic use of language as therapeutic tool exemplified by role of affective processes in the structure of dialogue.

In this arena many things that take place in the relationship between patient and analyst at the unconscious level of feelings and affects cannot be completely referred to by name, distinguished, and consolidated in experiencing (see Bucci, 1988, 1997a, 1998, 2005). Intentions that are prelinguistic and that consciousness cannot recognize can only be imprecisely verbalized. Thus, in fact much more happens between the patient and analyst than just an exchange of words. Freud's "nothing else" must be understood as a challenge for the patient to reveal his thoughts and feelings as thoroughly as possible. The analyst is called upon to intervene in the dialogue by making interpretations using mainly linguistic means. Of course, it makes a big difference if the analyst conducts a dialogue, which always refers to a two-sided relationship, or if he makes interpretations that expose the latent meanings in a patient's quasi-monological free associations.

Although it has become customary to emphasize the difference between the therapeutic interview and everyday conversation (Leavy, 1980), we feel compelled to warn against an overly naive differentiation since everyday dialogues often are:

> ... characterized by only apparent understanding, by only apparent cooperation, by apparent symmetry in the dialogue and in the strategies pursued in the conversation, and that in reality intersubjectivity often remains an assertion that does not necessarily lead to significant changes, to dramatic conflicts, or to a consciousness of a "pseudo-understanding...." In everyday dialogues something is acted out and silently negotiated that in therapeutic dialogues is verbalized in a systematic manner. (Klann, 1979, p. 128)

Flader and Wodak-Leodolter (1979) collected these first German studies on processes of therapeutic communication. Some years later these researchers discovered the rich material available at the Ulm textbank (Flader, Grodzicki, & Schröter, 1982). This was probably not surprising because the availability of original transcripts for linguists was at the time very limited. Among others, the opening phase of Amalia X's treatment—that phase of familiarizing the patient into the analytical dialogue and the transition from day-to-day discourse into the analytical discourse—was examined (Koerfer & Neumann, 1982):

Towards the end of the second (recorded) session Amalia X complains about the unusual dialogic situation in the following way: "alas, I find this is quite a different kind of talk as I am used to it."

This kind of difficulty is described by Lakoff (1981, p. 7) succinctly: "The therapeutic situation itself comprises a context, distinct from the context of 'ordinary conversation,' and that distinction occasions ambiguity and attendant confusion." In fact we are dealing with a learning situation comparable to learning a foreign language though less demanding:

> If in fact psychotherapeutic discourse were radically different in structure from ordinary conversation, we should expect something quite different: a long period of training for the patient, in which frequent gross errors were made through sheer ignorance of the communicative system, in which he had time after time to be carefully coached and corrected. (p. 8)

This perspective supports our maxim of the treatment technique: as much day-to-day dialogue as necessary to correspond to the safety needs of the patient to allow this learning process and as much analytical dialogue as possible to further the exploration of unconscious meanings in intra and interpersonal dimensions (Thomä & Kächele, 1994b, pp. 251ff).

In the following years, the "linguistic turn"—the inclusion of pragmalinguistic tools into the study of the psychoanalytical discourse—gained considerable momentum (Russell, 1989, 1993). For example, Harvey Sacks (1992a) describes "conversational analysis" (CA) that put "coherence" in the center, which also plays a central role in attachment research. Lepper and Mergenthaler (2005) could show in a group therapy setting and recently in a psychodynamic short therapy (Lepper & Mergenthaler, 2007) that the "topic coherence" stands in a close connection with clinically important moments, insights, and changes.

Systematic investigations on the special conversational nature of the psychoanalytic technique have become more diversified. The linguist Streeck (1989) illustrates how powerful conversational techniques were even in identifying prognostic factors for shared focus formulation in short-term therapy related to positive outcome where psychometric instruments failed. The role of metaphor in therapeutic dialogues has developed into a field of its own (Buchholz, 2007; Carveth, 1984; Casonato and Kächele, 2007; Lakoff, 1997; Spence, 1987). Intersubjective conceived treatment research enlarges the empirical frame by including dimensions of conversational practice, narrative representation, and use of metaphor. Is it too far fetched to connect the development of the relational perspective in psychoanalysis with the rise of narrative treatment research focusing on what happens between patient and analyst in great details as Buchholz (2006, p. 307) does?

The mechanism of psychoanalytic interpretation had been the object of an early discourse-analytic case study by Flader and Grodzicki (1982), recently followed by a larger sample studied by Peräkylä (2004). The issue of whether discourse in psychoanalysis proper is different from discourse in psychotherapy might be no longer in the center of interest. The more empirical material is studied the less these differences show up. Patients and their analysts display a range of conversational strategies in the diverse therapeutic situations as Streeck (2004) illustrates.

Long before we have seen the development of a conversation-analytical methodology for the study of verbatim protocols, the implementation of social science-based content analysis technique had fertilized the field of psychotherapy process research (Mowrer, 1953b). Ever since Dittmann and Wynne (1961) suggested studying emotionality in initial interviews the technique of content analysis was at the fore of process research.

The motherground of content analysis was the area of the mass communication and media research; all the more astonishing is the historical role Silbermann (1974) attributes in his handbook article to the author of the "Dream Interpretation," Sigmund Freud:

> If one would try to investigate the developmental history of the content analysis in all its details back to the times in which this term was not yet coined, so one would have to begin with the scientist who prepared the way for the scientific study of the soul. However, at least the name of Sigmund Freud would have to be mentioned and in particular his book "Dream Interpretation" from the year 1900. Here, for the first time, a summarized work is presented. It tries, in an experimental fashion, with the exclusion of philosophical thought processes, to cast light onto the irrational elements of human behavior, particularly in reference to symbolism, language and myth. The conceptual analysis of symbolic forms, as it stood in the foreground of Ernst Cassirer's "Philosophy of Symbolic Forms" (1923), is already abandoned here to give way for an analysis that tries to show the meaning of symbols concerning the social life. (p. 253)

Crucial for the classification of the technique of dream interpretation by Freud as the precursor of the content analysis is the demonstration of relationships between symbol and social communications structure. So following Silberman (1974) it was social scientists who first studied the communicative function of symbols in the social structure.

As one of the first, Lasswell (1933) mediates between the psychoanalytical and the social scientific methodology. In his work about "Psychoanalysis and Socioanalysis," he discusses the relationship between the extensive observation method of the social science and the intensive method of psychoanalysis and thus comes to speak about the meaning of the psychoanalytical symbol science:

> The fruitful dialectic relationship between intensive and extensive observation methods can be viewed through a short reference on the meaning of the psychoanalysis for general theory of social happenings. Psychoanalysis has broadened our knowledge of dialectic relationships among symbols.... Psychoanalysis mainly provides contributions for the dialectic handling of symbol to symbol and complements therewith the dialectic procedure that up to now only enclosed material-symbol and symbol-material relations. (p. 380)

The development of content analysis led to a scientific interpretation technique, which tried to differentiate itself from the hermeneutic interpretation method essentially in that the interpretative process had to be conducted according to prior set rules and specifications. This scientific attitude was found in the first fundamental definition of the content analysis as it was presented by Berelson (1952, p. 18): "The content analysis is an examination technique that serves the objective, systematic and quantitative description of the obvious content of information of all kinds."

This early definition has been since then extended and changed in a manifold way. Berelson's (1952) commitment to manifest contents was particularly outdated through the inclusion of the properties of transmitter and receiver in the research processes. Stone et al. (1966) underline in the framework of mechanical content analysis its deductive character: "Content analysis is every research technique for the set up of conclusions in which systematically and objectively, individually defined properties within a text are identified" (p. 5).

From the mere descriptive intentions of Berelson (1952) content analysis developed to a concluding observational method. In this development, the theory-related character of all scientific questioning is more visible than ever, which is emphasized particularly in the discussion of the content analytical dictionaries in the framework of mechanical text analysis (Gerbner, Holsti, Krippendorf, Paisley, & Stone, 1969). The very first effort to bridge between linguistics and content analysis studying "pathological and normal language" (Laffal, 1965) paved the way for further developments.

The pace-setting "Reader" by Gottschalk and Auerbach (1966) represented, at the time, important works concerning content analysis of psychotherapeutic protocols. Soon after, the first volume of the "Handbook of Psychotherapy and Behavior Change" (Bergin & Garfield, 1971) summarized the contributions of content-analytic studies to the growing field (Marsden, 1971), and Luborsky and Spence (1971) pointed to the new possibilities of computer based technology. Our early familiarity with the works of Dahl (1972, 1974) and Spence (1968, 1969) was crucial for the further methodological development in Ulm (Kächele, 1976; Kächele & Mergenthaler, 1983, 1984). Fertile collaboration with Bucci linking verbal and nonverbal representations using computer analysis of referential activity (Mergenthaler & Bucci, 1999) and development of the therapeutic cycles model (TCM; Mergenthaler, 1996, 2008) mark the state of the art in this technology for process research.

Computerized linguistic indicators have been developed (Bucci & Maskit, 2007) that are associated with each phase of the referential process that includes Arousal, Imagery and Narrative, Emotional Reflection, and Process of Change. Referential Activity, one of Bucci's (2007) major linguistic indicators, has been shown to be higher in A sessions as opposed to Z sessions. With the concept of A and Z sessions Bucci refers to Freedman, Lasky, and Hurvich (2003). A sessions "generally represent processes of integration, consolidation, developmental progression, and relatively stable exploration" and Z sessions have qualities that indicate "non-integration, regression, and destabilization" (Bucci, 2007, p. 185).

With the verbatim protocols of Amalia X various exploratory linguistic studies were conducted. Schafer's (1976) ideas concerning the language in action prompted a student of the Department of Linguistics in Hamburg, Beermann (1983), to study syntactic variations of the usage of active and passive voice in the text of our four tape-recorded analytic patients' protocols. Identifying neurotic disorder as a relationship disturbance she decided to characterize a neurotic speaker as a user of frequent passive sentence constructions in order not to appear as active agency and as not being able to thematize the very own interest in relationships. A neurotic person—so her assumption—compensates the limited capacity for metacommunicative expression by a forced strategy using passive sentence constructions. Studying four sessions of Amalia X she identified significant, case-specific increase of active syntactic constructions in the course of the treatment. Of interest was her finding that the quantitative analysis of the analyst's language identified a lesser use of passive constructions throughout the analysis.

Another pilot study tested how the change of latent speech structures could be measured (Mergenthaler & Kächele, 1985). Using computer-based vocabulary methods the body-related vocabulary of Amalia X and Christian Y was compared (Schors et al., 1982). These encouraging results led to the development of the *Ulm Body Dictionary* (Schors & Mergenthaler, 1994), which has already been applied to four short-term therapies; studies with this dictionary of Amalia X's protocols are not yet completed.

To develop computer-based strategies of analyzing the bodily representations of Amalia X has been one avenue of research. The same line of investigatory efforts was also taken by Maldavsky (2005) and his group from

Buenos Aires applying the David Liberman algorithm to sessions of Amalia X. A totally different road was taken by von Wyl and Boothe (2003) using a qualitative approach to understand Amalia X's way of constructing her gender-related body experiences. Their psychodynamic interpretations of results of a narrative methodology—known as JAKOB (Boothe, 2000)—aim to reconstruct the organization of individual experience, subjective involvement, and personal relationships. The systematic unfolding of the plots involved allows conflict and defense impulses to be modeled within the intersubjectively testable context of communication. The Zurich group directed by Boothe extensively applied this qualitative technique to study many facets of Amalia X's in-treatment patterns (Luder, 2006).

In summary the diversity of techniques that are available for studying verbatim recorded sessions opens a wide field for research. But we also agree with Bucci (2007) that a theory is needed that allows to demonstrate "the validity of the concepts of the metapsychology essentially as defined a century ago" (p. 203) and, as we may add, allows to integrate the findings from the disparate empirical approaches presented elsewhere and in this book for the case of Amalia X.

6.2   THE ULM TEXTBANK*

Introduction

Extensive verbatim transcribed protocols of psychoanalytic treatments demanded by Luborsky and Spence (1971) have established themselves as an important source of data in psychoanalytical research. From today's point of view it clearly shows that it was overdue—because of the manifold expectations—to develop, for the application in the area of psychotherapy, proper and user-friendly methods intended for the handling of a text corpus. Beyond this, it also became apparent how important it was to develop meaningful methods for the description of such texts or to learn from linguistic data processing. To solve the problems 30 years ago in Ulm, an interdisciplinary approach was chosen that connects the psychotherapy-related questions with scientific methods of informatics and linguistics.

Historical Summary

Since 1968 the Department of Psychotherapy of the University of Ulm has focused on the development of a methodology for psychoanalytic process research. Within this framework producing audio and video recordings of psychoanalytic long-term treatments provided an essential methodological

---

* Adapted and shortened version based on Mergenthaler and Kächele (1993).

step that inevitably led to a great collection of verbatim transcripts. In the course of the first decade we realized the necessity of developing a computer-based databank for our research. Thus began, within the "Special Research Collaboration 129" (SFB 129) of the German Research Foundation, the development of the Ulm Textbank Management System. During this period of development it became further apparent that such a databank* would also serve other scientists who are interested in process research and in analyzing of linguistic material. The final design of the system was therefore characterized strongly by the orientation of a manifoldness of users with very differing methodological approaches (Mergenthaler, 1985). With the conclusion of the SFB 129 in 1988, this task was completed. Since then the Ulm Textbank has been a public institution available for psychotherapy research.

General Aims

One of the main goals in the development of the Textbank was to make available linguistic material of psychotherapeutic sessions and also of neighboring areas, to researchers in order to save time and money for research endeavors that can be conducted with the already accessible material (archival function). A further goal was also to create availability for computer-based text analyses for all the scientists who do not have resources of this kind of their own. A third goal consisted of connecting the results that were gained in preceding analyses in order to facilitate a rediscovery of text on the basis of already available results. Thus, the Textbank Management System was designed to facilitate the following tasks:

1. Recording and processing of texts under manifold points of view
2. Management of an unlimited number of text units on various data media
3. Management of an unlimited amount of information on text units and their authors and their conducted text analyses
4. Management of an open-ended amount of methods for editing and analysis of stored text units
5. Support of interfaces for statistical and other user software
6. Support of a simple interactive user interface in the utilization of the aforementioned, from (1) to (5) mentioned tasks.

The Textbank Management System is thereby an information system that can manage texts and information about texts and integrates processing of linguistic data processing as well as text processing for the analysis of texts.

---

* In the conceptualization, the example of routine services provided by a medical blood bank were helpful in many lectures to spread the steering idea of the project.

It features a uniform user interface that assists in the input, processing, output, and analyses of text units.

The documents stored in the Ulm Textbank represent an open collection of texts. The main character of such data collections is that they can be extended continuously. The measure of completeness of a database, however, influences the strategies in which the research results concerning these texts are handled. Two approaches can be discerned: (1) All available data are stored together with the texts itself, and (2) the analyses are being conducted anew according to need.

The Textbank project provides the realization of tools for informatics in psychotherapy research. Special interest was given to the acceptance and performance of the, at the time, rather new approach. During the phase of the gathering of texts, the field had to be acquainted with a new fact: namely the shared usage of primary data. Soon a rapidly increasing number of colleagues understood our goals and joined generously in contributing to the success by making their data sources available.*

Methods

Clientele and Samples

The optimal display of a Textbank Managing System needs to be open for processing scientific questions that are hard to predict at the time of its inception. Therefore, it is particularly important that individual text collections can be put together as subdivisions in the Textbank. In this context two important working emphases have crystalized, which at the same time correspond to two different research approaches: longitudinal studies and cross-section studies.

Longitudinal studies concentrate on the materials from psychotherapeutic and psychoanalytic treatments. Their goal is to investigate changes through the therapeutic process. To collect large numbers of tape-recorded psychoanalytic treatments is still a dream. Therefore, the study of single cases and their evaluation concerning the manifold aspects have remained in the foreground.

Naturally there are also questions that can be studied in cross-sectional designs, for example in the initial interview texts. In these studies different populations of patients are examined. In this way it is possible to observe the influence of variables such as sex or diagnosis (Parra et al., 1988). Sometimes it is useful to keep separate text collections for special studies such as studies of Balint groups (Rosin, 1989), the linguistic behavior of doctors and patients during the ward rounds (Westphale & Köhle, 1982),

---

* We extend our thanks to our many colleagues who have given us their trust and cooperation.

or the linguistic exchange in family therapies (Brunner, Brunner-Wörner, & Odronitz-Dieterle, 1984).

The texts that correspond to the main goals of the Ulm Textbank are sampled as potential users come along. Meanwhile the archive contains, besides several completely available short therapies, also extensive samples on four psychoanalytical treatments. The initial interview corpus consists of several hundred different interviews and is balanced in view of the sex of the patient and that of the therapist, respectively; and further in terms of the diagnostic differentiation, neurosis, or psychosomatic disorder. The kinds of texts that are found in the Textbank also determine the goals, questions, and scientific interests of the other supporting facilities. The creation of such a publicly available research basis is likewise useful for clinical education and supervision.

At present about two-thirds of the stock of the Ulm Textbank dates from investigations we have performed in Ulm itself. The other texts were gained as a result of scientific contacts and joint research projects in facilities outside of Ulm. In most cases these texts were handed over with the agreement to be utilized by other users as well. Many users are psychotherapists themselves; the other users predominantly belong to the fields of linguistics and social sciences. Presently there are contacts with about 30 institutes in Germany, four in the United States, two in Sweden, two in Switzerland, and one in Austria.

Altogether, the electronically stored texts comprise 10 million words generating a basic vocabulary of 180,000 different German words. Thus, the Ulm Textbank can also provide statements on the frequency of words in spoken German such as Dahl (1979) shows, solely relying on his database of Mrs. C.

Questions concerning the degree of representativeness of the collected materials are rather difficult to answer. We tried to keep an eye out to include a variety of therapists, to include different diagnostic categories, and to get hold of shorter and longer treatments. Still, the psychoanalytic corpus in Ulm can be viewed as representative only for specific questions. Table 6.1 provides an overview of the material at the end of 2006.

Instruments

Departing from a semiotic view of language, as can be traced back to Charles S. Peirce, the founder of semiotics, and its further development by Charles Morris, language is understood as a system of symbols whose structure is ascertained through rules concerning the relation between form and content.

Correspondingly, it is possible to distinguish among the following text measures:

Table 6.1 The Stock of the Ulm Textbank*

Type	Available As	Sessions
1. Consultation		
	Transcript, Audio and Video	4
	Audio	1
	Video	1
2. Short-Term Therapy		
	Transcript, Audio	153
	Transcript, Audio and Video	17
	Transcript only	2
	Audio	584
	Video	314
	No Information	5
3. Analytical Psychotherapy		
	Transcript, Audio	27
	Transcript, Video	19
	Transcript only	91
	Audio	1484
	No Information	14
4. Psychoanalyses		
	Transcript, Audio	1023
	Transcript only	214
	Audio	5662
	Video	13
	No Information	58
5. Couples Therapy		
	Transcript only	2
	Audio	37
6. Family Therapy		
	Transcript, Audio	31
	Transcript only	28
	Audio	11
7. Group Therapy		
	Transcript only	26
	Audio	140
	Video	21

Table 6.1 The Stock of the Ulm Textbank* (continued)

Type	Available As	Sessions
8. Supportive Psychotherapy		
	Transcript, Audio	1
9. Group Work		
	Transcript only	3
10. Client-Centered Therapy		
	Video	3
11. Behavioral Therapy		
	Transcript, Audio	6
	Audio	32
	Video	1
12. Initial Interview		
	Transcript, Audio	127
	Transcript, Audio and Video	23
	Transcript, Video	3
	Transcript only	232
	Audio	180
	Video	73
	No Information	8
13. Initial Interview Report		
	Text, Audio	8
	Text	365
14. Report of Psychotherapy Session		
	Text	19
	Audio	57
15. Report of Psychoanalysis Session		
	Text, Audio	7
	Text	153
	Audio	163
16. General Lectures		
	Audio	14
	No Information	3
18. Balint Group		
	Transcript only	53
	Audio	89
	No Information	3

Table 6.1 The Stock of the Ulm Textbank* (continued)

Type	Available As	Sessions
19. Gestalt Therapy		
	Transcript only	46
	Audio	2
20. Dreams		
	Transcript, Audio	128
	Transcript only	91
22. Psychodiagnostics		
	Transcript, Audio	128
	Transcript only	104
	Audio	40
23. Follow-up Interview		
	Transcript, Audio	41
	Transcript only	15
	Audio	7
	Video	7
24. TAT (Thematic Apperception Test)		
	Transcript only	183
25. Language Sample		
	Transcript only	74
26. Genetic Consultation		
	Transcript only	37
28. HIT (Holzmann Inkblot Test)		
	Text	19
29. Psychotherapy Session Report		
	Text	19
32. Cognitive Behavioral Therapy		
	Transcript, Audio	20
	Audio	19
33. Supervision		
	Transcript, Audio	16
	Audio	5
34. Psychiatric Treatment		
	Transcript only	24

Table 6.1 The Stock of the Ulm Textbank* (continued)

Type	Available As	Sessions
36. Family Interview		
	Transcript, Audio	2
	Transcript only	47
37. Interactional Psychotherapy		
	Transcript, Video	28
	Transcript only	1
38. Half Standardized Interview		
	Transcript, Audio	21
	Transcript only	5
	Audio	44

*Overview of text units December 31 2002.

1. Formal
2. Grammatical
3. Content

Each of these measuring methods can be differentiated further in view of focusing on an individual speaker or on the text as a whole, as a dialogue. Therefore, one can speak of monadic or dyadic measurement values. Further, it can be differentiated according to the kind of measurement values. Well known are the simple measurements of the frequency of appearance of tokens, which are the basis for proportional data and their distribution. Moreover, one should heed that some of the formal measures require knowledge of content—for example, the denotative meaning of a word.

The formal measurements can generally be generated in a very simple way. In computer-based approaches, simply the ability of segmenting of symbol sequences (i.e., letters, digits, and special characters) concerning words and punctuation can be examined. The effort for programming is comparatively small; recoding or precoding is not necessary. Formal measurements that are available encompass the following:

- Text size (tokens)
- Vocabulary (types)
- Type–token ratio
- Redundancy
- Change of speaker in family and group conversations

The simplest and most elementary measurement is the number of words spoken by the therapist and the patient. This will be illustrated in section 6.3 using the example of the treatment of Amalia X.

Redundancy is a text measure that derives from information theory. Spence (1968) suggests that redundancy would increase during psychodynamic treatment without providing an empirical demonstration. Thus, we confirmed one of his hypotheses, namely that the redundancy of the patient (frequent repetition of words) during the treatment of the patient Christian Y increased stepwise. The values of the analyst, however, remained constant (Kächele & Mergenthaler, 1984).

Grammatical measures demand linguistic knowledge about the examined language—for example, about German grammar. The programming and coding effort for computer-based procedures for such measures remains quite considerable. Yet many questions cannot be performed completely automatically. An example is the lemmatization that is the automatic back-tracing of an inflected word form to its basic form, which today, depending on the kind of text, has a degree of effect between 50% and 95%. Psychotherapeutic conversation that displays many syntactic deviations (e.g., incomplete words and phrases) is typical for spontaneously spoken language and therefore ranges in the lower area. Correspondingly, there are few computer-based analyses of psychotherapeutic texts that are based on grammatical measurements (Mergenthaler & Pokorny, 1989). The Ulm Textbank provides the following measures:

- Distribution of word types
- Diminution and comparison
- Interjection

The connection between the choice of a type of word and the semantic class to which it belongs was already shown by Busemann (1925) in an examination of child language. He spoke of an "active" and "quantitative" style in relation to verbs and adjectives, respectively. He furthermore showed that these stylistic differences are only minimally dependent on the topic of the spoken word and should rather be seen as being personality related. Using a computer-based approach, Mergenthaler and Kächele (1985) analyze a psychoanalytical session of Amalia X and demonstrate that the choice of the type of word definitely depends on the content of the report. However, this microanalytical view does not exclude the possibility that, viewed at a macrolevel, variables of the personality, as they are described by Busemann, can have an influence.

The role of personal pronouns for the structuring of self and object relationships in spoken language is analyzed by Schaumburg (1980) on the four extensively recorded psychoanalytic cases of the Ulm Textbank.

Measures of content have been "types of anxiety" or "primary/secondary" processes. Measures of content demand additional detailed expertise in terms of the referential content: What concept does a word stand for? Computer-based procedures can, in this case, only deliver approximate results and are limited in the frame of narrowly sketched working models. Convincing examples have been delivered by the analysis of working and resistance sessions in the case of Mrs. C (Reynes, Martindale, & Dahl, 1984). Based on a German adaptation of the Harvard III Psychosocial Dictionary, Kächele (1976) could demonstrate that linear combinations of content categories and complex clinical concepts, such as positive and negative transference constellations in connection with selected anxiety topics, could be predicted. His results are based on a single case study of the patient Christian Y, in a sample of 55 sessions; correlations between the clinical concepts and the Harvard III Dictionary Categories were amazingly high, varying between .77 and .91.

Large amounts of text, but also selected segments from treatment protocols, can thus be examined with the help of computer-based text analysis as a tool in psychoanalytical process research. This will be illustrated in the following contributions.

These approaches, however, demand that the available methods are further developed, that basic research is furthered, and that newer techniques of related scientific disciplines, such as informatics and linguistics, are continuously implemented.

Requirements

In order to include a text into the Textbank it is necessary to remove personal names, names of location, and otherwise personal features using cryptographic procedures or even to replace them by pseudonyms to keep the text more readable. These personal data are stored on computers, which are exclusively at the disposal of the Ulm Textbank management staff. This separate data storing, as well as extensive control mechanisms, protect the Ulm Textbank extensively against misuse. The personnel of the Textbank is obligated to abide by the rules of the government-controlled data-protection regulations.

New Research Fields and Directions

Further methodological progress can only be reached by overcoming the weak points of present research techniques. This begins with the process of collecting data, which is still tied to laborious transcript writing; however, in the meantime this can be conducted more efficiently and reliably because of the development of standards (Mergenthaler & Stinson, 1992). Further steps of qualitative and quantitative text essentially improved through multimedia approaches by which very comfortable forms of tools are available for archiving, retrieval, analyzing, and attributing of texts.

The Ulm Textbank began in the eighties as a "big science" enterprise in the mainframe computer world. The successful evolution of the PC provides that text analysis systems are by now established in the daily routine of the scientist and offer themselves for defined analyses. However, it remains desirable that individual research groups push ahead for further development. An example for this is the software CM, which allows features of the therapeutic cycle model (Mergenthaler, 1996) to be measured.* CM is a text-analyzing tool that produces, for a text transcript, a graphical representation of the emotional and cognitive processes taking place during the session (see also section 6.6).

The Relation to Other Research Programs

The services of the Ulm Textbank are available for other scientific institutes for a small fee. Fees are asked particularly for work-intensive tasks such as the transcribing of texts of tape-recorded conversations as well as for material. However, it is expected that texts that find their way into the Textbank in this way are also available for other scientists in the future. In view of the material that is being handed out by the Textbank a copy of the report or the publication made with the help of this material should be given in return. Thereby, in addition to the texts, a growing stock of knowledge by various scientific disciplines about the texts can be stored and made available for others. The Ulm Textbank is open to all researchers who want to store their texts there. The possibility of routine or specialized text analyses, the simple type of text management, or the possibilities for multiple prints are reason enough to utilize these services.

As a final remark there remains the fact that, due to recent laws concerning data protection, only text material can be admitted to the Textbank or borrowed from it if it is factually anonymous so that there is no indication as to the identity of the participating speakers. This is often difficult to do without changing the content or partially even distorting it. When dealing with older material another difficulty arises: The law does not allow asking the patient for consent at a later time for further questions or for the handling by another research team. The emphasis of the Ulm Textbank therefore lies now rather in the consulting and cooperation with interested scientists of various disciplines and in the work with material in which the parameters of the recent valid data protection are given. Table 6.1 reflects in its overview the stock of the Ulm Textbank prior to the last decisive change of the data protection law (federal and state).

---

* For technical details go to: http://inf.medizin.uni-ulm.de.

6.3   VERBAL ACTIVITY IN THE
          PSYCHOANALYTIC DIALOGUE*

Therapeutic Dialogues

In his paper on the "Question of Lay Analysis" Freud (1926e, p. 187) characterizes the psychoanalytic dialogue in the following way: "Nothing takes place between them except that they talk to each other." The dialogic situation that constitutes the psychoanalytic treatment is not as specific as it often is portrayed. It may be useful to ask—whether the psychoanalytic dialogue is clearly distinguished from other, philosophical, or literary forms of dialogue—how it can be distinguished from everyday dialogues and how it differs from the dialogues of other forms of psychotherapy (Streeck, 2004).

We may start by stating that at first the patient is invited to talk, to freely associate. At a later point always uncertain for the patient in time the analyst may come in and add his points of view. From the first opinion poll that Glover and Brierley (1940) performed among the members of the British Society, we learn that the most frequent question of younger colleagues addressing the more experienced were not so much concerned with criteria of interpretation but were directed as to the issue of quantity, shape, and timing of the analyst's talk (Glover, 1955b, p. 269). The question, "Do you tend to talk little or more during a session?," led to the findings that the majority of analysts rather tended to fewer interpretative activity than talking too much (ibid., p. 274). However, the cliché that the analyst only uses interpretations never has done justice to his discursive activities. Simple questions, confrontations, clarifications, and even supportive comments belong to his technical armamentarium. The most common feature seems to be a certain asymmetry of the dialogue that reflects the different tasks of patient and analyst. Patients react to this constitutional asymmetry of the psychoanalytic situation: "The patient may respond with various forms of explicit or veiled anger to the initial lack of verbal response" (Shapiro, 2002, p. 206). How the analyst can help him is crucial in the warming-up phase of analysis. And the longer the analysis runs "even the most monological of analysts become more of a participant," writes Shapiro with a sober view on the real world (p. 208). There are a number of formal features that characterize dialogue—like turn taking, topic maintenance, gestures, mimesis, and even kinetics—and in psychoanalytic dialogues many more (Streeck, 2004). We first decided to study the most elementary of all issues: to talk or not to talk—that was the question.

---

* Horst Kächele and Erhard Mergenthaler; adapted from Kächele (1983b).

How Much Talking Do Amalia X and Her Analyst Do?

As the dialogic situation is placed into a more or less fixed frame of temporal limitation one has to take into account a bilateral dependency. Except for short periods of time either one of the two participants is talking or both are silent (Kächele, 1983b). Neglecting the usually small amount of simultaneous talking, it has been worth studying the distribution of speech and silence activity in analytic dyads.

Extensive empirical data on verbal activity levels in such therapeutic encounters are virtually absent. There are some opinions saying that the relationship of verbal activity of patient to analyst is approximately 4 to 1 (Garduk & Haggard, 1972). We have recorded and transcribed large samples of four psychoanalytic treatments, two each from two analysts.

Patients Amalia X and Christian Y were treated by an experienced analyst (H. Thomä) and patients Franziska X and Gustav Y by a candidate (H. Kächele). Table 6.2 shows that in three of the four treatments the ratio P:A is between 3.0:1 up to 5.0:1. The analytic treatment of Christian Y displays a rather unusual ratio of 1.1:1; these figures account for the fact that handling of this chronic silent patient caused the analyst to be verbally involved much more than one would expect (see the clinical account of this patient in Thomä & Kächele, 1994b). However, this finding is only characteristic for the first half of this long analytic treatment; after about 500 sessions the patient's average amount of speech reached that of the three other patients, and the analyst could return to his usual level of verbal activity (Kächele, 1983b).

Regarding the verbal exchange processes in the course of the analysis of the patient Amalia X one can see an impressive difference in degree of the analyst's verbal activity level and that of the patient. Of her treatment after 14 preparatory sessions, 517 sessions have been tape recorded and by now more than 50% of all recorded sessions have been transcribed. One fifth of all recorded sessions have been included in this study representing an adequate sample of all (recorded) sessions over the time of treatment.

Table 6.2 Verbal Activity in Four Psychoanalytic Treatments: Mean Number of Words per Session

	Patient	Analyst	Ratio P:A	Number of Sessions
Amalia X	2,921.2	780.3	3.7 : 1	113
Christian Y	1,353.7	1,200.4	1.1 : 1	110
Franziska X	2,483.6	817.8	3.0 : 1	93
Gustav Y	3,595.0	718.0	5.0 : 1	50

Adapted with permission from *Psychotherapy Research*.

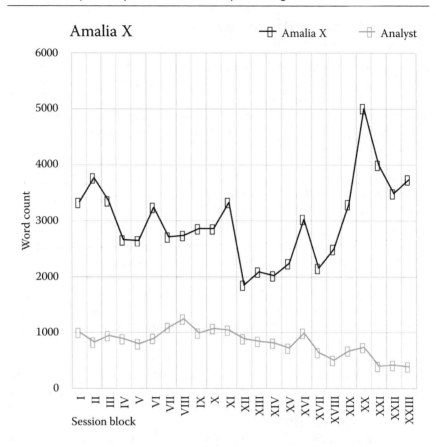

Figure 6.1 The development of verbal activity along the course of treatment.

Across the 113 sessions of the time-related sample the patient displays a broad spectrum of verbal activity. She takes part in the analytic dialogue in quite variable ways. Sometimes she talks a lot, and at other times she is quite silent. The analyst, however, shows a narrow band of verbal activity averaging about one-third of the patient's verbal activity. Compared with our other cases Amalia X starts at a medium level—and moves down in verbal activity until the midpoint of the treatment. Then her verbal activity reaches a peak toward the end (period XX, sessions 476–480). The analyst's activity shows a peak around the sessions of period VIII (176–180) in the first third of the treatment; then he slowly but steadily reduces his amount of verbal participation in the dialogue.

Discussion

One might ask whether this course of verbal exchange represents a typical pattern. To be fair we do not know. We know, however, that there is no significant statistical relationship between the degree of verbal activity of the two participants; this means each of them in each session regulated his or her verbal activity on their own. We surmise that this independence of talking participation should be expected in a well-running psychoanalytic treatment where each of both participants partially has his or her own agenda to follow. Or would it be more appropriate to characterize this feature of nonsignificant verbal activity relations a coproduced agenda? Measuring verbal activity is but an indirect measure of the degree of silence which is a shared discursive activity. It is only the recommendation of "free association" that has been conveyed to the patient in the beginning, that one usually attributes silence to the responsibility of the patient. The open space of silent moments in the analytic session is regarded as an invitation to the patient to use this space or not to use it. In everyday communication silence can be the speaker's silence, it can be the listener's silence, and only rarely it can be both. Usually participants in everyday talk know whose silence it is, and they conduct their interaction on the basis of this knowledge. Therefore, the study of verbal exchange raises the issue of how much everyday communicative activity and how much of analytic communicative activity is useful for a patient at any moment during the analytic treatment.

6.4   THE EMOTIONAL VOCABULARY*

Vocabulary Analyses

Words, nothing but words; how can we produce change just with words? This question is at the center of the psychoanalytic treatment technique because, beyond all of the rules concerning the setting, significant meaning is given to the gestalt of the psychoanalytical dialogue. Even if the verbalization in the psychoanalytical situation does not encompass the whole interaction, we can again refer to Freud's (1933a) comment from the "Introductory Lectures" as a motto, since the exchange of thoughts and feelings through verbal action plays a critical role in psychoanalysis. The Argentine psychoanalyst Liberman (1970) suggests in a three-volume work *Linguistica, Interaccion Comunicativa y Proceso Psicoanalitico* (1970) the linguistic foundation of psychoanalytic action. North American authors have connected language structure and psychoanalysis (Shapiro, 1988; 1999) demonstrating how the representational world needs to be translated into the linguistic idiom. Feelings have to be reformatted into words in the psychoanalytic dialogue which, according to Shapiro (1999), amounts to a semiotic transformation (p. 108). Empirical studies on the role of giving words to affective processes on the basis of transcripts highlight the

---

* Michael Hölzer, Dan Pokorny, Nicola Scheytt, and Horst Kächele.

fine-grained understanding of therapeutic operations in the dialogues of psychoanalysis and psychotherapy (Kemmler, Schelp, & Mecheril, 1991).

The vocabulary of patients was an early topic of an, at first, psychopathologic diagnostic orientated research (Johnson, 1944). Mowrer (1953b) shows that linguistic variability increases in manifold ways with the success of the psychotherapy. Linguistic variability is calculated by dividing the number of the different words (types) by the whole number of the words in a text (token). The relation of these two indices is generally viewed as an indicator of the diversification of a text (Jaffe, 1958). However, this measure is not independent of the proportion of the text, so Herdan (1966) suggests using a logarithmic type–token ratio (TTR). These early studies on the TTR generated enthusiasm that did not hold up. What Jaffe (1958) describes as "language of the dyad" could not be replicated: Schaumburg (1980) analyzes the interactive patterns of personal pronouns in four psychoanalytic treatments and could not confirm earlier findings about interpersonal tracking phenomena. Thus, the once promising lead of his sample may have been a random finding. The relevant literature for a lexical usage as an expression of psychopathology was first summarized by Vetter (1969).

In the same vein the general notion, measured in whatever way, that a greater linguistic variety could be a sign of working through, as Spence (1969) argues, has not been substantiated to date. We have ourselves performed a study concerning the aspect of formal redundancies—however, not for the patient Amalia X. In this study we have identified in the text of the patient Christian Y—not in the case of the analyst—that indeed a phase-like course of redundancies could be linked to the process of working through (Kächele & Mergenthaler, 1984).

Vocabulary analyses, as they have been detailed in the field of lexical statistics for a long time, were rarely considered in psychotherapeutic research to be a worthwhile effort; in psychoanalytic research they are absent. Studies concerning the connection of expressivity and form of neurosis dominated the first relevant studies (Lorenz, 1953).* Mahl's (1959, 1961) studies about paraverbal aspects of the spoken language received lively attention for some time. However, lexicographic statistics were bypassed last but not least due to the immense manual labor work necessary. In the late sixties the capacities of computers to handle not only numbers but also alphanumeric data and language was discovered in various fields in the humanities (Gerbner et al., 1969). Harting, Dahl, Spence and Donald have been the forerunners to apply the new technology in psychotherapy research. At the first European conference of SPR in 1981 we were able to present our own developments in "computer-aided analysis of psychotherapeutic discourse" (Kächele & Mergenthaler, 1983).

---

* Many years later this author discussed "Language and a woman's place" in society (Lorenz & Cobb, 1975).

If one would examine the vocabulary of an analyst, what would we expect? Would we have an assimilation of the linguistic world of the patient? Would we expect that the adherence to a certain school of psychoanalysis expresses itself in the vocabulary and that after longer time of professional experience of an analyst one would find a freer vocabulary independent of his theoretical orientation? One thing is certain, as Laffal (1967) shows: The effect of situational factors on the linguistic world is considerable. Therefore, the question of which characteristics and dimensions of the vocabulary should be examined is not trivial.

Even before the establishment of the machine supported content analysis in Ulm (Kächele, 1976), we demonstrated the change of the topic-related classes of nouns as a process characteristic in a single case study (Kächele, Thomä, & Schaumburg, 1975). Later, with the establishment of the Ulm Textbank and its methodological tools, we could embark toward more systematic vocabulary analyses.

A first vocabulary analysis of transcripts from the Penn Psychotherapy Project (Luborsky et al., 1980) demonstrated that "successful therapy" correlated indeed significantly with the simple vocabulary measurements such as the "private" (i.e., words used only by one of the speakers) and the "common" vocabulary (i.e., words used by both speakers). There were indications that in successful treatments the therapists adapted to the linguistic behavior of their patients, on the level of the vocabulary, to a greater degree than "nonsuccessful" therapists do. The analysis of the various subvocabularies examined indicated that the adaptive performance of the therapists in respect to the affective part of the vocabulary was particularly prominent. Words of patients that express feelings and moods seemed to be systematically responded by successful therapists (Hölzer, Mergenthaler, Pokorny, Kächele, & Luborsky, 1996). This led to the development of an instrument for the systematic analysis of the affective vocabulary (Hölzer, Pokorny, Kächele, & Luborsky, 1997).

By investigating affective vocabularies it became possible to grasp the linguistic exchange of patients and analysts in order to examine it directly with respect to the creation of a shared linguistic world. The following report gives a first impression of the possibilities of this approach.

Affective Dictionary Ulm (ADU)

The authors' construction of the Affective Dictionary (Hölzer et al., 1997) had the goal of using a classification schema of emotions that would be close to analytical thinking and at the same time, thanks to a simple classification algorithm, also of practical use in empirical research. The first steps were based on the thoughts of de Rivera, who proposed a six-dimensional schema with 64 theoretically possible categories. De Rivera's schema was theoretically comprehensive, but the high number of categories prevented its practical application decisively. Dahl and Stengel (1978) simplify the construction to a three-dimensional schema with eight categories. The classification procedure takes place according to Dahl, Hölzer, and Berry (1992) in four steps:

1. Is the given word principally of emotional nature or not?
2. Does the emotional word express a positive or negative emotion?
3. Does the emotional concept describe a feeling that refers to a relation (and a wish characteristic for this particular relation) of the subject to an object ("it" or also object-emotion, prototypically: anger or affection), or does it describe an emotional condition of the subject without a direct object relation ("me" or self-emotion, which are seen as beliefs in the status of wish fulfillment, prototypically: contentment or depression)?
4. In the case of the object emotions another dimensional direction is estimated: from the subject acting *toward* the object ("to" 1 = love; 5 = rage), or the other way around: *from* the object to the subject ("from" 2 = enthusiasm; 6 = fear). In the self-emotions *passive* (3 = contentment; 7 = depressivity) and *active* emotions (4 = joy; 8 = anxiety) are differentiated.

The first dimension has central meaning differentiate positive and negative and especially also the second dimension (object/self) that grasps a psychoanalytic meaningful quality of the emotions: for example, in negative emotions, the negative self emotions (e.g., anxiety and depression) are being differentiated from object emotions (e.g., rage and fear). The aim of the analytic therapeutic work is generally not to replace step by step the negative by the positive emotions but to transform "complaints" (i.e., negative self-emotions such as depressivity or anxiety) into "accuses" (rage, fear)—that is, to support a patient in becoming conscious of repressed attachment-regulating feelings through corresponding interpretations. Clinically valid subcategories were added later (Hölzer, 1996) to the four self-emotions: relief, pride, shame, and guilt. With the studies using the Affective Dictionary Ulm (ADU) one now has the choice between the basic system with 8 or an extended system with 12 categories. Figure 6.2 illustrates the basic eight categories of the ADU (and in addition frequently used entries of Amalia X).

On the basis of this theoretical classification procedure a German and an English version of the dictionary were created; an encompassing list of all words with the corresponding affective connotations of the 8 (or 12) categories was made. This classification could not be conducted mechanically, since the meaning of the words strongly depends on the context, which, however, can be examined only empirically. This was possible in a row series of studies on the basis of the available psychotherapy verbatim protocols texts in the Ulm Textbank and by the work of many graduate

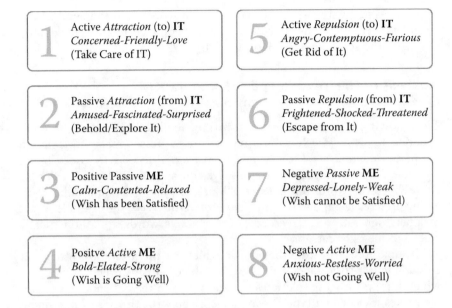

1 Active *Attraction* (to) **IT**
   Concerned-Friendly-Love
   (Take Care of IT)

5 Active *Repulsion* (to) **IT**
   Angry-Contemptuous-Furious
   (Get Rid of It)

2 Passive *Attraction* (from) **IT**
   Amused-Fascinated-Surprised
   (Behold/Explore It)

6 Passive *Repulsion* (from) **IT**
   Frightened-Shocked-Threatened
   (Escape from It)

3 Positive Passive **ME**
   Calm-Contented-Relaxed
   (Wish has been Satisfied)

7 Negative *Passive* **ME**
   Depressed-Lonely-Weak
   (Wish cannot be Satisfied)

4 Positve *Active* **ME**
   Bold-Elated-Strong
   (Wish is Going Well)

8 Negative *Active* **ME**
   Anxious-Restless-Worried
   (Wish not Going Well)

Figure 6.2 This schema shows the eight main emotion categories based on the independent decisions on the three dimensions—each with three emotion labels empirically shown to be prototypes of the category (Dahl and Stengel, 1978). In brackets, either generic consummatory acts ("it" emotions) that fulfill implicit wishes or generic beliefs in the status of wish fulfillment ("me" emotions) are depicted (Hölzer & Dahl, 1996).

and doctorate students. Presently the ADU encompasses 2,046 affective words in the basic grammatical form that, with the help of a linguistic tool, can be expanded to 26,823 potential complete forms (Pokorny, 2000). In the analysis of the verbatim protocols of therapy sessions, the program processes word by word, but free of context. This leads inevitably to some faulty evaluations. A greater exactness could therefore only be achieved by an additional manual evaluation that requires a considerable effort.

Among the successful studies made with the ADU, the aforementioned investigation of the transcripts, stemming from the Penn Psychotherapy Project, is of particular relevance. In outpatient analytically oriented therapies Luborsky et al. (1988) distinguishes, by means of a differentiated outcome assessment, "successful" from "not successful" psychotherapies. Later the "helping alliance" was extracted from the results of this study as a predictor for therapy success. Not only could the extensive verbatim protocols of this study be made available to the Ulm Textbank, but also the ADU could, with the help of native speakers, be transformed from the German version into an English one. The study of the Penn Transcripts in two consecutive steps brought forth the expected results: Successful therapies were associated with the number of emotion words, and the emphasis of negative object emotions at the end of the therapy correlated particularly high with the good outcome (Hölzer et al., 1997).

Analysis of the Text Corpus of Amalia X: Qualitative Analysis by Examples

The following examples portray the working mode of the ADU. It becomes apparent that many feelings and moods are expressed metaphorically, in the phrase context respectively, and they are not necessarily coded by an individual expression. Also false-positive coding is possible as in example B, in which the words *am liebsten* ("liking the most") should indicate an acting preference but not an actual emotion. Otherwise, the examples show a rather high rate of correctness; most emotive words are automatically placed in the right categories.

Example A derives from the hour in which the therapist most often uses emotion words from category 1 ("love"), which is in any event the category which significantly differentiates the analyst from the patient. This example makes it clear in a typical way not only how the therapist takes up an affective term of the patient and verbalizes it but also how the therapist puts into relation the "loving daughter" immediately to "love in return" and in this case especially to the absence of this "love in return" (i.e., unrequited love, which would be a negative object emotion). There are many similar examples for this transformation process found in this analysis.

Example A: The Analyst's Work with Category I—Love (Session II)*

> Patient (P): I still did want to say something about the father. Yesterday I said that I would have liked to be **loving** (1) daughter. That is obviously two sided; I naturally would also have a normal relationship from the inside.
>
> Analyst (A): A **loving** (1) father. You would like to be a **loving** (1) daughter, in order to also ...
>
> ...
>
> A: Yes, that is also the origin of the tears, hm.
>
> ...

---

* Boldface indicates words are captured by the ADU.

A: Yes respectively, there was in earlier times one, as I believe you have described, that he has favored her which however obviously in a way that did not correspond to what looks to you like **love (1)**, **attention (1)**, **and affection (1)**.

...

A: Yes, it is such a trying once and again, to be a **loving (1)** daughter, to then go empty handed.

...

A: You have said now that you are also searching for something then. You go home or so, or travel with the parents, so as if there you have the only chance as a **loving (1)** daughter to receive still some **love in return (1)**, there and nowhere else. I am exaggerating now.

...

A: Well on the other hand you said before, you would not search for them because it is so **frustrating (7)** to be a **loving (1)** daughter without finding any **love in return (1)** and now one could then say, so, instead you have then nonetheless the mother who cares for you, who is nice then, who also **spoils (2)** you somewhat.

...

A: That then however means, not only to renounce from him on the **hope (4)**, respectively; that they not realistic, as you are describing, that also he could be different sometimes, for this is an old **longing (1)** that did not receive any **love in return (1)**, but instead then also on the mother, so, that is a ... that would then mean renouncing on all tracks.

Example B: Category 5—Rage on the Therapist (Session 172)

Example B begins with the aforementioned faulty positive coding ("... would have liked the most to kill him"). Ironically, the patient expresses with this, in the beginning of the session, the opposite meaning of the coding, grasped by the ADU. The remaining coding is, however, correct: The leading theme of the whole hour was on how to handle hatred. In this sense it concerns a typical sequence, since the therapist takes almost every chance in the course of the further therapy to take up strong feelings on the part of the patient (here in particularly those from the category 5 [rage]) and if possible to also relate them onto himself in order to enable a working through of impulses that have so far been repressed.

A: Yes? (Very, very long pause). Is something special?

P: Hm. (Very long pause) I do not know, maybe.

A: Hmhm.

P: I believe I would have **liked** (1) to kill you yesterday.

A: Mh. (Very long pause) at the end, ah, of the session, or?

P: Mh.

A: Mh.

P: Afterward.

A: As you left, or?

P: Yes. (Very long pause).

...

P: I do not know whether I am **angry** (5); I do not believe that I am **angry** (5). (...) I know, for example, exactly why it touches you if I would be **angry** (5).

A: Yes, maybe that, ah, also the **hatred** (5), ah, has to do with, that so going according to the clock.

...

P: What do I mean?

A: **Hatred** (5).

P: Yes, something as that (pause 0:10). There are two levels. You are talking to me as a therapist, but you are at the same time also a certain human; and ...

A: Mh.

P: I am not quite sure toward whom the **hatred** (5) is directed.

A: Yes, toward the one; it is the **hatred** (5) toward the one who has the **power** (4), has **power** (4).

P: No; I rather believe toward you yourself.

...

P: I believe that I know this very well, how that is from secondhand.

A: Mh.

P: That is.

A: Yes, second hand, that means I can, you mean, I can talk, talk well.

P: Mh.

A: Mh. He can say whatever he wants.

P: Yes, so; and from this also the **hatred** (5) stems.

A: Mh.

P: Or the **envy** (5) or; I also do not know (pause 2:10).

Example C: Category 7—Depression and Enduring of Helplessness (Session 175)

Example C: Three hours later the line of interpretation and the recognizable strategy of the transformation of negative self-emotions into negative object-emotions proves successful. First the patient speaks about depression and helplessness (here by the example of a movie as a departing point of her associations) so, at the end of the sequence (however, not anymore recorded by the ADU) she finds the courage for open critique—even an ambush—against the analyst (category 5: "Do you even listen?").

P: Did you perhaps see the movie about these convicts; about prisoners for life, yesterday?

A: No.

P: No, hm. (pause 0:15).

A: That is **moving (2)** you and still **moves (2)**.

P: Yes, it was very **depressing (7)**. ... **horribly (6) depressing (7)**; ... so **gruesome (6)**, so (pause) the phrase about **helplessness (7)** came back to my mind; that one would have to endure it, which is unthinkable.... There one would *lieber* (**rather like 1**) do something and then I do not know what and then I feel really **helpless (7)**.

...

P: That there are humans who are there for enduring **helplessness (7)** and, and the others, ah, they tralala, have it well.

A: Yes, that, in any event. The phrase was generalized by you, not so as if I would have meant it.

P: Probably.

A: That one has to do in any case; that is wonderful.

P: Ah no; oh no, wait, no; I actually wanted to say to you today.

A: Mh.

P: I very often have the feeling, you demand from me, demand is said a bit **strongly (4)** now, rather change and do something and, and.

A: Mh.

P: And, yes, mainly (not understandable: talks very fast) and I also wanted to say something against this; does one always, always, always have to change and, and, yes, I immediately say in which context I mean it, completely. There actually the alternative enduring of **help-lessness (7)** was not so convenient for me; but let us say into this direction that one occasionally also waits or really endures something. I certainly do not reject this and I also did not want to generalize it like this, but yesterday and today, as I read something like that in the newspaper (not understandable) there it appeared to me when there would be human groups who could do what they wanted; they are somehow for this, ah, I would have almost said, damned to endure helplessness (7) and the others are **active** (4) and with **success** (4) or also **passive** (7) with **success** (4). That is really generalized, I know; and that I have also made it to be this way. That I also know (pause 0:10). And sent them into the other camp and that I have also done; into the camp of the **successful ones** (4) (pause 0:45). Now you have not listened to me at all (pause 0:15).

A: At which part not?

P: Yes, departing from the last phrase that you have spoken.

Example D: Relationship Reflections at the End of the Therapy (Session 502)

Example D should not so much depict the assumed therapeutic strategies of the verbalization or show the interpreting transformation itself but rather show the resulting emotional manifoldness with which the patient, in an advanced phase of her analysis, describes attachment episodes. In terms of the dual code theory of Bucci (1997a), the patient deepened her emotional experience; she describes particularly on the level of emotion, many-faceted and vivid, her inner experiences. From our view such episodes, at the end of therapies, speak for therapeutic success in the sense of a generalized emotional blooming—however, not in the sense of a "superficial" accumulation of positive self-emotions.

P: But otherwise I will have no more material; if I do not dream and if my friend *D is no more there; although he still exists. He still exists more than ever. He still covers everything. It is **horrible** (6) and I cannot be **angry** (5) at him. Sometimes I try in a **cramping** (8) manner to add up all his **bad** (7) things and it has no effect. On the contrary; it is such a stage where I, if I would not find it **embarrassing** (8) or almost sentimental, I could write a letter every day. Ah; I could write ten letters, not only one. But a lot is keeping me from this. Mostly, the awareness that this will **bother** (6) him and that it is altogether not true what I write. And then it is **overwhelmingly** (2) true again; that is completely **crazy** (8). But that is.

(...)

P: There are such humans who, I remember a primeval forest scene, **horrible** (6). We walked for an hour, a good hour through the fog. Through thick forests and with really roaring stags; it was almost **uncanny** (6). Nothing came except this night and this forest and it was miles away; walked completely **lonely** (7) there. And we walked together, but it was absolutely the distance. We also had not talked, but D is, yes, like a little boy who is on his sand pile and builds his castles and bakes his cakes and does not need anyone for this; because he does not need anyone there. (Grasp). But in, he is in everything very **lonely** (7); in grasping and with the whole way in which he lives. He once had such a breakdown of perception; that is **frightening** (6). There he also looks at you; there you think that he had fallen onto the world for the first time. He is a *single player* (i.e., one that plays alone). I do not know if one can play along with him, if there are bridges where one plays along. Actually, if one looks at him; that is mostly such a tragic look or such a grandiose look, or, I do not remember a, a long looking or **tender** (1) or so. It always was very, somehow very **hard** (5); must have also lived as a child very locked up.

A: Although he is a *single player* (i.e., one that plays alone), ah, as you say, he could also awake very much playing passion, ah, within you.

P: Yes all. However, this has nothing to do with him, but only with myself.

A: Yes.

P: Yes, yes, all. Yes, oh. That is the point, at which I never get further; because I assume that the point makes for, ah, the whole **fascination** (2).

Quantitative Analysis of the Text Corpus

This study was based on 219 (of 517 transcribed) sessions of the analysis of Amalia X. Since the results of our former study with data from the Penn Psychotherapy Project showed the interdependence of the emotional vocabulary of patient and therapist, we assumed that the corresponding emotional vocabularies should also correlate with one another as it would make little sense to bypass the feelings of a patient. Our data analysis also provided evidence, as described already, on a systematic transformation of negative self-emotions into negative object emotions in the course of analytic treatment. Correspondingly, hypotheses for the examination of the corpus of Amalia X could be formulated as follows:

H1: The corresponding emotional vocabulary categories of patient and therapist should quantitatively correlate positively with one another.
H2: For both speakers there should be an increase of negative object-emotions (particularly in the category "rage") in the course of the

treatment and with it a corresponding decrease of negative self-emotions.

The absolute and the relative frequencies of the affective vocabulary (related to the "tokens," i.e., on the whole amount of words) and their subcategories were calculated. For both speakers a rate of approximately 1.8% of emotion words in the spoken text was found. The comparison of the realized vocabulary—that is, the frequency of their usage (see Table 6.3)—shows a certain correspondence of the word usage, since the distribution of the affective words on the categories are strongly similar to one another. However, it is also not very astonishing that the patient—contrary to the therapist—shows increases in the categories of negative self-emotions and especially in the negative object category "fear" as well. The therapist's emphasis on the category 1 ("love") is discussed later in the text. H1, in view of the interdependence of the linguistic expression of emotions with which we assumed a positive correlation of the affective expressions of the patient and therapist on the level of words, could be proven.

Amalia X and her analyst correlate with one another significantly positively in all corresponding categories of the ADU (Table 6.4). However, it remains open whether this adaptation reflects a particular understanding (and linguistically documented) of in-therapy behavior. It is at least possible that the analyst takes up the affective expressions of his patient and reverbalizes them. However, it is also possible that Amalia X processes for herself, in a reflecting way, affective focused interventions of her analyst and therefore similarities in the linguistic usage result. One can, however, assume that it is clinically a commonly created process-like dialogue in which both "directions" are integrated.

Table 6.3 Comparison of Frequency of Emotional Vocabulary (Percentage of Total Vocabulary)

Emotion	Analyst %	Patient %	ES
Love	.25	.14	+.56
Surprise	.15	.14	+.05
Contentment	.10	.08	+.12
Joy	.32	.28	+.19
Anger	.17	.16	+.08
Fear	.26	.32	−.54
Depression	.29	.34	−.20
Anxiety	.32	.33	−.05
Total	1.8	1.78	+.03
T-Test, p twofold	.05	.01	.001

ES: effect size, d according to Cohen

Table 6.4 Positive Correlations of Emotional Categories of Analyst and Patient

N =219 Sessions	P1	P2	P3	P4	P5	P6	P7	P8
	Love	Surprise	Content-ment	Joy	Anger	Fear	Depression	Anxiety
A1 Love	.35	.11	.05	.08	.11	−.06	.05	−.06
A2 Surprise	.07	.23	−.10	−.12	−.07	.10	−.28	.04
A3 Contentment	.01	.03	.28	−.03	.05	.02	−.08	−.02
A4 Joy	.16	.06	.04	.33	−.08	.01	.15	−.03
A5 Anger	.01	−.07	.15	−.06	.39	.03	.05	−.10
A6 Fear	−.04	.05	.13	−.04	−.19	.30	−.07	.23
A7 Depression	−.02	−.07	.13	−.04	.01	.09	.22	.04
A8 Anxiety	−.01	.01	.10	−.07	−.09	.15	.01	.33
Spearman-correlation, p onefold			.05		.01			.001

"Complaints in Accusations"

H2, with which we assumed an increase of the negative object-emotions and a simultaneous decrease of negative self-emotions, could be partially confirmed. The increase of the negative object emotion "anger" is found in the vocabulary of Amalia X but not in the vocabulary of the analyst (Table 6.5). However, he focuses in the course less on negative self-emotions—in our view, because of a more and more relationship-oriented interpretational activity. The fact that the detected correlations are rather weak effects does not speak against the principal truth of the theoretical assumptions but rather that the structural change, aspired in the analysis, is a difficult and time-consuming process.

Coda

In conclusion, it is worthwhile to pay attention to subvocabularies; hereby we can particularly emphasize, on the basis of our results in short- and long-term therapies, the area of the affective vocabulary. This makes intuitive sense for clinical reasons. Krause (1997) claims that there is no relevant psychological disorder that would not also be an affective disorder. Therefore, affect theories in the understanding of the genesis of psychological and psychosomatic developments of symptoms thus rightfully take a prominent place (Stephan & Walter, 2003).

That the ADU delivers only a relatively rough analysis and that the more subtle metaphoric expressions are, to a great extent, not grasped has become clear in the above examples. However, this is not the intention of this method. According to our research policy, such methods should be indicators of the therapeutic process in order that it can later be applied as a screening procedure. If the interest is directed to microprocesses one must examine the text qualitatively for its subtle verbalization of emotions.

Table 6.5 Time-Related Development of Frequency of Negative Self—and Object
Emotions of Analyst and Patient

N = 219 sessions	C1	C2	C3	C4	C5	C6	C7	C8
Analyst	-.02	-.05	-.11	-.07	.01	-.03	-.18	-.18
Amalie X	.05	.15	-.12	.07	.15	-.17	.04	.03
Spearman-correlation, p twofold				.05		.01		.001

C = emotion category of the ADU: C1 = love, C2 = surprise, C3 = contentment, C4 = joy, C5 = anger, C6 = fear, C7 = depression, C 8 = anxiety

Dahl et al. (1992) work out a manual for this, which connects theory and category schema with the ADU. The study exemplifies Freud's viewpoint that the therapeutic task consists in the transformation of "complaints" (negative self-emotions) into "accusations" (negative object-emotions). This formula might sound simple; it is our opinion that this transformation significantly correlates with the success of psychoanalytical therapy, which, alas, remains to be shown in a larger sample.

6.5 THE CHARACTERISTIC VOCABULARY OF AN ANALYST*

Introduction

Discussions about an analyst's official and private theories tend to limit themselves to the process of listening: "The psychoanalyst who knows and uses psychoanalytic theories ... listen to the patient, enriched by an associative context that includes the shared experiences of the entire community of psychoanalysts, past and present, as well as the psychoanalyst's own clinical and personal experience" (Michels, 1999, p. 193). Apart from the various influences on the receiving process that Spence and Lugo (1972) studied in an experimental fashion little is said or written about the impact of an analyst's theories on his way of implementing them by specific vocabulary (Hamilton, 1996). How does this cognitive background influence the analyst's way of talking; how does one transform one's understanding into an intervention? Approaches for elucidating the analyst's role in creating the uniqueness of the patient–analyst pair (Kantrowitz, 1993) have been rare although the formative influence of the analyst's feeling and thinking may well be crucial. Is it possible to study the lexical usage of an analyst at work?

Verbal activity is among other aspects constituted by vocabulary. Operational measures for the vocabulary have to distinguish between formal and substantial aspects. The term *vocabulary* refers to the number of different words (types) that are used by a speaker. Measures of types are interesting,

* Horst Kächele, Michael Hölzer, Erhard Mergenthaler; adapted from Kächele et al. (1999).

since words stand for concepts (and therapy has essentially to do with an exchange of concepts and beliefs, with assimilation of new material and accommodation of previous schemata). So the analyst's vocabulary at the beginning of the analysis will both shape and reflect the patient's experiential world. During the analysis its evolution might run parallel or at least partly reflect the conceptual and emotional learning processes that take place (French, 1937).

As we have mentioned above, a variety of computer-aided methods for the evaluation of psychotherapy process have been suggested during the last decades. Promising in many respects are vocabulary measures that are rarely mentioned explicitly in literature on computer-aided strategies in the field of psychotherapy research. Systematic studies of the size of vocabulary of an analyst or of the change of vocabulary during therapy are still lacking partly due to the fact that the computer-supported search for linguistic markers as indicators for therapeutic processes faces a general dilemma: While the rather mechanical way of analyzing data by means of computerized methods paves the way for a host of various procedures, the selection of the variables to be investigated is often restricted to formal criteria lacking clinical relevance.

Our studies show that the investigation of vocabulary and certain features of vocabularies can well be linked to clinically relevant aspects of process and outcome of psychotherapy. Since psychotherapeutic treatment can well be seen as the development of a shared language (Gedo, 1984) it seemed to be a straightforward hypothesis that exchange processes like those in psychotherapy and psychoanalytic therapy should somehow be reflected in the vocabulary of the speakers involved.

As opposed to verbal activity measures (see above), formal vocabulary measures do not belong to the current battery of psychotherapeutic research tools although they might well help fill the gap between formal and content related approaches. From a research perspective, vocabulary measures defined in terms of types are interesting, because they are easily and objectively obtained. Since words stand for concepts (and therapy has essentially to do with an exchange of concepts and beliefs, with assimilation of new material and accommodation of previous schemata), changes in the vocabulary during treatment might parallel or at least partly reflect such exchange processes.

In a therapeutic dialogue different kinds of vocabulary can be distinguished as follows:

1. The "Private Vocabulary" (PV)—that is, the set of words (types) that are only used by one of the speakers.
2. The "Intersectional Vocabulary" (IV), the set of words (types) that are used by both patient and therapist.

In this study we examine a third kind: the "Characteristic Vocabulary" of Amalia X's analyst. Since there are many constraints operating in the use of language in actual discourse we focused on a specific interactive, hence, "characteristic," subset of the analyst's vocabulary, that part he is actively implementing within the dialogues not merely following the patient's lead. Here the decision as to whether a certain type belongs to the "Characteristic Vocabulary" is based on frequency of occurrence.

A word has to occur in the text of one speaker significantly more often compared with the text of the other speaker to be incorporated in this "Characteristic Vocabulary." Depending on the chosen level of significance, the magnitude of the "Characteristic Vocabulary" may differ considerably. The characteristic vocabulary does not include words used by just one speaker; these would belong to the realm of the Private Vocabulary.

An Analyst's Characteristic Vocabulary

We identified the analyst's characteristic vocabulary at the beginning of the analysis of patient Amalia X based on 18 sessions. Based on a total of 13,311 tokens we found 1,480 types. The analyst's characteristic vocabulary comprised 36 nouns and 80 other words; this is about 10% of his vocabulary. Discussing the results of this study we reproduce the English translation and then the original German word and the frequency of occurrence in parentheses. This data analysis used a "lemmatized" version of the text. This means that all inflected words have been reduced to their basic form; for example, the plural form "women/Frauen" has been replaced by the singular form "woman/Frau."

It is no surprise that the famous "uhm/hm" used by analysts all over the world came out as the most frequent and the most characteristic (976). There are any number of words that betray the analyst's so-called minor encoding habits like "yes/ja" (678), the dysfluency indicator once studied by George Mahl "ah/äh" (395), "also/auch" (238), "that/dass"(200), "something/etwas" (66), "this/dieser, dieses" (60), "than/als" (58), and "uhuh/aha"(31). Analyzing a second set of 18 sessions at the end of the analysis and checking these characteristics again, we did not find much change with these particles; they remain the linguistic fingerprints of any speaker out of conscious control. They are bad, but minor, encoding habits. However, some of them make for the tedious reading of transcripts. These particles are in no way specific to the analyst's task, though they may be used for detective reasons especially when countertransference issues are the focus of an investigation (Dahl, Teller, Moss & Truillo, 1978).

Nouns as elements of style inform us about the subject of a dialogue; they tell what the two participants were conversing about and how one of them tried to shape it (Kächele et al., 1975). Therefore, the characteristic vocabulary of the analyst in terms of his nouns is very telling. In the 18 sessions from the beginning of the analysis we found the following nouns as being highly characteristic ($p \leq 0.01$) for the analyst:

- Dream (Traum 88)
- Woman (Frau 31)
- Theme (Thema 18)
- Thought (Gedanke 17)
- Question (Frage 16)
- Anxiety (Angst 16)
- Hair (Haar 13)
- Cousin (Cousin 9)
- Demand (Anspruch 8)
- Madonna (Madonna 8)
- Notary (Notar 7)
- Insecurity (Unsicherheit 7)
- Seduction (Verführung 7)
- Comparison (Vergleich 7)
- Claim (Forderung 5)
- Mortification (Kränkung 5)
- Relief (Entlastung 5)
- Spinster (Jungfer 5)
- Tampon (Tampon 5)
- Breakout (Ausbruch 4)
- Conviction (Überzeugung 4)
- Dog (Hund 4)
- Intensity (Intensität 4)
- Lawyer (Jurist 4)
- Toilet (Klo 4)
- Uneasiness (Beunruhigung 3)
- Candidate (Prüfling 3)
- Shyness (Scheu 3)

Ordering the nouns into semantic fields we may distinguish the following:

- *Technical items:* dream theme thought question demand comparison claim conviction
- *Emotional items:* anxiety breakout mortification relief insecurity intensity uneasiness shyness
- *Sexual/bodily items:* woman seduction spinster tampon toilet madonna hair
- *Topical items:* cousin notary dog lawyer

From this tabulation we may infer that the analyst in these first 18 sessions characteristically emphasizes in his interventions four classes of nouns:

1. *Technical nouns,* which are part of his task to invite the patient's participation in the special analytic point of view
2. *Emotional nouns,* which are part of the analyst's technique to intensify emotions
3. *Sexual/bodily linked nouns,* which clearly refer to the patient's embarrassing sexual self-concept
4. *Topical nouns,* which are stimulated by the patient's life situation as reported in the first sessions.

To deepen our understanding we next subjected the use of the noun *dream* to a more thorough examination. In the beginning of an analysis the analyst conveyed to the patient that the analytic dialogue is an unusual dialogue insofar that the analyst may use highlighting certain words as a style of interventions. As the word *dream* was a prominent characteristic part of the analyst's vocabulary compared with the patient, we hypothesized that the analyst tried to intensify the patient curiosity about dreams as a special class of reported material.

Hypothetically we assumed that in each of the sessions when the patient reports or speaks about a dream the analyst focuses his verbal activity using the noun *dream* relatively more frequently than the patient. To avoid circularity—our hypothesis is built on the findings from the 18 sessions—we extended the database from the original 18 sessions to include 29 sessions that cover the period from the first 100 sessions. The results confirmed our hypothesis: In 25 out of 29 sessions the analyst uses the noun *dream* more often than the patient, relative to the proportion of his speech activity.

The patient's use of the noun *dream* has a mean of 0.13% (s = +0.02) of all words; the analyst's use has a mean of 0.57% (s = +0.35) The t-test for paired samples proves the significant difference ($p \leq 0.000$). The result may be partially explained by the fact that the analyst uses shorter interventions, while the patient details his material.

Based on these findings we assume that in the opening phase of the analysis there is a systematic relationship between the patient talking about dreams and the analyst's efforts to stay close and even sometimes to intensify the work on the reported dream. Whenever the patient uses the noun *dream* there is a variable response of the analyst that is in the majority of instances even numerically above the level of the patient's use. This may mean that within a few sentences the analyst will point to the phenomena more explicitly. Analyzing a new sample of sessions at the end of the treatment the noun *dream* no longer was part of the characteristic vocabulary of the analyst.

Discussion

Techniques of lexical investigation allow us to identify the analyst's preferred conceptual tools as far as they are expressed in words. The analyst's vocabulary is a part of a complex linguistic task in a specially designed setting. Its study may help us to better understand what "analysts at work" are doing. There is no standard vocabulary, but there might be components of verbalization that are an essential part of the analytic technology for its task to transform theory into practice.

To work on the patient's communications with interpretations requires empathy and introspection. They alone would not lead the analyst to his specific form of understanding. He also needs theoretical knowledge that he has obtained by training, be it as part of his own analytic experience or by studying what other psychoanalysts have already described. About the process of how these two domains of knowledge are interwoven in the actual therapeutic operation we know very little. For many years we only had available armchair speculation on how the mind of the analyst works (Ramzy, 1974). The few empirical studies that have been performed on how analysts' minds work have only opened a first glance at the immense variability of reasons for actual performance.

One fruitful approach to study personal concepts of individual analysts about a specific etiological topic—psychic trauma—was launched by Sandler's (1983) putting into operational terms his own reflections on the relation of concepts to practice. The study group at the Sigmund Freud Institut in Frankfurt opened one way of exploring the unknown realm of what analysts think about their practice (Sandler, Dreher, & Drews, 1991). An empirical approach was established by Meyer (1988), who studied tape-recorded postsession reflections of three German analysts on a larger sample of recorded sessions.

Clearly the relation of theory and practice is mediated by the analyst's mental operations. Our concepts shape our actual therapeutic practice; however, we know very little about how this is executed. The very existence of different schools in psychoanalysis raises the question of to what extent these theoretical orientations influence the daily practice. One can safely assume that the complexity of the human mind allows for quite a few divergent theoretical constructions that are all viable within the psychoanalytic frame of reference (Hamilton, 1996); however, it has not yet been demonstrated with respect to results that in psychoanalysis "all are equal and all must have prizes" (Luborsky et al., 1975, p. 995).

6.6   EMOTIONAL AND COGNITIVE REGULATION IN THE PSYCHOANALYTICAL PROCESS: A MICROANALYTICAL STUDY*

The Therapeutic Cycles Model

The TCM was developed for verbal therapy forms and is based on two variables of change: emotional experiencing and cognitive mastery, which is measurable in transcripts as a relative proportion of emotional tinged words and abstract words. Dependent on the quantitative emphasis of both variables, four emotion abstraction patterns are differentiated. The pattern A, Relaxing, is marked by little emotion, little abstraction. It often describes the condition of patients when they feel relaxed or do not speak about any topic related to illness. Pattern B, Reflecting, marks a condition when patients reflect but without being simultaneously emotionally involved. A high measure of abstraction can also be interpreted as an expression of defense, as it is described by the defense mechanisms of rationalizing and intellectualizing. Pattern C, Experiencing, shows an above-average emotional participation whereas there is little manifestation of abstraction. In pattern D, Connecting, both variables are manifested above average. The patient has access to feelings and can, at the same time, reflect upon them. This pattern serves as an indicator for key sessions within a therapy; within individual sessions it stands for moments that are clinically particularly meaningful and are related to change. In psychodynamic orientated therapies it appears predominately when patients work through conflict topics and through this also experience emotional insight.

Next to the emotional and the cognitive processes in psychoanalysis, aspects of the behavior are of meaning as well. Even without a limitation on transcripts and particularly in psychoanalytical therapy, the observation of the behavior is generally not possible immediately but is developable merely by recounts. However, recounts are basically nothing other than "actions turned into words." Beyond this, the course of the recount has the effect of structuring the conversation as well. When a story is told, the listeners are silent; they are listening. As soon as the story is over a high character of demand develops upon the listener to respond to the story and to comment the recounted events. The "narrative style," a measure for the appearance of a story in the speech, therefore emerges as a third variable—a structure variable. In texts the narrative style concerning the appearance of markers is measured as, for example, prepositions.

After the TCM, the four emotion abstraction patterns and the narrative style appear during the therapeutic process in a specific sequence of five phases. The idealistically typical course begins with the pattern A, Relaxing

* Erhard Mergenthaler and Friedemann Pfäfflin.

(e.g., the patient does not know what to talk about). It is followed by a report of a negative emotional experience (measurable as negative experiencing), frequently followed or mixed in by recounts (measurable as narrative style). This goes along with an increase of positive emotional tone (measurable as positive experiencing). Thereafter there should be found a phase of working through with insight processes (measurable through connecting). The individual phases or sequences of phases can also repeat. The cycle ends with the pattern A, Relaxing. One or more successful run-throughs of the cycle within a therapy session lead to a "Mini-Outcome." The repetition of these "local" cycles finally leads to a "global" change and a positive "Macro-Outcome." Therewith this model is suited for the description of complete therapy courses (macroprocess) as well as for the description of individual therapy sessions (microprocess). The meaning of the cycle and particularly the pattern D, Connecting, for a favorable therapy course and therapy outcome is shown by Mergenthaler (1996) in a cross-sectional study with 20 patients and in the meantime also in subsequent studies (Fontao, 2004; Lepper & Mergenthaler, 2005, 2007; Mergenthaler, 2000).

However, for the application of the model in empirical studies it is expected that the therapeutic cycle does not appear, as previously described, in an ideal typical form. For practical application, therefore, the appearance of a cycle and, with it the proof of a therapeutic advance, is simplified and is defined as follows: A cycle is every sequence of emotion abstraction patterns that contains at least one Connecting pattern and is limited to the left and to the right by Relaxing (beginning and end of a session always are considered to be Relaxing). As another additional condition it demands that in the Connecting pattern at least one of the two variables reach an emotional tone or abstraction with a value greater than half a standard deviation. The cycles are generally preceded by so-called shift events—that is, linguistic as well as nonlinguistic events that allow an increase and the dominance of positive emotion after a negative dominating phase. Typical examples for shift events are the reporting of childhood memories and dreams in the analytical therapy or imagination exercises; the Gestalt two-chair technique, and the like in other therapeutic orientations.

Example from Session 152 of Amalia X

After a short banter about the rescheduling of a session quite in the beginning of the session, the patient recounts a dream (at the transition of WB 1 to WB 2). This is reported here:

P: Mhm (pause 2:00) (moans). Tonight I have dreamed, this morning as long as the alarm clock rang. I was murdered by a dagger.

A: Mhm.

P: And it was however like in a movie—and I had to lie on my stomach very long and had a dagger in the back and then many people came—and, I do not know any more exactly, holding the hand very calmly, somehow //

A: Mhm.

P: It was very embarrassing to me that the skirt has slid so far up in the back.

A: Mhm.

P: And then came a colleague, very clearly visible also *5382 (a town), this was my very first work place, and he then also pulled out the dagger from my back and took it with him and I know (1) it was then like a souvenir. And then came a young couple—I only know that he was black. And they have cut off my hair and indeed wanted to make a wig of it I believe. And that I found very horrible. Simply all down and they have then also started to cut. And, I then got up—and went to the hair stylist. And there I still had // I am /.

The dream is put here at the beginning to explain the clinical context. What would an analysis be without dreams and dream interpretation? Certainly one waits with the dream interpretation for the ideas of the patient. However, one cannot avoid that, during the telling of the story or the reading of it, respectively, one develops one's own interpretations, even if they are trivial: Also the dagger is a sharp instrument; the patient has it in her "back"—that is, there where the analyst usually sits. In the tape recording the passage with the "slid up skirt" is acoustically barely understandable, and one will see as follows that the analyst does not get involved with this aspect for a long time—probably because he could not decipher it acoustically. Later in the dream, the patient is exposed (her hair is cut off), and the dream ends with the attempt of reconciling this intervention (going to the hairstylist).

From the relative spoken shares of the patient and the analyst in Figure 6.3, it is shown that the analyst is a lot more active than one can observe in many other protocols. The chart above the graph for verbal activity shows the course of the positive (black) and negative (gray) emotional tone, and notice that these two variables depict only very discrete varying with three high points of the positive valence in WB 10–11, WB 16–17, and WB 20–21. The upper graph shows the patient's text. One sees the typical fluctuations of the narrative style with a maximum in WB 2, the dream report. There is a cycle with the pattern Connecting in WB 13 and WB 17. The lower part of the graphic documents the common text of the patient and the therapist, which shows in this session two cycles. The first is mostly the same with the cycle in the text of the patient; however, the Connecting moments are weakened by the contribution of the analyst. In addition, there is a second cycle with Connecting in WB 21, which is essentially dominated by the spoken share of the analyst and becomes clearer through him.

The content of the dream is followed first by the associations of the patient concerning the dream she experienced, "as in a theater." She talks about nonchalance; everything is so unimportant to her, which she associates at the same time with fearlessness. She ponders to sell her vehicle, to go to a convent, feels dirty. In WB 4 and in the following word blocks there is no Connecting, because—in dependence on the model of the emotion/abstraction pattern, the hypothesis—the psychoanalyst only verbalizes the negative feelings of the patient, for example, her restlessness, her feeling to not get ahead, her impression to be rather dead than alive. Although the patient has emphasized several times before that she was still alive after the dagger hit her and afterward (in the dream) she still went to the hair stylist. Several times the analyst begins his phrases with contradiction: "But ... you have this and that...." He says she would be afraid; she would do everything wrong. If one wants one can understand this taking up of negative emotions of a dagger stabbing. The expressed experience in the dream of the patient seems to be subsequently confirmed in the behavior of the analyst.

In WB 6 the patient says that she would like to rush to the analyst, grab him by the neck, and hold him very tight; however, she fears that he would not endure this and would then suddenly drop dead. Again, he verbalizes her negative emotions (fears) and interprets the dream as a "struggle down to the knife."

In WB 8 with a high shaping of abstraction in the patient's spoken share she talks about how she wants to measure the head of the analyst, wants to know what is inside this head, what he thinks about her, whether he laughs over her, and so forth.

In WB 10–11 the positive emotional tone increases. The content is about the analyst's laughing, about the false laughing of the patient's father in earlier times as well as frequent laughing of the patient in earlier sessions. Very empathically and reassuring the analyst says, "Naturally I find it good that you can laugh.... I laugh too little." After this intervention it comes in WB 13 to Connecting. This 13th word block is introduced by the analyst with a long interpretation:

> A: Yes, yes, mhm. Yes, you meant whether I now—why I do Jung and not Freud ah or, more Freud than Jung. Now ah, without that I that, that from—I do not believe out of practical reasons, but I believe that you in your occupation with my head are not only concerned with—

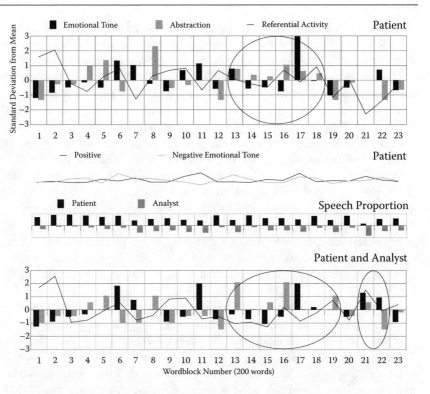

Figure 6.3 Application of the Therapeutic Cycle Model for the microanalysis of the hour 152. The two upper graphics concern the spoken shares of only the patient; the other two graphics relate to the spoken share of the patient as well as that of the analyst. Cycles are marked by an ellipse.

the occupation with maleness, with my male head and a principle; but that you are possibly also—concerned with very concrete matters, which you have thought about before with the knife. Not so, not in vain your girlfriend has spoken about shrink heads.

P: Yes. But I can do this; I have because of this also interrupted the thought.

A: Yes, yes.

P: Because, because momentarily this appeared to me so stupid.

About the understanding of this passage one must know the association field of the word shrink heads, which the two speakers—patient and analyst—have developed in earlier sessions. The patient has recounted about a girlfriend who, with this word, has brought her experiences with fellatio to this term, which means that the analyst must have understood, at least unconsciously, the in the tape recording barely understandable dream passage with the "slid up skirt" and the associated sexual connotation.

The patient reacts in an irritated fashion: "That you have brought me out of my concept, now I am thoroughly lost...." "You want to find out and think about it, maybe start with something innocuous, but it is really your head" (WB 14). She gets up, closes the window of the treatment room, lies back on the couch, and continues to talk about the head of the analyst, which she wants to measure (WB 15) and of which she is envious.

In WB 16 and 17 in which the positive valence rises again the remarks of the patient about the head of the analyst are tied in with the shrinking heads of which her girlfriend had talked about, and she differentiates that it is not their nonsexual meaning that fascinates but the hands-on approach of her girlfriend fascinates her. In a very intimate dialogue the analyst takes up her earlier association that she herself would like to take a hands-on approach, grab him by the neck, but had doubts whether he would endure this.

She wishes to be allowed to be able to knock a little hole into the head of the analyst in order to put some of her own thoughts in there, which the analyst takes up very sympathetically (WB 18–20). It is a relaxed dialogue. The positive emotional tone rises again (WB 20–21) and leads in (WB 21) to Connecting, which in its content culminates with a wonderful metaphor, namely in the wish of the patient to be able to stroll in the head of the analyst:

> P: No, because you, because it appeared to me as if everything (20) which you have done here, nonsense and, and, and generally was useless, wasn't it?
>
> A: Mhm.
>
> P: I was simply—ah—yes, to be surpassed.
>
> A: Yes, yes, I wanted to say, now it is; you have yourself now I believe so ah, a—ah found a solution for this, namely you would like, you have struggled yourself through that you entrust so much stability in me that I would overcome a little hole.
>
> P: Yes.
>
> A: True, and—
>
> P: Mhm.

A: And you stick it in there. But you naturally want—hm—no little hole. You do not want to put in a little, but a lot.

P: Probably yes.

A: You have made a timid try, but—

P: Probably.

A: To try out the stability of the head, with the thought, of how big and small to make the hole, true?

P: Mhm.

A: But you want to make a big one.

P: Mhm.

A: Have an easy entrance.

P: Mhm.

A: Not a difficult entrance, you would like, with the hand—ah, also touch this which is there, not only see it with the eyes. One also does not see well with the eyes when a hole is only small, true. So, ah, I believe you want a big hole as—

P: I even want your (21) be able to go for a stroll in your head.

A: Yes, mhm.

P: I would like that. I.

A: Yes, mhm.

P: And I would also like a bench.

A: Yes, yes.

P: Not only in the park.—And well that is, I believe, easier—understand what else I would like.

A: Yes, more calmness of the head ah—

P: Yes.

A: The calmness that I have here! Here I am calm, aren't I? This is; this is also searched for, true?

P: Yes, I have thought before that when you die then you can say I have had a wonderful working place; that is very funny.

Discussion and Conclusions

Session 152 is mainly marked by the dream reported at the outset of the session. At this time the patient was, from an emotional viewpoint, in a neutral condition: neither the negative nor the positive shares predominated. Therefore, there was first the need of an amplification of negative feelings and the leading toward a problem, which was to be worked through. This succeeds in several approaches in which it followed that two cycles came about. Thus, one can assume that in this session a Mini-Outcome was reached and contributed to therapeutic change.

The formal evaluation of protocols made by tape recordings and transcribed psychotherapeutic sessions with the dictionaries concerning emotional tone and abstraction shows processes that are clinically plausible. Particularly noticeable is that this is valid although with the two variables emotion and abstraction only less than altogether 10% of the spoken words in the sessions are being grasped. By the concrete material one can—in our view provable—follow why a psychotherapeutic process either gets going or stagnates. Regardless of these impressive results, many questions remain open; however, here only one should be mentioned. The TCM is based on the assumption that the interchange of the valence of the emotions has an essential part in the processes of insight. Yet also other dichotomies in the emotional happening are thinkable as, for example, rapprochement versus avoidance (desire and death; rage and sadness; it versus me), that can contribute as a shift event in the therapeutic change. Interventions such as interpretation or confrontation can, under this aspect, play an essential role. This will need to be clarified in further detailed examinations that lead to cycles. It is also thinkable that both aspects are taking part in a specific manner, since a large part of the positive emotions go along with rapprochement and many of the negative feelings with avoidance.

Looking ahead, it can be ascertained that the microscopic analysis in the sense of the TCM seems to be suitable for the examination of the quality of psychoanalytic sessions as well as for the didactic purposes in the framework of the education.

6.7   ATTACHMENT AND LOSS*

Introduction

As discussed in the first part of this chapter, linguistic measures cover a wide range of qualitative and quantitative methods. One of the methods relying heavily on a cognitive-affective view of language is the Adult Attachment Interview (AAI) developed by George, Kaplan, and Main (1985).

The AAI is designed to elicit thoughts, feelings, and memories about early attachment experiences and to assess the individual's state of mind in respect to attachment. Eighteen questions (semistructured format) are about the relationship with parents in childhood, sorrow, illness, first separations, losses of significant others, and threatening experiences like sexual or physical abuse. The interviews, transcribed literally, are rated along different scales, such as loving relationship with mother and father, quality of recall, idealization and derogation of relationships, and, most importantly, coherence (Grice, 1975) of the narrative. The AAI measures the current representation of attachment experiences in terms of past and present on the basis of narratives. The questioning technique aims at the extent to which a speaker is capable of spontaneously recounting his or her childhood history in a cooperative, coherent, and plausible way.

Therefore, the AAI elucidates the construction of "attachment representation" and its linguistic characteristics. Its strength is that it does not generalize to representations or mental strategies related to other relevant areas of life. That is, the AAI captures representation of attachment and not the mental representation of sexuality, aggression, or vocation. The AAI uses specification and concretization as the questioning technique to produce stress. In the AAI, the stress is specifically attachment-related stress; the AAI is said to activate the attachment behavioral system through questions that "surprise the unconscious" (Main & Goldwyn, 1996).

From a conversational stance, an interview is a dyadic event. In the AAI, the interviewer's questions and specifications are not considered as a component of the text analysis of the transcript. The working assumption, an assumption that has been supported empirically, is that the interviewee's answers and way of speaking are not understood as an individual reaction to the interviewer's probing. AAI questions and probes are carefully designed to activate the interviewee's attachment system and thus produce memories without interference from the interviewer. AAI probes are neutral, and interaction with the interviewer does not include interpretation, exploration, or reflection; therefore, the interviewee's memories are "uncontaminated" by the interviewer's interaction.

---

* Anna Buchheim and Horst Kächele; based on Buchheim and Kächele (2007).

The coherence of the discourse provides the leading criterion for the evaluation of the AAI. Main and Goldwyn (1996) define coherence for the purpose of evaluating the AAI transcript following linguistic communications maxims as formulated by Grice (1975). Following these maxims, coherence in the AAI assesses the extent a speaker is able to respond cooperatively to the interviewer's questions and is able to give a true (quality), adequately informative (quantity), relevant (relevance), and comprehensible (manner) portrayal of childhood experience. Therefore, the central interest in the AAI is evaluation of the story as a coherent whole versus only fragments of that story. The AAI also evaluates the interview discourse using rating scales for reported real experience (e.g., parent as loving, rejecting) and representational transformations of experience (e.g., idealization, involving anger, derogation of the attachment figure). The final product of the AAI, derived from evaluations of the interview patterns of these three categories of discourse evaluation (coherence, real experience, transformations) results in a classification that represents the individual's representational status regarding attachment: secure, dismissing, preoccupied, unresolved, or cannot classify (Main & Goldwyn, 1996).

The "unresolved" classification is designated based on evaluations of the interviewee's transient mental disorientation when describing experiences of loss through death or physical/sexual abuse. This discourse pattern suggests that these experiences are accessible to memory but not yet integrated to create a whole sense of self-representation. Sometimes references to or descriptions of elements pertaining to these traumatic events literally "erupt" during portions of the interview in which these memories are not relevant. Sometimes these memories have a spectral quality in which events are described as if the interviewee has returned to the scene, so to speak. Sometimes descriptions contain irrational convictions of the interviewee's own guilt or confusion (e.g., speaks as if the deceased is alive) (Main & Goldwyn, 1996). In sum adults with the classification unresolved show temporary lapses in the monitoring of reasoning or discourse during discussion of potentially traumatic events. Specifically, lapses in reasoning—for example, indications that a speaker believes that a deceased person is both dead and not dead—may indicate parallel, incompatible belief and memory systems regarding a traumatic event that have become dissociated.

George and Solomon (1999) propose that a major difference between psychoanalysis and attachment theory lies in the description of the defensive processes themselves. Traditional psychoanalytic models provide a complex constellation of defenses to interpret a broad range of intrapsychic phenomenon, including fantasy, dream, wish, and impulse (e.g., Horowitz, 1988; Kernberg, 1994). According to George and Solomon (1999) Bowlby's perspective conceives defensive exclusion in terms of two qualitatively distinct forms of information processing: *deactivation* (similar to repression) and *cognitive disconnection* (similar to splitting). These two defensive strategies provide the individual (infant and adult) with an *organized* form of excluding information from conscious awareness or separating affect from a situation or person eliciting it. Regarding severe psychopathology Bowlby (1980) suggests that under certain circumstances these two forms of exclusion can lead to a *disorganized form* of representation, what he calls *segregated systems*. This is operationalized in the unresolved attachment status with respect to trauma and loss. George and West (1999, p. 295) conclude, "In order to understand the relationship between adult attachment and mental health risk we need to examine the attachment concepts of defense and segregated systems, the mental processes that define disorganization." Suggesting that these representational structures have developed under conditions of attachment trauma (abuse, loss) the concept of segregated systems is fruitful to explain some forms of relationship-based psychopathology in adults (Kächele et al., 2001).

The Adult Attachment Interview with Amalia X

To clarify some current personal problem, the now 65-year-old lady contacted our department where her former analyst had been the head of the department. Referring her to a colleague in private practice to work through her current problem, she was willing to take part in an investigation with the AAI. We did not have an AAI from the time when her analysis started 30 years ago, nor had we an AAI from the time of termination 25 years ago.

In the countertransference the interviewer (A.B.) felt overwhelmed by the speed of Amalia's ability to remember many details of her childhood memories. She was clearly dominating, and the interviewer had a hard job to structure the interview. There was no AAI question where Amalia hesitated or made a pause in order to think about what she wanted to say. Sometimes she gave consistent summaries of her childhood experiences with an amazing metacognitive knowledge; then she skipped into a somewhat "crazy" voice with an exaggerated, partly irrational quality, which was frightening. In the end of the AAI the interviewer could join Amalia's self-description as being a kind of "witch." She came as a sophisticated old lady and went away somewhat like a ghost. This countertransference was influenced strongly by the last part of the interview, where Amalia was talking about the losses of her mother and her father. This part definitely had a spooky quality.

In this interview the descriptions of her parents were quite contradictory. Amazingly she described her mother as "very, very caring" and a "beautiful woman" who was much more interesting and attractive to her than her father. She remembers having "adored" and "courted" her mother. As a child Amalia always wanted to *please* her, and she became extremely sensitive what her mother needed ("I was there for her; she could use me").

Her father was described by her as "weak," saying, "Of course I was his darling"; he was "caring" but "not interesting at all in me," "he couldn't be sufficient for us," and "there was cotton wool between us." The grandmother was described as "stern" and "strict" but much more supporting, encouraging, and not as intrusive as her mother.

Analyzing the transcript with respect to discourse quality and coherence criteria, there is considerable evidence for a contradictory picture of her childhood experiences, which indicates a preoccupied state of mind. Amalia is oscillating between an extraordinary positive evaluation of her mother's caring qualities, and at other parts of the interview she is talking about abandonment, cruel separations, and long-lasting tormenting fantasies about being in hell as a child. Sometimes Amalia values the integrity of her father ("He always supported me when I had troubles at school"); then she skips into a devaluating, derogating speech ("I didn't like his lovely care when I was ill, and his way of asking me 'How is my little patient today?' I hated that."). Amalia seemed to be unable to move beyond a sense of the self as entangled in the early relationship with her mother. She presents a passive speech with run-on sentences, interruptions, and the inability to complete sentences. In consequence there is a notable lack of a sense of personal identity in the first half of the interview and an inability to focus fruitfully, objectively during the interview. Sometimes Amalia seems caught up in memories of youth and childhood and unable to move beyond these episodes to an objective overview at the semantic or abstract level. Her overview is characterized by oscillatory tendencies (see above). She sometimes has a hallowed view of her childhood, and negative evaluations may disappear in contradictions. On the other hand she sometimes impresses the interviewer with transgenerational knowledge, when being asked about the influence of childhood experiences on her personality development or about why she believes that her parents behaved like they did. Though she has obvious capacities, like "mind reading" regarding her mother, the overall evaluation leads to a "preoccupied" state of mind with respect to attachment. In the end of the interview her lifelong struggle for autonomy leads to unusual attempts to become an autonomous adult person, starting an inner dialogue with her dead parents in the present tense.

We cite some typical statement from the transcript the kind of which lead to this "preoccupied" classification:

Interviewer (I): How would you describe the relationship with your mother, when you were a child?

Amalia (A): I have adored her, this feeling lasted long after her death, I have adored her, I wanted to do all the best for her.... I always tried to find out, what she wants.... She needed me, she has loved me very very warmly, as a child I always felt everything is ok, what she is doing.... She was there for us in an extraordinary way, she was the untouchable.... I loved to learn at school, and wanted to show her how I learned to write an "A", and I wanted to be praised by her, ... and she reacted kind of angry and told me that such a daughter doesn't fit to her, I was hurt by that, and at the same time provoked to try to get some praise from her.

I: You said your mother was extremely caring, could you remember a specific event from your childhood?

A: I can't describe, nobody will believe me. My mother always asked me (when she was an adult) "May I cook for you?" and when I had back problems, she took the next train and brought me sacks of potatoes, though we had potatoes, and she said "No."

I: Are there some memories from earlier stages of your childhood, where your mother was very very caring?

A: Yes for us all. She has collected fir cones for us in the forest. She had a lady bicycle, and she drove into the forest with my brother and came back with a very big bag, we had two fire places at home, and she collected these fir cones, and now there was the question how to handle it? And I still see her coming with this bag, we were standing at the window, and then she has cooked for her children, such things, she always was full of fantasy, and has cared for us extremely well.

This characteristic passage about the relationship with her mother shows her ambivalence. On the one hand Amalia gives examples where her mother was caring, though with a functional quality (e.g., cooking, potatoes, collecting of fir cones) and intrusive elements; on the other hand, she had to struggle as a child to be recognized and accepted by her. Amalia's speech is exaggerated ("very, very") and does not seem objective. She is not really able to integrate positive and negative feelings in a convincing manner, due to the defensive cognitive disconnection (i.e., the splitting of good and bad). There are positive wrap-ups and subtle negativity at the same time without direct expressions of anger.

According to Main and Goldwyn's (1996) criteria, an individual should be classified as "unresolved," when during discussions of loss (or abuse), he shows striking lapses in the monitoring of reasoning or discourse.

The category "Unresolved" in the AAI is given when the following coding criteria are fulfilled pertaining to loss:

- Indication of disbelief that the person is dead
- Indication of confusion between self and dead person

- Disorientation with respect to time and space
- Psychologically confused statements
- Extreme behavioral reaction to a loss

Amalia shows two parts of these aspects in the AAI, which are an indicator of her unresolved state of mind: She shows many indications of disbelief that her parents are dead, and at the same time there are psychologically confused statements in the discourse spoken with a spooky voice.

> A: Hm, very strange was, my father was dying in 1996, and then he was flying with me one night long to his Italian favorite places, and I had a terrible night full of guilt feelings. And then he was away. Then my mother was living a while and was not talking about him at all. And I tried to pamper her a bit and go on journey with her, and so. And when she was dead, I suffered a lot, and I had to sell the house, everything was very bad.

> I: How old were you?

> A: I was in the end of my fifties, and she was dying before I became 60 years old. In any case she died in 1998 in spring time, and I was fighting with her and had struggles with her over nearly 4 years, that was so cruel, and when I was beginning to fight with her, then he came wonderfully and he protected me and gave me advice, that was like a dialogue and I have seen him, now he is away again. And then I said this year to my mother: Now I am fed up, finally, it has to have an end with this competition.

> I: And you have talked with her internally?

> A: ... Since this year I am able to be myself and since that time there is peace.... I have fighted with my mother when I was an adult, but I never believed that it will be as cruel after her death.... I am talking with my parents wherever I am, and graves don't mean anything to me. ...Now I am peaceful. And sometimes she smiles at me, and after her death she suddenly told me: "Let me alone" and she was driving fast somewhere in the sky; my father was traveling with me one night long, but at the same time these guilt feelings, but it was just one night long. And then, she was living, and the father was away. And this came after her death. That was ... And now in 2002 she begins to talk with me in a friendly manner, and now I don't need it so much any more.

Evidence for the continuing unresolved/disorganized responses to loss are characterized by lapses of monitoring of reasoning and discourse or reports of extreme behavioral reactions. Main and Hesse (1990) link lapses in *monitoring*—and this is what Amalia has shown in the passages about loss—to the possible intrusion of dissociated or partially dissociated ideation. George and West (2001) state that across methodological contexts, unresolved attachment has been linked to the expression of not integrated attachment trauma that is ascribed to the underlying dynamic of segregated systems (George & Solomon, 1999) or multiple models of attachment (Liotti, 1999; Main, 1991). Unresolved attachment has been consistently associated with the sudden, "unmetabolized" emergence of disorganized thought. In the AAI, individuals must demonstrate a moderate to high degree of unresolved thinking in order to be judged unresolved; minor lapses in monitoring traumatic material do not automatically yield an unresolved designation.

Amalia describes herself as a witch and that she has had spiritual qualities since she was a child. The expression of religious beliefs in the context of loss experiences deserves special consideration. If it is presumed that the dead person is in heaven or will be met again in another life with the convincing knowledge that the person is truly dead now, this is coded as a metaphysical consideration, which is not unresolved. In Amalia's case there are no indications for the interviewer that she shows cooperation (Grice, 1975) or metacognitive monitoring (Main, 1991) to perceive how strange it must be for the interviewer to listen to such psychological confusing phrases without any objectivity. This kind of long and repetitive passages of "making the dead parents alive" is quite rare.

In the clinical context we would have to discuss what this could mean for this special person.

What Amalia probably wanted to say was that all the fights with her dead mother in the present time lead to a new autonomy and inner peace. Clinically we might conclude that she found her way as an older, sophisticated lady, who at least has achieved an internal independence from a dominant, intrusive mother. But the way she describes this struggle is strange; it has a somewhat psychotic or dissociative quality and induced in the interviewer a mixed feeling of being amused and frightened at the same time. We can raise the question: How can we understand this disorganized discourse with respect to a clinician's impression of Amalia's mental development up to now?

Although unconscious and deactivated, Bowlby (1980) emphasizes that segregated systems (threatening experiences like losses) are, in and of themselves, organized representational systems that can, when activated, frame and execute plans. *Upon activation*, however, behavior, feeling, and thought are likely to appear *chaotic and disorganized*. This is what probably happened with Amalia: Unconsciously she has found a way to master the traumatic experience of having lost her parents without having resolved her painful feelings of abandonment and intrusive interactions with them when they were alive. From an attachment point of view we should examine when and how this "dissociative mastering" becomes maladaptive.

Chapter 7

A Summary and Implications of Research for Psychoanalytic Practice

INTRODUCTION

The Ulm Psychoanalytic Process Research Study Group, embedded within a university department and thanks to the long-standing support of the German Research Foundation (DFG), started, developed, and differentiated the multidimensional project of research on the course of a single psychoanalytic case. Now we can look back on the successful implementation and discuss the implications of this program for clinical work and consider further perspectives.

The studies of Amalia X, probably one of the most intensive empirical examinations of the materials of one patient ever conducted, reliably identified numerous indicators of change in directions that were specified a priori. Does this allow us to say we identified mutative factors? Working with conditional predictions of the format, "If this patient will be treated sufficiently long, working through her core conflictual problem areas using a patient-oriented technique then specific changes in various areas are to be expected," we are now in a position to positively answer that under these conditions of a long-term intensive treatment with an experienced psychoanalyst the patient showed clear unequivocal signs of improvement as specified beforehand.

We acknowledge the unresolved epistemological problem of psychoanalysis that we have no consensually agreed, independent criteria for psychoanalysis. Lacking that, the judgment of the treating senior psychoanalyst that the treatment is psychoanalysis is the closest approximation any research group can provide. This criterion was also used by Schachter (2005c) when selecting the cases for his clinical reports on how analyst and patient view the power of the psychoanalytic treatments that transformed their lives. We think that short-term intervention which makes up the bulk of today's clinical practice would not have been able to free this patient from her characterological constrictions, although we cannot prove that. In any case, a clinical case report of this specific analytic treatment, unaided

392 From Psychoanalytic Narrative to Empirical Single Case Research

by empirical studies, given the patient's and analyst's uniqueness, could not have specified these change processes with the same degree of certainty.

In order to map what the naked eye cannot see, in Chapter 5 we looked at the pre- and postchange of emotional insight, recorded the systematic change of self-esteem, analyzed the patient's suffering, traced the patient's intrapsychic development in her dream material, identified the fate of her core conflictual conflicts across the treatment, and followed the patient's capacity to overcome separation issues. Studying the patient's unconscious plan for dealing with personal and social experiences added to our psychodynamic understanding and generated a partially alternative view of the patient's pre-oedipal experiences. Applying Blatt's (2004) distinction of analytic and introjective personality organization we would classify Amalia X as belonging to the introjective type and thus are in agreement with his recent conclusion (Blatt, 2006) that psychoanalytic work in contrast to supportive treatment is optimal for this personality organization. These approaches using the technique of guided clinical judgments were enriched by the availability of a descriptive map on the clinical course of the analysis—a map that could have been even more detailed but was good enough to convey a thorough and detailed understanding of the clinical development (Chapter 4).

In Chapter 6, after a short introduction on the relationship of psychoanalysis to linguistic research, we have presented the Ulm Textbank as the first instrument of its kind. It is no longer unique, which demonstrates that such a tool is a sine qua non to further basic treatment research. Various studies of exploratory character testing out the potentials of computer-based approaches point to the possibilities of studying microprocesses where we always felt in good company with researchers like Dahl, Spence, and some others. When the patient returned 25 years after having terminated her analysis she allowed us to assess the impact of her parents' death on her attachment representations, a topic that is fairly new in the field.

The question of determining on which level of the material so-called mutative factors operate, remains a difficult one. Our tentative work on the linguistic level points to the potential richness of such material that cannot be seen by the unaided eye. Current microscopic analysis in anatomy and pathology has moved to the level of cells and their infrastructures in order to identify causal mechanisms. Clinical concepts are but stakeholders waiting to be dissected into microscopic processes (Luborsky & Crits-Christoph, 1988). Today familiar concepts like "helping alliance" (Luborsky, 1976, 2000) raise new issues: How is this experience generated, by what mechanisms, and on what level? They may reflect the outcome of bits of interactive behavior that intuitively has to be staged by the two participants in order to generate a productive therapeutic process (Hatcher & Barends, 2006). Research has to go "beneath the surface of the therapeutic interaction" (Bucci & Maskit, 2007, p. 1355). Working with unconscious material like dreams may lead to subtle change in mentation reflecting activation of right brain processes as Schiffer (1998) and Mergenthaler (2008) point out. The regulation of verbal and nonverbal activities in itself may be responsible for a satisfying experience for the patient who feels contained in a precise fitting interactive synchronization (Knoblauch, 2000).

We did not attempt to explore the various roles of the analyst's suggestion. In order to clarify the issue we have to remind the reader of Freud's (1921c) discussion of suggestion. He refers to the English meaning of the word that is equivalent to the German *anregen*—to stimulate (p. 89). It may be feasible to study the impact of direct and indirect suggestive elements in the analyst's activities, to identify moments of his tonality where his subjective convictions may have played an overriding role, and we invite potential researchers to examine our audio records for such subtle effects. This also would be an excellent arena of discourse-analytic studies. Although it is very likely that personal influence—for example, the analyst's position as a university professor—played some role in Amalia X's analytic treatment, as it does in all other medical treatments, research on such impact would have to focus on microanalytic interaction patterns and require innovative research designs. This is certainly not to deny that the analyst's optimism and confidence may have contributed to the patient's therapeutic benefit from treatment.

The same is true for suggestion. One possible clue that the analyst, outside of awareness, may be shaping the patient's productions by implicit suggestions would be that none of the patient's productions in the sessions 152 and 153 seem a surprise to the analyst. This should give the analyst pause and should lead him to explore whether he may have been making covert suggestions, perhaps outside of his awareness. The methodological approach to research this issue could be using symptom-context technique as described by Luborsky (1996).

The role of the placebo effect deserves a different discussion. For good reasons, there has never been an empirical study of this mechanism as an explanatory concept for analytic treatments, which is in contrast to the study of time-limited psychotherapies (Prioleau, Murdoch, & Brody, 1983). The explanation for some of the impressive findings in those placebo studies is that what serves as placebo therapy is in fact minimal treatment groups, for which certain treatment benefits may be expected (Luborsky, Docherty, Barber, & Miller, 1993, p. 505). Obviously it would be hard to construct a convincing alternative treatment modality lasting five years without the patient recognizing the true nature of its being only a control condition. Therefore, Grünbaum (1986b) rightfully doubts whether the placebo concept has a place in psychotherapy at all, since social interaction cannot be circumvented; no "empty pill" is available. Therefore the placebo effect is confined to pharmacological therapies and ultimately makes sense only in connection with the possibility of double-blind controlled studies. In any kind of psychotherapy to imagine a double-blind control condition is absurd.

Grünbaum's (1984) philosophical challenge is that psychotherapy sessions cannot be used "probatively," meaning that data for sessions cannot be used to prove any hypothesis but only to suggest hypotheses. Luborsky et al. (1993, p. xxiii) points out that Grünbaum's thinking has not been sufficiently influenced by the probability theory that forms the basis of most current statistics. There is a significant probability that the patterns we identified are not entirely based on suggestion by the analyst. To explore "what can change in a good analysis" (Fonagy, 1999b, p. 1) we quoted the analyst's conviction based on his understanding of the initial situation: The analyst offered to treat this woman, who was hard-working in her career, cultivated, single, and quite feminine despite the way she felt about her stigma, because he was relatively sure and confident that it would be possible to change the significations she attributed to her stigma (Chapter 4).

We have shown that such research is feasible, provided that enough devotion, passion, and financial resources are provided. Psychoanalytic clinical work can be the subject of objectifying and methodologically sophisticated research. The inspection of the analytical process from an external view leads to empirical results that a treating analyst cannot achieve. Extraclinical or so-called off-line research can contribute to an understanding of change mechanisms that cannot be gained in any other way. We recommend that the analyst should be involved adding his clinical perspective in such a research process, articulating his subjective responses, participating in clinical examinations or bringing in critical comments to the formal findings.

On the basis of our experiences, however, we once recommended that during the course of the treatment neither the analyst nor the patient should expect to participate in anything additional to and external to the treatment. The experience of other researchers, however, has shown that establishing a parallel domain by postal interviewing a patient in analytic treatment by a research group has been demonstrated not to negatively influence the process (Grande et al., 2003; Huber & Klug, 2003). The often heard argument that interventions during treatment would be necessarily deleterious has not been confirmed. It seems more appropriate to experiment with such additional research parameters and evaluate whether they are damaging or helpful to the dyad. Our long-term experiences with tape-recorded treatments have shown us that the initial approval of the patient for additional research interventions is absolutely necessary for legal reasons but that the patient and the analyst must feel free to revoke this decision at any time. The more intrusive such interventions are, such as placing patients before and during analytic treatment in a neuro-scientific research framework, the more a careful clinical recording of its potential impact on the process is to be recommended. In our most recent study patients with chronic depression (Buchheim et al., 2008) are investigated at the opening of their psychoanalytic treatments and in regular intervals three times more by EEG and fMRI in a laboratory environment while presenting highly structured cues distilled from diagnostic interviews with the patients. A study group of the involved analysts share and discuss their clinical experience, functioning as a reflective environment to understand the responses of patients and analysts to this challenge (Taubner, Bruns, & Kächele, 2007).

We plead strongly for a multidimensionality of empirical approaches to the subject of psychoanalysis—namely to conduct research on the impact of unconscious processes on conscious experience and behavior. In relation to this research process the systematic single case study takes it proper place—next to other ways of access.

Although a generational approach to the development of psychotherapy research (Wallerstein, 2001) is adequate to plot main lines of research activities, we prefer a conception in which six stages of therapeutic research are differentiated (Kächele, 2005). Then the systematic single case study is to be assigned on the one hand to the descriptive stage I in which careful, reliable descriptions are required (Messer, 2007). On the other hand, the single case study can, as the studies in this volume show, in a diverse way generate experimental data belonging to stage II that allow confirmation or disconfirmation of single case–oriented hypotheses (Figure 7.1).

Therefore, we are of the opinion that the model case Amalia X represents an example of a research-based case study that Grawe (1992) marks as an especially successful and promising way for future process research:

> Such "research informed case studies" … that is case studies in which extensive process and measured change on the basis of an elaborated clinical case conception are interpreted in their entire context and in which every statement can be traced back to the base in the recorded measuring, can be viewed as a particularly promising way for future research of process. Because of the interpretation in the context of the understanding of a clinical case, the results make clinical sense; however they differ from clinical fiction in that they have a close comprehensible relation on a basis of objective measuring data, which is independent from the interpretation. (p. 140)

These studies we have reported not only support the finding that this treatment led to a diversity of changes in the experience and behavior of the patient Amalia X but also demonstrate the benefit of research techniques in which the findings contribute to the understanding of change processes. Research techniques provide the essential reliability of observations that are lacking in clinical inferences. The number of descriptive dimensions, which can be examined by means of a transcribed corpus, is hugely dependent only on the availability of suitable process measures. However, we can

Stages of treatment research

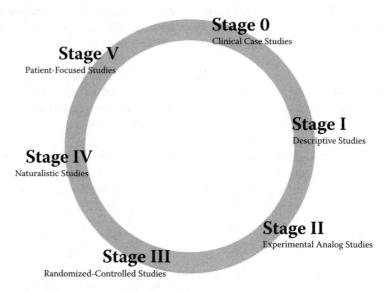

Figure 7.1 Six stages of treatment research.

conclude that change processes exist and that these can be recorded reliably and validly. We find these in interactive dialogical exchange as well as in basic changes in the personality of the patient. These often show a linear trend. This leads us back to our metatheoretical discussion:

> Possibly, from a logical point of view, the objection could be raised that, instead of the concept of strict causality, a statistical relation should be applied to the interdependencies indicated by psychoanalysis— perhaps in the sense that persons under the influence of certain engrams are more inclined toward Freudian slips, nervous symptoms, and dream pictures than others who are free of them, just as a dice that has been tampered with shows more sixes on the average than an unbiased one.... It is a reasonable conjecture that psychoanalytic theory would have received a more correct form, modified in this sense, if at the time of its creation the deterministic conception of all natural occurrences had not been so absolutely predominant in sciences.

> Psychoanalysis comprises the scientific theory of a specific area of psychological occurrences: on the grounds of objective observations it constructs a hypothetical causal connection between certain

symptoms and the latent remainders of earlier experiences. Almost all objections raised against it so far are of an extralogical nature. But it seems justified to point out that the totality of observations in this field seems to correspond more to the assumption of a statistical than of a strictly causal correlation. (von Mises, 1951, p. 238)

Therewith, the statement that psychoanalytic therapy occupies itself with probabilistic states of a person is supported; in other words, the object of therapeutic efforts is the patient's response tendencies that in the beginning show great stability (in the sense of persistent templates; Chapter 2), which in the course of the treatment become more and more unstable and through which changes of the system become possible. When the conditions by which a system of response tendencies is supported are known, then clinically typical statements of probability are permitted. Due to uniqueness in each individual case these conditions can also be completely different; consequently, the necessity of single case studies arises as well as the known problems of generalization (Midgley, 2006).

The formalized evaluation of treatment reports goes beyond the heuristic function of clinical description and can secure statistically significant correlations. Schneider (1983, p. 2) propagates this "way toward a new understanding of the psychotherapeutic process" theoretically into therapy research by utilizing on to biological change models. Our findings show that such changes of the probability of the behavior and the experience of a patient can hardly be reliably identified in individual sessions and need instead to be observed on the macrosystematic level of multiple sessions over time. Our empirical studies of our model case Amalia X emphasize that a long-term view of the course of treatment is essential to identify structural changes of the patient. Short-term assessments using a few sessions may be useful for understanding the current interactions, but they do not provide reliable information about enduring changes in feeling and behavior. In our view only a long-term perspective over the course of the treatment can be the arbiter of success. This necessity for a longitudinal approach was also demonstrated by a number of controlled single case studies that have been published in the last years (Joseph et al., 2004; Waldron et al., 2004a, b; Lingiardi et al., 2006; Porcerelli et al., 2007).

The long-standing research model dominant in clinical psychoanalysis "Testing an Interpretation Within a Session" (Wisdom, 1967) is critically undermined if one keeps in mind that one session is but part of a series of sessions in which at each different time different conditions exist and therewith a great openness for possible reactions of a patient exists ("like in weather conditions"). The suggestions of the Boston Change Process Study Group (BPCSG) (BPCSG, 2005; BPCSG et al., 1998) about "moment-to-moment changes" are presently being discussed very vigorously (Litowitz, 2005; Mayes, 2005); however, according to our experience structurally relevant processes of change only can be identified over a longer time span of the treatment. The single response of a patient to an intervention is open to a diversity of theoretical attributions. It needs not only contextual knowledge but also "general interpretations" (in the sense of Habermas). These are the unavoidable theoretical models in the mind of an analyst (e.g., Kleinian, Bionian, Kohutian, Lacanian, Relational, etc.; see Hamilton, 1996) that back up the handling of contextual information. This bidirectional process increases the subjective plausibility of an interpretation. Following Bowlby (1979) there is no way to bypass this process for any involved clinician. In order to overcome the self-sufficiency of an understanding that confirms itself in subjective evidence, we recommend a critical attitude that might be acquired in interaction with researchers or even by finding one's own field of clinical research.

We recommend discontinuing unending discussions of the validity of specific individual interventions and interpretations as they are only part of a larger game as implied in Freud's metaphor of chess where a single move's value only can be determined by the state of the game. Interventions derive their status from their functional utility at any moment in the process. As has been illustrated in the microanalysis of two sessions, an analyst's intervention strategies can be demonstrated to be successful in furthering the patient's insight in a problematic area (Chapter 5.1). However, as the presentation of this material at the New Orleans International Psychoanalytic Congress in 2004 again has demonstrated (Ireland, 2004; Wilson, 2004) alternative, divergent views are easily brought forward. Presenting the clinical material in verbatim recorded details allows comparative, even competitive discussions that do not transgress matters of opinion, however sophisticated the clinical expertise of the proponents. In order to judge the success of a psychoanalytic treatment general statements about the treatment have to be measured objectively. Only on that level would we venture to estimate the probability of validity of our findings.

Long-term course observations are essential (Thomä, 1996); only then comparative examinations can be evaluated meaningfully. The individual session can, to an outside person, certainly convey quite a lot about the applied technique and the up-to-date standing of transference and countertransference, but, as with a magnifying glass, one easily loses the view of the whole matter. Only the systematic examination of the process generates demonstrable statements that can also withstand the critical view of outsiders.

In order to identify such effects we need sophisticated measurement techniques reaching beyond the ones Galatzer-Levy, Bachrach, Skolnikoff, and Waldron (2001) list. As Bucci (2007, p. 200) points out we need in addition to the clinical evaluations by external observers a broad range of reliable and valid empirical process measures: "These will include measures to be applied to the verbatim transcripts and also measures applied to tape recordings that examine the nonverbal aspects of the clinical

interaction, including emotive and other paralinguistic vocalizations, paus-
ing, vocal tone and modulation." New technologies like phonological
analysis based on voice recordings have hardly been tried; they might be
attractive supplemental approaches especially for the detection of countertransference responses (Dahl, Teller, Moss & Trujillo, 1978). Recordings of
facial activity only work in a face-to-face setting. In the couch setting mimic
expression is hardly used as a communicative channel. Linguistic techniques
in all their diversity are still the best way to tap these microprocesses.

We quoted Habermas (1971a), who states that individual interpretations
cannot be supported or rejected; they only can be applied by the patient to
himself leading to that kind of narrative truth which makes up the intrigu-
ing quality of psychoanalytic experience. "General interpretative strategies," however, may fail or not in the long run. In this vein our theories,
like old soldiers, never die—they just wither away.

For example, in the context of existing pluralism in psychoanalysis we
are witnessing changes in paradigmatic frames of references. Interpretative
activities based on the conception of drive psychology or ego psychology are
on the decline; intersubjectivity is on the rise—for better or worse. These
changes in the psychoanalytic intellectual climate are not research based
or evidence based but may reflect societal change. It is part and parcel of
research to open the questioning as to what is specific to psychoanalytic
theory and technique, recognize the theoretical vacuum that still exists in
psychoanalysis which Thomä and Kächele (1987), Holt (1985), and others
have referred, and work through its implications" (Bucci, 2007, p. 203).

Scientific results must be repeated in order to establish their value. In this
sense we hope that there will be subsequent examinations of individual psychoanalytic cases. However, at this time the impact of conducting our own
research efforts on our own psychoanalytic thinking has been enormous.
Nothing enriched our thinking and doing as much as the discussion of our
detailed reports by friendly critics and critical friends.

Investigations that relate to what happens in psychoanalytic treatment
are presently highly important, and "quantitative research" is no longer
a stepchild of the psychoanalytic profession, as Luborsky and Spence
(1971) write. The successful launching of an IPA Committee on Research,
research sections in our journals, and annual poster sessions at meetings
of the American Psychoanalytical Association (APsaA) signal a definite
change in climate toward empirical research. Still one encounters a common response to quantitative research: "Does this finding agree with clinical knowledge?" This skepticism may contribute to the fact that although
the leadership of the APsaA increasingly verbalizes about the importance
of analytic research, the allocation to research of the association remains at
3% to 4% with some current increases in funds.

We do not share the position of Mijolla (2003), a historian of psychoanalysis, claiming that the phase of objective research ended when Freud

began his self-analysis. Even a perfunctory view of the 100-year-old history of psychoanalytic research shows that neither training analysis nor the subsequent self-analysis can replace scientific thinking and acting. We definitely prefer Bowlby's (1979) admonition that differentiates the role of the scientist and the clinician:

> In his day work it is necessary for a scientist to exercise a high degree of criticism and self-criticism: and in the world he inhabits neither the data nor the theories of a leader, however admired personally he may be, are exempt from challenge and criticism. There is no place for authority. The same is not true in the practice of a profession. If he is to be effective a practitioner must be prepared to act as though certain principles and certain theories were valid; and in deciding which to adopt he is likely to be guided by those with experience from whom he learns. Since, moreover, there is a tendency in all of us to be impressed whenever the application of a theory appears to have been successful, practitioners are at special risk of placing greater confidence in a theory than the evidence available may justify. (p. 4)

IMPLICATIONS FOR PSYCHOANALYTIC PRACTICE

From decades of intensive study of many facets of treatment, what stands out the most is the limitations of our clinical knowledge about analytic treatments. This is the lesson we would like to impart to practitioners. As Bowlby (1979) notes, analysts are inclined to place greater confidence in their theories and analytic views than are warranted; this, indeed, is risky. In conclusion, the most salient implication for psychoanalytic practice that we can identify from our empirical study case is that rather than the analyst making sweeping inferences and drawing strong conclusions, we urgently suggest that humility and tentativeness in all interventions are optimal. Analysts' need for confidence and conviction may expose them to a tendency toward arrogance, often more covert than overt, for at least hypothetically understandable reasons.

This need for certainty may arise from analysts having underlying feelings of uncertainty—probably unconscious—about the difficult work they do with treatment guidelines less and less clear and widespread unresolved diversity of views about analytic theory and practice. Too often this uncertainty is defended against by compensatory feelings of knowing all about analytic treatment or, as Jonathan Lear (1998) terms it, "Knowingness." This view is also supported by Casement (2007, p. 1): "The more experienced we are, we need to be able to recover a position of non-certainty. For in my opinion, it is only thus that we can keep the analytic space free from preconception." Thus, the analyst needs enough confidence to be effective in treatment, but not so much confidence that it merges into arrogance—a challenging dialectic for an "impossible profession" (Malcolm, 1980).

The current unresolved differences about what constitutes the fundamental tenets of psychoanalysis strongly suggests, and is supported by empirical data (Schachter, 2002), that none of the conflicting psychoanalytic theories have been validated. If that is the case, to view with "certainty" any particular analytic theory and to base the analyst's confidence upon that theory is misplaced and self-deceiving. Such "certainty" can provide only a spurious feeling of confidence about analytic work for the analyst.

However, despite conflicting theories of treatment, available evidence on symptomatic outcome may provide analysts with a necessary sense of confidence about their work. Leichsenring (2008), recently reviewing the literature, concludes: several controlled quasi-experimental effectiveness studies showed that psychoanalytic therapies fulfill the criteria (A) [A treatment has proved to be superior to a control condition – placebo or no treatment] or (B) [To be as effective as an already established treatment]. These studies included control groups for which comparability with the psychoanalytic treatment groups was ensured by measures of matching, stratifying or statistical control of initial differences. In all these studies, psychoanalytic therapy was significantly superior to the respective control condition, including shorter forms of psychodynamic therapy.

At a more personal level, the analyst may have found that his/her own training analysis produced therapeutically helpful changes. In addition, the analyst probably had succeeded in being helpful to prior patients. Therefore, this empirical and experiential evidence, taken together, makes it plausible and realistic to believe that if the analyst is concerned about and cares about the patient, and is genuinely trying to be helpful (as Thomä was with Amalia X) the analyst can be reasonably confident that he/she will succeed in being helpful to many of his/her patients.

Psychoanalytic treatment, however, is a difficult enterprise under the best of circumstances, in part because the personality of the analyst is so intrinsically involved in the process. The context within which the treatment is conducted is likely to influence its course, whether it is the personal context of analyst or patient or the societal context. Germany, where Amalia X was treated, provides an unusually supportive context for analytic treatment. It is no accident that the intensive, long-term, multidisciplinary, expensive studies of Amalia X were possible in Germany. In other countries, the societal context is less supportive. Probably the greatest contrast is with the United States, where psychoanalysis has been steadily declining in status and prestige. The U.S. government provides no reimbursement, directly or indirectly, for psychoanalytic treatment, and private insurance provides little reimbursement. The number of patients in psychoanalytic treatment has been slowly but continuously decreasing. We estimate that currently the 3,500 members of the APsaA have in psychoanalytic treatment at four or more sessions per week a total of 6,000 patients in a nation of 300 million people. In contrast, in Germany there are approximately 400,000 patients in psychodynamic psychotherapy of one session per week and about 40,000 patients in psychoanalytic therapies of two, three, or four sessions per week in a nation of 80 million people. It should come as no surprise to psychoanalysts that conducting analytic treatment in a context or atmosphere of criticism and depreciation, whether at a societal or personal level, is apt to intensify defensiveness both of analyst and patient. In the case of the patient, the parents or the spouse may oppose analytic treatment and ridicule it. It is our impression that conducting analytic treatment in a context or atmosphere lacking support and including active hostility and criticism increases the risk that both analyst and patient will become defensive. For the analyst, this increased defensiveness is likely to include conviction about knowing exactly how psychoanalytic treatment should be conducted (Schachter, 2005b). Such "knowingness" will most probably be deleterious to the treatment. It is imperative that we remain open to innovative ideas and approaches to analytic practice.

European outcome studies on psychoanalytic therapies (Richardson, Kächele, & Renlund, 2004) point in a direction "that many of the traditional ideas concerning psychoanalytic psychotherapy will need to be revised" (Fonagy, 2004). The German studies (Huber & Klug, 2003, 2007; Leichsenring, Biskup, Kreische, & Staats, 2005; Leuzinger-Bohleber, Stuhr, Rüger & Bentil, 2003; Grande et al., 2003, 2006) show that little differences in symptomatic improvements between low and high dose of treatment can be ascertained but that the gains in structural changes are the field where the battle will be won or lost (Jakobsen et al., 2007).

CONCLUSION

Presentation of our studies and their results may be of differing relevance for clinicians. "Bridging the gap" between practice and research has long been called for (Talley, Forrest, Strupp, & Butler, 1994). The controversy should not center around "clinical conviction or empirical evidence?" (Dahlbender & Kächele, 1999); instead the crucial demanding task consists of reconciling empirical knowledge and clinical experience (Soldz & McCullough, 1999). We want to encourage other psychoanalysts to make their private work accessible to the scientific public. We also strongly recommend educating young scientists in acquiring sufficient clinical experience, as has been recommended by Kernberg (1986), Thomä (1993), and Thomä and Kächele (1999). At the same time, the training of experienced clinicians in quantitative and qualitative research methods is necessary (Teller & Dahl, 1995). The success of the Research Training Program initiated by the Research

Committee of the International Psychoanalytic Association demonstrated the feasibility and acceptance by younger and more senior analysts. We need psychoanalysts as clinicians and researchers who bring with them the strength to make steady and cumulative progress. We need institutions that make such scientific teams possible. To produce a cadre of researchers sufficient in numbers to address empirically the scope of unresolved analytic principles, it may be necessary fundamentally to transform psychoanalytic education. All teaching of candidates should be done jointly by researchers as well as clinicians, and candidates should be expected to become knowledgeable about analytic research as well as knowledgeable about analytic practice. Admittedly, this would constitute a drastic transformation in psychoanalytic education. We believe that the worldwide scope of stress on psychoanalysis and the trajectory of decline in status and prestige constitute a drastic situation, and drastic situations require drastic changes. The broad implementation of such scientific activities will decisively enrich psychoanalysis and will foster its growth and development. Some years ago the editors of an important handbook for clinical practice on "Psychodynamic Treatment Research" promised to their readers that this volume would inform about the manner in which Freud's treatment concepts have been ingeniously operationalized and validated: "The translation of rich, multifaceted clinical phenomena into definable variables amenable to precise and reliable measurement constitutes a critical milestone in the scientific evaluation of our field" (Luborsky, Docherty, Barber, & Miller, 1993, p. xv).

This kind of work has been the shibboleth of our own efforts. In this handbook Wallerstein (1993, p. 102) reminds the readers of our position on testing psychoanalytic propositions:

Thomä and Kächele (1975, p. 63) note that, in addition, extraclinical testing carries its own severe limitations. They state: "If the psychoanalytic method is not employed, and the process takes place outside of the treatment situation, only those parts of the theory can be tested that do not need a special interpersonal relationship as a basis of experience, and whose statements are not immediately related to clinical practice".

This statement obviously endorses the view that psychoanalytic practice must be the crucial place where the proof of its explanatory theories is to be rendered . It really is a matter of ecological validity.

We hope that we have been able to at least partially having fulfilled this claim.

References

Abel, T. (1953). *The operation called Verstehen*. New York: Appleton-Century-Crofts.

Abelin, E. F. (1971). Role of the father in the separation-individuation process. In McDevitt, J. B., & Settlage, C. F. (Eds.), *Separation-Individuation: Essays in honor of Margaret S. Mahler*. New York: International Universities Press, pp. 229–52.

Ablon, J. S., & Jones, E. E. (1998). How expert clinicians' prototypes of an ideal treatment correlate with outcome in psychodynamic and cognitive-behavioral therapy. *Psychotherapy Research*, 8, 71–83.

Ablon, J. S., & Jones, E. E. (1999). Psychotherapy process in the NIMH Treatment of Depression Collaborative Research Program. *Journal of Consulting and Clinical Psychology*, 67, 64–75.

Ablon, J. S., & Jones, E. E. (2005). On analytic process. *Journal of the American Psychoanalytic Association*, 53, 541–68.

Abraham, K. (1914). Über Einschränkungen und Umwandlungen der Schaulust bei Psychoneurotikern nebst Bemerkungen über analoge Erscheinungen in der Völkerpsychologie [On limitations and transformations of scoptophilia in psychoneurotics supplemented by remarks on analogous phenomena in the psychology of nations]. In Abraham, K. (Ed.), *Psychoanalytische Studien zur Charakterbildung*. Frankfurt: Fischer, pp. 324–81.

Abraham, K. (1924). *Versuch einer Entwicklungsgeschichte der Libido auf Grund der Psychoanalyse seelischer Störungen* [Sketch of a history of libido based on psychoanalysis of psychic disorder]. Leipzig Wien Zürich: Internationaler Psychoanalytischer Verlag.

Adler, A. (1928). *Die Technik der Individualpsychologie. Band 1: Die Kunst eine Lebens- und Krankengeschichte zu lesen* [The technique of individual psychology. Vol. 1: The art of reading a life and patient history]. München: Bergmann.

Adorno, T. W., Dahrendorf, R., Pilot, H., Albert, H., Habermas, J., & Popper, K. (1969). *Der Positivismusstreit in der deutschen Soziologie* [The battle on positivism in German sociology]. Neuwied, Germany: Luchterhand.

Akhtar, S. (2007). Diversity without fanfare: Some reflections on contemporary psychoanalytic technique. *Psychoanalytic Inquiry*, 27:690–704.

Albani, C., Blaser, G., Jacobs, U., Jones, E. E., Thomä, H., & Kächele, H. (2002). Amalia X's psychoanalytic therapy in the light of Jones's Psychotherapy Process Q-Sort. In Leuzinger-Bohleber, M., & Target, M. (Eds.), *Outcomes of psychoanalytic treatments. Perspectives for therapists and researchers*. London: Whurr Publishers, pp. 294–302.

Albani, C., Pokorny, D., Blaser, G., Grüninger, S., König, S., Marschke, F., et al. (2002). Re-formulation of Core Conflictual Relationship Theme (CCRT) categories: The CCRT-LU category system. *Psychotherapy Research*, 12, 319–38.

Albani, C., Pokorny, D., Blaser, G., & Kächele, H. (2008). *Beziehungsmuster und Beziehungskonflikte. Theorie, Klinik und Forschung* [Relationship patterns and relationship conflicts. Theory, clinic and research]. Göttingen: Vandenhoeck & Ruprecht.

Albani, C., Pokorny, D., Blaser, G., König, S., Thomä, H., & Kächele, H. (2003). Study of a psychoanalytic process using the Core Conflictual Relationship Theme (CCRT) Method according to the Ulm Process Model. *European Psychotherapy*, 4, 11–32.

Albani, C., Pokorny, D., Dahlbender, R. W., & Kächele, H. (1994). Vom Zentralen Beziehungs-Konflikt-Thema (ZBKT) zu Zentralen Beziehungsmustern (ZBM). Eine methodenkritische Weiterentwicklung der Methode des "Zentralen Beziehungs-Konflikt-Themas" [Moving from the CCRT to the CRP. A methodological critique of the CCRT]. *Psychotherapie Psychosomatik Medizinische Psychologie*, 44, 89–98.

Albani, C., Villmann, B., Villmann, T., Körner, A., Geyer, M., Pokorny, D., et al. (1999). Kritik der kategorialen Strukturen der Methode des Zentralen Beziehungs-Konflikt-Themas (ZBKT) [A critique of the categorical structures of the CCRT]. *Psychotherapie Psychosomatik Medizinische Psychologie*, 49, 408–21.

Albani, C., Volkart, R., Humbel, J., Blaser, G., Geyer, M., & Kächele, H. (2000). Die Methode der Plan-Formulierung: Eine exemplarische deutschsprachige Anwendung zur "Control Mastery Theory" von Joseph Weiss [The method of plan formulation: An exemplary German application of the "Control-Mastery Theory"]. *Psychotherapie Psychosomatik Medizinische Psychologie*, 50, 470–81.

Albert, H. (1968). Theorie und Prognose in den Sozialwissenschaften [Theory and prognosis in social sciences]. In Topitsch, E. (Ed.), *Logik der Sozialwissenschaften*. Köln: Kiepenheuer & Witsch, pp. 126–43.

Albert, H. (1969). Im Rücken des Positivismus? [The backside of positivism]. In Adorno, T. W., Dahrendorf, R., Pilot, H., Albert, H., Habermas, J., & Popper, K. R. (Eds.), *Der Positivismusstreit in der deutschen Soziologie*. Neuwied & Berlin: Luchterhand, pp. 267–305.

Albert, H. (1971). *Plädoyer für kritischen Rationalismus* [Plea for a critical rationalism]. München: Piper.

Albert, H. (Ed.) (1972). *Theorie und Realität* [Theory and reality]. Tübingen: Mohr/Siebeck.

Alexander, F. (1937). *Five year report of the Chicago Institute for Psychoanalysis, 1932–1937*. Chicago: Institute for Psychoanalysis.

Alexander, F., & French, T. M. (1974). *Psychoanalytic therapy. Principles and applications*. New York: Wiley. (Original work published 1946.)

Allport, G. W. (1937). *Personality: A psychological interpretation.* New York: Holt.

Allport, G. W. (1942). The use of personal documents in psychological science. *New York Social Science Research Council Bulletin*, 49.

Anonymous (1988). The specimen hour. In Dahl, H., Kächele, H., & Thomä, H. (Eds.), *Psychoanalytic process research strategies.* Berlin: Springer, pp. 15–28.

Anstadt, T., Merten, J., Ullrich, B., & Krause, R. (1996). Erinnern und Agieren [Remembering and acting-out]. *Zeitschrift für Psychosomatische Medizin und Psychoanalyse*, 42, 34–55.

Anthony, E. L. (1974). Review of F. Dolto: Dominique. The analysis of an adolescent. New York 1971. *Psychoanalytic Quarterly*, 43, 681–84.

Anzieu, A. (1977). Review of D.W. Winnicott: Fragment d'une analyse. Payot, Paris 1975. *Bulletin European Psychoanalytic Federation*, 11, 25–9.

Apel, K. O. (1955). Das Verstehen [Understanding]. *Archiv für Begriffsgeschichte*, 1, 142–99.

Apel, K. O. (1965). Die Entfaltung der "sprachanalytischen Philosophie" und das Problem der "Geisteswissenschaften" [The development of analytic philosophy and the problem of the "humanities"]. *Philosophisches Jahrbuch*, 72, 239–89.

Apel, K. O. (1966). Wittgenstein und das Problem des hermeneutischen Verstehens [Wittgenstein and the problem of hermeneutic understanding]. *Zeitschrift für Theologie und Kirche*, 63, 49–87.

Apel, K.O. (1967) Analytic philosophy of language and the Geisteswissenschaften. Dordrecht: Reidel.

Apel, K. O. (1971). Szientistik, Hermeneutik, Ideologiekritik [Scientism, hermeneutics, critique of ideology]. In *Hermeneutik und Ideologiekritik* (Ed.). Frankfurt am Main: Suhrkamp, pp. 7–44.

Appignanesi, L., & Forrester, J. (1992). *Freud's women.* London: Weidenfeld & Nicolson.

Argelander, H. (1971). *Der Flieger* [The pilot]. Frankfurt am Main: Suhrkamp.

Arlow, J. A. (1979). Metaphor and the psychoanalytic situation. *Psychoanalytic Quarterly*, 48, 363–85.

Arlow, J. A. (1982). Psychoanalytic education: A psychoanalytic perspective. *Annals of the New York Academy of Sciences*, 10, 5–20.

Arnold, E. G., Farber, B. A., & Geller, J. D. (2004). Termination, posttermination, and internalization of therapy and the therapist: Internal representation and psychotherapy outcome. In Charman, D. P. (Ed.), *Core processes in brief psychodynamic psychotherapy.* Mahwah, NJ: Erlbaum, pp. 289–308.

Asendorpf, J., & Walbott, H. G. (1979). Maße der Beobachterübereinstimmung: Ein systematischer Vergleich [Measures of observer agreement: A systematic comparison]. *Zeitschrift für Sozialpsychologie*, 10, 243–52.

Austin, J. L. (1962). *How to do things with words.* Oxford: Clarendon Press.

Bales, R. F. (1950). *Interaction process analysis: A method for the study of small groups.* Cambridge, MA: Addison-Wesley.

Balint, M. (1950). Changing therapeutical aims and techniques in psycho-analysis. *International Journal of Psychoanalysis*, 31, 117–24.

Balint, M. (1968). *The basic fault. Therapeutic aspects of regression.* London: Tavistock.

Balint, M., Ornstein, P. H., & Balint, E. (1972). *Focal psychotherapy. An example of applied psychoanalysis.* London: Tavistock Publications.

Balter, L., Lothane, Z., James, H., & Spencer, J. R. (1980). On the analyzing instrument. *Psychoanalytic Quarterly*, 49, 474–504.

Bandura, A. (1977). Self-efficacy: Toward a unifying theory of behavior change. *Psychological Review*, 84, 191–215.

Barnes, M. (1971). *Two accounts of a journey through madness*. London: Harcourt, Brace & Jovanovich.

Baumeyer, F. (1952). Bemerkungen zur Krankengeschichte des "Kleinen Hans" [Some remarks on the case history of "Little Hans"]. *Praxis der Kinderpsychologie und Kinderpsychiatrie*, 1, 129–33.

Baumeyer, F. (1956). The Schreber case. *International Journal of Psychoanalysis*, 37, 61–74.

Baumeyer, F. (1970). Noch ein Nachtrag zu Freuds Arbeit über Schreber [Once more an addendum to Freud's study on Schreber]. *Zeitschrift für Psychosomatische Medizin und Psychoanalyse*, 16, 243–45.

Beck, A. T. (1967). *Depression: Clinical, experimental, and theoretical aspects*. New York: Harper & Row.

Beck, A. T., & Hurvich, M. (1959). Psychological correlates of depression. I Frequency of "masochistic" dream content in a private practice sample. *Psychosomatic Medicine*, 21, 50–55.

Beck, A. T., & Ward, C. (1961). Dreams of depressed patients: Characteristic themes in manifest contents. *Archives of General Psychiatry*, 5, 462–67.

Beckmann, D., & Richter, H. E. (1972). *Gießen-Test. Ein Test für Individual- und Gruppendiagnostik* [Giessen Test: A test for individual and group diagnostics]. Bern: Huber.

Beckmann, D., Richter, H. E., & Scheer, J. W. (1969). Kontrolle von Psychotherapieresultaten [Evaluation of psychotherapy outcomes]. *Psyche - Zeitschrift für Psychoanalyse*, 23, 805–23.

Beermann, S. (1983). *Linguistische Analyse psychoanalytischer Therapiedialoge unter besonderer Berücksichtigung passivischer Sprechmuster* [Linguistic analysis of psychoanalytic dialogues with regard to pattern of passive syntax construction]. Ph.D. dissertation, Universität Hamburg.

Beigler, J. S. (1975). A commentary on Freud's treatment of the rat man. *Annual of Psychoanalysis*, 3, 271–85.

Bellak, L., & Chassan, J. B. (1964). An approach to the evaluation of drug effects during psychotherapy. *Journal of Nervous and Mental Disease*, 139, 20–30.

Bellak, L., & Smith, M. B. (1956). An experimental exploration of the psychoanalytic process. *Psychoanalytic Quarterly*, 25, 385–414.

Benjamin, J. D. (1950). Methodological considerations in the validation and elaboration of psychoanalytical personality theory. *American Journal of Orthopsychiatry*, 20, 139–56.

Benjamin, J. D. (1959). Prediction and psychopathological theory. In Jessner, L., & Pavenstedt, E. (Eds.), *Dynamic pathology in childhood*. New York: Grune & Stratton, pp. 6–77.

Benjamin, L. S. (1974). Structural analysis of social behavior (SASB). *Psychological Review*, 81, 392–425.

Benjamin, L. S. (1985). *From interpersonal diagnosis and treatment, the SASB approach*. New York: Guilford Press.

Berelson, B. (1952). *Content analysis in communications research*. Glencoe, IL: Free Press.

Berg, C. (1946). *Deep analysis: The clinical study of an individual case*. London: Allen & Urwin.

Bergin, A. E., & Garfield, S. L. (Eds.) (1971). *Handbook of psychotherapy and behavior change. An empirical analysis, 1st ed.* New York: Wiley & Sons.

Bergmann, P. (1966). An experiment in filmed psychotherapy. In Gottschalk, L. A., & Auerbach, H. A. (Eds.), *Methods of research in psychotherapy*. New York: Appleton-Century-Crofts, pp. 35–49.

Bernfeld. S., & Feidelberg, S. (1930) Über psychische Energie, Libido und deren Messbarkeit (On psychic engery, libido and its measurement). Imago 16: 66–118.

Bernfeld, S. (1934). Die Gestalttheorie [Theory of Gestalt]. *Imago*, 20, 32–77.

Bernfeld, S. (1949). Freud' s scientific beginnings. *American Imago*, 6, 165–96.

Bibring, E. (1937). Versuch einer allgemeinen Theorie der Heilung [Approaching a general theory of healing]. *Internationale Zeitschrift für Psychoanalyse*, 23, 18–42.

Binswanger, L. (1955). Zur Problematik der psychiatrischen Forschung und zum Problem der Psychiatrie [On the problem of psychiatric research and on the problem of psychiatry]. In Binswanger, L. (Ed.), *Ausgewählte Vorträge und Aufsätze* [Selected papers and lectures] (vol. 2). Bern: Francke.

Bion, W. R. (1967). Notes on memory and desire. In Bott Spillius, E. (Ed.), *Melanie Klein today*. London: Tavistock 1988, pp. 17–21.

Blacker, K. H. (1981). Insight. Clinical conceptualizations. *Journal of the American Psychoanalytic Association*, 29, 659–71.

Blanck, G., & Blanck, R. (1988). The contribution of ego psychology to understanding the process of termination in psychoanalysis and psychotherapy. *Journal of the American Psychoanalytic Association*, 36, 961–84.

Blanton, S. (1971). *Diary of my analysis with Sigmund Freud*. New York: Hawthorn Books.

Blatt, S. J. (2004). *Experiences of depression. Theoretical, clinical and research perspectives*. Washington, DC: American Psychological Association.

Blatt, S. J. (2005). Commentary on Ablon and Jones. *Journal of the American Psychoanalytic Association*, 53, 569–78.

Blatt, S. J. (2006). A fundamental polarity in psychoanalysis: Implications for personality development, psychopathology, and the therapeutic process. *Psychoanalytic Inquiry*, 26, 494–520.

Blatt, S. J., & Auerbach, J. S. (2003). Psychodynamic measures of change. *Psychoanalytic Inquiry*, 23, 268–307.

Blatt, S. J., & Behrends, R. S. (1987). Internalization, separation-individuation and the nature of therapeutic action. *International Journal of Psychoanalysis*, 68, 279–97.

Blatt S. J., & Sharar G. (2004) Psychoanalysis: For what, with whom and how. A comparison with psychotherapy. J Am Psychoanal Ass 52: 393–447.

Blos, P. (1970). *The young adolescent. Clinical studies*. New York: Free Press.

Blum, H. P. (2007). Little Hans: A centennial review and reconsideration. *Journal of the American Psychoanalytic Association*, 55, 749–65.

Boehm, F. (1923). Review von Sadger: Die Lehre von den Geschlechtsverirrungen auf psychoanalytischer Grundlage [Review of Sadger: The theory of sexual aberrations on psychoanalytic grounds]. *Internationale Zeitschrift für Psychoanalyse*, 9, 535–39.

Boesky, D. (2005). Psychoanalytic controversies contextualized. *Journal of the American Psychoanalytic Association*, 53, 853–63.

Bolland, J., & Sandler, J. (1965). *The Hampstead Psychoanalytic Index. A study of the psychoanalytic case material of a two-year old child*. New York: International Universities Press.

Bonaparte, M. (1927). *Der Fall Lefevre: Zur Psychoanalyse einer Mörderin* [The case Levevre: On the psychoanalysis of a murderess]. Leipzig: Internationaler Psychoanalytischer Verlag.

Bonaparte, M. (1945). Notes on the analytic discovery of a primal scene. *Psychoanalytic Study of the Child*, 1, 119–25.

Bonaparte, M. (1949). *The life and work of Edgar Allen Poe*. London: Imago Publishing.

Boothe, B. (2000). *Manual der Erzählanalyse JAKOB. Version 2000* [Manual of narrative analysis JAKOB.Version 2000]. Berichte aus der Abteilung Klinische Psychologie, Psychologisches Institut der Universität Zürich.

Bortz, J., & Döring, N. (1995). *Forschungsmethoden und Evaluation für Sozialwissenschaftler* [Methods of research and evaluation for social scientists] (2d ed.). Berlin: Springer.

Boston Process Change Study Group (BPCSG) (2005). The "something more" than interpretation revisited: Sloppiness and co-creativity in the psychoanalytic encounter. *Journal of the American Psychoanalytic Association*, 53, 693–729.

Boston Process Change Study Group (BPCSG), Stern, D. N., Sander, L. W., Nahum, J. P., Harrison, A. M., Lyons-Ruth, K., et al. (1998). Non-interpretative mechanisms in psychoanalytic therapy. *International Journal of Psychoanalysis*, 79, 903–1006.

Bouchard, M. A., Normandin, L., & Seguin, M. H. (1995). Countertransference as instrument and obstacle: A comprehensive and descriptive framework. *Psychoanalytic Quarterly*, 64, 717–45.

Bowlby, J. (1969). *Attachment and loss. Vol. 1: Attachment*. New York: Basic Books.

Bowlby, J. (1973). *Attachment and loss. Vol. 2:. Separation. Anxiety and anger*. New York: Basic Books.

Bowlby, J. (1979). Psychoanalysis as art and science. *International Review of Psychoanalysis*, 6, 3–14.

Bowlby, J. (1980). *Attachment and loss: Vol.3: Loss, sadness and depression*. New York: Basic Books.

Box, G. E. P., & Jenkins, G. M. (1976). *Time-series analysis: Forecasting and control*. San Francisco: Holden-Day Inc.

Bracken, B. A. (Ed.) (1996). *Handbook of self-concept: Developmental, social and clinical considerations*. New York: Wiley.

Brenner, C. (1939). On the genesis of a case of paranoid dementia praecox. *Journal of Nervous and Mental Disease*, 90, 483–88.

Breuer, J., & Freud, S. (1895). *Studien über Hysterie* [Studies on hysteria]. Leipzig: Deuticke.

Brody, B. (1970). Freud's case load. *Psychotherapy: Theory, Research and Practice*, 7, 8–12.

Brody, B. (1976). Freud's case load and social class. *Psychotherapy: Theory, Research and Practice*, 13, 196–97.

Bromley, D. B. (1986). *The case-study method in psychology and related disciplines.* New York: Wiley.

Brunner, E. J., Brunner-Wörner, R., & Odronitz-Dieterle, A. (1984). Methodische Grundlagen zur Analyse familialer Kommunikation [Methodological foundations for the analysis of familial communication]. In Brunner, E. J. (Ed.), *Interaktion in der Familie.* Berlin: Springer, pp. 89–104.

Bucci, W. (1988). Converging evidence for emotional structures: Theory and method. In Dahl, H., Kächele, H., & Thomä, H. (Eds.), *Psychoanalytic process research strategies.* Berlin: Springer, pp. 29–49.

Bucci, W. (1997a). Pattern of discourse in good and troubled hours. *Journal of the American Psychoanalytic Association*, 45, 155–88.

Bucci, W. (1997b). *Psychoanalysis & cognitive science.* New York: Guilford Press.

Bucci, W. (1998). Transformation of meanings in the analytic discourse; A strategy for research. *Canadian Journal of Psychoanalysis*, 6, 233–60.

Bucci, W. (2005). Process research. In Person, E. S., Cooper, A. M., & Gabbard, G. O. (Eds.), *Textbook of Psychoanalysis.* Washington, DC: American Psychiatric Press, pp. 317–33.

Bucci, W. (2007). Building the research-practice interface: Achievements and unresolved questions. In Bucci, W., & Freedman, N. (Eds.), *From impression to inquiry: A tribute to the work of Robert Wallerstein.* London: International Psychoanalytical Association, pp. 175–204.

Bucci, W., & Freedman, N. (Eds.). (2007). *From impression to inquiry: A tribute to the work of Robert Wallerstein.* London: International Psychoanalytical Association.

Bucci, W., & Maskit, B. (2007). Beneath the surface of the therapeutic interaction; The psychoanalytic method in modern dress. *Journal of American Psychoanalytic Association*, 55, 1355–1997.

Buchheim, A., & Kächele, H. (2007). Nach dem Tode der Eltern. Bindung und Trauerprozesse [After parents' death. Attachment and mourning]. *Forum der Psychoanalyse*, 23, 149–60.

Buchheim, A., Kächele, H., Cierpka, M., & et al. (2008). Psychoanalyse und Neurowissenschaften: Neurobiologische Veränderungsprozesse bei psychoanalytischen Behandlungen von depressiven Patienten—Entwicklung eines Paradigmas [Psychoanalysis and neuroscience: Neurobiological change processes in psychoanalytic treatment of depressive patients]. *Nervenheilkunde*, in press.

Buchholz, M. B. (2006). Konversation, Erzählung, Metapher. Der Beitrag qualitativer Forschung zu einem relationalen Paradigma der Psychoanalyse [Conversation, story telling, metaphor. The contribution of qualitative research to a relational paradigm of psychoanalysis]. In Altmeyer, M., & Thomä, H. (Eds.), *Die vernetzte Seele. Die intersubjektive Wende in der Psychoanalyse.* Stuttgart: Klett-Cotta, pp. 282–313.

Buchholz, M. B. (2007). Listening to words, seeing images. Metaphors of emotional movement. *International Forum of Psychoanalysis*, 16, in press.

Bühler, K. (1927). *Die Krise der Psychologie* [The crisis of psychology]. Jena: Fischer.

Burnes, E., Moore, M. D., & Fine, B. D. (1968). *A glossary of psychoanalytic terms and concepts*. Washington, DC: American Psychoanalytic Association.

Busemann, A. (1925). *Die Sprache der Jugend als Ausdruck der Entwicklungsrhythmik* [The language of youth as expression of developmental dynamics]. Jena: Gustav Fischer.

Bush, M., & Gassner, S. (1986). Plan compatibility scale. In Weiss, J., Sampson, H., & Mount Zion Psychotherapy Research Group (Eds.), *The psychoanalytic process: Theory, clinical observation, and empirical research*. New York: Guilford Press, pp. 277–98.

Campbell, D. T. (1967). From description to experimentation: Interpreting trends as quasi-experiments. In Harris, C. W. (Ed.), *Problems in measuring change*. Madison: Univeristy of Wisconsin Press, pp. 212–42.

Campbell, D. T., & Stanley, J. C. (1966). *Experimental and quasi-experimental designs for research*. New York: Rand MacNally.

Canetti, E. (1962). *Crowds and power*. New York: Viking Press.

Cardinale, M. (1983). *The words to say*. Cambridge, MA: Van Vactor and Goodheart.

Carmichael, H. T. (1966). Sound-film recording of psychoanalytic therapy: A therapist's experience and reactions. In Gottschalk, L. A., & Auerbach, A. H. (Eds.), *Methods of research in psychotherapy*. New York: Appleton-Century-Crofts, pp. 50–59.

Carnap, R. (1950). *The logical foundations of probability*. Chicago: University of Chicago Press.

Carveth, D. L. (1984). The analyst's metaphors. A deconstructionist perspective. *Psychoanalysis and Contemporary Thought*, 7, 491–560.

Casement, A. (Ed.) (2004). *Who owns psychoanalysis?* London: Karnac Books.

Casement, P. (1982). Some pressures on the analyst for physical contact during the reliving of an early trauma. *International Review of Psychoanalysis*, 9, 279–86.

Casement, P. (1985). *Learning from the patient. Part I*. London: Tavistock.

Casement, P. (1990). *Learning from the patient. Part II*. London: Routledge.

Casement, P. (2000). The issue of touch: A retrospective overview. *Psychoanalytic Inquiry*, 20, 160–84.

Casement, P. (2007). *Learning from life*. London: Routledge.

Casement, P. (2007, July). *Some problems with training analysis*. International Psychoanalytical Association, IPA News, eNewsletter.

Casonato, M., & Kächele, H. (2007). Le metaphore di Amalie X (Amalia X's metaphors). In Kächele, H., & Thomä, H. (Eds.), *La ricerca in psicoanalisi. Lo studio del "caso empirico."* Urbino: Quattro Venti, pp. 195–204.

Caspar, F. (1995). *Plan analysis. Toward optimizing psychotherapy*. Seattle: Hogrefe-Huber.

Caspar, F. M., & Berger, T. (2007). Insight and cognitive psychology. In Castonguay, L. G., & Hill, C. (Eds.), *Insight in psychotherapy*. Washington, DC: American Psychological Association, pp. 375–99.

Cassirer, E. (1923). *Philosophie der symbolischen Formen* [Philosophy of symbolic forms] *Vol. 1: Die Sprache*. Darmstadt: Wissenschaftliche Buchgemeinschaft.

Caston, J. (1977). Manual on how to diagnose the plan. In Weiss, J., Sampson, H., Caston, J., & Silberschatz, G. (Eds.), *Research on the psychoanalytic process— A comparison of two theories about analytic neutrality.* San Francisco: The Psychotherapy Research Group, Department of Psychiatry, Mount Zion Hospital and Medical Center San Francisco, pp. 15–21.

Caston, J., Goldman, R. K., & McClure, M. M. (1986). The immediate effects of psychoanalytic interventions. In Weiss, J., Sampson, H., & and the Mount Zion Psychotherapy Research Group (Eds.), *The psychoanalytic process: Theory, clinical observation, and empirical research.* New York: Guilford Press, pp. 277–98.

Cattell, R. B., Coulter, M. A., & Tsujioka, B. (1966). The taxonometric recognition of types and functional emergents. In Cattell, R. B. (Ed.), *Handbook of multivariate experimental psychology.* Chicago: Rand McNally, pp. 288–329.

Caws, P. (1991). Das Gerüst der Psychoanalyse [The framework of psychoanalysis]. In Grünbaum, A. (Ed.), *Kritische Betrachtungen zur Psychoanalyse. Adolf Grünbaums "Grundlagen" in der Diskussion* [Critical comments on psychoanalysis. A. Grünbaum's "foundations" in discussion]. Berlin: Springer, pp. 39–41.

Caws, P. (2003). Psychoanalysis as the idiosyncratic science of the individual subject. *Psychoanalytic Psychology,* 20, 618–634.

Chassan, J. B. (1979). *Research design in clinical psychology and psychiatry* (2d ed.). New York: Appleton-Century-Crofts.

Cheshire, N. M. (1975). *The nature of psychodynamic interpretation.* London: Wiley.

Cheshire, N. M., & Thomä, H. (1987a). General factors and specific techniques in self-concept therapy. In N. M. Cheshire, & H. Thomä (Eds.), *Self, symptoms and psychotherapy.* New York: John Wiley & Sons, pp. 115–47.

Cheshire, N. M., & Thomä, H. (Eds.) (1987b). *Self, symptoms and psychotherapy.* New York: John Wiley & Sons.

Cheshire, N. M., & Thomä, H. (1987c). The rehabilitation of the self. In Cheshire, N. M., & Thomä, H. (Eds.), *Self, symptoms and psychotherapy.* New York: John Wiley & Sons, pp. 19–42.

Clippinger, J. (1977). *Meaning and discourse: A computer model of psychoanalytic speech and cognition.* Baltimore: Johns Hopkins University Press.

Cochrane, W. G. (1954). Some methods for strengthening common chi-squared tests. *Biometries,* 10, 417–51.

Cohen, J. (1960). A coefficient of agreement for nominal scales. *Educational and Psychological Measurement,* 20, 37–46.

Cohen, R., & Laudan, L. (Eds.) (1983). *Physics, philosophy and psychoanalytic essays in honor of Adolf Grünbaum.* Dordrecht: Reidel.

Cohen, R. S. (1959). Adolf Grünbau: A memoir. In: Cohen, R. S. and Laudan, L., *Physics, Philosophy and Psychoanalysis.* Reidel: Dordrecht, ix–xviii.

Colby, K. M., & Stoller, R. J. (1988). *Cognitive science and psychoanalysis.* Hillsdale, NJ: Lawrence Erlbaum.

Collins, W. D., & Messer, S. B. (1991). Extending the plan formulation method to an object relations perspective: Reliability, stability, and adaptability. *Psychological Assessment,* 3, 75–81.

Compton, A. (1972). The study of the psychoanalytic theory of anxiety. *Journal of the American Psychoanalytic Association,* 20, 3–44, 341–94.

Compton, A. (1990). Psychoanalytic process. *Psychoanalytic Quarterly*, 59, 585–98.

Connolly Gibbons, M. B., Crits-Christoph, P., Barber, J. P., & Schamberger, M. (2007). A review of empirical literature. In Castonguay, L. G., & Hill, C. E. (Eds.), *Insight in psychotherapy*. Washington, DC: American Psychological Association, pp. 143–65.

Cooke, T., & Campbell, D. T. (1979). *Quasi-Experimentation. Design and analysis issues for field settings*. Boston: Houghton Mifflin.

Crits-Christoph, P., Barber, J., & Kurcias, J. S. (1993). The accuracy of therapists' interpretations and the development of the therapeutic alliance. *Psychotherapy Research*, 3, 25–35.

Crits-Christoph, P., Cooper, A., & Luborsky, L. (1998). The measurement of accuracy of interpretations. In Luborsky, L., & Crits-Christoph, P. (Eds.), *Understanding transference*. New York: Basic Books (2d ed.), pp. 197–212.

Crits-Christoph, P., & Demorest, A. (1991). Quantitative assessment of relationship theme components. In Horowitz, M. (Ed.), *Person schemas and maladaptive interpersonal patterns*. Chicago: University of Chicago Press, pp. 197–212.

Curtis, J. T., Ransohoff, P., Sampson, F., Brumer, S., & Bronstein, A. A. (1986). Expressing warded-off contents in behavior. In Weiss, J., Sampson, H., & and the Mount Zion Psychotherapy Research Group (Eds.), *The psychoanalytic process: Theory, clinical observation, and empirical research*. New York: Guilford Press, pp. 187–205.

Curtis, J. T., & Silberschatz, G. (1986). Clinical implications of research on brief dynamic psychotherapy: I. Formulating the patient's problems and goals. *Psychoanalytic Psychology*, 3, 13–25.

Curtis, J. T., Silberschatz, G., Sampson, H., & Weiss, J. (1994). The plan formulation method. *Psychotherapy Research*, 4, 197–207.

Curtis, J. T., Silberschatz, G., Sampson, H., Weiss, J., & Rosenberg, S. E. (1988). Developing reliable psychodynamic case formulations: An illustration of the plan diagnosis method. *Psychotherapy*, 25, 256–65.

Curtius, M. (1976). Rezension von Yalom & Elkin (1975). *Psyche - Zeitschrift für Psychoanalyse*, 30, 643–46.

Czogalik, D., & Russell, R. L. (1995). Interactional structures of therapist and client participation in adult psychotherapy: P-technique and chronography. *Journal of Consulting and Clinical Psychology*, 63, 28–36.

Dahl, H. (1972). A quantitative study of psychoanalysis. In Holt, R. R., & Peterfreund, E. (Eds.), *Psychoanalysis and contemporary science*. New York: International Universities Press, pp. 237–57.

Dahl, H. (1974). The measurement of meaning in psychoanalysis by computer analysis of verbal context. *Journal of the American Psychoanalytic Association*, 22, 37–57.

Dahl, H. (1979). *Word frequencies of spoken American English*. Essex: Verbatim.

Dahl, H. (1983). On the definition and measurement of wishes. In Masling, J. (Ed.), *Empirical studies of psychoanalytical theories* (vol. 1). New York: Lawrence Erlbaum Associates, Hillsdale, pp. 39–67.

Dahl, H. (1988). Frames of mind. In Dahl, H., Kächele, H., & Thomä, H. (Eds.), *Psychoanalytic process research strategies*. Berlin: Springer, pp. 51–66.

Dahl, H. (1988). Introduction. In Dahl, H., Kächele, H., & Thomä, H. (Eds.), *Psychoanalytic process research strategies*. Berlin: Springer, pp. vii–xvi.

Dahl, H., Hölzer, M., & Berry, J. W. (1992). *How to classify emotions for psychotherapy research*. Ulm: Ulmer Textbank.

Dahl, H., Kächele, H., & Thomä, H. (Eds.) (1988). *Psychoanalytic process research strategies*. Berlin: Springer.

Dahl, H., Rubinstein, B., & Teller, V. (1978). *A study of psychoanalytical clinical inference as interpretive competence and performance*. Proposal to the Fund for Psychoanalytic Research. Unpublished manuscript.

Dahl, H., & Stengel, B. (1978). A classification of emotion words: A modification and partial test of de Rivera's decision theory of emotions. *Psychoanalysis and Contemporary Thought*, 1, 269–312.

Dahl, H., Teller, V., Moss, D., & Trujillo, M. (1978). Countertransference examples of the syntactic expression of warded-off contents. *Psychoanalytic Quarterly*, 47, 339–63.

Dahlbender, R. W., Albani, C., Pokorny, D., & Kächele, H. (1998). The Connected Central Relationship Patterns (CCRP): A structural version of the CCRT. *Psychotherapy Research*, 8, 408–25.

Dahlbender, R. W., & Kächele, H. (1999). What do you believe in? Clinical conviction or empirical evidence ? In Soldz, S., & McCullough, L. (Eds.), *Reconciling empirical knowledge and clinical experience. The art and science of psychotherapy*. Washington, DC: American Psychological Association, pp. 151–66.

Dahmer, H. (1973). *Libido und Gesellschaft* [Libido and society]. Frankfurt am Main: Suhrkamp.

Danto, A. C. (1965). *Analytical philosophy of history*. Cambridge, England: Cambridge University Press.

Dare, C., & Holder, A. (1981). Developmental aspects of the interaction between narcissism, self esteem and object relations. *International Journal of Psychoanalysis*, 62, 323–37.

Davison, G. C., & Lazarus, A. A. (1994). Clinical innovation and evaluation. *Clinical Psychology: Science and Practice*, 1, 157–67.

De Boor, C. (1965). *Zur Psychosomatik der Allergie, besonders der Asthma bronchiale* [On psychosomatics of allergy, especially bronchial asthma]. Bern: Huber/Klett.

De la Parra, G., Mergenthaler, E., & Kächele, H. (1988). Analisis computerizado de la conducta verbal de pacientes y terapeutas en la primera entrevista diagnostica [Computer based analysis of verbal communications of patients and therapists]. *Acta Psiquiatrica y Psicologica de America Latina*, 34, 309–20.

de Swaan, A. (1980). On the sociogenesis of the psychoanalytic situation. *Psychoanalysis and Contemporary Thought*, 3, 381–413.

Deutsch, F. (1949).

Deutsch, F. (1957). A footnote to Freud's "Fragment of an analysis of a case of hysteria." *Psychoanalytic Quarterly*, 26, 159–67.

Deutsch, H. (1928). Ein Frauenschicksal—George Sand [A woman's fate—George Sand]. *Imago*, 14, 334–57.

Devereux, G. (1951). Some criteria for the timing of confrontations and interpretations. *International Journal of Psychoanalysis*, 32, 19–24.

Dewald, P. A. (1972). *The psychoanalytic process. A case illustration*. New York London: Basic Books.

Dilthey, W. (1894). Ideen über eine beschreibende und zergliedernde Psychologie [Ideas on a descriptive and dissecting psychology]. In Dilthey, W. (Ed.), *Gesammelte Schriften*: 5. Leipzig: Teubner, pp. 139–240.

Dilthey, W. (1900). Die Entstehung der Hermeneutik [The origin of hermeneutics]. In Dilthey, W. (Ed.), *Gesammelte Schriften Bd 5*: Bd.5. Leipzig: Teubner, pp. 317–38.

Dilthey, W. (1924). Beiträge zum Studium der Individualität [Contributions to a study of individuality]. In Dilthey, W. (Ed.), *Gesammelte Schriften 5*. Leipzig: Teubner Verlag, pp. 241–316.

Dittmann, A. T., & Wynne, L. C. (1961). Linguistic techniques and the analysis of emotionality in interviews. *Journal of Abnormal and Social Psychology*, 63, 201–4.

Döll-Hentschker, S. (2008). *Die Veränderung von Träumen in psychoanalytischen Behandlungen. Affekttheorie, Affektregulierung und Traumkodierung* [Change of dreams in psychoanalytic treatments. Affect theory, affect regulation and coding of dreams]. Frankfurt am Main: Brandes & Apsel.

Dollard, J., & Auld, F. (1959). *Scoring human motives: A manual*. New Haven, CT: Yale University Press.

Dollard, J., & Mowrer, O. H. (1947). A method of measuring tension in written documents. *Journal of Abnormal and Social Psychology*, 42, 3–32.

Dolto, F. (1971). *Le cas Dominique*. Paris: Edition du Seuil. eng. (1973) Dominique: analysis of an adolescent. Outerbridge and Lazard, New York.

Donnellan, G. J. (1978). Single-subject research and psychoanalytic theory. *Bulletin of the Menninger Clinic*, 42, 352–57.

Doolittle, H. (1956). *Tribute to Freud*. New York: Pantheon Books.

Dorpat, T. L. (1973). Research on the therapeutic process. Panel report. *Journal of the American Psychoanalytic Association*, 21, 168–81.

Dreher, A. U. (2000). *Foundations for conceptual research in psychoanalysis*. London: Karnac.

Dreher, A. U. (2005). Conceptual research. In Person, E. S., Cooper, A. M., & Gabbard, G. O. (Eds.), *Textbook of psychoanalysis*. Washington, DC: American Psychiatric Press, pp. 361–72.

Drews, S. (1978). *Provokation und Toleranz—Alexander Mitscherlich zum 70. Geburtstag* [Festschrift for Alexander Mitscherlich]. Frankfurt: Suhrkamp.

Eagle, M. (1973). Sherwood on the logic of explanation in psychoanalysis. In Rubinstein, B. B. (Ed.), *Psychoanalysis and contemporary science*: 2. New York: International Universities Press, pp. 331–37.

Eagle, M. (1984). *Recent developments in psychoanalysis. A critical evaluation*. New York: McGraw-Hill.

Eagle, M. N. and Wakefield, J. (2004). How NOT to escape from Grünbaum Syndrome: A critique of the "new view" of psychoanalysis. In Casement, A. (Ed.), *Who Owns Psychoanalysis?* Karnac Books: London, p. 343–361.

Edelheit, H. (1968). Language and the development of the ego. *Journal of the American Psychoanalytic Association*, 16, 113–22.

Edelson, M. (1972). Language and dreams: The interpretation of dreams revisited. *Psychoanalytic Study of the Child*, 27, 203–82.

Edelson, M. (1983). Is testing psychoanalytic hypotheses in the psychoanalytical situation really impossible? *Psychoanalytic Study of the Child*, 38, 61–109.

Edelson, M. (1984). *Hypothesis and evidence in psychoanalysis.* Chicago: University of Chicago Press.

Edelson, M. (1985). The hermeneutic turn and the single case study in psychoanalysis. *Psychoanalysis and Contemporary Thought,* 8, 567–614.

Edelson, M. (1986a). Causal explanation in science and psychoanalysis. *Psychoanalytic Study of the Child,* 41, 89–127.

Edelson, M. (1986b). The convergence of psychoanalysis and neuroscience: Illusion and reality. *Contemporary Psychoanalysis,* 22, 479–519.

Edelson, M. (1988). *Psychoanalysis—A theory in crisis.* Chicago: University of Chicago Press.

Edwards, A. L., & Cronbach, L. J. (1952). Experimental design for research in psychotherapy. *Journal of Clinical Psychology,* 8, 51–59.

Eissler, K. R. (1968). The relation of explaining and understanding in psychoanalysis. Demonstrated by one aspect of Freud's approach to literature. *Psychoanalytic Study of the Child,* 23, 141–77.

Eissler, K. R. (1971). Death drive, ambivalence, and narcissism. *Psychoanalytic Study of the Child,* 26, 25–78.

Ekman, P., & Friesen, W. V. (1978). *Manual for the facial action coding system.* Palo Alto, CA: Consulting Psychologists Press.

Ellis, A. (1956). An operational reformulation of some of the basic principles of psychoanalysis. In Feigl, H., & Scriven, M. (Eds.), *Minnesota studies in the philosophy of science I. The foundations of science and the concepts of psychology and psychoanalysis.* Minneapolis: University of Minnesota Press, pp. 131–54.

Epstein, S. (1979). The ecological study of emotions in humans. In Pliner, P. (Ed.), *Advances in the study of communication and affect.* New York: Plenum Press, pp. 47–83.

Erikson, E. H. (1954). The dream specimen of psychoanalysis. *Journal of the American Psychoanalytic Association,* 2, 5–56.

Erikson, E. H. (1962). Reality and actuality. *Journal of the American Psychoanalytic Association,* 11, 451–74.

Erikson, E. H. (1964). *Insight and responsibility. Lectures on the ethical implications of psychoanalytic insight.* New York: Norton.

Escalona, S. (1952). Problems in psychoanalytic research. *International Journal of Psychoanalysis,* 33, 11–21.

Etchegoyen, H. R. (1991). *The fundamentals of psychoanalytic technique.* London: Karnac Books.

Etchegoyen, H. R. (1986). *Los fundamentos de la técnica psicoanalitica.* Buenos Aires: Amorrortu editores. engl. (1991) The fundamentals of psychoanalytic technique. Karnac Books, London.

Fahrenberg, J. (1975). Die Freiburger Beschwerdeliste [The Freiburg list of complaints]. *Zeitschrift für Klinische Psychologie,* 4, 79–100.

Fahrenberg, J., Selg, H., & Hampel, R. (1978). *Das Freiburger Persönlichkeitsinventar* [The Freiburg Personality Inventory]. Göttingen: Verlag für Psychologie.

Fairbairn, W. R. (1952). *Psychoanalytic studies of personality.* London: Tavistock.

Farrell, B. A. (1961). Can psychoanalysis be refuted? *Inquiry,* 4, 16–36.

Farrell, B. A. (1964). The criteria for a psychoanalytic interpretation. In Gustavson, D. F. (Ed.), *Essays in philosophical psychology.* Garden City, NJ: Doubleday.

Farrell, B. A. (1981). *The standing of psychoanalysis*. Oxford: Oxford University Press.

Fava, G., & Sonino, N. (2000). Psychosomatic medicine: Emerging trends and perspectives. *Psychotherapy and Psychosomatics*, 69, 184–97.

Fenichel, O. (1931). *Perversionen, Psychosen, Charakterstörung* [Perversions, psychoses, character disorder]. Darmstadt, 1992 [1931]: Wissenschaftliche Buchgemeinschaft.

Ferenczi, S. (1927 [1964]). *Bausteine zur Psychoanalyse* [Fundamentals of psychoanalysis], *vol. 2, Praxis* [Practice]. Wien: Internationaler Psychoanalytischer Verlag.

Fingert Chused, J. (2007). Little Hans "analyzed" in the twenty-first century. *Journal of the American Psychoanalytic Association*, 55, 767–78.

Firestein, S. K. (1978). *Termination in psychoanalysis*. New York: International Universities Press.

Firestein, S. K. (1982). Termination of psychoanalysis. Theoretical, clinical, and pedagogic considerations. *Psychoanalytic Inquiry*, 2, 473–97.

Fisher, C., & Greenberg, R. P. (1977). *The scientific credibility of Freud's theories and therapies*. New York: Basic Books.

Fisher, S., & Greenberg, R. P. (1996). *Freud scientifically reappraised: Testing the theories and therapy*. New York: John Wiley & Sons.

Flader, D., & Grodzicki, W. D. (1982). Die psychoanalytische Deutung. Eine diskursanalytische Fallstudie [The psychoanalytic interpretation. A discourse-analytic case study]. In Flader, D., Grodzicki, W. D., & Schröter, K. (Eds.), *Psychoanalyse als Gespräch* [Psychoanalysis as discourse]. Frankfurt am Main: Suhrkamp, pp. 138–93.

Flader, D., Grodzicki, W. D., & Schröter, K. (Eds.) (1982). *Psychoanalyse als Gespräch* [Psychoanalysis as discourse]. Frankfurt am Main: Suhrkamp.

Flader, D., & Schröter, K. (1982). Interaktionsanalytische Ansätze der Therapiegesprächsforschung [Interaction analytic approaches to therapeutic discourse analysis]. In Flader, D., Grodzicki, W., & Schröter, K. (Eds.), *Psychoanalyse als Gespräch* [Psychoanalysis as discourse]. Frankfurt: Suhrkamp, pp. 7–15.

Flader, D., & Wodak-Leodolter, R. (1979). *Therapeutische Kommunikation* [Therapeutic communication]. Königstein: Scriptor.

Flarsheim, A., & Giovacchini, P. L. (1972). Introductory note to Winnicott D. Fragment of an analysis. In Giovacchini, P. (Ed) Tactics and techniques in psychoanalytic therapy. London: Hogarth. p.455–456.

Fliess, R. (1953). *The revival of interest in the dream*. New York: International Universities Press.

Fónagy, I., & Fonagy, P. (1995). Communications with pretend actions in language, literature and psychoanalysis. *Psychoanalysis and Contemporary Thought*, 18, 363–418.

Fonagy, P. (1999a). Memory and therapeutic action. *International Journal of Psychoanalysis*, 80, 215–23.

Fonagy, P. (1999b, April 16). *The process of change and the change of processes: What can change in a good analysis*. Paper presented at the Spring meeting of Division 39 of the American Psychological Association, New York.

Fonagy, P. (2001). *Attachment theory and psychoanalysis*. New York: Other Press.

Fonagy, P. (2002). Epistemological and methodological background: Reflections on psychoanalytic research problems—An Anglo-Saxon view. In Fonagy, P. (Ed.), *An open door review of outcome studies in psychoanalysis*. London: International Psychoanalytic Association, pp. 10–29.

Fonagy, P. (2003). Some complexities in the relationship of psychoanalytic theory to technique. *Psychoanalytic Quarterly*, 72, 13–47.

Fonagy, P. (2004). Foreword. In Richardson, P., Kächele, H., & Renlund, C. (Eds.), *Research on psychoanalytic psychotherapy with adults*. London: Karnac, pp. xix–xxvii.

Fonagy, P. (2005). In praise of simplicity: Commentary on Ablon and Jones. *Journal of the American Psychoanalytic Association*, 53, 579–89.

Fonagy, P., Gergely, G., Jurist, E., & Target, M. (2002). *Affect regulation, mentalization, and the development of the self*. New York: Other Press.

Fonagy, P., Jones, E. E., Kächele, H., Krause, R., Clarkin, J. F., Perron, R., et al. (2002a). *An open door review of outcome studies in psychoanalysis* (2d ed.). London: International Psychoanalytical Association.

Fonagy, P., & Moran, G. (1993). Selecting single case research designs for clinicians. In Miller, N., Luborsky, L., Barber, J., & Docherty, J. (Eds.), *Handbook of psychodynamic treatment research*. New York: Basic Books, pp. 62–95.

Fontao, M. I. (2004). *Emotion, Abstraktion und Wirkfaktoren in der Gruppentherapie: eine Einzelfallstudie an Patientinnen mit Essstörungen* [Emotion, abstraction and effective ingredients in group therapy: a single case study with eating disordered patients]. Ph.D. dissertation, Universität Ulm, Sektion Informatik in der Psychotherapie.

Forrester, J. (1980). *Language and the origins of psychoanalysis*. London: Macmillan.

Forster, G. F., & Stuart, A. (1954). Distribution-free test in time-series. *Journal of the Royal Statistical Society*, 16, 1–22.

Fosshage, J. L. (1990). Clinical protocol: How theory shapes technique: Perspectives on a self-psychological clinical presentation. *Psychoanalytic Inquiry*, 10, 461–77.

Freedman, N., Lasky, R., & Hurvich, M. (2003). Two pathways towards knowing psychoanalytic process. In Leuzinger-Bohleber, M., Dreher, A. U., & Canestri, J. (Eds.), *Pluralism and unity? Methods of research in psychoanalysis*. London: International Psychoanalytical Association, pp. 207–21.

French, T. M. (1937). Klinische Untersuchung über das Lernen im Verlaufe einer psychoanalytischen Behandlung [Clinical investigation about learning during psychoanalysis]. *Internationale Zeitschrift für Psychoanalyse*, 23, 96–132.

French, T. M. (1952). *The integration of behavior. Vol. I: Basic postulates*. Chicago: University of Chicago Press.

French, T. M. (1954). *The integration of behavior. Vol. II: The integrative process in dreams*. Chicago: University of Chicago Press.

French, T. M. (1958). *The integration of behavior. Vol. III: The reintegrative process in a psychoanalytic treatment*. Chicago: University of Chicago Press.

Frenkel-Brunswik, E. (1949). Intolerance of ambiguity as emotional and perceptual personality variable. *Journal of Personality*, 18, 108–43.

Frenkel-Brunswik, E. (1954). Meaning of psychoanalytic concepts and confirmation of psychoanalytic theories. *Scientific Monthly*, 79, 293–300.

Freud, A. (1936). *The ego and the mechanisms of defense*. London: Hogarth.

Freud, A. (1958). Child observation and prediction of development. *Psychoanalytic Study of the Child*, 13, 92–116.

Freud, S. (1893f). Charcot. In *Standard edition* 3. London: Hogarth Press, pp. 11–23.

Freud, S. (1895). A project for a scientific psychology. In Bonaparte, M., Freud, A., & Kris, E. (Eds.), *The origins of psycho-analysis*. London: Basic Books, pp. 347–445.

Freud, S. (1895f). A reply to criticisms of my paper on anxiety neurosis. In *Standard edition* 2. London: Hogarth Press, pp. 123–39.

Freud, S. (1895d). Studies on hysteria. In *Standard edition* 2. London: Hogarth Press.

Freud, S. (1896c). The etiology of hysteria. In *Standard edition* 3. London: Hogarth Press, pp. 191–221.

Freud, S. (1900a). The interpretation of dreams. In *Standard edition* 4–5. London: Hogarth Press.

Freud, S. (1901b). The psychopathology of everyday life. In *Standard edition* 6. London: Hogarth Press.

Freud, S. (1905e). Fragment of an analysis of a case of hysteria. In *Standard edition* 7. London: Hogarth Press, pp. 7–122.

Freud, S. (1905c). Jokes and their relation to the unconscious. In *Standard edition* 8. London: Hogarth Press.

Freud, S. (1905d). Three essays on the theory of sexuality. In *Standard edition* 7. London: Hogarth Press, pp. 135–243.

Freud, S. (1909b). Analysis of a phobia in a five-year-old boy. In *Standard edition* 10. London: Hogarth Press, pp. 5–147.

Freud, S. (1909d). Notes on a case of obsessional neurosis. In *Standard edition* 10. London: Hogarth Press, pp. 151–318.

Freud, S. (1910a). Five lectures on psycho-analysis. In *Standard edition* 11. London: Hogarth Press, pp. 7–55.

Freud, S. (1911c). Psychoanalytic notes on an autobiographical account of a case of paranoia (Dementia Paranoides). In *Standard edition* 12. London: Hogarth Press, pp. 9–79.

Freud, S. (1912d). On the universal tendency to debasement in the sphere of love (Contributions to the psychology of love). In *Standard edition* 11. London: Hogarth Press, pp. 231–38.

Freud, S. (1912e). Recommendations to physicians practising psycho-analysis. In *Standard edition* 12. London: Hogarth Press, pp. 111–20.

Freud, S. (1912b). The dynamics of transference. In *Standard edition* 12. London: Hogarth Press, pp. 97–108.

Freud, S. (1913c). On beginning the treatment (Further recommendations on the technique of psychoanalysis). In *Standard edition* 12. London: Hogarth Press, pp. 123–44.

Freud, S. (1914c). On narcissism: An introduction. In *Standard edition* 14. London: Hogarth Press, pp. 73–102.

Freud, S. (1914d). On the history of the psycho-analytic movement. In *Standard edition* 14. London: Hogarth Press, pp. 7–66.

Freud, S. (1914g). Remembering, repeating, and working-through. In *Standard edition* 12. London: Hogarth Press, pp. 147–56.

Freud, S. (1915f). A case of paranoia running counter to the psycho-analytic theory of disease. In *Standard edition* 14. London: Hogarth Press, pp. 263–72.

Freud, S. (1915a). Observations on transference-love. In *Standard edition* 12. London: Hogarth Press, pp. 157–71.

Freud, S. (1915e). The unconscious. In *Standard edition* 14. London: Hogarth Press, pp. 159–215.

Freud, S. (1915b). Thoughts for the times on war and death. In *Standard edition* 14. London: Hogarth Press, pp. 275–300.

Freud, S. (1917). Introductory lectures on psychoanalysis. In *Standard edition* 15–16. London: Hogarth Press.

Freud, S. (1918b). From the history of an infantile neurosis. In *Standard edition* 17. London: Hogarth Press, pp. 7–122.

Freud, S. (1919a). Lines of advance in psycho-analytic therapy. In *Standard edition* 17. London: Hogarth Press, pp. 159–68.

Freud, S. (1920b). A note on the prehistory of the technique of analysis. In *Standard edition* 18. London: Hogarth Press, pp. 263–65.

Freud, S. (1920g). Beyond the pleasure principle. In *Standard edition* 18. London: Hogarth Press, pp. 7–64.

Freud, S. (1920a). The psychogenesis of a case of female homosexuality. In *Standard edition* 18. London: Hogarth Press, pp. 147–72.

Freud, S. (1921c). Group psychology and the analysis of the ego. In *Standard edition* 18. London: Hogarth Press, pp. 69–143.

Freud, S. (1923b). The ego and the id. In *Standard edition* 19. London: Hogarth Press, pp. 12–59.

Freud, S. (1925d). An autobiographical study. In *Standard edition* 20. London: Hogarth Press, pp. 7–70.

Freud, S. (1926d). Inhibitions, symptoms, and anxiety. In *Standard edition* 20. London: Hogarth Press, pp. 87–172.

Freud, S. (1926e). The question of lay analysis. In *Standard edition* 20. London: Hogarth Press, pp. 183–250.

Freud, S. (1927a). Postscript to "The question of lay analysis." In *Standard edition* 20. London: Hogarth Press, pp. 251–58.

Freud, S. (1928b). Dostoevsky and parricide. In *Standard edition* 21. London: Hogarth Press, pp. 177–94.

Freud, S. (1930a). Civilizations and its discontent. In *Standard edition* 21. London: Hogarth Press, pp. 64–145.

Freud, S. (1933a). New introductory lectures on psycho-analysis. In *Standard edition* 22. London: Hogarth Press, pp. 5–182.

Freud, S. (1937c). Analysis terminable and interminable. In *Standard edition* 23. London: Hogarth Press, pp. 216–53.

Freud, S. (1937d). Constructions in analysis. In *Standard edition* 23. London: Hogarth Press, pp. 257–69.

Freud, S. (1940a [1938]). An outline of psycho-analysis. In *Standard edition* 23. London: Hogarth Press, pp. 144–207.

Freud, A. (1965). Preface. In J. Bolland, & J. Sandler (Eds.), The Hampstead Psychoanalytic Index. A study of the psychoanalytic case material of a two-year old child. New York: International Universities Press. pp ix–x.

Frommer, J., & Langenbach, M. (2001). The psychoanalytic case study as a source of epistemic knowledge. In Frommer, J., & Rennie, D. L. (Eds.), *Qualitative psychotherapy research. Methods and methodology.* Lengerich: Pabst, pp. 50–68.

Frommer, J., & Rennie, D. L. (Eds.) (2001). *Qualitative psychotherapy research. Methods and methodology.* Lengerich: Pabst.

Gabbard, G. O. (1995). Countertransference: The emerging common ground. *International Journal of Psychoanalysis, 76,* 475–85.

Gabbard, G. O., & Westen, D. (2003). Rethinking therapeutic action. *International Journal of Psychoanalysis, 84,* 823–42.

Gadamer, H. G. (1959). Vom Zirkel des Verstehens [On circularity of understanding]. In *Festschrift für M. Heidegger.* Pfullingen: Neske, pp. 24–34.

Gadamer, H. G. (1965). *Wahrheit und Methode. Anwendung einer philosophischen Hermeneutik* [Truth and method. Application of a philosophical hermeneutic]. Tübingen: Mohr.

Gadamer, H. G. (1971a). Replik [A replique]. In *Hermeneutik und Ideologiekritik.* Frankfurt: Suhrkamp, pp. 283–317.

Gadamer, H. G. (1971b). Rhetorik, Hermeneutik und Ideologiekritik [Rhetoric, hermeneutics and critique of ideology]. In *Hermeneutik und Ideologiekritik.* Frankfurt: Suhrkamp, pp. 57–82.

Galatzer-Levi, R. M., Bachrach, H., Skolnikoff, A., & Waldron, W. (2001). *Does psychoanalysis work?* New Haven, CT: Yale University Press.

Gardiner, M. (1971). *The Wolf-man.* New York: Basic Books.

Gardner, R. A. (1972). Little Hans—The most famous boy in child psychotherapy literature. *International Journal of Child Psychotherapy, 1,* 24–50.

Garduk, E. L., & Haggard, E. A. (1972). *Immediate effects on patients of psychoanalytic interpretations.* New York: International Universities Press.

Gebhardt, F. (1967a). *FAST. Vergleich von Faktorstrukturen* [FAST: Comparison of factor structures]. Deusches Rechenzentrum Darmstadt.

Gebhardt, F. (1967b). Über die Ähnlichkeit von Faktormatrizen [On the similarity of factor matrices]. *Psychologische Beiträge, 10,* 591–99.

Gedo, J., Sabshin, M., Sadow, L., & Schlessinger, N. (1964). Studies on hysteria: A methodological evaluation. *Journal of the American Psychoanalytic Association, 12,* 734–51.

Gedo, J. E. (1984). *Psychoanalysis and its discontents.* New York: Guilford Press.

Geist, W. B., & Kächele, H. (1979). Zwei Traumserien in einer psychoanalytischen Behandlung [Two dream series in a psychoanalytic treatment]. *Jahrbuch der Psychoanalyse, 11,* 138–65.

Geleerd, E. (1963). Evaluation of Melanie Klein's "Narrative of a child analysis." *International Journal of Psychoanalysis, 44,* 493–506.

Gendlin, E. T., & Tomlinson, T. M. (1962). *The experiencing scale.* University of Wisconsin.

George, C., Kaplan, N., & Main, M. (1985). *The Attachment Interview for Adults.* Unpublished manuscript. University of California, Berkeley.

George, C., & Solomon, J. (1999). The development of caregiving: A comparison of attachment theory and psychoanalytic approaches to mothering. *Psychoanalytic Quarterly, 19,* 618–46.

George, C., & West, M. (1999). Developmental vs. social personality models of adult attachment and mental ill health. *British Journal of Medical Psychology*, 72, 285–303.

George, C., & West, M. (2001). The development and preliminary validation of a new measure of adult attachment: The Adult Attachment Projective. *Attachment and Human Development*, 3, 30–61.

Gerbner, G., Holsti, O. R., Krippendorf, K., Paisley, W., & Stone, P. (Eds.) (1969). *The analysis of communication content. Developments in scientific theories and computer techniques*. New York: John Wiley.

Gergen, K. J. (1985). The social constructionist movement in modern psychology. *American Psychologist*, 40, 266–75.

Gill, M. M. (Ed.) (1967). *The collected papers of David Rapaport*. New York: Basic Books.

Gill, M. M. (1982). *Analysis of transference. Vol. 1: Theory and technique*. New York: International Universities Press.

Gill, M. M. (1983). The point of view of psychoanalysis. Energy discharge or person. *Psychoanalysis and Contemporary Thought*, 6, 523–51.

Gill, M. M. (1984). Psychoanalysis and psychotherapy: A revision. *International Review of Psycho-Analysis*, 11, 161–79.

Gill, M. M. (1991). Indirect suggestion: A response to Oremland's "Interpretation and Interaction." In Oremland, J. D. (Ed.), *Interpretation and interaction. Psychoanalysis or psychotherapy*. Hilldsdale, NJ: Analytic Press, pp. 137–63.

Gill, M. M. (1994). *Psychoanalysis in transition: A personal view*. Hillsdale, NJ: Analytic Press.

Gill, M. M., & Hoffman, I. Z. (1982). A method for studying the analysis of aspects of the patient's experience in psychoanalysis and psychotherapy. *Journal of the American Psychoanalytic Association*, 30, 137–67.

Gill, M. M., Simon, J., Fink, G., Endicott, N. A., & Paul, I. H. (1968). Studies in audio-recorded psychoanalysis. I. General considerations. *Journal of the American Psychoanalytic Association*, 16, 230–44.

Giovacchini, P. L. (1972). *Tactics and techniques in psychoanalytic therapy*, International Psychoanalytic Library. London: Hogarth.

Glover, E. (1947). Basic mental concepts: Their clinical and theoretical value. *Psychoanalytic Quarterly*, 16, 482–506.

Glover, E. (1955a). Common technical practices: A research questionaire. In Glover, E. (Ed.), *The technique of psychoanalysis*. London: Baillière Tindall & Cox, pp. 259–350.

Glover, E. (1955b). *The technique of psychoanalysis*. New York: International Universities Press.

Glover, E., & Brierley, M. (Eds.) (1940). *An investigation of the technique of psychoanalysis*. London: Baillière, Tindall & Cox.

Goffman, E. (1974). *Stigma. Notes on the management of spoiled identity*. New York: Jason Aronson.

Goldberg, A. (1978). *The psychology of the self—A casebook*. New York: International Universities Press.

Gottschalk, L. A., & Auerbach, A. (Eds.) (1966). *Methods of research in psychotherapy*. New York: Appleton-Century-Crofts.

Gottschalk, L. A., & Gleser, G. C. (1969). *The measurement of psychological states through the content analysis of verbal behaviour*. Berkeley: University of California Press.

Grabhorn, R., Overbeck, G., Kernhof, K., Jordan, J., & Mueller, T. (1994). Veränderung der Selbst-Objekt-Abgrenzung einer eßgestörten Patientin im stationären Therapieverlauf [Changes in self-object differentiation of an eating disordered patient in inpatient treatment]. *Psychotherapie, Psychosomatik, Medizinische Psychologie*, 44, 273–83.

Graff, H., & Luborsky, L. (1977). Long-term trends in transference and resistance: A quantitative analytic method applied to four psychoanalyses. *Journal of the American Psychoanalytic Association*, 25, 471–90.

Grande, T., Dilg, R., Jakobsen, T., Keller, W., Krawietz, B., Langer, M., et al. (2006). Differential effects of two forms of psycho-analytic psychotherapy. Results from the Heidelberg-Berlin Study. *Psychotherapy Research*, 16, 470–85.

Grande, T., Rudolf, G., Oberbracht, C., Jakobsen, T., & Keller, W. (2003). Investigating structural change in the process and outcome of psychoanalytic treatment—The Heidelberg-Berlin Study. In Richardson, P., Kächele, H., & Renlund, C. (Eds.), *Research on psychoanalytic psychotherapy with adults*. London: Karnac, pp. 35–61.

Grawe, K. (1988). Zurück zur psychotherapeutischen Einzelfallforschung [Back to psychotherapeutic single case research]. *Zeitschrift für Klinische Psychologie*, 17, 4–5.

Grawe, K. (1992). Psychotherapieforschung zu Beginn der neunziger Jahre [Psychotherapy research at the beginning of the nineties]. *Psychologische Rundschau*, 43, 132–62.

Green, A. (1996). What kind of research for psychoanalysis. *International Psychoanalysis*, 5, 8–9.

Green, A. (2000). Science and science fiction in infant research. In Sandler, J., Sandler, A.-M., & Davies, R. (Eds.), *Clinical and observational research: Roots of a controversy*. London: Karnac Books, pp. 41–72.

Green, A. (2005). The illusion of common ground and mythical pluralism. *International Journal of Psychoanalysis*, 86, 627–32.

Green, H. (1964). *I never promised you a rosegarden*. London: Gollancz.

Greenberg, L., & Safran, J. (1987). *Emotion in psychotherapy. Affect, cognition, and the process of change*. New York: Guilford Press.

Greenson, R. R. (1960). Empathy and its vicissitudes. *International Journal of Psychoanalysis*, 41, 418–24.

Greenson, R. R. (1965). The problem of working through. In Schur, M. (Ed.), *Drives, affects, behavior* (vol. 2). New York: International Universities Press, pp. 277–314.

Greenson, R. R. (1967). *The technique and practice of psychoanalysis, vol. I*. New York: International Universities Press.

Grice, H. P. (1975). Logic and conversation. In Cole, P., & Morgan, J. L. (Eds.), *Speech acts: Syntax and semantics*. New York: Seminar Press, pp. 41–58.

Grünbaum, A. (1982a). Can psychoanalytic theory be cogently tested "on the couch"? Part I. *Psychoanalysis and Contemporary Thought*, 5, 155–255.

Grünbaum, A. (1982b). Can psychoanalytic theory be cogently tested "on the couch"? Part II. *Psychoanalysis and Contemporary Thought*, 5, 311–436.

Grünbaum, A. (1984). *The foundations of psychoanalysis. A philosophical critique.* Berkeley: University of California Press.

Grünbaum, A. (1986a). Précis of the foundations of psychoanalysis. A philosophical critique, and author's response to 39 reviewers: "Is Freud's theory well-founded." *Behavioral and Brain Sciences*, 9, 217–84.

Grünbaum, A. (1987a). *Psychoanalyse in wissenschaftstheoretischer Sicht. Zum Werk Sigmund Freuds und seiner Rezeption* [Psychoanalysis in epistemic perspective. On the work of Sigmund Freud and its reception]. Konstanz: Universitätsverlag.

Grünbaum, A. (1986b). The notion of placebo in psychotherapy. *Psychological Medicine*, 16, 19–38.

Grünbaum, A. (1988a). *Die Grundlagen der Psychoanalyse* [The foundations of psychoanalysis]. Stuttgart: Reclam.

Grünbaum, A. (1988b). The role of the case study method in the foundations of psychoanalysis. In Vetter, H., & Nagl, L. (Eds.), *Die Philosophen und Freud.* Wien: Oldenburg, pp. 134–74.

Grünbaum, A. (Ed.) (1991). *Kritische Betrachtungen zur Psychoanalyse* [Critical remarks on psychoanalysis]. Berlin: Springer.

Grünbaum, A. (1993a). The placebo concept in psychiatry and medicine. In: *Validation in the clinical theory of psychoanalysis. A study in the philosophy of psychoanalysis.* Madison, CT: International Universities Press, 69–108.

Grünbaum, A. (1993b). *Validation in the clinical theory of psychoanalysis. A study in the philosophy of psychoanalysis.* New York: International Universities Press.

Grünbaum, A. (2001). A century of psychoanalysis: Critical retrospect and prospect. *International Forum of Psychoanalysis*, 10, 105–12.

Grünbaum, A. (2006). Is Sigmund Freud's psychoanalytic edifice relevant to the 21st century? *Psychoanalytic Psychology*, 23, 257–84.

Grünbaum, A. (2007). The reception of my Freud-critique in the psychoanalytic literature. *Psychoanalytic Psychology*, 24, 545–76.

Grünzig, H. J. (1988). Time-series analysis of psychoanalytic treatment processes: Sampling problems and first findings in a single case. In Dahl, H., Kächele, H., & Thomä, H. (Eds.), *Psychoanalytic process research strategies.* Berlin: Springer, pp. 213–26.

Guntrip, H. (1961). *Personality structure and human interaction.* New York: International Universities Press.

Guntrip, H. (1975). My experience of analysis with Fairbairn and Winnicott. *International Revue of Psychoanalysis*, 2, 145–56.

Haas, E. (1976). Rezension of F. Dolto: Le cas Dominique [Review of F. Dolto]. *Psyche - Zeitschrift für Psychoanalyse*, 30, 353–55.

Habermas, J. (1963). Analytische Wissenschaftstheorie und Dialektik (Analytic metascience and dialectics). In Horkheimer, M. (Ed.) *Zeugnisse. Theodor W. Adorno zum sechzigsten Geburtstag.* Frankfurt am Main: Europäische Verlagsanstalt, pp. 473–501.

Habermas, J. (1967). *Zur Logik der Sozialwissenschaften* [On the logic of social sciences]. Beiheft 5: Philosophische Rundschau.

Habermas, J. (1968). *Erkenntnis und Interesse* [Knowledge and human interest]. Frankfurt am Main: Suhrkamp.

Habermas, J. (1969). Gegen einen positivistisch halbierten Rationalismus [Against a positivistic splitted rationalism]. In Adorno, T. W., Dahrendorf, R., Pilot, H., Albert, H., Habermas, J., & Popper, K. (Eds.), *Der Positivismus Streit in der deutschen Soziologie*. Neuwied: Luchterhand, pp. 235–68.

Habermas, J. (1971a). *Knowledge and human interests*. Boston: Beacon Press.

Habermas, J. (1971b). Zu Gadamers "Wahrheit und Methode" [On Gadamer's "Truth and method"]. In *Hermeneutik und Ideologiekritik*. Frankfurt: Suhrkamp, pp. 45–56.

Haldane, J. B. S., & Smith, C. A. B. (1947–1949). A simple exact test for birth-order effect. *Annals of Eugenics*, 14, 117–24.

Hall, C. S., & van de Castle, R. L. (1966). *The content analysis of dreams*. New York: Appleton-Century-Crofts.

Hall, C. S., & Lindzey, G. (1968). The relevance of Freudian psychology and related viewpoints for the social sciences. In Lindzey, G., & Aronson, E. (Eds.), *Historical introduction. Systematic positions: The handbook of social psychology* (2d ed.). Reading, PA: Addison-Wesley, pp. 245–319.

Hamilton, V. (1996). *The analyst's preconscious*. Hillsdale, NJ: Analytic Press.

Hanly, C. (1992). Inductive reasoning in clinical psychoanalysis. *International Journal of Psychoanalysis*, 73, 293–301.

Hartmann, H. (1972). *Die Grundlagen der Psychoanalyse* [The foundations of psychoanalysis]. Leipzig: Thieme. Neuauflage 1972.

Hartmann, H. (1958). Discussion of A. Freud. *Psychoanalytic Study of the Child*, 13, 120–22.

Hatcher, R., & Barends, A. W. (2006). How a return to theory could help alliance research. *Psychotherapy: Theory, Research, and Practice*, 43, 292–99.

Hauser, S. T. (2002). The future of psychoanalytic research: Turning points and opportunities. *Journal of the American Psychoanalytic Association*, 50, 395–405.

Hauser, S. T. (2004). Creative alliances: Enhancing the interface between psychoanalysis and research. *Journal of the American Psychoanalytic Association*, 52, 385–91.

Heimann, P. (1969). Gedanken zum Erkenntnisprozeß des Psychoanalytikers [Thoughts on knowledge formation of the psychoanalyst]. *Psyche - Zeitschrift für Psychoanalyse*, 23, 2–24.

Heimann, P. (1977). Further observations on the analyst's cognitive process. *Journal of the American Psychoanalytic Association*, 25, 313–33.

Hempel, C. (1952). Problems of concept and theory formation in the social sciences. In American Philosophical Association—Eastern Division (Ed.), *Science, language, and human rights*. Philadelphia: University of Pennsylvania Press, pp. 65–86.

Hempel, C. (1965). *Aspects of scientific explanation*. Glencoe, IL: Free Press.

Hempel, C., & Oppenheim, P. (1953). The logic of explanation. In Feigl, H., & Brodbeck, M. (Eds.), *Readings in the philosophy of science*. New York: Appelton, pp. 319–52.

Herdan, G. (1966). *The advanced theory of language as choice and chance*. Wien: Springer.

Herold, G. (1995). *Übertragung und Widerstand* [Transference and resistance]. Ulm: Ulmer Textbank.

Hertz, N. (1983). Dora's secrets, Freud's techniques. In *Diacritics*, 65–83.

Hilgard, E. R. (1952). Experimental approaches to psychoanalysis. In Pumpian-Mindlin, E. (Ed.), *Psychoanalysis as science*. Stanford: Stanford University Press, pp. 2–45.

Hill, C., Castonguay, L. G., & Angus, L. (2007). Insight in psychotherapy: Definitions, processes, consequences, and research directions. In Castonguay, L. G., & Hill, C. (Eds.), *Insight in psychotherapy*. Washington, DC: American Psychological Association, pp. 441–54.

Hill, R. D., & Lambert, M. J. (2004). Methodological issues in studying psychotherapy processes and outcomes. In Lambert, M. J. (Ed.), *Bergin and Garfield's Handbook of psychotherapy and behavior change*. New York: John Wiley & Sons, pp. 84–135.

Hilliard, R. B. (1993). Single case methodology in psychotherapy process and outcome research. *Journal of Consulting and Clinical Psychology*, 61, 373–80.

Hinshelwood, R. D. (1989). *A dictionary of Kleinian thought*. London: Free Association Books.

Hohage, R. (1986). *Empirische Untersuchungen zur Theorie der emotionalen Einsicht* [Empirical studies on the theory of emotional insight]. Retrieved from http://sip.medizin.uni-ulm.de/ abteilung/buecher.detail.html

Hohage, R., & Kübler, J. C. (1987). Die Veränderung von emotionaler Einsicht im Verlauf einer Psychoanalyse [The change of emotional insight during a psychoanalysis]. *Zeitschrift für Psychosomatische Medizin und Psychoanalyse*, 33, 145–54.

Hohage, R., & Kübler, J. C. (1988). The emotional insight rating scale. In Dahl, H., Kächele, H., & Thomä, H. (Eds.), *Psychoanalytic process research strategies*. Berlin: Springer, pp. 243–55.

Holland, N. N. (1975). An identity for the Rat Man. *International Revue of Psychoanalysis*, 2, 157–69.

Holt, R. R. (1958). Clinical and statistical prediction. *Journal of Abnormal and Social Psychology*, 56, 1–12.

Holt, R. R. (1962). A critical examination of Freud's concept of bounds vs. free cathexis. *Journal of the American Psychoanalytic Association*, 10, 475–525.

Holt, R. R. (1965). A review of some of Freud's biological assumptions and their influence on his theories. In Greenfield, N. S., & Lewis, W. C. (Eds.), *Psychoanalysis and current biological thought*. Madison: University of Wisconsin Press, pp. 475–525.

Holt, R. R. (2002). Quantitative research on the primary process: Method and findings. *Journal of the American Psychoanalytic Association*, 50, 457–82.

Holt, R. R. (2005). A lifelong attempt to understand and assess personality. *Journal of Personality Assessment*, 84, 3–13.

Hölzer, M. (1996). Das *"Affektive Diktionär Ulm": Eine Methode zur computerunterstützten Erfassung psychotherapeutischer Emotionsverarbeitung* [The "affective dictionary Ulm": A method for computer assisted analysis of emotions]. Habilitation. Universität Ulm, Abteilung Psychotherapie.

Hölzer, M., Aeschelmann, D., Schwilk, C., & Kächele, H. (1993). Defense mechanisms and linguistic styles. *New Trends in Experimental and Clinical Psychiatry*, 9, 15–22.

Hölzer, M., & Dahl, H. (1996). How to find frames. *Psychotherapy Research*, 6, 177–97.

Hölzer, M., Dahl, H., Pokorny, D., & Kächele, H. (2007). A basic interpretative strategy in psychoanalytic treatments. *Psychotherapy Research*, submitted.

Hölzer, M., Mergenthaler, E., Pokorny, D., Kächele, H., & Luborsky, L. (1996). Vocabulary measures for the evaluation of therapy outcome: Re-studying the transcripts from the Penn Psychotherapy Project (PPP). *Psychotherapy Research*, 6, 95–108.

Hölzer, M., Pokorny, D., Kächele, H., & Luborsky, L. (1997). The verbalization of emotions in the therapeutic dialogue—A correlate of therapy outcome? *Psychotherapy Research*, 7, 261–73.

Hölzer, M., Scheytt, N., Pokorny, D., & Kächele, H. (1990). The "Affective Dictionary." A comparison between the Student and the Forward their emotional vocabulary. *Psychotherapie Psychosomatik Medizinische Psychologie Disk-Journal*, 1, 1.

Hook, S. (1959a). *Psychoanalysis. Scientific method and philosophy*. New York: International Universities Press.

Hook, S. (1959b). Science and mythology in psychoanalysis. In Hook, S. (Ed.), *Psychoanalysis. Scientific method and philosophy*. New York: International Universities Press, pp. 212–24.

Horowitz, L. (1977). Two classes of concomitant change in psychotherapy. In Freedman, N. & Grand, S. (Eds.), *Communicative structures and psychic structures*. New York: Plenum Press, pp. 419–40.

Horowitz, M. J. (1988). *Introduction to psychodynamics. A new synthesis*. New York: Basic Books.

Huber, D., & Klug, G. (2003). Contributions to the measurement of mode-specific effects in long-term psychoanalytic therapy. In Richardson, P., Kächele, H., & Renlund, C. (Eds.), *Research on psychoanalytic psychotherapy with adults*. London: Karnac, pp. 63–80.

Huber, D., & Klug, G. (2007). Scales of psychological capacities: The Munich contribution to their psychometric qualities. In Bucci, W., & Freedman, N. (Eds.), *From impression to inquiry: A tribute to the work of Robert Wallerstein*. London: International Psychoanalytical Association, pp. 97–134.

Ireland, M. S. (2004). Freudian and Lacanian approaches to the clinical case: Listening, interpretation, transference and countertransference. *International Journal of Psychoanalysis*, 85, 1251–55.

Isaacs, S. (1939). Criteria for interpretation. *International Journal of Psychoanalysis*, 20, 853–80.

Isaacs, K., & Haggard, E. A. (1966). Some methods used in the study of affect in psychotherapy. In Gottschalk, L. A., & Auerbach, A. H. (Eds.), *Methods of research in psychotherapy*. New York: Appleton-Century-Crofts, pp. 226–39.

Israels, H. (1989). *Schreber: Vater und Sohn. Eine Biographie* [Schreber: father and son. A biography]. München: Internationaler Psychoanalytischer Verlag.

Jaffe, D. (1958). Language of the dyad. A method of interaction analysis in psychiatric interviews. *Psychiatry*, 21, 249–58.

Jakobsen, T., Rudolf, G., Brockmann, J., Eckert, J., Huber, D., Klug, G., et al. (2007). Ergebnisse analytischer Langzeitpsychotherapie bei spezifischen psychischen Störungen: Verbesserungen in der Symptomatik und in interpersonellen Beziehungen [Results of psychoanalytic long term treatments with specific psychic disorders: Improvements in symptomatology and in interpersonal relationships]. *Zeitschrift für Psychosomatische Medizin und Psychotherapie*, 53, 87–110.

James, H. (1979). Review: Winnicott's piggle. *International Journal of Psychoanalysis*, 60, 130–39.

Jaspers, K. (1948). *Allgemeine Psychopathologie* [General psychopathology]. Berlin: Springer.

Jiménez, J. P. (2007). Can research influence clinical practice? *International Journal of Psychoanalysis*, 88, 661–79.

Johnson, W. (1944). Studies in language behavior: I. A program of research. *Psychological Monographs*, 56, 1–15.

Jones, E. (Ed.) (1949). *Selected papers of Karl Abraham*. London: Hogarth Press.

Jones, E. (1953). *The life and work of Sigmund Freud, vol. I*. New York: Basic Books.

Jones, E. (1955). *The life and work of Sigmund Freud, vol. II*. New York: Basic Books.

Jones, E. E. (1993). How will psychoanalysis study itself? *Journal of the American Psychoanalytic Association*, 41, 91–108.

Jones, E. E. (2000). *Therapeutic action: A guide to psychoanalytic therapy*. Northvale, NJ: Jason Aronson.

Jones, E. E., Hall, S. A., & Parke, L. A. (1991). The process of change: The Berkeley Psychotherapy Research Group. In Beutler, L. E., & Crago, M. (Eds.), *Psychotherapy research: An international review of programmatic studies*. Washington, DC: American Psychological Association, pp. 99–106.

Jones, E. E., & Price, P. B. (1998). Interaction structure and change in psychoanalytic psychotherapy. In Bornstein, R. F., & Masling, J. M. (Eds.), *Empirical studies of the therapeutic hour*. Washington, DC: American Psychological Association, pp. 27–62.

Jones, E. E., & Pulos, S. M. (1993). Comparing the process in psychodynamic and cognitive-behavioral therapies. *Journal of Consulting and Clinical Psychology*, 61, 985–1015.

Jones, E. E., & Windholz, M. (1990). The psychoanalytic case study: Toward a method for systematic inquiry. *Journal of the American Psychoanalytic Association*, 38, 985–1016.

Joseph, L., Anderson, E., Bernard, A., Father, K., & Streich, J. (2004). Assessing progress in analysis interminable. *Journal of the American Psychoanalytic Association*, 52, 1185–214.

Kächele, H. (1976). *Maschinelle Inhaltsanalyse in der psychoanalytischen Prozessforschung* [Computer based content analysis for psychoanalytic process research]. *Habilitationsschrift Medizinische Fakultät Universität Ulm*. Ulm: second ed. 1988 in PSZ-Verlag.

Kächele, H. (1981). Zur Bedeutung der Krankengeschichte in der klinisch-psychoanalytischen Forschung [On the relevance of case history in clinical psychoanalytic research]. *Jahrbuch der Psychoanalyse*, 12, 118–77.

Kächele, H. (1983a). Sprache im psychoanalytischen Dialog [Language in the psychoanalytic dialogue]. *Texte - Zur Theorie und Praxis der Psychoanalyse*, 3, 309–27.

Kächele, H. (1983b). Verbal activity level of therapists in initial interviews and long-term psychoanalysis. In Minsel, W. R., & Herff, W. (Eds.), *Methodology in psychotherapy research*. Frankfurt: Lang, pp. 125–29.

Kächele, H. (1986). Validating psychoanalysis: What methods for which task? *Behavioral and Brain Sciences*, 9, 2–44.

Kächele, H. (1988). Clinical and scientific aspects of the Ulm process model of psychoanalysis. *International Journal of Psychoanalysis*, 69, 65–73.

Kächele, H. (1990). Welche Methoden für welche Fragen? [What methods for which question?]. In Argelander, H. (Ed.), *Empirische Forschung in der Psychoanalyse* (vol. 10). Frankfurt: Sigmund Freud Institut, pp. 73–89.

Kächele, H. (1992). Psychoanalytische Therapieforschung, 1930–1990 [Psychoanalytic treatment research, 1930–1990]. *Psyche - Zeitschrift für Psychoanalyse*, 46, 259–85.

Kächele, H. (1995). Klaus Grawes Konfession und die psychoanalytische Profession [Klaus Grawe's confession and the psychoanalytic profession]. *Psyche - Zeitschrift für Psychoanalyse*, 5, 481–92.

Kächele, H. (2001). Book Review: Does psychoanalysis work? By Robert M. Galatzer-Levi, Henry Bachrach, Alan Skolnikoff, and Sherwood Waldron, New Haven, Yale University Press. *Journal of the American Psychoanalytic Association*, 49, 1041–47.

Kächele, H. (2005). The role of psychoanalytic treatment research in psychoanalytic training. Twenty good reasons. *International Journal of Psychotherapy*, 9, 53–60.

Kächele, H., Buchheim, A., Schmücker, G., & Brisch, K. H. (2001). Development, attachment and relationship: New psychoanalytic concepts. In Henn, F. A., Sartorius, N., Helmchen, H., & Lauter, H. (Eds.), *Contemporary psychiatry* (vol. 3). Berlin: Springer, pp. 358–70.

Kächele, H., Eberhardt, J., & Leuzinger-Bohleber, M. (1999). Expressed relationships, dream atmosphere & problem solving in Amalia's dreams—Dream series as process tool to investigate cognitive changes—A single case study. In Kächele, H., Mergenthaler, E., & Krause, R. (Eds.), *Psychoanalytic process research strategies II*. Retrieved from: http://sip.medizin.uni-ulm.de/abteilung/buecher.html

Kächele, H., Ehlers, W., & Hölzer, M. (1991). Experiment und Empirie in der Psychoanalyse [Experiment and empirical studies in psychoanalysis]. In Schneider, F., Bartels, M., Foerster, K., & Gaertner, H. J. (Eds.), *Perspektiven der Psychiatrie. Forschung—Diagnostik—Therapie*. Stuttgart: Gustav Fischer, pp. 129–42.

Kächele, H., Hölzer, M., & Mergenthaler, E. (1999). The analyst's vocabulary. In Fonagy, P., Cooper, A. M., & Wallerstein, R. S. (Eds.), *Psychoanalysis on the move: The work of Joseph Sandler*. London: Routledge, pp. 217–29.

Kächele, H., & Mergenthaler, E. (1983). Computer-aided analysis of psychotherapeutic discourse—A workshop. In Minsel, W.-R., & Herff, W. (Eds.), *Methodology in psychotherapy research. Proceedings of the 1st European Conference on Psychotherapy Research*. Frankfurt: Lang, pp. 116–61.

Kächele, H., & Mergenthaler, E. (1984). Auf dem Wege zur computerunterstützen Textanalyse in der psychotherapeutischen Prozessforschung [On the way to computer-assisted psychotherapeutic process research]. In Baumann, U. (Ed.), *Psychotherapie: Makro/Mikroperspektive*. Göttingen: Verlag für Psychologie Dr. Hogrefe, C J, pp. 223–39.

Kächele, H., Schaumburg, C., & Thomä, H. (1973). Verbatimprotokolle als Mittel in der psychotherapeutischen Verlaufsforschung [Transcripts as means in psychotherapeutic process research]. *Psyche - Zeitschrift für Psychoanalyse*, 27, 902–27.

Kächele, H., Schinkel, A., Schmieder, B., Leuzinger-Bohleber, M., & Thomä, H. (1999). Amalie X—Verlauf einer psychoanalytischen Therapie [Amalia X—The course of a psychoanalytic therapy]. *Colloquium Psychoanalyse*, 4, 67–83.

Kächele, H., & Thomä, H. (1993). Psychoanalytic process research: Methods and achievements. *Journal of the American Psychoanalytic Association*, 41, 109–29 Suppl.

Kächele, H., Thomä, H., Ruberg, W., & Grünzig, H.-J. (1988). Audio-recordings of the psychoanalytic dialogue: Scientific, clinical and ethical problems. In Dahl, H., Kächele, H., & Thomä, H. (Eds.), *Psychoanalytic process research strategies*. Berlin: Springer, pp. 179–94.

Kächele, H., Thomä, H., & Schaumburg, C. (1975). Veränderungen des Sprachinhaltes in einem psychoanalytischen Prozeß [Change of speech content in a psychoanalytic process]. *Schweizer Archiv für Neurologie, Neurochirurgie und Psychiatrie*, 116, 197–228.

Kafka, E. (2004). Book review: Bergmann M (Ed.), *The Hartmann era*. *Psychoanalytic Quarterly*, 73, 836–51.

Kafka, J. S. (1971). Ambiguity for individuation. *Archives of General Psychiatry*, 25, 232–39.

Kafka, J. S. (1989). How do we change? In Kafka, J. S. (Ed.), *Multiple realities in clinical practice*. New Haven, CT: Yale University Press, pp. 79–105.

Kaminski, G. (1970). *Verhaltenstheorie und Verhaltensmodifikation* [Theory of behavior and modification of behavior]. Stuttgart: Klett.

Kantrowitz, J. L. (1993). The uniqueness of the patient–analyst pair. Approaches for elucidating the analyst's role. *International Journal of Psychoanalysis*, 77, 893–904.

Kanzer, M. (1955). The communicative function of the dream. *International Journal of Psychoanalysis*, 36, 260–66.

Kanzer, M. (1966). The motor sphere of transference. *Psychoanalytic Quarterly*, 35, 522–39.

Kanzer, M. (1972). Book review: Muriel Gardiner (Ed.): *The Wolf-Man by the Wolf-Man*. Basic Books, New York. *International Journal of Psychoanalysis*, 53, 419–22.

Kaplan, A. (1964). *The conduct of inquiry*. San Francisco: Chandler.

Kardiner, A. (1957). The man I knew, the scientist, and his influence. In B. Nelson (Ed.), Freud and the twentieth century. New York: Jason Aronson. pp 46–58.

Katan, M. (1959). Schreber's hereafter. Its building-up and its downfall. *Psychoanalytic Study of the Child*, 14, 314–82.

Kazdin, A. E. (1982). *Single case research designs: Methods for clinical and applied settings*. Oxford: Oxford University Press.

Kazdin, A. E. (1994). Methodology, design, and evaluation in psychotherapy research. In Bergin, A. E., & Garfield, S. L. (Eds.), *Handbook of Psychotherapy and Behavior Change* (4th ed.). New York: John Wiley & Sons, pp. 19–71.

Kazdin, A. E. (2003) Research design in clinical psychology. Needham Heights, MA: Allyn & Bacon.

Kemmler, L., Schelp, T., & Mecheril, P. (1991). *Sprachgebrauch in der Psychotherapie. Emotionales Geschehen in vier Therapieschulen* [Use of language in psychotherapy. Emotionality in four schools of psychotherapy]. Bern: Huber.

Kernberg, O. F. (1986). Institutional problems of psychoanalytic education. *Journal of the American Psychoanalytic Association, 34,* 799–834.

Kernberg, P. (1994). Mechanisms of defense: Development and research perspectives. *Bulletin of the Menninger Clinic, 58,* 55–58.

Klann, G. (1977). Psychoanalyse und Sprachwissenschaft [Psychoanalysis and science of language]. In Hager, F. (Ed.), *Die Sache der Sprache* [The issue of language]. Stuttgart: Metzler'sche Verlagsbuchhandung, pp. 129–67.

Klann, G. (1979). Die Rolle affektiver Prozesse in der Dialogstruktur [The role of affective processes in the structure of dialogue]. In Flader, D., & Wodak-Leodolter, R. (Eds.), *Therapeutische Kommunikation.* Königstein: Scriptor, pp. 117–55.

Klauber, J. (1968). On the dual use of historical and scientific method in psychoanalysis. *International Journal of Psychoanalysis, 49,* 80–87.

Klein, G. S. (1976). *Psychoanalytic theory. An exploration of essentials.* New York: International Universities Press.

Klein, M. (1961). *Narrative of a child analysis.* London: Hogarth.

Klein, M., Mathieu, P. L., Gendlin, E. T., & Kiesler, D. J. (1970). *The experiencing scale: A research and training manual* (vol. 1 and 2). Madison, WI: Psychiatric Institute, Bureau of Audio Visual Instruction.

Kline, P. (1981). *Fact and fantasy in Freudian theory* (2d. ed.). London: Methuen.

Klumpner, G. H. (1992). *A guide to the language of psychoanalysis: An empirical study of the relationships among psychoanalytic terms and concepts.* Madison, CT: International Universities Press.

Klumpner, G. H. (2007). The Open Access project: origins and new directions. In Bucci, W., & Freedman, N. (Eds.), *From impression to inquiry.* London: International Psychoanalytical Association, pp. 137–51.

Klumpner, G. H., & Frank, A. (1991). On methods of reporting clinical material. *Journal of the American Psychoanalytic Association, 39,* 537–51.

Knapp, P. H., Greenberg, R. P., Pearlman, C. H., Cohen, M., Kantrowitz, J., & Sashin, J. (1975). Clinical measurement in psychoanalysis: An approach. *Psychoanalytic Quarterly, 44,* 404–30.

Knapp, P. H., Mushatt, C., & Nemetz, S. J. (1966). Collection and utilization of data in a psychoanalytic psychosomatic study. In Gottschalk, L. A., & Auerbach, A. H. (Eds.), *Methods of research in psychotherapy.* New York: Appleton-Century-Crofts, pp. 401–22.

Knoblauch, S. (2000). *The musical edge of therapeutic dialogue.* Hillsdale, NJ: Analytic Press.

Koerfer, A., & Neumann, C. (1982). Alltagsdiskurs und psychoanalytischer Diskurs [Everyday discourse and psychoanalytic discourse]. In Flader, D., Grodizcki, W.-D., & Schröter, K. (Eds.), *Psychoanalyse als Gespräch. Interaktionsanalytische Untersuchungen über Therapie und Supervision.* Frankfurt: Suhrkamp, pp. 96–137.

Kohut, H. (1959). Introspection, empathy, and psychoanalysis. An examination of the relationship between mode of observation and theory. *Journal of the American Psychoanalytic Association, 7,* 459–83.

Kohut, H. (1971). *The analysis of the self. A systematic approach to the psychoanalytic treatment of narcissistic personality disorders.* New York: International Universities Press.

Kohut, H. (1977). *The restoration of the self.* New York: International Universities Press.

Kohut, H. (1979a). The two analyses of Mr. Z. *International Journal of Psychoanalysis,* 60, 3–27.

Kohut, H. (1979b). *Die Heilung des Selbst (The restoration of the self)* (1st ed.). Frankfurt am Main: Suhrkamp.

Kohut, H. (1984). *How does analysis cure?* Chicago: University of Chicago Press.

König, H. (1993). *Zur Naturalisierung psychoanalytischer Prozesse* [On the naturalization of psychoanalytic processes]. Promotion (Dr. phil.). Universität Tübingen.

Koppe, F. (1979). Hermeneutik der Lebensformen—Hermeneutik als Lebensform. Zur Sozialphilosophie Peter Winschs [Hermeneutics of forms of living—Hermeneutics as form of living. On the social philosophy of Peter Winsch]. In Mittelstraß, J. (Ed.), *Methodenprobleme der Wissenschaften vom gesellschaftlichen Handeln* [Problems of method in the sciences of social action]. Frankfurt am Main: Suhrkamp, pp. 223–72.

Krause, R. (1997). *Allgemeine psychoanalytische Krankheitslehre: Band 1 Grundlagen* [General psychoanalytic theory of disorder, Vol. 1 Basic principles]. Stuttgart: Kohlhammer.

Krause, R., & Lütolf, P. (1988). Facial indicators of transference processes within psychoanalytic treatment. In Dahl, H., Kächele, H., & Thomä, H. (Eds.), *Psychoanalytic process research strategies.* Berlin: Springer, pp. 241–56.

Krause, R., Steimer-Krause, E., & Ulrich, B. (1992). Use of affect research in dynamic psychotherapy. In Leuzinger-Bohleber, M., Schneider, H., & Pfeifer, R. (Eds.), *"Two Butterflies on my Head ..." Psychoanalysis in the interdisciplinary dialogue.* Berlin: Springer, pp. 277–91.

Kris, E. (1951). Ego psychology and interpretation in psychoanalytic therapy. *Psychoanalytic Quarterly,* 20, 15–30.

Kris, E. (1954). Introduction. In Bonaparte, M. F. A., & Kris, E. (Eds.) *S. Freud: The origins of psycho-analyis.* London: Imago Publishing Company, pp. 1–47.

Kris, E. (1956). On some vicissitudes of insight in psychoanalysis. *International Journal of Psychoanalysis,* 37, 445–55.

Krugmann, P. (2007, February 15). Who was Milton Friedman? *New York Review of Books,* 54, 27–30.

Kubie, L. S. (1952). Problems and techniques of psychoanalytic validation and progress. In Pumpian-Mindlin, E. (Ed.), *Psychoanalysis as science. The Hixon lectures on the scientific status of psychoanalysis.* New York: Basic Books, pp. 46–124.

Kubie, L. S. (1958). Research into the process of supervision in psychoanalysis. *Psychoanalytic Quarterly,* 27, 226–36.

Kubie, L. S. (1974). The drive to become both sexes. *Psychoanalytic Quarterly,* 43, 349–426.

Kuhn, T. S. (1962). *The structure of scientific revolutions.* Chicago: University of Chicago Press.

Kuiper, P. C. (1964). Verstehende Psychologie und Psychoanalyse [Hermeneutic psychology and psychoanalysis]. *Psyche -Zeitschrift für Psychoanalyse*, 18, 15–32.

Kuiper, P. C. (1965). Diltheys Psychologie und ihre Beziehung zur Psychoanalyse [The psychology of Dilthey and its relation to psychoanalysis]. *Psyche - Zeitschrift für Psychoanalyse*, 19, 241–49.

Kunz, H. (1975). Die Erweiterung des Menschenbildes in der Psychoanalyse Sigmund Freuds [The expansion of the image of man by psychoanalysis]. In Gadamer, H. G., & Vogler, P. (Eds.), *Neue Anthropologie*. Stuttgart: Thieme, pp. 44–113.

Labov, W., & Fanshel, D. (1977). *Therapeutic discourse. Psychotherapy as conversation*. New York: Academic Press.

Lacan, J. (1953). Fonction et champ de la parole et du langage en psychanalyse. In Lacan, J. (Ed.), *Écrits*. Paris: Éditions du Seuil, pp. 237–322.

Lacan, J. (1959). D'une question préliminaire à tout traitement possible de la psychose. In Lacan, J. (Ed.), *Ecrits*. Paris: Editions du Seuil. 1966, pp. 531–83.

Laffal, J. (1965). *Pathological and normal language*. New York: Atherton Press.

Laffal, J. (1967). Characteristics of the three-person conversation. *Journal of Verbal Learning and Verbal Behavior*, 6, 555–s9.

Laffal, J. (1976). Schreber's memoirs and content analysis. *Journal of Nervous and Mental Disease*, 162, 385–90.

Lakoff, G. (1997). How unconscious metaphorical thought shapes dreams. In Stein, D. (Ed.), *Cognitive science and the unconscious*. New York: American Psychoanalytic Association, pp. 89–120.

Lakoff, R. T. (1981). *The rationale of psychotherapeutic discourse*. Berkeley: mimeo.

Lambert, M. J. (Ed.) (2004). *Bergin and Garfield's Handbook of psychotherapy and behavior change* (5th ed.). New York: John Wiley and Sons.

Langs, R. (1976). The misalliance dimension in Freud's case histories: I. The case of Dora. *International Journal of Psychoanalytic Psychotherapy*, 5, 301–17.

Laplanche, J., & Pontalis, J. B. (1967). *Vocabulaire de la psychanalyse*. Paris: Presses Universitaires de France.

Lasswell, H. D. (1933). Psychoanalyse und Sozioanalyse [Psychoanalysis and socioanalysis]. *Imago*, 19, 378–83.

Lear, J. (1998). Open minded: Working out the logic of the soul. Cambridge, MA: Harvard University Press.

Leavy, S. A. (1980). *The psychoanalytic dialogue*. New Haven, CT: Yale University Press.

Lebovici, S., & Soulé, M. (1970). *La connaissance de l'enfant par la psychanalyse*. Paris: Presses Universitaires de France.

Leichsenring, F. (2008). Efficacy, indications and applications of psychodynamic psychotherapy to specific disorders. In Gabbard, G. (Ed.), *Psychiatry*. New York: American Psychiatric Publishing. In press.

Leichsenring, F., Biskup, J., Kreische, R., & Staats, H. (2005). The Göttingen study of psychoanalytic therapy. *International Journal of Psychoanalysis*, 86, 433–55.

Lepper, G., & Mergenthaler, E. (2005). Exploring group process. *Psychotherapy Research*, 15, 433–44.

Lepper, G., & Mergenthaler, E. (2007). Therapeutic collaboration: How does it work? *Psychotherapy Research*, 17, 576–87.

Leuschner, W., & Hau, S. (Eds.) (1995). *Traum und Gedächtnis* [Dream and memory]. Münster: LIT Verlag.

Leuzinger, M. (1984). *Psychotherapeutische Denkprozesse* [Psychotherapeutic thought processes]. Ulm: PSZ-Verlag.

Leuzinger-Bohleber, M. (1989). *Veränderung kognitiver Prozesse in Psychoanalysen. Bd 2: Eine gruppen-statistische Untersuchung [Change of cognitive processes in psychoanalyses. Vol. 2 A group-statistical study].* Berlin: Springer.

Leuzinger-Bohleber, M. (1995). Die Einzelfallstudie als psychoanalytisches Forschungsinstrument [The single case study as psychoanalytic research instrument]. *Psyche - Zeitschrift für Psychoanalyse, 49,* 434–80.

Leuzinger-Bohleber, M., Dreher, A. U., & Canestri, J. (Eds.) (2003). *Pluralism and unity? Methods of research in psychoanalysis.* London: International Psychoanalytical Association.

Leuzinger-Bohleber, M., & Fischmann, T. (2006). What is conceptual research in psychoanalysis? *International Journal of Psychoanalysis, 87,* 1355–86.

Leuzinger-Bohleber, M., & Kächele, H. (1988). From Calvin to Freud: Using an artificial intelligence model to investigate cognitive changes during psychoanalysis. In Dahl, H., Kächele, H., & Thomä, H. (Eds.), *Psychoanalytic process research strategies.* Berlin: Springer, pp. 291–306.

Leuzinger-Bohleber, M., Stuhr, U., Rüger, B., & Beutel, M. (2003). How to study the quality of psychoanalytic treatments and their long term effects on patients' well-being. A representative multiperspective follow-up study. *International Journal of Psychoanalysis, 84,* 263–90.

Levi, L. H. (1963). *Psychological interpretation.* New York: Holt, Reinhart and Winston.

Levine, S. (2005). Freud and Dora: 100 years later. *Psychoanalytic Inquiry, 25,* 1–115.

Lewin, K. (1937). Psychoanalysis and topological psychology. *Bulletin of the Menninger Clinic, 1,* 202–12.

Libermann, D. (1970). *Linguistica, interaccion comunicativa y proceso psicoanalitico, vol 1–3.* Buenos Aires: Galerna.

Lichtenstein, H. (1961). Identity and sexuality. *Journal of the American Psychoanalytic Association, 9,* 179–260.

Lienert, G. (1969). *Testaufbau und Testanalyse* [The construction of tests and its analysis]. Weinheim: Beltz.

Lingiardi, V., Shedler, J., & Gazillo, F. (2006). Assessing personality change in psychotherapy with the SWAP-200: A case study. *Journal of Personality Assessment, 86,* 23–32.

Liotti, G. (1999). Understanding the dissociative process: The contribution of attachment theory. *Psychoanalytic Inquiry, 19,* 757–83.

Lipton, S. (1977). Freud's technique and the Rat Man. *International Journal of Psychoanalysis, 58,* 255–74.

Litowitz, B. E. (2005). When "something more" is less: Commentary on the Boston Change Process Study Group. *Journal of the American Psychoanalytic Association, 53,* 751–59.

Little, M. (1990). *Psychotic anxieties and containment. A personal record of an analysis with Winnicott.* Northvale, NJ: Jason Aronson.

Loch, W. (1965). *Voraussetzungen, Mechanismen und Grenzen des psychoanaly-tischen Prozesses* [Preconceptions, mechanisms and limitations of the psycho-analytic process]. Bern: Huber.

Loch, W., & Jappe, G. (1974). Die Konstruktion der Wirklichkeit und die Phanta-sien [On the construction of reality and the phantasies]. *Psyche -Zeitschrift für Psychoanalyse*, 28, 1–31.

Loewald, H. W. (1960). On the therapeutic action of psychoanalysis. *International Journal of Psychoanalysis*, 41, 16–33.

Loewald, H. W. (1971). On motivation and instinct theory. *Psychoanalytic Study of the Child*, 26, 91–128.

Loewenstein, R. M. (1951). The problem of interpretation. *Psychoanalytic Quar-terly*, 20, 1–14.

Lorenz, M. (1953). Language as expressive behavior. *Archives of Neurology and Psychiatry*, 70, 277–85.

Lorenz, M., & Cobb, S. (1975). *Language and a woman's place*. New York: Harper & Row.

Lorenzer, A. (1970). *Sprachzerstörung und Rekonstruktion. Vorarbeiten zu einer Metatheorie der Psychoanalyse* [Language destruction and its reconstruction. Studies on a metatheory of psychoanalysis]. Frankfurt am Main: Suhrkamp.

Lorenzer, A. (1985). Das Verhältnis der Psychoanalyse zu ihren Nachbarsdisziplinen [The relationship of psychoanalysis to its neighbouring disciplines]. *Fragmente*, 14–15, 8–22.

Lothane, Z. (2005). Daniel Paul Schreber on his own terms: Or how interpretative fictions are converted into historical facts. In Steinberg, H. (Ed.), *Leipziger Psychiatriegeschichtliche Vorlesungen. Reihe B Band 7*. Leipzig: Evangelische Verlagsanstalt, pp. 129–56.

Lowenfeld, Y. (1975). Rezension T. Moser: Lehrjahre auf der Couch [Review of T. Moser: Years of apprenticeship on the couch]. *Psyche - Zeitschrift für Psycho-analyse*, 29, 186–88.

Luborsky, L. (1953). Intraindividual repetitive measurements (P-technique) in under-standing psychotherapeutic change. In Mowrer, O. H. (Ed.), *Psychotherapy—Theory and research*. New York: Ronald Press, pp. 389–413.

Luborsky, L. (1967). Momentary forgetting during psychotherapy and psychoanaly-sis: a theory and research method. In R. R. Holt (Ed), Motives and thought: Psychoanalytic essays in honor of David Rapaport. New York: International University Press. pp 177–217.

Luborsky, L. (1976). Helping alliance in psychotherapy: the groundwork for a study of their relationship to its outcome. In Claghorn, J. L. (Ed.), *Successful psycho-therapy*. New York: Brunner, Mazel, pp. 92–116.

Luborsky, L. (1977). Measuring a pervasive psychic structure in psychotherapy: The core conflictual relationship theme. In Freedman, N., & Grand, S. (Eds.), *Com-municative structures and psychic structures*. New York: Plenum Press, pp. 367–95.

Luborsky, L. (1984). *Principles of psychoanalytic psychotherapy. A manual for sup-portive-expressive treatment*. New York: Basic Books.

Luborsky, L. (1995). The first trial of P-technique in psychotherapy research. A still-lively legacy. *Journal of Consulting and Clinical Psychology*, 63, 6–14.

Luborsky, L. (Ed.) (1996). *The Symptom-Context Method. Symptoms as opportunities in psychotherapy*. Washington, DC: American Psychological Association.

Luborsky, L. (2000). A pattern-setting therapeutic alliance study revisited. *Psychotherapy Research*, 10, 17–29.

Luborsky, L., Albani, C., & Eckert, R. (1992). Manual zur ZBKT-Methode [German Manual of the CCRT-method]. *Psychotherapie Psychosomatik Medizinische Psychologie - DiskJournal*, 5.

Luborsky, L., & Crits-Christoph, P. (1988). Measures of psychoanalytic concepts— The last decade of research from the "The Penn Studies." *International Journal of Psychoanalysis*, 69, 75–86.

Luborsky, L., & Crits-Christoph, P. (1998). *Understanding transference* (2d ed.). New York: Basic Books.

Luborsky, L., Crits-Christoph, P., Friedman, S. H., Mark, D., & Schaffler, P. (1991). Freud's transference template compared with the Core Conflictual Relationship Theme (CCRT): Illustrations by the two specimen cases. In Horowitz, M. J. (Ed.), *Person schemas and maladaptive interpersonal behavior*. Chicago: University of Chicago Press, pp. 167–95.

Luborsky, L., Crits-Christoph, P., Mintz, J., & Auerbach, A. H. (1988). *Who will benefit from psychotherapy?* New York: Basic Books.

Luborsky, L., & Diguer, L. (1990). The reliability of the CCRT measure: Results from eight samples. In Luborsky, L., & Crits-Christoph, P. (Eds.), *Understanding transference: The CCRT method*. New York: Basic Books, pp. 97–108.

Luborsky, L., Diguer, L., Kächele, H., et al. (1999). A guide to the CCRT's methods, discoveries and future. http://sip.medizin.uni-ulm.de/abteilung/buecher.html

Luborsky, L., Docherty, J. P., Barber, J. P., & Miller, N. E. (1993). How this basic handbook helps the partnership of clinicians and clinical researchers: Preface. In Miller, N. E., Luborsky, L., Barber, J. P., & Docherty, J. P. (Eds.), *Psychodynamic treatment research. A handbook for clinical practice*. New York: Basic Books, pp. ix–xxvi.

Luborsky, L., Mintz, J., Auerbach, A. H., & et al. (1980). Predicting the outcomes of psychotherapy. Findings of the Penn psychotherapy project. *Archives of General Psychiatry*, 37, 471–81.

Luborsky, L., & Schimek, J. (1964). Psychoanalytic theories of therapeutic and developmental change implications for assessment. In Worchel, P., & Byrne, D. (Eds.), *Personality change*. New York: Wiley, pp. 73–99.

Luborsky, L., Singer, B., & Luborsky, L. (1975). Comparative studies of psychotherapy: Is it true that "Everybody has won and all must have prizes?" *Archives of General Psychiatry*, 32, 995–1008.

Luborsky, L., & Spence, D. P. (1971). Quantitative research on psychoanalytic therapy. In Bergin, A., & Garfield, S. (Eds.), *Handbook of psychotherapy and behavior change*. New York: John Wiley and Sons, pp. 408–38.

Luborsky, L., & Spence, D. P. (1978). Quantitative research on psychoanalytic therapy. In Garfield, S. L., & Bergin, A. E. (Eds.), *Handbook of psychotherapy and behavior change* (2d ed.). New York: John Wiley and Sons, pp. 331–68.

Luborsky, L., Stuart, J., Friedman, S. H., Diguer, L., Seligman, D. A., Bucci, W., et al. (2001). The Penn Psychoanalytic Treatment Collection: A set of complete and recorded psychoanalyses as a research resource. *Journal of the American Psychoanalytic Association*, 49, 217–34.

Luder, M. (2006). *JAKOB Report 2005. Die Entwicklung der Erzählanalyse JAKOB von 1989 bis 2005* [The development of the narrative analysis JAKOB from 1989 until 2005]. Psychologisches Institut Zürich: Klinische Psychologie, Psychotherapie und Psychoanalyse.

Luyten, P., Blatt, S. J., & Corveleyn, J. (2006). Minding the gap between positivism and hermeneutics in psychoanalytic research. *Journal of the American Psychoanalytic Association, 54*, 571–610.

MacAlpine, I. (1953). The Schreber-Case: A contribution to schizophrenia, hypochondria and psychosomatic symptom formation. *Psychoanalytic Quarterly, 22*, 328–71.

MacAlpine, I., & Hunter, R. A. (Eds.) (1955). *D. P. Schreber: Memoirs of my illness.* London: Dawson and Sons.

MacIntyre, A. C. (1958). *The unconscious. A conceptual analysis.* London: Routledge.

Mack-Brunswik, R. (1928). A supplement to Freud's "History of an infantile neurosis." *International Journal of Psychoanalysis, 9*, 439–76.

Madison, P. (1961). *Freud's concept of repression and defense, its theoretical and observational language.* Minneapolis: University of Minnesota Press.

Mahl, G. F. (1959). Exploring emotional states by content analysis. In Pool, I. (Ed.), *Trends in content analysis.* Urbana: University of Illinois Press.

Mahl, G. F. (1961). Measures of two expressive aspects of patient's speech in two psychotherapeutic interviews. In Gottschalk, L. A. (Ed.), *Comparative psycholinguistic analysis of two psychotherapeutic interviews.* New York: International Universities Press, pp. 91–114.

Mahler, M. S. (1969). On human symbiosis and the vicissitudes of individuation. London: Hogarth.

Mahony, P. J. (1977). The place of psychoanalytic treatment in the history of discourse. *Psychoanalysis and Contempory Thought, 2*, 77–111.

Mahony, P. J. (1982). *Freud as a writer.* New York: International Universities Press.

Mahony, P. J. (1984). *Cries of the Wolf Man.* New York: International Universities Press.

Mahony, P. J. (1986). *Freud and the Rat Man.* New Haven, CT: Yale University Press.

Mahony, P. J. (2005). Freud's unadorned and unadorable: A case history terminable and unterminable. *Psychoanalytic Inquiry, 25*, 27–44.

Main, M. (1991). Metacognitive knowledge, metacognitive monitoring, and singular (coherent) vs. multiple models (incoherent) of attachment. In Parkes, C. M., Stevenson-Hinde, J., & Marris, P. (Eds.), *Attachment across life cycle.* London, New York: Tavistock, pp. 127–59.

Main, M. (1995). Recent studies in attachment: Overview, with selected implications for clinical work. In Goldberg, S., Muir, R., & Kerr, J. (Eds.), *Attachment theory: Social, developmental, and clinical perspectives.* Hilldale, NJ: Analytic Press, Inc. pp 407–474.

Main, M., & Goldwyn, R. (1996). *Adult attachment scoring and classification systems.* Unpublished manuscript. University of California, Berkeley.

Main, M., & Hesse, E. (1990). Parents' unresolved traumatic experiences are related to infant disorganized attachment status: is frightened and/or frightening parental behavior the linking mechanism? In Greenberg, M. T., Cicchetti, D., & Cummings, E. M. (Eds.), *Attachment in the preschool years.* Chicago: University of Chicago Press, pp. 161–84.

Malan, D. H. (1963). *A study of brief psychotherapy*. London: Tavistock.

Malan, D. H. (1975). Book review: Focal psychotherapy: An example of applied psychoanalysis. By M Balint, P. H. Ornstein and E. Balint. *International Journal of Psychoanalysis*, 56, 115–17.

Malcolm, J. (1980). *Psychoanalysis: The impossible profession*. New York: Knopf.

Maldavsky, D. (Ed.) (2005). *Systematic research on psychoanalytic concepts and clinical practice*. Buenos Aires: UCES.

Marcus, S. (1976). Freud and Dora: story, history, case history. In Shapiro, T. (Ed.), *Psychoanalysis and contemporary science*: 5. New York: International Universities Press, pp. 389–442.

Marsden, G. (1971). Content analysis studies of psychotherapies. In Bergin, A. E., & Garfield, S. L. (Eds.), *Handbook of psychotherapy and behavior change*. New York: John Wiley and Sons, pp. 345–407.

Masling, J. M. (Ed.) (1983). *Empirical studies of psychoanalytical theories* (vol. 1). Hillsdale, NJ: Analytic Press.

Masling, J. M. (Ed.) (1986). *Empirical studies of psychoanalytical theories* (vol. 2). Hillsdale, NJ: Analytic Press.

Masling, J. M., & Bornstein, R. F. (Eds.) (1996). *Empirical studies of psychoanalytical theories: Psychoanalytic perspectives on developmental psychology* (vol. 6). Washington, DC: American Psychological Association.

Masling, J., & Cohen, J. (1987). Psychotherapy, clinical evidence and the self-fulfilling prophecy. *Psychoanalytic Psychology*, 4, 65–79.

Mayes, L. C. (2005). Something is different but what or why is unclear: Commentary on the Boston Change Process Study Group. *Journal of the American Psychoanalytic Association*, 53, 745–50.

Mayman, M. (Ed.) (1973). *Psychoanalytic research. Three approaches to the experimental study of subliminal processes*. New York: International Universities Press.

Mayman, M. (1973). Reflections on psychoanalytic research. In Mayman, M. (Ed.), *Psychoanalytic research. Three approaches to the experimental study of subliminal processes*. New York: International Universities Press, pp. 1–10.

Mayring, P. (1993). *Qualitative Inhaltsanalyse. Grundlagen und Techniken* [Qualitative content analysis. Foundations and techniques]. Weinheim: Beltz.

McDougall, J., & Lebovici, S. (1969). *Dialogue with Sammy*. London: Hogarth.

Meehl, P. E. (1963). *Clinical versus statistical prediction*. Minneapolis: University of Minnesota Press.

Meehl, P. E. (1973). Some methodological reflections of the difficulties of psychoanalytic research. In Mayman, H. (Ed.), *Psychoanalytic research. Three approaches to the experimental study of subliminal processes*. New York: International Universities Press, pp. 104–17.

Meehl, P. E. (1983). Subjectivity in psychoanalytic inference: The nagging persistence of Wilhelm Fliess's Achensee question. In Earman, J. (Ed.), *Testing scientific theories. Minnesota studies in the philosophy of science* (vol. 10). Minneapolis: University of Minnesota Press, pp. 349–411.

Meissner, W. W. (1971). Freud's methodology. *Journal of the American Psychoanalytic Association*, 19, 265–309.

Meissner, W. W. (1976). Schreber and the paranoid process. *Annual of Psychoanalysis*, 4, 3–40.

Meissner, W. W. (1983). Values in the psychoanalytic situation. *Psychoanalytic Inquiry*, 3, 577–98.

Meltzer, D. (1967). *The psychoanalytic process*. London: Heinemann.

Meltzer, D. (1978). *The Kleinian development: Part II, Richard week-by-week*. Perthshire: Clunie.

Menaker, A. (1995). *The relationship between attributional style and interpersonal guilt*. Unpublished doctoral dissertation, California School of Professional Psychology, Alameda.

Mergenthaler, E. (1985). *Textbank systems. Computer science applied in the field of psychoanalysis*. Berlin: Springer.

Mergenthaler, E. (1996). Emotion-abstraction patterns in verbatim protocols: A new way of describing psychotherapeutic processes. *Journal of Consulting and Clinical Psychology*, 64, 1306–15.

Mergenthaler, E. (2000). The Therapeutic Cycle Model in Psychotherapy Research: Theory, measurement, and clinical application. *Ricerche sui Gruppi*, 10, 34–40.

Mergenthaler , E. (2008). Resonating minds. Presidential address to the Society for Psychotherapy Research. Madison 2007. *Psychotherapy Research*, in press.

Mergenthaler, E., & Bucci, W. (1999). Linking verbal and non-verbal representations: Computer analysis of referential activity. *British Journal of Medical Psychology*, 72, 339–54.

Mergenthaler, E., & Kächele, H. (1985). Changes of latent meaning structures in psychoanalysis. *Sprache und Datenverarbeitung*, 9, 21–28.

Mergenthaler, E., & Kächele, H. (1988). The Ulm Textbank management system: A tool for psychotherapy research. In Dahl, H., Kächele, H., & Thomä, H. (Eds.), *Psychoanalytic process research strategies*. Berlin: Springer, pp. 195–212.

Mergenthaler, E., & Kächele, H. (1993). Locating text archives for psychotherapy research. In Miller, N., Luborsky, L., Barber, J., & Docherty, J. (Eds.), *Psychodynamic treatment research—A guide for clinical practice*. New York: Basic Books, pp. 54–62.

Mergenthaler, E., & Pokorny, D. (1989). Die Wortarten-Verteilung: eine linguo-statistische Textanalyse [The distribution of text types: a linguo-statistical text analysis]. In Faulbaum, F., Haux, R., & Jöckel, H. (Eds.), *SoftStat 89. Fortschritte der Statistik- Software 2*. Stuttgart: Fischer, pp. 512–21.

Mergenthaler, E., & Stinson, C. H. (1992). Transcription standards. *Psychotherapy Research*, 2, 125–42.

Merkle, G. (1987). *Veränderungen des Trauminhaltes während einer Psychoanalyse: Veränderungen des Mozart-Kontextes im Modell kognitiver Prozesse* [Change of dream content during a psychoanalytic treatment: Changes in the MOZART-context in a model of cognitive processes]. Medizinische Dissertation. Universität Ulm, Abteilung Psychotherapie.

Merton, R. K. (1957). The self-fulfilling prophecy. In Merton, R. K. (Ed.), *Social theory and social structure*. (Enl. Ed.). New York: The Free Press of Glencoe, pp. 475–90.

Messer, S. B. (2007). Psychoanalytic case studies and the pragmatic case study method. *Pragmatic Case Studies in Psychotherapy*, 3, 55–58.

Messer, S. B., & McCann, L. (2005). Research perspectives on the case study: Single-case study method. In J. S. Auerbach, K. N. Levy, & E. C. Schaffer (Eds.), *Relatedness, self-definition and mental representation: Essays in honor of Sidney J. Blatt*. New York: Routledge. pp. 222–37.

Messer, S. B., & McWilliams, N. (2007). Insight in psychodynamic therapy: Theory and assessment. In Castonguay, L. G., & Hill, C. (Eds.), *Insight in psychotherapy*. Washington, DC: American Psychological Association, pp. 9–29.

Meyer, A. E. (1963). *Zur Endokrinologie und Psychologie intersexueller Frauen* [On the endocrinology and psychology of intersexual women]. Stuttgart: Enke.

Meyer, A. E. (1981). Psychoanalytische Prozessforschung zwischen der Skylla der "Verkürzung" und der Charybdis der "systematischen akustischen Lücke" [Psychoanalytic process research between the scylla of shortening and the deep blue sea of "systematical acoustical gap"]. *Zeitschrift für Psychosomatische Medizin und Psychoanalyse*, 27, 103–16.

Meyer, A. E. (1988). What makes psychoanalysts tick? In Dahl, H., Kächele, H., & Thomä, H. (Eds.), *Psychoanalytic process research strategies*. Berlin: Springer, pp. 273–90.

Meyer, A. E. (1994). Nieder mit der Novelle als Psychoanalysedarstellung—Hoch lebe die Interaktionsgeschichte [To hell with the novella as means of representing psychoanalytic treatments—Let us praise the report of interactions]. *Zeitschrift für Psychosomatische Medizin und Psychoanalyse*, 40, 77–98.

Meyer, A. E., & von Zerssen, D. (1960). Psychologische Untersuchungen an Frauen mit Hirsutismus [Psychological studies on women with hirsutism]. *Journal of Psychosomatic Research*, 4, 206–35.

Michels, R. (1999). Psychoanalysts' theories. In Fonagy, P., Cooper, A. M., & Wallerstein, R. S. (Eds.), *Psychoanalysis on the move: The work of Joseph Sandler*. London: Routledge, pp. 187–200.

Michels, R. (2000). The case history. With commentaries by Sydney Pulver, Stephen B. Bernstein, Philip Rubovits-Seitz, Imre Szecsödy, David Tuckett, Arnold Wilson. *Journal of the American Psychoanalytic Association*, 48, 355–75.

Midgley, N. (2006). The "inseparable bond between cure and research": Clinical case study as a method of psychoanalytic inquiry. *Journal of Child Psychotherapy*, 32, 122–47.

Mijolla, A. (2003). Freud and psychoanalytic research: a brief historical overview. In Leuzinger-Bohleber, M., Dreher, A. U., & Canestri, J. (Eds.), *Pluralism and unity? Methods of research in psychoanalysis*. London: International Psychoanalytical Association, pp. 81–96.

Miller, N. E., Luborsky, L., Barber, J. P., & Docherty, J. P. (Eds.) (1993). *Psychodynamic treatment research. A handbook for clinical practice*. New York: Basic Books.

Mills, J. (2007). A response to Grünbaum's refutation of psychoanalysis. *Psychoanalytic Psychology*, 24, 539–44.

Milner, M. (1969). *The hands of the living god. An account of a psychoanalytic treatment*. London: Hogarth.

Mitchell, S. A. (1998). The analyst's knowledge and authority. *Psychoanalytic Quarterly*, 67, 1–31.

Mitscherlich, A. (1947). Vom Ursprung der Sucht [The origin of addiction]. In Mitscherlich, A. (Ed.), *Gesammelte Schriften, Vol. 1: Psychosomatik*. Frankfurt: Suhrkamp, pp. 141–404.

Mitscherlich, A., & Vogel, H. (1965). Psychoanalytische Motivationstheorie [Psychoanalytic theories of motivation]. In Thomae, H. (Ed.), *Handbuch der Psychologie. 2. Band Allgemeine Psychologie. II. Motivation*. Göttingen: Hogrefe, pp. 759–93.

Modell, A. H. (1965). On having the right to a life: An aspect of the superego's development. *International Journal of Psychoanalysis*, 46, 323–31.

Moore, G. E. (1955). Wittgenstein's lectures in 1930–1933. In Moore, G. E. (Ed.), *Philosophical papers*. London: Allen & Unwin, pp. 252–324.

Moran, G., & Fonagy, P. (1987). Psychoanalysis and diabetes: An experiment in single case methodology. *British Journal of Medical Psychology*, 60, 357–72.

Moser, T. (1974). *Lehrjahre auf der Couch. Bruckstücke meiner Psychoanalyse* [Apprenticeship on the couch. Fragments of my analysis]. Frankfurt am Main: Suhrkamp.

Moser, U. (1991). On-Line und Off-Line, Praxis und Forschung, eine Bilanz [On-line and off-line, practice and research, drawing a balance]. *Psyche - Zeitschrift für Psychoanalyse*, 45, 315–34.

Moser, U., & von Zeppelin, I. (1996). Der geträumte Traum. Wie Träume entstehen und sich verändern (How dreams are generated and how they change). 2nd ed. Stuttgart: Kohlhammer.

Moser, U., Pfeifer, R., Schneider, W., & von Zeppelin, I. (1980). Experiences with computer simulation of dream processes. In Koella, W. (Ed.), *Sleep 1982. Sixth European Congres on Sleep Research Zürich*. Basel: Karger, pp. 30–44.

Mowrer, O. H. (1953a). Changes in verbal behavior during psychotherapy. In Mowrer, O. H. (Ed.), *Psychotherapy: Theory and research*. New York: Ronald Press, pp. 463–545.

Mowrer, O. H. (Ed.) (1953b). *Psychotherapy: Theory and research*. New York: Ronald Press.

Munder Ross, J. (2007). Trauma and abuse in the case of Little Hans: A contemporary perspective. *Journal of the American Psychoanalytic Association*, 55, 779–98.

Muschg, W. (1930). Freud als Schriftsteller [Freud as a writer]. *Die psychoanalytische Bewegung*, 2, 467–509.

Myerson, P. G. (1965). Modes of insight. *Journal of the American Psychoanalytic Association*, 13, 771–92.

Neudert, L., & Grünzig, H. J. (1983). *Beurteilungsmanual für Selbstgefühlveränderung* [Coding manual for changes in self-esteem]. Ulm: Abteilung Psychotherapie, Universität Ulm. Unpub. Manuscript.

Neudert, L., Grünzig, H. J., & Thomä, H. (1987). Change in self-esteem during psychoanalysis: A single case study. In Cheshire, N. M., & Thomä, H. (Eds.), *Self, symptoms and psychotherapy*. New York: Wiley & Sons, pp. 243–65.

Neudert, L., & Hohage, R. (1988). Different types of suffering during a psychoanalysis. In Dahl, H., Kächele, H., & Thomä, H. (Eds.), *Psychoanalytic process research strategies*. Berlin: Springer, pp. 227–41.

Neudert, L., Kübler, J. C., & Schors, R. (1985). Die inhaltsanalytische Erfassung von Leiden im psychotherapeutischen Prozeß [Content-analytic measurement of suffering in the psychoanalytic process]. In Czogalik, D., Ehlers, W., & Teufel, R. (Eds.), *Perspektiven der Psychotherapieforschung. Einzelfall, Gruppe, Institution*. Freiburg: Hochschulverlag, pp. 120–34.

Nichols, C. (1972). Science or reflection: Habermas on Freud. *Philosophy of the Social Sciences*, 2, 261–70.

Niederland, W. G. (1974). *The Schreber case. Psychoanalytic profile of a paranoid personality*. New York: Quadrangle/ New York Times Book Co.

Niederland, W. G. (1981). The survivor syndrome: Further observations and dimensions. *Journal of the American Psychoanalytic Association*, 29, 413–25.

Norville, R., Sampson, H., & Weiss, J. (1996). Accurate interpretations and brief psychotherapy outcome. *Psychotherapy Research*, 6, 16–29.

Nunberg, H. (1952). Discussion of Katan's paper on Schreber's hallucinations. *International Journal of Psychoanalysis*, 33, 454–56.

O'Connor, L. E., Berry, J. W., Inaba, D., Weiss, J., & Morrison, A. (1994). Shame, guilt, and depression in men and women in recovery from addiction. *Journal of Substance Abuse Treatment*, 11, 503–10.

O'Connor, L. E., Berry, J., Weiss, J., Bush, M., & Sampson, H. (1997). Interpersonal guilt: The development of a new measure. *Journal of Clinical Psychology*, 53, 73–89.

Orlinsky, D. E., & Geller, J. D. (1993). Patients' representations of their therapists and therapy: A new research focus. In Miller, N., L, L., Barber, J., & Docherty, J. (Eds.), *Psychodynamic treatment research. A handbook for clinical practice*. New York: Basic Books, pp. 423–66.

Orlinsky, D. E., Rønnestad, M. H., & Willutzki, U. (2004). Fifty years of psychotherapy process-outcome research: Continuity and change. In Lambert, M. J. (Ed.), *Handbook of psychotherapy and behavior change* (5th ed.). New York: John Wiley and Sons, pp. 307–89.

Ornstein, P. H. (1972). Preface. In Balint, M., Ornstein, P. H., & Balint, E. (Eds.), *Focal psychotherapy. An example of applied psychoanalysis*. London: Tavistock Publications, p. vii.

Parker, B. (1962). *My language is me*. New York: Basic Books.

Pauker, S., Gorry, G., Kassirer, J., & Schwartz, W. (1976). Towards a simulation of clinical cognition. *American Journal of Medicine*, 60, 981–96.

Pearson, G. H. (1968). *A handbook of child psychoanalysis*. New York: Basic Books.

Peräkylä, A. (2004). Making links in psychoanalytic interpretations: A conversation analytical perspective. *Psychotherapy Research*, 14, 289–307.

Perrez, M. (1971). Zur wissenschaftlichen Theoriebildung und zum Bewährungsproblem in der Psychoanalyse [On the formation of scientific theories and on the problem of validation in psychoanalysis]. *Zeitschrift für Klinische Psychotherapie*, 19, 221–42.

Perrez, M. (1972). *Ist die Psychoanalyse eine Wissenschaft?* [Is psychoanalysis a science?]. Bern: Huber.

Perron, R. (2003). What are we looking for? How? In Leuzinger-Bohleber, M., Dreher, U., & Canestri, J. (Eds.), *Pluralism and unity? Methods of research in psychoanalysis*. London: International Psychoanalytical Association, pp. 97–108.

Perron, R. (2006). How to do research? Reply to Otto Kernberg. *International Journal of Psychoanalysis*, 87, 927–32.

Person, E. S., Cooper, A. M., & Gabbard, G. O. (Eds.) (2005). *Textbook of psychoanalysis*. Washington, DC: American Psychiatric Press.

Persons, J. B., Curtis, J. T., & Silberschatz, G. (1991). Psychodynamic and cognitive-behavioral formulations of a single case. *Psychotherapy*, 28, 608–17.

Peterfreund, E. (1975). How does the analyst listen? On models and strategies in the psychoanalytic process. *Psychoanalysis and Contemporary Science*, 4, 59–101.

Pfeifer, R., & Leuzinger-Bohleber, M. (1986). An application of cognitive science methods to psychoanalysis: A case study and some theory. *International Review of Psychoanalysis*, 13, 221–40.

Pine, F. (2006). The psychoanalytic dictionary: A position paper on diversity and its unifiers. *Journal of the American Psychoanalytic Association*, 54, 463–91.

Pokorny, D. (2000). A successful therapy of Mr. H (Hamlet). *A sample application of a computer program HILI for the computer assisted content analysis of emotions.* unveröff. Manuskript, Universitätsklinik Psychosomatische Medizin und Psychotherapie, Universität Ulm.

Pokorny, D. (2007). Datenanalyse mit CCRT-LU [Data analysis with CCRT-LU]. In Albani, C., Pokorny, D., Blaser, G., & Kächele , H. (Eds.), *Beziehungsmuster und Beziehungskonflikte* [Relationship pattern and relationship conflicts]. Göttingen: Vandenhoeck & Ruprecht, in press.

Popp, C., Luborsky, L., & Crits-Christoph, C. (1990). The parallel of the CCRT from therapy narratives with the CCRT from dreams. In L. Luborsky & P. Crits-Christoph (Eds.), Understanding Transference. New York: Basic Books. pp 158–172.

Popper, K. R. (1944). *The open society and its enemies* (vol. 2). Princeton, NJ: Princeton University Press.

Popper, K. R. (1957). *The poverty of historicism* (2d ed.). Boston: Beacon Press.

Popper, K. R. (1959). *The logic of scientific discovery*. New York: Basic Books.

Popper, K. R. (1963a). *Conjectures and refutations*. London: Routledge and Kegan Paul.

Popper, K. R. (1963b). Prediction and prophesy in the social sciences. In Popper, K. R. (Ed.), *Conjectures and refutations*. London: Routledge & Kegan Paul, pp. 336–46.

Popper, K. R. (1972). Die Zielsetzung der Erfahrungwissenschaft [The goal of empirical science]. In Albert, H. (Ed.), *Theorie und Realität*. Tübingen: J.C. B. Mohr, pp. 29–41.

Porcerelli, J. H., Dauphin, V. B., Ablon, J. S., & Leitman, S. (2007). Psychoanalysis with avoidant personality disorder: a systematic case study. *Psychotherapy: Theory, Research, Practice, Training*, 44, 1–13.

Prioleau, L., Murdoch, M., & Brody, N. (1983). An analysis of psychotherapy versus placebo studies. *Behavioral and Brain Sciences*, 6, 275–310.

Pulver, S. E. (1987a). Epilogue to "How theory shapes technique: perspectives on a clinical study." *Psychoanalytic Inquiry*, 7, 289–99.

Pulver, S. E. (1987b). How theory shapes technique: perspectives on a clinical study. *Psychoanalytic Inquiry*, 7, 141–299.

Pulver, S. E. (1987c). Prologue to "How theory shapes technique: perspectives on a clinical study." *Psychoanalytic Inquiry*, 7, 141–45.

Pumpian-Mindlin, E. (Ed.) (1952). *Psychoanalysis as science. The Hixon lectures on the scientific status of psychoanalysis.* New York: Basic Books.

Radnitzky, G. (1973). *Contemporary schools of metascience*. Chicago: Henry Regnery Company.

Ramzy, I. (1974). How the mind of the psychoanalyst works. An essay on psychoanalytic inference. The International Journal of Psychoanalysis, 55, 543–550.

Rapaport, D. (1967). The scientific methodology of psychoanalysis. In Gill, M. M. (Ed.), *The collected papers of David Rapaport*. New York: Basic Books, pp. 165–220.

Rapaport, D. (1960). *The structure of psychoanalytic theory. A systematizing attempt.* New York: International Universities Press.

Rapaport, D. (1967). On the psychoanalytic theory of motivation. In Gill, M. M. (Ed.), *The collected papers of David Rapaport*. New York: Basic Books, pp. 853–915.

Rapaport, D., & Gill, M. M. (1959). The points of view and assumptions of metapsychology. *International Journal of Psychoanalysis*, 40, 153–62.

Renik, O. (1998). The analyst's subjectivity and the analyst's objectivity. *International Journal of Psychoanalysis*, 79, 487–97.

Renik, O. (2004). Intersubjectivity in psychoanalysis. *International Journal of Psychoanalysis*, 85, 1053–56.

Reynes, R., Martindale, C., & Dahl, H. (1984). Lexical differences between working and resistance sessions in psychoanalysis. *Journal of Clinical Psychology*, 40, 733–37.

Richardson, P., Kächele, H., & Renlund, C. (Eds.) (2004). *Research on psychoanalytic psychotherapy with adults*. London: Karnac.

Rickman, J. (1950). On the criteria for the termination of an analysis. *International Journal of Psychoanalysis*, 31, 200–01.

Ricoeur, P. (1970). *Freud and philosophy: An essay on interpretation.* New Haven, CT: Yale University Press.

Ricoeur, P. (1981). *Hermeneutics and the human sciences.* New York: Cambridge University Press.

Roback, H. B. (1974). Insight. A bridging of the theoretical and research literature. *Canadian Psychologist*, 15, 61–88.

Rogers, C. R. (1959). A theory of therapy, personality and interpersonal relationships. In Koch, S. (Ed.), *Psychology: A study of a science*. New York: McGraw Hill, pp. 184–256.

Rosch, E. (1978). Principles of categorization. In Rosch, E., & Lloyd, B. (Eds.), *Cognition and categorization*. Hillsdale, NJ: Erlbaum, pp. 27–48.

Rosen, V. H. (1969). Sign phenomena and their relationship to unconscious meaning. *International Journal of Psychoanalysis*, 50, 197–207.

Rosenberg, S., Silberschatz, G., Curtis, J. T., Sampson, H., & Weiss, J. (1986). A method for establishing reliability of statements from psychodynamic case formulations. *American Journal of Psychiatry*, 143, 1454–56.

Rosenblatt, A. D., & Thickstun, J. T. (1970). The concept of psychic energy. *International Journal of Psychoanalysis*, 51, 265–78.

Rosenfeld, H. A. (1987). *Impasse and interpretation. Therapeutic and anti-therapeutic factors in the psychoanalytic treatment of psychotic, borderline, and neurotic patients.* London: Tavistock.

Rosin, U. (1989). *Balint-Gruppen: Konzeption. Forschung. Ergebnisse* [Balint-Groups: Concept. Research. Findings]. *Die Balint-Gruppe in Klinik und Praxis: 3.* Berlin: Springer.

Ruben, D. H. (Ed.) (1993). *Explanation.* Oxford: Oxford University Press.

Rubinstein, B. B. (1973). On the logic of explanation in psychoanalysis. In Rubinstein, B. B. (Ed.), *Psychoanalysis and Contemporary Science* (vol. 2). New
York: International Universities Press, pp. 338–58.

Rubinstein, B. B. (1980). The self and its brain. An argument for interactionism.
By Karl Popper and John C. Eccles. *Journal of the American Psychoanalytic
Association*, 28, 210–19.

Rubovitz-Seitz, P. (1998). *Depth-psychological understanding. The methodological
grounding of clinical interpretations.* Hillsdale, NJ: Analytic Press.

Russell, R. L. (1989). Language and psychotherapy. *Clinical Psychology Review*, 9,
505–19.

Russell, R. L. (Ed.) (1993). *Language in psychotherapy. Strategies of discovery.* New
York: Plenum Press.

Ryle, G. (1949). *The concept of mind.* New York: Barnes & Noble 1960.

Sacks, D. (2005). Reflections on Freud's Dora case after 48 years. *Psychoanalytic
Inquiry*, 25, 45–53.

Sacks, H. (1992a). *Lectures in conversation* (vol. 1). Oxford: Blackwell.

Sacks, H. (1992b). *Lectures in conversation* (vol. 2). Oxford: Blackwell.

Sacks, H., Schegloff, E. A., & Jefferson, G. (1974). A simplest systematics for the
organization of turn-taking for conversation. *Language*, 50, 696–735.

Sadger, I. (1921). *Die Lehre von den Geschlechtsverirrungen auf psychoanalytischer
Grundlage (Theory of sexual aberrations on a psychoanalytic foundation).*
Leipzig: Deuticke.

Sampson, H., Weiss, J., Mlodnosky, L., & Hause, E. (1972). Defense analysis and
the emergence of warded off mental contents. *Archives of General Psychiatry*,
26, 524–32.

Sandell, R., Lazar, A., Grant, J., Carlson, J., Schubert, J., & Broberg, J. (2007). Therapists' attitudes and patient outcomes: II. Therapist attitudes influence change
during treatment. *Psychotherapy Research*, 17, 201–11.

Sandler, J. (1962). The Hampstead Index as an instrument of psychoanalytic research.
International Journal of Psychoanalysis, 43, 289–91.

Sandler, J. (1976). Countertransference and role-responsiveness. *International
Review of Psychoanalysis*, 3, 43–47.

Sandler, J. (1983). Reflections on some relations between psychoanalytic concepts
and psychoanalytic practice. *International Journal of Psychoanalysis*, 64,
35–45.

Sandler, J., Dreher, A. U., & Drews, S. (1991). An approach to conceptual research in
psychoanalysis illustrated by a consideration of psychic trauma. *Interntional
Review of Psychoanalysis*, 18, 133–42.

Sandler, J., Kawenoka, M., Neurath, L., Rosenblatt, B., Schnurmann, A., & Sigal, J.
(1962). The classification of superego material in the Hampstead Index. *Psychoanalytic Study of the Child*, 17, 107–27.

Sandler, J., & Sandler, A.-M. (1984). The past unconscious, the present unconscious
and interpretation of the transference. *Psychoanalytic Inquiry*, 4, 367–99.

Sargent, H. D. (1961). Intrapsychic change: Methodological problems in psychotherapy research. *Psychiatry*, 24, 93–108.

Sargent, H. D., Horwitz, L., Wallerstein, R. S., & Appelbaum, A. (1968). *Prediction
in psychotherapy research. Method for the transformation of clinical judge-
ments into testable hypothesis.* New York: International Universities Press.

Sarnoff, I. (1971). *Testing Freudian concepts: An experimental approach*. New York: Springer.

Saul, L. (1940). Utilization of early current dreams in formulating psychoanalytic cases. *Psychoanalytic Quarterly*, 9, 453–69.

Saul, L., & Sheppard, E. (1954). The quantification of hostility in dreams with reference to essential hypertension. *Science*, 119, 382–83.

Saul, L., & Sheppard, E. (1956). An attempt to quantify emotional forces using manifest dreams; A preliminary study. *Journal of the American Psychoanalytic Association*, 4, 486–502.

Scarfone, D. (2002). Commentary to first interview and one session with Anna. *International Journal of Psychoanalysis*, 83, 575–77.

Schachter, J. (2005a). An early psychoanalytic success: Freud's treatment of the "Rat Man." In Schachter, J. (Ed.), *Transforming lives. Analyst and patient view the power of psychoanalytic treatment*. New York: Jason Aronson, pp. 9–15.

Schachter, J. (2005b). Contemporary American psychoanalysis: A profession? Increasing the role of research in psychoanalysis. *Psychoanalytic Psychology*, 22, 473–92.

Schachter, J. (Ed.) (2005c). *Transforming lives. Analyst and patient view the power of psychoanalytic treatment*. New York: Jason Aronson.

Schachter, J., & Kächele, H. (2007). The analyst's role in healing: Psychoanalysis-PLUS. *Psychoanalytic Psychology*, 34, 429–44.

Schafer, R. (1976). *A new language for psychoanalysis*. New Haven, CT: Yale University Press.

Schalmey, P. (1977). *Die Bewährung psychoanalytischer Hypothesen* [The confirmation of psychoanalytic hypotheses]. Kronberg/Ts: Scriptor.

Schaumburg, C. (1980). *Personalpronomina als Indikatoren interpersonaler Beziehungen* [Personal pronouns as indicators of interpersonal relationships]. Dr. rer. biol. hum. Universität Ulm, Abteilung Psychotherapie.

Schaumburg, C., Kächele, H., & Thomä, H. (1974). Methodische und statistische Probleme bei Einzelfallstudien in der psychoanalytischen Forschung [Methodical and statistical problems in psychoanalytic research]. *Psyche - Zeitschrift für Psychoanalyse*, 28, 353–74.

Schiffer, F. (1998). *Of two minds—The revolutionary science of dual-brain psychology*. New York: Free Press.

Schilder, P. (1927). Über eine Psychose nach einer Staroperation [On a psychotic episode after an eye operation]. *Internationale Zeitschrift für Psychoanalyse*, 8, 35–44.

Schlesinger, H. J. (1974). Problems of doing research on the therapeutic process. *Journal of the American Psychoanalytic Association*, 22, 3–13.

Schlessinger, N., Gedo, J., Miller, J., Pollock, G., Sabshin, M., & Sadow, I. (1967). The scientific style of Breuer and Freud in the origins of psychoanalysis. *Journal of the American Psychoanalytic Association*, 15, 404–22.

Schmidl, S. (1955). The problem of scientific validation in psychoanalytic interpretation. *International Journal of Psychoanalysis*, 36, 105–13.

Schneider, H. (1983). *Auf dem Weg zu einem neuen Verständnis des psychotherapeutischen Prozesses* [On a way to a new understanding of the psychotherapeutic process]. Bern: Huber.

Schönau, W. (1968). *Sigmund Freud's Prosa* [Sigmund Freud's prose]. Stuttgart: Metzlersche Verlagsbuchhandlung.

Schors, R., Mergenthaler, E., & Kächele, H. (1982). Computer-aided content analysis in the study of body concepts. *European Congress of Psychosomatic Research in*. Noorwijkerhout, Holland, Sept 1982.

Schors, R., & Mergenthaler, E. (1994). Sprachinhaltsanalytische Untersuchungen zum Körperbild mit dem Ulmer Körperwörterbuch [Content-analytic studies on the body image by the Ulm body dictionary]. In Dyck, J., Jens, W., & Ueding, G. (Eds.), *Jahrbuch Rhetorik, Vol. 13: Körper und Sprache*. Tübingen: Niemeyer, pp. 119–29.

Schreber, D. P. (1903). *Denkwürdigkeiten eines Nervenkranken* [Memoirs of my illness]. Leipzig: Mutze.

Schwartz, M. A., & Wiggings, O. P. (1987). Typification: The first step for clinical diagnosis in psychiatry. *Journal of Nervous and Mental Disease*, 175, 65–77.

Scriven, M. (1959). Explanation and prediction in evolutionary theory. *Science*, 130, 477–82.

Sechehaye, M. (1947). *La réalisation symbolique*. Bern: Huber.

Sechehaye, M. (1950). *Reality lost and regained: Autobiography of a schizophrenic girl*. New York: Grune & Stratton.

Segal, H. (1962). The curative factors in psycho-analysis. *International Journal of Psychoanalysis*, 43, 212–17.

Seitz, P. (1966). The consensus problem in psychoanalysis. In Gottschalk, L. A., & Auerbach, A. H. (Eds.), *Methods of research in psychotherapy*. New York: Appleton Century Crofts, pp. 209–25.

Shakow, D. (1960). The recorded psychoanalytic interview as an objective approach to research in psychoanalysis. *Psychoanalytic Quarterly*, 29, 82–97.

Shapiro, T. (1988). Language structure and psychoanalysis. *Journal of the American Psychoanalytic Association*, 36 (supplement), 339–58.

Shapiro, T. (1999). The representational word and the linguistic idiom. In Fonagy, P., Cooper, A. M., & Wallerstein, R. S. (Eds.), *Psychoanalysis on the move: The work of Joseph Sandler*. London: Routledge, pp. 105–17.

Shapiro, T. (2002). From monologue to dialogue. *Journal of the American Psychoanalytic Association*, 50, 199–219.

Shengold, L. (1971). More about rats and rat people. *International Journal of Psychoanalysis*, 52, 277–88.

Sherwood, M. (1969). *The logic of explanation in psychoanalysis*. New York: Academic Press.

Sherwood, M. (1973). Another look at the logic of explanation in psychoanalysis. In Benjamin, R. B. (Ed.), *Psychoanalysis and Contemporary Science* (vol. 2). New York: International Universities Press, pp. 359–66.

Shevrin, H. (2000). The experimental investigation of unconscious conflict, unconscious signal anxiety. In Velmans, M. (Ed.), *Investigating phenomenal consciousness. New methodologies and maps*. Amsterdam: Benjamins, pp. 33–65.

Shevrin, H. (2005). Toward a theory on consciousness based on recent developments in subliminal research. In Giampieri-Deutsch, P. (Ed.), *Psychoanalysis as an empirical, interdisciplinary science. Collected papers on contemporary psychoanalytic research*. Wien: Verlag der Österreichischen Akademie der Wissenschaften, pp. 57–74.

Shope, R. K. (1971). Physical and psychic energy. *Philosophy of Science*, 38, 1–12.

Shrout, P. E., & Fleiss, J. L. (1979). Intraclass correlations: Uses in assessing rater reliability. *Psychological Bulletin*, 86, 420–28.

Shulman, D. G. (1990). The investigation of psychoanalytic theory by means of the experimental method. *International Journal of Psychoanalysis*, 71, 487–98.

Silbermann, A. (1974). Systematische Inhaltsanalyse [Systematic content analysis]. In König, R. (Ed.), *Handbuch der empirischen Sozialforschung, Vol. 4: Komplexe Forschungsansätze*. Stuttgart: Enke, pp. 253–339.

Silberschatz, G. (1986). Testing pathogenic belief. In Weiss, J., Sampson, H., and the Mount Zion Psychotherapy Research Group (Eds.), *The psychoanalytic process: Theory, clinical observation, and empirical research*. New York: Guilford, pp. 256–66.

Silberschatz, G., & Curtis, J. T. (1986). Clinical implications of research on brief dynamic psychotherapy. II. How the therapist helps or hinders therapeutic progress. *Psychoanalytic Psychology*, 27–37.

Silberschatz, G., & Curtis, J. T. (1993). Measuring the therapist's impact on the patient's therapeutic process. *Journal of Consulting and Clinical Psychology*, 61, 403–11.

Silberschatz, G., Curtis, J. T., & Nathans, S. (1989). Using the patient's plan to assess progress in psychotherapy. *Psychotherapy*, 26, 40–46.

Silberschatz, G., Curtis, J. T., Sampson, H., & Weiss, J. (1991). Mount Zion Hospital and Medical Center: Research on the process of change in psychotherapy. In Beutler, L. E., & Crago, M. (Eds.), *Psychotherapy research. An international review of programmatic studies*. Washington, DC: American Psychological Association.

Silberschatz, G., Fretter, P. B., & Curtis, J. T. (1986). How do interpretations influence the process of psychotherapy? *Journal of Consulting and Clinical Psychology*, 54, 646–52.

Silberschatz, G., Sampson, H., & Weiss, J. (1986). Testing pathogenic beliefs versus seeking transference gratifications. In Weiss, J., Sampson, H., & the Mount Zion Psychotherapy Research Group (Eds.), *The psychoanalytic process: Theory, clinical observation, and empirical research*. New York: Guilford Press, pp. 267–76.

Simon, J., Fink, G., & Endicott, N. A. (1967). A study of silence. *Journal of the Hillside Hospital*, 16, 224–33.

Soldz, S., & McCullough, L. (Eds.) (1999). *Reconciling empirical knowledge and clinical experience. The art and science of psychotherapy*. Washington, DC: American Psychological Association.

Solomon, J., & George, C. (Eds.) (1999). *Attachment disorganization*. New York: Guilford.

Speidel, H. (1979). *Entwicklung und Validierung eines Wörterbuches zur maschinell-inhaltsanalytischen Erfassung psychoanalytischer Angstthemen* [Development and validation of a dictionary for computer-assisted content analysis of psychoanalytic anxiety themes]. Psychol Dipl. Arbeit. Konstanz und Ulm: Universität Ulm.

Spence, D. P. (1968). The processing of meaning in psychotherapy: Some links with psycholinguistics and information theory. *Behavioral Science*, 13, 349–61.

Spence, D. P. (1969). Computer measurement of process and content in psychoanalysis. *Transactions of the New York Academy of Science*, 31, 828–41.

Spence, D. P. (1973). Tracing a thought stream by computer. In Rubinstein, B. (Ed.), *Psychoanalysis and contemporary science* (vol. 2). New York: Macmillan Company, pp. 109–31.

Spence, D. P. (1982). *Narrative truth and historical truth. Meaning and interpretation in psychoanalysis.* New York: Norton.

Spence, D. P. (1986). When interpretation masquerades as explanation. *Journal of the American Psychoanalytic Association*, 34, 3–22.

Spence, D. P. (1987). *The Freudian metaphor. Towards paradigm change in psychoanalysis.* New York London: W.W. Norton.

Spence, D. P. (1992). The virtual case report. *Psychoanalytic Quarterly*, 71, 679–98.

Spence, D. P. (1994). *The rhetorical voice of psychoanalysis: Displacement of evidence by theory.* Cambridge, MA: Harvard University Press.

Spence, D. P. (1998). Rain forest or mud field? *International Journal of Psychoanalysis*, 79, 643–47.

Spence, D. P., Dahl, H., & Jones, E. E. (1993). Impact of interpretation on associative freedom. *Journal of Consulting and Clinical Psychology*, 61, 395–402.

Spence, D. P., & Lugo, M. (1972). The role of verbal clues in clinical listening. In Holt, R. R., & Peterfreund, E. (Eds.), *Psychoanalysis and contemporary science* (vol. 1). New York: Macmillan Company, pp. 109–31.

Spence, D. P., Mayes, L. C., & Dahl, H. (1994). Monitoring the analytic surface. *Journal of the American Psychoanalytic Association*, 42, 43–64.

Spiegel, U., & Boothe, B. (2006). Dream as prototypes of the "polyphonic novel of self"— A single case study (Amalia). *Society for Psychotherapy Research.* Edinburgh.

Spielrein, S. (1912). Über den psychologischen Inhalt eines Falles von Schizophrenie [On the psychological content of a case of schizophrenia]. *Jahrbuch für Psychoanalyse und Psychopathologische Forschung*, 3, 329–400.

Spitzer, M. (1999). *The Mind within the net: Models of learning, thinking, and acting.* Cambridge, MA: MIT Press.

Stegmüller, W. (1969). *Probleme und Resultate der Wissenschaftstheorie und analytischen Philosophie. Bd II: Theorie und Erfahrung* [Problems and results of the theory of science and of analytical philosophy]. Berlin: Springer.

Stekel, W. (1935). *Fortschritte und Technik der Traumdeutung* [Progress and technique of dream interpretation]. Wien: Verlag für Medizin.

Stephan, A., & Walter, H. (Eds.) (2003). *Natur und Theorie der Emotion* [Nature and theory of emotion]. Paderborn: Mentis Verlag.

Stern, D. N. (1985). *The interpersonal world of the infant: A view from psychoanalysis and developmental psychiatry.* New York: Basic Books.

Stern, D. N. (1998). The process of therapeutic change involving implicit knowledge: Some implications of developmental observations for adult psychotherapy. *Infant Mental Health*, 19, 300–08.

Stern, D. N. (2000). The relevance of empirical infant research to psychoanalytic theory and practice. In Sandler, J., Sandler, A.-M., & Davies, R. (Eds.), *Clinical and observational research: Roots of a controversy.* London: Karnac Books, pp. 27–31.

Stierlin, H. (1972). Review of "Sprachzerstörung und Rekonstruktion" von A. Lorenzer. *International Journal of Psychoanalysis*, 53, 422–25.

Stoller, R. J. (1968). *Sex and gender. Vol. I: On the development of masculinity and feminity.* London: Hogarth.

Stoller, R. J. (1974). *Splitting. A case of female masculinity.* London: Hogarth Press.

Stoller, R. J. (1988). Patients' responses to their own case reports. *Journal of the American Psychoanalytic Association*, 36, 371–92.

Stone, L. (1961). *The psychoanalytic situation. An examination of its development and essential nature.* New York: International Universities Press.

Stone, L. (1981). Notes on the noninterpretive elements in the psychoanalytic situation and process. *Journal of the American Psychoanalytic Association*, 29, 89–118.

Stone, P. J., Dunphy, D. C., Smith, M. S., & Ogilvie, D. M. (1966). *The General Inquirer: A computer approach to content analysis.* Cambridge, MA: MIT Press.

Storch, A. (1922). *Das archaisch-primitive Erleben und Denken der* Schizophrenen [The archaic-primitive experience and thinking of schizophrenics]. Berlin: Springer.

Streeck, S. (1989). *Die Fokusierung in Kurzzeittherapien* [Focusing in short term therapies]. *Beiträge zur psychologischen Forschung Band 16.* Opladen: Westdeutscher Verlag.

Streeck, U. (1994). Psychoanalytiker interpretieren "das Gespräch, in dem die psychoanalytische Behandung besteht" [Psychoanalysts interpret "the talk which makes up the psychoanalytic treatment"]. In Buchholz, M. B., & Streeck, U. (Eds.), *Heilen, Forschen, Interaktion. Psychotherapie und qualitative Sozialforschung.* Opladen: Westdeutscher Verlag, pp. 29–47.

Streeck, U. (2004). *Auf den ersten Blick—Psychotherapeutische Beziehungen unter dem Mikroskop* [On a first glance—Psychotherapeutic relationships under the microscope]. Stuttgart: Klett-Cotta.

Strenger, C. (1991). *Between hermeneutics and science. An essay on the epistemology of psychoanalysis.* Psychological Issues Monographs 59. Madison: International Universities Press.

Strozier, C. B. (2001). *Heinz Kohut. The making of a psychoanalyst.* New York: Farrar, Strauss and Giroux.

Strupp, H. H. (1957). A multidimensional system for analyzing psychotherapy techniques. *Psychiatry*, 20, 293–306.

Strupp, H. H. (1960). *Psychotherapists in action: Explorations of the therapist's contribution to the treatment process.* New York: Grune & Stratton.

Strupp, H. H., Chassan, J. B., & Ewing, J. A. (1966). Toward the longitudinal study of the psychotherapeutic process. In Gottschalk, L. A., & Auerbach, A. H. (Eds.), *Methods of research in psychotherapy.* New York: Appleton-Century-Crofts, pp. 361–400.

Stuart, J. (2007). Hans and Freud's self-analysis: A biographical view of clinical theory in the making. *Journal of the American Psychoanalytic Association*, 55, 799–820.

Sullivan, H. S. (1940). Conceptions of modern psychiatry: The first William Alanson White Memorial Lectures. *Psychiatry*, 3, 1–117.

Szczepanski, J. (1974). Die biographische Methode [The biographical method]. In König, R. (Ed.), *Handbuch der empirischen Sozialforschung, Bd 4 Komplexe Forschungsansätze.* Stuttgart: Enke, pp. 226–52.

Taft, J. (1933). *The dynamics of therapy.* New York: Macmillan Comp.

Talley, P., Forrest, P., Strupp, H. H., & Butler, S. F. (Eds.) (1994). *Psychotherapy research and practice. Bridging the gap.* New York: Basic Books.

Taubner, S., Bruns, G., & Kächele, H. (2007). Studienpatienten gesucht [Recruiting patients for treatment studies]. *Psychotherapeut, 52,* 236–38.

Teller, V., & Dahl, H. (1995). What psychoanalysis needs is more empirical research. In Shapiro, T., & Emde, R. (Eds.), *Research in psychoanalysis: Process, development, outcome.* Madison, CT: International Universities Press, pp. 31–49.

Thomä, H. (1954). Über die psychoanalytische Behandlung eines Ulcuskranken [On the psychoanalytic treatment of a patient with gastric ulcer]. *Psyche -Zeitschrift für Psychoanalyse, 9,* 92–125.

Thomä, H. 1958). Exploration und Interview [Exploration and interview]. *Psychoanalytische Klinik Heidelberg,* unpublished manuscript.

Thomä, H. (1961). *Anorexia nervosa. Geschichte, Klinik und Theorie der Pubertätsmagersucht.* Bern/Stuttgart; engl. (1967) Anorexia nervosa. International Universities Press, New York: Huber/Klett.

Thomä, H. (1967). Konversionshysterie und weiblicher Kastrationskomplex [Conversion hysteria and female castration complex]. *Psyche - Zeitschrift für Psychoanalyse, 21,* 827–47.

Thomä, H. (1968). *Über einige Probleme und Ergebnisse der psychoanalytischen Prozessforschung* [Some problems and results of psychoanalytic process research]. Paper presented at the annual meeting of the German Psychoanalytic Association, Ulm., June

Thomä, H. (1974). Zur Rolle des Psychoanalytikers in psychotherapeutischen Interaktionen [On the role of the psychoanalyst in psychotherapeutic interactions]. *Psyche - Zeitschrift für Psychoanalyse, 28,* 381–94.

Thomä, H. (1977). Psychoanalyse und Suggestion [Psychoanalysis and suggestion]. *Zeitschrift für Psychosomatische Medizin und Psychoanalyse, 23,* 35–56.

Thomä, H. (1978). Von der "biographischen Anamnese" zur "systematischen Krankengeschichte" [From the "biographical anamnesis" to the "systematic case history"]. In Drews, S., Klüver, R., Köhler-Weisker, A., Krüger-Zeul, M., Menne, K., & Vogel, H. (Eds.), *Provokation und Toleranz. Alexander Mitscherlich zu ehren. Festschrift für Alexander Mitscherlich zum 70. Geburtstag.* Frankfurt am Main: Suhrkamp, pp. 254–77.

Thomä, H. (1980). Auf dem Weg zum "Selbst." Einige Bemerkungen zur psychoanalytischen Theorieentwicklung in den letzten Jahrzehnten. [On the way to the "self": Some remarks on the development of psychoanalytic theory in the last decades]. *Psyche - Zeitschrift für Psychoanalyse, 34,* 221–45.

Thomä, H. (Ed.) (1981a). *Schriften zur Praxis der Psychoanalyse: Vom spiegelnden zum aktiven Psychoanalytiker* [Collected papers on the practice of psychoanalysis]. Frankfurt: Suhrkamp.

Thomä, H. (1981b). Über die Identifizierung des Patienten mit dem Psychoanalytiker und seinen Funktionen [On the identification of the patient with the analyst and his functions]. In Thomä, H. (Ed.), *Schriften zur Praxis der Psychoanalyse: Vom spiegelnden zum aktiven Psychoanalytiker.* Frankfurt: Suhrkamp, pp. 122–39.

Thomä, H. (1993). Training analysis and psychoanalytic education: Proposals for reform. *Annual of Psychoanalysis, 21,* 3–75.

Thomä, H. (1996). Validierung psychoanalytischer Deutungen (1965–1995) [On the validation of psychoanalytic dialogues]. *Psychotherapie Psychosomatik Medizinische Psychologie, 46,* 234–40.

Thomä, H. (2005). Psychoanalysts without a specific professional identity—A utopian dream? *International Forum of Psychoanalysis*, 13, 213–36.

Thomä, H., Grünzig, H. J., Böckenförder, H., & Kächele, H. (1976). Das Konsensusproblem in der Psychoanalyse [The consensus problem in psychoanalysis]. *Psyche - Zeitschrift für Psychoanalyse*, 30, 978–1027.

Thomä, H., & Houben, A. (1967). Über die Validierung psychoanalytischer Theorien durch die Untersuchung von Deutungsaktionen [On the validation of psychoanalytic theories by the investigation of interpretative actions]. *Psyche - Zeitschrift für Psychoanalyse*, 21, 664–92.

Thomä, H., & Kächele, H. (1975). Problems of metascience and methodology in clinical psychoanalytic research. *Annual of Psychoanalysis*, 3, 49–119.

Thomä, H., & Kächele, H. (1985). *Lehrbuch der psychoanalytischen Therapie, Vol. 1: Grundlagen.* Berlin: Springer.

Thomä, H., & Kächele, H. (1987). *Psychoanalytic practice. Vol. 1: Principles.* Berlin: Springer.

Thomä, H., & Kächele, H. (1992). *Psychoanalytic practice. Vol. 2: Clinical studies.* Berlin: Springer.

Thomä, H., & Kächele, H. (1994a). *Psychoanalytic practice. Vol 1: Principles.* Paperback edition. New York: Jason Aronson.

Thomä, H., & Kächele, H. (1994b). *Psychoanalytic practice. Vol. 2: Clinical studies.* Paperback edition. New York: Jason Aronson.

Thomä, H., & Kächele, H. (1999). Memorandum on a reform of psychoanalytic education. *International Psychoanalysis News*, 8, 33–35.

Thomä, H., & Kächele, H. (2000). On the devaluation of the Eitingon-Freud model of psychoanalytic educuation. Letters to the editor. *International Journal of Psychoanalysis*, 81, 806–08.

Thomä, H., & Kächele, H. (2007). Comparative psychoanalysis on the basis of a new form of treatment reports. *Psychoanaytic Inquiry*, 27: 650–689.

Thomä, H., & Rosenkötter, L. (1970). Über die Verwendung audiovisueller Hilfsmittel in der psychotherapeutischen Ausbildung [On the use of audio-visual technology in the training of psychotherapists]. *Didacta Medica*, 4, 108–12.

Thorner, H. A. (1963). Ursache, Grund und Motiv. Ein psychoanalytischer Beitrag zum Verständnis psychosomatischer Phänomene [Cause, reason and motive]. *Psyche - Zeitschrift für Psychoanalyse*, 15, 487–93.

Tolstoy, L. (1868). *War and peace* (2d ed.). Edited and translated by G. Gibian. New York: Norton 1996 [1868].

Tuckett, D. (1994). The conceptualization and communication of clinical facts in psychoanalysis. *International Journal of Psychoanalysis*, 75, 865–70.

Ullrich, R., & Ullrich, R. (1975). Das Emotionalitätsinventar (EMI) [The inventory of emotions]. *Diagnostika*, 21, 84–95.

Vaughan, S. C., Spitzer, R., Davies, M., & Roose, S. (1997). The definition and assessment of analytic process. Can analysts agree? *International Journal of Psychoanalysis*, 78, 959–73.

Vetter, H. U. (1969). *Language behavior and psychopathology.* Chicago: Rand McNally & Comp.

Volkart, R. (1995). *Fiebriges Drängen, erstarrender Rückzug. Emotionen, Fantasien und Beziehungen bei Borderline-Persönlichkeitsstörung und Depression* [Feverish pushing, freezing retreat. Emotions, phantasies and relationship in patients with borderline-personality disorder and affective disorders]. Bern: Peter Lang.

Volkart, R., & Heri, I. (1998). Kann man "die Spirale aus Scham, Wut und Schuldgefühlen durch Lachen auflösen"? [Is it possible to dissolve the spiral of shame, anger and guiltfeelings by laughter?]. *Psychotherapeut*, 43, 179–91.

Volkart, R., & Walser, B. (2000). Patient's nonverbal reactions after therapeutic interventions: A pilot study based on the Control-Mastery Theory of the psychotherapeutic process. *European Psychotherapy*, 1, 70–80.

Von Bormann, C. (1971). Die Zweideutigkeit der hermeneutischen Erfahrung [The ambiguity of hermeneutic experience]. In *Hermeneutik und Ideologiekritik* [Hermeneutics and critique of ideology]. Frankfurt: Suhrkamp, pp. 83–119.

Von Mises, R. (1939). *Kleines Lehrbuch des Positivismus*. The Hague. (1951). *Positivism. A study in human understanding*. Boston: Harvard University Press.

Von Weizsäcker, C. F. (1971). *Die Einheit der Natur* [The unity of nature]. München: Hanser.

Von Weizsäcker, V. (1935). *Studien zur Pathogenese* [Studies on pathogenesis]. Leipzig: Thieme.

Von Wright, G. (1994). *Normen, Werte, Handlungen* [Norms, values, actions]. Frankfurt: Suhrkamp.

von Wyl, A., & Boothe, B. (2003). Weibliches Leiden an der Anatomie. Der Körper als Feind im Spiegel des Alltags—und Traumnarrativs [Female suffering from anatomy. The body as enemy in the mirror of every day and dream narratives]. *Zeitschrift für qualitative Bildungs-, Beratungs- und Sozialforschung*, 4, 61–79.

Wachholz, S., & Stuhr, U. (1999). The concept of ideal types in psychoanalytic follow up research. *Psychotherapy Research*, 9, 327–41.

Waelder, R. (1962). Psychoanalysis, scientific method and philosophy. *Journal of the American Psychoanalytic Association*, 10, 617–37.

Waelder, R. (1963). Psychic determinism and the possibility of predictions. *Psychoanalytic Quarterly*, 32, 15–42.

Waelder, R. (1967). *Progress and revolution. A study of the issues of our age*. New York: International Universities Press.

Wakefield, J. C. (2007). Attachment and sibling rivalry in Little Hans: The fantasy of the two giraffes revisited. *Journal of the American Psychoanalytic Association*, 55, 821–849.

Waldron, S., Scharf, R. D., Crouse, J., Firestein, S. K., Burton, A., & Hurst, D. (2004a). Saying the right thing at the right time: A view through the lens of the analytic Process Scales (APS). *Psychoanalytic Quarterly*, 73, 1079–125.

Waldron, S., Scharf, R. D., Hurst, D., Crouse, J., Firestein, S. K., & Burton, A. (2004b). What happens in a psychoanalysis? A view through the lens of the Analytic Process Scales. *International Journal of Psychoanalysis*, 85, 443–66.

Waldron, W. (1989). *Psychoanalytic research consortium*. New York Psychoanalytic Institute. New York.

Wallerstein, R. S. (1988). One psychoanalysis or many? *International Journal of Psychoanalysis*, 69, 5–21.

Wallerstein, R. S. (1990). Psychoanalysis. The common ground. *International Journal of Psychoanalysis*, 71, 3–20.

Wallerstein, R. S. (1991). Assessment of structural change in psychoanalytic therapy and research. In Shapiro, T. (Ed.), *The concept of structure in psychoanalysis*. Madison, CT: International Universities Press.

Wallerstein, R. S. (1993). Psychoanalysis as science: Challenges to the data of psychoanalytic research. In Miller, N. E., Luborsky, L., Barber, J. P., & Docherty, J. (Eds.), *Psychodynamic treatment research—A guide for clinical practice*. New York: Basic Books, pp. 96–106.

Wallerstein, R. S. (1995). *The talking cures. The psychoanalyses and the psychotherapies*. New Haven, CT: Yale University Press.

Wallerstein, R. S. (2001). The generations of psychotherapy research. An overview. *Psychoanalytic Psychology*, 18, 243–67.

Wallerstein, R. S. (2002). The trajectory of psychoanalysis: A prognostication. *International Journal of Psychoanalysis*, 83, 1247–67.

Wallerstein, R. S. (2003). Psychoanalytic therapy research: Its coming of age. *Psychoanalytic Inquiry*, 23, 375–404.

Wallerstein, R. S. (2005a). Dialogue or illusion? How do we go from here? *International Journal of Psychoanalysis*, 86, 633–38.

Wallerstein, R. S. (2005b). Will psychoanalytic pluralism be an enduring state of our discipline? *International Journal of Psychoanalysis*, 86, 623–26.

Wallerstein, R. S. (2007). The vision of CAMP and the future of psychoanalytic therapy research. In Bucci, W., & Freedman, N. (Eds.), *From impression to inquiry: A tribute to the work of Robert Wallerstein*. London: International Psychoanalytical Association, pp. 207–24.

Wallerstein, R. S., & Sampson, H. (1971). Issues in research in the psychoanalytic process. *International Journal of Psychoanalysis*, 52, 11–50.

Weber, M. (1949). *The methodology of social sciences* (2d ed.). New York: Free Press.

Weiss, J. (1971). The emergence of new themes. A contribution to the psychoanalytic theory of therapy. *International Journal of Psychoanalysis*, 52, 459–67.

Weiss, J. (1993). *How psychotherapy works. Process and technique*. New York: Guilford Press.

Weiss, J. (1994). The analyst's task: To help the patient carry out his plan. *Contemporary Psychoanalysis*, 30, 236–54.

Weiss, J., & Sampson, H. (1982). *Psychotherapy research: Theory and findings (Bulletin 5)*. San Francisco: Mont Zion Hospital and Medical Center.

Weiss, J., Sampson, H., & The Mount Zion Psychotherapy Research Group (Eds.) (1986). *The psychoanalytic process: Theory, clinical observation, and empirical research*. New York: Guilford Press.

Welsen, P. (1987). "Freudlektüre" und "philosophische Freudinterpretationen" ["Reading Freud" and "philosophical interpretations of Freud"]. *Psyche - Zeitschrift für Psychoanalyse*, 41, 699–716.

Welsen, P. (1988). "Subjekt und sein Anderes"—Subversion und Wiederaneignung des Subjektes bei Paul Ricoeur und Jacques Lacan ["The subject and the other"—Subversion and regaining of the subjects in Ricoeur and Lacan]. *Philosophisches Jahrbuch*, 95, 307–21.

Westphale, C., & Köhle, K. (1982). Gesprächssituation und Informationsaustausch während der Visite auf einer internistisch-psychosomatischen Krankenstation [Discourse and information exchange during ward rounds]. In Köhle, K., & Raspe, H. H. (Eds.), *Das Gespräch während der ärztlichen Visite. Empirische Untersuchungen*. München: Urban & Schwarzenberg, pp. 102–39.

Wexler, D. A. (1974). A cognitive theory of experiencing, self actualisation and therapeutic process. In Wexler, D. A., & Rice, L. N. (Eds.), *Innovations in client-centered therapy*. New York: Wiley, pp. 49–116.

White, R. B. (1961). The mother-conflict in Schreber's psychosis. *International Journal of Psychoanalysis*, 42, 55–73.

White, R. B. (1963). The Schreber case reconsidered in the light of psychosocial concepts. *International Journal of Psychoanalysis*, 44, 213–21.

Widmer-Perrenoud, M. (1975). Review von E. Kestemberg u S. Decobert (1972) "La faim et le corps". *Psyche - Zeitschrift für Psychoanalyse*, 29, 581–87.

Wilson, A. (2004). Multiple approaches to a single case: Conclusions. *International Journal of Psychoanalysis*, 85, 1269–71.

Winnicott, D. W. (1954). Withdrawal and regression. In Winnicott, D. W. (Ed.), *Collected papers: Through pediatrics to psychoanalysis*. London: Tavistock, pp. 205–15.

Winnicott, D. W. (1956). Zustände von Entrückung und Regression [States of withdrawal and regression]. *Psyche - Zeitschrift für Psychoanalyse*, 10, 205–15.

Winnicott, D. W. (1965). *The maturational processes and the facilitating environment. Studies in the theory of emotional development*. New York: International Universities Press.

Winnicott, D. W. (1972). Fragment of an analysis. In Giovaccini, P. L. (Ed.), *Tactics and techniques in psychoanalytic therapy*. London: Hogarth Press, pp. 455–693.

Winnicott, D. W. (1975). Fragment d'une analyse. Paris: Payot.

Winnicott, D. W. (1978). *Piggle. An account of the psychoanalytic treatment of a little girl*. London: Hogarth Press.

Winnicott, D. W. (1982). Bruchstücke einer Psychoanalyse. Stuttgart: Klett-Cotta.

Wisdom, J. O. (1967). Testing an interpretation within a session. *International Journal of Psychoanalysis*, 48, 44–52.

Wisdom, J. O. (1970). Freud and Melanie Klein. Psychology, ontology, Weltanschauung. In Hanly, C., & Lazerowitz, M. (Eds.), *Psychoanalysis and philosophy*. New York: International Universities Press, pp. 327–62.

Wisdom, J. O. (1972). A graduated map of psychoanalytic theories. *Monist*, 56, 376–412.

Wisdom, J. O. (1984). What is left of psychoanalytic theory? *International Review of Psychoanalysis*, 11, 313–26.

Wittels, F. (1924). *Der Mann, die Lehre, die Schule*. Leipzig: Tal. engl. Sigmund Freud: His personality, his teaching, and his school. London: George Allen & Unwin 1924.

Wolberg, L. R. (1945). *Hypnoanalysis*. New York: Grune & Stratton.

Wolpe, J., & Rachman, S. (1960). Psychoanalytic evidence: A critique based on Freud's case of Little Hans. In Rachman, S. (Ed.), *Critical essays on psychoanalysis*. Oxford: Pergamon, pp. 198–220.

Wortis, J. (1954). *Fragments of an analysis with Freud*. New York: Simon & Schuster.

Wundt, W. (1910). *Völkerpsychologie* [Psychology of nations]. Weinheim 1987: Beltz.

Wyss, D. (1961). *Die tiefenpsychologischen Schulen von den Anfängen bis zur Gegenwart* [The depth-psychological schools from the beginnings until present]. Göttingen: Vandenhoeck & Ruprecht.

Yalom, I. D., & Elkin, G. (1974). *Every day gets a little closer. A twice-told therapy.* New York: Basic Books.

Zenz, H., Brähler, E., & Braun, P. (1975). Persönlichkeitsaspekte des Kommunikationserlebens im Erstinterview [Aspects of personality in communicative experiences in the initial interview]. *Zeitschrift für Psychosomatische Medizin und Psychoanalyse*, 21, 376–89.

Zetzel, E. R. (1966). Additional notes upon a case of obsessional neurosis: Freud 1909. *International Journal of Psychoanalysis*, 47, 123–29.

Zielke, M., & Kopf-Mehnert, C. (1978). *Veränderungsfragebogen des Erlebens und Verhaltens* [Questionnaire on changes of experience and behavior]. Weinheim: Beltz Test GmbH.

Index